THE MIDDLE AGES

The Middle Ages

395-1500

Fifth Edition

JOSEPH R. STRAYER

DANA C. MUNRO

APPLETON-CENTURY-CROFTS
Educational Division
MEREDITH CORPORATION

New York

NOTE TO THE FIFTH EDITION

This is an updating of the last edition to make it conform to the results of recent research. The most extensive changes are in the chapters dealing with the later Middle Ages, a period which is being more carefully studied than it used to be. There is also some new material on economic history which reflects our greatly expanded knowledge of this field. I am grateful to readers who called attention to errors in the last edition and so made it possible to make a number of small corrections.

J.R.S.

Princeton

PREFACE TO FOURTH EDITION

This book has had a long history. The first version was written by the late Professor Dana Carleton Munro in 1921. Professor Munro believed, with some justice, that ideas and institutions which were typical of the Middle Ages became so distorted after 1270 that the ensuing period could hardly be called medieval; he therefore ended his book with the thirteenth century. This unusual chronological division did not fit very well into the normal pattern of undergraduate courses; it left the fourteenth and fifteenth centuries in a sort of limbo, attached to neither medieval nor modern history. For this reason, chapters on the period between 1300 and 1500, written by Professor Raymond James Sontag, were added to the 1928 edition of the book. By the late 1930's, when it became apparent that a third edition was necessary, Professor Munro was dead and Professor Sontag's interests had shifted to the field of diplomatic history. The publisher suggested that I prepare a completely revised text, drawing on the older material only where it seemed appropriate. Professor Sontag and the heirs of Professor Munro very generously agreed to this arrangement. The result was the completely reorganized and rewritten version of 1942.

The changes in this, the fourth edition, are not as great as those made in

1942. I have rewritten some sections, such as the one on feudalism, which seemed inadequate in the 1942 text. I have corrected mistakes which were called to my attention by readers of the book; I have also changed some passages to make them conform to the results of recent research. I have attempted to make the book more usable for teaching purposes by breaking up the chapters into short subtopics. I have also added genealogical tables and a list of important dates, and have revised the list of suggested readings. An entirely new set of maps has been prepared which should make it easier to visualize the geographic setting. Finally, some illustrations have been included to give the student a sample of medieval artistic achievements.

No changes or additions can entirely solve the basic problem—that of covering a very long period in a relatively short book. Much has had to be omitted and many complex problems have been simplified. In making these condensations and excisions I have been guided by two main ideas. In the first place, the Middle Ages are one of the great creative periods in the history of our civilization. They are a period in which Western Europe was relatively isolated and largely dependent on its own resources; they are therefore a period in which the people of Western Europe were forced to develop their own ideas, institutions, and artistic and literary forms. I have tried to emphasize the growth of those elements which gave Western European civilization its unique characteristics and which are living realities today. In the second place, the Middle Ages offer an almost unique opportunity to study over a long period the interaction between a lofty set of ideals and the often conflicting demands of practical life. The tension between the ideal and the actual is always important in determining the development of a civilization; it is seldom seen as clearly as it was in the Middle Ages. For this reason, I have given a large amount of space to the rise and decline of the medieval Church, and to the effects which its rise and decline had on medieval civilization.

Medieval history is the history of our own ancestors who had to deal with the same problems which confront us—the problem of organizing an economy which would give them an adequate material basis for life, of building governments which would give them both security and an opportunity to live the good life, of creating ideals which would make life meaningful. We can learn both from their successes and their failure. If this book encourages some students to read more about the Middle Ages—one of the most interesting periods in human history—it will have served its purpose.

J.R.S.

Princeton

CONTENTS

ILLUSTRATIONS

MAPS

(Maps drawn by Theodore R. Miller)

I

->>>->>>->>>->>)<<<-<<<-<<<-<<<-

The Roman World in the
Fourth Century

THE GOVERNMENT

AT THE BEGINNING of the history of medieval Europe lies the Roman Empire, half of which was not European at all. The population and wealth of the Empire were concentrated on the shores of the Mediterranean Sea—on the Asiatic and African shores as well as on the European. Asia Minor and Syria, Egypt and North Africa were Roman, and Rome was heir to the ancient civilizations of those lands. If Rome borrowed her literature and art from Greece, she took her religions, much of her economic organization, and some of her political ideas from Asia and Africa. What Rome borrowed from the South and East she passed on, in Latin forms, to the North and West—to north Italy, Spain, Gaul and Britain. Thus, regions which we think of as very different today were united politically and culturally. England and Egypt, Spain and Syria, France and Turkey, to use modern equivalents, were under the same government and partook of the same civilization.

The Roman citizen of the year 300 A. D. was in some respects a very fortunate person. He did not have to fear international rivalries; there were no nations, there was only Rome. He did not worry about the sinister influence of alien civilizations; there was only one civilization, and that was his. Within the sure boundaries of the western ocean, the northern wilderness, the southern and eastern deserts, were all the people who really counted. It did not matter whether they were Latins or Celts, Greeks, or Egyptians—they were all citizens of the Empire. The men who lived outside these limits were unimportant. Beyond the Rhine-Danube frontier on the north were only the barbarous Germans. Across the Sahara were half-known Negro tribes, and in the Syrian desert were the

1

scattered Arabs. In the East were great civilizations, but while the Romans were vaguely conscious that they existed, they thought little about them. The Sassanid kingdom of Persia was the nearest thing to another state which Rome knew. Sassanid rulers had defeated Roman armies, and Roman traders imported most of their Eastern goods through Persia. Yet even this strong, civilized people made little impression on the Romans. China and India interested them even less. The Roman Empire was the world, and Roman civilization was the only civilization.

It was fitting that the Roman Empire, which was a world, should be ruled by a god. Such was the case in the fourth century when the emperor was "divine," everything pertaining to him "sacred," and his word had the force of law. But the emperor had not always been so exalted a personage. Rome had once been a republic, ruled by an aristocratic Senate whose power could be checked only by uprisings of the city mob. In the first century B.C. this political system caused so much disorder that the citizens of Rome allowed power to be concentrated in the hands of one man—a boss or a dictator. Octavian, the last of the bosses, became Augustus, the first emperor. His powers, however, were not much greater than those of a strong American president. He was commander of the army and head of the administration; he made policy and proposed laws, but he was supposed to act with the advice of the Senate. Augustus' successors, however, assumed much more power. Frequent civil wars and the necessity of protecting the frontiers made their military functions more important and decreased the power of the Senate. Then came a long period of anarchy in the middle of the third century. When a strong emperor, Diocletian, finally emerged in 285, the condition of the Empire was so bad that every one acquiesced in his assumption of absolute authority. Diocletian and his successors named all officials and levied taxes at will. They were the supreme judges and court of last appeal of the Empire; they had the power of life and death over every citizen. It was an accepted maxim that "the will of the prince has the force of law, since the Roman people by law have transferred to their prince the full extent of their power and sovereignty."

With this actual power it is not surprising that Diocletian acted more like an Eastern king than a Roman magistrate. Eastern ideas had penetrated all parts of the Roman Empire and no one was greatly shocked when he adopted the costume and ceremonial of an Oriental despot. The emperor was now a semi-divine monarch, to be addressed with reverence and awe. He wore a diadem and sat on a throne; he lived in a vast, rambling palace, secluded from the people. His officials, basking in reflected glory, formed a palace nobility with high-sounding titles such as "most perfect," "most illustrious," and "most eminent."

The emperor had become an Oriental king but he had not ceased to be a general. More than ever, in the fourth century, his primary duty was to command the army. The fact that the Empire was built around the Mediterranean made it hard to defend. It had the shape of a long oval, hollow in the middle. Most of its richest provinces were within easy striking distance of outside enemies, and it had extraordinarily long frontiers in proportion to its area and population. Barbarian tribes of the North carried on constant guerilla warfare against the Romans. After quick raids on Roman territory they hid in their forests and swamps, while punitive expeditions had to content themselves with destroying huts and burning crops. The Sassanid kings of Persia were a constant threat to the rich provinces of Syria. During the fourth century it became clear that one commander could not guard the whole frontier; two or more were necessary. But command of the army was a sign of imperial power, and if there were two commanders there were bound to be two emperors. From 300 on, most emperors, much as they disliked sharing their power, faced the facts and accepted one or more of their fellow-generals as their colleagues. But while there were usually two or more emperors, there was only one empire. In theory they ruled jointly, though in practice they often divided their duties to secure greater efficiency. Thus one emperor was often responsible for the Danube frontier and the East, while another guarded the boundary of the Rhine. Such arrangements were usually temporary and division of the high command did not mean division of the Empire.

The divine, all-powerful emperor needed the aid of thousands of men in his work of ruling. There were great government bureaus at his capital, just as there are in modern states. For example, there was a treasury department headed by a high official, the "count of the sacred largesses." Yet, on the whole, the central administration employed fewer people, and those people had less specialized functions than in any modern state. The Empire performed few services for its subjects besides the elementary one of keeping peace. There was no system of general public education, no provision for public health; there were no separate bureaus to aid or to regulate commerce and agriculture. There was almost no need for a department of foreign affairs. Supplies for the army and navy were provided by men who had many other administrative duties. The primary duty of the central administration was to see that local authorities received and obeyed the emperor's orders and collected the taxes which he imposed. It also settled disputes between local officials and heard appeals from their judicial or administrative decisions.

From this central bureaucracy depended a whole hierarchy of lesser officials. The Empire was divided into four great divisions called prefectures, each with a prefect at its head. A prefecture was divided into dioceses, ruled by vicars. In each diocese were several provinces, each with its own governor. For example, the Prefecture of the Gauls included the Dioceses of Britain, Gaul, and Spain; the Diocese of Britain

York
Lincoln
Chester

DIOCESE OF
BRITAIN

London

Cologne
Tournai
Soissons
Reims
Mainz
Paris
Chalons
Tours
Orleans
Poitiers
DIOCESE OF
GAUL

PREFECTURE OF
GAUL

Lyons

Toulouse
Narbonne
Arles
Saragossa

DIOCESE OF
SPAIN
Toledo
Barcelona

Valencia

Cadiz

DIOCESE ITALY

Milan
Pavia
Genoa
Bologna
Ravenna

Rome
DIOCESE OF
ROME
Naples

PREFECTURE OF
ITALY

Syracuse

Hippo
Regius
Carthage

DIOCESE OF AFRICA

ROMAN EMPIRE

DIOCESES
AND
PREFECTURES

TRM

500 MILES

PREFECTURE OF
ILLYRICUM

DIOCESE OF
THRACE

DIOCESE
OF
DACIA

Adrianople

DIOCESE OF
PONTUS

Constantinople

Thessalonica

DIOCESE OF
MACEDONIA

DIOCESE OF
ASIA

Ephesus

Antioch

Athens

DIOCESE
OF
THE
EAST

Damascus

PREFECTURE OF
THE EAST

Jerusalem

Alexandria

DIOCESE OF
EGYPT

was made up of five provinces, and so on. The heads of these administrative divisions had general supervisory functions. Beneath them was a mass of fiscal agents, legal advisers, and special investigators. Yet what was said of the central government is also true of the local administration. Considering the size of the provinces, there were few government employees, and their functions were not highly specialized.

The central government and the prefectorial and provincial governments were supervising and coördinating organisms. The basic unit of government was the *civitas,* a term which may be translated as "city-state" if equal emphasis is given to both halves of the English equivalent. The *civitas* was sometimes as large as a small American state, such as Delaware, although it was more often the size of a county. Like an American state, it was the unit of government which dealt directly with the individual. It collected the taxes and controlled the police and the courts of first instance. But it was a *city-*state. Rural districts and even large villages were completely subject to an urban center. The city was dominant politically and its officials governed the adjacent rural areas as well as the urban center.

The *civitas* seemed the natural form of political organization for the ancient world. It arose spontaneously in Greece and Italy, and the Romans had no trouble in introducing it in regions where it had not yet developed, such as Gaul. In the early centuries of the Empire, the central government merely laid down general rules of administration and law, and entrusted most of the actual work of governing to the city-states. At first they performed their functions admirably. But the city was the essential part of the city-state and by 300 A. D. the cities of the Roman Empire were approaching economic collapse. Many city governments were bankrupt; many city officials were faced with personal financial difficulties. City government became inefficient and corrupt, and the central government had to interfere more and more in local affairs. This was unfortunate in an age in which communications were slow; in which a day's journey was measured in tens rather than in hundreds of miles. Only the rich and the lawless profit by delay. As we shall see, conditions in the late Roman Empire favored these two groups at the expense of every one else.

This administrative system was not unduly complicated or excessively expensive, considering the area of the Roman Empire. Nor was the army as large in proportion to total population, or as expensive in proportion to total wealth, as it would be in a modern European state. Its equipment was cheap and durable—there were no guns, high explosives, tanks or airplanes to be purchased. The imperial court was luxurious, but at its worst it was no Versailles. Salaries and supplies for administration, army, and court were the chief expenses of the government, and by modern standards they were not very high.

Taxes were not numerous and the rate of taxation seems to have been, at least in theory, rather low. Yet all during the last centuries of the Empire there were repeated complaints about the extravagance of the government and the intolerable burden of taxation. The most productive tax was on land, graduated according to the fertility of the soil and the number of workmen on the estate. There were also minor levies, such as an occupational tax on merchants and artisans. Burdensome services were imposed on many people, such as the duty of maintaining roads and bridges, or of furnishing transport and provisions for the army. The worst thing about the tax system was the method of assessment. Each *civitas* was responsible for a lump sum, and if some inhabitants of the district were unable to pay, the burden fell on their fellows. Wealthy land-owners were often able to avoid paying their full share of taxes by bribing or intimidating the tax-collectors. Moreover, while the original assessment on a *civitas* was based on careful investigation of its resources, allowances were not always made for a decline in its economic activity. Some districts were certainly overtaxed, and some tax-collectors used the most oppressive methods to make up their quotas. Lactantius, a Christian living in Gaul, gives this description of their activity in seeking hidden resources:

> Slaves were dealt with to accuse their masters, and wives to accuse their husbands. When no sort of evidence could be found, men were forced by torture to accuse themselves. . . . After all men were thus listed, then so much money was laid upon every man's head, as if it had been to pay so much for his life. Yet this matter was not trusted to the first tax-men, but new sets of them, one after another were sent about, that new men might always find new matter to work upon; and though they could not really discover anything, yet they increased the numbers in the lists they made, so that it might not be said that they had been sent to no purpose. By means of these oppressions the stock of cattle was much diminished and many men died; and yet the taxes continued still to be levied, even for those that were dead.

When moderate taxes could be collected only by such methods, there must have been something seriously wrong with the economic condition of the Empire.

Lactantius' description of tax-collectors represents the worst side of Roman government. Some Roman officials were corrupt, inefficient, and arbitrary, though they were seldom bloodthirsty. These faults were probably increasing during the fourth century, when it seemed that the Empire could be held together only by despotic rule. Yet at its best the Roman government was inspired by a love of justice which few of its predecessors had possessed. It had developed an excellent legal system; most disputes were settled by law and not by the whim of irresponsible officials. It gave centuries of peace to regions which have known little but war since. It implanted the idea of the unity of the civilized world so strongly in men's minds that it remained a dominant force in European thought for a thousand years after the Empire had collapsed.

ECONOMIC AND SOCIAL CONDITIONS

The Empire was united politically. However, it had little economic unity, and this perhaps was its greatest weakness. In spite of its size, population, and wealth, there was no large-scale industry in the Roman Empire and comparatively little commerce that was more than local. Most men in the Roman world made their living by agriculture, and Roman methods of agriculture tended to make each region self-sufficient. The staples were grain, olive oil, and wine. These products could be grown almost everywhere in the Mediterranean basin. Ordinary Roman cities were very small and were supplied with food from the immediate neighborhood. The two capitals, Rome and Constantinople, had to draw their food from more distant regions, but the bulk of their supplies came from the great imperial estates in Africa and Egypt. Even food for the army was often obtained from taxes paid in kind, and was not purchased in the open market.

Altogether, there was relatively little trade in foodstuffs and the ordinary farmer could sell his products only in the local market. Clothing, furniture, tools, and almost all other manufactured goods were made either at home or by local artisans. There was no mass-production and no empire-wide commerce in articles of common use.[1] There was a luxury trade, based primarily on importations from the East—silk, ivory, spices, jewels —but a luxury trade gives employment to very few people. In fact, the Roman luxury trade was probably harmful, since the Romans produced little that the Easterners desired, and hence had to pay for most of their purchases with gold. Rome had little enough gold as it was, and since all money at that time had to be actual metal, loss of gold made it hard to do business. As the supply of money decreased, prices fell, and it became even harder to find a market for ordinary products.

The failure of the Romans to take full advantage of the world market which they had created is puzzling. It can be explained only by remembering that both the Greeks and the Romans considered business, and especially manufacturing, degrading. The highest social group in Rome, the senatorial class, was definitely forbidden to engage in trade. Practically all group labor, such as mining or pottery-making, was done by slaves. Slave labor was cheap, at least in the early centuries of the Empire, and no one was greatly interested in inventing labor-saving ma-

[1] In the first and second centuries there had been a manufacturing center around the Bay of Naples, the most important product of which was pottery. It declined during the third century when other regions found that it was easy to imitate this ware

chinery. The Romans knew that steam would perform work, but they never made any serious effort to use it. They knew that grain could be ground more quickly by water power than by hand, yet there were very few water-mills in the Empire in the fourth century. Only in the Middle Ages did the water-mill become common and displace the hand-mortar. Since most work was done by hand, there was little to be gained by centralizing production in one place. Each town—and in some cases each farm—could make cloth, pottery, leather goods and tools as cheaply as the next. Even an advantage in raw materials was of little use. Transportation by land was very inefficient. Carts were clumsy and small, and with their usual disregard for saving power, the Romans harnessed their horses so badly that they could pull only very light loads. Under such conditions the costs of transportation ate up the profits on most objects sent more than a hundred miles. Transport by sea was less expensive, but Roman ships were small and navigation practically ceased from late fall to late spring. For all ordinary purposes, each part of the Empire had to be self-sufficient.

This tendency toward local self-sufficiency was accentuated by the way in which Roman agriculture had developed. As a general rule, the small farmer thrives only in a primitive society. As economic life becomes more complex, as the demands of the state for services and taxes increase, the small farmer gets into trouble. Bad judgment or bad crops force him to borrow money, which he is seldom able to repay. Thus more and more farm land falls into the hands of the creditor—be he great landlord or banker. This process had been going on in Roman territory since the second century B. C., and by 300 A. D. no one could remember when Rome had not had a farm problem. Every one bewailed the decline of the small farmer but, except for the unsuccessful movement of the Gracchi, no one did anything about it. In fact, by barring the aristocracy from trade, the state practically forced them to put all their capital in land, and so encouraged the tendency to build up great estates.

By the fourth century, the small farmer had no economic importance. Most of the farming population lived on large estates, and large estates were responsible for most of the agricultural production of the Empire. The large estate, with its thousands of acres and hundreds of workers, was naturally a much more self-sufficient unit than a small farm could be. It became a sort of fad for the wealthy to derive everything they needed from their own lands. Trade within the Empire was still further discouraged by this tendency.

It seems that what commerce there was in the Roman Empire declined steadily during the fourth century. The reasons for this decline are obscure, although loss of gold, impoverishment of the small farmer, and growth of the self-sufficient great estate undoubtedly played a part. Some economists have also suggested that the Roman world had never had a healthy economic life, since it had been living on its capital for centuries. After the first century its capital ceased to be replenished by successful foreign wars, and from that time decline was inevitable. Whatever the causes, the decline of commerce had dangerous results. There were no common economic interests to supplement the political ties which held the Empire together. Gaul profited little from being in the same empire as Italy, and Britain sold few of its products to Spain. Most men derived no economic benefits from being citizens of a world-state, and this may be one cause of the indifference to the fate of the Empire which is such a striking feature of the fourth and fifth centuries. The same situation occurred in the United States early in the nineteenth century, when absence of a nation-wide market coincided with a certain distrust of the federal government. Another result of the decline of Roman commerce was the weakening of the cities, which, as we have seen, were the most important units of government in the Empire. Finally, almost all classes except the very rich were degraded politically and economically, as a result of the collapse of the economic system.

Roman society was divided by sharp class distinctions in the fourth century. At the top were the senators. They were not necessarily members of the senate which sat at Rome, nor of the newly formed senate at Constantinople. Many senators seldom, if ever, visited either one of the capital cities. The rank of senator had become merely a title of nobility which might be conferred upon any wealthy person by the emperor. The dignity was greatly desired, as it conferred not only prestige but also important immunities for which candidates were willing to pay; consequently, almost all very wealthy men were senators. They possessed most of the land and from their number were drawn many of the higher imperial officials. When not holding office the senators preferred to live in the country on their estates. They were uncomfortable in the cities, where rigid etiquette compelled them to spend much of their time in social formalities, where government officials might interfere with them, where they felt crowded behind the narrow limits of the city wall. Moreover, their estates demanded constant supervision.

The great estate owned by a noble was called a *villa*. Such estates were very large; one which contained about fifteen hundred acres was described as rather small. They usually included cultivated lands, meadows, vineyards and woods. On the *villa* lived farm-laborers, shepherds, vinedressers, bakers, millers, carpenters, masons, smiths, weavers, tailors and other workmen as well as tenants who farmed part of the land on their own account. By the end of the fourth century some estates had their own chapels and priests. Often the owner settled all disputes among his dependents and discouraged the intervention of government officials in any of their affairs. Thus the great estates tended to be self-sufficient and had only limited contacts with the outside world.

The life of a noble on one of these great estates was very like that of a country gentleman in England during the last century. The houses were large and comfortable, with picture galleries, libraries, spacious dining halls, and elaborate baths. The letters of Apollinaris Sidonius (430–487 A. D.) are full of details about the life of the Roman nobles in Gaul. In one letter he describes a week's visit with some friends. In the morning some played tennis or backgammon while others read religious books or the Latin classics. The noonday meal was rather light and was enlivened by many stories. Next they took a siesta, followed by horseback riding and several hours spent in the bath, while they engaged in pleasant and witty talk. The day ended with a luxurious and protracted supper. Other passages in his letters show the pleasure taken by the nobles in games, hunting, reading, and telling anecdotes. Yet it should not be forgotten that Sidonius and the friends whose life he described held high offices in the church and in the state and managed large properties, and therefore could not have spent all their time in this leisurely manner.

The laboring population of a *villa* was divided into two classes, slaves and freemen, although the line between the two was gradually becoming effaced. The slaves included the household servants, who were very numerous, and most of the laborers who worked on the portion of the land cultivated directly by the master. The proportion of slaves to free laborers was decreasing, partly because the Empire was no longer waging wars of conquest and gaining new supplies of slaves, partly because Roman slave-owners were rather generous with manumissions. The condition of the remaining slaves had been greatly improved as a result of the influence of the humanitarian ideas of the great lawyers of the early centuries of the Empire. A master no longer had the legal right to kill a slave at his pleasure, and they were seldom confined in underground prisons at night, as had once been customary. Many owners found that slaves worked better if they were given a separate hut and land to cultivate on shares. Since these "hut-slaves" increased the value of the land, the government enrolled them on its tax-registers, and forbade selling land without the hut-slaves who belonged on it. Yet even these slaves, who had gained a certain degree of security and independence, were subject to heavy burdens and could not legally accumulate any property of their own. It was only by slow changes that they rose to a position equal to that of the *coloni.*

The *coloni* formed the bulk of the agricultural population of the *villa.* They were a class of farmers who had a hereditary right to cultivate small plots of land which they did not actually own. The legal owner of these lands was the proprietor of the *villa,* and he received a rent in money or kind from each plot. As long as he paid his rent, the *colonus* could not lose his land, but he was forbidden by law to leave his land or to change his occupation. If a *colonus* fled from his land he was brought back by force and might be reduced to slavery. If the land was sold he went with it, and his children held it after him on the same terms. He had a master, the owner of the estate, to whom he owed obedience. In other respects he was free, and the law, while speaking of him as his master's *man*, carefully distinguished him from a slave. He could contract a legal marriage, bring suit at law, own personal property, and leave it to his children.

The *coloni* had come from several different classes. Some, though probably not the most numerous group, had been German barbarians subdued or captured in war. At times whole tribes had been brought into the Empire. These had been distributed as *coloni* or agricultural laborers, not slaves, among the landed proprietors. Each one had been assigned to some piece of land and had been enrolled in a government register. Since the state was anxious to increase the population of thinly settled districts and encourage agricultural production, it insisted that *coloni* of this type and their descendants remain on the farms where they had been placed.

It is probable that rules made for these *coloni*, in whom the state had a special interest, were gradually extended to other men in the same economic position. Every great land-owner had many dependents to whom he had given pieces of land in an effort to make them self-supporting. When a slave was freed he still owed lifelong reverence to his master, and his master still owed him protection. Both obligations were fulfilled if, as frequently happened, the freedman assumed the status of a *colonus*.

Finally, many *coloni* were recruited from the class of small, free farmers. These small farmers, as we have seen, were in a bad position in the last centuries of the Roman Empire. Overwhelmed with debts, deprived of markets, they often sought the protection of the great landlords. They might abandon their land and receive new holdings from their patrons; their creditors might foreclose their land and let them stay on it as lease-holders. In either case they soon became indistinguishable from the *coloni*, even in the eyes of the law.

Almost the only landholders left with small properties were the *curiales*. These ranked next below the senators and formed the hereditary governing body in the *civitas*. They were not paid for their work but they had various privileges which had once made men eager to obtain the position of curial. But during the fourth century their situation became worse and worse. They had always been responsible for collecting taxes in their districts, and if they failed to obtain the quota due, they had to make up the difference from their own fortunes. The general impoverishment of the Empire in the fourth century made tax-collection difficult, and many *curiales* were ruined. Moreover, municipal officeholders were supposed to give games to amuse the populace, which meant heavy expenses. Naturally, no one wanted to be a curial under these conditions, but the government forced every one with sufficient wealth to enter the class, unless he were a senator. The *curiales* tried hard to escape from their hereditary occupations, but the government made every possible effort to prevent this. They were not allowed to reside outside their city, and their sons were forbidden to enter the army, the civil service or the church. In spite of repressive laws many *curiales* did escape and by the fifth century this class had disintegrated. A law of 458 A. D. states:

> We must consider the *curiæ* . . . as the souls of the cities and the sinews of the republic. Nevertheless they have been so oppressed . . . that most of their numbers have resigned their offices, expatriated themselves, and sought an obscure asylum in some distant province.

Town-dwellers who engaged in industry or commerce were also in a difficult position. Decline of trade and the growing self-sufficiency of great estates made it difficult for the ordinary artisan or small business man to make a profit. The government had to force men to remain in occupations essential to the welfare of the towns. Thus transport workers, bakers, and others engaged in the preparation of food were forbidden to leave their calling unless they could supply a substitute. Their sons were obliged by law to follow their father's trade. In the cities, as in the country districts, there was little opportunity and less freedom.

The emperors of the fourth and fifth centuries have often been blamed for their policy of regimentation. It may be admitted that economic revival was not stimulated by forcing men to remain in unprofitable occupations, or by making most jobs hereditary. Yet it is hard to see what else the emperors could have done. They were aware that something was wrong with the economic organization of the Empire, but they were soldiers, not economists, and they had pressing military problems to consider. There were no economic experts to advise them, even if they had had time to conduct a thorough investigation. The emperors knew that production was declining, that many men were deserting their lands or their occupations, and that these tendencies weakened the cities and lowered the income from taxes. But the cities were essential units of government, and loss of revenue might make it impossible to defend the frontiers. Regimentation seemed the only answer: force men to do their work, force the cities to perform their functions. The emperors could not allow economic forces to have free play, for those forces were destroying the Empire. It is probably true that the Empire was too large, that the burden of supporting a world government was not compensated for by increased economic opportunity. But it was the duty of the emperors to preserve the Empire, and their policy of regimentation held it together for at least a century after collapse seemed inevitable.

The effects of regimentation on the ordinary citizen were very bad.

There was little opportunity for even the ablest man to improve his condition, and ambition was crushed. Men worked without enthusiasm and felt no interest in the general welfare. The average man is always suspicious of a far-off, centralized government. Regulations and taxes imposed by the central government are present realities; benefits obtained by being a member of a large political unit are indefinite and intangible. This natural distrust of elaborate political organization increased greatly in the last centuries of Roman rule. The burden of government was great and the benefits of government went only to the very wealthy. The ordinary man had lost income, opportunity, and freedom. In the end the Empire fell because most of its subjects were unwilling to make any great effort to preserve it.

LITERATURE, EDUCATION, AND ART

The decadence of late Roman society is reflected in the literature, educational methods, and art of the fourth and fifth centuries. It has been well said that the Romans were becoming barbarized long before the barbarian invasions. In literature the Christian writings are the only works which display vigor of thought and energy of style. Secular literature was turgid, rhetorical, and imitative. The great classical writers of the first century were taken as models; their thoughts and their style were copied, and nothing was added except adjectives. In education a definite breach was opened between Greek and Latin learning. The Romans had conquered the East but they had never imposed their language there as they did in the West. This lack of uniformity had at first no bad effects —in the great centuries of the Empire all educated men knew both Greek and Latin. Growing localism caused Western students to neglect Greek in the fourth and fifth centuries and contacts between the two cultures became less frequent. This was especially bad for the West. Greek literature had always been more original than Latin and the Greeks had a scientific tradition which could not be matched in the West. The Romans had done almost no work in science and had translated few of the scientific treatises of the Greeks. Thus, when knowledge of Greek died out, knowledge of Eastern science also vanished and was not regained until the twelfth century. Roman education in the late Empire was based on compends and compilations from the earlier Latin authors. The emphasis was on poetry and rhetoric. Some attention was given to philosophy, but history and science were neglected.

A good example of the intellectual interests of the Romans of the late Empire is furnished by Martianus Capella's *Marriage of Mercury and Philology*. This is an encyclopedic textbook, thinly disguised as an allegory. The first two books describe the marriage, in rather wearisome detail, and then the bride's attendants, the seven liberal arts, begin to discuss their accomplishments. The idea of summarizing all knowledge in seven categories was not original with Martianus, but his arrangement became so popular that it furnished a framework for all advanced study for centuries to come. The seven liberal arts were grammar, rhetoric, and logic, which were later known as the *trivium* or language studies, and arithmetic, geometry, astronomy and music, which were eventually grouped as the *quadrivium* or scientific subjects. Some of these categories had a wider content than might be expected; thus grammar involved the study of Latin literature, and geometry included some geography and natural history. Music, on the other hand, meant primarily the study of mathematical relationships between tones. The book is one long series of facts, with almost no interpretation of their significance. Martianus tried to include everything which he thought a well-educated man should know, but in spite of his efforts he failed to touch on many important topics. Trivial details were given as much space as the most significant items of information, and the book as a whole is dull and uninteresting. However, it did give, within its limits, a fairly accurate summary of the knowledge possessed by classical writers, and this knowledge made it very popular throughout the middle ages. For many generations this little volume—it occupies only 422 small-octavo pages in the Teubner edition—represented the limits of human knowledge.

In Roman art there was a marked decline of the old classical style. Imitators of this style had little skill; when Constantine built a triumphal arch he had to pillage earlier monuments in order to obtain most of the sculpture which decorated it. Less formal art of the imperial period had developed a rather successful representational technique, but this style was also declining in the late Empire. Christian artists did not wish to represent the fleeting appearance of this world, but rather the eternal verities of the faith. This shift in interest required a shift in style from realism to symbolism and while the shift was taking place the level of art remained low. It was only after the Empire had been seriously weakened that the first masterpieces of Christian art were produced.

RELIGION

The men of the late Empire were deprived of economic opportunity; they took little interest in politics, and their intellectual and artistic work was unimaginative and imitative. But they were tremendously interested in religion and most of their energy was devoted to this field. This tendency began as early as the first century, when growing cosmopolitanism and sophistication made belief in the old Roman gods seem ridiculous. It is probable that the steady decline in political and economic freedom made men turn more and more to religion for assurance that the individual was important in the eternal scheme of things, however unimportant he might seem in the actual world.

Among the upper classes the old religion was usually replaced by Stoicism. This philosophy taught that human happiness and dignity came from voluntary obedience to the universal law. The good life was based on self-control and love of justice and truth. External circumstances which could not be controlled were to be disregarded. Illness, poverty and death were not real evils for a man with a clear conscience. Political and social distinctions were unimportant; all men were equal under the eternal law. Stoics paid equal honor to the slave Epictetus and to the emperor Marcus Aurelius for their writings, and for the dignity and honesty of their lives. Stoicism had a tremendous influence on Roman law and government, since many high officials were Stoics. Roman law became more humane, more willing to recognize the rights of all men. For example, we have seen that the slave gained some protection against his master. The idea of the brotherhood of all men, a favorite Stoic doctrine, received political recognition when all subjects of the Empire received citizenship.

Yet Stoicism could not appeal to many people; it was too intellectual, too impersonal. Ordinary men wanted the warm assurance of the existence of a god interested in their individual troubles, instead of a statement of abstract principles of an eternal law. They doubted greatly that the good life was possible in this world; they felt that the imperfections and injustices of this life must be remedied in a future state. So they turned to the Oriental mystery religions, such as Mithraism, or the worship of Isis and Osiris. Most of these religions had some form of communion service, whereby the believer was placed in direct contact with the divinity. Most of them believed in a redeemer-god who saved mankind by his death. They all emphasized the importance of the future life, in which men were rewarded or punished for their deeds on earth.

In the eyes of the Romans, Christianity was only one of the Oriental religions competing for their favor. At first it was by no means the most popular. Christianity was exclusive and unwilling to compromise. Other religions were tolerant of each other, and were quite ready to conform to any requirements laid upon them by the state. The Romans were annoyed by the Christians' lack of respect for other men's beliefs. They were outraged by the Christians' apparent lack of loyalty to Rome and the emperor. The Christians would not take part in civic celebrations in which the old gods were honored, and they would not sacrifice to the emperor. Most Romans thought of these ceremonies as mere patriotic observances, with no more religious significance than we find in pledging allegiance to the flag. The emperor was the symbol of the unity of the civilized world; it was his power which held together men of widely differing origins and beliefs. It did not seem unreasonable to pay him divine honors. The Roman government could not forget that the official reason for executing the founder of Christianity had been that he was accused of plotting a rebellion against the state. The Christians were a secret society; they recruited almost all their adherents from the lowest classes, and many of their doctrines seemed anti-social. It was easy to accuse them of plotting the overthrow of government and civilization. Hence Christianity was outlawed, while other Oriental religions were warmly welcomed in the West. At a time when a priest of the Sun-God sat on the imperial throne, when followers of Mithra held high commands in the army, the Christians were still persecuted.

Yet persecution had not been continuous. In actual practice it was found that the Christians were not very dangerous to the state. Only the most conscientious or the most despotic emperors felt that it was worth while to make an effort to destroy Christianity. And while thorough and persistent persecution can destroy a belief, spasmodic attacks usually strengthen the faith of the survivors. The membership of the church in its early days was composed of men and women who were profoundly in earnest, ready to risk their lives for their faith, and usually of high character and excellent morals.

Men of this sort naturally attracted others. The very exclusiveness of Christianity became an advantage. In the growing depression and uncertainty it was a relief to find a faith which was absolute and uncompromising. Other religions had absorbed superstitions and practices from their competitors which were inconsistent with their own basic beliefs. Once its first premises were accepted, Christianity was logical and coherent. It could be expressed in terms which were acceptable to men who knew Greek philosophy and Roman law. Christianity was also free of the crudities which marred some of its most dangerous rivals. For example, in Mithraism the initiate was cleansed of his sins by being drenched with the blood of a slaughtered bull. Christianity could offer everything found in other religions in a purer, more consistent, and more attractive form.

The number of Christians increased rapidly during the third century. Yet most authorities agree that in 300 A. D. the Christians formed only a small minority of the total population. They were stronger in certain provinces, particularly Asia Minor, and everywhere they were concentrated in the cities. This made their influence more noticeable and their earnestness, zeal, and high moral character gave them strength entirely disproportionate to their numbers.

Diocletian, who restored the Empire on an authoritarian basis after the anarchy of the third century, naturally resented the growing power of the Christians and tried to exterminate them. One of his successors followed the same policy. But Constantine, who was emperor in the

West at the same time, was less hostile from the beginning of his reign, and eventually became the champion of the Christians against his pagan co-rulers. It is difficult to find any adequate material explanation for Constantine's attitude. His part of the Empire was the least Christian section and the dominant religion in his army was Mithraism. He may have dreamed of conquering the East from his rivals by gaining the support of the Christians, who were more numerous there, but he must have known that the Christians were of little use in military operations. He may have felt that the state needed the energy and ability of the Christians; that to outlaw them was to waste the scanty human resources of the Empire. But there seems to be more than policy in his acts; there was an element of personal belief, however superstitious it was at first. He felt that the Christian God had power and he invoked that power in a campaign against his most dangerous rival. His famous victory at the Mulvian Bridge was won in the name of the Christian God, and confirmed his belief. All penalties against Christians were removed in 312. Christianity was not only tolerated, it was favored by the emperor. When Constantine had eliminated the last of his rivals, he made Christianity the state religion, although he himself was baptized only on his deathbed. Other religions were forbidden in 353 A. D. by Constantine's descendants, but there was no serious attempt to enforce this edict until the end of the century. Pagan practices persisted in the West well into the fifth century, but their survival had no great importance. From the time of Constantine's conversion, Christianity was the dominant religion.

The triumph of Christianity made it possible to perfect the organization of the Church. Even in the period of persecution the faithful had formed local units under the headship of a bishop, but much of the Empire had never been formed into bishoprics, and there was no agreement as to the size of the district which a bishop should control. In Africa and the East, where there were more Christians, bishops were very numerous, while they were rare in the West. Gradually the idea was established that the bishop's district, or diocese, should correspond to the *civitas*. This correspondence was fairly complete in the West by the beginning of the fifth century, but it was never fully achieved in the East. There the territorial jurisdiction of the numerous bishops was often restricted to the limits of a single small town.

The power of the bishops was greatly increased by imperial privileges. The clergy as a whole were partially exempted from the jurisdiction of the civil courts, so that cases in which they were concerned might be tried in ecclesiastical courts presided over by the bishops. In certain cases, such as offenses against religion, even laymen were tried in the courts of the Church. Moreover, the state recognized the ecclesiastical penalty of excommunication, which barred the offender from all acts of Christian worship and even from social relations with any Christian. It was ruled that excommunication from the church in one place excluded the excommunicated from all orthodox churches. This weapon gave the bishops great power over all members of their churches.

There was no doubt that the bishop was head of all the faithful of his diocese, but what were to be the relations between bishops? Here the establishment of a definite hierarchy was slower. It was, however, clear that the bishops of the larger towns would have a certain prestige which might become authority. This was especially true of the bishops in large towns whose churches had been founded by the apostles. Thus, in the East, the three patriarchs of Antioch, Alexandria, and Constantinople had great power. The last, although he did not claim apostolic origin, gradually came to be recognized as superior in authority to the other two. This was due mainly to the importance of his position as bishop of the imperial city.

While the organization of the Eastern Church was delayed by the rivalry of the three patriarchs, the supremacy of the bishop of Rome was unchallenged in the West. In the early centuries the Church of Rome was the only one in the West which claimed apostolic foundation. Moreover, an apparently authentic tradition stated that the Roman Church had been founded by Peter, the chief of the apostles, to whom had been given power to bind and to loose on earth and in heaven. The bishops of Rome were supposed to have inherited their authority from their great predecessor. In addition, the prestige of Rome, the capital of the world, to which people were accustomed to look for laws and guidance, naturally gave its bishops great authority. They increased this power by using it wisely. They were "always to be found on the side of a staunch but liberal orthodoxy." By the beginning of the fifth century their decisions in matters of faith were accepted without question in the West and usually prevailed, though with more difficulty, in the East. Their power in administration was not nearly so great; each diocese still chose its own bishop and managed its own property without much outside supervision. Yet the bishops of Rome already held a unique position, from which the powers of the medieval papacy were easily developed.

The Christian emperors of the fourth century caused the triumph of the faith, but they very nearly brought about the enslavement of the Church. They felt responsible for the guidance of the Church as well as of the state, and believed it their duty to decide what was orthodox Christianity, to summon general councils, and to enforce the laws of the Church. They even made laws on purely ecclesiastical matters, such as the provisions forbidding rebaptism in the Theodosian Code. Bishops of the most important towns were often deposed and appointed by the emperor without ceremony. Except in matters of conscience, the emperor's right to direct ecclesiastical affairs was not questioned, and even in matters of conscience few men dared oppose him. Only the collapse of the Empire in the West, freed the Roman Church from the control of the monarch. In the East, where the Empire survived, the Church remained subservient to the state.

The Church was threatened, not only by the influence of lay authorities, but also by the growth of heresy. In the beginning the simplest statement of the faith had been enough, but as time went on men began to worry more about the exact meaning of basic doctrines and the logical relationship among them. The tendency to engage in theological arguments grew as members of the upper classes, trained in the subtleties of Roman law and Greek philosophy, entered the Church. Naturally there was disagreement among the theologians and it was not always easy to decide who was teaching orthodox doctrine. Those who deviated too far from generally accepted authorities were denounced as heretics, but it was difficult to silence such men or to persuade their followers to abandon them. During the fourth century heresy threatened to split the Christians into dozens of warring sects, and the unity of faith was achieved only after a long struggle.

Many heresies naturally centered around the mysterious nature of Jesus Christ, the Man-God. Was Jesus wholly human, or wholly divine? If neither, were the two natures mixed, or did each exist separately in him? If Jesus were the Son of God was he equal to or less than the Father? Was the Trinity a unity, a partnership, or a hierarchy? Dozens of heresies arose from these questions; one was especially important in later history. This was Arianism, the belief taught by Arius and his followers that Jesus, while God, was a lesser God created by the Father and not of the same substance or co-eternal with him. Arianism was strong in the East and for a while it almost caused civil war in the Empire. There were riots over the question in the streets of eastern cities, and co-emperors became bitter rivals as they took sides in the quarrel. In an attempt to settle the dispute, Constantine called the first general council of the Church at Nicæa in 325, and his practice was followed by his successors. In these councils the orthodox creed was defined, and finally triumphed, thanks to the unity of the West under the leadership of Rome. Although Arianism was eventually outlawed, Arian missionaries had been sent to the Germans during the struggle. They were entirely too successful for the future peace of Europe, for when these heretical Germans entered the Empire in the fifth century, the battle for orthodoxy had to be waged again.

Another heresy, or rather, a rival religion which was a recurrent danger to the Church, was the belief of the Manicheans. This sect took its name from Mani, who taught in Persia in the third century. Since the Manicheans were the most successfully persecuted of all the heretics, it is difficult to describe their doctrine. Written records of their beliefs were carefully destroyed and descriptions of their faith given by Christian opponents are naturally biased. The Manichean religion seems to have been a mixture of old Persian beliefs with Christianity and a few other elements, but Christianity was not dominant in the final blend. For example, a fundamental Manichean belief was in the existence of the two eternal principles of good and evil. This world was the creation of the spirit of evil, whom they identified with the God of the Old Testament. Jesus represented the principle of good, but he was killed by the jealousy of Jehovah. This part of their creed appealed strongly to many men in the fourth century. It was difficult to reconcile the obvious existence of evil with the Christian conception of an all-powerful God. This problem caused as able a man as Augustine to accept the Manichean faith for nine years before he turned to orthodox Christianity. Manichean beliefs seemed almost dead at the end of the fifth century but they had a surprising revival after 1000, when they again threatened Christianity.

The Church was endangered not only by heresy and state interference, but also by the indifference and immorality of some of its own members. When Christianity became the state religion many ambitious men joined the Church to secure the emperor's favor. Indifferent and immoral people became nominal Christians because it was easier to drift with the majority. The growing wealth and power of the Church attracted time-servers and politicians. The worldly bishop, more interested in easy living and intrigue than in his spiritual duties, was a not uncommon figure by the end of the fourth century. In short, now that the Church was identified with Roman society it suffered from many of the defects of Roman society. It could not force the mass of new converts to observe the high standards which had prevailed during the era of persecution. If the world had become Christian, Christianity was becoming worldly.

A natural reaction was that many earnest Christians sought to put a new barrier between themselves and the world. Since mere profession of the Christian faith no longer insulated them from the temptations of the flesh, more drastic steps were needed. They renounced all secular occupations and interests, in order to prepare themselves for the next world. To avoid all distractions they retired to deserted or secluded places, where they often joined together to form groups devoted to the religious life. Thus the monastic ideal arose.

This withdrawal from the world commenced in lower Egypt. The legends of the hermit saints give a good idea of the first stages of the movement. The most renowned of the early ascetics was Anthony, who sold all his property and retired to the desert. At first he lived alone, combating the temptations which tormented him for fifteen years. Later others gathered around him, and he became the head of a community which supported itself by manual labor and engaged in works of charity. Twice he visited the great city of Alexandria, once to seek martyrdom during a persecution, and a second time, at the head of an army of monks, to fight Arianism. He won great popular veneration, but was eager to return to the desert. "The fish die," he said, "when they are drawn to land, and the monks lose their strength in towns."

By the middle of the fourth century there were thousands of hermits in the East. Some led a simple life of toil and prayer, others went to almost insane extremes of asceticism. A few were hypocrites who found that in their new way of life they could avoid work and enjoy the esteem of the people. Most of the monks, like Anthony, were fiercely orthodox and were very helpful in combating the Arians. Athanasius, a vigorous opponent of Arianism, took two monks with him on a visit to Rome, and thus induced the West to take an interest in monasticism. Some ascetic communities were formed in Rome, under the guidance of Jerome, who was not only a great Christian writer, but also an enthusiastic advocate of monasticism. But Jerome himself, with many of his adherents, retired to Palestine, and other Western churchmen were not so well disposed toward the movement. Monasteries established in the West followed Eastern usages and had little influence during the fourth, and even most of the fifth centuries. Only in the sixth century, when Benedict had organized Western monasticism, did it become the Christian ideal in the West.

Heresy and worldliness in the Church were combated not only by the monks but also by the great theologians of the fourth century. Of these, Augustine was probably the most influential, and his life illustrates many of the conflicts of the period. He was born in 354 in northern Africa. His mother was a Christian, but he received a pagan education, first in the classics and then in law. He had a reasonably happy and secure life for some years, during which time he acquired a mistress and a son. Yet he felt the same need for religious assurance experienced by others less fortunate than himself, and as a young man became a Manichean. This doctrine, in the end, failed to satisfy him, and he was equally disappointed with other pagan philosophies and creeds. Augustine then turned toward Christianity, but it took two years of study and self-examination before he was converted. In 387 he and his son were baptized at Milan by Ambrose, one of the most influential bishops of the Western church. For the rest of his long life, Augustine used his great talents as a scholar and writer to defend Christianity. He attacked the chief heresies of his time, and in the process defined many Christian doctrines. With his Manichean background, it is natural that he was interested in the problem of reconciling the presence of evil with the existence of an omnipotent and omniscient God. He solved the problem by denying the existence of an independent evil power. Evil was merely the absence of good, resulting from human unwillingness to accept the grace and guidance of God. In attacking the Pelagian heresy, which denied original sin, stressed free will, and minimized the importance of predestination, he had to clarify these essential doctrines of the Church. He believed both in original sin (man's inborn tendency to reject divine law) and in predestination, but he insisted that man also had free will and full responsibility for his acts. When the pagan minority blamed the collapse of the Empire on Christianity, Augustine pointed out in one of his most famous books, the *City of God*, that the old gods had not always preserved Rome from disaster, and that in any case the future life was more important than earthly prosperity. His *Confessions*, which are a sort of autobiography, describe his intellectual and spiritual experiences, and should be read by every one who wishes to understand the life of the late Roman Empire. His collected writings are so voluminous that a medieval scholar said no one could ever hope to read them all, but through them Augustine became the spiritual guide of Western Christendom.

Augustine died as bishop of Hippo, a town in North Africa, while the city was being besieged by a group of German invaders. The circumstances of his death symbolize the changes which were taking place in the Roman world in the fifth century. The Empire was declining, but Christianity was strong enough to survive this decline. Wherever we look, in social organization and in popular leadership, in literature and in art, the really vital work of the period was being done under the auspices of the Church. The ablest, most intelligent, most energetic men in the fourth and fifth centuries were the leaders of the Church. There was passionate interest in and passionate devotion to Christianity at a time when few men were interested in preserving the economic and political institutions of the Empire. Loyalty to Christianity was taking the place of loyalty to the decaying Roman state; it was to be the medieval equivalent of patriotism. It was clear by the end of the fourth century that Christianity was the most vital element in Roman civilization, and that Roman civilization would survive only as far as it was taken over by Christianity.

II

->>>->>>->>>->>>-(((-(((-(((-(((-

The Decay of the Roman World
in the West

THE EARLY GERMANS

ACROSS THE RHINE and the Danube lived the Germans, who were to replace the Romans as the rulers of the western world. The Romans fought with them frequently and traded with them intermittently, but they were not greatly interested in their customs and institutions. The Germans were barbarians, and they lived in a barbarous country; that was all the average Roman wanted to know. "Who, indeed," wrote Tacitus, "would leave Asia, or Africa or Italy to seek Germany, with its desert scenery, its harsh climate, its sullen manners and aspect?"

As a result of this attitude we have very little information about the early Germans. Most classical authors dismiss them with a few brief sentences. Medieval accounts of their laws and history were written long after they entered the Empire and cannot be relied on as evidence of their original condition. Archeological research has supplied some useful data, but most of what has been written on the early Germans (which is far too much) is derived from one little pamphlet, Tacitus' *Germania*. Tacitus was no anthropologist and as far as we know he never visited Germany. His pamphlet was about the equivalent of a modern newspaper article; he wanted to amuse as well as to give some rudimentary information. He wrote at the end of the first century A. D., and there is no reason to suppose that the Germans of the fourth century were exactly like those whom he describes.

In Tacitus' time, the Germans were just beginning the transition from a pastoral to an agricultural economy. They knew how to raise grain and had cleared fields here and there, but Tacitus thought that most of the country was "covered over with wild forests and filthy swamps."

24

There were not many acres under cultivation and the yield per acre was low. The Germans had to rely on hunting and grazing to get an adequate diet; they kept great herds of cattle and swine that roamed through the wastelands and forests. Emphasis on hunting and grazing meant that the population was thin and scattered and that migration was easy. It was only after they entered the Empire that the Germans became completely sedentary, and even then their laws indicate that they thought of cattle as a more important type of property than land.

The Germans had skilled craftsmen, especially in metalworking. Their goldsmiths made elaborate, and often very beautiful, ornaments; their blacksmiths made fairly effective weapons and rather less effective tools. The women wove linen and woolen cloth and made earthenware vessels. The Germans were, however, very backward in the building crafts. They made almost no use of brick and stone, and the Romans despised their rough wooden houses.

Though the Germans carried on trade with each other and with their more civilized neighbors, they had no cities. They lived in villages or hamlets, with each house separated from the others by open spaces. Villages were widely dispersed; often there were extensive tracts of forest between each settlement.

Living as they did in scattered villages, with each community almost self-sufficient, the Germans naturally had no need for an elaborate political organization. A few thousand fighting men and their dependents formed a "folk." The folk's chief function was to make war on its neighbors or to defend itself from their attacks. In time of peace it had few political responsibilities; only on rare occasions did it try to settle disputes among its members. Normally each family had the duty of protecting and answering for the behavior of its members. Since a family of those days included very remote kinsmen it might be involved in a long series of unending disputes. A man was responsible for the acts of his second or third cousins or his relatives by marriage and he expected assistance from them in return. A powerful family, with many able-bodied men, could usually take care of itself and avenge its injuries without asking for outside assistance. If, however, the family were weak, or if for some other reason it did not want to start a feud, it could bring its grievances before a neighborhood assembly. The accused probably tried to establish his innocence by oaths of his friends or by undergoing an ordeal.[1] If he failed, he paid a fine, with the assistance of his relatives. Even homicide could be atoned for by money. But resort to a neighborhood court was entirely voluntary. The community could not force a family to settle its disputes in court, though public opinion gradually began to favor this means of ending quarrels.

[1] For these procedures see below, p. 57.

The folk had its recognized leaders, men who were descended from families that were considered noble. Often, but not always, there was a king who came from a particularly distinguished family that claimed descent from the gods. Such a king represented his people in the literal meaning of the word. He spoke for them before the gods; he dealt with strangers on their behalf; he led them in war. But neither king nor noble leaders had judicial or administrative power. They could influence men by their prestige, their wealth and their fighting ability, but they could not coerce them.

Important decisions, usually those concerning war and peace, were made in public assemblies. All free men of military age had a right to be present, but they could do little except to pass on propositions laid before them by their leaders. The king and the chiefs had usually agreed on the policy to be adopted before the meeting and in such a case approval was almost automatic. If there had been a disagreement, each leader presented his case; the people then clashed their arms to show agreement with a speaker and shouted him down if they disapproved. The assemblies sometimes acted as a court for very important cases and witnessed formal acts, such as the investing of young men with arms. This was a sign that the youth had reached the age of manhood and made him a full-fledged member of the folk.

One of the most important Germanic institutions was the war-band, or *comitatus,* as the Romans called it. Young men who sought adventure and glory often became the followers of a leader renowned in war. The leader gave his dependents food, shelter, weapons and presents. In return they owed him absolute fidelity and support in all his undertakings. In war, it was a disgrace for any retainer to survive his chief. A late Roman historian, Ammianus Marcellinus, tells of a German king who surrendered after a defeat at Strasburg. "His followers, two hundred in number, and his three most intimate friends, thinking that it would be a crime in them to survive their king, or not to die for him if occasion required, gave themselves up as prisoners." This devotion of the *comitatus* to its leader was one of the strongest forces in German political life. It persisted in the barbarian kingdoms that grew out of the wreckage of the Late Roman Empire and was one of the sources of feudalism.

As this example shows, loyalty to persons was far more important among the Germans than loyalty to institutions. The most binding obligations were to the family or to the chief to whom allegiance had been sworn. The power of a ruler depended more on his personal ability than on the position that he held. The Germans had no idea of the state, no conception of remote and impersonal authority. For this reason it was difficult to delegate power. Men feared and obeyed a ruler only when he was present. A weak deputy was ignored; a strong one usurped the place of his superior without effort. This inability to conceive of political relationships except in terms of personal contacts and loyalties long remained a weakness of the Germanic kingdoms.

The nineteenth-century idea that the early Germans formed a sort of primitive democracy is almost completely false. As we have seen, men of some families were considered noble, and they were wealthier and had greater influence than the ordinary freemen. They were the leaders, perhaps the masters, of the communities in which they lived. Even among the freemen there were great variations in wealth and prestige. And below the freemen were the half-free—perhaps remnants of conquered tribes—and the slaves. The half-free received smaller sums when they sued for compensation for their injuries in community courts; otherwise they seem to have had about the same status as the poorer freemen. The slaves tended the herds or worked small plots of lands for their neighbors; they were treated in somewhat the same way as the Roman *colonus*.

The Germans had a fairly elaborate mythology, with a dozen or so principal gods and innumerable spirits of the water and the woods. They do not, however, seem to have worried much about religious problems. A royal family gained prestige by claiming descent from a god such as Woden (Odin) but a member of such a family was not a sacred personage; he could be attacked and killed like any other man. It was prudent to reverence sacred groves and sacred trees, and to pay honor to the gods by sacrificing animals to them,[2] but the sacrifice was usually to avoid bad luck, rather than to obtain divine aid. The gods were not all-powerful, and they themselves were faced by dangerous enemies. The Germans had no strong attachment to their religion and were easily converted to other faiths. On the other hand, some of their superstitions about spirits associated with sacred wells, or sacred groves lingered on for centuries.

Eking out a bare existence in a half-cleared, thinly occupied land, subject to endless hardship and danger, the German could hardly be a cheerful, easygoing man. Even his amusements were reckless and violent. In time of peace the men loved to gather together for great drinking and gambling parties. It was no disgrace to drink for a night and a day, and they would stake all their property and even their liberty on a throw of the dice. But the great amusement was war, and courage was the great virtue, just as cowardice was the unpardonable sin. Cowards were loaded with stones and sunk in miry swamps so that their infamy might be hidden forever from human sight. Next to courage, hospitality was the

[2] Horses were the most common sacrifice, and since the sacrifice was eaten by the worshippers, in Christian times the eating of horseflesh was considered infallible evidence of pagan beliefs. This helps explain the popular prejudice against eating horsemeat.

most important virtue. It was a crime for a German to turn any man away from his door and almost as bad to be stingy with entertainment.

Some German territories, notably the region that lies in the angle between the headwaters of the Rhine and the Danube, were occupied by Rome for several centuries. Traders from the Empire visited the Germans regularly and the two peoples mixed freely in frontier districts. There was no racial hostility; individual Germans rose to high positions in Roman society and marriages between Romans and Germans were not uncommon. It is probable that the Germans became more interested and more skillful in agriculture as a result of observing Roman practices and that the area under cultivation in Germany increased. They certainly developed a taste for Roman luxuries and an admiration for the civilization that could produce them.

Border raids were frequent, and more serious incursions took place when the Empire was weak, as it was in the third century. But centuries of sporadic fighting left surprisingly little ill-feeling on either side. Until the very end of the Empire the Germans were usually defeated in any prolonged campaign, but they learned from their defeats.

Such were the Germans of the age of Tacitus. During the next three centuries they seem to have become somewhat more advanced in political and economic organization. This is not surprising, since they were in constant contact with the Romans during this time. There was an old tradition of hostility between the two peoples, going back to the first century B. C., but even in war the Germans learned from the Romans. By the end of the fourth century, they were as good soldiers as the Romans, and their commanders were not inferior to imperial generals. To hold their own with the Romans they had had to form larger political units and place more power in the hands of one man. Small groups coalesced to form great confederations, and most of the confederations were ruled by a single king instead of a group of chiefs. For example, the Alamanni, whom the Romans fought steadily in the fourth century, were a confederation whose name means simply "all men." They seem to have had only one leader, or king, in time of war. The more famous Franks, or "freemen," were also a confederation which developed rather late in German history. Even peoples who were not in direct contact with the Romans had to combine in order to protect themselves from such confederations.

Finally, there were many Germans living in the Empire temporarily or permanently. It was a regular Roman practice to demand that the leading families of defeated peoples send hostages to Rome. These hostages were shown the splendor of Roman civilization; the younger ones received a Roman education, and when they returned home they introduced Roman ideas and frequently supported Roman policy. There were also many Germanic peoples settled within the Empire. The lands held by the Romans were very thinly populated by our standards, and there seems to have been an actual decline in population during the last centuries of the Empire. The emperors felt keenly the shortage of manpower and saw no danger in admitting Germanic groups which had been weakened by defeats inflicted on them by the Romans or by fellow-Germans. These groups were settled in exposed regions where Roman farmers had been discouraged by constant raids. They cultivated the fields and formed a sort of border militia which protected the Empire against the attacks of their kinsmen. As the number of Romans available for military service decreased, the regular army also became Germanized. By the fourth century the bulk of the army, including the highest officers, was composed of Germans. Here also the Empire was barbarized long before the so-called "barbarian invasions."

The Germans were more powerful and better organized in the fourth century than they had been before; the Empire was undoubtedly weaker. Yet the Germans had no idea of uniting to overthrow Rome. They still hated each other as much, if not more, than they did the Romans. German soldiers served Rome faithfully against their fellow-Germans. The prestige of Rome was still great, and Roman diplomacy was very active among the Germans. Many leaders received regular subventions from the imperial government, conditional on their good behavior. Roman agents persuaded dangerous federations to make war on each other. Thus Ammianus Marcellinus tells us that the emperor Julian, threatened with attacks from the Alamanni, "decided to weaken them by stirring up against them the Burgundians, a warlike people, whose flourishing condition was due to the immense number of their young men, and who were therefore to be feared by all their neighbors."

The Germans probably had a higher opinion of Roman civilization than many Romans. They wished to enjoy it, not to destroy it. If they could obtain the advantages of Roman civilization by settling in the Empire and serving Rome, they were glad to do so. If not, they could at least obtain a few Roman luxuries by border raids. Their deliberate policy hardly went further than this, and had it not been for outside forces, the old relations between Romans and Germans might have continued for many more years.

THE MIGRATIONS

For many generations Germanic groups had been slowly migrating, usually toward the south. A folk defeated in war would seek to put more distance between itself and its enemies. Victorious peoples needed more space for their growing population. Even if the population remained stationary, a folk might have to change its home because primitive methods of agriculture had exhausted the soil, or because pasture for cattle was inadequate. There was a general desire to move to the sunny southern lands where the winter cold was not so severe, and where the ground was not encumbered by forests and swamps. Thus, in the first century B.C. the Cimbri and the Teutons had tried to seize the Po Valley, and the Helvetians had sought the fertile fields of Burgundy. These movements into the Roman sphere of influence had failed, and later direct attacks on the Empire had gained comparatively little territory. Therefore the stronger groups turned southeastward toward the Russian plains. Here there was little resistance, for the Slavs at this time were weak and unorganized. They were a fluid, unresisting people, able to fight only when led by foreigners, holding only the lands which no one else wanted. The easternmost Germans, the Ostrogoths, pushed far out into the plains above the Black Sea. Next to them were the Visigoths; and near the Visigoths, on the middle Danube between the present sites of Vienna and Budapest, were the Vandals. These three east German peoples had moved considerable distances, and had naturally caused other migrations as they seized new territories and abandoned old ones.

The western Germans never moved as far as those of the East, but the federations that they had formed pressed heavily on Gaul and Britain. Furthest south were the Alamanni in the angle formed by the Rhine and the Danube. The Burgundians were located in the region of the middle Rhine and the Ripuarian (river) Franks held lands along the lower Rhine. Just across the Rhine in the lowlands of northern Gaul were the Salian (seacoast) Franks, who had been given lands in this deserted corner of the Empire by the emperor Julian. The Angles and the Saxons, less unified than the groups mentioned above, lived on the shores of the North Sea between the Rhine and the Elbe. Further to the east were the Lombards, about whom little is known at this time. There were other Germanic groups in the interior, but the people named above were the ones who played the largest role in partitioning the Empire.

The expansion of the eastern Germans toward the Black Sea region might eventually have relieved pressure on the Roman frontiers if Europe had been insulated from Asia. But there is no geographic barrier between Europe and Asia, and until the creation of a strong Russian state there was no political barrier to protect the West from the shock of Asian invasions. The Urals are no great obstacle and in any case there is a wide corridor between the Urals and the Caspian Sea through which successive hordes have driven into the heart of Europe. From the fourth to the thirteenth century, Huns and Hungarians, Avars and Bulgars, Petchenegs and Mongols poured through that gateway, and did untold harm to the civilizations of eastern Europe.

These invaders all belonged to the same general stock, the Ural-Altaian. They were the nomads who lived on the roof of the world, the great plateaus of central Asia. Excellent horsemen, inured to extremes of heat and cold, used to traveling a thousand miles between summer and winter pastures, it was no great effort for them to raid a people who lived three thousand miles away. Fortunately for their neighbors, their nomadic habits made it difficult to organize them into an effective fighting force; ordinarily they were divided into small groups which had little contact with each other. But this lack of organization made it easy for a great warrior to gain power with a handful of men. The scattered nomads could not resist even a small army and most of them would rush to join the conqueror to avoid the penalties of a defeat. The nomad armies grew like avalanches, and like avalanches they descended with terrifying speed on the coastal civilizations of China, India, or Europe. In this way an empire greater than that of Rome might be created in twenty years.

The nomads were expanding in the fourth century. One group was attacking China; another group, the Huns, was moving toward the west, picking up the remnants of tribes which had failed to join the attack on China. Their army grew in the usual snowballing way, and when they burst out on the Russian plains about 370 A.D. no German people could stand against them. The Ostrogoths, who were the first to meet them, suffered a crushing defeat, and the other Germans became panic-stricken. The terror caused by the Huns drove the Germans back against the Empire. and each other. The resulting pressures were too great to be resisted by the weakened Roman state, and many of the German peoples crossed the frontier, either with or without the consent of the imperial government.

Most terrified of all were the Visigoths, since the collapse of the Ostrogothic kingdom left them exposed to the Huns. They felt that it was hopeless to fight and humbly begged the emperor to protect them by allowing them to cross the Danube and settle in Roman territory. They were already allies of the Romans and received a regular subsidy for guarding their side of the river, so there was nothing strange in their request. Many other Germans had been admitted to the Empire in similar circumstances. Moreover, the Visigoths had absorbed a great deal of Roman civilization, and some of them were Christians even before the Council of Nicaea (325 A.D.), since a Gothic bishop attended that meeting. Many more converts were made by Ulfilas, the great missionary to the Goths. He was born about 311 A.D. and was sent to Constantinople in his youth, probably as a hostage. There he learned Greek and Latin and was converted to Arian Christianity. He was consecrated as a missionary bishop in 341 and for the next forty years worked among his countrymen. For their sake he translated most of the Bible into Gothic, omitting the books of Samuel and Kings, which are so full of fighting. As he said, "The nation was already very fond of war, and needed the bit rather than the spur, so far as fighting was concerned." In order to make his translation, Ulfilas had to invent an alphabet, based on Greek letters, with some additional forms borrowed from old Gothic runes or the Roman alphabet. A large portion of his version has been preserved and forms the chief basis for the study of the early Germanic languages. Through his efforts the Arian form of Christianity was adopted by many of the Visigoths and from them it spread to other Germanic peoples. Unfortunately, the Arian creed which he taught had been condemned as heretical by the orthodox church, and many Germans who considered themselves good Christians received a rude shock when they entered the Empire.

Thus the Goths, who were Christians and allies, might well have seemed sufficiently civilized to be no danger to the Empire. Yet the emperor hesitated before admitting them, perhaps on account of their numbers. They were one of the larger Germanic peoples. One estimate, certainly exaggerated, puts the total at a million. However, in 376 the emperor Valens finally gave them permission to cross the Danube, but ordered that all their weapons must be surrendered. Unfortunately, the Roman troops sent to enforce this order were more interested in rape and robbery than in depriving the warriors of their swords and shields. They seized the young women, sold children into slavery, and plundered the wagons in which the Goths had stored their property. Once the Germans had crossed the river, there was difficulty in finding food for them at reasonable prices. According to one chronicler, Roman officials traded dogs for German slaves.

Germanic warriors were easily angered, and the Visigoths certainly had grievances against imperial officials. They began to plunder the countryside in order to meet their needs. After some indecisive fighting, the emperor Valens attempted to crush them. In a pitched battle near Adrianople, 9 August 378, "the lines dashed against each other, like the beaks of ships." After a hard fight the Romans were routed. The emperor was slain, with almost two-thirds of his army, and for a short time the East was almost without protection.

The soldiers lost at Adrianople were never fully replaced, and from that time on Rome could not guard her outlying frontiers. Yet the immediate results of the battle were not disastrous. The Goths were rather puzzled as to what to do with their victory; they needed an emperor to use them and to pay them. They wandered about plundering, but made no effort to set up an independent government. When Valens was replaced by Theodosius, the last of the great emperors, they made peace with him quickly and fought loyally for him during his reign. Until his death in 395, Theodosius held the Empire together by his military ability and his skill in dealing with the Germans.

Theodosius left the Empire to his two sons, Arcadius and Honorius, the former ruling from Constantinople and the latter from Ravenna. Both were under age and actual power was in the hands of their ministers. The most important of these ministers was Stilicho the Vandal, who was the real ruler of the West. Other officials were jealous of him and he was often too busy defending himself to defend the Empire. Alaric, the leader of the Visigoths, hoped to profit from this dissension and asked for a high command in the Roman army. When his request was refused he persuaded his people to revolt. Thus the great migration of the Visigoths began, which was to last more than a generation.

The first move of the Visigoths was to pillage Thessaly and Greece. Stilicho pursued them and apparently had them trapped, but they escaped his army either through his carelessness or by his collusion. He may have felt it foolish to destroy good soldiers whom he hoped to control. After this episode Alaric was made governor of Illyricum, and the Visigoths settled down there for four years. Then in 401 they invaded Italy and fought an indecisive campaign with Stilicho during the next two years. In spite of the invasion they were again enrolled in the Roman army when the fighting was over. But the emperor Honorius was jealous of Stilicho and in 408 had him put to death on charges of treason and collusion with the barbarians. It seems quite possible that Stilicho was using the Visigoths for his own purposes, but at least he was able to hold them in check, a feat of which his successors were incapable.

As soon as he heard of Stilicho's death Alaric began to threaten Rome. He seems to have hoped to blackmail Honorius into giving him an annual subsidy in grain and money, and recognizing him as ruler of the country around the head of the Adriatic. Honorius was safe in impregnable Ravenna and was rather slow in meeting Alaric's terms. The Visigoths finally lost patience and marched on Rome, capturing the city in August, 410. The Romans were robbed, but the lives of most of the population were spared and little permanent damage was done to the city. Nobles from Gaul who visited Rome after 410 still spoke of it as a great and flourishing city.

The capture of Rome did not disturb the incompetent emperor, who seems to have been incapable of any deeper emotions than fear and jealousy, but it was a tremendous shock to other Romans, and it dealt another blow to Roman prestige among the Germans. The pagan minority attributed the fate of Rome to the anger of the gods whose altars had been deserted. It was in answer to these critics that St. Augustine wrote his great book on *The City of God*. His central idea was: "The City of God abideth forever, though the greatest city of the world has fallen in ruin."

Alaric died soon after the capture of Rome. As before, the Goths seemed to have little idea of what to do with their victory. Food was scarce in Italy and the Goths showed no desire to found an independent kingdom in the peninsula. Finally, Alaric's successor led them out of Italy through southern Gaul to Spain. There they defeated a small Germanic group (the Suevi), who had occupied much of Spain while the Goths were distracting the attention of the central authorities. After disposing of these rivals, the Visigoths finally settled down and established a kingdom that included most of Spain and the southwestern portion of Gaul. They had complete control of the government of these regions, yet they still claimed to be soldiers of the Empire. This was not mere pretense; they fought for the Empire under the command of a Roman general in the great battle against the Huns in 451. They remained faithful to Alaric's plan of making the Goths an autonomous people *within* the Empire—a people which would have full powers of government in its own territory, while respecting the unity of the Roman world and the preëminence of the emperor.

The curious relationship between Goths and Romans may be illustrated by a romantic story which, strangely enough, has been overlooked by the historical novelist. The incompetent emperors Honorius and Arcadius had a sister, Galla Placidia, who seems to have been the best man of the family. This lady was captured by the Visigoths during an attack on Rome. She was well treated, but was kept a prisoner while Alaric tried to extort favorable terms from Honorius as a condition of her return. After Alaric's death his brother Athaulf fell in love with Placidia and they were eventually married. A year later Placidia was left a widow by the murder of her husband. She was treated with great ignominy by his successor, who, fortunately for her, lived only a few days. The next Gothic ruler sent her back to her brother in order to get supplies and recognition of his position in Gaul. Once in Italy, she married a former suitor, an able Roman general, who eventually became co-emperor with Honorius. By him she became the mother of the future Valentinian III, but soon after the child's birth both her husband and her brother died. She knew another period of adversity during the brief reign of a usurper, but Valentinian was soon recognized as emperor. Since he was only seven, Galla Placidia became regent and for the next twenty-five years, from 425 to 450, she was the actual ruler in the West. This is the barest outline of the story of this remarkable woman who was queen of the Goths and empress of Rome.[3]

When Alaric began the invasion of Italy, Roman troops had to be recalled from the Rhine and upper Danube frontiers. The Germans

---

[3] The tomb of Galla Placidia at Ravenna is one of the most important architectural monuments of the period. The body of the empress was embalmed, dressed in royal robes and placed in a sitting position in the tomb. For over a thousand years she could be seen there, but unfortunately some children, playing with a torch, set fire to the body and burned it to ashes. See Hodgkin, *Italy and Her Invaders,* I, 888.

massed in this region seized the opportunity to enter the Empire. Among the first of these people to move were the Vandals, accompanied by smaller groups from other tribes. After crossing Gaul, they tried to take over Spain, but could not hold it against the Visigoths, who were theoretically acting in behalf of the legitimate emperor. While the Vandals retained the southern part of Spain until 428 or 429, they were harassed by their northern neighbors, and eventually their leader Gaiseric decided to move to Africa. Before crossing the straits, Gaiseric ordered his people to be counted and is said to have found that there were eighty thousand males, including old men and babies.[4] Probably no more than half of these could be counted on for fighting. This gives a rough indication of how insignificant the Germans were in relation to the total Roman population. If the Romans could have used all their manpower against the Germans, the barbarians would have been in a hopeless position.

Roman Africa was no more united in opposition to the Germans than was Spain or Gaul. There were jealousies among imperial officials, and one group allied themselves with the Vandals. Gaiseric and his followers moved along slowly, taking one Roman province after another. They were momentarily checked at Augustine's city of Hippo, which they besieged in vain for fourteen months. The aged bishop finished his last book during the siege, but died before the Vandals abandoned the attack. However, when Carthage fell in 439, the Vandals were masters of all of North Africa. From this base they turned to the sea and soon became noted pirates. In 455 they made a famous raid on Rome which has given them undeserved notoriety. As in Africa, they were called in by one faction of Romans eager for revenge on their opponents. The Vandals found the city defenseless and they sacked it thoroughly and leisurely for fourteen days. They had promised Pope Leo, who had tried to restrain them, that there would be no murder, no torture, and no arson, and on the whole they kept their word. They did little wanton damage; they were guilty of systematic robbery rather than of "vandalism." Later Roman emperors did much more harm to the city by removing the metal roofs of public buildings to make armor and weapons.

In Africa the Vandals ruined many rich Romans by seizing much of their land and imposing heavy taxes on the rest. They were Arians, and frequently destroyed Catholic churches, or handed them over to heretical congregations. But they did not oppress the poor as the Romans had done, and a Catholic contemporary admits that they raised the standard of morality in the kingdom.

While the great Gaiseric lived, the Vandals were a power in Mediter-

---

[4] The eighty thousand may even have included all the people; numerical statements at this time are never clear and can seldom be trusted completely.

ranean politics. After his death in 477, they declined rapidly. They had never been very numerous, and as they mixed with the Romans they lost their fighting ability. Probably, in absorbing Roman civilization, they absorbed its political and economic weaknesses. In 534 the Vandal kingdom was conquered in a single campaign by a Roman general sent out from Constantinople, and the Vandals ceased to exist as a separate people. It is interesting to note that the inhabitants of North Africa regretted the easy rule of the Vandals when Roman methods of taxation were reintroduced after the conquest.

The migrations of the Visigoths and the Vandals are especially interesting because these two peoples passed through all sections of the Empire except Britain and the extreme East. They showed that everywhere the Empire was weak; Roman officials were jealous of each other, and the population was indifferent to a change of rulers. The other migrations may be dealt with more summarily, as they merely illustrate the same points.

The Burgundians became restive when they saw the march of the Visigoths and the Vandals, and they were allowed by Honorius to enter the Empire. When they seized too much territory, they were badly defeated by a Roman army, but the remnant of the people were allowed to keep the land near the lake of Geneva. From this base they pushed forward again into the valley of the Rhône, where they formed a Burgundian kingdom. The Franks, who already had a foothold in the Low Countries, were allowed to cross the Rhine and to settle in northeastern Gaul. Here another barbarian kingdom arose, eventually to be the strongest of all. A little later the Angles, Saxons, and Jutes began the conquest of Britain. The Roman garrison had been withdrawn from the island soon after 400 by generals who were fighting for the imperial title. Britain, left to its own devices, seems to have split into petty states which could not coöperate with each other. As a result there was no central authority to deal with the invading Germans, and Britain suffered more from them than any other province.

On the continent the position of the Germans was regularized by officials of the dying Empire. The barbarians were enrolled as soldiers in the imperial army, they were assigned lands for settlement, and they were accepted as lawful rulers by the Roman population. They did not have to act as conquerors and they did very little damage to Roman civilization. But in Britain no one had authority to make arrangements with the Angles and Saxons, who seem to have been more ferocious and less Romanized than other Germans. As a result the island had to be conquered foot by foot; after a century and a half of fighting the native population was still holding out in the West. Roman civilization, Roman cities, and the Christian religion practically disappeared in England.

While the outlying provinces dropped off one by one, Italy remained subject to the emperor. During the long reign of the weak Valentinian III, court politics were dominated by the emperor's mother, Galla Placidia, while the army was controlled by Aëtius. Aëtius, the last great Roman general in the West, was of barbarian descent, and his childhood was spend as a hostage among the Huns. By skilfully playing off one barbarian people against another he maintained the balance of power in the West, and preserved a semblance of imperial suzerainty even in the abandoned provinces. He succeeded in making the Vandals agree to pay tribute in 435; he checked the Burgundians in 437; he restricted the Franks to a relatively small part of Gaul, and even checked the powerful Visigoths. Because of his early life among the Huns, he was on friendly terms with that people, and frequently used Hunnish troops in his operations against the Germans. Yet when the Huns became dangerous, he was able to use German troops to defeat them. In short, he had mastered the Roman principle of "divide and rule," and if he had had equally able successors, the Empire might have retained Italy and even part of Gaul.

The importance of the victory won by Aëtius over the Huns has often been exaggerated. While the Huns dominated many German tribes of central Europe, their chief strength was in the East, and the eastern part of the Empire had suffered more from their raids than the West. They were showing a tendency to break up into small groups when they were united by Attila, "the scourge of God" (434–453). He first raided the East and forced the emperor at Constantinople to pay a large sum of gold and promise an annual tribute in return for peace. He then turned to the West and invaded Gaul with a force which included many Germans. Aëtius met him near Troyes in the summer of 451 with an army which was also largely German. Attila was defeated, largely by the bravery of the Visigoths who were fighting for Rome, but his army was by no means destroyed. The next year he invaded Italy, razed Aquilea to the ground, and plundered or took ransom from many other cities. Venice is said to have been founded at this time by fugitives who fled to its mud-banks in terror at the approach of the Huns. Attila approached Rome, but was persuaded to make peace and withdraw by Pope Leo. The troops of the Huns were suffering from disease and famine and were harassed by a Roman army, so that the efficacy of Pope Leo's action does not have to be explained, as it later was, by a miracle. Nevertheless, it should be noted that the pope, and not the emperor, protected Rome. Attila died the next year, and with his death the empire of the Huns crumbled to pieces.

It should be clear from the sketch above that Aëtius did not give Attila a decisive defeat, that the collapse of Attila's empire was not due

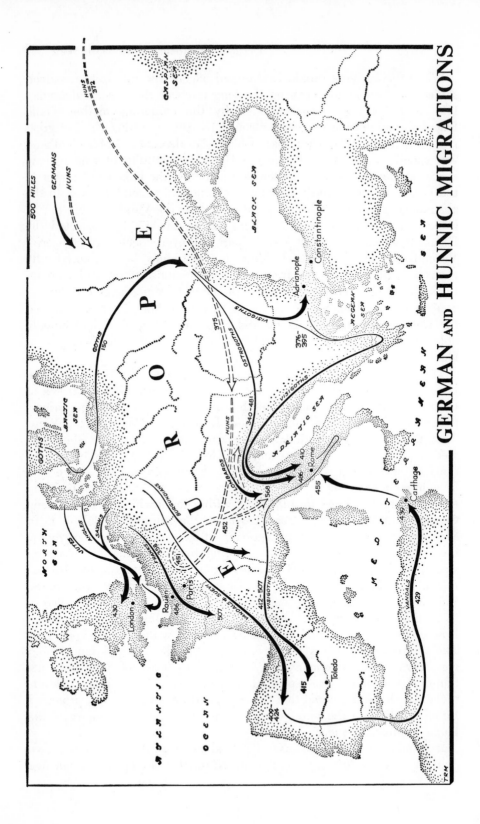

GERMAN AND HUNNIC MIGRATIONS

to the efforts of Roman army, and that European civilization, such as it was at the time, was not greatly endangered by the Huns. The Huns had already passed the peak of their power in Attila's day and were depending on their German subjects and allies. Regions occupied by the Huns for a century did not become Asiatic in civilization. Even if Attila had conquered Gaul, his successors would have lost it in a few years, as they lost most of his other territories.

Aëtius' victory over the Huns gained him little favor with the emperor. Valentinian naturally distrusted a general who was too clever, and Aëtius had a bad record of political intrigues. The emperor was easily persuaded that Aëtius was a traitor and murdered him with his own hands. Aëtius was avenged, curiously enough, by two Huns who had been in his service and who seized the first opportunity of murdering Valentinian. This double assassination was followed by the Vandal sack of Rome in 455. If any date can be taken to mark the end of Roman political power in the West this year has as good a claim as any. After 455 neither the emperors nor their generals had much influence outside Italy.

The list of ephemeral emperors after Valentinian has no significance. These rulers were puppets; the remains of the Roman Empire in the West were controlled by the commanders of the army. Unfortunately, none of these men were as able as Stilicho or Aëtius, and their attention was absorbed by political intrigues in Italy. In 475 one of these generals had his little son, Romulus, proclaimed emperor. Romulus was called Augustulus, "the baby emperor," and before he could live down the title, the barbarian troops revolted against his father. The leader of the uprising, Odovacar the German, deposed Romulus, "but granted him his life, pitying his infancy, and because he was comely." Odovacar did not replace Romulus with a new puppet. Instead he had the Roman Senate write to Constantinople that a separate emperor in the West was no longer necessary. One emperor was enough; Italy would be under his suzerainty; and Odovacar was just the man to rule Italy for him.

This is what happened in the year 476, and it has frequently been called the "fall of the Roman Empire." This seems to exaggerate the importance of an event which was neither unique nor catastrophic. Another province had come under the control of a German king, that was all. It was shocking, perhaps, that this new German kingdom was in Italy, the old center of the Empire, but even for this there were precedents. Italy had in fact been controlled by barbarian or semi-barbarian generals ever since the time of Stilicho, and there had been years before 476 when there was no emperor in the West. Rome and Italy had been declining in importance for the last three centuries, especially since Constantine had founded his new capital on the Bosporus. The strength of the Empire was in the East in the fifth century and Odovacar's act did not injure the power of the emperor at Constantinople. No one felt that the Empire ended in 476, or that Italy was outside the Empire after that date. There was only one Empire, whether there were one, two, or four emperors; there was only one Empire, even if barbarian peoples within the Empire claimed autonomy. The emperor at Constantinople asserted his authority in the West as soon as possible after Odovacar's seizure of power.

To regain control of the West he adopted the old policy of setting one German people against another. The East at this time was suffering from a rebellion of the Ostrogoths. The remnant of this people, after escaping from the Huns, had entered and served the Empire, but as they grew stronger they became unruly. They had a remarkable leader, Theodoric, who had been a hostage at Constantinople, and later a commander in the imperial army. He was a great admirer of Roman civilization and had received the high Roman titles of senator, patrician, and consul. Yet, like most Germans in the service of Rome, he felt that he and his people deserved more political power and a greater share of Roman wealth than they were given. He started a rebellion and had reached the gates of Constantinople when the emperor succeeded in making terms with him. It was agreed that Theodoric was to subdue Odovacar and act as the emperor's representative in the West. Thus the authority of the Empire would be reasserted where it was weakest, and the dangerous Ostrogoths would be removed from the neighborhood of the capital.

The plan worked to the satisfaction of both parties. After some hard fighting, Odovacar was defeated and killed, and Theodoric became master of Italy in 493. He founded an Ostrogothic kingdom which preserved Roman civilization as far as was possible. The suzerainty of the emperor was admitted; his image was placed on coins; the Roman administrative system was preserved. Yet in actual practice Theodoric had independent power in Italy. His policy toward the other German kings was very like that of Aëtius. By skilful diplomacy and threats of force he kept the balance of power and preserved at least the memory of imperial unity among the peoples of the West. But with all his reverence for Roman tradition Theodoric was a German king rather than an imperial general, and his triumph meant that all the West was now subject to barbarian rulers.

THE GERMANIC KINGDOM OF ITALY

In spite of Theodoric's success, or rather, because of it, the Roman Empire was dead as a political organization in the West by the year 500. It did survive as a political ideal, and its culture and economic organization remained dominant everywhere except in Britain. But the political history of the West after 500 is the history of the barbarian kingdoms rather than the history of the Empire. Theodoric's presence in Italy prevented the emperor from intervening directly in the West, and to other rulers Theodoric's position as king of the Ostrogoths was more important than his position as representative of imperial authority.

This division of the West into separate kingdoms ruled by barbarians shows again the fundamental weakness of the Empire. The Germans were a minority, usually a very small minority, everywhere. Yet the Roman population acquiesced in their rule, and does not seem to have regretted either the loss of political unity or the collapse of the imperial administrative system. Political unity had not made the West economically interdependent, and the division of that region into separate kingdoms does not seem to have made the economic situation any worse than it was. Ordinary trade was already on a local basis, and the luxury trade with the East was not greatly affected by the loss of political unity. There was no reason for the inhabitants of the West to regret the imperial government, which had given neither prosperity nor protection in recent years in return for the taxes it collected. Men who had lost their freedom took no interest in politics; political life in the cities was dead; and the land-owning class, secluded on its estates, seems to have hoped that the new rulers would not interfere with a comfortable, gentlemanly life.

In short, the inhabitants of the West felt that the Empire was not worth making an effort to preserve. There were many contributory reasons for this feeling. Declining population made it hard to support an elaborate administrative system or to defend the frontiers. Lack of original ideas and excessive veneration of the past made the upper classes indifferent to and ignorant of contemporary conditions. Preoccupation with religion took the place of patriotism among the lower classes. Yet it is hard to avoid the conclusion that all these phenomena were surface manifestations of a profound economic maladjustment which was responsible for loss of initiative, declining population, and general discontent and unhappiness. The best proof of this statement lies in the fact that the Empire survived in the East. The East suffered from most of the weaknesses of the West. It was as badly governed and as heavily taxed; its population was even more mixed and its basic culture was older; it was even more interested in religion and the future life. The one great contrast between the East and the West was economic. The East had an active trade and a certain amount of industry. Eastern merchants were middlemen between Persia, India and China, and the West. Eastern cities were prosperous when Western towns were ruined. As we shall see later, the East had other things in its favor, including a certain amount of pure luck, but the economic advantage seems to have been the most important.

The West was ready to abandon Roman political organization, while preserving Roman culture and most of the Roman economic system. This seems to have been the desire of both Germans and Romans. The Germans wanted to enjoy the Roman standard of living without subjecting themselves to the emperor. The Romans wanted to live on as Romans without supporting the burden of taxes and the bureaucracy. This attitude appears everywhere, but is most marked in Italy under the rule of Theodoric.

Under Theodoric the Romans preserved their own system of law, their own courts, and their own administrative system. High officials were named by the king, but since Romans of good family were ready to serve him, this worked no hardship on the native population. In fact, the government seems to have been more honest and more efficient at this time than under the last western emperors. The Goths had complete control of the army, and they were tried by their own law in their own courts, but since they were not numerous this caused no more confusion than the existence of military courts does today. Suits between Romans and Goths were tried in mixed courts. The Goths received a share, perhaps as much as one-third, of the lands in Italy, but the distribution was made by Roman officials, apparently without violence. Italy was one of the regions where it seems most certain that the population had declined, and for this reason there should have been plenty of land. It is also possible that earlier German armies, such as that of Odovacar, had received lands, and that the Goths merely took over these holdings. They seem to have adopted Roman agricultural practices, including the *villa* system.

It will be remembered that Theodoric was a great admirer of Roman learning. He tried to encourage intellectual work by attracting leading Roman writers to his court. Thus his secretary was Cassiodorus, a Roman of illustrious descent, and one of the most learned men of his day. The letters which Cassiodorus wrote are curious productions by our standards, for he could not issue the simplest administrative order without displaying his rhetorical skill and his stock of recondite information. When Theodoric had to decide what was to be done with a murderer who had taken refuge in a church, Cassiodorus' version of the sentence was as follows:

We decide that capital punishment shall be remitted out of reverence for his place of refuge, but he shall be banished to the Vulcanian (Lipari) islands, there to live away from the paternal hearth, but ever in the midst of burning, like a salamander, which is a small and subtile beast, of kin to the slippery worm, clothed with a yellow color. The substance of volcanoes, which is perpetually destroyed, is by the inexplicable power of nature perpetually renewed. The Vulcanian islands are named for Vulcan, the god of fire, and burst into eruption on the day when Hannibal took poison at the court of Prusias. It is especially wonderful that a mountain kindling into such a multitude of flames, should be half-hidden by the waves of the sea.[5]

It must have been a consolation to the murderer to receive such an interesting sentence. But while Cassiodorus was something of a pedant, he had a real desire to preserve, as far as he could, the old Roman learning. When he retired from public life he founded a monastery on his ancestral estate in southern Italy, and drew up an elaborate program of reading in both secular and religious literature for his monks. It was far too ambitious to be fully carried out, but it certainly encouraged scholarship in an age in which scholarship was difficult, and it may have helped to preserve certain classical works. The idea that a monastery should be a center of learning owes much to Cassiodorus.

Another Roman scholar in the service of Theodoric was Boëthius. Like Cassiodorus he came of a good family and received an excellent education. He held high office under Theodoric, but his chief interest seems to have been his literary work. Unlike most of his contemporaries, he was well aware of the value of Greek learning, and he developed the ambitious plan of translating all the key works of Greek science and logic into Latin. Unfortunately, he was able to complete only a few of these translations: some elementary Aristotelian works on logic, an arithmetic, a tract on music, and perhaps one or two other mathematical treatises. This was a mere fragment of Greek science, but it was enough to keep alive some interest in these subjects, and eventually to stimulate an effort to recover more Greek knowledge.

Just at the height of his career, Boëthius was accused of treason, whether justly or not, it is now impossible to decide, and was cast into prison. There he composed the last great work of Roman eloquence, *The Consolation of Philosophy,* a book which remained popular for over a thousand years, and was translated by both Alfred the Great and Chaucer. As its title suggests, Boëthius attempted to console himself in his misfortune by meditations on philosophical, or rather ethical, topics. Though Boëthius was a Christian, the tone of the work is that of the old Roman Stoics. Worldly riches and honors are unimportant; the wise and self-controlled man can rise above all misfortune and draw an inner strength from his understanding of the vanity of human desires. Soon after finishing the book Boëthius was condemned by the senate at the behest of Theodoric and was executed in 524.

Theodoric tried to preserve other elements of Roman civilization in addition to literature. He fostered agriculture, repaired the roads, and kept up the aqueducts. He gave careful attention to the preservation of public buildings and monuments and built new ones. He even continued the old tradition of "bread and games" for the proletariat at Rome. He

[5] As translated by Hodgkin, in *Letters of Cassiodorus.*

gave Italy the last long period of peace it was to know for centuries and established his frontiers on the Danube and the Rhône. Yet he was unable to establish an enduring state or to ensure future prosperity for the civilization he so admired.

Theodoric's great difficulty seems to have been that both he and most of his people were Arians. Personally he was quite tolerant, as is shown by letters which he dictated:

> We cannot order a religion because no one is forced to believe against his will. . . . To pretend to rule over the spirits is to usurp the rights of the Divinity. The power of the greatest sovereigns is limited to exterior police. They have a right to punish only the disturbers of the public order, which is placed under their guard, and the most dangerous heresy is that of a prince who separates from him a part of his subjects simply because they do not believe what he does.

Following these principles, Theodoric gave gifts to the Roman Church and for many years left it independent, except when a contested papal election caused disorder and bloodshed. Then he suppressed the disorder, but refused to intervene further. But the Eastern emperors were not so tolerant and persecuted Arians with increasing severity. Theodoric could not endure this attack on his fellow-religionists and toward the end of his life became much more hostile to Catholics. He grew suspicious of his Roman officials, and this very suspicion may have caused them to plot against him. Boëthius and other Roman nobles were victims of this unfortunate state of affairs, and Theodoric's last years saw a growing breach between Goth and Roman, Arian and Catholic.

Theodoric's immediate successors were incompetent and the Goths were so weakened by factional strife that they seemed to invite conquest. The emperor at Constantinople at this time was Justinian, a very ambitious ruler who dreamed of regaining all the territory which the Empire had lost in the West. His first campaign against the Vandal kingdom in Africa was a complete success, and this encouraged him to send his victorious general Belisarius against the Goths in Italy. But the Goths fought with more vigor than the Vandals, and the native population does not seem to have given much help to the imperial general. The war began in 536, but not until 554 was the last Gothic king killed, and the last Gothic army destroyed. Meanwhile there had been years of terrible fighting. Rome had endured three exhausting sieges, and other barbarians had poured across the unguarded northern frontiers. Italy suffered more from the reconquest by the Empire than it had from any of the barbarian "invasions."

Justinian regained not only Italy and Africa, but also the Mediterranean islands and, thanks to civil strife among the Visigoths, the southeastern corner of Spain. He had made great progress in his plan for reviving the Empire in the West. But he had succeeded only by imposing unendurable burdens on his subjects in the East and by destroying the most civilized and promising of the Germanic kingdoms. Worse still, his revived Empire was no more able to gain the loyalty and promote the welfare of its subjects than its predecessor had been. Italy, suffering once more from heavy taxes, misgovernment, and political intrigues, regretted the rule of the Goths. The eunuch Narses, who had succeeded Belisarius as commander of Justinian's army during the Gothic war, ruled Italy with absolute power and accumulated an enormous private fortune while he was in office. It is not surprising that there was little resistance to the new wave of German invaders.

The new invaders were the Lombards, a German people who had originally lived far from the Roman frontier, but who had moved down to the Danube border during the great migrations. There they had become allies of the Empire, and some of them had served in Italy under Narses during the final campaigns against the Goths. They had conquered a rival tribe, the Gepidæ, and had gained valuable reinforcements by absorbing fragments of other peoples, notably a large group of Saxons. Compared to the Goths, they had had little contact with Roman civilization, and they seem to have been less interested in it, or less able to adapt themselves to it.

The Lombards entered Italy in 586 under the leadership of their king Alboin. Italy, exhausted by the Gothic war, and disgusted with the imperial administration, could offer little resistance to the new invaders. All the northern part of the peninsula was overrun by the barbarians; only Rome and a few other fortified towns held out. Alboin was murdered soon after his army had overcome the last resistance in the North, and since no one was strong enough to take his place, the invaders were divided under the leadership of thirty-five dukes. This stopped their progress toward the South, and the Empire was able to preserve a few fragments of Italy, some of which it kept for centuries. These territories included Genoa, Rome, and Naples on the west coast, Venice with its hinterland, Ravenna, and the region around Ancona on the east coast, Perugia and surrounding lands in the center, and the whole heel and toe of the peninsula.

This division of Italy between Lombard and imperial holdings influenced the political and social development of the country down to the present day. From the Lombard invasion to the reign of Victor Emmanuel II, Italy was never united under one government. The invaders were numerous in the North, especially in the region which is now known as Lombardy, and their customs and laws had great influence there. In the South, the population was predominantly Roman, or at least non-Germanic, and remained under Roman organization.

Thus each region developed its own characteristics and the difference between them is still noticeable. The Lombards were weakened by their failure to gain all Italy, and especially by the fact that Rome itself remained in the hands of their enemies. If they could have taken Rome in their first rush into the peninsula, there would have been few protests, but later attacks on Rome were always denounced by other rulers as attacks on the pope and the Church. Even when it was reunited under a single king, the Lombard state was never very strong, since it lacked some of the chief cities of Italy and was on bad terms with the papacy. Yet, if the Lombards were weakened by the Empire's retention of part of Italy, the Empire had great difficulties in protecting its holdings. The emperor's representative, the exarch of Ravenna, was badly placed to govern and defend such widely separated lands, most of which he could reach only by sea. The emperor tended to concentrate his efforts on South Italy, the largest and wealthiest of the districts still under his control. The papacy profited from these conditions. The pope usually had greater prestige than any official in Rome, and he was frequently the outstanding representative of Roman authority in all North Italy. As a result, the pope became temporal ruler of the city of Rome with its dependent territories and gradually developed claims to other imperial lands in the North, especially the strip running across the peninsula through Perugia to Ancona and Ravenna. Thus began the political power of the papacy and the first idea of a papal state.

THE RISE OF THE FRANKS

Had it not been for Justinian's attack, the Ostrogoths might have formed the dominant Germanic kingdom. As it was, the leadership of the West, which they had unquestionably possessed under Theodoric, passed to the Franks. This people had not been very important during the early migrations, and we have little authentic information about their early history. Our best source is the *History of the Franks* written by Bishop Gregory of Tours, in the latter half of the sixth century. But while Gregory was fairly accurate about events of his own time, he could not differentiate between legend and fact in the earlier period. About all that can safely be said of the Franks during their first migration is that they settled in northern and eastern Gaul, that they occupied comparatively little territory, and that they were divided into several petty kingdoms.

About 481, a boy named Clovis became king of one of these little Frankish states. His people lived in the valley of the upper Scheldt, grouped around Tournai. They were still pagan, rather backward in civilization, but excellent fighters. Clovis first led them against the Romans living in the region between the Seine and the Loire. This part of Gaul had never been occupied by Germans, but since it had been cut off from the imperial government it had fallen under the rule of a Roman noble named Syagrius. Clovis defeated him in 486, and occupied all his territories, including Paris and Orleans. Then he turned on the other Frankish kings, most of whom were his kinsmen and all of whom were potential rivals. He slew one, who had aided him in the campaign against Syagrius, for demanding a share in the spoils. He killed another for failing to aid him. A master of intrigue, perfectly unscrupulous, he soon destroyed all his relatives who were, or might be, rulers.

> Nevertheless [says Gregory], in a general assemblage he is said to have spoken concerning the kinsmen whom he had himself destroyed: "Woe is me, who have remained like a pilgrim among foreigners, and have no kinsmen to aid me, if adversity befall me." But he said this not because he grieved at their death, but with the cunning thought that he might perhaps find one still alive whom he could kill.

In 496 he subdued the Alamanni, a victory that gave him control of much of southwestern Germany. Then came a crucial campaign against the Visigoths, who held almost as much territory in the south of Gaul as Clovis possessed in the north, and in addition ruled most of Spain. In spite of their greater resources, the Visigoths were decisively defeated by the Franks at the battle of Vouillé in 507. Theodoric the Ostrogoth intervened to keep the balance of power and saved the extreme south of Gaul for the Visigoths, but they were no longer a power in the country. Clovis now ruled most of Gaul; only the Mediterranean coast and the Rhône Valley were in the hands of other rulers. No king north of the Alps was as strong as he, and the last possible danger to his leadership of his own people was ended when he succeeded in destroying the ruling family of the Ripuarian Franks soon after the victory over the Visigoths. Thus, in a quarter of a century, the insignificant kinglet of a petty tribe had become one of the most powerful men in Europe.

The most important event in the life of this bloodthirsty barbarian was his conversion to Christianity. He had married a Burgundian princess, named Clotilda, who happened to be a Catholic, although most of the Burgundians were Arians.

> Queen Clotilda did not cease to urge him to know the true God and leave his idols. But he could in no wise be moved to believe these things till at last he once on a time fell into a war against the Alamanni. When the two armies met, there was a fierce and bloody struggle, and the host of Clovis was on the point of being destroyed. Seeing this, he raised his eyes to heaven, his heart was touched, and with tearful eyes he said: "Jesus Christ, Clotilda says that you are the son of the living God, and that you give help to those in trouble, and victory to those who put their hope in you: I pray you humbly for the honor of your aid. If you will now grant me victory

over these my enemies, and if I thus experience that power which the people devoted to your name claim to have tested, I too will believe in you and be baptized in your name. For I have called on my own gods; but, as I find, they have forsaken me with their help." [6]

He won the victory and kept his promise; three thousand of his warriors were baptized at the same time. The rest of the Frankish people soon followed the example of their king and accepted the Catholic faith.

The consequences of this conversion were far-reaching, especially in political affairs. The mass baptism had little effect on the morals of Clovis and his warriors; they remained as violent and treacherous as ever. In fact, it might be said that the real work of converting the Franks to Christianity began after their baptism, and that the task took about two hundred years. But in the political sphere, Clovis' act brought immediate results. He was the first German king to become a Catholic; all his rivals were pagans or Arians. Consequently, he seemed a God-sent champion to many Catholics under Arian domination. This attitude was counteracted to some extent by the fact that both the Visigoths and Ostrogoths, who were the leading Arian peoples, were more Romanized than the barbarous Franks. A group of Romans fought for the Visigoths at Vouillé, and hostility to Frankish rule persisted in southern Gaul for many years. Yet it is true that the only equivalent for patriotism at this time was religion, and that a king who held a belief different from that of the majority of his subjects could not count on their support. We have seen how Theodoric, with all his excellent qualities, was weakened by the Arian-Catholic controversy. Other German kings had the same trouble; at best they could count on the neutrality, but not the active support of most of their Roman subjects. The Catholic Franks, on the other hand, despite their lack of Roman culture, soon gained the support of the papacy and of the bishops in Gaul, and this gave them great influence over all their subjects. Their barbarism was forgotten because of their orthodoxy. Thus Gregory of Tours sums up Clovis' career as follows: "The Lord cast his enemies under his power day after day, and increased his kingdom, because he walked with a right heart before Him, and did that which was pleasing in his sight." Such is the language used by a conscientious and upright bishop concerning a king whose hands were red with the blood of his kinsmen, treacherously slain. Clovis' orthodoxy probably played a part in inducing the emperor to confer upon him the title of consul, thus making his rule more legitimate in the eyes of his Roman subjects. Clovis also used his religion as an excuse for wars of conquest. He is said to have announced his attack on the Visigoths in these words: "I cannot endure that those Arians should

[6] Gregory of Tours' account, translated by Burr.

possess any part of Gaul. With God's aid we will go against them and conquer their lands."

Clovis died in 511, and the kingdom was divided among his four sons. They and their descendants ruled Gaul for the next two centuries. This dynasty is usually called the Merovingian, after a more or less mythical ancestor of Clovis named Meroweg. There has seldom been a ruling family whose members hated each other as bitterly, and attacked each other as treacherously, as the Merovingian. The fundamental reason for these family quarrels was the Frankish custom of dividing the kingdom among the sons of the last ruler. Each king then sought to deprive his kinsmen of their share, and battles and assassinations ended only when a lucky survivor had eliminated all his rivals. Thus Chlotar or Lothair, the youngest son of Clovis, succeeded in getting the whole kingdom into his hands by 558. In the process he murdered two of his young nephews and got rid of a rebellious son by burning him and his family alive. Even the Franks felt that this was going too far, and there was general relief when Chlotar died in 561. However, Chlotar's sons were no great improvement on their father and commenced a bloody series of civil wars which lasted until 613, when only one king was left.

In spite of the division of the kingdom and the bad feeling among members of the royal family, the Franks continued to gain power in the sixth century. This was especially true during the reigns of the sons of Clovis, who were occasionally able to coöperate. Even during the worst of the civil wars the Franks lost no territory and remained the strongest German people in the West. Their first conquest after Clovis was that of the Burgundian kingdom in the Rhône Valley. While the king of the Burgundians was a Catholic, most of his warriors were Arian, so the religious excuse could be invoked again. Provence was seized when the Ostrogothic kingdom collapsed. Across the Rhine, Bavaria and southern Thuringia were added to the Frankish domains. These successes of the Franks may seem surprising, in view of their domestic difficulties, but they had great advantages over their rivals. As we have seen, they were favored by the Church, and in the long run they obtained more active support from their Roman subjects than the other Germans. They were also aided by their geographical position. They never lost touch with Germany or with their old homes on the Rhine. They avoided the terrific wastage of manpower incurred in migrations such as those of the Goths or the Vandals; they could always replace the warriors they had lost by drawing on Germany. They balanced their acquisitions of Roman territory with conquests in Germany, thus increasing their potential manpower to meet their new defense problems. Even more important was the fact that their strength lay in the North. Thus they were shielded from the attacks which rolled up from the East and the South. The Empire under Justinian destroyed the Vandal and Ostrogothic kingdoms; the

Moslems, striking from Africa, ended the Visigothic power in Spain; but the Franks were never seriously threatened by either offensive. Finally, the division of the kingdom was not always a handicap. It was still difficult for a German ruler to govern wide territories and to keep control over distant subordinates. The Frankish kingdom was too large for any but the most able king to rule successfully; the average monarch was better obeyed and made more effective use of his resources when he had less land. After Clovis' death the Merovingian kingdom was often weakest when it was united under one ruler.

A famous historian has said that Merovingian government was "despotism tempered by assassination." The king was controlled only by his fear of his more powerful subjects. The old assembly of free men no longer met, and all decisions were made by the king alone. He was the law-giver, the supreme judge, and the head of the army. But even when divided, the Frankish kingdoms were too large for the king to enforce all his orders in person, and when he tried to delegate authority all the old political weaknesses of the Germans reappeared. The Frankish kings, unlike Theodoric, made no effort to preserve the old Roman administrative system, and their Gallo-Roman subjects seem to have had no great desire to save the old forms of government.

Instead of an elaborate hierarchy of administrators, judges, treasury agents, civil and military commanders, the kings delegated all local authority in each district to a count or a duke. These were military titles, taken over from the late Roman Empire, and one of the chief duties of the Frankish counts and dukes was to command the fighting men of their districts. They also presided in courts, where they could inflict the death sentence, and they collected all the king's local revenue. The districts which they ruled were large enough to give them a good deal of authority. A county was often an old Roman *civitas* or, in Germany, the territory which had been held by a tribe. A duchy might include several frontier counties united for purposes of defense. This concentration of power in the hands of local officials was dangerous, given the German tendency to obey the immediate, visible authority rather than a remote superior, and to be loyal to men rather than to institutions. Even worse was the fact that the counts and the dukes received no salary. They supported themselves from great estates which they inherited, or which were given them by the king. This tended to identify their interests with those of other great land-owners, who were usually very hostile to the central government. The counts and dukes also received a share of the fines they levied, which meant that they had a constant incentive to extortion and injustice. Altogether, local officials were an independent and rebellious group, and the Merovingian kings had difficulty in keeping any sort of control over them. After 600, the power of the counts, dukes, and great land-owners was usually greater than that of the king.

Only the strongest sort of central government could have controlled such powerful local officials, and the central government of the Merovingians was rudimentary and unorganized. It was composed of the men who happened to be living with the king, and any one of those men might be called on for any sort of work. There was no distinction between personal service rendered the king and political service due to the state. Thus members of the king's bodyguard might be sent on important missions to outlying provinces and frequently became counts after a certain length of service. The count of the stables, or constable, acted as a high military official. The most important member of the household was the *major domo,* a term which really means no more than "steward," but which is usually translated as "mayor of the palace." As head of the household, the mayor of the palace was also head of the administration, and he could act as the king's deputy for any purpose. Naturally, the aristocracy coveted this office and they eventually succeeded in making the mayor of the palace their representative rather than the king's. Thus the central government, which had never had adequate control over the magnates, was weakened still further.

The Frankish government performed few services for its subjects. The counts held courts in which disputes might be settled if the parties did not prefer to fight it out, and the king organized the army, for defense or attack. In contrast to the Ostrogoths, neither king nor counts were much interested in such things as education, upkeep of the roads, or public buildings. Neither the central nor the local governments spent much money. With few paid officials, administrative and judicial services cost almost nothing. All free men owed military service, and on expeditions they had to furnish their own food and equipment. Such public services were personal obligations, and men sought public office for the power it conferred, rather than for the salary attached to it. These conditions were to be typical in feudalism, and they were an important factor in bringing feudalism into existence. The fact that the government needed little money reinforced the old Roman hatred of taxation and built up such formidable prejudices that for centuries taxation was impossible. The personal expenses of the king could be met by income from his lands; there were almost no public expenses; therefore any king who asked for taxes was a bloodsucking miser. Some of the most popular saints of the Merovingian age were those who worked unpleasant miracles on tax-collectors. Some of the most unpopular kings were rulers who tried to revise the old Roman tax-lists, now sadly out of date. A story told of Chilperic, one of the strongest and most unscrupulous Merovingian kings, illustrates both these attitudes. He tried to increase his income from taxation, but his subjects rebelled and his sons fell ill. Every one was sure that this was divine vengeance on the avaricious monarch, and Chilperic, urged by his wife, finally agreed to burn the tax-registers. In the face of such beliefs, which were supported by clergy and aristocracy, general taxes could not be collected. By the end of the seventh century, taxation had ceased to be an important source of revenue for the government.

THE CIVILIZATION OF THE FRANKISH KINGDOM

The Franks were less Romanized than the Ostrogoths, especially in details of their political organization, but this does not mean that they were impervious to all Roman influences. The great majority of the population of Gaul was composed of Romanized Celts, the old senatorial aristocracy remained an important land-owning class, and the Latin language survived everywhere except in the extreme northeast. The Germans did not like to live in the cities, and the urban centers were left to the Gallo-Romans, so that at first there was comparatively little change in the life of the town-dwellers. Local administration remained in the hands of the same men, trade with the East continued, and there was no marked decrease in population. However, the new masters did nothing to improve economic conditions, and the towns continued their slow decline under Merovingian rule. After a while it seemed unnecessary to keep up the machinery of city government; the bishop became the leader of the townsmen instead of the old local officials. The counts also interfered more and more in urban affairs, and by the seventh century the town was no longer an important unit of government.

More significant than the temporary survival of the towns was the survival of the *villa* system. As in the last centuries of the Empire, the great estate remained the dominant feature of economic life. This is not surprising, since the old senatorial aristocracy survived the invasions and kept most of its prestige and much of its land. Many places in France still bear the name of the Roman who owned them when they were *villae* and show how the estate remained a unit during all the confusion of the early Middle Ages. For example, the suburbs of Passy and Clichy near Paris are the former estates of the Gallo-Romans Paccius and Clipius. The owners of these estates naturally preserved the old organization of their lands as far as possible, and the Franks imitated them. Thus, under the Merovingians, agriculture was still the chief occupation of the people, and most labor was performed by unfree or semi-free men working on the estates of great land-owners.

Another factor which tended to preserve some features of the old civilization was the use of Roman law. The Germans, when they entered the Empire, were in the stage of personal law; that is, they believed that a man, wherever he might chance to live, should be subject to the penalties and entitled to the benefits of the law of his people. Consequently, all relations between Romans continued to be regulated by Roman law. However, neither the Romans nor their German rulers had sufficient energy to master the enormous mass of Latin legal literature, so brief summaries of the law were used instead. The Visigothic king had such a compilation made for his Roman subjects about the year 506, a work known as the *Breviary of Alaric,* and other rulers followed his example. The Germans began to write down their own laws only after becoming aware of the existence of the Roman law. They also tended to adopt provisions of Roman law regulating activities with which they had been unfamiliar when they entered the Empire. Thus even the earliest German codes, such as those of the Salian Franks and the Burgundians, show some Roman influence.

The most important agency in preserving Roman civilization was the Church. Its organization continued while the old political organization slowly disintegrated. The heads of the Church were taken at first from the leading Roman families; thus Gregory of Tours boasts both of his senatorial ancestry and of the number of bishops in his family. The Church was the one institution which exercised any real restraint upon the barbarian kings and leaders, though it did not always succeed in curbing them. During the seventh century the influence of the Church became weaker. The German aristocracy began to seek high places in the Church because they conferred wealth and power; the morals and education of the clergy declined, and general councils ceased to meet because of chronic civil war. Yet, even at its worst, the Church preserved the prestige of the Roman name and did much to bring Roman and German together. The bishops were the natural intercessors between the Roman population and the German kings; the church edifice was the common asylum for all who needed protection; the monastery welcomed both Germans and Romans as members.

Latin was the language of the Church, and it was also the language of most of the population. Even the German kings used Latin in their official correspondence. Their secretaries were Romans, and, at first, laymen, which shows that some town schools must have survived the invasions. However, the great majority of the population was uneducated and spoke a vulgar Latin which was more simple and direct than the literary language. This vulgar Latin gradually replaced both the Germanic dialects spoken by the small group of invaders, and the correct Latin spoken by the educated class. Gregory of Tours, in apologizing for the rusticity of his Latin, is consoled by the fact that the ordinary man will understand him better than if he wrote really good

Latin. All the Romance (or Roman) languages—Italian, French, Provençal, Spanish, and Portuguese, are descended from the vulgar Latin. Variations among them are due partly to the isolation of one region from another while the languages were being formed, and partly also to the differences in the number and provenance of the Germans who dwelt there. But the variations do not hide the resemblances, and all these languages betray, even to the casual observer, their Latin origin.

While lay education persisted for a time, the most important schools were already controlled by the Church. As Roman civilization continued to decline, the Church gained a practical monopoly of education, at least north of the Alps. All teaching was in Latin, and since much of the old literature had been preserved by the Church, educated men were still able to read the most important works of Roman authors. But the tendency to epitomize and condense continued, and in the schools extracts rather than whole works were studied. The seven liberal arts were still taught, but in abbreviated form. For the language studies—grammar, rhetoric and logic—there were fairly good textbooks and collections of extracts, so that the student could hope to attain some proficiency in Latin. Mathematics and science, on the other hand, were often slighted, and at best were taught at a very elementary level. After the study of seven liberal arts, students might proceed to theology, which included the study of the scriptures and the church fathers.

Certain textbooks used at this time remained in favor for centuries, so that it is possible to form some conception of the basic scholastic training of medieval students. The first study was naturally the alphabet, and for this pupils were given tablets in which the individual letters were written. As soon as they had learned the alphabet, they began to read in psalters written in large letters. Sometimes they learned to read the psalter glibly without understanding a word of it. After the psalter, *Cato* was the favorite reading book. The author of *Cato* is unknown, but he lived in the third or fourth century and his little book retained its popularity for over a thousand years.[7] It contained about a hundred and fifty couplets, many of which have become common proverbs. As examples may be cited: "The chief virtue is to know how to hold your tongue." "In good fortune beware of evil, as the outcome is often different from the beginning." "Bear poverty patiently since you came into the world naked."

In connection with reading, writing was taught. Sometimes the teachers seem to have used blocks into which letters were cut deeply. The pupil followed the lines in the block with his pen until his hand was accustomed to the form of the letters. After that, or sometimes first of all, tablets covered with wax were used. At the top the teacher wrote

[7] The copy from which I am quoting was printed in 1766 in Germany. It contains the Latin distichs and, below, translations into various German meters of each couplet.

the copy, and then guided the pupil's hand while the latter formed the letters. Finally, the ablest pupils were given practice in fine writing on parchment; but as parchment was expensive, many never attained to this height.

The elementary textbook in grammar was the work of Donatus, who lived in the fourth century and may have been the teacher of St. Jerome. He wrote two books on grammar, the *Ars Minor* and the *Ars Major*. The first occupies only twelve pages in a modern printed edition and consists of elementary questions and answers, with some declensions and conjugations. It was highly appreciated in the early middle ages and remained in use for several hundred years. Of the larger work only the last part, which treated of rhetoric, was commonly used in the schools. A more advanced textbook in grammar was that of Priscian, which was full of quotations from classical authors [8] and gave some training in literature, history, and mythology.

After they had been *donatistæ*, or grammar-grade pupils, the bright boys might be introduced to Martianus Capella and his *Marriage of Mercury and Philology*. It will be remembered that this was an encyclopedic textbook, thinly disguised under the forms of allegory. Gregory of Tours praised this work highly as containing all the knowledge needful for education. Yet comparatively few students mastered even this inadequate summary of the seven liberal arts. The decline in learning, begun under the Empire, continued under the Merovingians, even though some of the sixth century kings were quite willing to patronize scholars and writers. Chilperic, who tried to restore the Roman tax system, also tried to reform spelling by inventing several new letters which he ordered to be used in all books, but he was no more successful in the field of orthography than he had been in the field of finance. Even this misguided interest in learning was lacking in the rulers of the seventh century.

Roman towns, the *villa* system, Roman law, the Catholic Church and Latin literature survived the Frankish conquest. But as time went on, the lack of vitality in Roman institutions was shown by an increasing influence of German customs. Roman forms of government gradually disappeared, and, what is even more surprising, Roman legal procedure was supplanted by the crude practices of the barbarians. Even in those regions where the substantive law remained essentially Roman, the method of trial was based on German ideas. The judicial procedure of the Franks is worth studying in some detail, since similar forms were used everywhere in the early Middle Ages. Few other activities show so clearly the low level to which civilization declined during this period.

[8] Priscian quotes the *Æneid* 721 times, Virgil's other writings 146 times, Terence, 225, Horace, 158, Juvenal, 121, Sallust, 80, Homer, 78, Ovid, 73, and Lucretius, 25 times. The preference for Virgil is noteworthy, and is continued throughout the Middle Ages.

The basic idea in Germanic procedure was not to do justice, but to stop a fight. Actual physical combat was to be transformed into a formalistic legal contest. The man who played the game with the fewest errors won the case. The court merely acted as umpire; it declared the rules of the game, announced when they had been broken, and certified the winner of the contest. The count presided in the court, but he was usually aided in his work of umpiring by the whole community, or by some of the leading citizens. The rules of the game were based on custom rather than legislation, and old inhabitants might know them much better than a newly appointed count.

The legal contest was based on the belief that God would not allow the innocent party to make errors which would cause him to lose the contest; it was an appeal to divine rather than human justice. Therefore it was considered reasonable to give the defendant an opportunity to prove his innocence, rather than to force the accuser to demonstrate his guilt. Since innocence could often be proved by relatively simple acts, it was usually advantageous for the defense to assume the burden of proof. The actual forms of proof probably go back to the pagan period, but they had been accepted and sanctified by the Church.

A defendant of high standing might be allowed to clear himself by his own oath. Thus, when Bishop Gregory of Tours was accused of calumniating the queen, he purged himself at three separate altars by performing mass and taking an oath that he was innocent. This completely cleared him, and the man who had accused Gregory was severely punished by the king. Relics were frequently used to enhance the value of an oath, and the strength of the oath varied with the sacredness of the relics. A man who perjured himself while invoking the witness of God and the saints was asking for eternal damnation. Usually, if the accused hesitated or made a slip of the tongue while reciting the words of the oath, he lost his case; God had caused him to stumble because he was a perjurer.

When the oath of the accused was deemed insufficient, other men might be required to swear that they believed he was telling the truth. This process was called compurgation and lasted in ecclesiastical courts down to modern times. At first the oath-helpers, or compurgators, were kinsmen, but later anyone who was willing could act in this capacity. The number required varied with the rank of the accused, the rank of the plaintiff, and the gravity of the crime. For example, if a noble were accused of slaying another noble he must obtain eleven compurgators; for a free man he needed only seven; and for a slave, three. A free man would need eleven compurgators if accused of the killing of another free man, seventeen for the killing of a noble, and five for the killing of a slave. In extraordinary cases, a much greater number might be required. When King Guntram announced that he doubted the legitimacy of the child

ARCH OF CONSTANTINE

•

An Early Christian Church
ST. PAUL'S-OUTSIDE-THE-WALLS

JUSTINIAN'S CHURCH OF HAGIA SOPHIA, INTERIOR

EMPRESS THEODORA
Mosaic Portraits at Ravenna, 6th Century
EMPEROR JUSTINIAN

PAGE FROM A GOTHIC BIBLE, *c.* 500

Christianity Comes to the Germans

KING ALFRED'S TRANSLATION OF POPE GREGORY'S *PASTORAL CARE*

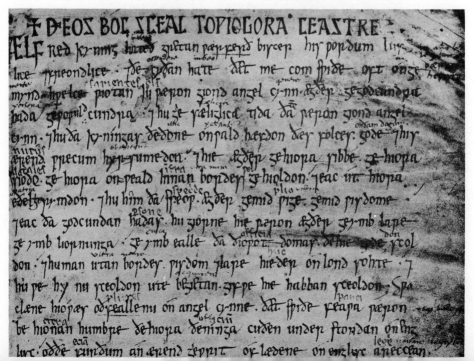

for whom his brother's kingdom was claimed, the accused queen satisfactorily established the paternity of her son by swearing with three
bishops and three hundred nobles that King Chilperic was his father.

Compurgation was usually allowed only when charges were based on
mere suspicion, or when the character of the accused made physical
tests undesirable. Thus churchmen and women were usually allowed to
clear themselves by compurgation. The physical tests were known as
ordeals; the most common were hot water, cold water, fire, or red-hot
iron. In the ordeal by hot water, a small object was dropped in a boiling
cauldron. The depth of the water often varied with the gravity of the
charge. The water was blessed, God was besought to show the right, and
the accused then took the object from the kettle. His hand was then
sealed up and left for three days or more, during which time salt and holy
water were mixed with his food. If, at the end of the period, his hand
was found "clean," that is, uninfected and with only a small scar, he was
judged innocent. The ordeal by red-hot iron was much the same. The
accused carried the hot iron a fixed number of paces and his innocence
was proved by the rapid healing of the burn. In the ordeal by cold water
the accused, after a preliminary hallowing of the water, was "bound by
a rope and cast into the water." If he floated he was considered guilty,
for, as Bishop Hincmar of Rheims claimed, "the pure nature of the
water recognizes as impure and therefore rejects as inconsistent with
itself such human nature as has once been regenerated by the waters
of baptism and is again infected by falsehood." Consequently, to prove
his innocence, the man had to sink. In the ordeal by fire, the accused
seems at first to have put his hand into the fire; later he was obliged
to walk between two burning piles of wood. The severity of the ordeal
was determined by the size of the piles and the distance between them.
These and other forms of the ordeal were frequently used, until the
custom was condemned by the Church in the thirteenth century.

A special form of ordeal which had an even longer life was the wager
of battle or judicial duel. This defense of one's honor by fighting naturally appealed to a barbarous people, and since they were sure that
God would protect the right, it seemed the most satisfactory way of
deciding important cases. It was used all over Europe to determine
purely legal questions regarding the inheritance of land. Once, in Gothic
Spain, wager of battle was used to decide which form of ritual should be
followed by the Church. Often an accused could avoid other forms of
proof by challenging his accuser to battle. Those unfit to fight, such as
women and children, were allowed to substitute champions who won or
lost in their place.

Historians have vainly sought to rationalize these methods of proof.
It may be admitted that some men were more afraid of perjury than
they were of losing a law-suit. This was by no means true of all; medieval

writers are bitter in their denunciations of the false swearing which went on every day. It may also be admitted that consciousness of guilt might lead to nervousness which would cause the accused to garble the words of an oath or lose his deftness in the physical tests. But the shock of a false accusation might cause very similar agitation. There is no reason to suppose that the Germanic methods of proof resulted in just decisions except by accident. Their one merit, as was said before, is that they stopped fights; any decision was better than a blood-feud.

When a man was convicted of wounding or killing a person, the penalty was a fine, as compensation to the injured party or his family. The amount of the fine varied according to the extent of the injury; many barbarian codes of law are nothing but long lists of offenses with their appropriate fines. One of the most detailed lists is to be found in the laws of Alfred the Great. He fixed the penalty for knocking out a front tooth at 8 shillings, a "cheek tooth" at 12 shillings, and a "man's tusk" at 15 shillings. The values of the fingers were respectively: the "shooting finger" (forefinger), 15 shillings; the middle, 12 shillings; the "gold finger" (ring finger), 17 shillings; the little finger, 9 shillings. The nails varied from 1 shilling for the little finger to 5 shillings for the thumb.

If a person were killed, the compensatory payment was called *wergeld,* and varied according to the rank of the victim. Among the Franks the *wergeld* for "a free Frank, or a barbarian living under the Salic law" was 200 shillings; for a free Roman, 100 shillings; for a Frank or a Roman in the service of the king, the respective penalties were multiplied by three. If the murderer attempted to conceal the body, the penalty was also tripled. Thus the fine was 1800 shillings when a free Frank in the service of the king had been killed and the murderer hid the body. A Roman who paid tribute was valued at only 63 shillings, while the slaying of a Frankish boy under ten years of age involved a fine of 600. The penalties for women varied not only according to rank but also according to the possibility of their having offspring. Thus a woman who had begun to bear children was valued at 600, one who was pregnant at 700, but one who had passed the child-bearing age at only 200 shillings. In connection with these penalties, it should be pointed out that the value of money at the time was so great that a fine of a few hundred shillings would ruin even a wealthy man. A poor man faced with a heavy fine would have to flee the country and become an outlaw.

While Romans had an inferior position in the Salic law, this did not keep them from rising to high positions under the Merovingians. The king's secretaries were almost always Gallo-Romans, and many counts, even in the sixth century, bear Roman names. At the beginning of the seventh century, a Roman reached the highest position in the kingdom by becoming mayor of the palace. Intermarriages were common, and the distinction between the two races was gradually effaced. The continuing decline of civilization in Gaul was not due to hostility between Franks and Romans, but to the weaknesses of both peoples. The Romans had lost both the ability and the desire to create and maintain civilization, and the Germans could not supply the necessary leadership. Frankish government was certainly more inefficient, and probably more corrupt, than that of the Romans, but the Roman government had not prevented violence and oppression. The Franks were not responsible for the enserfment of the great mass of the population; serfdom was created in the last days of the Empire. There is no doubt that there was an intellectual and moral decline in the sixth century; the best educated men were often ignorant and superstitious, while the leaders of society were cruel and treacherous. This would seem to indicate a weakness in the Romans rather than the Franks. The invaders were always greatly outnumbered, and they were not fundamentally hostile to Roman civilization. Their mere presence could not have destroyed learning and morality if the great mass of the population had been interested in preserving its traditions. But the discouraging fact about the Merovingian period is that it did nothing to relieve the stagnation of the late Roman Empire. Most men were still indifferent to political conditions and had no hope of improving their economic situation. Their interests were purely local; they saw no benefit in large-scale organizations or in specialized activities such as science and the arts. Historians have often spoken of the vigor and new interest in life brought into the Empire by the fresh and unspoiled Germanic peoples. There is little evidence of this new vitality in Merovingian Gaul.

THE CHURCH IN THE GERMANIC KINGDOMS

The idea of imperial unity persisted in the West long after it had actually been broken up into separate kingdoms. But the one institution in which that unity was still a fact rather than a memory, was the Church. The Church was the heir of Rome in the West, and during the sixth and seventh centuries it began to profit from the legacy. It became an independent political power, the greatest landlord in the West, and the center of learning and the arts.

The Lombard conquest of Italy furnished the papacy with its opportunity for achieving independence. The Ostrogoths, although Arians, had exercised some control over the popes and papal elections. Thus Theodoric had interfered in the case of a disputed election; he had sent a pope to Constantinople to demand that the emperor cease persecuting Arians; and later he had nominated a pope who was duly accepted. After the conquest of the Goths, Justinian interfered even more with the Roman Church. "No Roman emperor so nearly assumed the position of a temporal pope." During his reign the Church was obliged to submit to his will; it did so, although sometimes unwillingly, because he frequently used the power of the state for the benefit of the Church. He gave great authority to the bishops and extensive privileges to the clergy. He recognized and increased the jurisdiction of the ecclesiastical courts. But "the bishop of Rome, before entering on his functions, must, like others, await the consent of the emperor or of the governor of Ravenna." Yet in the end the pope profited from the imperial reconquest of Rome.

> The emperor was far away at Constantinople, the Byzantine governor held his court in Ravenna, the senate was a pithless shadow. The few subordinate officials who occupied the Palatine were not of such standing as seriously to interfere with him. The pope was the man of highest rank in Rome, and he represented the only Roman institution which yet retained vitality, the only one which in an age of universal corruption and decay continued fresh and vigorous. To the Church men looked for maintenance and guidance, and the pope was head of the Church.

The invasion by the Lombards accentuated these conditions. The people in Rome needed assistance and defense more than ever, and the emperor and his officials were unable to give aid, since the city was almost completely cut off from other imperial territories. The senate at Rome, if still in existence, was of no importance; it was not even mentioned in treaties with the Lombards. By the close of the sixth century, therefore, the pope was the virtual ruler of Rome.

The authority of the papacy, already increased by the isolation of Rome from the rest of the Empire, was still further advanced by pope Gregory the Great. The career of this pontiff illustrates perfectly the way in which Roman administrative traditions were combined with Christian ideals to form the organization of the medieval Church. Gregory was born of an illustrious senatorial family, and was given a good education, with special training in law. He entered the imperial civil service and, while still a young man, was given the high position of prefect of the city of Rome. There was much surprise when he withdrew abruptly from the world and devoted his great wealth to the foundation of monasteries. Gregory became a simple monk in one of these foundations and spent three very happy years practising the most rigorous asceticism. Later, when pope, he wrote: "I remember longingly what I once was in the monastery; how I rose in contemplation above all changeable and decaying things, and thought of nothing but the things of heaven; how my soul, though pent within the body, soared beyond its fleshly prison, and looked with longing upon death itself as the means of entering into life." But the pope felt that Gregory was far too useful a man to be permitted to spend his life in seclusion. He made him first one of the Seven Deacons charged with the administration of the Church of Rome, and a little later sent him to be the papal representative at the imperial court in Constantinople. This stay at the capital was very distasteful to Gregory, but it completed his political education. He took as little part as possible in the life of the court and did not even learn Greek, but he did see the imperial administrative system working under more favorable conditions than in Italy, and he made some useful friends. Yet even in Constantinople he lived an ascetic life, spending all the time he could in study, meditation, or prayer.

During this period Gregory wrote the *Magna Moralia,* or commentary on the Book of Job. Like most of the important books of the sixth century this was really a summary and a condensation of earlier works, but it was to have great influence throughout the Middle Ages. In long commentaries on each verse, Gregory introduced all the important theological ideas of his predecessors in simple and uncompromising form. Earlier writers, such as Augustine, had reached their conclusions only after arduous mental and emotional struggles. Gregory had no such problem; he was interested in the facts of doctrine rather than in the logical steps by which they had been discovered. He wanted definite statements, not hypotheses and qualified assertions. For example, Gregory made the doctrine of Purgatory, which was rather vague in earlier writers, perfectly clear and explicit. By abandoning the intellectual subtleties of his predecessors, by emphasizing allegory and miracle, Gregory made it easier for theology to survive during the period when European intellectual activity was at a low ebb.

After returning from Constantinople, Gregory was elected abbot of his old monastery. In 589 and 590 a terrible plague swept over Rome, the pope died, and Gregory was unanimously chosen as his successor. In such a time of peril the strong man was needed and, although unwilling, Gregory was forced to accept the office. In their trouble the electors did not wait to consult the emperor, but Gregory delayed his consecration for six months until the imperial assent was given. The first duty of the new pope was to defend his city against the Lombards. The emperor and the exarch gave little help, but by skilful diplomacy Gregory prevented another sack of Rome and finally, in 599, concluded a treaty of peace which put an end to the Lombard war that had been going on for thirty years. This greatly increased the pope's prestige and made him the leader of all the Romans in Central Italy. Gregory was even more interested in his spiritual position as head of Western Christendom and worked steadily to preserve the unity of the Church. He successfully reasserted his authority in Africa, a land troubled by persistent heresy. He aided a growing Catholic party among the Arian Lombards. One of his friends converted the king of the Visigoths and so brought Spain back to the Catholic faith. Gregory also sent a mission to England and began the process of bringing that country under the sway of the Roman Church. Even in Gaul, where the Merovingians considered Church offices as political spoils to be distributed among their dependents, Gregory asserted his authority with some success. It cannot be said that he was able to raise the standard of morality among the Frankish clergy, but his requests were never officially rejected, and he established useful precedents for his successors when they wanted to intervene in ecclesiastical affairs of the kingdom. By the time of his death in 604, he had increased both the temporal and spiritual power of his office.

Another aid to the Church at this time was the great improvement in the organization of monasticism. As we have seen, Gregory himself was a monk, and the monks were very useful to him in his attempts to increase his control of outlying churches. Monasticism had made rapid progress in the West during the fifth and early sixth centuries, but it was still modeled upon Eastern usages and it lacked the discipline and order which were to make it a great instrument of Christian unity. To create a type of monasticism adapted to the needs of the Western Church was the work of St. Benedict of Nursia.

Benedict was born about 480 of a noble Italian family which had furnished many consuls to the state and more virgins to the Church. At the age of twelve he was sent to Rome to be educated. He soon became disgusted with the corrupt society of the city and at the age of fourteen withdrew, in the words of his biographer, Gregory the Great, "learnedly ignorant and wisely untaught." He found a retreat at Subiaco, a lovely spot in the Apennines, in the midst of "a frightful and terrible silence which was broken only by the cries of the wild beasts." There he dwelt in a cave for three years. A friendly hermit, who was unable to reach his almost inaccessible retreat, let down each day a loaf of bread on a cord, and Benedict shared "not so much the repast as the fast of his benefactor." At first the boy was sorely tempted by the lusts of the world, but he overcame his temptations by rolling in a bed of thorns until the pain stifled all other sensation. Eventually his retreat was discovered by shepherds, people flocked to him for comfort and advice, and he became the leader of other hermits who gathered around him. After some years Benedict found that his work at Subiaco was hampered by the jealousy of other monks in the neighborhood. So with a few associates, he wandered south to Monte Cassino, an isolated mountain-top between Rome and Naples. There he found peasants still worshiping Apollo, and he had the satisfaction of teaching them the Christian religion. Many soon came to him to be enrolled as monks, and his monastery became a peaceful, well-ordered community where Roman and Goth, noble and peasant, worked and prayed side by side. There Benedict made his home until his death in 543.

For the government of his monks, St. Benedict wrote the famous Benedictine rule, based on the three fundamental vows of monasticism: poverty, chastity, and obedience. The monks were not allowed to have any property of their own but were to be given all necessities from the common stock. Clothing was to be furnished in conformity to their needs and to the climatic conditions. When they had to go on a journey, they were to have better garments than usual; when their gowns became worn they were to receive new ones, and the old were to be given to the poor. Bedding, utensils, and other needful objects were to be supplied with a like liberality. Absolute obedience was required. If an impossible task was enjoined upon a brother, he might humbly suggest the causes of the impossibility. "But if, after his suggestion, the command of the superior continue according to his first opinion, the junior shall know that it is expedient for him; and in all love, trusting in the aid of God, he shall obey." The monastery was ruled by an abbot, who was elected by his fellow-monks, but who had absolute authority once he had taken office. However, in all important matters he was to ask the whole congregation for counsel before making his own decision. In less weighty affairs, the advice of the elders was sufficient.

The great weakness of early monasticism had been its lack of discipline, which allowed individuals to go to extremes of idleness or asceticism. St. Benedict's rule had a definite occupation for each hour of the day. First, and most important, was the "work of God," or prayer. Eight times a day the monks were to assemble and hold brief services; on Sundays and holy days they increased the length of their devotions. Then the monastery was to be self-sufficient and supply its own needs as far as possible. Ordinary monks worked in the fields while those with special skills produced the manufactured goods which the brothers needed. If there were a surplus it might be sold outside the monastery at a price slightly lower than that asked by laymen who made similar wares. Such manual labor took about seven hours a day. During their rest periods, especially in the afternoon, the monks were to spend their time in reading. They had two hours for this in ordinary seasons and somewhat longer in Lent. The books which they read were usually on religious topics, but a few of the wealthier monasteries gradually acquired important collections of secular works. In this way some monasteries, though by no means the majority, became important centers of learning, since, as Roman civilization continued to decline, few books survived outside monastic libraries.

St. Benedict guarded against extreme asceticism just as he guarded against idleness, and made great allowance for human frailty. There were two meals a day, and at each there were to be two different kinds of food "so that if any one perchance may not be able to eat one he may partake of the other." Vegetables were allowed in addition to the main dishes, but meat was forbidden except for those who were ill. St. Benedict believed that it was better to abstain from drinking wine, but because of the weakness of the flesh he arranged that each brother might have a moderate amount daily. The prior, who was the abbot's lieutenant, might increase the allowance in summer, or when the monks were doing especially hard work. Old men and young boys were not bound to observe the rules about food as strictly as the others, and seem to have been permitted to eat between meals.

While the monks sought seclusion from the world and felt that the chief service which they could render their fellow-men was to pray for their souls, they were bound to aid those who came to them for help. The poor were to be fed and travelers were to be lodged, for the rule said: "All guests who come shall be received as though they were Christ. . . . Chiefly in the reception of the poor and of pilgrims shall care be most anxiously exhibited: for in them Christ is received the more." This noble standard of hospitality was of the utmost importance during the Middle Ages when there were very few inns, and traveling was both expensive and dangerous.

Life in a monastery, as far as its physical aspects went, was probably no harder than the life of a peasant on a great estate. The hours of labor were not long and the diet was as varied as that of the ordinary poor man. Richer men who entered monastic life must have found it hard at first, and the rigorous discipline, with its insistence on humility, was a stumbling-block to many novices. Every monk had to give up not only his selfish desires but even his pride in his special abilities and skills; a craftsman who gloried in his work was to be transferred to other tasks. The monk was to think of nothing but the service of God. Some men could never conform to these standards; others needed a long period of initiation. So the regulations for admission to the order were very strict. Only those candidates were to be admitted who seemed fit for the life, and a year's probation was required before the novice was allowed to take the final vows.

The number of monks observing the Benedictine rule grew rapidly during the sixth and seventh centuries. Most monasteries founded before St. Benedict began his work either accepted his reform, or had it thrust upon them by pious kings and bishops. Hundreds of new monasteries were founded, almost all of them on the basis of Benedict's rule. Civilization was still declining in the West, and most men saw no hope for the return of prosperity or good government. The monastery sheltered those who merely sought refuge from violence and disorder, and it afforded an almost unique opportunity, in that age of decay, to serve God and mankind. The strongest, as well as the weakest, became monks, and the monastery was probably the most useful institution in the West during the early centuries of the Middle Ages. Sometimes it was a center of learning and always it performed essential charitable services. More important was the fact that the monks made a real effort to live up to Christian ideals in an age when most laymen, and even some bishops and priests, paid them only lip-service. The monastery set an example of disciplined, organized work in a time when most men seemed incapable of discipline and organization. It was the most efficient economic unit; monastic property became more valuable as other estates went down-hill. By the eighth century the monks had the best buildings and the best agricultural practices; the backward peoples of England and Germany learned much from them. The monastery was also the most efficient religious unit; from the time of Gregory the Great on, the popes depended increasingly upon the monks for missionary work and support of their policy of centralization. Class distinctions, which were so important in the outside world, were ignored in monasteries. The ablest men could rise to the top, even if they were of humble origin, and this contributed greatly to the efficiency of monastic organization.

The conversion of England shows how useful the monks were to the papacy. In the time of Gregory the Great, the Angles and Saxons who had conquered the eastern half of the country were still pagan. The old Celtic population, which had been driven into Cornwall, Wales, and Scotland, was Christian, but had lost touch with Rome during the long agony of the conquest. The British Christians were not exactly heretics, but they had a number of peculiar observances which distinguished them from their brethren on the Continent. They tended to lessen the power of bishops; they observed Easter at a different date; their priests had a strange form of tonsure. Ireland had been converted by St. Patrick, who followed Celtic usages, and Scotland had been converted from Ireland, so that the Christians of the British Isles formed a powerful, coherent group, very independent of papal authority.

The Celtic Christians were zealous missionaries—as we shall see, they tried to reform the Church in Gaul—but they found it difficult to convert their hereditary enemies, the Anglo-Saxons. The Frankish church was too corrupt to do its duty by its own members, much less to send missionaries across the Channel. It was left for the distant pope to undertake the conversion of England. Gregory the Great could not overlook such an opportunity to assert his leadership. He sent his friend, the abbot Augustine,[9] with a party of monks, to introduce Christianity into southern Britain. They landed in Kent in 597, and won some important successes almost immediately. The king of Kent, Ethelbert, had married a Frankish Christian princess, and was quite ready to hear about the new religion. He was soon converted and allowed Augustine to build churches in all lands acknowledging his authority. Since Ethelbert was the most influential of the ten or so petty kings who were ruling the Anglo-Saxons, his support gave the mission a chance to work beyond the narrow limits of Kent. Augustine was made archbishop of the Eng-

[9] This is *not* the St. Augustine mentioned previously, who was a great theologian and died in 430.

lish, with his seat at Canterbury, and a rudimentary church organization was planned.

After the death of Ethelbert, the progress of conversion in the south was checked by the collapse of the hegemony of Kent and the opposition of other rulers. But soon an opportunity in the north was afforded the Romans. A king of Northumbria had married a Kentish princess and the Christian bride took with her Paulinus, whom Gregory had sent to aid Augustine in 601. Moved by his preaching and the queen's prayers, the king vowed to adopt Christianity if he were successful in an attack on Wessex. He won a complete victory, and then a council was held in order to win over his followers. Bede, the earliest of English historians, has left us an account of this meeting which may not be entirely accurate, but which illustrates the two arguments which were most convincing among the Germans. One was the certainty of the Christians regarding the future life; the other was the powerlessness of pagan divinities. At the gathering, after the Christians had had their say, one of the aged councilors spoke:

> So seems the life of man, O King, as a sparrow's flight through the hall when a man is sitting at meat in wintertide, with a warm fire burning on the hearth but the chill rain storm without. The sparrow flies in at one door and tarries for a moment in the light and heat of the hearth-fire, and then, flying forth from the other, vanishes into the wintry darkness whence it came. So tarries for a moment the life of man in our sight, but what goes before, or what comes after, we know not. If this new teaching tells us aught certainly of these, let us follow it.

Then a pagan priest declared that he had served his gods faithfully and they had done nothing for him in return. Therefore he repudiated them and hurled a spear against their shrine. As the insult to the heathen deities remained unavenged, the elders assented to the arguments and the wishes of the king and accepted Christianity. Paulinus became the first archbishop of York, as Augustine had been first archbishop of Canterbury.

A pagan reaction soon drove Paulinus back to Kent, but Celtic missionaries now took up the work of converting the north of England. In spite of temporary setbacks, most of England was Christianized by the middle of the seventh century. But the influence of the Celtic church was still strong, and it was doubtful whether England would eventually accept the leadership of Rome or remain isolated with the Celtic Christians. The matter was brought to an issue at the Synod of Whitby in 664. The half-whimsical decision of the king that he would follow St. Peter, since even the Irish missionaries admitted that St. Peter held the keys of heaven, gave the victory to Rome. A few years later Theodore of Tarsus, a great administrator, was sent to England as archbishop of Canterbury. He perfected the organization of the English church, and

Celtic Christianity began to lose ground. Gradually, Roman customs were adopted everywhere in England and eventually in Scotland, Wales, and even in Ireland.

Even in Gaul, Rome was threatened by the zeal of Celtic missionaries. Ireland was the backbone of the Celtic church, and in the sixth and seventh centuries many Irish scholars and monks worked among the Germans of the Continent. With Christianity, Ireland had received the Roman learning which survived in Britain, and the Irish preserved that learning more carefully and intelligently than other northern peoples. As a result, the Irish clergy were well trained and well educated and were a civilizing influence wherever they went. The life of Columban, the greatest of the Irish missionaries, illustrates their influence. He had studied the classics and the sciences, as well as theology, and had spent many years in a monastery. He had always "longed to go into strange lands," as his biographer wrote, and finally sailed for Brittany with twelve companions. He found that in Gaul "the Christian faith had almost departed from the country, the creed alone remained; but the saving grace of penance and the longing to root out the lusts of the flesh were to be found only in a few."

Columban and his followers won the favor of the kings by their preaching and example and were allowed to found monasteries in the forests and hills of eastern France. Many converts joined them, and the growing influence of the Irish monks soon aroused the hostility of the Frankish bishops. Columban made matters worse by his fearless denunciations of the king's vices and he was ordered to return to Ireland. However, he took refuge with rival rulers, who received him well and allowed him to continue his missionary work among the Alamanni and the Lombards. Columban did not follow the Benedictine rule, but instead imposed a somewhat stricter code of his own on his monks. At the same time he and his followers preserved the Irish tradition of scholarship, and the monasteries which they founded, such as Luxeuil in the Vosges, St. Gall near the Lake of Constance, and Bobbio in the northern Apennines, were important centers of learning. Thus, while the Roman Church was getting control of England, the Celtic church was extending its influence in Gaul. During the eighth century, however, the Irish monasteries on the Continent were forced to accept the Benedictine rule. Curiously enough, most of them were brought under the control of Rome by an English monk, Boniface. As we shall see, eighth century England sent out missionaries who wrought a great reform of the Church and a great increase of papal authority north of the Alps, so that in the long run Augustine's mission had more enduring results than Columban's.

III

-»-»-»-»<<-<<-<<-<<-

The Decay of the Roman World
in the East

THE FAILURE OF JUSTINIAN'S REVIVAL

ONE OF THE greatest difficulties in explaining the fall of the Roman Empire in the West is that the Empire survived in the East. The East suffered from misgovernment, heavy taxes, and barbarian inroads just as much as the West did. The East had seemed tired and indifferent as early as the first century B. C., when it was conqured by Rome. If Latin civilization was decadent by the fourth century A.D., Greek civilization, which was older, should have been in an even worse condition. Yet the East showed amazing energy and an almost miraculous power of revival as the West sank further and further into barbarism.

Perhaps the greatest advantage which the East had over the West was its active commerce. The Greeks and the Syrians had always been more interested in business than the Italians, and their geographic position gave them a practical monopoly of the luxury trade from the Orient. So the East was held together by commercial ties, while the West was breaking up into little local units. Eastern cities were prosperous, while Western ones were a burden on the government. Many men in the East benefited by the large market which the Empire gave them; they paid their taxes more readily, and the emperor at Constantinople had more money for his army than the ruler at Ravenna.

Geography favored the Empire in the East. Its richest provinces were protected by the sea; the Germans who crossed the Danube line had only the Balkans as a field of settlement. It was not difficult to persuade them to move on to the more fertile lands of the West. They could not reach the rich trading cities of Syria and Egypt without taking Con-

stantinople, and Constantinople was the nearest thing to an impregnable city that was ever built. With the inlet of the Golden Horn on
the north, the Sea of Marmora on the south, and the swift current of
the Bosporus on the east, it was almost surrounded by water. On the
west, or land side, a short wall was enough to bar invaders. It is not
surprising that Constantine, seeking a capital in the East, should have
picked this site, and rebuilt the little town of Byzantium into a new
Rome. His successors improved the fortifications, and from that time to
the present Constantinople has been the key position in the Near East.
It was a strong fortress and a wealthy trading city. The possession of
Constantinople alone gave the Eastern emperors a great advantage
over their co-rulers in the West. Moreover, from Constantinople, Asia
Minor could be controlled, and in Asia Minor, as the Eastern emperors
slowly discovered, were peasants who still made good soldiers. The
barbarians had dominated the army in the East as in the West, but they
were gradually replaced by levies from the Anatolian highlands. The
process was never entirely completed; to the very end the Eastern
Empire used foreign mercenaries, but there was always a strong contingent of native troops to keep the foreigners from seizing control. As
long as the emperors held Constantinople and Asia Minor, they could
never be entirely vanquished.

Finally, the East was more fortunate in its rulers than the West. The
fifth century emperors at Constantinople were not great men, but they
were not as incompetent as Honorius or Valentinian III. They knew
how to play the old Roman game of setting the barbarians against each
other; they had enough ready money so that they could buy peace when
they could not secure it by intrigues. In their rather plodding and un-
heroic way, they held the East together and kept civilization at a fairly
high level in their territories.

In fact, relieved of the dead weight of the West, the East even showed
signs of a revival. The frozen Græco-Roman tradition began to crack,
while ancient Oriental influences which had been suppressed for centuries began to be felt again. New ideas and new combinations were possible; slavish imitation of the past was no longer required. This was
especially noticeable in the arts, where the Christians finally found
forms to express their ideas. Thus a new style of church architecture was
developed which owed much to Syrian influences as well as to older
Roman models. There was more respect for tradition in economics and
politics, but even in these fields the eastern fragment of the Roman
Empire was ceasing to be a fragment and was developing its own institutions and its own techniques. The late Roman Empire was becoming
the Byzantine Empire.

Yet it should be remembered that the Byzantine Empire always called
itself the Roman Empire, and that the old tradition of a world-state

died hard. In the sixth century this tradition was revived by Justinian, the last Latin-speaking emperor. Much more ambitious than his fifth century predecessors, he dreamed of regaining all the Western territories which had once been ruled by Rome. Since he was the real power during the brief reign of his uncle Justin (518–527), who was a good but rather illiterate general, and since his own reign lasted from 527 to 565, he had almost half a century to carry out his plans. During this period, as we have seen, he regained most of North Africa, all of Italy south of the Alps, and the southeastern corner of Spain. In spite of these successes, the Empire was weaker at his death than at his accession. Within a century it was to lose not only Justinian's conquests but some of its richest eastern provinces.

As in the fourth century, a state covering most of the Mediterranean basin was an economic mistake. Even though the West was taxed until its inhabitants regretted the easier rule of the barbarians, it remained a burden on the East. The armies which took and held Italy, Africa, and the Spanish coast were raised in the East and paid for by the East. The conquests of Justinian dissipated rather than increased the military and financial resources of the Empire. The emperor's best generals were in the West, and the East was bled dry to support their armies at a time when both the money and the armies were needed nearer home.

On the eastern frontier of the Empire was the Sassanid kingdom of Persia, which had been a match for Rome in its greatest days. It was even more dangerous in Justinian's day, and it could always find excuses for war in the undetermined boundary between the two states. Again and again it attacked the eastern provinces of the Empire, but Justinian was so determined on the conquest of the West that he contented himself with fighting a defensive war against Persia. As a result, Syria suffered horribly from Sassanid raids, and the important silk trade with the Orient was frequently interrupted. Justinian strove to find routes to India and China which Persia could not block, but he had little success. So the Persian war not only necessitated heavier taxes but also impoverished the great trading cities on which the welfare of the Empire depended.

Justinian, in his early years, had recognized the weakness of the Roman financial and administrative system. He had hoped that he could reduce the burden of taxes and improve the standard of honesty of the civil service. Instead, he had to ask more and more money from his subjects, and he allowed his agents to collect that money by the most oppressive means. High officials at court might be dishonest and tyrannical, but as long as they produced the required sums, no questions were asked. The loyalty of the eastern provinces to the Empire, which had been unquestioned during the crisis of the migrations, was weakened by the strain of Justinian's demands.

This was especially true in Egypt and Syria, where the native population had never been completely assimilated, in spite of eight centuries of Greek and Roman rule. As we have seen, the old traditions of these people were beginning to work their way through the threadbare fabric of Græco-Roman culture. By the sixth century, the Egyptians and the Syrians had a tendency to feel that their interests were quite distinct from those of the Greeks, who held most of the important positions in the imperial civil service. This tendency was stimulated by the conquest of the West, which benefited the officials who got jobs there rather than the people of the Oriental provinces who had to pay heavy taxes.

Religious differences widened the breach between the native populations and the emperor's officials. The dispute was over the old question of the relation between the divine and the human elements in Christ. Did Christ have two natures—that is, was he completely human and completely divine at the same time—or did the divine nature predominate? Many people in the East, especially in Egypt and Syria, favored the latter interpretation, which had been condemned as heretical. The West, as usual, had accepted the orthodox doctrine whole-heartedly. A difference of this sort was serious at a time when men were ready to defy all lay authority to maintain their religious beliefs. Justinian worked desperately to impose a compromise which would satisfy all parts of the Empire, but he found, as many men since his day have found, that of all disputes a religious one is the hardest to compromise. The pope accepted his settlement only after threats and imprisonment, while a large part of the population of Egypt and Syria never accepted it at all. Since the Greek ruling class adhered to the emperor's creed, a new distinction was drawn between them and the natives, and soon each group was supporting its own church.

Some of Justinian's advisers urged that further concessions should be made to the eastern heretics, even at the cost of offending the Roman Church. This policy was advocated by the empress Theodora, who probably had more political insight than her husband. She had been the Byzantine equivalent of a chorus girl before she married the young Justinian, and her early experiences, while not particularly edifying, had acquainted her with all classes of people and many parts of the Empire. In personal courage she was superior to Justinian. During the famous Nika riots, when the mob of Constantinople besieged the emperor in his own palace, Theodora persuaded him to resist, instead of fleeing as he had first planned. The advice of such a woman was worth considering, but Justinian could not accept it as long as he hoped to gain territories adhering to the Roman Church.

Justinian weakened the Empire in two-thirds of the East in order to gain lands in the West which his successors could not hold. But all the dangers in his policy were not apparent at once; to contemporaries his reign was a magnificent demonstration of the eternal power of Rome. This magnificence was especially noticeable in the heart of the Empire, the Greek-speaking districts centering in Constantinople. These regions suffered less from war and profited more from Justinian's extraordinary expenditures than any other region. It was at this time that Constantinople became the greatest trading city in the Mediterranean region. Its old rival, Antioch, was weakened by the Persian war. The Syrian hinterland was devastated by the enemy and Antioch itself was held for a short time by an invading army in 540. Constantinople, however, was out of the danger zone and traders naturally centered their business there. Justinian was a great builder, and his capital benefited especially from this interest. Everywhere in the Empire new public buildings and churches rose, but the crowning achievement of the reign was Santa Sophia in Constantinople. Here the new architectural style, which had been growing up in the East, revealed all its possibilities. The great dome of the church and the colorful mosaics which adorned the walls showed that Byzantium had succeeded in creating art forms which were not classical, and yet were neither barbarous nor decadent.

Santa Sophia is one of Justinian's chief monuments—the other is his summary of Roman law, the *Corpus Juris Civilis*. The Romans' greatest achievement was their law, but the law lay scattered in thousands of fragments—acts of the Senate, imperial administrative orders, judicial decisions, official books of jurisprudence, and so on. Some earlier attempts had been made to organize this material, but no one had succeeded in doing the whole job. In his plans for administrative reform, Justinian included the restatement of the law and, unlike most of his other projects, this one was accomplished. Much of the credit should go to Tribonian, who headed the commission which did the actual work, but the emperor applied the pressure which made the commission finish its task with amazing rapidity. The laws were codified (the *Code*); interpretations of the law were classified and harmonized (the *Digest*) and a manual explaining the principles of the law was written (the *Institutes*). Some valuable material was lost in the attempt to eliminate contradictions, repetitions, and archaic elements, but the essential parts of Roman law were preserved as they never would have been if we had had to rely on the survival of the hundreds of manuscripts which Tribonian and his fellows abridged.

It is hard to overestimate the influence of this work in the late medieval and early modern periods; at times it was second only to that of the Bible. Here was a summary of the legal knowledge of the most legal-minded people of antiquity. Here was the law of a great civilization, ready to be used by the men who were trying to build a great civilization anew. There was no problem of human relations which the Roman lawyers had not discussed, and their solutions were always worthy of respectful consideration. The *Digest*, which included extracts from works in which Roman lawyers had tried to state the basic principles of law, was especially influential in European thought. And since lawyers were to play a leading role in the new states which eventually emerged in the West, Justinian's work affected the whole political future of Western Europe. In the end, all Western countries, except England, eventually adopted the principles of Roman law, and even the English organized their law in Roman categories.

MOHAMMED AND HIS RELIGION

Soon after the death of the aged Justinian, a child was born in Arabia who was to change the history of the world. This child, Mohammed, was to establish the religion which became the chief rival of Christianity; he was to found an empire which became larger than that of Rome. Yet, in the sixth century, any one born in Arabia seemed condemned to obscurity, however great his ability. The huge peninsula, about a third the size of the United States, was like a wedge driven into the civilizations of the East. On the west, across the Red Sea and the Sinai Desert, was Egypt; to the north lay Palestine and Syria; the northeastern frontier touched Mesopotamia; and across the eastern ocean was India. Yet most of the trade-routes passed by, rather than through Arabia. Travelers skirted its deserts on the north; they sailed past its forbidding coasts on the west and east. For Arabia, in spite of its size and strategic location, was a dry, barren country which supported only a small population. Mountain chains or hills, running parallel to the coast, shut out the sea breezes and cut off the rainfall from the high plateau of the interior. There were no forests, the rivers dried up in the summer, and only in the oases was agriculture possible. The extreme south, the frankincense country, was somewhat more fertile, but in most of the peninsula nothing grew except scanty desert grasses.

The Arabs were Semites, closely related to the Jews, the Syrians, and the ancient Babylonians and Phœnicians. At the time of Mohammed most of the Arabs were Bedouins, or nomads, who made a living by grazing their animals over immense ranges in the arid interior. In the south and along the western coast were town-dwellers, who supported themselves by trading and such agriculture as was possible. Frankincense, which grew in South Arabia, was carried by land, up the west coast, to the Mediterranean. Some dealers in Oriental goods, who feared the difficult passage up the Red Sea, landed their cargoes at Arabian ports and let them take the same route. This trade had once been important enough to support a fairly advanced civilization in South Arabia, but after the Romans occupied Egypt, traders from India landed their goods on the western side of the Red Sea rather than on the Arabian coast.

As a result, the towns of Arabia declined, and by the seventh century many of their inhabitants had reverted to the nomadic life of the desert.

Along the coasts and in the extreme north, the Arabs had formed some rather loosely organized kingdoms. Elsewhere, there was no central government, and even the tribes had little coherence. In times of peace each family, or wandering group of a few families, took care of its own affairs. Only in case of war did the head of the tribe have any real authority. This lack of organization made it easy for a strong leader with a few devoted followers to dominate a wide area. On some occasions in the past, the desert Semites had pushed into the richer countries of the North, probably as a result of overpopulation or temporary union under a powerful ruler. The Phœnician and Jewish settlements in Palestine are examples of such movements. But since the rise of Rome, the Arabs had been unable to do anything more than raid border towns, and in the sixth century no one considered them a menace.

The Arabs were a sensitive, imaginative people, very fond of poetry and deeply interested in religious problems. Yet in their relations with each other they were rather brutal, and their religion had little effect on their conduct. Men who could afford it had several wives; others found it possible to arrange temporary marriages. Weak and superfluous children were killed. Widows and orphans had no rights and were treated as beggars or slaves. Each family avenged its own injuries and, in the process, tried to do more damage than it had received, so that feuds once started were hard to stop. The aggrieved family might accept money instead of using its right of vengeance, but no outside authority could force it to do so. Intertribal wars were common, and raiding parties made travel unsafe during most of the year. The religion of the Arabs consisted almost entirely of external observances and was in a state of great confusion. They had succeeded in discovering several hundred gods, and each tribe had its favorite deities. In addition, they had to propitiate the innumerable tribes of *djinns,* spirits intermediate between gods and men. Christian and Persian beliefs had also entered the country, while some northern Arabs had accepted Judaism. The influence of these three religions, and especially that of Judaism, was felt even by Arabs who remained loyal to their old faith. In spite of all this divergence there were religious practices common to all the Arabs, a fact which was very helpful to Mohammed in securing unity of faith among his people. There were, for example, three sacred months during which all feuds and wars were suspended and men could attend fairs and religious ceremonies without danger. Mecca, a fairly important trading center near the Red Sea, was recognized as the religious center and enjoyed permanent neutrality. In Mecca was the great Arabian sanctuary, the Kaaba, a square stone house which held 360 idols, including an image of Christ. The most revered object in the Kaaba was the famous black stone which had fallen from heaven, probably as a meteorite, and had been adored by the Arabs for centuries. These common beliefs were not enough to form a national religion, but they made the task of the prophet easier. He was also aided by the fact that the excessive number of deities and the new ideas coming in from foreign lands were weakening the old faith in idols.

Mohammed was born about the year 571 of our era. In early childhood he was left an orphan with very little property. There is little contemporary evidence about his early years. His utterances in the Koran contain only one reference to this period:

> Did He not find thee an orphan, and sheltered thee?
> And found thee erring, and guided thee?
> And found thee poor and enriched thee?

The traditions handed down by the prophet's followers relate that he grew up as a shepherd boy and later entered the service of a rich widow, his cousin Khadija. While in charge of her affairs he made several long journeys, during which he may have met Arabs who knew something of the Jewish and Christian faiths. At the age of twenty-five he married his employer, though she is said to have been about fifteen years older. This marriage gave him wealth, position, and leisure.

From childhood Mohammed had been subject to peculiar seizures, and as he grew older the attacks became more frequent. During these paroxysms he was completely unconscious of what he said, and showed many of the symptoms of a man with a violent fever. His followers have naturally regarded these attacks as holy trances; Christian writers, seeking a rational explanation, have called them fits of hysteria. They certainly inclined Mohammed toward religious meditation; after his marriage he spent a month each year in retirement and prayer. But until he was about forty years of age his inspiration was not clear, and he was uncertain as to what he was to do. Then he had a vision in which he believed that the angel Gabriel came down to the lowest heaven and commanded him to preach.

> Cry, in the name of thy Lord, who created—
> Created man from blood.
> Cry! for thy Lord is the bountifulest!
> Who taught the pen,
> Taught man what he did not know.

Mohammed was still doubtful that he was really called to a prophetic career, but Khadija comforted him and believed in him. Gradually he became filled with the vision of the one, eternal God and began to plead with his countrymen to abandon their multitude of deities. To this period belong the great poetic passages of the Koran, the appeals to "the wonders of nature, the stars in their courses, the sun and the moon, the dawn cleaving asunder the dark veil of night, the life-giving rain, the fruits of the earth, life and death, change and decay—'all are signs of God's power, if only ye would understand.'" This earliest portion of the Koran is one long blazonry of nature's beauty. "How can you believe in aught but the one, omnipotent God, when you see this glorious world around you and this wondrous tent of heaven above you?" is Mohammed's frequent question to his countrymen.

The prophet was not without honor among his immediate associates, for his first followers were his wife, his servant, and his cousin Ali; but progress was very slow, and it is said that in three years he made but fourteen converts. While Mohammed insisted that he was the prophet of God, he did not claim supernatural powers or worship for himself. "I am no more than man; when I order you anything with respect to religion, receive it, and when I order you about the affairs of the world then I am nothing more than man." Throughout his life he always denied that he could work a miracle. His fellow-citizens were not impressed by a prophet without magical gifts. Abu-Bekr, Othman, Omar and Ali were almost the only men of good family who believed in him, and his followers were mainly from the lower classes, especially slaves. When he began to preach against the idols, violent opposition was aroused, since the prosperity of Mecca was based on the pilgrimages made to its shrine. First the prophet's lowly followers were persecuted and then his own life was threatened. He made one unsuccessful attempt to withdraw to another city, but was stoned from its gates. Then he fled with his supporters to Yatrib, which was renamed Medinet-en-Nabi, the City of the Prophet, now Medina. This hegira, or flight, was in the year 622 A. D., and from it the Mohammedans reckon the beginning of their era.

Medina was the center of the Arabs who had accepted the Jewish faith, and so was less hostile to monotheism than Mecca. Mohammed seems to have hoped to persuade the Jews to accept him as a successor to their prophets. While he failed in this attempt, he made many converts among the pagan Arabs and soon found himself at the head of a large community. This involved him in endless political difficulties. He had to keep peace among his own followers; he had to keep them from quarreling with the natives of Medina; and he had to carry on a desultory war with his enemies at Mecca. These preoccupations are reflected in the revelations which Mohammed received during this period; there is a great deal less poetry, and a great deal more law. Rules regarding the punishment of criminals, the division of inheritances, and the forms of marriage were laid down during the sojourn at Medina. At the same time, definite religious observances were imposed.

There are many traditions regarding the prophet's life at Medina, and they seem more authentic than the stories of his early years. He led a simple life, avoiding both luxury and asceticism. His regular food was dates, or barley bread and water; he seldom allowed himself the pleasures of eating milk and honey. His clothes were plain but exquisitely neat; when they wore out he mended them himself. At home he kindled the fire, swept the floor, milked the goats, and did other work when it was necessary. He was fond of animals and children. He loved to take part in the children's games; after he had married the child Aisheh, he frequently helped her play with her dolls. A bench always stood before his door on which any poor man might rest and share his food. He inspired the deepest devotion in his followers, and he never lost the friendship of one whom he trusted. And with all his power and authority he was, as Aisheh said, as "bashful as a veiled virgin."

During the long stay at Medina, Mohammed's power increased steadily. He had the best of the sporadic fighting with the Meccans, and finally gained so many allies that in 630 he could attempt a direct attack on the city. Mecca fell without much opposition, and Mohammed immediately purified the Kaaba of its idols so that it could be a fitting center for his religion. He had claimed from the beginning that the Kaaba and the black stone were remnants of a temple built by Abraham, and that the line of prophetic succession, which commenced with Abraham, was to end with himself. Thus he was able to take over the most venerated object in Mecca for his religion and preserve the city's position as the religious center of Arabia. The fall of Mecca greatly impressed the Arabs, and most of the tribes of the peninsula immediately acknowledged Mohammed's spiritual and political leadership. Yet Arabia was still far from being a unified state when the prophet died in 632.

However, Mohammed had left behind him the Koran, the collected body of his revelations, and his followers could still guide themselves by his principles. The prophet had said: "Let the Koran ever be your guide. Do what it commands or permits; shun what it forbids." The Arabs believed that the Koran contained all that man needed to know. God had prepared this guide for the human race; it had always existed in heaven; but no one had been worthy of receiving it before Mohammed. It was revealed to him piece by piece, as he became capable of understanding it, or as circumstances made it applicable, but it formed a coherent and consistent whole. From the beginning of the prophet's mission his associates had tried to preserve his words, writing them down on whatever was handy, paper, parchment, palm leaves, bones or stones. This confused mass of Mohammed's sayings was collected and arranged by Abu-Bekr (632–634). But other copies of the prophet's utterances were still in existence, and disputes soon arose as to what were the correct readings. This difficulty was eventually ended by the caliph Othman (644–656), who had an authoritative collection made and ordered all other copies to be destroyed. Othman's collection has remained practically unchanged down to the present day. In no other religion is there such complete contemporary evidence as to what the founder said, nor such early agreement on the authentic version of his remarks. On the other hand, the Koran was put together so hurriedly that its arrangement is very bad. The first revelation, in which he was commanded to begin his mission, is in chapter ninety-six, and, in general, the earliest utterances come late in the book, while the long Medina passages come in the first chapters. Many crudities, repetitions, contradictory statements, and purely contemporary decisions were preserved which might have dropped out if the authorized version had not been made so soon. Yet, as it stands, orthodox Moslems consider it perfect in form and content—a great piece of literature, as well as the most important revelation ever made to man.

The religion taught in the Koran was easy to comprehend, and easy to follow. "There is no God but Allah. . . . God is one and omnipotent. . . . He begetteth not nor is He begotten, nor is there one like unto Him. . . . Mohammed is His prophet. . . . Verily they only are true believers who believe in God and His apostle." The faithful must also believe in the resurrection and the day of judgment, when every man will be rewarded according to his merits. Mohammed likewise enjoined respect for earlier prophets, such as Adam, Noah, Abraham, Moses and Jesus, although their revelations had been superseded by the Koran. Many stories from the Old and New Testaments were inserted in the Koran, often in such an inaccurate form that it is clear that Mohammed was quoting legends circulating among the Arabs, rather than actual written texts. Yet in spite of misquotation, many Jewish religious precepts are recognizable in the Koran, and the Mohammedan conception of the last judgment is very like the Christian. Besides strict monotheism, belief in a future life, and respect for the prophetic tradition, the Koran emphasizes predestination. Mohammed's own name for his religion was Islam, "submission to the will of God," and the Koran says: "Every man's fate have we bound about his neck."

The principal religious practices enjoined by the prophet are equally simple: prayer, fasting, almsgiving, and pilgrimage. A good Moslem must pray five times a day: at daybreak, just after noon, in the middle of the afternoon, at sunset, and at nightfall. Prayer is preceded by purification with water, or in the desert with sand. Throughout the month of Ramadan, believers must fast during the hours of daylight; at night they may eat and drink until they can discern a black thread from a white thread by the light of day. Almsgiving was especially emphasized; "Ye will never attain to righteousness until ye give in alms of that which ye love." A favorite saying of one of the caliphs was: "Prayer carries us half way to God; fasting brings us to the door of His palace; and alms procure us admission." Every believer, unless prevented by insurmountable difficulties, must make a pilgrimage to Mecca at least once in his lifetime. But "he only shall visit the Mosque of God who believes in God and the Last Day, and is instant in prayer, and payeth the alms, and feareth God only."

Besides these religious principles, the Koran also contained moral precepts and a rudimentary code of law. Wine-drinking and gambling, "abominations of the devil's making," were prohibited. A dietary law, somewhat like that of the Jews, banned certain foods, especially pork. More important were the rules designed to curb the violence and brutality of the Arabs. Disputes among followers of the prophet were to be arbitrated instead of being allowed to grow into blood-feuds. Elaborate rules of inheritance were revealed, which greatly increased the rights of orphans and female relatives. Infanticide was severely condemned. An effort was made to improve the position of women. Temporary unions were frowned upon, and no man might have more than four legitimate wives. Divorce was still easy, but the divorced wife could no longer be sent away penniless. On the whole, Mohammed succeeded in abolishing the worst abuses of Arab society and made possible the formation of a much more unified and coöperative community.

While the religion of Islam borrowed much from its Christian and Jewish predecessors, in one important respect it was unique. In Mohammedanism there was no need for an organized priesthood, nor for a sacramental system. Each individual believer had to assure his own salvation by his own good conduct. Every essential act of the religion could be performed by a man living alone. It was customary for the faithful to assemble together on Friday for prayers; it was common for certain men to devote themselves to explanation of the holy book; but neither the assembly nor the theologian were necessary. The simplicity of the Moslem faith, the absence of church organization and ritual, made it easy to spread. Any true believer could preach the faith; any one could accept it immediately, without waiting for the creation of a local church. This often gave Moslems a great advantage in missionary competition with Christianity. On the other hand, Islam could easily become a religion of pure external observance, because its very simplicity barred it from certain emotional appeals.

THE ARAB CONQUESTS

Mohammed had thought of many things, but he had made no plans for a successor when he died. Yet a strong leader was necessary; Arabia was still very imperfectly consolidated, and many Bedouin tribes still resented the supremacy of the prophet. Revolts broke out as soon as Mohammed died, and his followers at first were bewildered and helpless. They finally decided to choose a caliph, or successor, who would take

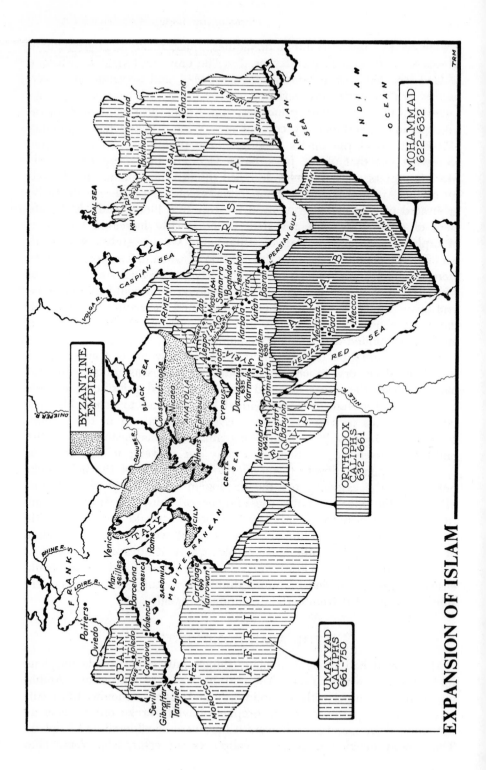

EXPANSION OF ISLAM

MOHAMMAD
622-632

BYZANTINE
EMPIRE

ORTHODOX
CALIPHS
632-661

UMAYYAD
CALIPHS
661-750

Mohammed's place as leader of the community of the faithful. Abu-Bekr, one of the earliest converts and most sincere believers, was given this office. He ruled only two years (632–634), but by his wisdom and boldness he managed to stem the crisis and complete the unification of Arabia. Under his successor, Omar (634–644) the wonderful conquests began. The Arabs had long envied the wealth of their neighbors. Now, united for the first time by the new religion, they found both Rome and Persia weakened by misgovernment and disastrous wars. We have already seen that the non-Greek inhabitants of the Eastern Empire were irritated by the taxes and disgusted with the religious policy of the government. They did nothing to oppose the Arab attack, since they felt that they might be better off under the new rulers. Without popular support the imperial armies could not hold the open country, and the few towns which they garrisoned could not hold out indefinitely when they were cut off from supplies. So between 634 and 649 Syria, Palestine, and Egypt were conquered by the Arabs. At the same time, a fleet was built which gained effective control of the Mediterranean and seized the important islands of Cyprus, Crete, and Rhodes. Persia was taken with almost equal ease between the years 632 and 642. Like the Syrians and Egyptians, the Persians were disgusted with their oppressive and incompetent rulers and made little resistance to the Arabs. Islam was now dominant from the eastern boundary of Persia to Tripoli in Africa. The Arabs were pushing onward in every direction, when their advance was interrupted by civil war at home.

The first two caliphs, Abu-Bekr and Omar, had been generally respected, but under Omar's successor, Othman (644–656), the believers gradually split into two parties. While Othman was one of the earliest converts to the faith, he did not have the intense feeling of hostility to the people of Mecca that was held by most of the old believers. He was accused of favoring his kinsmen, the Ommiads, who were one of the leading families of Mecca and had at one time bitterly opposed the prophet. The old believers resented the frequent assigning of high positions to recent converts, and feeling became so intense that Othman was assassinated in 656. Matters were made worse by the election of Ali, the son-in-law and adopted son of Mohammed, to succeed Othman. Ali did nothing to punish the murderers of his predecessor and was suspected of being an accomplice. Opposition arose within his own party and a rebellion was led by Aisheh, widow of the prophet. No sooner was she captured than Ali had to face a new uprising, led by the Ommiads. After some fighting, the whole matter was submitted to arbitration, and the decision went against Ali. One of the Ommiads was proclaimed caliph, but Ali refused to submit and held Persia and Mesopotamia for a short time. He was assassinated in 661 by a member of a new sect which opposed all caliphs, and sought democratic government. This sect was itself unimportant; however, the removal of Ali ended opposition to the Ommiad caliph, who soon restored the unity of the Moslem world.

This first Ommiad ruler took the decisive step of moving the capital of the Arab Empire from Mecca to Damascus. Damascus occupied a more central position and it was also removed from the narrow influence of those who wished to keep all power in the hands of the first converts and their families. The Ommiads wished to make the loosely organized Arab Empire into a real state. They employed many Syrians and Egyptians, who put their knowledge of Roman administrative techniques at the service of the new government. Centralization increased; regular taxes were introduced, and the office of caliph was made hereditary.

The "old believers" in Mecca and Medina were scandalized by these innovations and tried to free themselves from the worldly rule of the Ommiads, but their rebellion was put down with great severity. The old Arab aristocracy, rather than the companions of the prophet, was now in control of the state. This gave the Ommiads the support of the military leaders, but at the same time it involved them in difficulties with their non-Arab subjects. Many of the conquered peoples accepted the new faith, both because it was attractive in itself and because the follower of Islam was exempt from the heavy tribute demanded from the unbeliever. These converts became so numerous that they threatened the dominant position of the Arabs, and the Ommiad caliphs did their best to keep them in an inferior position. They were forced to pay heavy land-tax from which the Arabs were exempt and they were seldom advanced to responsible positions. In fact, Christians often had a better chance of attaining high office than converts. Thus, far from forcing Mohammedanism on their subjects, the Ommiad caliphs adopted a rather discouraging attitude toward converts and in Syria, where their influence was greatest, it was several centuries before Islam became the dominant religion among the non-Arabs. In the old Persian kingdom there were more converts, and their bitter resentment over their inferior position led to constant rebellions. Moslem sects which resented what they called the usurpation of the Ommiads could always find allies among the Persians.

While the Ommiads wished to keep political power in the hands of the Arabs, they had no objections to profiting from the superior civilization of their non-Arab subjects. Their administration was based on Roman and Persian models, and they were even more willing to absorb the art and learning of their predecessors. Christian and Persian scholars were welcomed at Damascus, and the great task of translating medical and scientific works into Arabic was begun. Beautiful mosques were built at Damascus and Jerusalem, in which Syrian architecture was adapted to the needs of the Mohammedan religion. A new civilization began to form around the Ommiad court at Damascus, a civilization in which Greek, Syrian, Persian, and Egyptian traditions played a greater part than Arab. Luxuries increased, and much of the old desert simplicity was lost. Unlike the Germans in the West, the Arab conquerors of the East were able to use their heritage from the old Mediterranean civilizations almost as soon as they occupied the country.

The end of civil war and the growing efficiency of Ommiad government soon made further conquests possible. The second great period of Moslem expansion began in the last decade of the seventh century and continued for about fifty years. North Africa was the first objective and here, as usual, the invaders benefited from the profound antagonism which existed between the Roman government and the native population. In Africa, as in Italy, Justinian's reconquest had been followed by heavy taxation and by persecution of heretics. The Romanized Africans were ruined and many of them left the country. The Berbers, natives who had not accepted Roman civilization, soon refused to obey imperial officials. A region so divided could not put up effective resistance. While the Berbers fought bravely to preserve their own independence, they lacked the support of the Roman cities, and the cities in turn were helpless without the support of the country people. Carthage fell in 697, and by 708 Africa, as far as the Straits of Gibraltar, was in the power of the Moslems.

From the Straits it was easy to pass over into Spain. The Visigothic kingdom was as badly governed as Merovingian Gaul; the nobles were ready to do anything to weaken royal power, and the common people had no love for a regime which was always inefficient and often tyrannical. A single victory, in 711, was enough to open the whole country to Tarik, who commanded the invading army, and from whom Gibraltar takes its name.[1] It is said that his forces numbered only twelve thousand, of whom all but three hundred were Berbers from newly conquered Africa. The figures may not be accurate, but the proportion of non-Arabs is probably not exaggerated. The handful of inhabitants of the Arabian peninsula could never have made their conquests had they not been able to enlist subject peoples in their army. The conquest of Spain is a striking illustration of this point. Not only was the invading army composed of Berbers, but in Spain itself many Visigothic nobles joined the conquerors. The whole peninsula, with the exception of the Galician mountains, was soon subject to the Moslems.

They pressed on across the Pyrenees into southern Gaul, but this country was not quite as disorganized as Spain. The south could not be protected, but when the raiders pushed north in 732, they were checked at Poitiers. Charles Martel, the mayor of the palace, had begun to reform the decadent Merovingian government, and he was able to as-

[1] *Gebel Tarik*—Tarik's hill.

semble an army which could hold its own against the invaders. The actual fighting at Poitiers was not very decisive; the Moslems were unable to push their raid farther, but their army withdrew in good order. Later legends embellished the victory, and recounted that 375,000 invaders, together with their king, had been killed, while the Frankish loss was only 1500. Even in modern times, the importance of this battle has been greatly overestimated. It did not free Gaul from danger, and raids on the south continued for some years. Lyons was pillaged in 743, and the invaders held Narbonne until 759. The most effective check to the Moslem advance was a revolt of the Berbers in Africa. This deprived the western Mohammedans of their best troops and cut them off from reinforcements from the East. Before this obstacle could be overcome, Charles Martel and his son had succeeded in reviving the power of the Frankish state and further conquests in Europe were impossible.

In the East, the Moslems made great advances during this same period. They captured Khiva, Bokhara, and Samarkand and advanced to the frontiers of China, thus gaining full control of one of the most important medieval trade-routes—the silk road from the East. They obtained a foothold in India by subjugating Afghanistan and the valley of the Indus. But, in spite of desperate efforts, they could not destroy the Eastern Empire. Asia Minor remained Byzantine, and the impregnable city of Constantinople resisted two prolonged sieges. The city on the Bosporus was then, as so often later, the bulwark of Europe. In spite of this failure, the caliphate reached its greatest extent under the Ommiads. In a hundred years the Moslems had created an empire far larger than Rome had ever ruled.

IV

The Attempted Revival Under
Pippin and Charlemagne

THE ANCESTORS OF CHARLEMAGNE

D URING the seventh century the kingdom of the Franks seemed to
be disintegrating as the other Germanic kingdoms had done. In
spite of all their efforts, the kings lost power steadily to the nobles. The
nobles were neither willing nor able to maintain the power of the central
government. It is true that the mayor of the palace, who controlled the
royal administration, usually represented the interests of the aristocracy,
but the mayor's authority was by no means unquestioned. The kings were
sometimes strong enough to get rid of an unpopular mayor; the nobles
were frequently jealous of his power, and since there was a mayor for
each division of Frankish territory, civil wars between them were frequent. One mayor in Austrasia (East Frankland) formed an exaggerated
idea of his own power and tried to make his son king, but he failed to
get enough support to carry out his plans and was tortured to death by
the king of Neustria (West Frankland). Authority was so divided that
no one could make effective use of the resources of the country. Outlying districts, such as Gascony and Bavaria, became practically independent, and peace and security were lacking even in the heart of the
kingdom.

The Frankish realm was rescued from this hopeless situation by a
remarkable family which succeeded in gaining hereditary control of the
mayorship. The first of these great mayors was Pippin, whose grandfather had held the same office in the early part of the century. Pippin
at first ruled only Austrasia, the eastern half of the kingdom, but in
687 he defeated the mayor of Neustria and gained control of the entire

realm. He succeeded in restoring some degree of order and in increasing Frankish influence in the turbulent frontier districts. Even more important was his encouragement of the missionary activity of the Church. Since Pippin came from the German part of the kingdom, he was especially interested in the conversion of the pagans who pressed on his eastern frontiers. He also seems to have been a sincere Christian, in contrast to most of the Merovingian rulers. One of his grandfathers had been a mayor of the palace, but the other had been a bishop and a saint. Pippin was especially interested in the conversion of the Frisians, a piratical people whom he had subdued. He felt that his conquest of their country would never be secure until they had become Christians and abandoned their pagan practices. Consequently, he encouraged the labors of the Irish missionaries, who still had almost a monopoly of the field. He also sought help from England, which still had all the zeal of a newly converted country. Through this close coöperation with the Church, Pippin laid the foundation for the alliance which was to bind together his family and the papacy and strengthen both parties greatly.

Pippin died in 714, leaving the mayorship to his young grandsons. But Pippin's real successor was to be his illegitimate son Charles, later known as Martel, or the "Hammer." The supporters of the young mayors feared Charles' ability, and had him imprisoned, but they were unable to repress other dangers. The nobles of Neustria at once took advantage of the opportunity offered by the rule of a minor to assert their independence. They were successful at first, but Charles escaped from prison and in 717 won a decisive victory which subjected Neustria to his rule. Austrasia had already recognized him as mayor, and thenceforth neither the Merovingian kinglets nor the nobles of Neustria attempted to dispute his supremacy.

After Charles acquired the mayorship, the authority of the Merovingian kings still further declined. Einhard, the secretary of Charles the Great, has left a well-known description of them which shows how useless they appeared to Franks of a later generation.

There was nothing left for the king to do but to be content with his name of king, his flowing hair, and long beard; to sit on the throne and play the ruler; to give ear to the ambassadors that came from all quarters, and to dismiss them, as if on his own responsibility, in words that were, in fact, suggested to him or even imposed upon him. He had nothing that he could call his own beyond this vain title of king and the precarious support allowed by the mayor of the palace in his discretion, except a single country-seat, that brought him but a very small income . . . When he had to go abroad, he used to ride in a cart, drawn by a yoke of oxen, driven, peasant-fashion, by a plowman; he rode in this way to the palace and to the general assembly of the people, that met once a year for the welfare of the kingdom, and he returned home in like manner. The mayor of the palace took charge of the government, and of everything that had to be planned or executed at home or abroad.

Charles Martel had to fight hard to maintain his power. After his father's death many outlying parts of the Frankish realm had reasserted their independence. In rapid succession Charles had to subdue Swabia, Bavaria, and Aquitaine. Later he had to defend the country from the Moslems, and his success in checking the invaders at Poitiers did much to consolidate his power over his subjects. Yet Charles realized that military victories were not enough. Like Pippin, he wanted the assistance of the Church in organizing and civilizing his people. He encouraged missionaries and reformers, and carried on his father's tradition by showing special favor to Englishmen engaged in this work.

The greatest of the missionaries was the Englishman Winfrith, or, to give him his monastic name, Boniface. He was educated in his native land, and lived for a long time in a secluded monastery before he felt the call to preach in strange countries. His first work was in Frisia in 716, when he was forty years old, but he found the people so hostile to his efforts that he soon returned to England. A year later Boniface went to Rome and was sent to Thuringia and Hesse where he had more success. Then he returned to Frisia, where the work of evangelization could now proceed, thanks to the victories and support of Charles Martel. By this time Boniface had gained such a reputation that he was summoned to Rome and consecrated as a bishop. This visit made him an enthusiastic champion of the Roman supremacy, and he took an oath to obey the Roman Church in everything, and to have no communion with priests who did not recognize the absolute authority of the pope. The latter gave him a letter to Charles Martel which secured for him full protection and assistance. Later Boniface wrote: "Without the aid of the prince of the Franks I should not be able to rule my church, nor to defend the lives of my priests and nuns, nor to keep my converts from lapsing into pagan rites and observances." Secure in the protection of Charles, Boniface could risk such acts as cutting down Odin's oak near Fritzlar and building a chapel from its timber. Paganism now survived only in Frisia, Saxony, and other remote corners of Germany.

An even greater problem than paganism was the lack of organization of the German Church. Many Germans were only nominal Christians, who had little contact with the clergy and seldom attended religious services. There were almost no bishops functioning east of the Rhine. Irish monks were probably the most influential Christian leaders in central Germany and they were almost independent of Rome. To overcome these difficulties, Boniface was made an archbishop, with full authority to organize the German Church. He divided Bavaria and eastern Austrasia into bishoprics, over which he set his own disciples.

He persuaded some of the Irish monks to conform to Roman usages; those who would not yield were driven out and replaced by Benedictines. Boniface also founded new monasteries of which Fulda, built in the wilderness near the land of the "wild Saxons," was the most important. Even more than in Gaul, the Benedictines in Germany acted as pioneers, clearing land and introducing advanced agricultural methods in backward and thinly settled regions.

Boniface was also worried by the lack of respect for Rome and the corruptness of the West Frankish clergy. With the aid of Charles Martel he strove in council after council to make them take their duties seriously and to lead moral lives. Boniface always insisted on complete recognition of the pope's authority in matters of administration as well as of doctrine. The oath taken by his own German bishops in 784 shows what entire submission to Rome he exacted:

> We have declared and decreed that we would maintain and protect, until the end of our lives, the Catholic faith and unity, and submission to the Roman Church, St. Peter, and his vicar; that we would meet together each year in a council; that the metropolitan should apply to the Roman See for the pallium [1] and that we would canonically follow all the precepts of St. Peter, in order that we might be numbered among his sheep. We have all consented and subscribed our names to this oath, and have sent it to be deposited on the tomb of St. Peter, prince of the apostles.

When the Roman supremacy had been accepted, Boniface felt that his great work had been completed. He returned to the scene of his early labors, seeking martyrdom, and soon found the death for which he longed. He and a band of his followers were killed by pagan Frisians in 754 or 755. In accordance with his wishes he was laid at rest in Fulda.

His work had been fully as important for the state as for the Church. The councils presided over by Boniface were summoned by the mayor, and in them bishops and nobles discussed together the welfare of the whole kingdom. The reform in the morals and organization of the Church had great civic importance at a time when churchmen held high offices in the state and when the Church performed many essential functions of government. The constant aid which Charles and his sons gave to the work of Boniface persuaded the Church to tolerate the use of its property for secular purposes. In order to raise a force of cavalry large enough to cope with the Saracens, Charles had seized lands belonging to the Church and distributed them among his followers. The Church retained title to these lands, and received a nominal rent from them, but most of the income was retained by the lay holder and was used for his military expenses. This arrangement seems to have played

---

[1] The metropolitan is the archbishop. The pallium is a narrow strip of cloth which is one of the distinguishing marks of the office and can be conferred only by the pope.

an important part in creating the feudal concept of the fief—a grant of the use of property in return for military service. Charles' sons followed his example and the Church submitted, under protest, because it needed the aid of the mayors. The pope himself in 739 sought support from Charles in his struggle with the Lombards. Charles refused to help him, but the pope did not despair of eventually securing Frankish aid, and meanwhile he was anxious to bind the Franks more closely to his cause.

When Charles Martel died in 741, he was succeeded by two sons, Pippin and Carloman. A third son felt himself slighted and attempted a rebellion. He was captured and imprisoned, but revolts continued and the brothers finally found it necessary to set up a Merovingian king. For some years before his death Charles had allowed the throne to remain vacant and they had at first followed the same policy. Now they determined to crown the heir of the Merovingian line, who was an insignificant man, but whose name gave a shadow of legitimate authority to the real rulers. The stratagem was successful and after three years of continuous fighting Pippin and Carloman succeeded in crushing all rebellion.

When their position had been firmly established Carloman withdrew to a monastery. Einhard says: "The causes no man knew, but it would seem that he was truly moved by a desire for the life of contemplation and for the love of God." It is significant of the man's character that he waited until order had been established before carrying out his desires. On Carloman's retirement the third brother again attempted to revolt, but Pippin put this down and "the whole land had peace for two years." Secure, because of this unusual peace, Pippin now determined to make himself king. But as he was desirous of moral support for his action, he sent an embassy to the pope to ask who ought to be king, the Merovingian or himself. The pope replied, "It is better that the man who has the real power should also have the title of king, rather than the man who has the mere title and no real power." This consultation of the pope was significant and its importance was later magnified into a claim that the pope, by his spiritual power, had deposed the Merovingian and given the throne to Pippin. Actually the final step in the substitution of the new line took place in an assembly of nobles. With their consent, the Merovingian king "was deposed, shaved, and thrust into a cloister," and Pippin became king of the Franks.

PIPPIN AND CHARLES THE GREAT

The close connection between the pope and the Frankish kingdom, brought about by the work of Boniface and Charles Martel, became a political alliance after the coronation of Pippin. The pope was in great difficulties, as the Lombards had conquered Ravenna and were threatening Rome. The emperor at Constantinople did nothing to aid Italy, and the pope was wholly unable to defend the menaced territory. On the other hand, Pippin's position was not entirely secure. There had been some rebellious movements and many of his subjects resented his seizure of the throne. In these circumstances, the pope felt that the appeal for aid against the Lombards might be renewed with greater success.

In 754, Pope Stephen II went to France to ask assistance from Pippin. He was well received and immediately began to beg for protection against the Lombards. Meanwhile he devoted himself to strengthening the position of the new royal family. The king was anointed, in a solemn religious ceremony, as the kings of Israel had been. In addition, Stephen forbade the Franks, under penalty of excommunication, ever to choose a king from another family. Thus Pippin and his descendants obtained a sanction which the Merovingians had never possessed. They were God's anointed, and rebellion against them was rebellion against the Church. The pope also gave Pippin and his two sons the title of "patricians of the Romans." This was an empty honor, conferring no power, and the king seems to have considered it unimportant. In return for all these favors, Stephen obtained a promise of aid against the Lombards. Pippin had difficulty in persuading the nobles to accept this decision, since they preferred Charles Martel's policy of alliance with the Lombards, but they were finally won over and two expeditions were made across the Alps. Each time the Franks were victorious, and each time the Lombards, yielding temporarily to force, gave up Ravenna and other cities, and promised not to attack Rome. On the second expedition, in 756, the keys to the surrendered cities were solemnly carried to Rome and placed with a deed of gift on St. Peter's tomb. This was the famous donation of Pippin. Until the Lombards were thoroughly subdued, the gift was of little value; but later it served as a very important precedent and helped to influence Charles the Great to make his donation.

Pippin carried on the family policy of regaining the outlying territories and improving the government of the Frankish kingdom. He expelled the Saracens from Narbonne in 759 and, after eight years of fighting, reduced all Aquitaine to submission, thus completing two tasks begun by Charles Martel. He put down a rebellion in Bavaria and began the long task of conquering the Saxons by successful campaigns against them in 753 and 758. His reforms in government were completed by Charlemagne and will be discussed in connection with the latter's work. Pippin prepared the way for his more famous son in all fields, but the renown of Charlemagne has obscured the great services of the father.

When Pippin died in 768 he was succeeded by his sons, Charles and Carloman, who divided the realm between them. Carloman, however, died after reigning only three years. He left two infant sons, but Charles

excluded them from the succession, and thus acquired the entire kingdom. Once established as sole ruler, he was free to carry on the work
begun by his father and grandfather. The peoples who were nominally
under Frankish rule had to be subdued, and hostile neighbors conquered.
His first war was occasioned by a revolt in Aquitaine, which had been
so recently subdued by his father; he was successful and the province
was firmly annexed. His second war continued Pippin's policy of aiding
the pope against the Lombards. Charles believed firmly in the papal
alliance, as is shown by an early act in which he entitled himself:
"Charles, by the grace of God, king and rector of the kingdom of the
Franks, devoted defender of the Holy Church and its aider in all things."
However, among the other Franks, and even among members of the
royal family, this policy was unpopular. Carloman had been a friend
of the Lombard king Desiderius, and Pippin's widow had married Charles
to a Lombard princess in spite of the pope's protests against the "diabolical
union." But Desiderius had aroused Charles' anger by reconquering
the cities surrendered to Pippin, and he soon made matters worse by
giving shelter to Carloman's widow, who was still hoping to regain her
husband's inheritance for her children. Charles angrily repudiated his
Lombard wife and welcomed the pope's appeal "to succor the church
of God as Pippin, his father of holy memory had done." To satisfy the
reluctant nobles, he proposed terms of peace, which the Lombards refused, and then declared war. Desiderius was taken prisoner and thrust
into a monastery, while Charles took his place as king of the Lombards
in 774. At the pope's request he renewed the donation made by Pippin
and even extended it, but Charles never relinquished his actual control
over most of the territory included in the grant.

The conquest of the Saxons, who held most of northwestern Germany,
was Charles' greatest military achievement. As one of Charles' own
officials [2] wrote:

> No war ever undertaken by the Frank nation was carried on with such
> persistence and bitterness, or cost so much labor, because the Saxons, like
> almost all the tribes of Germany, were a fierce people, given to the worship
> of devils, and hostile to our religion, and did not consider it dishonorable
> to transgress and violate all law, human and divine. Then there were
> peculiar circumstances, that tended to cause a breach of the peace every
> day. Except in a few places, where large forests or mountain-ridges inter-
> vened and made the bounds certain, the line between ourselves and the
> Saxons passed almost in its whole extent through an open country, so that
> there was no end to the murders, thefts, and arsons on both sides. In this
> way the Franks became so embittered that they at last resolved to make
> reprisals no longer, but to open war with the Saxons. Accordingly war was
> begun against them and was waged for thirty-three successive years with

[2] Einhard, Turner's translation.

great fury; more however to the disadvantage of the Saxons than of the Franks. It could doubtless have been brought to an end sooner, had it not been for the faithlessness of the Saxons. It is hard to say how often they were conquered, and humbly submitting to the king promised to do what was enjoined upon them, giving without hesitation the required hostages and receiving the officers sent them from the king. They were sometimes so much weakened and reduced that they promised to renounce the worship of devils and to adopt Christianity: but they were no less ready to violate these terms than prompt to accept them, so that it is impossible to tell which came easier to them to do; scarcely a year passed from the beginning of the war without such changes on their part. But the king did not suffer his high purpose and steadfastness—firm alike in good and evil fortune—to be wearied by any fickleness on their part, or to be turned from the task that he had undertaken; on the contrary, he never allowed their faithless behavior to go unpunished, but either took the field against them in person, or sent his counts with an army to wreak vengeance and exact righteous satisfaction. At last, after conquering and subduing all who had offered resistance, he took ten thousand of those that lived on the banks of the Elbe, and settled them, with their wives and children, in many different bodies here and there in Gaul and Germany. The war that had lasted so many years was at length ended by their acceding to the terms offered by the king; which were renunciation of their national religious customs and the worship of devils, acceptance of the sacraments of the Christian faith and religion and union with the Franks to form one people.

While it took years to subdue the Saxons, there were periods in which they were relatively quiescent, and Charles had plenty of time for other wars. He destroyed the powers of the Avars, a nomad people who had penetrated to the region of the middle Danube, and gained great wealth in sacking their camp. With the collapse of the Avars many of the Slavic tribes living in what is now eastern Germany recognized Charles' suzerainty and paid him tribute. At the other end of the kingdom, Charles attempted to take advantage of disputes among the Mohammedan rulers of Spain by occupying the region between the Ebro and the Pyrenees. He was obliged to retreat hastily, and in the valley of Roncesvalles his rearguard, commanded by Count Roland,[3] was annihilated by a sudden Gascon attack. In spite of the defeat, Charles retained possession of a strip of land beyond the Pyrenees. This expedition, of little actual importance, was to be remembered as the most famous episode of Charles' career. When Europe became enthusiastic over the Crusades, Charles was represented as having spent his life in fighting the Saracens, and Roland became the hero of a great medieval epic.

His conquests had made Charles ruler over many nations. He had

---

[3] Nothing else is known of Roland; a fact which made it easy for him to become a legendary hero.

doubled the size of the old kingdom of the Franks, and his territories could well be described as an empire. Yet every one still believed in the unity of the Christian world and in the continued existence of the Roman Empire. As long as the ruler at Constantinople did nothing to forfeit the respect of the West, he was accepted without question as the head of Christendom. In the eighth century, however, the Byzantine rulers had not only failed to protect the pope from Lombard attacks; they had also forbidden sacred images in the churches. This policy offended the pope, who felt that it was an attack on the orthodoxy which the Roman Church had always defended. Matters were made worse when the empress Irene blinded her son and assumed the throne. No woman had ever ruled the Roman state and many people, unwilling to recognize Irene, considered that the Empire had no legal head. At the same time the pope, Leo III, was greatly in need of a protector. In 799 his enemies had attacked him in the streets of Rome and had attempted to blind him. He fled to Charles, who furnished him with a guard which enabled him to reëstablish himself in the city. But there was no assurance that the guard would remain and legally it had no right to interfere in the government of Rome. The pope felt that he was at the mercy of his enemies unless Charles could be given permanent legal authority in the city. Consequently, when Charles visited Rome in the following year:

> It seemed both to Leo the pope himself, and to all the holy fathers who were present in the self-same council, as well as to the rest of the Christian people, that they ought to take to be emperor Charles king of the Franks, who held Rome herself, where the Cæsars had always been wont to sit, and all the other regions which he ruled through Italy and Gaul and Germany; and, inasmuch as God had given all these lands into his hands, it seemed right that with the help of God and at the prayer of the whole Christian people he should have the name of emperor also.[4]

On Christmas Day, 800, as Charles knelt in prayer before the altar in the old church of St. Peter, Pope Leo suddenly placed upon his head a crown, and the people acclaimed him as emperor. If we can trust an account written a little later they cried three times: "To Charles, the most pious Augustus, crowned of God, the great and peace-giving emperor, be life and victory." [5]

Einhard, Charles' secretary and biographer, says that Charles declared that he would not have entered the church the day he was crowned if he had known of the pope's plan. This is difficult to understand, since it is inconceivable that a man in Leo's position would have risked annoying his protector by conferring on him an unwanted title. Moreover, the

[4] Translation from the Annales Laureshamenses, by James Bryce (*Holy Roman Empire,* ch. V).
[5] From the *Life of Leo III.*

ceremony seems to have been carefully prepared, and it is hard to believe that the royal household remained ignorant of the plans. Charles' remark may have arisen from the same false modesty which forced every bishop-elect to protest his unworthiness. Or, when he began negotiations with the Eastern Empire for recognition of his title, he may have wished to represent the pope as solely responsible for the coronation. In any case, there is no doubt that Charles wished to be emperor; in spite of protests from Constantinople he used the title for the rest of his life.

When he was crowned emperor Charles was about fifty-eight years of age. Einhard describes him as follows:

> . . . large and strong and of lofty stature, though not disproportionately tall. . . . The upper part of his head was round, his eyes very large and animated, nose a little long, hair fair, and face laughing and merry. Thus his appearance was always stately and dignified, whether he was standing or sitting; although his neck was thick and somewhat short, and his belly rather prominent; but the symmetry of the rest of his body concealed these defects. His gait was firm, his whole carriage manly, and his voice clear, but not so strong as his size led one to expect. His health was excellent. . . . In accordance with the national custom, he took frequent exercise on horseback and in the chase. . . . He enjoyed the exhalations from natural warm springs and often practised swimming, in which he was such an adept that none could surpass him; and hence it was that he built his palace at Aix-la-Chapelle, and lived there constantly during his later years until his death. He used not only to invite his sons to his bath, but his nobles and friends, and now and then a troop of his retinue or bodyguards, so that a hundred or more persons sometimes bathed with him.
>
> Charles was temperate in eating, and particularly so in drinking, for he abominated drunkenness in anybody, much more in himself and those of his household; but he could not easily abstain from food, and often complained that fasts injured his health. His meals ordinarily consisted of four courses, not counting the roast, which his huntsmen used to bring in on the spit; he was more fond of this than of any other dish. While at table he listened to reading or music. The subjects of the readings were the stories and deeds of olden times: he was fond, too, of St. Augustine's books, and especially of the one entitled the *City of God*. He was so moderate in the use of wine and all sorts of drinks that he rarely allowed himself more than three cups in the course of a meal. In summer, after the midday meal, he would eat some fruit, drain a single cup, put off his clothes and shoes, just as he did for the night, and rest for two or three hours.

In governing his empire Charles made few innovations; he simply developed the system which had been used by his predecessors. His real ability was shown, not in creating new institutions, but in making old institutions work. The Merovingians, ruling a much smaller kingdom, had been unable to secure obedience from the counts and local magnates. Charles' authority was respected everywhere, and, while he did not succeed in eliminating all bad officials and lawless nobles, there was greater security and better government in western Europe during his reign than there had been for centuries. Charles had the great quality of persistence, a quality which so many otherwise able medieval rulers lacked. It was shown in his long war with the Saxons; it appeared equally in his attention to the details of government. For example, since most of the emperor's income came from his estates, he required his stewards to send him every year a detailed report of the income and resources of each villa. The stewards were ordered to describe the amount of land cultivated, the status of the laborers, the number of farm animals, the amount of food, wool, soap and lumber produced, and the furniture, tools, and farm equipment available. In his laws Charles attacked the same abuses again and again. While this shows that he did not succeed in eradicating them, it also shows that he did not forget them; he seldom abandoned a plan which he had conceived.

Charles relied heavily on the *missi dominici*, agents of the central administration send out to investigate the conduct of the counts. *Missi* had been employed by earlier kings, but Charles used them far more extensively than his predecessors had done. The Empire was divided into districts, and every year two *missi*, one a layman and the other a cleric, were sent to each district. They held a court in which any one could complain about misconduct of the local authorities and when they finished their work they were required to send written reports to the emperor. In this way he was able to retain some control over the counts and nobles, even though the *missi* were not always as efficient or as honest as they might have been.

While Charles restricted the power of the nobles by his use of the *missi*, he was obliged to recognize their growing importance in military affairs. Theoretically, every free man owed service in the army whenever it was summoned, but since there was a war in almost every year of Charles' reign, rigid enforcement of this rule would have worked intolerable hardship. Usually only the men of the districts near the seat of the war were summoned, but even this limited service was a burden to the poorer landholders. They had to furnish their own equipment and food for three months, and had to abandon their farms during the growing season. Gradually a rule was evolved whereby only the wealthy land-owners owed personal service, while the poorer men clubbed together and sent one of their number to represent the group. In 808, for example, men with more than four *mansi* [6] served in person; those with less were grouped so that they sent one representative as soon as their farms added up to four *mansi*, and so in proportion. At the same time Charles realized that many great land-owners were building up private

* The *mansus* was, in theory, the amount of land which could support one family.

bodyguards and that many poor men, seeking the protection of the wealthy, had become bound to them by personal ties. Consequently, permission was given to all men to come to the army in the contingent led by their lord rather than in the local force led by the count. By these two measures the greater land-owners became the most important element in the army.

In spite of his power, Charles could not free himself from dependence on the counts and great land-owners. The government still had no important sources of revenue; its income was derived almost entirely from estates held by the emperor, from a share of the fines levied in local courts, and from the "free gifts" which officials and magnates had to make when they visited the court. Thus there was not enough money to pay for an elaborate administrative system and Charles depended almost entirely upon the unpaid services of wealthy men. His prestige was great enough to keep them obedient, but their power in local affairs increased even during his reign, and it was evident that a weaker ruler would have trouble in keeping them under control. The interests of most men were still confined to their own localities, and the restoration of order and political unity in the West brought no corresponding economic revival.[7] Under Charles, as under the last Western emperors, there were few economic ties to supplement the political bond of the Empire.

Perhaps Charles' greatest service to Europe was his interest in the revival of education, and his continued support of the reform of the Church. Both these movements had originated in England, but their success was ensured by the fact that Charles favored them. As Einhard says:

> He most zealously cultivated the liberal arts, held those who taught them in great esteem, and conferred great honors upon them. He took lessons in grammar of the deacon Peter of Pisa, at that time an aged man. Another deacon, Albin of Britain, surnamed Alcuin, . . . who was the greatest scholar of the day, was his teacher in other branches of learning. The king spent much time and labor with him studying rhetoric, dialectics, and especially astronomy; he learned to reckon, and used to investigate the motions of the heavenly bodies most curiously, with an intelligent scrutiny. He also tried to write, and used to keep tablets and blanks in bed under his pillow, that at leisure hours he might accustom his hand to form the letters; however as he did not begin his efforts in due season, but late in life, they met with ill success.

Alcuin was the teacher, not only of Charles, but also of the palace school, which was attended by the children of the emperor and of lead-

---

[7] This would be denied by Dopsch and other German historians. There is little evidence of any sort about economic activity under Charlemagne; a fact which suggests that it was not very intense.

ing nobles. Other schools were established and were open to the nobles and to bright youths of humble birth. Charles also tried to assemble at his court learned men from all parts of western Europe. Alcuin was from the episcopal school at York in the Anglo-Saxon kingdom of Northumbria; Paul the Deacon was a Lombard from Friuli; Theodulf was a Goth; Angilbert was a Frank; Peter was from Pisa; Paulinus was from Aquitaine; Einhard, who has been quoted so extensively, was a Frank. These men, together with Charles and others, formed a so-called academy. They assumed names drawn from the Bible or the classics; thus Charles was known as David, Alcuin as Horace, and Angilbert as Homer. The members of this academy discussed all kinds of questions and prided themselves on their learning. An admiring biographer writing some years later says that "the Gauls and the Franks were then the equals of the old Romans and Athenians."

Much of the work that these men did was imitative and unoriginal, yet they rendered great services to learning. By bringing together men from all parts of the West, it became possible to reunite the scattered fragments of classical knowledge. The common culture of the West, which had been threatened by the anarchy of the seventh century, was reëstablished. While Charles' scholars added little new knowledge, they made it much easier to discover and assimilate the knowledge which already existed. Moreover, for the first time, the Germans took part in this culture as equals, instead of looking to the Romans as masters. Thanks to the conquest and conversion of most of Germany by Charles and his father, the Latin tradition could now spread to parts of the world where Rome had never ruled. Perhaps the most visible evidence of the influence of the new learning may be seen in handwriting. The Romans had used only capitals. In the Merovingian period small letters were introduced, but the books of that age were very badly written and are very hard to read. Charles ordered that all books used in the church service be revised, since men often prayed to God badly because of the illegible script and the errors of careless copyists. He then entrusted to Alcuin the reformation of handwriting and the results may be seen in the beautiful manuscripts written at Tours while the Englishman was abbot there. These manuscripts are perfectly legible at the present day, and most of our small letters are derived from the reformed handwriting of Alcuin. This interest in learning also led to the copying of important works. Since earlier examples of these works have since been lost, we owe much of our knowledge of the ancient world to the scholars who worked under Charles.

Like all his family, Charles was interested in the reform of the Church. He wanted his state to be a Christian kingdom, and he felt that it was just as much his duty to make it Christian as it was to strengthen the monarchy. This tendency became especially marked after his coronation as emperor. In fact, Charles seems to have desired the title primarily because it gave him greater power over the Church. He took over the traditions of the old Roman emperors and frequently interfered in religious affairs. For example, in the general instructions which he issued in 802, Charles ordered all subjects over the age of twelve to take an oath of fidelity to him as emperor. Then he defined this fidelity to include living a highly moral life, as well as the fulfilment of the ordinary duties of the subject. There was special emphasis on the morals of the clergy:

> Bishops and priests shall live according to the canons [law of the Church] and shall teach others to do the same . . . monks shall live firmly and strictly according to the rule . . . monasteries for women shall be strictly ruled . . . no bishops, abbots, priests, deacons, or other members of the clergy shall presume to have dogs for hunting, or hawks, falcons and sparrow hawks . . . the canonical clergy shall observe fully the canonical life, and shall be instructed at the episcopal residence or in the monastery with all diligence.

Charles failed to create a lasting government, largely because economic conditions still favored localism rather than centralization. But much of his other work endured. In his reign the long decline of civilization which had begun in the third century was halted and the foundations of a new Europe were laid. The sharp distinction between Roman and German vanished; men of all races coöperated in scholarship and in religion. The old tribal laws were overridden by imperial capitularies, or ordinances, which applied to the whole realm. The reformed Church, which owed so much to Charles and his family, made the nominal Christians of northern Europe take their faith more seriously. There was an optimism, a hopefulness, in Charles' reign which had not been known for centuries. Even though there was a decline after Charles' death, conditions were never quite so bad again as they had been in the seventh century. Europe had passed the turning point; it no longer suffered from the death agony of the ancient world, but from the birth pangs of the new civilization. The fact that Europe had a common culture is due as much to Charles as to the Roman Empire. This is why men have agreed to call him great, so that his name is commonly written Charlemagne, Charles the Great.

V

The Collapse
of the Carolingian Empire

THE SUCCESSORS OF CHARLEMAGNE

WHEN CHARLEMAGNE died in 814, the difficult problems of govern-ment which had been masked by his personal ability became in-creasingly apparent. The Empire was very large, communications were slow, and the old tendency to local self-sufficiency was stronger than ever. Wars between Byzantium and the Arabs had interfered with Mediter-ranean trade and had probably diminished the flow of goods from the East. The decreased supply of luxury articles caused a decline in Western commerce and there were few economic bonds between different parts of the Empire. The free German warriors, who had been the chief sup-port of the Frankish kings, were impoverished by the endless wars and many of them had become dependents of the wealthy land-owners. These land-owners were resentful of central control, yet the whole government depended upon their support. They controlled the county courts, were the dominant element in the army, and practically monopolized the offices of count and bishop. The counts who were the greatest land-owners, were more interested in building up their local power than in obeying the orders of the emperor. Einhard says that most of the counts were corrupt and dishonest and that even the *missi* had to be closely watched. Charlemagne himself had not been able to protect ambassadors from ill-treatment by his own counts. Only a very strong ruler could keep any semblance of order and unity under such conditions. Charlemagne's successors, while they were of more than average ability, lacked his remarkable energy and perseverance. It is only fair to add that even the great Charles might have found it hard to keep the Empire together during the strains of the ninth century. The fatal disease of localism, which began in the last days of Rome, had not been checked, and a new wave of barbarian invasions increased the difficulty of maintaining central authority.

Charles' heir was his one surviving son, Louis the Pious, as he is usually called. There have been great differences of opinion with regard to his character, but all historians have agreed that he was a far weaker man than Charlemagne. In a less responsible position he might have made a good ruler. He had been made king of Aquitaine while his father was still alive and had won praise for the excellence of his government there. He was much better educated than his father had been and he was also more pious, as he had been trained by the leading churchmen of the time. When he succeeded to the throne he dismissed all the councilors of his father who had led immoral lives. This alienated some of the strongest supporters of the monarchy and caused an opposition party to rise. The feeling against him was intensified by the fact that he had lived long in Aquitaine and had little in common with the East Frankish nobles who had been so influential at his father's court. His piety made him subservient to the pope and to other officials of the Church. During his father's lifetime he had been directed to crown himself emperor, but after Charles' death he had had himself recrowned by the pope. By this act the pope helped to lay a foundation for the theory that a new emperor had to be approved by the Church; a theory which Charles had probably wished to contradict by ordering Louis to crown himself.

Louis' respect for the Church weakened his imperial authority, but his final downfall was caused by family difficulties. He was easily influenced by those whom he loved and trusted: unfortunately it was never possible to satisfy all of these people at the same time. His whole reign was made miserable by the attempt to find a solution to the problem of the succession which would preserve the Empire without irritating his family. The old Frankish custom of dividing a kingdom among all the sons of a ruler, as if it were a piece of private property, had never been forgotten, but the bad consequences of this policy had been avoided for a century by a series of fortunate accidents. Charles Martel had left two sons, but one of them entered a monastery. Pippin had divided his kingdom between Charles and Carloman, but Carloman soon died. Charles the Great had planned a division of the Empire, but Louis was the only one of his sons to survive. Now Louis, who had three sons, was faced with the problem of division. In 817 he marked out the portion which each was to have, but at the same time he tried to preserve the unity of the Empire by subordinating the two younger brothers to the eldest. Lothair was to be emperor and was to supervise the government of his brothers in the small portions of the realm which they were to receive.

He was immediately associated with his father in the rule of the Empire, in order to gain experience. This plan entirely neglected the claims of Bernard, a nephew of Louis who had been ruling over a part of Italy which Charlemagne had assigned to his father. Bernard naturally felt much aggrieved and, supported by the opposition, attempted to set himself up as an independent king. The rebellion was quickly put down; Bernard's allies were executed, and Bernard himself was sentenced to be blinded. Although he had come to his uncle's court under a safe-conduct, the sentence was carried out, and so clumsily that Bernard died from the shock.

Louis was filled with remorse as a consequence of this act and when his wife died the following year he looked upon her death as a sign of the displeasure of heaven. Regret preyed on his mind until in 822 he did public penance in his palace at Attigny, where he confessed that "he had shown himself so often guilty, in his life, in his faith, and his duties, that it would be impossible for him to enumerate all the circumstances in which he had been at fault." This public humiliation shows Louis' piety, and also the difference between him and his father; it is impossible to imagine Charlemagne humbling himself before his subjects. The act hurt Louis' prestige and probably encouraged his sons to rebel against him.

Shortly before the penance at Attigny, Louis had made another serious mistake by marrying again. The new empress Judith was as strong-minded as she was beautiful and soon gained control over her husband. When a son, Charles, was born to Judith and Louis, she forced the emperor to spend the rest of his life preparing a suitable kingdom for the boy. Louis' other sons resented any favors given to their half-brother and despised their father for his weakness. At the same time the whole family disliked Lothair, the eldest son, who was taking his position as co-emperor too seriously. An endless series of family quarrels eventually turned into civil wars. At times the three elder sons combined against Louis and held him prisoner; at other times Louis succeeded in uniting his younger sons against Lothair and regained his power. The only ones to profit from these senseless struggles were the nobles, who became more and more independent as their masters quarreled. Finally, in 838, one of the sons died, and another, Louis the German, was in disgrace, so the emperor turned again to Lothair, offering him forgiveness and half the kingdom if he would protect Charles and aid him in keeping possession of the other half. Lothair accepted, and Louis the Pious drew up a final treaty of division which embodied these terms.

Louis died in 840, hoping that he had finally ended the quarrel over the succession. Instead it soon became worse than before. Lothair did not keep the agreement which he had just made, but claimed the whole Empire in accordance with the constitution of 817. Charles, later called the Bald, naturally resented this and allied himself with the disinherited Louis the German. So "the war of the three brothers" began. The nobles of the Empire made the most of this new opportunity to extort concessions and served whichever party promised them the most. It was not to their interest to have any brother win a decisive victory, and both parties had to contend with disloyalty within their own ranks. The one great battle of the war, at Fontenay in 841, was inconclusive, though each side made exaggerated claims about the slaughter of their opponents. Contemporaries, unable to understand the increasing success of Viking raids, believed that so many Franks were killed in the battle that there were no longer enough men to guard the frontiers. There is no proof of such serious decrease in manpower, and the success of the Northmen may be ascribed rather to the growing weakness of the central government.

Soon after the battle Charles and Louis separated, but they were helpless against Lothair when they split their combined force. In February, 842, they met at Strasburg and renewed their alliance. Each one took a public oath to support the other, using the vernacular languages which were understood by the soldiers. Since Charles had been assigned Gaul at various times, and Louis had ruled a portion of Germany for many years, the bulk of their followers came from these two regions. Consequently, the oaths give us early examples of the dialects which developed into French and German. The oath ran as follows:

> For the love of God and the common salvation of the Christian people and ourselves, from this day forth, as far as God gives me wisdom and power, I will treat this my brother as one should rightfully treat a brother, on condition that he does the same by me. And with Lothair I will not willingly enter into any agreement which might injure this, my brother.

The Romance form was:

> Pro Deo amur et pro Christian poblo et nostro commun salvament, dist di in avant, in quant Deus savir et podir me dunat, si salvarai eo cist meon fradre Karlo et in adiudha et in cadhuna cosa si cum om per dreit son fradra salvar dift, in o quid il mi altresi fazet; et ab Ludher nul plaid numquam prindrai, qui meon vol cist meon fradre Karlo in damno sit.

The German version was:

> In Godes minna ind in thes Christianes folches ind unser bedhero gehaltnissi, fon thesemo dage frammordes, so fram so mir Got gewizci indi madh furgibit, so haldih thesan minan bruodher, soso man mit rehtu sinan bruher scal, in thiu, thaz er mig so sama duo; indi mit Ludheren in nohheinin thing ne gegango, the minan willon imo ce scadhen werden.

This union of the two brothers forced Lothair to terms and in 843 he accepted the treaty of Verdun, dividing the Empire into three portions. Lothair retained the title of emperor and received the largest share of the lands. But his portion was a long, central strip, extending from the mouth of the Rhine to Rome, and touching the Rhône on the west and the Rhine on the east. This territory included the two capitals of Aix-la-Chapelle and Rome, and the majority of the emperor's estates, but it had neither political, geographic, nor linguistic unity. It was exposed to attack from either side, since the boundaries were not very clearly marked out and were not protected by natural defenses. The creation of such an artificial unit shows how little the Franks understood the real nature of a state. To them a kingdom was merely an assemblage of counties obeying the same master or a large enough group of royal estates to support a king; they never felt that other bonds were necessary. Lothair's possession of the central strip determined the location of the shares of his brothers. Louis the German received almost all the eastern lands beyond the Rhine, while Charles the Bald was given the western portion of the Empire. This division led the way to the formation of the modern nations, since France was clearly separated from Germany, and Italy soon fell away from the central kingdom. The rest of the middle lands never achieved political stability and were destined to be the eternal battleground of Europe. The struggles for possession of Belgium and Lorraine in recent wars are simply the latest phases of a conflict which began in the ninth century.

The middle kingdom was inherently weak, and the old policy of dividing the family possessions among the sons of the ruler soon led to its complete collapse. The emperor Lothair, who died in 855, gave each of his three sons a share of his lands. The eldest, Louis, received Italy with the imperial title, an honor which by this time was almost meaningless. Another son was given the territory lying between the Rhône and the Alps, a region known as the kingdom of Burgundy. The second son, who bore his father's name of Lothair, took over the northernmost lands, which soon became known as Lothair's kingdom, Lotharingia or Lorraine. It should be noticed that the Lorraine of this period was far larger than the present district of that name; it included Alsace, the Low Countries and much of eastern France and western Germany. The second Lothair died without heirs in 869 and his uncles, Charles the Bald and Louis the German, immediately began quarreling over the heritage. By the treaty of Mersen, 870, Lorraine was divided between the two rulers, but this settlement was no more lasting than earlier ones, and the two brothers remained on very bad terms. When the emperor Louis II, who had been vainly struggling to maintain order in the Italian kingdom, died in 875, Charles and Louis the German had a new cause for disputes. Each wanted the imperial title, but Charles reached Rome first and was crowned on Christmas Day, 875. It was the anniversary of the coronation of Charles the Great, but that was the only resemblance between the two ceremonies. In the brief space of

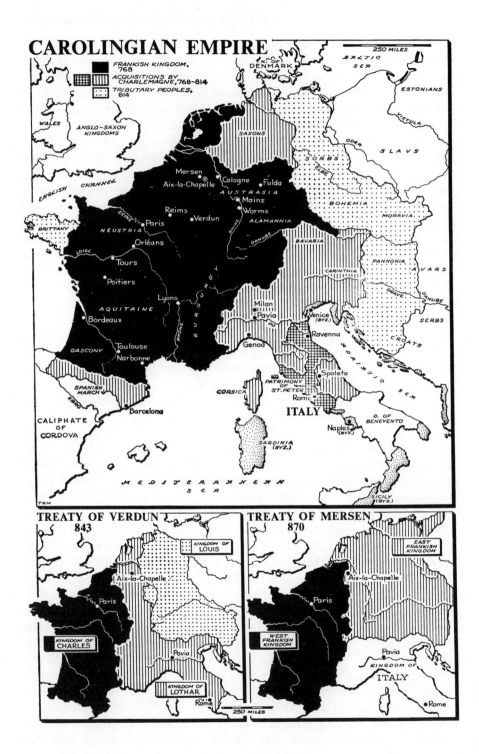

CAROLINGIAN EMPIRE

- ■ FRANKISH KINGDOM, 768
- ▦ ACQUISITIONS BY CHARLEMAGNE, 768-814
- ⠿ TRIBUTARY PEOPLES, 814

250 MILES

DENMARK
BALTIC SEA
ESTONIANS
WALES
ANGLO-SAXON KINGDOMS
VISTULA
SLAVS
ENGLISH CHANNEL
SAXONS
ODER
SORBS
ELBE
Mersen
Cologne
Fulda
BRITTANY
Aix-la-Chapelle
AUSTRASIA
BOHEMIA
MORAVIA
SEINE
Mainz
Reims
Worms
Paris
Verdun
ALAMANNIA
NEUSTRIA
RHINE
Orléans
LOIRE
DANUBE
BAVARIA
PANNONIA
AVARS
Tours
CARINTHIA
DANUBE
Poitiers
DRAVE
Lyons
AQUITAINE
RHONE
Milan (BYZ.)
Venice (BYZ.)
SERBS
Bordeaux
BURGUNDY
Pavia
Ravenna
CROATS
GASCONY
Genoa
ADRIATIC SEA
Toulouse
Narbonne
SPANISH MARCH
CORSICA
PATRIMONY OF ST. PETER
Spoleto
CALIPHATE OF CORDOVA
Barcelona
Rome
ITALY
D. OF BENEVENTO
Naples (BYZ.)
SARDINIA (BYZ.)
MEDITERRANEAN SEA
SICILY (BYZ.)
TRM

TREATY OF VERDUN 843

KINGDOM OF LOUIS
Aix-la-Chapelle
Paris
KINGDOM OF CHARLES
Pavia
KINGDOM OF LOTHAR
Rome
250 MILES

TREATY OF MERSEN 870

EAST FRANKISH KINGDOM
Aix-la-Chapelle
Paris
WEST FRANKISH KINGDOM
Pavia
KINGDOM OF ITALY
Rome

seventy-five years the Empire had become a fiction; Charles the Bald returned to France as soon as he received the title and left the pope and Italy to their fate.

Louis the German died in 876, and Charles the Bald in 881. Their descendants were remarkably short-lived. By 884 only two legitimate Carolingians were left, Charles the Fat, son of Louis the German, and Charles the Simple, grandson of Charles the Bald. Since the latter was a child of five, the French nobles decided to accept Charles the Fat as their ruler. He was already king of Germany and had been crowned emperor in 881, so that his accession to the throne of France reunited all the old Carolingian lands under one ruler. This is his only claim to distinction. He was utterly incompetent as a ruler, and was deposed in 887, dying three months later. With his abdication the power of the Carolingians came to an end. Powerful nobles created new royal dynasties in France, Germany and Italy, while Burgundy, Provence, and Brittany became independent kingdoms. It is true that Charles the Simple regained the throne of France in 898, and that he and his descendants retained a precarious hold on the country for another century, but their position was never secure. The rival royal family, descended from the counts of Paris, was always ready to seize the throne, and the great nobles demanded such concessions in return for their support that very little authority was left the king.

THE NEW INVASIONS

Family quarrels, divisions of the Empire, and personal incompetence had marked the reigns of the last Carolingians. The counts and dukes had taken full advantage of the weaknesses of their kings to make themselves practically independent rulers of the districts in which they lived. There had been surprisingly little loyalty among any class of the population to the ideal of the unity of Christendom, as expressed in the Frankish Empire. Only the great churchmen of the ninth century realized the dangers inherent in the breakdown of central government. The Church could not function effectively if Europe were to be split up among quarrelsome petty tyrants. Its centralized organization would inevitably suffer from local jealousies and endangered communications. Local rulers would seek to make their own favorites bishops and abbots and the reforms of the eighth century would be swept away. The Church as an international organization could do its work only in a united Europe. Moreover, the leaders of the Church, who were the most enlightened and civilized men of the ninth century, were appalled by the growth of war, disorder, and misgovernment. Under the leadership of such men as Hincmar, bishop of Rheims, they strove desperately to preserve the unity of Europe. Again and again they made the quarreling Carolingians swear to live in peace with each other and aid each other in defending and ruling their lands. Again and again this family league to keep peace was broken by the greediness and jealousy of its members. Yet the Church could not abandon the Carolingians. Bad as they were, they had some understanding of the methods and values of large-scale political organization, an idea which their opponents completely lacked. But the Church, in its dual campaign to preserve the unity of Europe and the authority of the Carolingians, had little success. The great mass of the people of Europe seemed quite resigned to the disintegration of the Empire and to the collapse of royal power. Like the Roman Empire, the Carolingian Empire fell because few men were willing to make any great effort to preserve it. Economic interests were local, and political loyalty was given to the local strong man rather than to the distant sovereign. Neither the Church nor the royal family could arrest the creeping paralysis of localism which had already destroyed the far stronger empire of Rome.

Yet the complete and rapid collapse of Charlemagne's Empire was not due solely to internal causes. Some semblance of unity might have been preserved, at least for a time, had it not been for a new series of invasions which began early in the ninth century and continued for over one hundred years. These new invasions were the worst which western Europe has ever had to face; they did far more damage than the German movements of the fifth century. Unlike the Germans, the new invaders were at first interested in plunder rather than settlement, and they struck at every part of the Empire in their search for spoils. The Carolingian kings were helpless against the fast-moving, widely scattered raiders; they could seldom move their armies fast enough to catch their elusive enemies. Communications became even worse than before, and each district had to see to its own defense. The local magnates assumed the task of protecting their weaker neighbors and in taking over the duties of the central government they also took over its powers. As a result, when the invasions finally ended, feudalism was firmly established in France and Italy and was growing in England and Germany.

The new invaders were the Saracens, the Northmen, and the Magyars. They ringed Europe on three sides, South, North, and East, and with their light ships and fast-moving cavalry they penetrated to every part of the continent. They raided every region from the British Isles to Sicily, and from the Bay of Biscay to the Black Sea. They stole everything which could be carried off—gold, silver, the base metals, cloth and even children, whom they sold as slaves. They destroyed everything which they could not steal, and slaughtered hundreds of thousands of men. To beat off or assimilate these invaders was one of the hardest tasks which Europe ever faced.

The Saracens came first, continued their raiding longest, and yet probably did the least damage. They confined their activities to a smaller area; only Italy and southern France suffered from their attacks. They became interested in conquest sooner than the other invaders, a fact which led them to concentrate their efforts on a few localities. They also suffered more from internal dissensions and so were more vulnerable to counterattacks. Nevertheless, they kept Italy in a turmoil for over a hundred years and hampered Mediterranean trade until the eleventh century.

The Saracen danger came from Africa rather than Spain. In their eagerness to strike at Gaul, the Moslems had never completed the conquest of the Iberian peninsula and some tiny Christian kingdoms survived in the northern mountains. Charlemagne prolonged the line of buffer states by his conquest of the Spanish March, and from his time on, Moslem Spain was insulated from the rest of Europe. The Saracens of the peninsula exhausted their strength in attacking the Christian states of the North and in quarreling with each other. They were not very dangerous to Europe in the ninth and tenth centuries.

The Saracens of Africa were far more of a menace. They became great seamen and great pirates; from the seventh to the nineteenth centuries Europe was troubled by the problem of the corsairs of North Africa. By the ninth century mere piracy was not enough; they began to establish themselves on the islands of the western Mediterranean as a preliminary to further raids. The conquest of Sicily, which began in 827, was completed by the middle of the century, and by 900 both Sardinia and Corsica were in Moslem hands. During the same period they attacked the Italian mainland, but with less success. They held some towns for seventy years, but they never gained enough territory to create an Italian Saracen state. However, from the bases which they had acquired, they were able to plunder and terrorize the whole peninsula. One Moslem outpost was established at the mouth of the Garigliano, between Rome and Naples, a strategic location which enabled the raiders to exact tribute from the pope and to plunder the mother abbey of Monte Cassino. Another robbers' nest was located at Garde Frainet, on the extreme north coast of Italy. From this fortress they struck far inland, robbing and holding for ransom travelers in the chief Alpine passes. The Carolingians of Italy exhausted themselves in fighting the Saracens, but they were never able to drive them entirely out of the peninsula. The dens of pirates were eliminated only when the local magnates became so alarmed that they forgot their differences and gave up their treasonable alliances with the infidels. The islands remained under Moslem rule until the eleventh century, when the Italian cities became strong enough to seize command of the sea and Norman adventurers drove the Saracens from Sicily.

The Northmen covered far more territory and did much more damage than the Saracens. They attacked every European country from Spain to Russia, though their most destructive raids were made on the British Isles and France. They pushed their peaceful settlement even farther afield, occupying the Orkneys, the Faroes, Iceland, Greenland and, temporarily, a part of the North American coast. Historians have not yet solved the problem of the expansion of the Northmen. How could the small, relatively poor Scandinavian countries send forth such hordes of warriors? Why did this great emigration come when it did? It seems likely that the population of Norway, Sweden, and Denmark grew steadily from the fifth century on, and that those who were too crowded at home moved to the empty lands around the Baltic which the Germans had deserted when they moved south. Only when all the unused land was occupied did the rest of Europe feel the pressure. It has also been suggested that, as the population increased, attempts were made to form larger and more powerful political units, and that local leaders, defeated by stronger opponents, emigrated rather than obey their rivals. This was true especially in Denmark, where the kings waged a long and, in the end, successful war against the nobles. But this does not explain why the population of the Scandinavian countries should have been increasing at a time when it was certainly no more than stationary in other regions, and this, after all, is the heart of the problem.

The Northmen knew Europe well. They were traders before they were pirates and had controlled one of the most important routes of European commerce. This route left the great overland road to the East at the Caspian Sea and went through the trading cities of the Volga to the rivers which flow into the Baltic. From the Baltic, goods could be shipped to England, Saxony, Flanders, and France. This route was especially important when Mediterranean commerce was harassed by the Byzantine-Moslem conflict, and the traders who used it became acquainted with every port and river of northern Europe.

The Northmen were already restless at the time of Charlemagne. The Danes raided the northern frontier of the Frankish Empire and a few tentative attacks were made on England, Ireland, and Frisia during the last decade of the eighth century. These first exploratory raids were relatively unsuccessful, but they did point out the weak spots in European defenses and demonstrated especially the poor political and military organization of the Irish. During the early years of the ninth century, Ireland alone suffered severely from the Northmen, while other countries experienced only desultory raids. But about 830 civil wars began to weaken the Frankish Empire, and at the same time the raiders from the North began to take their work more seriously. They established permanent bases in enemy territory and began to make raiding a permanent profession instead of a sporadic adventure. Their bases were usually islands at the mouths of great rivers—places which could be easily defended by the Viking rulers of the sea, and which were equally convenient for drives into the interior. Such islands were Noirmoutier at the mouth of the Loire, Oissel at the mouth of the Seine, and Sheppey at the mouth of the Thames. These permanent bases for raiding were established first in Ireland about 831, then in France in 843, and finally in England in 851. Once they had been set up, no place in Europe was safe from attack. The ships of the Vikings were shallow-draft rowboats holding twenty to forty men; they could ascend not only the main rivers but also their tributaries, and few places in Europe are far removed from running water. It is true that European rivers were probably deeper then than they are now, after years of deforestation and diversion of water, but nevertheless it is amazing to see how far inland the Northmen could take their ships. And yet those same ships could cross the North Atlantic to Iceland, Greenland, and America!

The Northmen were not completely dependent upon ships. When they were blocked by fortified bridges or shallow water they beached their boats, stole horses, and continued their raiding as cavalry. In fact, in countries in which they were numerous, as in England, they gave up the use of ships almost entirely and marched the length and breadth of the land as a conquering army. Their reputation for ferocious bravery became so great that many rulers, and even Carolingian emperors, paid them bribes to avoid their attacks.

Viking activity reached its peak during the years from 850 to 860. During those years their armies held more than half of Ireland and England. The southern part of Frisia was granted to a Viking chief. All the river towns in France were attacked by the Vikings: Beauvais, Amiens, Therouanne and St. Omer in the North; Tours, Nantes, Blois and Orleans on the Loire, and smaller towns in the Seine and Garonne valleys. (Rouen, Paris, and Bordeaux had already been sacked between 841 and 846.) At the same time, the towns of Utrecht and Bremen in northern Germany were pillaged and Viking raiders, in sheer bravado, entered the Mediterranean. This foray, made in 860, was not very profitable, but it shows the territory which could be threatened by a single expedition: Christian Spain, Moslem Spain, Morocco, and the Rhône delta were all attacked. The raid ended with the sack of the little town of Luna in Italy, a place which the invaders are said to have mistaken for Rome.

By this time the raiders were becoming conquerors. The permanent camp in enemy territory was developing into a Viking kingdom or dukedom. There was little left to steal except the land itself, so the Northmen took that. This change came first in Ireland, the region which had suffered most from Viking attacks. At times the Viking kingdoms in Ireland covered half the island, but they fell on evil days in the eleventh century. The Irish, with their usual obstinacy, refused to stay conquered, and the Viking rulers wasted their strength in quarreling with each other, instead of uniting to suppress the natives. The North-men eventually lost everything except some small kingdoms on the east coast, around Dublin and Waterford, which continued to exist until the English conquest in the twelfth century.

The Vikings had even less success in establishing a permanent home in Germany. They were granted Frisia in 855, and might have created a sort of German Normandy there, had it not been for the bad judg-ment of their leader. He became involved in the political quarrels of the German kingdom, chose the wrong side, and was assassinated. His fol-lowers were almost exterminated by the victorious king, and Frisia was lost to the Northmen.

At about the same time the Northmen, and especially the Danes, turned to England. The northern part of the country was seized without much trouble and was intensively colonized. Traces of the Danes are still evident in the place-names, language, agricultural methods, and local government of the region. They not only seized the North, but they came very close to taking the kingdom of Wessex in the South as well. The heroic efforts of Alfred kept them north of the Thames, and Alfred's successors gradually reconquered the Danelaw—the region held by the invaders in the North. However, they never succeeded in gaining the complete loyalty of the Danish colonists, and a second wave of invasion in the eleventh century made England, for a time, a Danish kingdom. The English seemed fated to be ruled by men of Viking blood, for it was only a few years after the collapse of this second Danish kingdom that the Norman Conquest took place.

After England came Normandy. The Vikings camped at the mouth of the Seine could not be driven away. On the other hand, they had plundered almost every town within easy reach and were meeting with increasing resistance on their drives into the interior. They were ready to settle down, and the French king felt that he might as well let them have a province which he could no longer defend. So in 911 (the tradi-tional date is as good as any) the land on both sides of the lower Seine was granted to the leader of the Northmen. They promptly set about enlarging their grant, and in the end more than doubled its size, reach-ing Brittany on the west and coming uncomfortably close to Paris on the south. This district, called Normandy after its new rulers, soon recovered from the disasters of the period of invasion and became rela-tively prosperous. The leaders of the Northmen, now dukes of Nor-mandy, devoted their remarkable abilities to building up a strong gov-ernment; Normandy was one of the best ruled lands in Europe in the eleventh century.

While the Norwegians had concentrated on Ireland, and the Danes had attacked England and France, the Swedes had been pushing east and south. The Slavs living on the great plains of eastern Europe had practically no political organization, and made little resistance to the invaders. In fact, at times they seem to have welcomed them as military leaders who would protect them against their neighbors. The first Swedish settlements on the eastern plains were founded at about the same time as the Norwegian kingdoms in Ireland; that is, about 830. By the ninth century most of Russia was dominated by a handful of Viking adventurers. The name "Russia" itself is of Swedish origin, and seems to be derived from a tribe which lived in the upper part of the Scandinavian peninsula.

Ninth-century Russia was a land of city-states, each ruled by a Viking prince and his war-band and linked together in a loose federation under the ruler of Kiev. Strange as it may seem, Russia at this time was predominantly urban, rather than rural. It has been pointed out that a great trade-route ran from the Black and Caspian seas through Russia to the Baltic. Much of the land was still covered with forests, which produced wild honey and furs—commodities which were greatly desired in western Europe. The wealthy traders were town-dwellers and dominated the scattered rural population. The Swedish rulers of Russia profited by the trade of their towns and became powerful enough to attempt the conquest of the great commercial city of Constantinople. They were beaten off with some difficulty, and the Eastern Empire granted them a very favorable commercial treaty in the hope of avoiding future attacks. During the eleventh century the Vikings were gradually assimilated by the Slavic population and lost some of their aggressiveness. Yet Russia remained a wealthy commercial country until a series of nomad invasions in the twelfth and thirteenth centuries cut it off from the trade-routes to the South and East.

During the tenth century, the raids of the Northmen became less annoying and gradually ceased. The growth of feudal states made raiding more dangerous, and with each successive attack there was less to steal. In France, local leaders had organized successful resistance during the last part of the ninth century. Thus a certain Robert the Strong, duke of the country between the Loire and the Seine, defeated the Northmen several times between 858 and 866. Robert's son, Eudes, defended Paris against a great Viking attack in 885, even though he received little help from the incompetent Charles the Fat, who ruled France at the time. The exploits of these men gave their family such prestige that it eventually took the place of the Carolingian dynasty on the throne of France. Even the Carolingians, weak as they were, won some important victories over the Northmen in the last quarter of the ninth century. The king of Germany annihilated the Vikings in his territory, and Alfred broke the power of the Danish army in England. It took more than one defeat to stop Viking invasions, but the cumulative effect of this series of battles was great. The Northmen were losing their warriors faster than they could be replaced. There simply were not enough of the Scandinavian peoples to conquer and settle Ireland, England, France, and Russia. So from 900 on, the Northmen tended to concentrate on holding what they already had, and abandoned their far-flung raids.

However, just as the danger from the North began to subside a new foe arose in the East. Like the Huns before them, the Magyars drove through the corridor between the Urals and the Caspian, along the Black Sea, and into the heart of the Danube Valley. Like the Huns, they were a nomad Ural-Altaian people, forced from their original homes by defeat, but able to turn retreat into a victorious advance. They were great horsemen, ferocious fighters, and merciless enemies. They appeared on the German frontier about 890, and for sixty years they devastated central Europe. Bavaria and Swabia suffered most from their raids, but northern Germany was not immune. Bremen, sacked once by the Northmen, was plundered again by the Magyars during an attack on Saxony. On the greatest raids, France and Italy suffered, too; the Magyars rode in a huge circle around the Alps, burning, robbing, and killing all along a circuit thousands of miles in length. Thus in 937 they passed through Bavaria, Swabia, Franconia and Lorraine, to Champagne in eastern France. From Champagne they moved down through Berry and Burgundy to Piedmont, in Italy. They went down the west coast through Tuscany, the duchy of Rome and Campania, and returned home by the east coast and the Istrian peninsula.

Although the Magyars inflicted serious damage on southern Germany and northern Italy, they were not as formidable enemies as the Northmen, and their power rapidly declined. Unlike the Huns, the Magyars had not been able to absorb all the western nomads in their drive on Europe. Unlike the Huns, they did not succeed in filling their army with conquered European peoples. No large group of Germans was ever forced to serve the Magyars, and even the weak Slavic peoples of the Danube basin were able to maintain a certain degree of independence. As a result the Magyars lacked manpower, and the rise of an able line of German kings soon put an end to their raids. Henry the Fowler (918–936) encouraged the building of forts along the frontier, and Henry's son Otto inflicted a crushing defeat on a Magyar army at the Lechfeld in 955. This defeat almost immediately stopped the raids. The Magyars settled down on the middle Danube, where they created the kingdom of Hungary. The most important result of their invasion was that a wedge was driven between two great groups of Slavs. The Poles and Czechs were separated from the Serbs and Croats by the Germans on the upper

Danube, and the Magyars in the plain of Hungary. This weakened both groups of Slavs, and led, eventually, to their conquest by Germans or Hungarians.

The new invasions had ended by the year 1000. Europe had finally beaten off the raiders; it had survived a series of attacks as dangerous as those which occurred when the Western Empire fell. On the whole, Europe resisted the new invasions more successfully than the migrations of the fifth century. There was less change between 800 and 1000 than between 400 and 600. Nevertheless, the Europe which emerged from the period of invasions was very different from the Europe of Charlemagne's day. A new form of government, a new organization of society, which we call feudal, had been created during a century of confusion and war. This background of violence and disorder should be kept in mind during the discussion of feudalism. Feudalism could not be a coherent, logical, uniform system because the society which created it had none of these characteristics. Feudalism was a desperate improvisation; it represented the last stand in the struggle against anarchy and invasion.

FEUDALISM

Feudalism was one of the most important forces in the history of the early Middle Ages. It helped shape the institutions and ideas of all the peoples of western Europe. Because it had such great influence, it is necessary to examine it closely, to see what it was, and, just as important, what it was not. For feudalism loses all precise meaning if it is made a label for all political, social, and economic activities from the ninth to the fifteenth century. The word should be used to describe the new conditions which existed after the break-up of the Carolingian Empire, not old relationships which had existed from time immemorial. And what was new in the society of this period was its political organization, not its economic or social organization. The great estates continued to exist, as they always had, but they were not the essential element in feudalism any more than the factory system is the essential element in democracy. The great estate is simply the normal form of concentration of wealth in a pre-industrial society; it can be and has been used as the basis for half a dozen different types of government. In the same way, the existence of a noble class was not the essential element in feudalism. Not all members of the nobility became feudal lords, and the knights, who were an essential part of feudalism, were not at first considered noble. The concept of nobility, like the system of great estates, has existed in many societies, and is compatible with many different types of government. But the peculiar set of political relationships which began to be prominent in the Europe of the ninth century had never existed before and has never been exactly duplicated since.

Feudalism was primarily a method of government, a way of getting essential political acts performed in a period of disorder and confusion. In order to get these acts accomplished, public authority had to be treated as a private possession, and public duties were performed as a result of private contracts. Thus the right to hold courts of justice became the private possession of certain lords. These lords expected to make a profit out of their courts; they also felt perfectly free to give away all or some of their jurisdiction. The lords had to defend the territories which they ruled; they did so not by calling on all free men to serve in the army, but by summoning their vassals, men who had made a private contract with them to perform military service. This lord-vassal relationship was now the basis of all governmental activities.

Feudalism preserved the memory of the larger political units out of which it had grown. Kingdoms persisted and the greatest lords were vassals of kings. But the kingdoms were without shape or structure and the kings had little power over the lords. Feudalism was an effective method of government primarily at the local level. A single knight or a petty lord could not be independent; he had to acknowledge the authority of the local strong man. But the local lord who had a castle and forty or fifty knights could be independent; he gave little service to the king and allowed no interference with his government. Each important lordship tended to develop its own laws and institutions since there was no effective supervision of local authority by the central government.

Because in feudalism political power was personal and local, it tended to be fragmented. The degree to which power was divided varied from place to place, but no lord had absolute authority over all his men in all matters. He could not do all the work of government himself; he had to share his authority with his vassals. Most feudal lordships rapidly became a patchwork of overlapping and incomplete rights of government. One vassal might have jurisdiction over a road, but not over the fields through which it ran, or jurisdiction over theft but not over murder. Moreover, no lord could demand unlimited services from his vassals; he was limited by the agreements he made with them or by ancient custom. Many feudal lords were inclined to be tyrants, but power was so fragmented that it was almost impossible for them to make themselves absolute rulers of their districts.

When feudalism was fully established the typical lord was a count, who had turned his office into an hereditary possession. He was the vassal of a king, but this gave him little trouble. At most he would attend the king's court once or twice in his lifetime, and fight for the king when the king's enemy happened to be the same as his own. If he lived far away he would not have even these contacts with the monarch. No royal agents interfered with the administration of the county or heard appeals from its courts. The county was a self-contained unit, run by the count and his vassals. The vassals furnished the count his army and garrisoned his castles; they helped with the work of local administration and justice. A strong count would have kept all important matters, such as trials for murder, in his own court, but most police-court work, simple assault, larceny, and the like, would be handled by the vassals. Here we see the three main elements of feudalism: public authority in private hands, the predominance of local government, and the fragmentation of political power.

The two chief factors in creating conditions which made political power a private possession were the collapse of central authority and the growth of a new system of personal relationships called vassalage. For centuries the state had slowly been losing control over wealthy and powerful subjects. The Roman emperors had been unable to keep members of the senatorial class from exercising police power on their estates. The authority of the imperial government was defied and its agents were excluded by many owners of villas. The Germans, who were backward politically when they entered the Empire, did nothing to strengthen central authority. Some of the kings may have grasped the Roman idea of the state, but the great body of immigrants understood only the old personal ties of a man to his folk, his family, and his lord. Even the kings tended to think of the kingdom as a private possession and had little hesitancy in granting away political power. Thus the Merovingians frequently conferred "immunities" on churchmen who were great landowners. The immunity was an order barring all local officials from the lands in question, especially when they came to collect money. All public revenues were turned over to the possessor of an immunity, and he gradually gained the right to hold a court for the men of his district. These privileges were frequently sought because of the tyranny of the king's local representative. Bishops and abbots wished to be dependent only upon the king and so to avoid the oppression of the count of their district. The king was usually willing to grant such requests because it restricted the power of his often unruly subordinates. Laymen were seldom granted immunities, but the more powerful usurped powers which were fully as great. As the Merovingian monarchy declined, most of these *de facto* jurisdictions were recognized by the king, notably in a lengthy edict extorted by the land-owners in 614.

While the proprietors of great estates were gaining political powers in their lands, counts and other officials were seeking to make their offices hereditary. As early as the seventh century there was a tendency to keep offices in the same family, but the advent of the strong Carolingian rulers kept this from developing into a definite hereditary right. As the royal power weakened under the strain of civil war and invasion, the hereditary principle again became very strong. At the assembly of Kiersy in 877, Charles the Bald officially recognized that the general rule was for the son of a count to succeed his father. By the tenth century counts regularly passed on their office to their direct descendants and ruled their counties for their own advantage with no regard for royal orders.

The growing power of the counts and great land-owners was based not only on public authority, delegated or usurped, but also on their control over large groups of dependent freemen. The king was always remote, and often feeble, so weak individuals sought the protection of powerful men in their own districts. In return for protection they agreed to aid the lord in all his undertakings, and to serve him faithfully all the days of their lives. This relationship between a lord and his followers was soon given legal recognition, under the name of commendation. It is clearly described in formulas of the seventh century, for example: [1]

> To that magnificent lord, so and so, I, so and so. Since it is known familiarly to all how little I have whence to feed and clothe myself, I have therefore petitioned your piety, and your good will has decreed to me that I should hand myself over or commend myself to your guardianship, which I have thereupon done; that is to say in this way, that you should aid and succor me as well with food as with clothing, according as I shall be able to serve you and deserve it. And as long as I shall live I ought to provide service and honor to you, suitably to my free condition; and I shall not during the time of my life have the ability to withdraw from your power or guardianship; but must remain during the days of my life under your power or defense.

It will be noted that this formula does not specify the services which are to be rendered; the lord may ask his follower to do anything which is not unworthy of a free man. Commended men were given a wide range of duties, depending upon their ability and social position. Some might perform important administrative functions, others were little better than household servants, and still others sank to a position indistinguishable from that of a peasant. But there was a special class of commended men, distinguished by the name of vassals, whose primary duty was to render military service. There has been a long argument among historians as to the origin of vassalage, but most scholars would now agree that it was derived from the German war-band or *comitatus*. It will be remembered that the members of the *comitatus* were free warriors, who lived in the household of their lord and were bound to fight for him until death. There was nothing degrading about such a relationship, and men of noble blood could serve in a *comitatus* without loss of dignity. On the other hand, service as a household warrior was primarily a career for young men without an established position. A man might rise to be a count through household military service, but most counts were descendants of great noble families, not members of the military household of the king.

[1] This, and other documents quoted below, are taken from E. P. Cheyney's excellent collection in the University of Pennsylvania *Translations and Reprints*, Vol. IV, no. 3.

We have only scanty information about household soldiers under the Merovingians, but the evidence which is available indicates that something like the *comitatus* continued to exist. In the eighth and ninth centuries, the reorganization of the Frankish state under the Carolingians cause a sharp increase in the number and importance of vassals. As we have seen, it was a real hardship for ordinary freemen to abandon their regular occupations and serve in campaigns on distant frontiers. Vassals, on the other hand, had few interests which could suffer from a prolonged absence. Their primary business was that of fighting and they had no reason to complain if they were kept in the army for long periods. At the same time, the growing importance of heavy-armed cavalry increased the need for a specialized military class. Sudden raids of Saracens or Northmen could not be met by slow-moving infantry and the ordinary freeman was in no position to equip himself for mounted service. Only the king and the greater lords could afford the cost of mounting and arming large cavalry forces, and they had no intention of giving expensive equipment to men whom they did not control. Thus an increase in the number of mounted soldiers meant an increase in the number of vassals. Finally, Charlemagne and his successors realized that the personal bond between a man and his lord was far stronger than the vague idea of allegiance to the state. They tried to shore up the shaky structure of public authority with a scaffolding of personal loyalties. Laws were promulgated urging ordinary freemen to commend themselves to the more powerful lords in their own districts. Thus in 847 the three sons of Louis the Pious issued the following order: "We will, moreover, that each free man in our kingdom shall choose a lord, from us or our faithful, such a one as he wishes. We command, moreover, that no man shall leave his lord without just cause, nor should anyone receive him . . ." This order, like most laws of the period, was not universally enforced, but it reflected both the tendency of the time and the policy of the government. In the long run the great majority of freemen did become dependents of lords, most of them as simple peasants. The few who had skill in fighting became vassals, a permanent military bodyguard for their lords.

At the same time the kings tried to secure the loyalty of the counts and other great men by making them royal vassals. This was an innovation; as we have seen, vassals had hitherto been rather undistinguished men, household servants of a special sort. The Carolingians hoped to receive the special devotion which had marked the relation of the retainer to the lord, but they were deceived in this expectation. There was a great difference between the vassalage of a count to a king and that of a simple fighting-man to a count. The count had few personal ties with the king; he saw him seldom and felt no great loyalty to him. The count had ample economic resources and strong local authority; he could be and usually was quite independent of the king. The simple mounted soldier, on the other hand, lived in his lord's house and might well be a personal friend. In any case, he was entirely dependent on his lord for protection and livelihood; he could not afford to be disobedient. This is why vassalage was so much more effective as a unifying force at the local than at the national level.

Vassalage was the essential element in feudalism, but fully developed feudalism did not appear until vassalage had been combined with fiefholding. The fief, like vassalage, seems to have been a specialized form of the relationship between a lord and his dependents which was so common in the later Frankish period. In times of disorder, weak individuals had to seek protection for their property as well as their persons. In order to gain the support of a powerful neighbor or to avoid his enmity, they frequently gave him title to their land and kept only the income. The lord received a small rent and some personal services from the holder of the land. In addition, it was usually agreed that the land should go to the lord on the death of the holder, or perhaps after the death of all his children. Such an arrangement was called a benefice, since the lord allowed his dependent the benefit of the use of the land. Frequently the small land-owner surrendered his property to a monastery, thus gaining spiritual benefits as well as the protection of the Church against his enemies. A typical seventh-century formula, which illustrates this practice, reads as follows:

> I have settled in my mind that I ought, for the good of my soul, to make a gift of something from my possessions, which I have therefore done. And this is what I hand over, in the district named so and so, in the place of which the name is such and such, all those possessions of mine which there my father left me at his death . . . or those which I was able afterward to add to them in any way, in their whole completeness, that is to say the courtyard with its buildings, with slaves, houses, lands cultivated and uncultivated, meadows, woods, waters, mills, etc. These, as I have said before, with all the things adjacent or appertenant to them, I hand over to the church which was built in honor of such and such a saint . . . on these conditions, viz.: That so long as life remains in my body, the possessions above described I shall receive from you as a benefice for usufruct, and the due payment I will make to you and your successors each year, that is so and so much. And my son shall have the same possessions for the days of his life only and shall make the above-named payment; *or* if my children should survive me they shall have the same possessions during the years of their life and shall make the same payment; *or* if God shall give me a son from a legitimate wife, he shall have the same possessions for the days of his life only; after the death of whom the same possessions with all their improvements shall return to your part to be held forever. . . .

The men who held benefices were not necessarily vassals, but there were excellent reasons for combining the two relationships. As the number of vassals increased, it became difficult for lords with a large following to provide food and shelter for all their men. Given the economic conditions of the period, it was impossible to pay vassals salaries which would have enabled them to set up their own households. The only solution was to grant them small estates which would provide the necessary income. Charles Martel set the example, when he endowed his soldiers with lands taken from the Church, which they held on condition of rendering service to the king and paying a small rent to the former ecclesiastical proprietor. Other lords, who could not seize Church lands, imitated this practice by granting portions of their own estates to their followers. At first only the older or more distinguished vassals received such grants. In the early period of feudalism it was not at all necessary to give every vassal a benefice, and household knights who possessed no land were numerous as late as the end of the eleventh century. However, the principle of making grants to vassals had been established, and eventually every retainer came to expect a benefice in return for his services. At the same time there was a tendency for the benefice to become hereditary, instead of reverting to the lord at the death of the holder or of his children. When this evolution was complete, the benefice became known as a fief and remained in the same family as long as there were legal heirs. Feudalism took its name from the *feudum* or fief, but it should not be forgotten that fief-holding developed later than vassalage, and that vassalage was the most important element in the feudal relationship.

The final stages in the development of feudalism took place during the disorders of the ninth and tenth centuries. Under Charlemagne, vassalage was still compatible with monarchy; it had not yet generated a rival system of government. It is true that control of the army and of local government was passing into the hands of the lords, but the lords were vassals of the king and at first were reasonably obedient to him. Only under the strain of civil war and foreign invasion did vassalage escape from the framework of Frankish monarchy and produce an independent, self-contained, political system. Charlemagne's successors, harassed by rebellions, bewildered by the widely scattered raids of the Northmen, could neither control the counts and other great men nor defend their subjects. Since the central government gave neither leadership nor protection, the people of each district naturally turned to neighboring lords for assistance, and these potentates soon became the real rulers of the country. They controlled the only effective fighting force through the system of vassalage, and they soon increased their military power by building castles at strategic points in their territories. Though these castles were mere wooden blockhouses, surrounded by a ditch and a log stockade, they could not easily be taken by armies which had neither the time nor the equipment for siege operations. They protected the local population against raiders; they also protected the lord against the king, or against rival lords in the same district. With this solid military foundation for their power, the lords found it easy to acquire all public authority in their territories. Those who held offices by royal appointment turned their offices into hereditary possessions; others usurped control over public courts and revenues. These men might be royal vassals; they might even render the king service when it suited their convenience or their political ambitions, but in actual fact they were independent rulers.

The basic unit of feudal government was the county, since the counts had been the most important local officials and were in the best position to seize governmental power as the Carolingian Empire disintegrated. But the early feudal age saw a wild scramble for power, in which many counts lost their lands either to greedy neighbors or to their own vassals. Some men, such as the counts of Flanders and Anjou, gained control over many counties and dominated many lesser lords. These vassals of the great counts might have soldiers, castles, and courts of their own, but they were forced to obey their powerful superiors. At the other extreme were districts in central France in which the authority of the count almost disappeared and every petty castle-holder was practically independent. There was no plan or system in early feudalism; every lord seized as much land and governmental authority as he could and was as independent of his nominal superiors as he dared be. For this reason it is a mistake to think of early feudalism as a pyramid, with every lord owing allegiance and service to a man just above him. Rather, it was an endless series of overlapping circles of influence. Some were large, some small, but no one included all the others. Each lord was well obeyed in his own immediate neighborhood; his power dwindled in more distant regions, until finally a zone was reached in which some other lord's influence began to be felt.

In the period when vassals were merely household retainers, there were no very definite rules as to the services which might be asked of them. They were to help the lord in any way that they could, and at any time. But when the vassal was given a fief, he could not be at the lord's beck and call continuously; he needed time to take care of his own affairs. Moreover, men of dignity and position were now becoming vassals; they could not be treated as personal retainers. So a tendency arose to define and limit the service which a vassal owed his lord, and in the end the obligations of the vassal were greatly reduced. This fixing of feudal customs naturally took place at different times in different localities, and the rules were not always the same. Yet a general description of feudalism as it existed in the twelfth century may be given which will be true in its main outlines. It will be most accurate for North France, the region in which feudalism was most complete, and will fit other regions only roughly.

CHARLEMAGNE'S THRONE IN HIS CHAPEL
AT AIX-LA-CHAPELLE

•

STATUETTE OF CHARLEMAGNE, 9th CENTURY

AN 11th-CENTURY SHIP FROM THE *BAYEUX TAPESTRY*

•

PAGE FROM THE BEGINNING OF *BEOWULF*, 10th CENTURY

PALACE OF THE GERMAN KINGS AT GOSLAR

ST. ÉTIENNE AT CAEN, 11th CENTURY

A vassal assumed his obligations by a solemn act of homage and fealty. He knelt before his lord bareheaded, without his sword, and placing his hands within the hands of the lord, made a formal promise. He declared that he became the lord's man or vassal, for all the days of his life, and that he would defend the lord against "all men who may live or die." The lord then raised him up, kissed him on the mouth, and declared that he accepted him as a vassal. This act of homage was usually followed by an oath of fidelity to the lord, sworn upon the gospels, or some other sacred object. Then, if the vassal were to receive a fief, he was invested with it by some symbolic act, such as a stroke "with a little rod."

This contract involved obligations for both parties. The lord, theoretically, was bound to protect his vassal, secure justice for him, and give him such aid as he might need. The vassal was bound to give "aid and counsel" to his lord; words which covered a great many political services.

"Aid" meant, primarily, military service. The vassal was required to serve in the lord's army for a fixed period every year, often forty days. He was obliged to equip himself and to pay his own expenses during this time. The lord often had the right to ask for a longer term of service, but in such cases he had to pay the expenses for the additional period. A vassal who had vassals of his own was expected to bring some of his retainers with him to the lord's army, but only the strongest feudal lords were able to define and enforce this obligation. In addition to service in the field, the vassal was frequently required to do castle-guard for a fixed time each year. Sometimes he had to bring his wife and children with him while on service in his lord's castle. In this way the lord would have a personal knowledge of the character and qualities of members of the family, which might be useful to him.

"Counsel" meant that the vassal was bound to advise and assist the lord in any of his governmental duties. He might be asked to help audit accounts; he might be requested to give his opinion about general policies, such as peace and war. But since the chief business of a feudal government was judicial, the service most frequently requested was to help the lord hear and determine cases in his court. Usually the lord was a mere presiding officer, and disputes over law and procedure were settled by the collective opinion of his vassals.

Theoretically, the vassal did not owe any money payments to his lord, but when the lord had extraordinary expenses every vassal who held a fief was expected to give him "aid." Aid in this case meant financial assistance, and the cases in which an aid could be required varied greatly according to the custom of each region. In Normandy and in England, twelfth-century custom held that aids were due when the lord's eldest son was knighted, when the lord's eldest daughter was married, and when the lord himself was taken prisoner. In these circumstances the lord would have to pay large sums for the festivities of the knighting, for the dowry settled on his daughter, or for his own ransom from captivity. In the period of the Crusades, vassals in France were frequently required to give the lord an aid when he went on an expedition to the Holy Land.

The lord also had the right to take money when a fief changed hands through inheritance. Originally, fiefs had not been hereditary, but reverted to the lord whenever the holder died. Therefore, if the son of a vassal wished to keep his father's fief he made a present to the lord in order to obtain a new grant of the property. In some regions the death of the lord also invalidated the contract, and the vassal was expected to make a payment to his new suzerain in order to retain his holding. These presents were called "relief," and were often very burdensome, since they were frequently fixed at a year's income from the fief. After the early period of feudalism, there was a tendency to make the relief somewhat smaller and to exact it only when the vassal died.

Besides these money payments, the lord had other valuable rights in the fiefs of his vassals. If a vassal died leaving a minor heir, the lord might take possession of the property and hold it until the end of the minority. In such a case, he was exercising the right of wardship. The theory was that the vassal owed service to the lord in return for his fief, and since a minor could not perform these services the lord had a right to the income of the fief. The lord was expected to pay the living expenses of the minor heir and to restore the fief to him when he came of age. At that time a relief might be demanded and frequently was.

Closely connected with the right of wardship was the right of marriage. The lord naturally did not want his vassals allied to families which were hostile to him, and his consent was frequently required before their children could marry. The lords were especially insistent on controlling the marriages of female heirs, since the husband would have full power over his wife's fief. This right of arranging marriages for the heirs of fiefs was lucrative and was frequently abused; a lord might sell the right to marry one of his wards, and then accept a payment from the ward for forbidding the marriage. Thus we find in the English Exchequer Rolls entries such as this: "Hawisa, who was wife of William Fitz Robert, renders account of 130 marks and 4 palfreys that she may have peace from Peter of Borough, to whom the king has given permission to marry her; and that she may not be compelled to marry."

Finally, the lord frequently had the right of purveyance. This meant that the vassal was required to board and lodge the lord and all his followers for a time. At first there was no limit to this right, but it was so burdensome that it had to be restricted. Often the lord could visit his vassal only once a year, and both the number of persons and animals he brought with him and the kinds of food and supplies they were to receive were carefully stipulated. Even this restricted right was annoying, and in the later Middle Ages a fixed sum of money was often substituted for purveyance.

With the aid and counsel of his vassals the feudal lord governed his territory. He had no professional administrators, no trained judges, no regular soldiers. All services were performed by vassals, who were jacks-of-all-trades, and who begrudged the time which they gave to their lords. As a result, while feudalism reduced the functions of government to the bare essentials, it was often difficult to get even the bare essentials done. The chief duties of a feudal lord were to keep invaders out of his district and to preserve order in his district by seeing that all disputes were settled in the courts. But it was not always easy to defend a district, since vassals frequently failed to give the military service which they owed, and since other lords frequently made alliances to crush their weaker neighbors. It was not easy to keep peace, since members of the feudal group tended to settle their differences by the sword. If his most powerful vassals decided to fight a private war, the lord was helpless; his remaining forces would not enable him to intervene and stop the quarrel. Moreover, no lord knew exactly which vassal he could trust, for as feudalism developed, vassals received fiefs from many lords and could play one off against another. In the last analysis, the power of a feudal lord was determined by his success in war. If he could defeat his enemies and suppress rebellions of his vassals, he was respected and obeyed; if not, his neighbors seized his lands, or his vassals became independent rulers. So the early period of feudalism was marked by a long series of petty wars which established the boundaries of feudal states and defined the powers of feudal lords.

Yet feudalism conferred definite political benefits on Europe, in spite of the wars and violence which accompanied its development. In regions which had able rulers, feudal states were created which were stronger than any political units which had existed since the fall of the Roman Empire. They were small and compact; their rulers could govern them personally without having to place too much power in the hands of unruly subordinates. They corresponded to the natural social and economic units of the period; the old strain of trying to maintain a political unit which was too large to appeal to the interests and loyalties of the people was removed. Feudal governments were simple and inexpensive; they demanded a minimum of services and payments from their subjects. It is true that they gave very little in return, but it was actually an advantage to Europe to be undergoverned rather than overgoverned. For centuries the ablest rulers of the West had been trying to arrest the decay of old institutions, trying to prevent the collapse of over-elaborate, over-extended political organizations. They had been unsuccessful; their energies had been wasted; and their repeated failures had created an atmosphere of hopelessness and apathy. The triumph of feudalism marked the end of the losing struggle. Political organization had been reduced to the simplest possible terms. There was nothing more left to lose, and men could devote themselves to the task of rebuilding effective governments within the limits of the feudal principality.

Feudalism, by its very nature, could not be a uniform system of government that affected all parts of western Europe equally. It developed its peculiar institutions most completely in northern France, and then, thanks to the Norman Conquest, in England. Germany west of the Rhine was feudalized at a fairly early date; east of the Rhine feudalism grew more slowly and assumed its final form only in the late twelfth century. Southern France was only partially feudalized; in Italy feudalism never struck deep roots because the towns offered an alternate base of power. Spain had its own brand of feudalism, in which, thanks to the constant danger from the Moors, the feudal principality played less of a role than it did in France. Generally speaking, the most thoroughly feudalized regions—northern France and England—were the first to develop new types of political organization, states which were the direct ancestors of the states of the early modern period. This fact supports the observation made in the last paragraph; feudalism was not just a stopgap, it offered real opportunities to improve the structure of government.

THE MEDIEVAL VILLAGE

Feudalism was a method of government, not a system of production. The relationship of lord and vassal was primarily political, not economic. The basic economic unit was the village, not the fief, and the peasants who produced the material necessities of life were villeins and not vassals. The medieval village resembled the Roman *villa* in many ways; a group of unfree or semi-free men cultivated land in behalf of a lord. Yet the medieval village was not a *villa;* the forces which created feudal government also modified agricultural organization. The Roman, and even the Merovingian, land-owner had been able to supervise the work of his estate, either personally, or through a steward. He determined what should be done with each piece of land, what crops should be planted, and what work should be performed by his laborers. But as the land-owners became involved in feudalism, as they had to spend more and more time in politics and war, they found it impossible to direct the exploitation of their estates. The estate had to run itself; the peasants fell into fixed habits which were passed on from one generation to the next. At the same time the growing disorder made it absolutely essential for each small district to be self-sufficient. By the tenth century travel had become so dangerous that no one could count on securing food from a distant source. All the necessities of life had to be produced within a small district and it was often impossible to use land efficiently. Wheat had to be raised in mountainous regions which were better suited for grazing, and grapes were grown in northern lands where they could never thrive. The great estate, run for profit, gradually developed into the medieval village, which merely tried to keep alive.

The medieval village was a very small economic unit to aspire to self-sufficiency. Great nations today find it almost impossible to supply all their own needs, even with strict regulation of all economic activity. The medieval village needed fewer products, but its resources were also much more limited. It had to regulate the use of those resources; it could survive only by rigid application of rules which seemed absurd and wasteful to later generations. It could not afford experiments; there was too narrow a margin between survival and starvation. People could not be very enthusiastic about the process of trial and error when one error might mean that no one would be left to make further trials. Medieval villages were conservative and inefficient, but they produced enough food to keep Europe alive, and that was all that they were trying to do. Mere survival was no easy task in a period of invasion and war.

First of all, whatever the nature of the soil and climate, the village had to produce grain. Bread was literally the staff of life, to an extent which we can hardly imagine. It was the basic food; there were no other cheap starches, such as potatoes and rice, to take its place. Almost all the arable land of a village was devoted to grain; other crops were grown only in little garden patches around the villagers' huts. And in order to secure an adequate supply of grain, the arable land had to be cultivated in a very peculiar way. As we shall see later, it was difficult for a village to support many working animals and those which it did possess were small and weak. It took eight oxen to plow a field, and it was a rare peasant who owned a full team. So the fields had to be cultivated in common; each peasant furnished one or two oxen to the village plows. Under this system individual, fenced-off parcels of land would have been a nuisance. Instead, all the arable land was divided up into a few great open fields, and each peasant possessed strips of land in each field. The lord also held strips scattered about the fields, just as a peasant did, except that he had more of them. This system not only made joint cultivation easier, but it also gave every one a chance to secure enough grain to live on, since no one had a monopoly of the good land.

There was almost no fertilizer; soil-restoring crops were unknown, and the lack of sufficient animal power made it difficult to cultivate the soil thoroughly. The only way to prevent exhaustion of the land was to allow each field to lie fallow at regular intervals. In northern Europe the so-called three-field system gradually developed. In this system a crop of winter wheat was followed by a crop of spring grain, and the third year the field was allowed to rest. Thus out of every three fields, two would be under cultivation, and the plowing and harvesting in each of these could be done at different times. In this cycle there were really two fallow periods, since the winter wheat was harvested by July and the field could then rest until the spring sowing of the next year. In southern Europe this relatively efficient system could not be followed, since there was not enough summer rain to permit the growth of spring grains. Here the two-field system was used; that is, each field was sown to winter wheat one year and allowed to lie fallow the next. Thus only half the land could be cultivated at a time, and production was correspondingly lower. Under either system, the yield per acre was very low, owing to lack of fertilizer and poor cultivation. A yield of eight bushels an acre was considered remarkable, so even a small village needed a great deal of land to ensure an adequate food supply.

It was hard enough to raise grain for humans, and little of it could be devoted to feeding the few work-animals they possessed. Grass grew only in natural meadows along water-courses; men had not yet learned how to raise hay in the uplands. So the problem of securing enough food for the animals was as acute as the problem of securing enough food for their masters. Natural meadows were exceedingly valuable and were divided in small strips among the villagers. In addition, extensive pastures were needed where the animals could seek their own food during all but the coldest part of the year. These pastures were often larger than all the rest of the village lands together, and were usually common to all the animals of the place. Even this was not enough, and the cultivated fields had to be thrown open to the animals as soon as harvesting was finished, so that they could graze among the stubble and perhaps secure a few mouthfuls of grain. But by winter all these sources of food were exhausted, and only a few animals could be kept alive until spring. Those that did survive were weak, runty, and incapable of heavy work.

Since it was so difficult to feed work-animals, it is easy to see that there were not many beef-cattle and milch-cows. The only time that the villagers tasted beef was at Martinmas, late in the fall, when animals that could not be kept through the winter were slaughtered. Yet some meat, or at least some fat, was essential in the damp, cold climate of northern Europe. This need was supplied from the forest. In the forest great herds of swine roamed about, feeding on acorns and anything else which they could find. Usually each villager was allowed a number of pigs proportionate to the size of his holding, the largest number, of course, being reserved for the lord. The lords also gained by degrees a complete monopoly of the right of hunting in the forests. Thus they were able to increase the amount of meat in their diets, while the ordinary peasant seldom tasted game. In the South forests were less common, but the need for fats was less acute. Moreover, the South had olive oil, which, to some extent, made up for the lack of meat.

The forest was important to the village because it fed the swine, and also as a source of building materials and fuel. The peasants were allowed to use soft-wood trees and fallen branches as they needed them, but hard wood was reserved for the lords. The usual peasant house was a wattled hut, made by intertwining branches or saplings and then covering them with clay. The chimney, if the hut had such a luxury, was made of the same materials, and was apt to catch fire easily. Roofs were made of thatch resting on branches fastened to a central ridge-pole. The houses of the lords were somewhat more solid, but not much more luxurious. Stone castles were rare until after 1000; before that time, the ordinary lord had nothing better than a two-story wooden house. The furniture owned by all classes was very simple, and was always made out of wood. A peasant might have a plank table, a couple of stools, and a wooden bedstead. A noble would have the additional luxury of an armchair, but even in a castle most of the occupants would sit on benches and sleep in the straw on the floor. All tools were made of wood as far as possible, since iron was rare and expensive. Some plows were made entirely of wood, and even the best had nothing more than a thin strip of iron covering the share. Cart-wheels were often of solid wood, since iron rims were rare. Wood, or charcoal, was the universal fuel, even for the smelting of metals. Thus it can be seen that a village which had no woodland would find it very hard to exist.

Medieval men were convinced that water-drinking was very dangerous to their health. Even monks felt ill-treated if they were deprived of their customary ration of wine or beer. Since there was general ignorance of the most elementary principles of sanitation, this prejudice against water-drinking was probably well founded. But this meant that every village had to raise its own drink as well as its own food. In the South this was not too difficult; a few acres of vineyard would supply enough wine for the community. In the North, where grapes would not grow, people drank cider or beer. This meant either that extensive areas of land had to be devoted to orchards, or that some of the scanty supply of grain had to be used for brewing. In famine years, the making of beer was forbidden in order to conserve the stock of cereals, but it was not always easy to enforce such prohibitions.

Thus we see that the medieval village depended upon balanced, regulated use of all its resources. There had to be enough arable land to feed the village; there had to be enough pasture to feed the animals which cultivated the arable land; there had to be enough woodland to supply building materials and fuel. The nature of the crops planted, and the times of sowing and harvesting, were determined by the custom of the village. The use of pastures and wood was likewise regulated by village custom. These regulations resulted in great inefficiency, by our standards, but they did conserve natural resources. And, considering the conditions of the period, intensive, individualistic use of the land was impossible.

The village had to support not only itself but also the upper classes which were charged with its spiritual and political welfare. During the Carolingian period tithes had become obligatory; each peasant was supposed to give 10 per cent of his vegetable and animal produce to the Church. Theoretically, these payments were for the support of the parish church and the parish priest, but during the confused period of the growth of feudalism tithes were often treated like secular revenues. Frequently, a lord had acquired the right to collect all or part of the tithes in a given parish, and this right could be granted to one of his followers as a fief. Even when the Church had retained possession of the tithes, they often went to a bishop or a great monastery instead of to the parish priest. Such changes were no concern of the village; tithes had to be paid under pain of excommunication, no matter who received them.

Even heavier were the obligations of the village to its lord. He received a confused mass of services and payments, some of which resembled rent, others taxes, and still others the duties owed by slaves. As we have seen, the lord had a share of the land of the village. He held strips scattered about in the open fields, and his animals roamed in the common pastures. The village had to cultivate the lord's land and take care of his animals; each man had to devote a certain number of days each year to these tasks. Free peasants might owe only a few days of plowing and harvesting, while the unfree serfs might owe two or three days' work a week, and even more at the busy seasons of the year. Then, since all the land of the village was held by the lord, each villager owed rent for his house and strips in the fields. Here again the rate varied according to the status of the peasant; freemen owed comparatively little, while serfs had to make heavy payments. Usually the lord received a certain amount of grain per acre, and in addition "presents" of eggs, fowl, and bread at Christmas and Easter. Often there were charges for the use of the common pasture and wood; for example, the lord might take one pig out of every ten in the forest. In addition to land-rents, the lord could often demand a share of the peasant's income or personal property. Freemen usually, though not always, escaped this levy, but serfs were forced to make relatively large payments. In some districts there was no limit to what the lord could demand of them; all that they had was his, and his exactions were limited only by his sense of expediency. Everywhere serfs had to pay for the right to marry a person from another estate and for permission to inherit their parents' property. All these disabilities were reminders that the serf had once been a slave who had no property of his own and who could not contract a legal marriage or have legal heirs. Finally, the lord usually had certain monopolies in the village. He owned the mill, the oven, and in the South the wine-press, and he permitted no competition with these establishments. A peasant who passed by his lord's mill and had his grain ground elsewhere could be severely punished.

It should be noted that the income which the lord received from a village in the early Middle Ages was almost entirely in kind. This was satisfactory when the lord held only one or two villages. He could live near them and feed and clothe himself and his retainers with the products furnished by his peasants. But a lord who possessed many villages could not consume all their produce personally, and there was not much of a market for the surplus. His distant villages were really of very little value to him, and it was easier to grant them out as fiefs than to worry about protecting them and collecting revenue from them. A very power-ful lord might possess very little land as a result of this policy.

It was quite possible for a village to have more than one lord. Acci-dents of inheritance, or the deliberate policy of the overlord might lead to its division among several men. But this usually meant merely a division of the revenues from the village; it remained an economic unit and its lands were cultivated as a whole, whether it had one lord or many. For the same reason there was usually no attempt to combine the resources of two villages even if they had the same lord. The village was the basic unit of production, and had to remain a unit in spite of changes in proprietorship.

Not all Europe was divided into villages of the type just described. In some regions, especially in the South, small independent farmers survived. In other districts the population lived in hamlets which were smaller, less self-sufficient, and less closely regulated than the vil-lages. In some very sterile regions fields were cultivated only for two or three years and were then abandoned, so that there was no need for regulation of the use of the land. But everywhere the crops were much the same, the dues paid to the lord were much the same, and there was some communal control of agricultural practices. Few peasants could stand by themselves; they needed the support and guidance of a com-munity.

There were, of course, great differences in the standard of living among the peasants. Some villages had better land than others; some districts were well governed and suffered little from war, while others were plundered year after year by hostile armies. Even in a single village there might be great inequality. A free peasant who had inherited a full share of land, and who had a capable wife and some unmarried sons might live very comfortably. He would owe relatively small payments to the lord; his sons would perform the labor services due from his land and his wife would raise chickens and cultivate the garden around the house. Such a man would have plenty of grain and pork, and could supplement his diet with fowl, eggs, peas, beans, turnips and cabbages. At the other extreme would be a serf who had had to divide his father's holding with several brothers. He would owe half his produce to his lord, he would have to spend half or a third of his time working for his lord, and his bit of land would be too small to support him even without these burdens. He would have to increase his income by doing odd jobs for his more prosperous neighbors, and even then he would be barely able to avoid starvation. While there was great inequality among villagers in normal times, they were all equally helpless in periods of misfortune. They all lived in unsanitary conditions; they had no doctors, and at times pestilence swept away whole communities. Few families could store grain; a year of flood or drouth created terrible famines. The peasants could not defend themselves against heavy-armed feudal cavalry, and if their lord became involved in a war they were almost sure to see their fields ravaged and their houses burned. It is not surprising that the span of life was short, that a man of forty was considered old. The amazing thing is that organized communities survived at all; that in spite of pestilence, famine, and war the medieval village continued to exist.

THE CHURCH UNDER THE LATER CAROLINGIANS

The decline of the Carolingian Empire led at first to a striking increase in the authority and prestige of the Church. As we have seen, during the troubled ninth century the Church alone stood for Christian unity, order, and peace. The Church maintained the ideals of the Empire better than the emperors themselves; it opposed localism and the selfish aims of the magnates. As a result the Church took over political leadership from the emperors; churchmen were the promoters of all the movements to save the Empire and to stop factional warfare. No one could openly deny the validity of the political objectives of the Church, whatever might be his secret desires. No one could disregard the admonitions of the bishops or reject their program. This meant that the subjection of the Church to secular authority, as achieved by Charlemagne, soon vanished. By the middle of the ninth century the tables were completely turned, and the Church was claiming authority over secular rulers. Frankish bishops asserted that the spiritual power was superior to the temporal power, since a bishop could consecrate an emperor, while an emperor could not consecrate a bishop. Consequently, they claimed the right to judge and punish lay rulers, and actually did so on several occasions. Charles the Bald admitted that his bishops could disregard any law which, in their opinion, infringed the rights of the Church.

At the same time many churchmen felt the need for strengthening the authority of the pope. As the Empire broke up, the bishops became subject to different authorities and it was increasingly difficult for them to meet together for concerted action. Individual bishops were often helpless before local tyrants; they needed the support and moral backing of the papacy. Moreover, the power of the archbishops had been increasing, and they were attempting to control and discipline the bishops. Many bishops resented these claims and felt that they should be subject only to the pope. The fact that the pope was distant and would interfere less with the affairs of their dioceses undoubtedly had something to do with this feeling, but it is true that the archbishop had always occupied a somewhat equivocal position and that his powers had never been carefully defined.

The ablest men in the Church were seeking freedom from lay control, the right to advise and punish lay rulers, and increased authority for the pope over bishops and archbishops. They would probably have attained these objectives in any case, but their task was made easier by a famous forgery, the Pseudo-Isidorian Decretals. This collection was composed about the middle of the ninth century, apparently by a Frankish monk. It included many genuine letters of popes and authentic canons of councils, but when these documents failed to give precedents which supported the policy of the ninth century Church, the compiler had no hesitation in adding spurious material. Thus ample support was found for the Church's claim to entire freedom from lay control, and also for the supremacy of the pope over all other officials. This collection was almost universally accepted as genuine throughout the Middle Ages, but at the present time no one would defend its authenticity. Early popes were made to use the title of *servus servorum Dei*, which we now know was first used by Gregory the Great (590–604), and were made to quote from books written centuries later. Yet while these forgeries were used for centuries by the Church, their importance should not be exaggerated. The Church had advanced many of its most extreme claims before the false decretals were composed, and papal power had been increasing for centuries. The popes of the ninth century were capable of making their own precedents and were not dependent on forgeries.

The pontificate of Nicholas I (858–867) illustrates many of the tendencies which we have been discussing. Nicholas was a man of noble family and great ability, who spent his entire reign in trying to impose his authority on powerful laymen and ecclesiastics. His first struggle was with the Eastern Empire. At Constantinople the orthodox patriarch had been deposed by the emperor Michael in 857, and in his place the learned Photius had been raised to be head of the Byzantine Church. Both disputants appealed to Rome, and the pope sent legates to investigate the case. They were bribed to support Photius, but when the pope learned of this treachery he deposed his faithless officials, and in 863 ordered Photius to resign his office. The latter, in turn, excommunicated the pope, and charged the Roman Church with heresy. He was able to maintain his position until 867, when he was deposed by Michael's successor. Nicholas had made good his claim to judge the Eastern Church, but the struggle alienated the Byzantines and was one of the links in the chain of events which finally brought about a schism between the East and the West.

A second struggle emphasized the pope's position as the moral arbiter over kings as well as over other members of the Church. Lothair, king of Lorraine and brother of the emperor, had put away his wife Theutberga, and had taken in her place a mistress, Waldrada. The papal legates who were sent to investigate this affair were bribed by Lothair, pronounced Theutberga's divorce legal, and recognized Waldrada as his wife. Nicholas was very indignant and in 863 deposed and excommunicated both the guilty legates and the bishops who had sanctioned the divorce. There was a long struggle, but Nicholas stood firm, and Lothair was compelled to take back his lawful wife. When he repudiated her again and returned to Waldrada, he was excommunicated by Nicholas. Finally, after the death of Nicholas, Lothair humbled himself and submitted to the commands of the next pope. In this matter, as frequently throughout the Middle Ages, the pope stood firm as the champion of the sanctity of the marriage ties, and used the weapon of excommunication in order to enforce morality. He established the fact that the king as a Christian was subject to the judgment of the Church if he did wrong.

The third important struggle which Nicholas was obliged to carry on was against Hincmar, archbishop of Rheims, one of the ablest and most powerful churchmen in France. Hincmar had arrested and deposed one of the bishops in his province and then imprisoned him in a monastery, whence he appealed to Rome. The archbishop claimed that he had supreme authority in his province and that no one could appeal from his decision. Nicholas insisted that the pope alone could condemn a bishop and denounced Hincmar's action. The pope secured the support of Charles the Bald, who needed papal aid in other affairs, and Hincmar was forced to justify himself. He argued that, while the pope was supreme over the whole Church in doctrine, he had no right to interfere with the administration of an archbishop's province. In his reply Nicholas quoted the Pseudo-Isidorian Decretals to show that he was completely within his right. Hincmar seems to have had some doubts about the authenticity of this collection, since he spoke of it as "a mouse-trap to catch the archbishops," but he was eventually forced to yield. Nicholas had won a significant victory and had established an important precedent for the administrative authority of the pope over the Church.

THE CHURCH IN THE FEUDAL AGE

The pontificate of Nicholas I was the high-water mark, for the time being, of papal authority. During his reign the Church seemed destined to inherit the power which was slipping from the nerveless hands of the Carolingians, but it was soon to suffer, in its turn, from the forces which were destroying the Empire. Civil war and foreign invasions were to turn bishops into feudal lords and make the papacy itself the prize of Italian nobles. The Church was less independent of lay authority than it believed; spiritual power was not enough to restrain the unscrupulous rulers of feudal states. During the anarchy of the tenth century the learning, the morality and the organization of the Church suffered a severe decline. The benefits of the Carolingian reform were not entirely lost, but in many ways the tenth century Church was as corrupt as it had been under the Merovingians.

The break-up of the Empire isolated Italy from the rest of Europe, and Italian rulers were no more successful than those of the North in preserving authority and order in their realm. The emperor Louis II, son of the emperor Lothair, was the last Italian monarch who had any real authority in the peninsula. Louis spent most of his time fighting the Saracens, and even in performing this public service he received only lukewarm assistance from the magnates. After his death in 875, all real power passed to the Frankish counts and marquesses of the North and the Lombard princes of the South. These men engaged in an endless round of wars, alliances, betrayals, and treaties. They made kings and deposed them as soon as they tried to exercise any real authority; often there were two kings, each supported by a temporary coalition of nobles. To make matters worse, the Saracens were threatening the entire coast, and by the end of the century the Magyars had begun their devastating raids in the interior. The Greeks, who still held the heel and toe of the peninsula, did not wish to have a strong power as a neighbor and often supported opponents of royal authority. In these circumstances it is not surprising that the papacy steadily lost power. The nobles of Italy had no great respect for the pope; they seized the lands of the Church and did not hesitate to march against Rome itself. The pope tried the old trick of calling in northern rulers against his Italian enemies, but times had changed since the days of Pippin and Charles the Great. A Charles the Bald might make a hasty dash to Rome to receive the imperial crown, but a ruler who could not keep order in his own country was not going to end the anarchy in Italy. In self-defense, the popes had to ally themselves with Italian factions; if they could not get help from outside they must find local protectors. This involved the papacy in the sordid game of Italian politics. It was blamed for the unscrupulous acts of its supporters and was soon completely discredited in the eyes of the Italians. Moreover, the protectors of the papacy naturally aspired to be its masters, and by the tenth century they achieved their ambition.

The case of Formosus, who was pope from 891 to 896, shows how the papacy suffered from anarchical conditions in Italy. Following earlier precedents, the pope had joined a party which invited the German king, Arnulf, to intervene in Italy. Arnulf came down and was duly crowned emperor, but, like most of his predecessors, he was unable to maintain his position in Italy. As soon as he left, the opposition party sought vengeance on his supporters. Formosus had died, but his enemies were not to be thwarted. With the approval of the new pope, they exhumed Formosus' body and placed it on trial, clad in papal vestments and seated on a throne. The corpse was duly convicted, the vestments torn from it, and the three fingers which had formerly given the pontifical blessing were hacked off. Then it was dragged through the streets and hurled into the Tiber.

After Formosus there were eight popes in eight years. A certain degree of stability was achieved when Rome and the papacy passed under the control of a local noble, Theophylact. He styled himself "Senator Romanorum," and Rome was practically independent of the rest of Italy under his rule. But his wife, Theodora, was almost as powerful as he, and both she and her daughter, Marozia, were very influential in creating and appointing popes. While they were able women, their moral standards were very low, and the papacy was never so degraded as during their ascendancy. Theodora first secured the position of pope for her former lover, John X, who did much for the defense of Italy. During his pontificate the last Saracens were expelled from the peninsula. But he quarreled with Marozia, was imprisoned, and died in captivity. Succeeding popes were appointees of Marozia; in 931 she had the dignity conferred on her son, John XI.

Marozia's influence was ended only when another one of her sons, Alberic, felt threatened by her policies. The lady, who had lost two husbands, offered her hand with Rome as a dowry to Hugh, who was maintaining himself with some difficulty as king of Italy. This marriage threatened Alberic's chances of succeeding to the domination of Rome and annoyed many nobles of the region because it made Hugh too powerful. So Alberic headed an uprising of the Romans against Marozia and Hugh and drove the king out of the city. Alberic imprisoned his mother and kept his brother, pope John XI, under close surveillance, while he himself ruled as "princeps atque omnium Romanorum Senator." For twenty-two years, from 932 to 954, Alberic was all-powerful in the Eternal City and restricted the activity of the pope wholly to spiritual affairs. Before he died, in 954, he secured the succession of his sixteen-year-old son Octavian to his position as "princeps" and also to the papacy. Octavian, who was made temporal ruler of Rome in 954, became Pope John XII a year later. Of all the popes of the tenth century, he was perhaps the most vicious and immoral.

Outside of Italy little was known of the degradation of the papacy, and the Christian West as a whole still revered the successor of Peter. But the weak popes of the tenth century could not exert much influence outside of Italy, and the Church ceased to function as an administrative unit. The clergy of each region had to defend their rights and privileges without much assistance from Rome, and most of them were unsuccessful in this task. Feudalism, which had destroyed the state, came very close to absorbing the Church.

The Church possessed enormous amounts of land in the West, as the result of gifts by successive generations of the faithful. Like most other property owners, it found that it could not keep its land without the protection of a feudal army. Churchmen had bands of armed retainers and, like other land-owners, they soon found it necessary to grant fiefs to their soldiers. Thus, much Church property passed into the hands of vassals and was completely secularized. These vassals had to have a leader in time of war, and this involved churchmen in further difficulties. It was hardly proper for a bishop or an abbot to charge into battle at the head of his troops, though many of them had no scruples in doing so. Bishops and abbots also had courts, which might at times be required to impose the death sentence; this also seemed inappropriate for clergymen. Therefore, the more pious churchmen had to ask some neighboring lord to perform these very secular duties, and these "advocates," as they were called, usually ended by considering the Church's vassals as their vassals, and the Church's land as their land. At the same time the great dukes and counts were anxious to bring the resources and vassals of the Church under their control. They demanded military assistance from bishops and abbots; they appropriated revenues from Church property, and they gradually gained control over appointments to most Church offices. Since Carolingian times the clergy had performed many public duties; they were the best educated, most capable administrators who could be found. Feudal lords needed their services, and they naturally wished to see Church offices filled with their own supporters. So, in many regions, bishops were treated as vassals. They did homage to the ruler of their district and received their bishopric from him, just as a lay vassal would have received a fief. They were usually more faithful to their feudal lord than lay vassals, since they owed their position to his choice and could claim nothing by hereditary right.

It is easy to imagine the evils caused by this state of affairs. As churchmen became more and more involved in feudalism they neglected their spiritual duties. They were entirely occupied with the services which they owed as vassals; they were soldiers and politicians rather than religious leaders. Feudal lords abused their control over church offices; they sold bishoprics to the highest bidder or reserved them for bastards and younger sons. One duke of Normandy made four members of his family bishops. A powerful southern family bought the archbishopric of Narbonne for a ten-year-old boy, and he later secured a bishopric for his younger brother by selling the chalices and altar-cloths of his church.

Yet the Church had not wholly forgotten its old ideals. Feudal lords were not completely impervious to religious sentiments; they sometimes appointed good bishops and often protected monasteries which tried to maintain high standards of conduct. On the whole, the monks were less corrupt than the secular clergy. They had less property and less political influence and escaped some of the worst evils of lay control. More than ever, the monasteries attracted able and honest men, who were disgusted with the anarchy and corruption of the outside world. During the darkest part of the tenth century certain monasteries were preparing a great reform movement which was to purify the Church, revive the pope's authority, and lessen lay control over ecclesiastical offices. At the same time, some of the better bishops were trying to protect the poorer people from the ravages of feudal warfare and to recall the military class to a sense of their Christian duties. Both these movements were to bear important fruit in the eleventh century.

VI

->>>->>>->>>->>>-<<<-<<<-<<<-<<<-

Bridges Across the
Dark Ages

WESTERN CIVILIZATION on the whole declined during the ninth and tenth centuries. Europeans seemed to have lost their ability to work together on a large scale. Throughout much of Europe, political organization and economic activity were reduced to the subsistence level of the feudal state and the agricultural village. Even the universal Church suffered from the evils of localism and its organization became weak and corrupt. A society which was barely keeping alive could devote little time and energy to the arts and learning; the Carolingian Renaissance decayed with the Carolingian Empire. Yet the heritage of the past was not lost in this difficult period, even if it could not be fully used by the men of the West. The Greeks and Arabs in the East preserved, and even added to, the knowledge which they had received from the ancient world. The ideals of the Carolingian Empire continued to exert a powerful influence in Germany, where the great Saxon kings tried to carry on the work of Charlemagne. The Byzantine Empire, the Moslem Caliphate, and the German-Roman Empire of the West were bridges across the Dark Ages.

BYZANTINE EMPIRE

The ninth and tenth centuries, which were so dark for western Europe, saw the height of Byzantine and Moslem civilization. Throughout this period Constantinople and Bagdad were centers of commerce and manufacturing, of art and intellectual activity. Western Europe was to profit greatly by the existence of these two advanced civilizations on its very borders. The intellectual and economic revival of the West after 1000 was greatly stimulated by contacts with the Greeks and the Moslems.

Gibbon described Byzantine history as "a tedious and uniform tale of weakness and misery." His great authority, and similar judgments by Voltaire, Montesquieu and Taine, caused this opinion to prevail until the middle of the last century. "Byzantine" even yet is too frequently used as a term of opprobrium. But scholars now realize the debt which we owe to the Eastern Empire. They realize that for eight centuries law, literature, art, industry and commerce flourished at Constantinople, and that this city not only preserved the remnants of classical civilization but also protected the rest of Europe from Eastern invaders, until the West was in a position to use this older culture. They have learned that the most important feature of the Byzantine Empire was "its constant vitality and power of revival," "its marvellous recuperative energy."

These qualities were needed at the end of the seventh century, for the Eastern Roman Empire had been almost overwhelmed by the first victories of the Arabs. It had lost two-thirds of its territory—Syria, Egypt, and North Africa—and for a time it seemed doubtful whether it could survive the shock of these amputations. Yet in the end the loss of these provinces was not an unmixed evil; the Empire was more vigorous in the tenth century than it had been in the seventh. As we have seen, Syria and Egypt resented the domination of Constantinople and their resentment frequently expressed itself in religious and political revolt. On the other hand, the emperors who attempted to placate Syria and Egypt were attacked by the orthodox Greeks of the capital. Moslem conquests ended these sectional quarrels; Constantinople now had no rivals for political and religious leadership. At the same time much of the trade which had passed through Antioch and Alexandria shifted to Constantinople, so that the emperors could still count on a large and regular income from taxes on commerce. Constantinople was unquestionably the greatest port in the Christian world, and one of the greatest known anywhere; no state could be entirely helpless with such an asset. The old civil service remained; the careful organization of the army was preserved, and its equipment was improved. Altogether, the situation of the Eastern or Byzantine Empire was far from hopeless.

Recovery from the disasters of the seventh century was, of course, slow. During the eighth century the Arabs were still dangerous, and again threatened Constantinople in the great siege of 717–718. At the same time the iconoclastic controversy, the last dangerous religious dispute in the Empire, caused a breach between the emperors and the people of the capital. The rulers, influenced by the puritanical sects of Asia Minor and perhaps by Moslem criticism, became iconoclasts; that is, they attempted to outlaw icons—pictures of sacred personages—on the grounds that people were worshipping the images, rather than treating them as symbols of divinity and holiness. This attack gained them the support of the army, which was drawn largely from regions which were opposed to the veneration of images. At the same time it weakened the monasteries, which were entirely too influential to suit the emperors, by depriving them of the possession of wonder-working images. But the people of Constantinople, led by the monks, bitterly opposed the policy of iconoclasm, and the Empire could not be strong without their support. The popes also attacked the icono-clastic emperors and turned to the kings of the Franks for support, so that imperial influence declined in Italy. In the ninth century the images were restored, and the emperors gained the undivided support of their sub-jects. From this time on, the Byzantine Empire remained fiercely and unswervingly orthodox. Frequent political upheavals never troubled its essential unity, since the state was based on religion rather than patriotism.

Once the iconoclastic controversy had ended, the emperors could take advantage of weaknesses which were appearing in the world of Islam. The rugged uplands of Asia Minor furnished them excellent soldiers and the fabulous wealth of Constantinople gave them resources for ex-tensive campaigns. By the end of the tenth century Crete, Antioch, and northern Syria had been reconquered, and Byzantine armies had threat-ened Jerusalem and Bagdad. At the same time the Bulgars were forced to acknowledge Byzantine supremacy. They were a Ural-Altaian people who had imposed themselves as rulers of the Slavic tribes which had wandered across the Danube during the period of Byzantine weakness. They had built up a strong state in the Balkan hinterland, but they could not resist the power of the revived Empire.

The cultural and religious influence of the Byzantine Empire went far beyond its boundaries. The Bulgars and Slavs of the Balkans were quickly converted to Christianity, and their civilization was based on that of Constantinople. Byzantine missionaries were also active among the Slavs of the middle Danube and Moravia, but their work, successful at first, was ruined by the Magyar invasion in the late ninth century. The Western Slavs, cut off from the Greeks by the fiercely hostile Magyars, turned to the Latin West for help. As a result the Czechs and Slovaks became Roman Catholics, and even in the Balkan peninsula the westernmost Slavs accepted the headship of the pope. But this failure was more than atoned for by Russian acceptance of the Greek faith. The first converts were made in the tenth century, and during the eleventh century all Russia became Christian. Here, as among the Slavs of the Balkans, acceptance of the Byzantine religion led to imitation of Byzan-tine civilization. Russian art and architecture still bear witness to the profound influence which Constantinople exerted upon the Eastern Slavs.

The revival of the Byzantine Empire was accompanied by a revival of classical studies at Constantinople. This revival was focused on Greek literature rather than on Greek science; on Homer and Plato rather than on Aristotle. For these reasons it interested the West less than the work of the Arabs, who shared the Western preference for science and for Aristotle. Nevertheless the influence of Constantinople on medieval Latin scholarship should not be underestimated. Many Western scholars visited Constantinople, and many Greek works were translated into Latin for their use. It was always possible to find manuscripts of Aristotle at Constantinople, even if they were not given the place of honor in the libraries. And in the period of the Renaissance Byzantine scholarship was at last recognized when the Italian humanists became intensely interested in the study of Greek literature. In the last years of the Empire Greek scholars found an eager welcome in Italy for their knowledge and their manuscripts.

Byzantine art shows the Eastern Empire at its best. In other fields there was apt to be undue conservatism, but in art the Byzantines created a new and vigorous style. Even in the dark days of the Empire good work was done, and the great tenth century revival stimulated art as it had stimulated scholarship. It is difficult to speak with any certainty of the influence of Byzantine art on the West. Venice, of course, copied Byzantine architecture in the great cathedral of St. Mark's, and Venice in turn may have influenced the building of the domed churches of southwestern France. Byzantine mosaic work was imitated in the southern half of Italy, and Byzantine manuscript illumination influenced Western artists. In general, however, the West developed its own style in the arts, and Byzantine influence was never dominant in any field.

On the other hand, the commercial revival of the West sprang directly from contact with Constantinople. All the wares of India and China could be found in the city on the Bosporus, and the Byzantines themselves were famous as producers of luxury goods. In the sixth century they had learned the secret of making silk, and from that time on their reputation as makers of fine textiles increased steadily. They had no superiors in manufacturing brocades, velvets, cloth of gold and cloth of silver, or in dyeing silks and fine linens. They were equally skilled as goldsmiths and jewelers, and their work in enamel and ivory was sought everywhere. The West, even when it was poorest, was always anxious to obtain Byzantine wares. Churchmen needed fine cloth for their vestments, jewels for their altar vessels, and incense for their services. Kings and princes sought these same products to add to the splendor of their courts. And in spite of war and piracy, the routes between the West and Constantinople were never blocked. Until the twelfth century northern Europe could secure Byzantine wares through Russia, and by the time this road was cut, the sea route through the Mediterranean was relatively safe. More important was the fact that the Moslems never succeeded in gaining permanent control of Italy and the Adriatic. Even in the darkest period of the invasions, Eastern goods could be shipped across the narrow sea to Italian towns which were still nominally subjects of the Empire. Venice profited especially from this trade; its island position protected it from the consequences of the wars which raged on the mainland, and it was well located for distributing Byzantine goods to transalpine peoples. It is true that these Italian towns also traded with the Moslems when they could, in spite of ecclesiastical prohibitions, but this trade was dangerous and uncertain. Italian cities continued to exist and to carry on international trade in the tenth century primarily because of their contacts with Constantinople. And Italian cities were among the most important factors in the great economic revival which began in the eleventh century in the West.

The strong Byzantine Empire of the tenth century was too successful for its own good. As security was restored in the outlying parts of the country, land-ownership once more became a source of power. Great landlords had not sought independence when they needed the protection of the state against an aggressive enemy, but once the Moslems had been driven out of Asia Minor, all the evils associated with great estates reappeared. As in the old Roman Empire, small land-owners became subject to the owners of great estates, and local officials were subservient to men with great wealth. This meant a revival of the old disease of localism and dislike of central authority. Unfortunately for the Empire, this landed aristocracy was especially strong in Asia Minor, which was precisely the region from which most of the imperial troops were drawn. The great landlords soon gained control over a large part of the army and did not hesitate to use this power against the authorities at Constantinople. The abler emperors of the tenth century realized the danger and attempted to break up the great estates and to limit the powers of the aristocracy. Their efforts were unsuccessful; men of wealth continued to invest it in land and to dominate local government. In the eleventh century there was a constant struggle between the office-holding class at Constantinople and the land-owning aristocracy This seriously weakened the Empire, since the emperors of this period represented only one faction or the other and never controlled the whole state.

Unfortunately for the Greeks, this weakening of the Empire coincided with the rise of a new Moslem power. Ever since the ninth century the Turks had played an important rôle in Moslem politics as mercenary soldiers and generals, but they had entered the lands of the caliphate only in small groups. Now a whole people, the Seljuk Turks, moved down from the northeast and became the dominant element in the armies of the Caliph. Soon the Caliph had only nominal authority; Turkish sultans were the real rulers of the Middle East. From their strong position in northern Syria and Mesopotamia, the Turks soon began to raid Asia Minor. They were so annoying that in 1071 the emperor Romanus IV led all available Byzantine troops against them. Romanus had a larger army than his opponents, but he was so anxious to end the Turkish menace that he forgot the most elementary rules of prudence and suffered a crushing defeat at Manzikert. His army was annihilated, he was taken prisoner, and the Turks occupied most of Asia Minor. The Byzantine Empire never fully recovered from this blow. It had depended on the wealth of Constantinople and the manpower of Asia Minor. Now the latter had been lost, and the Byzantine army was never again large enough to be really effective. Even when part of Asia Minor was reconquered in the twelfth century the loss of manpower was not made good. The Turks were a pastoral, not an agricultural people; they had neglected irrigation works and had allowed some of the land to revert to semi-desert conditions, so that the population was greatly reduced. After 1071 the Byzantine Empire included little more than the city of Constantinople, with a strip of land on each side of the Straits. It continued to exist until 1453, but its greatest days had passed.

THE MOSLEM CALIPHATE

Moslem civilization had flourished under the Ommiad caliphs, but it reached an even higher point under their Abbasid successors. Abu'l Abbas, the founder of the new dynasty, appealed to all the groups who were discontented with Ommiad rule. He claimed an uncle of Mohammed as his ancestor, and thus satisfied to some extent the demands of the legitimists who insisted that only the close relatives of the prophet should rule. Outwardly, he was more pious than the worldly Ommiads, who had shocked the more puritanical Arabs by their indifference to religion. Most important of all, he succeeded in gaining the support of recent converts, especially in Persia, and thus identified himself with the growing opposition to the dominance of the Arab aristocracy of Syria. By the middle of the eighth century the Abbasid claimant was strong enough to risk a rebellion. The Ommiad caliph was decisively defeated in 750, and the new ruler tried to exterminate all members of the rival family. One Ommiad escaped to Spain, where he founded an independent state in 755, but the rest of the Moslem world recognized the authority of the Abbasid caliph. The Persians and other Eastern converts were rewarded for their support by the removal of the capital from Damascus to Mesopotamia. Here, on the banks of the Tigris, rose the new city of Bagdad, which was to become the center of Middle Eastern civilization.

The triumph of the Abbasids meant the end of Arab supremacy. Henceforth all Moslems were equal, and the non-Arabs rapidly gained political power. The Mohammedan Empire had been held together by the Arab aristocracy and with their eclipse it began to disintegrate. Submerged local patriotisms began to revive, and by the middle of the ninth century the caliph had only nominal authority in outlying districts. As we have seen, Spain became independent in 755. Morocco followed suit in 788, and the rest of North Africa broke away in 800. Egypt fell away after 868, and the northern and eastern regions of Persia became practically autonomous at about the same time. Even in regions nearer Bagdad the caliph was troubled by the tendency of provincial governors to found independent states. He became more and more dependent upon his generals, and after 900 the territories which still acknowledged his rule were actually governed by the commander of the army.

Yet the decline of the caliphate was very gradual, and during the first century of their rule the Abbasids were powerful and wealthy sovereigns. The provinces of the Far West, which were the first to break away, had added little to their military and financial resources. As long as the Middle East gave them obedience and taxes, they were strong. Perhaps the reign of the famous Haroun Al-Rashid (786–809) marks the height of Abbasid splendor, but his immediate successors were almost as magnificent. And even when the caliphate declined, civilization continued to flourish. Political unity was gone, but the Moslem world was still held together by many bonds. There was the common religion, Islam, and the common language of government and learning, Arabic. Most important of all, there was a network of commercial relations which stretched from Spain to India. The ordinary Moslem was not greatly troubled by political differences; he moved about freely in all regions which acknowledged Islam. Bagdad remained the cultural center of the Moslem world long after its political supremacy was gone.

The Ommiads had been interested in Greek and Persian learning and had welcomed scholars at their court. Unfortunately, almost no works exist which can be ascribed with certainty to the Ommiad period and it is impossible to judge how much progress was made at that time. Yet, whatever the achievements of earlier scholars, there is no doubt that the great period of Arabic learning came under the Abbasid caliphs. There was tremendous eagerness to acquire all the knowledge of earlier civilizations. Practically the entire body of Greek scientific treatises was translated into Arabic. Persian and Hindu works were also translated, and thus a great mass of scientific materials was made available to students who understood Arabic. At first the scholars of the caliphate merely restated and synthesized the work of their predecessors, but they soon began to make original contributions. Their greatest achievements were in the field of mathematics. The Greeks had known the fundamental principles of algebra and trigonometry, but they had expressed them in rather cumbersome forms. The Arabs improved the system of notation and developed new applications of both sciences. Most important of all, they borrowed the Hindu numerals, including the zero, and likewise the Hindu idea of arranging numbers by units, tens, and hundreds. Thus arithmetic became an elementary school subject, instead of an abstruse science which only advanced scholars could understand. The value of this contribution can be estimated only if the reader will try to perform a few simple arithmetical operations with Roman numerals. In astronomy, the Arab contribution was less remarkable. They preserved the observations and theories of the Greeks at a time when few other people were interested in them and added many facts, though few hypotheses, of their own. The great number of star-names of Arabic origin testifies to the thoroughness of their study of the heavens. While the Moslems did little original work in astronomy, it should not be forgotten that the caliph's scientists were able to make a reasonably accurate estimate of the circumference of the earth at a time when the greatest astronomers in Christian Europe could do little more than predict the date of Easter.

In medicine, Moslem contribution was much like that in astronomy. The basic theories remained Greek, though many new facts were observed. For example, there are excellent discussions of the symptoms of smallpox and measles in Arabic medical works. The most notable work was in ophthalmology, a field in which there were extensive opportunities for practice, owing to the prevalence of eye diseases in the East. Surgery could advance but little beyond Greek, since dissection was forbidden by the law of Islam. Yet in medicine, as in astronomy, the Arabic-speaking world was making effective use of its knowledge during the centuries when western Europe had not assimilated the most elementary treatises on the subject. Hospitals were established in the leading cities of the East, and doctors were examined and licensed in ninth-century Bagdad. Moslem chemistry was almost entirely alchemy—that is, an attempt to transform the base elements into gold. In the effort they were forced to extensive experimentation and discovered many important chemical reactions. Such words as alcohol, alembic, alkali, benzine, and nitre show the Arabic influence in this field. Yet while they discovered many useful facts, they added little to the theories which they had received from their predecessors.

Moslem scholars were attracted by Greek philosophy, especially by the work of Aristotle. They also received a mass of Neo-Platonic literature, some of which masqueraded under Aristotle's name. Thus they became involved in the great and hopeless task of trying to reconcile Aristotle and Plato, a task which was to absorb the energies of countless Christian scholars in later centuries. Their interest in philosophy involved them in a still more persistent problem, that of reconciling faith and reason. Aristotle had perfected a system of logic which was apparently applicable to any sort of data. By the use of his logical method he had worked out certain theories which contradicted the dogmas of both Christianity and Islam; for example, the theory that the world had not been created but had always existed. Respect for Aristotle was too great to allow his opinions to be rejected, and yet the teachings of the faith could not be set aside. Was it possible to reconcile the two, or must it be admitted that philosophical truth and religious truth were not identical? No completely satisfactory solution was ever found, but Moslem discussions of the problem were eagerly studied by Christian scholars who found themselves faced with the same difficulty in the twelfth and thirteenth centuries.

The attitude of the Moslem world toward science presents a sharp contrast to that of their Christian contemporaries. Western Europe had lost most of its scientific knowledge before the fall of the Roman Empire, and the Byzantines were not greatly interested in this heritage from the past. Only in Moslem countries was there deep interest in scientific problems; only in Moslem countries were scientists encouraged and supported by rulers. This interest in science overrode all religious and racial prejudices. Christian doctors attended the caliphs; Jews wrote some of the most important Arabic philosophical treatises. A surprising amount of free-thinking was tolerated in scientists, in spite of the protests of orthodox theologians. This conviction that scientific speculation was valuable was perhaps the most important contribution of the Moslems.

Art and literature flourished during the Abbasid period, but in these fields the Moslems had less influence on Christian Europe. Yet the pointed arch, which is typical of Gothic architecture, seems to have been first developed in Moslem countries. And it is very possible that the emphasis on love themes in Moslem poetry affected European writers. The poetry of the late Roman Empire had been narrative and didactic, and the theme of the lover sighing for his lady was almost unknown in the early Middle Ages. The earliest troubadours in southern France seem to have modeled their work on lyrics written in Moorish Spain. Arabic literature also served as a source of the romantic and marvelous to Christian writers. It was not the only source—Celtic legends were probably more important—but it contributed to the formation of the romantic tradition in European literature.

Agriculture was an activity in which the Moslems were greatly interested. Here they could profit both by their scientific approach and by their contacts with the East. They rapidly learned the methods which had been practiced in Mesopotamia, Syria, and Egypt. They studied old treatises and wrote new and more scientific works on the use of manure and irrigation, on grafting, on plant diseases and insect pests. Whenever they found a new vegetable, flower, or fruit, they attempted to grow it in their gardens and thence to transplant it to other lands. As a result many Eastern products were introduced into the regions of Europe which they conquered. For example, the Ommiad refugee, Abderrahman, is said to have brought with him to Spain a palm-sprout which he had carefully tended. The palm-trees of Spain and Portugal still bear witness to the exile's longing for his old surroundings. Our information about the introduction of other vegetable products is not so definite, and it is possible that some of them may have been known before the coming of the Arabs. We do know that in Sicily and Spain they raised rice and sugar-cane, which probably came from India; silk-worms and mulberry trees from Persia; apricots, peaches, and lemons from Syria, and bananas from Arabia. They also introduced cotton, pomegranates, saffron, and many flowers, including the rose and the morning-glory.[1]

Moslem commerce was active and well balanced. Luxury goods, such as silk, jewels, and spices, were imported from the Far East, but the Moslems themselves produced valuable articles which could be shipped back in exchange. Their textiles were especially famous, and in at least one field, that of rug-making, they have kept their supremacy to the present day. The steel of Damascus and Toledo, the leather of Cordova, the glass of Syria were also marketable almost anywhere in the world. In the ninth and tenth centuries trade between Moslems and Christians was still irregular and on a small scale, but even under these conditions a taste for goods produced or imported by the infidel arose in Christian Europe. Like the Byzantines, the Moslems supplied an important stimulus to European trade.

THE REVIVAL OF THE WESTERN EMPIRE

During the ninth century the Carolingian Empire disintegrated and the rulers of each portion proved unable to defend their people against invasions and internal disorders. At first the decline seemed equally rapid in all parts of Europe. By the middle of the tenth century, however, it was evident that Germany was suffering less from the common difficulties than other regions. For a time it seemed that the German king-

[1] This subject has not been thoroughly studied and further research may prove that some of the plants listed above came to Europe through other peoples. But there can be no doubt that the agricultural habits of southern Europe were profoundly modified by contacts with the Moslems.

dom might develop into a strong state which would be the leader of European civilization. This hope was never realized; Germany postponed, but did not avert collapse. For over a century, however, Germany was the strongest kingdom in Europe and preserved more than any other country the ideals and activities of the Carolingian Empire.

It may seem strange that Germany proved to be the strongest part of Charlemagne's state. The kingdom which Louis the German received in 843 was small, poor, and thinly settled. It had never been as well organized as the western lands: many districts had not been subjected to counts or other royal officials. It was also the least civilized part of the Frankish realm; most of Germany had never been included in the Roman Empire. But some of these defects were actually advantages in the dark years of the tenth century. German poverty may have been one reason why the Northmen concentrated their attack on France. The German people were less Romanized than those of France and Italy, but they were more warlike. Roman civilization had so depressed the masses in the countries where it was strong that they took little interest in military affairs. In Germany, on the other hand, the old tradition that all freemen served in the army was still alive as late as the eleventh century. The whole responsibility for defense was not thrust on the shoulders of a small military caste, and this may explain why Germany was more successful than France or Italy in beating off invaders. It may also explain why feudalism developed comparatively slowly in Germany. There were feudal lords in the eastern kingdom, but it took them a long time to obtain a monopoly of military and political power in a land where most freemen could defend themselves. Meanwhile, the German king was able to keep a certain degree of control over the entire country and hence to wield greater power than any other Western ruler.

The Germans were also more fortunate in their kings than either France or Italy. After the deposition of Charles the Fat in 887, France experienced a century of civil war between the Carolingians and the family of the count of Paris, while the kingdom of Italy was destroyed by the quarrels of the great men. But in Germany the nobles elected Arnulf, an illegitimate grandson of Louis the German, as their ruler. This revival of the old German principle of election was eventually to strengthen the nobles and weaken the kingship, but the immediate effect was to give Germany a strong ruler at a time when he was badly needed. Arnulf checked the raids of the Slavs on his eastern frontier and ended a dangerous Danish invasion by a great victory on the river Dyle in 891. This battle added greatly to Arnulf's prestige and gave him such authority in his own kingdom that he was able to revive the Carolingian claims to Italy. He conquered the Po Valley in 894 and in the following year forced his way to Rome where Pope Formosus crowned him emperor. Then, like so many other German conquerors, he and his army were stricken with disease and had to hasten back across the Alps. The brutality of his soldiers and his own severity had so angered the Romans that the opposition soon got control of the city and Arnulf was never able to return to restore order. The whole episode would have been unimportant had it not furnished a precedent for German intervention in Italy.

When Arnulf died in 899 he was succeeded by his six-year-old son Louis. During the brief reign of this last German Carolingian all the dangers which Arnulf had averted returned to plague the kingdom. The nobles fought with each other while the Slavs, the Danes, and the Hungarians harassed the frontiers. The collapse of the central government encouraged localism in Germany as it did in France and Italy, but the local units which emerged during the reign of Louis were not exactly like those of the other kingdoms. The different Germanic peoples were still conscious of their identity, and there was a tendency to form units based on tribal groups. Feudalism was weak in Germany and of little aid in building up local authority. The powerful men who arose tried to make themselves leaders of a people rather than to become lords of many vassals. As a result of these influences, Germany was divided into five great duchies, and the rulers of these districts had much more power than an ordinary feudal lord.

The strongest of these local rulers was the duke of Saxony, whose lands stretched clear across the north of Germany. In spite of the conquest by Charlemagne, the Saxons had never lost their sense of nationality. They remained warlike and independent, and most of them accepted the leadership of the duke, at least in relations with other peoples. The duke of Bavaria, the most powerful lord in the southeast, also profited from tribal feeling. Like the Saxons, the Bavarians had retained their identity in spite of the Frankish conquest. The Swabians, who inhabited the old territories of the Alamanni in the elbow of the upper Rhine, also had a duke, but in the early tenth century he had much less power than the dukes of Saxony or Bavaria. There was also a duchy of Franconia on the middle Rhine but no one family was dominant there, and there were bitter fights for leadership of the district during the early years of the tenth century. The fifth great duchy was Lorraine, which became definitely a part of Germany in 925 after swinging back and forth between the eastern and western kingdoms for half a century. Lorraine had less racial unity and more feudalism than any of the other duchies, and its duke had little power over other lords.

When the dukes first became strong during the reign of Louis the Child, it seemed as if they might dominate Germany for years to come. They possessed great wealth, effective military power, and had the support of such tribal patriotism as had survived the work of Charlemagne. Their authority, however, depended on their personal ability and private possessions, and their attempts to dominate their duchies were frequently resented by the counts and other nobles. Moreover, weak as the kings were, they still retained some authority over the dukes. The king controlled the Church, except in Bavaria, and often used it against the dukes. In addition the dukes, like all other officials, were theoretically royal servants, removable at pleasure, and later kings were able to exercise this right. Thus no duke could gain complete control of his own duchy, or complete independence of the king.

When Louis the Child died in 911 the nobles again asserted their right of election. The claims of the western Carolingians were ignored and Conrad, duke of Franconia, was chosen king. He had little power outside his own duchy, and during his reign the dukes continued to gain strength. He did not even succeed in founding a dynasty, for when he died in 918 the duke of Saxony was elected king. With the advent of the Saxon house the decline of the German monarchy was halted. During the century that this family held the throne (919–1024) they pushed back the Slavs in the East, gained the crown of Italy, and checked the growing power of the dukes.

The first of these Saxon kings was Henry I, later called the Fowler (919–936). At his election he was recognized only by Franconia and Saxony, but he soon forced Swabia and Bavaria to accept him as king. He also succeeded in incorporating Lorraine in the German kingdom, thus ending the disputes over this region for several centuries. He protected the eastern frontier by building a line of forts which he then used as bases for an attack on the Slavs who lived between the Elbe and the Oder. This great task, "the conquest of three-fifths of modern Germany," [2] could not be completed in his lifetime, or even in his century, but Henry did make the *Drang nach Osten,* "the push to the East," a permanent German policy. Fighting the Slavs was like cutting into water; they slipped away or yielded to the invader's blow, always ready to flow back and drown out isolated German detachments. The Slavs could not be conquered; they had to be displaced, and only the pressure of generations of German colonists could do this. Henry began the work of colonizing Slavic lands, though he could not finish it. More spectacular than the slow pushing back of the Slavs were Henry's two great victories over Magyar invaders in 933. These victories, following the one which Arnulf had gained over the Danes, did much to maintain the German monarchy and to slow down the growth of feudalism. In France and Italy, where the kings had little success against invaders, men turned to the local nobles for protection. In Germany and England, where the

---

[2] Lamprecht, as quoted by Thompson, *Feudal Germany,* p. xviii. It should be added that Lamprecht was speaking of the Germany of 1914. Since then, the two World Wars have cost Germany much of its eastern lands, although the lands between the Elbe and the Oder are still German.

kings were better generals, there was less reason for giving all power to the local strong man. Yet, while Henry gained prestige for his family, he, like his predecessor, lacked direct authority outside his own duchy. He was suspicious of the Church, which was the only force which he could have used against the nobles in their own territories, and he interfered very little with the local government of the dukes and counts.

Henry was succeeded by his son Otto (936–973), usually called the Great because under him the Saxon house reached the height of its power. Like so many famous kings, Otto built on the foundations created by a less ambitious father. It was the loyalty of Saxony which saved him during the first troubled years of his reign, when his own brothers joined the dukes in rebellion. But from the moment of his accession Otto showed that he was not going to be content with being merely the ruler of Saxony. At his coronation he gave a large place to the Church and emphasized his position as head of all the Christians of the kingdom. This was a revival of Charlemagne's old alliance between Church and state, and it proved as useful to Otto as it had to Charles. When secular lords failed to serve him, Otto could always raise a large army from the lands of the bishops and abbots who were his faithful supporters. At the same time that he sought the aid of the Church, Otto turned the administration of his Saxon duchy over to two of his subordinates, thus freeing himself for larger tasks. These moves, which indicated that he was planning to rule all Germany, caused a series of uprisings which were much more dangerous than those which usually occurred at the beginning of a reign. It was customary for the nobles to test the power of a new ruler by rebelling, but the attacks on Otto were so persistent that they showed definite understanding and fear of his policies. Not until 941 was the last threat ended, and only in that year was Otto master of the whole kingdom.

Otto's victories over the rebels greatly strengthened his power. The dukes of Lorraine and Franconia were killed during the wars, and the power of the dukes of Swabia and Bavaria was greatly weakened. This gave Otto a chance to get all the duchies in the hands of his family. He kept Franconia under his own control and gave Lorraine to a loyal noble who soon became his son-in-law. His brother and son married ladies of the ducal houses of Bavaria and Swabia and succeeded the reigning dukes in 947 and 949, respectively. At the same time Otto made important grants of lands and governmental powers to the Church. This actually strengthened the monarchy, since Otto felt that church lands were still his property and was able to treat the bishops and abbots as royal administrative officials. This policy of controlling Germany through family alliances and the Church was fairly successful during Otto's lifetime; royal power increased and the growth of ducal authority was definitely arrested. Yet the system was hardly adapted to the permanent maintenance of a strong kingship. There was no loyalty to the state or to the monarchy; the only ties which counted were religious and personal. Neither of these could be relied on over a long period; the Church was apt to pursue an independent policy, while the bonds of kinship could not bear much strain. Even in Otto's lifetime his son and son-in-law, the dukes of Swabia and Lorraine, rebelled, and the passage of one or two generations made the degrees of relationship too remote to be of much help.

Whatever the inherent weaknesses of his internal policies, Otto was the strongest ruler in the West. He was able to dominate most of the countries on his frontiers and to extend German power in central Europe. His foreign policy became a model for most of his successors. His basic ideas seem to have been (1) to keep France weak, but to seek no additional territory in the West; (2) to encourage his subordinates to conquer and settle Slavic territory in the East; and (3) to concentrate his own energy on gaining and keeping control of Italy. He was eminently successful in all these policies, and his success greatly influenced the later history of Europe.

In dealing with France, Otto had the advantage of being the brother-in-law both of the Carolingian king and of the head of the rival Robertian family. He was frequently asked to intervene in the quarrels between the two and used his power to keep either side from gaining a decisive victory. Thus France was kept weak and divided, and the desperate efforts of the last Carolingians to restore their authority were blocked. This meant that Otto's western lands, and especially the recently acquired duchy of Lorraine, were safe. More than this he did not want.

In the East, Otto had to meet for the last time the menace of a Hungarian invasion. He broke the Magyar forces on the Lechfeld in 955, a defeat which so discouraged them that they made no further raids on Germany. The Slavs beyond the Elbe were also troublesome, and Otto made several expeditions against them. On the whole, however, he could leave the eastern frontier to his representatives in Saxony, Herman Billung and Gero. These men kept up the steady pressure which was necessary to push back the Slavs, without letting themselves be discouraged by the difficulties of guerilla warfare. Thanks to their efforts, the region between Elbe and Oder became more and more German. Otto aided the work of Germanization by securing the foundation of new bishoprics in the occupied territory, once more showing how he hoped to use the Church to aid his political plans.

This need for the support of the Church may explain why Otto concentrated his efforts on the conquest of Italy during the last years of his reign. He had control of the German church; his brother was archbishop of Cologne, and one of his sons became archbishop of Mainz. But the German church was closely connected to Rome, thanks to the work of

St. Boniface, and no one could be sure that the Roman popes would always be as weak as they were in the first half of the tenth century. If the German kingdom could exist only with the aid of the Church, then it was wise for the German king to control the head of the Church. It is also true that Italy was so divided that it offered a constant temptation to ambitious northern lords. If Otto had not moved into Italy the duke of Bavaria probably would have done so, and a union of North Italy and Bavaria would have endangered Otto's position in Germany. Whatever his reasons, the fact that Otto spent ten of the last twelve years of his reign in Italy shows that he felt it essential to gain control of the country.

Otto's connection with Italy began when Adelaide, widow of one of the shadowy Italian kings, appealed to him for help against the new king, who was trying to force her into marriage with his son. Otto made a triumphant expedition to Italy and rescued and married the queen in 951. He was unable to establish his authority at this time, owing to the rebellion of his son in Germany, but he had shown his willingness to intervene in the tangled affairs of the peninsula. His victory over the Hungarians, who had been as great a scourge to Italy as to Germany, increased his prestige with the Italians. Both the pope and the nominal king were weak, corrupt, and unable to keep any order in the country, and a new appeal for aid was sent to Otto in 960. He was quite ready to act and in 961 entered Italy, where he was recognized as king by most of the magnates. He proceeded to Rome, where he was crowned emperor on February 2, 962. After the coronation, Otto renewed and expanded the donations of Pippin and Charlemagne, but at the same time he insisted that future popes must be approved by the emperor before they could be consecrated. He acted almost immediately to show that imperial control of the papacy was to be more than a mere form. The reigning pope, John XII, was generally disliked; as an eminent English historian has said, "no gleam of competence redeemed his debauchery." [3] Otto was not greatly shocked by the pope's dissolute life, but he was annoyed when John began to negotiate with his enemies. He summoned a synod at Rome to try the pope on charges of murder, perjury, robbery and other grave crimes. This was an action of more than doubtful legality. But Otto was strong and John was unpopular, so the synod deposed the pope and elected a man who was better disposed to the emperor. This set a precedent, and during the next hundred years the popes were often selected by the emperors, in spite of repeated protests by the people of Rome.

Otto had revived the Empire again and his act was almost as significant as the first renewal under Charlemagne. It had been almost a century since an emperor had had any real power, and there had not even

[3] Previté-Orton in *Cambridge Medieval History,* III, 161.

been titular emperors after 924. Otto claimed to be the successor of Augustus, Constantine, and Charles the Great, but in reality his empire was very different from any which had gone before. The name by which it was later known, "the Roman Empire of the German Nation," was very fitting, because it was really the union of the Roman imperial title with the German kingship. It included only Germany and two-thirds of Italy; it was neither as Roman nor as European as Charles' empire had been. Like Charles' empire it was based on an alliance of Church and state, but the union was no longer as perfect as it had been, for the interests of the two partners no longer seemed identical. Otto had no interest in the morals of his subjects; he thought of the Church as a political force which he must control. The popes no longer believed that they must follow the emperor's wishes in order to preserve Christianity; they felt quite capable of forming their own political plans. On the whole, the Ottonian empire was weaker and less well organized than the Carolingian; it was even more dependent upon the personality of the ruler.

Yet with all its weaknesses, the revived Empire bore the great name of Rome and men's imaginations still kindled at the sound. Long after the failure of Otto's policy was apparent, German rulers stubbornly refused to admit that it was wrong. It seemed essential to have political as well as religious unity in Christendom. How could men act as Christians if they were divided by the quarrels of petty states? It is easy enough to show the disasters caused by these beliefs; neither Germany nor Italy could become a strong, united nation as long as they were linked together by the tenuous, yet unbreakable idea of the Empire. German emperors wasted their energy in expeditions to Italy, instead of building a strong kingdom in their own land. Italy could not develop a national life of its own because of constant intervention by the German ruler. Both countries fell behind the more nationalistic and better organized states of the West, and Europe has been severely shaken by their frantic efforts to catch up with the procession. But looking at the matter from the viewpoint of the tenth century, it is hard to see how Otto could have acted otherwise. No one then believed that the development of national states was the chief end of man. Most rulers would have done what Otto did, if they had had the power. Every lay ruler needed the support of the Church to govern and would have been glad to get the support of the head of the Church. Otto's policies worked well for over a century, and few statesmen have seen much farther ahead than that.

Otto spent the last years of his life in extending his control over Italy. He followed the same policy there which he had applied in Germany— the policy of giving political power to the Church in order to counterbalance the strength of secular lords. Most of the North Italian bishops were given control of their cities and the surrounding territories, with the understanding that they would use these resources to support the emperor. The Church supplied Otto with the officials, the money, and the troops which he lacked, and thus disguised the fact that the empire had no central institutions, no bureaucracy and no adequate financial resources. In Italy, as in Germany, the support of the Church made it possible for Otto to control the higher nobility and to preserve the fiction that they were public officials, subject to the ruler.

THE EMPIRE AND THE CHURCH

Otto was succeeded by his son Otto II (973–983). In spite of the fact that the new emperor was the son of the Italian Queen Adelaide, and the husband of the Byzantine princess Theophano, he did not allow these Mediterranean connections to distract him from his work in Germany. He had to face the usual rebellion of the dukes, even though most of them were his relatives, and in suppressing it he inaugurated a new policy which was to end their power. The center of rebellion had been Bavaria, and Otto II tried to weaken the hostile duchy by giving large portions of it to his adherents. The southeastern section which controlled the approaches to Italy was made the duchy of Carinthia, and the eastern region, bordering on Hungary, became the East Mark or Austria. At the same time he regained control of Church appointments in Bavaria and greatly increased the territories of Bavarian bishops. This policy of weakening the dukes by setting up rival authorities in their duchies was followed by later emperors and was completely successful as far as its immediate objective was concerned. Yet in the end it merely multiplied the number of men who had sufficiently high rank to oppose the emperor.

After settling the affairs of Bavaria, Otto II felt strong enough to turn to Italy. In a rash attempt to conquer the southern third of the peninsula he suffered a disastrous defeat in 982. Disappointed and weakened by disease, he died in the following year, leaving a three-year-old son as his heir.

Otto the Great had established his family so firmly on the throne that his grandson, Otto III (983–1002), was recognized as king of Germany and Italy without serious opposition, even though the Germans had an understandable prejudice against kings who were minors. A further break with custom was made when the boy's mother, the Byzantine princess Theophano, was accepted as regent. She was an able and learned woman, but she had little respect for Germans and filled her son's head full of Byzantine ideas of imperial power. Young Otto learned Greek and Latin and prided himself on his Greek subtlety, in comparison with the barbarism of the Germans. He had as his tutor Gerbert,[4] the most

---

[4] See below, pp. 171–172.

learned man in the West, and he soon became known as the "wonder of the world" because of his wide learning and great ambitions. With this training it is not surprising that he concentrated on the Roman rather than the German aspect of his Empire. His great ideal was his predecessor Charlemagne, and one chronicler reports that in the year 1000 he solemnly opened the tomb of the great emperor and took from his finger a ring which he wore until his death. Otto the Great's imitation of Charlemagne may have been unconscious, but Otto III seems to have imitated him deliberately.

As might have been expected, Otto III, dazzled by the past, was not very successful in seeing the present clearly. He proudly bore the titles of *Italicus, Saxonicus, Romanus,* and *servus Apostolorum, servus J. Christi,* the first group in imitation of the pagan emperors and the second in imitation of his Frankish predecessors. But these titles had little connection with reality. In Germany the nobles increased their power and continued the slow work of building up feudal relationships which escaped imperial control. Even worse was a resurgence of Slavic power which undid much of the work which had been accomplished on the eastern frontier in the time of Otto the Great. Poland and Bohemia had accepted Christianity and had gained some degree of political organization. Thus the religious excuse for attacking these Slavic peoples was gone, and at the same time their military power had increased. The Germans never succeeded in conquering Poland, and Bohemia accepted the status of a vassal kingdom only after repeated wars which lasted well into the eleventh century. The immediate result of the Slavic resurgence was a rebellion of the Slavs in the lands between Elbe and Oder. They were assisted by the Poles and profited by the absences of Otto II and Otto III in Italy. As a result, the Germans lost for a century more than half of the territory which they had earlier gained in the East. These losses in Germany were not compensated for by an increase of imperial power in Italy. The Italians did not like Otto III, even though he sacrificed his health by living in Rome. In the last year of his reign they were plotting against him, and at his death there was a rebellion against German domination.

Only in his relations with the papacy did the young emperor have complete success. His father and grandfather had allowed the papacy to remain in the hands of the Romans, even though they insisted that the pope swear allegiance to the emperor. This practice had given bad results; the Romans were fundamentally opposed to outside control and several popes proved unfriendly to the Empire. During the minority of Otto III the Roman nobles tried to regain their old control of the papacy. Almost as soon as he came of age, Otto III tried to end these difficulties by securing the election of men who were not Romans or even Italians. First he had his cousin Bruno elevated to the papacy as Gregory V, and on Gregory's death he replaced him with his old tutor Gerbert. Gerbert took the title of Sylvester II and during his brief pontificate the medieval ideal of harmonious coöperation between pope and emperor was close to being a reality. Otto's selection of German and French popes not only strengthened his position as emperor, but also had important results in the history of the papacy. For two hundred and fifty years there had been only two popes who were not born in Rome or the immediate vicinity but from this time on popes were chosen from all parts of the Christian world. The change emphasized the universal character of the papacy and freed it from the evil influence of the Roman nobles. It is true that when Otto and Sylvester died the old conditions returned, and the papacy again became the prey of local factions. But the precedent was not forgotten and the next powerful German ruler followed the example of Otto III and secured a real reform in the Roman Church.

When Otto III died in 1002 "it seemed as if the life-work of his grandfather Otto the Great had been completely undone." [5] A rebellion broke out in Italy, and the German nobles revived their old claim to elect their king. Yet the Saxon house still kept some of its prestige, for the successful candidate, Henry of Bavaria, was a direct descendant of the first Otto. And Henry II (1002–1024), while weak physically and unfortunate in warfare, had the intelligence and persistence which marked the abler members of his family. He had the usual difficulties—a rebellion in the early years of his reign, opposition to German rule in Italy, wars with the Slavs on his eastern frontier—but by careful diplomacy and by keeping steady pressure on his enemies he succeeded in restoring the Empire and in regaining much of the power which had been lost during the reign of Otto III. He reconquered Italy, regained a little territory from the Slavs, and kept some degree of control over the nobles of Germany. Like all his family, he depended upon the aid of the Church in carrying out his policies, and like all his family, he tried to strengthen the Church by giving it generous grants of land and offices. Vacant counties were regularly given to churchmen, and bishops and abbots who did not receive counties were freed from the control of the nobles. Yet Henry II did not look on the Church merely as a political tool; he was sincerely interested in its welfare. As we shall see later, a great movement for reform in the Church had begun in certain monasteries in the late tenth century. Henry encouraged this movement, thus unwittingly preparing the way for the destruction of the Empire. Neither he nor the reformers foresaw that a reformed Church would be bound to break with the emperor because it could not reconcile its spiritual ideals with the political duties imposed on it under the Ottonian system.

Henry II left no direct heir when he died in 1024, and once again the

[5] E. H. Holthouse, in *Cambridge Medieval History*, III, 215.

nobles chose a descendant of the Saxon family as king. This time they selected Conrad of Franconia, who was related to the Ottos only in the female line, and whose policy was very different from that of his predecessors. Feudalism had been growing for several generations in Germany, but even in 1024 it was still far from being complete. Many men and lands were not included in feudal relationships, and the hereditary quality of offices and fiefs was not fully established. This was due in part to the survival of tribal ideas among the Germans, and in part to the strength of the Saxon rulers, who had insisted on their authority in all parts of the realm, and on their right to disregard hereditary claims in bestowing duchies and counties. Conrad II (1024–1039) seems to have sought deliberately to strengthen hereditary titles to offices and fiefs, especially among the lesser nobility. Perhaps this was due to the fact that his own immediate ancestors had lost important rights which they would have inherited under strict feudal law, or perhaps Conrad was worried by the dependence of the government upon Church support and was seeking new allies. He seems to have distrusted churchmen, and he certainly found the lesser nobles very useful in suppressing the inevitable rebellions of the first years of his reign. When order was restored, Conrad tried to make the lesser nobles into hereditary servants of the crown. This enabled him to dispense, to some extent, with the services of churchmen in his administration, though he still kept close control over appointments to high ecclesiastical offices. He still further weakened the bishops by favoring the exemption of monasteries from their control, thus reversing another policy of Henry II. By balancing laymen against churchmen, lesser nobles against the greater, and abbots against bishops, Conrad secured a high degree of peace and order in his country. But his power was based on a precarious equilibrium of forces which he did not fully control. If the bishops should unite with the abbots, or the lesser nobles with the magnates, it would be evident that the king had little power of his own. All local government and most of the resources of the kingdom were in the hands of churchmen or nobles; there were almost no institutions of central government, and everything depended upon the king's ability to keep a certain proportion of great men on his side.

Conrad maintained a loose control over Italy, as Henry II had done, and gained some successes over the eastern Slavs, but his real contribution in foreign affairs was the acquisition of the kingdom of Burgundy. This fragment of the old middle kingdom included western Switzerland and the lands between the Rhône and the Alps. It had suffered severely from the disintegrating tendencies of feudalism, and the kings of Burgundy had lost power steadily. The only important act in the reign of Rudolph III, the last of the line, was his decision to leave his title to Conrad. Conrad's claim was challenged by distant relatives of the Burgundian king, but he succeeded in taking possession of his new realm in

1033. However, both Conrad and his successors had so much else to do that they were never able to restore royal authority in the disorganized kingdom. The one advantage which the German kings gained from the possession of Burgundy was the control of the western passes into Italy.

Some writers have claimed that the medieval German Empire reached its height in the reign of Henry III (1039–1056), the son of Conrad II. Certainly Henry was an able and successful ruler, but the inherent weakness of the Empire became even more apparent during his reign. He had endless difficulties with the magnates, especially in the border region of Lorraine, where every subordinate noble tried to set himself up as an independent ruler. He had to establish new ducal families in the duchies which were in his hands in order to preserve any degree of order. By repeated military expeditions he was able to maintain the old policy of eastern expansion and to force the rulers of Poland, Bohemia, and Hungary to become vassals of the Empire, but of the three only the duke of Bohemia was really loyal to him. Henry succeeded in gaining the support of the Church by assisting the reformers, but in so doing he strengthened the Church so that it was soon able to declare its independence of the Empire. Moreover, in carrying out his ecclesiastical policy Henry once more involved Germany deeply in the affairs of Italy.

Henry II and Conrad II had made expeditions to Italy and had exercised a loose supervision over Italian affairs, especially in the northern plain. Conrad had gained the support of the lesser nobles in Italy as in Germany, by recognizing the hereditary quality of their fiefs. But neither Henry nor Conrad had tried to maintain the policy of Otto III toward the papacy. As a result, the leaders of the Roman nobility had regained their control over papal elections. When Henry III became king, the counts of Tusculum, descended from Marozia and Theodora, controlled both the city and the papacy. Three popes had been chosen from this family and, while the first had been an able and honest reformer, the reigning pope, Benedict IX, was noted for his vicious conduct. A later pope, Victor III (1086–1087), said that robbery and murder were among the least of his crimes. In the winter of 1044–1045 the people of Rome drove Benedict from the city and elected a new pope, Sylvester III. Benedict was soon restored by his supporters, but as he was in constant danger, he sold the papal office to a member of the reforming party who took the name of Gregory VI. It is eloquent of the distress of the Church that a reformer should take this desperate step, and that other reformers should openly rejoice at the act. But Benedict soon attempted to regain his position and Sylvester still claimed to be the rightful pope, so that in 1046 Rome was divided among the three rivals.

Such a state of affairs was intolerable, and Henry III was summoned to Italy to straighten out matters. He accepted gladly, not only because he wanted to revive all the rights of the Empire, but also because he was sincerely interested in reform of the Church. Some historians have blamed Henry for his support of the reformers, claiming that it was evident from the beginning that they wished to free the Church from all lay control. This is not entirely fair criticism. Henry, unlike Conrad, was anxious to secure the aid of the Church for his government, and the reforming party was already so strong that a lay ruler who opposed it would have lost the support of leading churchmen. Moreover, the reformers were not at first hostile to coöperation with secular rulers. They were interested primarily in restoring monastic discipline, in preventing the purchase or inheritance of church offices, and in purging the clergy of its evil members. This was a program designed to improve the character of churchmen rather than one directed against the emperor. It might injure feudal lords who had been filling the Church with worldly and corrupt men, but it could easily be advantageous to Henry. He needed able men in important ecclesiastical offices if he was to run his government through bishops and abbots. On the other hand, it is true that by the middle of Henry's reign, the leaders of the German clergy were beginning to show unusual independence and were insisting that the emperor should not interfere in purely ecclesiastical affairs.

In his own lifetime, however, Henry's policy seemed reasonably successful. He crossed the Alps in 1046 with an army composed largely of troops furnished by the German church. At Pavia he gained the good will of the reformers by holding a synod in which the practice of simony [6] was condemned. Henry bound himself to enforce this rule in his own dominions, and thereby deprived the crown of a considerable revenue, since bishops and other high officials had been expected to pay for their nominations. From Pavia, Henry moved to Sutri, where a council was held to settle the disputed title to the papacy. Gregory and Sylvester appeared, admitted that they were guilty of simony, and were deposed. Benedict, who refused to attend, was deposed by a council held at Rome a little later. Henry then succeeded in getting the Roman nobles to delegate to him their power of nominating the pope. He selected a German bishop, and on Christmas Day had him consecrated as Clement II. The new pope immediately crowned Henry emperor. But when Clement died ten months later, the deposed Benedict IX was able to force his way into Rome and to take over the papacy. He was driven out the next year, and Henry selected a second German pope who died almost as soon as he had assumed office. Henry's third choice was the bishop of Toul, who was an ardent member of the reforming party and who accepted the nomination only on condition that it be approved by the clergy and

[6] Simony was the act of buying or selling sacred offices or prerogatives. It takes its name from Simon Magus. See *Acts* 8.

people of Rome. When he reached the city in 1049 he was favorably received and became Pope Leo IX.

Leo was determined to reform the Church and especially to root out simony and marriage of the clergy. To do this it was necessary to reestablish the authority of the pope north of the Alps, where it had been almost forgotten during the disorders of the tenth century. One of Leo's first acts was to hold a great council at Rheims to discuss the problems of reform. This annoyed the French king, since the pope had not asked his permission to hold the council in his lands, and he tried to prevent French bishops and abbots from attending by summoning them to a feudal levy. This put them in a difficult position; they must either break their obligations as vassals or fail in their duty as churchmen. About one-third of the French bishops and abbots attended the councils; those who failed to come were excommunicated by the pope. Then Leo took up cases of simony and other crimes and discovered that several high officers of the Church were accused of very serious offenses. Leo did not go to extremes, but adjourned all the cases to his own court at Rome. Thus he restored the ties between Rome and the North without forcing his opponents into desperate resistance.

Leo was greatly aided by Henry III, with whom he worked apparently in complete concord. But many of the pope's supporters felt that the clergy must be freed from all lay domination if the Church was to be really reformed. Leo died in 1054 and Henry in 1056, before the issue became acute, but it is doubtful that these able men, even if they had lived longer, could have avoided the conflict which was rising. Henry III had completed the work of the Ottos; he had definitely freed the papacy from the mire of Roman politics. The pope no longer needed the aid of the German king and could be more independent. Leo IX had completed the work of Gregory the Great and Nicholas; the pope was now really head of the Church, in administration as well as in doctrine. Churchmen were now to devote their energies to serving the pope rather than the emperor. These changes undermined the whole structure of the Empire and were bound to cause trouble.

On the whole, the revived Empire of the Ottos had passed the period of its greatest usefulness by 1056. It was not one of the institutions which created the new civilization of Europe; its chief service was to preserve the old civilization during a period of disorder. It was based on the ideas of the Carolingian Empire—ideas which were out of date by the eleventh century. Like Charlemagne, the German emperors considered feudalism a purely private arrangement among their subjects, instead of a rival type of government. Like Charlemagne, they felt that they could control the magnates through their own personal authority, without an army or a civil service of their own. Like Charlemagne, they based their government on the resources and the personnel of the Church and tried to identify faith in Christianity with loyalty to the Empire. As a result the revived Empire had only one bond of unity and one institution of central government—the person of the emperor. There were no central courts and professional officials to supervise the work of local government; there were few political or economic activities which made one part of the Empire dependent on another. The personality of the emperor determined the strength of the Empire; the energy of the emperor determined the degree of activity of his government. But the Empire was too large, too disunited in language, race, and economic interests to be held together by loyalty to one man. These inherent weaknesses were disguised for a while by the extraordinary energy and ability of the rulers; they did so well with their limited resources that they failed to realize the need for increasing them. It may even be argued that it was a misfortune for Germany that her rulers from 919 to 1056 were so able, since their remarkable feat of preserving the old system of government stunted the growth of new forms which might have been better adapted to medieval conditions. In any case, the German Empire had done important work in the tenth and eleventh centuries. It had held back the Slavs and Hungarians and had begun the process of converting them to Western civilization. It had repeatedly saved the papacy from becoming the property of the petty barons of Rome. In spite of its demands on the clergy, it had kept the German Church at a higher level of learning and morality than that of any other European country. And by saving the papacy and the German Church it had preserved the most vital elements of earlier civilizations. All this it had done, but it could not adjust itself to the new conditions of the late eleventh century. After 1056 the Empire began to decline and, in spite of brilliant rulers and momentary revivals, the decline could not be permanently halted. After 1056 the Empire is no longer the central fact in European history.

VII

->>->>->>->> <<<-<<<-<<<-<<<-

The Revival
of Western Civilization

B Y THE ELEVENTH CENTURY, western Europe had survived its greatest
dangers. It had been plundered, but not conquered, by the Northmen, Saracens, and Magyars. The collapse of political authority had ended
with the establishment of feudalism, which, with all its emphasis on war,
was far from being a system of pure anarchy. But in order to survive,
Europe had had to abandon everything except the essentials of life.
Political organizations did little but assure defense; economic organizations did little but assure subsistence. It seemed as though civilization
could be rebuilt in Europe only by centuries of slow and painful effort.
Strangely enough, it took less time to rebuild than it had to destroy.
By 1150 a great renaissance, the truest renaissance Europe has ever
known, was in full swing. Political and economic organizations were
being reconstructed on a large scale; art, literature, and learning were
flourishing. In another hundred years medieval civilization had reached
its height, and had surpassed in many ways the Roman civilization which
had collapsed so many centuries ago.

The reason for this rapid revival of Western civilization is one of the
great problems of history, a problem which in many ways is more difficult to solve than that of the fall of Rome. It is easy enough to see weaknesses in an advanced and complicated civilization, even though historians may be unable to agree as to which was the fundamental cause of
the final collapse. But it is extraordinarily difficult to find the seeds of
future greatness in a primitive civilization which seems barely able to
exist. In what ways was Europe of the eleventh century different from
Europe of the seventh and eighth centuries, when the most that could

be hoped for was to arrest the decline of civilization? What were the hidden forces which made the great work of reconstruction possible?

Some of the causes of the revival were primarily negative. The gradual ending of the invasions relieved both the mental strain and the physical wastage caused by the destruction of life and property. If Europe had hit rock-bottom in political and economic organization at least it could sink no lower; if things could not get worse they might get better. Now that there was little left to destroy, almost any activity had to be constructive; even the strife of belligerent feudal lords could create only larger and stronger political units. The storms of the tenth century had leveled the ruins of old empires; the ground was cleared and ready for rebuilding.

But the removal of some of the old obstacles did not mean that civilization would spring up automatically. It was the conscious effort of thousands of men which caused the revival of the eleventh century. Their activity manifested itself in many fields, and each man's work strengthened his fellow's so that it is impossible to say that any one movement was the cause of the revival. We can sum up this activity under the heads of the religious revival, the political revival, and the economic revival. But we must remember that these are not exclusive categories. The religious revival aided the political revival by inspiring respect for law and desire for peace, but the religious revival would have been impossible without the aid of secular rulers. In the same way the economic revival benefited from the greater security preached by the Church and secured by the governments, while it helped to produce that security by giving Church and state new sources of power. It may be argued that no advance was possible in political or economic life until the Church had softened the hearts of the people of Europe. It may be argued that no religious or economic revival was possible until kings and feudal lords had secured a minimum degree of security for life and property. It may be argued that religious and secular rulers were powerless until increased economic activity had produced the surplus of men and goods which made possible advances in other fields. But the safest course is to admit that all three movements were going on simultaneously, and that no one of them was the cause of the other two.

THE RELIGIOUS REVIVAL

In discussing the revived empire of the Ottos and the Henries, we mentioned briefly a reform movement in the Church which was becoming very powerful by the middle of the eleventh century. The roots of this movement go back into the tenth century, to the period when the Church, like all other organizations, seemed to be disintegrating. As we saw, the tenth century Church was becoming feudalized, and many members of

EUROPE AT THE TIME OF
THE FIRST CRUSADE

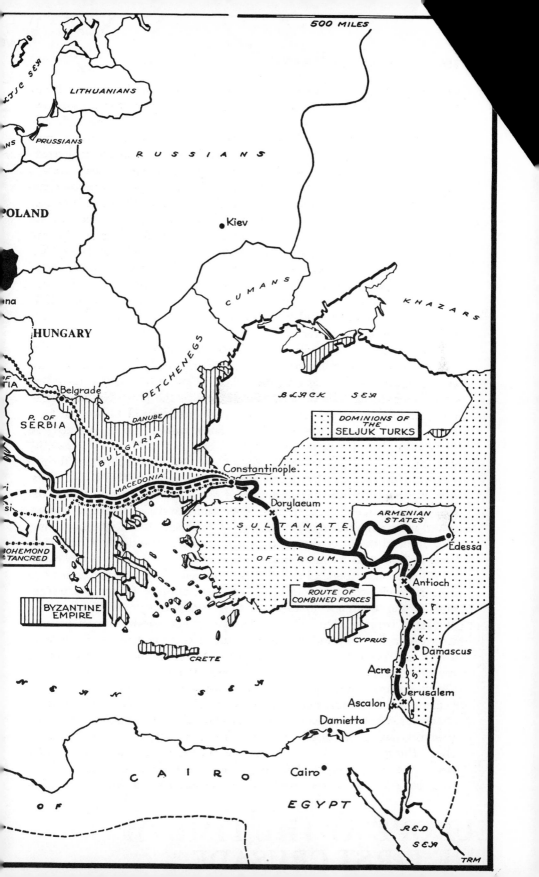

500 MILES

LITHUANIANS

PRUSSIANS

POLAND

R U S S I A N S

•Kiev

C U M A N S

K H A Z A R S

HUNGARY

P E T C H E N E G S

B L A C K   S E A

Belgrade

DOMINIONS OF
THE
SELJUK TURKS

P. OF
SERBIA

DANUBE

B U L G A R I A

M A C E D O N I A

Constantinople.

Dorylaeum

ARMENIAN
STATES

S U L T A N A T E

Edessa

BOHEMOND
& TANCRED

O F   R O U M

Antioch

ROUTE OF
COMBINED FORCES

BYZANTINE
EMPIRE

CYPRUS

Damascus

CRETE

Acre

Jerusalem

Ascalon

Damietta

C A I R O

Cairo•

O F

E G Y P T

R E D
S E A

TRM

ought only wealth and power. Yet the ideals of the Church
ompletely forgotten and many men protested against the
into which it had fallen. These protests were especially frequent in the monasteries, which, on the whole, attracted a better type
of men than those to be found in the secular clergy. Ordinary monks did
not have much chance of reaching high positions in the Church, and so
merely ambitious men shunned the monasteries. At the same time the
old belief that monasticism was the highest form of Christian life persisted, and humane and pious men were drawn to the monasteries. Thus
it is not surprising that the tenth century movement for reforming the
Church should have begun in the monasteries rather than among the
secular clergy. This reform movement started almost simultaneously
in many widely separated districts. However, the monastery of Cluny
in Burgundy soon became the most important center of reform, thanks
to its central location and remarkable organization. A study of Cluny
will illustrate many of the characteristics of the movement.

Cluny was founded in 910 by William, duke of Aquitaine. Like many
intelligent laymen of his day, he recognized the chief reasons for the
corruption of the Church, and he took great pains to free his monastery
from evil influences by subjecting it directly to the pope. Neither neighboring feudal lords, nor the almost equally feudalized bishops of Burgundy could intervene in its affairs. Cluny was fortunate, not only in
its founder, but also in its first abbots. They combined personal sanctity
with remarkable administrative ability and were more influential than
many of the popes of the tenth and early eleventh century. Their first
step was to adopt an interpretation of the Benedictine rule which decreased the emphasis on manual labor and physical hardships, and allowed more time for intellectual and religious activity. At the same time
they insisted on strict discipline and high moral standards. Cluny soon
became known as a model monastery, and monks of Cluny were called
in, often by lay rulers, to reform other houses. They naturally remained
in close touch with their old home, and the abbots of Cluny took advantage of this tendency to create a new ecclesiastical organization, the
monastic "congregation." The weakness of other reform movements was
their dependence on individuals and their lack of coherence. Each monastery had been treated as a separate unit; when the reforming abbot
died or was called to another establishment his work often collapsed.
Cluny, however, annexed the monasteries which it reformed; their abbots
became simple priors, appointed by the abbot of Cluny and subject to
his orders. Periodic assemblies were held at which the affairs of the congregation were discussed; between the meetings, the abbot traveled
about Europe inspecting the houses of his order. Scores of monasteries
joined the congregation of Cluny, either voluntarily, or under pressure
from lay rulers who were well disposed to the reform. Many new mon-

asteries were founded by monks of Cluny with the aid of pious laymen. These Cluniac priories were not confined to France; they were to be found in England, Germany, Spain and Italy as well. At the height of its power, Cluny is said to have had hundreds of affiliated houses. It is obvious that this great organization offered a remarkable opportunity for the spread of new ideas through Europe. The influence of Cluny in such incidental matters as architecture and literature can be traced all over the continent; how much greater, then, must its influence have been in its chief objective, the reform of the Church.

Cluny, of course, concentrated on the reform of monasteries rather than on the reform of the secular clergy. The chief interest of the abbots of Cluny was in restoring monastic life to its old standards and in making monks an example of Christian living to all the faithful. But the reform of one branch of the clergy could hardly fail to influence the other, and many of the ideals of Cluny applied as well to bishops and priests as to monks. There would probably have been a reform movement among the secular clergy in any case, but the success of Cluny and other re- formed monasteries greatly encouraged the leaders who wished to im- prove the character of bishops and priests.

The chief difficulty with the secular clergy was feudal and family influence. Powerful feudal lords named bishops; lesser lords named priests, and such appointments were either sold to the highest bidder, or were given to relatives and friends as a sort of pension. In either case the clergyman was not apt to pay much attention to his religious duties. Sometimes the bishop himself was a powerful feudal lord and then he tried to keep his bishopric in his family and to acquire other benefices for his retainers. Many parish priests were married and endeavored to pass their churches on to their sons. Thus church offices were treated as private property, and it seemed impossible for the secular clergy to function properly until these conditions were changed.

The reformers attacked these evils vigorously. Their program was to free the Church entirely from lay control and to reduce to a minimum the secular interests of the clergy. The sale of church offices was denounced as simony, and the most radical leaders soon extended this term to cover all appointments by laymen, even if no actual payment were made. The marriage of the clergy was condemned, and eventually it was ruled that all marriages of priests were invalid. The reformers won a great victory when the intervention of Henry III gave them control of the papacy, and by the end of the eleventh century they had gained many of their objectives. The worst forms of lay interference with church appointments were abolished; open buying and selling of church offices almost ceased. The danger that bishoprics would become hereditary fiefs was averted. The veto on the marriage of the clergy was successfully enforced, and sons of clergymen found it difficult to obtain positions in the Church. It is true that in spite of the bitter conflicts of the investiture struggle [1] the reformers found it impossible to deprive the more powerful lay rulers of all influence over appointments, but at least that influence could no longer be exercised in a totally irresponsible way. Moreover, the great increase in papal power under Leo IX and his successors made it possible for the popes to control bishops named by lay rulers in a way which had been impossible in the tenth century. The victory of the reformers was not complete, but they had made the Church more united and more powerful than it had ever been before. Feudal lords and kings still annoyed the Church, but they could no longer use it for their own purposes. Worldly bishops and incontinent priests still existed, but the clergy in general were respected by laymen. The Church, by 1100, had more influence than it had ever possessed in Europe. It was better organized than it had ever been, and there was no universal monarch, such as Constantine or Charlemagne, to control it. The Church was now free to pursue its own objectives, and its policies were sure to make a deep impression on all Europe. What influence did the Church have on the development of a new civilization?

In the first place, a popular religious revival accompanied the ecclesiastical one. The reformers had to appeal to laymen to gain their objectives, and in the process they greatly stimulated religious feeling. The better organization of the Church, the ending of the invasions, and the conversion of Vikings and Magyars also meant that more people were in regular contact with the clergy. In many parts of Europe parish priests were established only in the tenth or eleventh centuries and it was only when they were established that Christianity began to influence daily life. This popular religious revival did not reach its height until the twelfth century, but even in the eleventh century it had important results. There was a deeper emotional response to the exhortations of religious leaders than there had been before; men began to make a real effort to practise the Christian virtues. In 700 or even in 800 Christianity had often been merely a matter of external observances. By the eleventh century it was, for more and more men, a deep individual conviction which had to be expressed in actual behavior. One of the most notable examples of this was the development of two closely related movements—the Peace of God and the Truce of God. The Church had always preached against violence; now it began to do something about it. Associations to keep the peace were formed under the leadership of bishops in the disorderly regions of central France in the tenth century. These associations, composed of all the men of a given district, levied regular assessments on their members and used the money to provide armed protection against evil-doers. This was fairly effective in suppressing bandits and restrain-

[1] See below, Chap. 8.

ing the violence of minor feudal lords, but the Peace associations could not prevent the great barons from waging private war. They did attempt, with some success, to humanize warfare by forbidding attacks on peasants, merchants, and other non-combatants and by denouncing the destruction of crops and unfortified houses. The Truce of God was a less successful attempt to lessen the evils of warfare by forbidding fighting on certain days and in certain seasons which were especially holy. If it had been observed, the open season for warfare would have been limited to about eighty days. However, there is no evidence that it was ever taken very seriously and it had no permanent effect on lay society. The Peace of God, on the other hand, had an important influence on the development of secular government. In central France, which was the classic region of feudal anarchy, the Peace retained its original coöperative form until the end of the thirteenth century. Elsewhere the movement was taken over in the eleventh century by kings and great feudal lords who were delighted to have an excuse to exercise their authority over unruly subordinates. Some scholars have claimed that the basic idea of punishing all breaches of the peace as offenses against the supreme political authority came solely from the Church. Others have thought that lay rulers developed the idea independently because it was an obvious way to increase their power and income. But even in the latter case the support of the Church must have been of great assistance in imposing such a revolutionary idea upon people who were suspicious of all centralizing tendencies. And in general it may be said that the Church aided rulers who were trying to establish orderly governments and to suppress private war.

The improvement in the lot of the common man, which began at this time, was probably due more to economic conditions than to the teachings of the Church. It is true that the Church suggested that freeing serfs was a pious work, but the gift of serfs to monasteries was equally acceptable. And while the Church reproved lords who fleeced their serfs and agricultural tenants, bishops and abbots never hesitated to exact their strict due from their subjects. The Church did contribute the idea of a written document which would define the duties of unfree or semi-free tenants and so save them from unlimited exactions. And the Church did preach the dignity of labor, the idea that a man of any condition may serve God by doing his work well. It is true that scorn for manual labor persisted through the Middle Ages, and yet the medieval attitude toward labor marks a great advance over that of the Romans. Slavery became almost extinct; the number of serfs was greatly reduced, and medieval men showed an interest in labor-saving devices which was unknown in Greece and Rome. Respect for labor, imperfect as it still is, is one of the distinguishing characteristics of our civilization, and the Church certainly aided in establishing it.

Other important results of the religious revival were the Crusades, the beginnings of a new style of architecture, and a new interest in learning. The Crusades will be discussed in a later chapter, but it may be said here that they are the most striking evidence of the influence which the Church had gained. Thousands of men, from all regions of Europe, abandoned their homes at the call of the pope and marched off on one of the most hazardous undertakings that was ever planned. This shows how the Church had overridden all localisms and had given the people of Europe a set of common interests such as they had never before possessed. The new style of architecture was likewise a result of the new respect in which the Church was held. Important gifts were being made to the Church, especially to the reformed monasteries, and with this increased wealth more could be spent on church buildings. This was especially true of the Cluniac monks, who rivaled each other in building great churches, and who were less scornful of earthly beauties than might be expected of men who had renounced the world. Naturally, with more building being done, and more resources available for each building, there was an advance in architecture. The details of this architectural revival will be discussed in a later chapter, but to show how important it was, even in the eleventh century, a famous passage of the chronicler Raoul Glaber may be cited:

> Soon after the year 1000 all over the world, and especially in Italy and France, people began to rebuild their churches. Most of them were well constructed and in no need of alterations, but all Christian countries were rivalling each other to see which should have the most beautiful temples. One would have said that the world was shaking itself and throwing off its old rags, to reclothe itself in a white robe of churches.

The influences which had produced a revival in architecture also worked toward a new interest in learning. The reformers attacked the ignorance, as well as the immorality, of the clergy, and greater prosperity and security encouraged the growth of institutions of learning. The cathedral schools, which went back to the Carolingian period, flourished as never before. The schools of monasteries such as Cluny and Bec were almost as important. The work done in these schools was neither very original nor very profound, but this does not mean that it was unimportant. The heritage of the past had to be mastered before anything else could be done and this was accomplished during the tenth and early eleventh centuries. Only when scholars were able to state, in their own words, the knowledge which they had received from Roman authors and the Church Fathers, were they ready to use that material for new purposes. Moreover, the acquisition of a thorough knowledge of Latin was necessary before any important intellectual work could be done. It is almost impossible to think without expressing the thought in words, and the vernacular languages at that time, and for centuries to come, were so limited in vocabulary and so incoherent in syntax that they could not be used for logical thought. Even in the age of Elizabeth, English was hardly adequate for scientific discussions, and the crude Romance and Germanic dialects of the tenth and eleventh centuries were much worse. Latin, on the other hand, with all its weaknesses, was a language which permitted precise definitions and logical sequences. Until the thirteenth century, no rational discussion of any problem, secular or religious, was possible without using Latin. The revival of science and law, as well as the revival of theology and philosophy, depended upon a mastery of Latin.

The growth of interest in learning, and the influence of learned men, are well illustrated by the career of Gerbert. He was born just before the middle of the tenth century, the son of a poor peasant of southern France. The monks of Aurillac noticed his natural ability and admitted him to their school where he soon distinguished himself. Some years later the count of the Spanish March came to Aurillac and was induced by the abbot to take Gerbert back with him to Spain. There Gerbert spent several years acquiring the mathematical and scientific knowledge which was later to give him his legendary reputation as a magician. Then he visited Rome and attracted the interest of the pope, who recommended him to the emperor Otto I. The emperor made him a member of his court, but after a year Gerbert asked permission to study philosophy at Rheims. There his learning won the favor of the archbishop, who made him master of the cathedral school. During the next ten years Gerbert's reputation increased steadily and students flocked to hear him. Even the emperor Otto II was interested in his work, and at one time arranged a debate between Gerbert and a German scholar who disagreed with him on some points of metaphysics. The debate was held in the presence of the emperor and his attendants, who listened all day to arguments which we would find rather dull. The problem was one of definition of philosophical terms, a sharpening of the tools of thought rather than the building of a new intellectual structure. Gerbert won the applause of the imperial court, and a little later Otto gave him the abbey of Bobbio. Unfortunately, he found the discipline of the monastery very lax, and much of the property dissipated. His attempts to restore order aroused opposition, and with the early death of Otto II, Gerbert lost his chief source of support. He soon found himself in such straits that he was forced to return to Rheims and resume his position as master of the schools. However, he retained his title of abbot of Bobbio and he remained a faithful supporter of the imperial family.

Gerbert now devoted much of his time to politics, and worked faithfully in the interests of the child Otto III. With his archbishop he helped to thwart French efforts to regain Lorraine during the troubled period of the minority. He also took part in the struggle between the last French Carolingians and their rivals and played an important part in securing the election of Hugh Capet as king. The grateful Hugh had him elected archbishop of Rheims. His position there, however, was not very secure, since his immediate predecessor had been deposed without the pope's sanction. Eventually his difficulties became so great that he withdrew to the court of Otto III, who rewarded his past loyalty by giving him the archbishopric of Ravenna, and then by making him pope in 999. He took the name of Sylvester II, and labored to strengthen both papacy and Empire. He and Otto had magnificent dreams of what might be done by a pope and an emperor working together, but death removed both in a very few years—Otto in 1002, and Gerbert in 1003. A curious fatality seized upon Gerbert's memory; his conduct as pope had been exemplary, but he became known in legend as a wizard, and even the more kindly disposed thought that he had been too devoted to secular learning. So the name of Sylvester has been shunned by later popes, with the single exception of the anti-pope Sylvester III, who took the name before the legend was established. As a matter of fact, Gerbert's learning was surpassed by many men of the next century, though it was marvelous for his own day. He mastered all that was then known and was especially interested in science, which had been so long neglected. He used globes and other instruments in studying astronomy and popularized the use of the abacus, which made it possible to solve simple arithmetical problems, even though the clumsy Roman numerals were retained. Gerbert was more important as a teacher than as a scholar, but even in this field he was not unique. Many other men, almost as famous in their own day, were doing much the same work, and the revival of learning was not confined to the schools of Rheims.

THE POLITICAL REVIVAL—FRANCE

In spite of the glamour and power of the tenth century German Empire, it had not solved the problem of political organization. As we have seen, it was based on archaic theories of government, which proved ill-adapted to the needs of the new civilization arising in Europe. We must turn to France to find constructive work in politics, and to see the origins of the type of government which was to prevail in western Europe.

There seemed to be little political stability or security in tenth century France. Until the very end of the century the country was torn by the feud between the Carolingian and Robertian families. The country was ruled by Robertian kings from 923 to the year 936, when the Carolingians were restored. Neither family, however, could rule unchallenged or secure permanent authority. The Carolingians held their place only through the grace of the greater feudal lords. They had no real power except when the nobles were willing to accept them as leaders in war, and they were always menaced by their Robertian rivals who had great influence in the North of France. The Robertians were not much better off. In theory they held most of the country between Seine and Loire, but actually they had had to surrender most of their lands to vassals in order to gain military support. In this situation both families sought German aid, and Otto I and Otto II were frequently asked to intervene in French affairs. They naturally sought to keep a balance between the rivals and thus leave France weak and divided; Gerbert played an important part in carrying out this policy. Royal authority declined steadily in the tenth century, although the last Carolingians were not weak men. On the whole they were energetic and persistent, but they adhered to the old traditions of their family instead of adapting themselves to new conditions. They tried to exert their authority over the whole kingdom, instead of concentrating it in one region; they tried to govern through the great feudal lords, instead of building up a body of officials who would be devoted to them. They cannot be blamed too harshly for adhering to the old system; it was still working in Germany, and the first Capetian kings did not immediately abandon it. But feudalism had developed so rapidly in France that the French kings could no longer secure the obedience of any large group of subjects. They had lost almost all their rights of justice, and all military power was in the hands of feudal lords. When they did raise an army it exhausted its strength in prolonged sieges of the innumerable castles which every powerful lord possessed. In short, at the end of the tenth century, feudalism had apparently won a definite triumph over the French monarchy.

France was saved from being permanently divided among warring feudal lords by the great Capetian kings of the twelfth and thirteenth centuries. But no one could have imagined in 987 that such a result would follow from the transfer of the crown to Hugh Capet. Hugh, as heir of the Robertian family, duke of "France," and ally of the greater lords, represented feudalism rather than monarchy. The circumstances of his election show that the nobles and leading churchmen were trying to limit royal power, not to establish a new and vigorous line of kings. When the Carolingian Louis V died without direct heirs, his only relative, the duke of Lorraine, was a subject of Otto III and on bad terms with many French lords. An assembly of nobles was held at Senlis to discuss the situation, and there the archbishop of Rheims made a speech insisting on the elective character of the French monarchy. The feudal lords welcomed the proposal, since it gave them a chance to demonstrate their power, and Hugh was chosen king with comparatively little opposition. There was nothing irrevocable about the decision, the Carolingians had been displaced before and might be recalled again, all to the profit of the nobility.

Hugh occupied the throne for only nine years and did little more than maintain himself against the Carolingian claimant. By the time he became king he had had to give up most of his lands to gain supporters, and his more important vassals were practically independent. He was no longer one of the greatest landholders of the kingdom; many of the men who had elected him had greater resources. Hugh's successors, Robert II and Henry I, did little to increase royal authority. Robert conquered Burgundy, but was promptly forced to surrender it by the jealousy of feudal lords. His prestige was further shaken by a long and losing quarrel with the papacy over his second marriage. According to canon law, he was too closely related to his wife for the marriage to be legitimate, and the fact that the pope succeeded in dissolving the union is another sign of the growing strength of the reform movement.

Henry I is a rather shadowy figure who seems to have had the least power of any of the early Capetians. These three kings were still bound by the Carolingian tradition; they paid slight attention to the few territories under their immediate control and instead tried to spread their little authority very thinly over the whole realm. Robert's useless conquest of Burgundy is an example of this attitude. However, these kings did preserve the theory that the king had rights over all of France. On the whole they had better relations with the Church than most of their vassals, and they established their dynasty firmly on the throne. This was due more to good fortune than good management; the Capetians became a habit with the people of France, because they lived long and always had male heirs. Between 987 and 1314 the average length of the reigns was 29 years, and every king was succeeded by a son. Thus there were so few chances for the nobles to discuss the question of the succession that the elective princple, so strongly championed in 987, was rapidly forgotten.

Henry's son Philip has the sorriest reputation of any of the early Capetians, but this is due mainly to his troubles with the Church. As a matter of fact, he was the first of his family to do anything which really strengthened the position of the monarchy. He does not seem to have been a very intelligent ruler, and at times he overestimated his power as badly as any of his predecessors, but he did try to increase and consolidate the royal domain. This region, a strip of land stretching from Paris to Orleans, was the remnant of the duchy of France which Hugh had once held, and it had been sadly neglected by Philip's predecessors. Petty lords, established in castles within a few miles of Paris, were as disobedient as the powerful rulers of Normandy or Aquitaine. Yet this strip of land in the heart of France had strategic possibilities which gave it a value far greater than its size would indicate. It separated the great fiefs of the North from each other and made it difficult to form effective combinations against the king. It lay on the main routes of communication and gave access to all parts of France. It is doubtful that Philip saw these advantages; in attempting to unify and pacify the domain he was merely imitating the work which had been done in other parts of France by the great feudal lords. He was less successful in this task than many of his vassals; until the very end of his reign he was defied by petty barons who would not have dared to stand out against a duke of Normandy or a count of Flanders. This is well illustrated by the value which he set on his acquisition of Montlhéry, a castle only a few miles from Paris which he captured shortly before his death. "Guard this tower carefully," he said to his heir, "it has made me old before my time; the wickedness and perfidy of those who held it have never left me a moment of rest." Although he lacked brilliant successes, Philip did increase the size of the domain and strengthened his authority within it. By strengthening his control of a definite, if restricted, region he made the monarchy more capable of holding its own with the great barons. This policy was continued by his successors, and Philip's reign therefore marks a turning-point in the history of the Capetian dynasty.

However, France during the eleventh century was actually governed by its feudal lords and not by its kings. There was a great difference in the power and policies of these rulers; some were even more helpless than the king, others were much more powerful, and were building up governments which were far superior to that of their overlord. The duchies of Aquitaine, Brittany, and Burgundy were rather weak. Aquitaine, in spite of the energy of its rulers, was too large for one man to handle, under the conditions of the time. The vassals of the duke of Aquitaine were warlike and rebellious; those in the mountainous interior were practically independent. The duke of Burgundy likewise had little authority over his vassals. Many of them took advantage of their position on the main route to Rome to become highway robbers; some of the dukes themselves were so poor that they imitated these robber barons. Brittany, isolated from the rest of the kingdom by language and geography, was a sad, desolate, rude land—a country which retained its Celtic piety and love of marvelous legends along with its Celtic fondness for savage civil wars. The greatest ambition of a duke of Brittany was to keep the title in his family, and frequent rebellions made it difficult to satisfy even this modest desire.

There were other rulers who had succeeded in establishing their personal authority without creating elaborate administrative systems. The count of Anjou had built up a compact little state in the rich valley of the Loire. He was able to rule this small district personally, and he had far greater military power than his neighbor, the duke of Brittany. The counties of Blois and Champagne, to the west and the east of the royal domain, were held by the same family and were fairly obedient to their lords. Both were constantly at war with their neighbors, but Champagne eventually survived these early troubles and became one of the stronger feudal states. Blois was so weakened by the excessive ambition of its early counts, one of whom claimed both the kingdom of Italy and the kingdom of Burgundy, that, after a brilliant beginning, it sank back to the level of a second-rate feudal principality. In the far south the count of Toulouse succeeded in dominating many of the lords in his immediate neighborhood, while profiting from the new wealth created by the revival of Mediterranean trade. But in spite of its prosperity, Toulouse had little influence on the rest of the country. There were few ties to bind it to the region north of the Loire, and in language, culture, and customs, it was far closer to Italy and Spain than to Normandy or the Ile de France.

Finally, in a few feudal states the rulers had developed institutions and customs which gave them something more than purely personal authority. Flanders and Normandy were outstanding examples of this type. In each, the ruler was able to delegate power without losing all that he delegated. The viscounts of the duke of Normandy, the castellans of the count of Flanders, served their lords as judicial and financial agents without ever becoming entirely independent. In each state the ruler retained important rights of justice which enabled him to hold courts and to try people in all parts of the country. The duke of Normandy, for example, reserved for himself most cases which might lead to the imposition of capital punishment. In each state the ruler had a large income, drawn from all parts of the duchy (or county), based on tolls and market-rights as well as land. Moreover, this income was usually paid in cash, not in kind, and this made the government much more flexible. Both the duke of Normandy and the count of Flanders tried, with some success, to repress violence and disorder. The duke of Normandy was not able to forbid private wars, but he did forbid attacks on non-combatants and pillaging of property, perhaps under the influence of the Peace of God. He had the best army in western Europe, due to the early establishment of definite rules for military service. Elsewhere the amount of service rendered by a vassal depended on his personal sentiments to his lord. If he were very loyal, or very much afraid, he might bring all his men to aid his superior. Usually he gave just as little help as he thought safe. But in Normandy, by the end of the eleventh century, definite amounts of service were fixed for all the great fiefs, amounts which were roughly proportionate to the resources of the vassal. Thus the very powerful and wealthy bishop of Bayeux owed the service of 120 knights, while the comparatively poor bishop of Avranches owed only 5. The fact that military service was required from ecclesiastical landholders as well as laymen was another source of the duke's strength. Even if most of his lay vassals turned against him, he could still raise a large army from his bishops and abbots. He was almost always sure of their support, for alone among the great feudal rulers of France, he had absolute control of the Church in his domains. Neither his superior, the king of France, nor his inferiors, the Norman nobles, could influence the choice of bishops or abbots of the greater monasteries. Altogether, the duke of Normandy could utilize the resources of his state more efficiently than any other ruler in France, and for many years he was the most powerful man in the kingdom.

By the end of the eleventh century a large part of France was under fairly stable governments and was enjoying relative freedom from violence and disorder. Most of the North—Anjou, Blois, Champagne, Normandy, Flanders and even the Ile de France—had passed through the worst period of feudal disorder. The South was more turbulent, but even in the South there were lords who were able to give their subjects a certain degree of security. Feudal wars were still common, but they no longer absorbed all the surplus energy and productivity of the country. Strong rulers were able to discourage private wars in their own lands, and when two great lords fought, the damage was often confined to the frontier districts of each state. It is hard to realize that there was much improvement when we read the chronicles of the eleventh century, with their constant descriptions of wars and devastation, yet two facts show that conditions were better. In the first place, during the latter part of the eleventh century there are unmistakable signs that the peasant population, which had long been stationary, if not actually declining, was increasing. The villages could no longer hold all their people; some men went out to clear new land while others became peddlers or artisans. In the second place, the class of fighting men gradually turned into a landed aristocracy. Most of the armed retainers of the great lords had received fiefs by 1100, and once they held land fighting was no longer their chief business, even though it remained a favorite pastime. Those who still loved fighting, those who had received less than they desired, those who had had to share small inheritances with their brothers, found that eleventh century France no longer offered unlimited opportunities to a man with a good sword-arm. They began to seek adventures or fortunes abroad, since they were no longer to be had at home, and the departure of the more pugnacious and greedy warriors aided the pacification of France. Curiously enough, the men who emigrated were unconsciously infected with the ideas which caused them to leave home: once they had established themselves in a foreign land they attempted to create stable feudal states like those of France. Thus the French type of feudalism spread all over Europe and even into the Near East. Its extension was made easy by the fact that, with all its faults, it was still the best type of government which existed in western Europe in the eleventh century. Europe was still too poor to support a professional bureaucracy and too disunited to obey kings or emperors. The feudal state provided the rudiments of government cheaply and was small enough to have a certain degree of cohesion.

The results of the emigration of French feudal lords and knights may be traced everywhere in Europe. They settled in Germany, Italy, and Anglo-Saxon England. They went in even greater numbers to Spain, to aid in the work of driving out the Saracens. Here they founded influential families; the first Christian rulers of Portugal were descendants of the duke of Burgundy. The two most striking examples of French feudal expansion were the conquest of southern Italy and the conquest of England. In both these countries French adventurers became the ruling class, and French feudalism was used as the basis for remarkably strong governments.

THE POLITICAL REVIVAL—SICILY

At the beginning of the eleventh century the political situation in southern Italy was so confused that it is almost impossible to describe it in a few sentences. The country was covered with the wreckage of old governments, and no one seemed to be able to clear away the debris. The Byzantine Empire nominally held the mainland almost as far north as Rome, but its actual power was confined to the heel and toe of the peninsula. Yet the Greek claim to authority, backed by Greek money and diplomacy, was enough to prevent the petty rulers of the South from building strong states of their own. The interior and the west coast were held by Lombard princes who spent most of their time trying to steal each other's territories. Naples and Amalfi were city-states, prospering from their trade with the East, but in constant danger from their more powerful neighbors. Sicily was held by the Saracens, but these former lords of the Mediterranean were frittering away their strength in a constant series of civil wars. No ruler, Christian or Moslem, in southern Italy could count on the loyalty of his subjects, his army, or even his own family. No ruler was strong enough to protect his own territories, much less to subjugate his more annoying neighbors.

This was the situation when, about 1016, a group of Norman knights who were performing a pilgrimage landed near Salerno. Their military ability was soon recognized, and one of the local rulers tried to hire them as soldiers. They refused the offer but promised to tell their friends of the opportunity. Soon a stream of poor knights, landless younger sons, outlaws, and enemies of the duke of Normandy began to trickle down into lower Italy. The Normans fought well, they changed sides at the right moment, and eventually one of them gained the county of Aversa as a reward for his services. Aversa became a sort of employment agency for Normans seeking service as mercenaries; a lord in need of fresh troops could always pick up some good material there.

Among the Normans who came to Aversa were the two eldest sons of Tancred de Hauteville, a poor vassal of the Cotentin, who was burdened with twelve sons and an unascertained number of daughters. These two men, William Iron-Arm and Drogo, soon became leaders of the Normans. After serving the Greeks against the Saracens, and the Lombards against the Greeks, they decided that they might as well try fighting for their own account. They gained the support of most of the other Normans, by promising them a share of the spoils, and began a persistent attack on Byzantine possessions. They were frequently defeated, they had to face revolts of their own men, but unlike any other leaders in southern Italy they never gave in. They always had an army in the field and kept up steady pressure on the Greeks. Byzantine governors, distracted by palace revolutions in Constantinople and Turkish attacks in Asia Minor, lost ground steadily. William and Drogo were at first little more than bandit chiefs, but before their deaths at the middle of the century they had begun to create something like a state in Apulia.

Meanwhile, their younger brothers had drifted down into Italy. William and Drogo were not entirely pleased to see them, and they were especially harsh to the children of their father's second wife. But it was hard to discourage an Hauteville, and two of the younger sons became bandit chiefs in their turn. Robert Guiscard established himself in Calabria, while the baby of the family, Roger, began the long, heartbreaking task of driving the Saracens out of Sicily. When William and Drogo died, Robert Guiscard was soon able to take their place as leader of the Normans, in spite of the opposition of some of his relatives. He kept up the pressure on the Greeks until the last Byzantine stronghold fell in 1071. This would have been enough to satisfy any ordinary conqueror, but Guiscard had the terrible energy and insatiable desires of his Viking ancestors. He may also have feared the marvelous recuperative power of the Eastern Empire and its tenacity in maintaining claims to its old provinces. Whatever the reason, he had no sooner driven the Greeks from Italy than he attempted the conquest of the Byzantine Empire. He never quite succeeded, owing largely to his lack of a good navy, but he gave the Greeks a terrible fright and held portions of Albania for several years. Meanwhile, Roger was conquering Sicily, mountain by mountain. The Saracens were too disunited to drive him out, but they resisted bravely in their individual strongholds and the last Saracen fort fell only in 1091. It was the same sort of war which William Iron-Arm and Robert Guiscard had had to wage on the mainland, a war in which persistence and the maintenance of a permanent army counted for more than military genius. Roger received aid from Guiscard at crucial moments, but during most of the struggle he had to rely on his own very limited forces. In many ways this Norman conquest of Sicily was a greater feat than the more famous conquest of England; the resistance was stiffer and the invading army was smaller.

Guiscard's descendants made a bad job of ruling the mainland, but the great count Roger left an heir, Roger II, capable of taking his place in Sicily. When Guiscard's grandson died without heirs in 1127, Roger II was able to occupy his lands and the Norman states were united. Count of Sicily, duke of Apulia—Roger coveted an even higher title. A contested papal election soon gave him the opportunity he needed. One candidate recognized him as king in 1130; the other was forced to do so after Roger defeated and captured him in 1139. The grandson of the poor knight of the Cotentin was now one of the most powerful rulers in Christendom.

One might have expected that a state founded by bandits and mercenaries would remain weak and disorderly. But the Hauteville brothers were determined that this should not happen. They had massacred and plundered, assassinated and betrayed, fought with and conquered all their neighbors on their road to greatness, and they could not risk allowing others to enter on the same path of fruitful lawlessness. They resolved to make their vassals obedient and useful servants; they resolved to put down private war. This was especially difficult on the mainland, where William, Drogo, and even Robert Guiscard had been little more than presidents of a joint-stock company formed for the conquest of Byzantine lands. It was not at all certain that the other Normans owed feudal service for the lands which they had seized, or that the position of leader of the Normans was hereditary. Hence there were repeated revolts when Guiscard and Roger II tried to extend their authority. In Sicily the situation was clearer. It had been conquered by mercenaries in the pay of Roger; no one could hold anything except as a gift of the count and on the terms which the count decided. It was his power in Sicily which enabled Roger II to gain effective control of the mainland. In the end, royal authority reached a higher point in the kingdom of Sicily than anywhere else in Europe. All the old rules which had made the duke of Normandy so powerful were adopted and extended in Sicily. There were the same definite quotas of military service which assured the ruler a large army. There were the same rules limiting, and in the end prohibiting, private war. Moreover, the Norman kings of Sicily had inherited the remnants of a bureaucracy from their Byzantine and Saracen predecessors, and they soon restored, and used successfully, many of the forms of the older government. The government of twelfth-century Sicily was one of the wonders of the medieval world, with its Arabian emirs, Greek logothetes, and Norman barons working in harmony under a powerful king. Sicily was the melting-pot of Europe, and the Normans were the flux which enabled the other ingredients to fuse.

THE POLITICAL REVIVAL—ENGLAND

In England there was a different story. Here the conquerors were much more disciplined, and the conquered country less disorganized. It took a century to create a strong kingdom in southern Italy; in England the essential work was done in a decade. Since there were no relics of the ancient imperial system left in England, feudalism played the greatest part in the creation of strong monarchy there. In fact, English government in the period immediately after the Conquest is the great example of how effective feudal institutions could be under able leaders.

As we have seen, England suffered more than the continent from the Germanic invasions. All traces of Roman civilization were wiped out and the island was divided into a score of petty kingdoms, Celtic and German. The weaker German kingdoms were gradually eliminated; the native Celts retained their independence only in Wales, but no one ruler succeeded in uniting all of England. The acceptance of Catholic Christianity which produced such striking results in France had few political effects in England; no king was able to use the orthodox faith as an excuse for conquest. Northumbria, Mercia, and Wessex, which were able to expand at the expense of the Celts, were larger and stronger than the petty coastal kingdoms of East Anglia, Essex, Kent, and Sussex, which were often vassal states of their more powerful neighbors. Yet even the larger states were small by continental standards; no one of them was too large to be ruled effectively by an able king. Thus there was no need in England for the development of powerful local officials such as the Frankish counts. Moreover, since the Roman *villa* system had been almost completely wiped out [2] there were fewer great landowners and they had less influence on the government than they did in France. As a result, England before the ninth century was much more like the primitive Germanic kingdoms than were France or Italy. There were still free villages and many small and middling free landowners. Courts were still aseemblies of people; the nobles had not destroyed the power of the king or the political importance of lesser landholders. This is not to say that there had been no changes in Anglo-Saxon institutions since the sixth century. Stimulated by the Church, the kings were taking more responsibility for the administration of justice. They issued laws clarifying doubtful points of custom; they tried to see that the local courts did their work fairly. At the same time, the institution of lordship was growing. Individuals and even whole villages sought the protection of powerful men and gave them in return services or payments in kind. Yet, in spite of this differentiation, the "folk," the community of the land, was still an important factor in England at a time when it had been forgotten in the empire of the Franks.

[2] Some scholars think that memories of the *villa* system, surviving in the subject Celtic population, may have influenced the development of Anglo-Saxon institutions. Any such survivals were not enough to make England a land of great estates in the seventh and eighth centuries.

150 MILES

SHETLAND
ISLANDS

ORKNEY
IS.

N O R T H

S E A

P I C T S

DALRIADA

FIRTH OF FORTH

FIRTH
OF CLYDE

STRATH CLYDE

SOLWAY FIRTH

NORTHUMBRIA

ISLE
OF MAN

IRISH
SEA

I R E L A N D

Jarrow
Durham

Whitby

York

HUMBER R.

THE WASH

Lincoln

Chester

Nottingham

Derby

Ely

EAST
ANGLIA

WALES

OFFA'S DYKE

M E R C I A

Bedford

Oxford

ESSEX

London

ISLE OF
THANET

THAMES R.

Canterbury

KENT

Dover

Winchester

SUSSEX

W E S S E X

Exeter

Dorchester

Hastings

A T L A N T I C

O C E A N

E N G L I S H   C H A N N E L

FRANCE

ANGLO-SAXON ENGLAND

TRM

The shock of the Danish invasions caused great changes in the pattern of English life. As we have seen, only one Anglo-Saxon state, the kingdom of Wessex, survived the Viking attack. Alfred of Wessex checked the Danes; his son and grandson reconquered all England from the invaders. Now there was a kingdom of England, a kingdom which had been made by the ruling family, and which needed institutions of a type which had not been essential before. The tenth century rulers of the House of Wessex had to create administrative subdivisions, for their kingdom was now too large to be ruled directly by the king and his immediate household. They had to perfect a military system to guard against Danish rebellions, for thousands of Danes still remained in the northeastern quarter of the island. They had to improve the administration of justice, not only because this would strengthen their authority, but also because the Church was urging them to enforce the ideals of Christianity. The most influential person in tenth century England, outside of the royal family, was St. Dunstan, archbishop of Canterbury, and St. Dunstan was working steadily for a reform in church and state. Like his contemporary, Gerbert, Dunstan felt that his goal could be achieved only by the intimate coöperation of lay and ecclesiastical powers. Great councils of nobles and bishops, guided by the king and Dunstan, made laws for the reform of the church and the strengthening of the state. Nowhere else in tenth century Europe was the union of the two powers quite so perfect, and this may be one reason for the success of the new institutions of the English kings.

The most important and enduring reforms were in local government. The old Anglo-Saxon kingdoms had been divided into districts of varying sizes and names, so that each neighborhood could have its own assembly and court. Now a uniform pattern was imposed on the whole country. England was divided into shires (later called counties) and the shires in turn were divided into hundreds, or, in the Danish region, wapentakes. Both shire and hundred had a court, composed of the free men of the district and presided over by royal officials. Theoretically the bishops and the aldermen (great nobles who were often members of the royal family) were responsible for the administration of the shires. But bishops and aldermen had many shires to care for and many other duties, so that in practice the king's reeve gradually took over most of the work of local government. The king's reeves had at first been rather humble officials who collected revenues from royal estates, but their power grew during the tenth century, and the shire-reeve, or sheriff, eventually became a very important official. He collected most of the king's revenues; he supervised the work of the local courts; he was responsible for arresting malefactors and he led the local troops in war. Yet with all his power he was unable to turn his office into a private possession, as the counts had in France. His authority was relatively recent compared to that of the aldermen and he was not their equal in social position. The sheriff was strong only through the king, and he had to remain loyal to the king to retain his position.

This system of local government was the greatest achievement of the Anglo-Saxon kings. It kept the nobles from annexing all powers of local government, and it gave the king a chance to exert his influence throughout the realm. In both respects it was far superior to anything on the continent, as William the Conqueror recognized when he took great pains to preserve the institutions of the county court and the sheriff. The Anglo-Saxon system of local government not only survived the Norman Conquest; it has endured to this day in the United States and England.

Closely connected with the new system of local government were reforms in the administration of justice. The tenth century kings began to feel that they were responsible for repressing violence, that they should aid injured parties to secure redress. This was a complete change from the old attitude that all offenses were private matters and that courts were mere tribunals of arbitration. Now the king held that certain serious crimes offended him as well as the victim, and he ordered special fines to be paid to him in such cases. He ordered the reeves and sheriffs to force men to come to court to answer complaints and he insisted that the sentences of the courts be enforced. The people of each district were organized in small units for the pursuit of malefactors, and men of bad reputation had to find securities for good behavior. As the government took over the task of pursuing and punishing the criminal, the blood-feud became very rare. This new concept of royal responsibility for justice did not, of course, end crime in England. It was still very difficult, given the state of communications, to arrest a criminal who was not caught in the act. It was still difficult, owing to the use of compurgation, to convict a hardened liar. Yet these new rules about criminal law are important because they greatly increased royal power. Justice was no longer the concern of the family and the community alone; it was becoming the concern of the king and his officials. Custom was no longer the only source of law; the king and his councillors could make laws in order to repress violence and theft. Control of the courts and control of the laws are the necessary foundations for any powerful, well-organized government. The Anglo-Saxon kings did not create such a government, but they established some very useful precedents for their more absolute Norman successors.

The tenth century kings of England probably did more constructive work in government than any of their European contemporaries, but there were two great weaknesses in their system. The first was military. In theory all freemen still owed military service, but this militia was not very effective. The ordinary freeman was now a peasant farmer, not a warrior; his weapons were poor, and he was not trained to use them.

The best troops were the household retainers of the king and the nobles, but there were not very many of these, and they were still used for many duties which were not primarily military. England had passed beyond the stage of the tribal army, and had not yet attained the military spe· cialization of feudalism. In this respect she was weaker than most of her neighbors.

The other weakness was in institutions of central government. The new system of local government, the new laws repressing crime, would work well only if local officials and courts were constantly supervised and inspected. But the central administration was not fully enough developed to undertake these tasks. The king's household was small and there was little specialization among its members; any man could perform any function. The secretarial service was rudimentary and few written records were kept. The best work was done in recording and checking income that was due to the king. On the other hand, there were no regular appeals from local courts to the king's court. As a result there was no routine supervision of local government; only crying cases of injustice came to the king's attention. Even more dangerous to royal authority was the fact that there was no means of controlling the great lords, who were becoming too powerful to be checked by local officials. As in France, lordship had grown as the kingdom expanded, and by 1000 most men in England were subjects of lords as well as subjects of the king. The king had encouraged this development, for it was easier to suppress crime if every man had a lord and the lord were made responsible for producing his men in court. The lords also furnished the best men for the army and were useful to the king in other ways. But they were guilty of many acts of injustice, and they often tried to increase their own power at the expense of the common welfare. Only a powerful king's court, meeting regularly and at frequent intervals, could have forced these men to obey all royal commands. Such a court did not exist. There was an assembly of the *witan*, or "wise men," which met at irregular intervals to discuss problems which the king laid before it, but this assembly could not exercise the constant supervision over local affairs which was necessary. The "wise men" were the bishops, the members of the royal family, and the great lay lords—men who were too important to be bothered with the details of administration. They could advise the king in matters of state, approve laws which he suggested, or act as judges in important cases, but they were useless for routine work. Yet it was only through the drudgery of routine work, through constant commands and reprimands, that local officials and potentates could be kept in order. The *witan* were of little assistance to a strong king and, while they might check a weak king, they could not hold the country together if he failed to do so.

These weaknesses of the newly formed kingdom of England became apparent in the eleventh century. A weak king, Ethelred the Ill-Counseled, found himself unable to check the growing power of the nobles or to put an end to their disputes. At this moment the Northmen renewed their raids. Ethelred could not make his subjects work together to repulse them, so he adopted the hopeless practice of buying them off. In order to obtain money for this blackmail he imposed a tax, the Danegeld, on the whole country. This was the first general tax in English history and formed a useful precedent for later kings, but it only encouraged the Danes. At first they had merely sought plunder, but in 1013, when they found how weak England was, they began the conquest of the country. Ethelred was unable to hold them off and fled to Normandy. His son, Edmund Ironsides, resisted bravely, but when he died in 1016 the Danish king Canute was recognized as ruler of all England.

Canute was able to restore the strong kingship of the tenth century and gave England a welcome interval of good government. He followed Anglo-Saxon precedents and appointed many Englishmen to office. Though he ruled Denmark, Norway, and other lands, he spent most of his time in England, and did not let the cares of his empire interfere with his attention to English affairs. He was able to leave the kingdom to his sons, but they had little of their father's ability, and after their death the country rejected the Danish dynasty. Edward, the younger son of Ethelred, was recalled from his exile in Normandy, and the line of Alfred the Great was restored.

Edward, later called the Confessor, was not a strong ruler, but, like many weak men, he was obstinate, and this trait involved him in many difficulties. He had grown up in Normandy (his mother was a sister of the Norman duke), and he preferred Norman ways. He brought many Normans to England and gave them important offices. This weakened the loyalty of his English subjects and strengthened the native nobles who were already anxious to diminish royal power. Edward's troubles, however, were not due entirely to his own defects. England in the eleventh century was in the same position as France in the tenth. The country was too large to be ruled directly by the king, and there were no adequate central institutions to aid him in the task. The power of the lords was increasing steadily and local officials could not check it. More and more men were becoming subjects of lords rather than the king. The earls, who had been set over groups of shires by the Danes, as the aldermen had been before them, were acting as independent rulers. Something very like feudalism was growing in England, though most English historians refuse to call it by this name. It is true that the fief had not yet appeared; most land was held in absolute proprietorship. But it should not be forgotten that the fief appeared comparatively late in the history of French and German feudalism. All the other signs of the first stages of feudalism were apparent in eleventh century England. The lords had private armies of household retainers which they did not hesitate to use against each other or the king. The earls were beginning to claim that their offices were hereditary and were seeking to increase their power in every possible way. Most lords had set up private courts for their men, and many had been given hundred courts by the king. Private armies, private courts, and hereditary offices, rather than the fief, were the basic elements of feudalism, and they were weakening Edward as they had weakened the last Carolingian rulers of France.

The parallel can be pushed even further, for in eleventh century England, as in tenth century France, there was a rival family which was rapidly becoming more powerful than the legitimate dynasty. This was the house of Godwin, which had risen to prominence under Canute. Earl Godwin was the chief English leader at Edward's accession, and he strengthened his power by marrying his daughter Edith to the king. For several years he and his sons dominated the country, much to the disgust of the other English magnates, not to mention the king's foreign favorites. In 1051, when Godwin refused to obey an unjust order given by Edward, his enemies united against him and forced him to go into exile. This victory profited only the Normans, who were now supreme at the English court. It was at this time that Duke William of Normandy paid Edward a visit and was probably promised the succession to the throne of the childless king. William was Edward's first cousin, but had no hereditary claim on England, since the relationship was through Edward's Norman mother. This promise may have become known among the English; in any case they were so annoyed by the king's Norman leanings that they made little resistance when Godwin and his sons attacked England in the following year. Godwin was reinstated in his possessions and gradually added to his power until a majority of the earldoms were held by members of his family. After his death, his son Harold took his place. Edward, on his death-bed, recognized Harold as successor to the throne, and on the following day he was accepted as king by the *witan*.

Theoretically, Harold, as head of the most powerful family in England, should have been stronger than the friendless Edward. But Harold, like Hugh Capet, found that his accession to the throne weakened, rather than strengthened his political position. His own earldom of Wessex was loyal, but everywhere else in England there was jealousy of the new ruler who was not a descendant of the old royal family. The great lords, and especially the northern earls, held aloof and were more than ever determined to preserve their independence.

Harold, like Hugh, might have preserved his royal title at the price of allowing England to break up into semi-independent provinces. But he never had a chance to establish his dynasty, for unlike Hugh, he was challenged at once by an able opponent who had overwhelming military power on his side. William of Normandy in 1066 was already one of the most powerful rulers in Europe. He had been duke of Normandy since his father's death in 1035, and had kept control of the duchy in spite of violent opposition. His mother was a tanner's daughter and he was known as "William the Bastard" until he won a more glorious title. Since he inherited the duchy while a mere child, and since his father's relatives were annoyed by the preference given to an illegitimate son, it is not surprising that his early years were disturbed by unruly vassals and frequent rebellions. However, in 1047 he won a brilliant victory over the rebels, with the effective if short-sighted assistance of the French king. Thereafter he kept peace and order in his duchy, dominating it even more thoroughly than had his predecessors. He not only perfected the peculiar system of Norman feudalism which gave the duke such great power, but also had the intelligence to align himself with the new forces in the Church. He did much to reform the Norman Church and selected able men for its higher offices, such as Lanfranc of Pavia, who made the monastery of Bec a noted center of learning. With full control of his own territories, William was able to defeat his suzerain, the French king, and his neighbor, the count of Anjou, and to add the county of Maine to his lands. Obviously, William in 1066 was no rash adventurer. He was a middle-aged man with thirty years of experience as a ruler, which had made him a remarkable diplomat, a shrewd politician, and an able general.

William had counted on succeeding Edward, and Harold's accession made him furiously angry. But he knew that rage and the resources of Normandy were not enough to win England; he had to make a case which would appeal to men throughout Europe. He argued that Edward had promised him the throne and that Harold had agreed to aid him to become king. The last statement may well have been true, since Harold had once been shipwrecked on the coast of Normandy and had had to make some kind of promise to get out of William's hands. At all events, William accused Harold of perjury, a charge whch gave him an excuse to ask the pope's aid. The latter was quite ready to aid the duke, because Godwin and Harold had opposed the reform party and had grievously violated the rights of the Church. In the campaign against Edward's favorites they had expelled the Norman archbishop of Canterbury and had installed Stigand, an Englishman, who made matters worse by receiving the pallium from an anti-pope. William's support of the reformers in Normandy was a sharp contrast to these proceedings and the pope gave him his whole-hearted support. By sending a consecrated banner, he gave William's expedition an air of legality and piety which attracted many men to the duke's ranks. To quote the Norman poet Wace:

> The duke rejoiced greatly at receiving the banner and the license which the pope gave him. He got together carpenters, smiths, and other workmen,

so that great stir was seen at all the ports of Normandy. . . . They spent all one summer and autumn in fitting up the fleet.

As William's vassals were not obliged to follow him overseas he had to offer great inducements to secure men:

There was no knight in the land, no good sergeant, archer, nor peasant of stout heart and of age for battle, that the duke did not summon to go with him to England, promising rents to the vassals and honors to the barons. . . . The fame of the Norman duke soon went forth through many lands— how he meant to cross the sea against Harold, who had taken England from him. Then soldiers came flocking to him . . . and he retained them all, giving them much and promising more. Many came by agreement made by them beforehand; many bargained for lands, if they should win England; some required pay, allowances and gifts; and the duke was often obliged to give at once to those who could not wait the result.

Thus an army of about six thousand men was slowly assembled, dominated by the Normans, but including large numbers of men from other French provinces. Hundreds of ships were gathered, but they could not embark until they had a favorable wind, which was slow in rising.

Harold, of course, knew of William's preparations and gathered such forces as he could from the part of England which was loyal to him. But as time dragged on he could not hold his army together. His own private bodyguard (the house-carls) was sure, the lesser nobles (the *thegns*) were not so dependable, and the *fyrd*, or militia of farmers, were anxious to get back to their neglected fields. As the attack was delayed, many of the *fyrd* began to go home to harvest their crops. Just then came the news that Harold Hardrada, king of Norway, had landed in Northumbria, claiming the crown of England as Canute's heir. When he defeated the northern earls and took York, Harold could no longer stay on guard in the South and had to hasten to the rescue with his house-carls and *thegns*. By forced marches he succeeded in surprising the enemy at Stamford Bridge, where he won an overwhelming victory. Harold Hardrada was killed in the battle, and the danger of a new conquest by the Northmen was ended forever. But while Harold was in the North the wind had shifted. William's fleet was able to cross the Channel and land at Pevensey.

Once more Harold rushed across England, but with insufficient forces. The northern earls furnished no aid and apparently felt no gratitude for their rescue. Harold had to depend almost entirely upon his personal following of house-carls and *thegns*, together with hasty levies from Wessex. He felt it necessary to act on the defensive and established himself upon the hill of Senlac, a few miles north of Hastings. There, on 14 October 1066, was fought the decisive battle. At first the Normans, though they were better armed and well supplied with cavalry and archers, were unable to break through the English shield-wall. The house-carls, with their great, two-handed Danish axes, stood firm about Harold and the dragon standard. But William was a skilful tactician and had a well-disciplined army. A flight, perhaps intentional, of part of the Norman army, led the English to break their ranks to pursue the enemy. Then the Norman cavalry cut off the pursuers and mopped up the light-armed shire levies. The picked troops about Harold were now surrounded, but they fought on steadily till evening. Then, when Harold and his brothers had fallen, resistance ceased.

The battle was won and Harold was dead, but the land was not conquered. London and the Southeast submitted quickly, since there were no available troops for their defense, and William was crowned in the city on Christmas Day, 1066. But elsewhere, especially in the North, there were repeated rebellions, and William's authority was not recognized over all England until 1072. The rebellions failed because they were all local risings, led by individual nobles who were often fighting for their own advantage. There was no national leader to rally all the discontented. In addition, William punished rebellious regions so severely that others were afraid to rise against him. Thus he devastated the Vale of York so completely that much of it was still desert twenty years later. As the chronicler says, "There was no one left to bury the dead, for all were wiped out with sword or famine, or had departed from their homes on account of hunger. The land was destitute of cultivation. . . . Between York and Durham nowhere was there an inhabited village, while the dens of wild beasts and robbers caused terror to travelers."

William had to guard not only against the English, but also against his own followers. His army was very mixed; many men had never been subject to him before, and even his Normans were fighting as volunteers, rather than as vassals. These men, who had conquered England, were anxious to increase their own power rather than William's, and some of them did not hesitate to join with the English in their rebellions. His real greatness was shown, not in his more or less accidental victory at Hastings, but in his ability to make a strong kingdom out of a hostile population and an unruly army.

William profited from having two sources of authority. He insisted that he was lawful king of England, as Edward's heir and as the choice of the *witan*. Thus he retained all the powers of an Anglo-Saxon king, which were still important, even though they had declined in the last reign. He preserved all the machinery of local government, particularly the office of sheriff, which he found very useful in checking his warriors. He retained all the rights of justice held by his predecessors, which were very like the rights which he possessed in Normandy as duke. But William was not only king of the English, he was also lord of the Normans. He introduced the Norman system of feudalism, with all the powers which it gave the overlord, and enforced it even more rigidly than he had in his old territories. The fixed amount of military service, the rules against private war, the insistence on obedience to the overlord were all in existence in England within a few years of the Conquest. Thus William stopped the gradual usurpation of local authority by creating definite feudal relationships between himself and all the powerful men of the realm. The local lord had only the powers which William allowed and he had to render important services in return for the grant. England passed at one jump from the anarchic early stage of feudalism to the orderly, smooth-running conditions which existed only in a few places in northern France. The combination of widely recognized royal authority with an advanced type of feudalism existed nowhere else, save perhaps in Sicily. England, which had always lagged behind the continent politically, now shot ahead, and was to retain her lead in the arts of government for centuries to come.

The Conquest was, of course, a great shock to the English, especially to the upper classes. Since William claimed to be lawful heir of Edward, all those who had supported Harold and all those who resisted the Conqueror after Harold's death were treated as rebels, and forfeited their lands. Practically all the land in England thus entered the king's hands, and he gave it away only as fiefs, never as private property. Thus private ownership of land ceased to exist in England, and the most complete system of feudal tenures in Europe took its place. Because the tenures were definite creations of the king, he was able to specify the terms on which they were held and to demand real service for them. Because the Conquest was piecemeal, the grants to important vassals were widely scattered; each man was given a share of each section of the country as it was conquered. This prevented, for the most part, the creation of compact, territorial fiefs which might have become dangerous, though William did not hesitate to create such fiefs on the Welsh and Scotch frontiers. The greater English land-owners were completely and rapidly dispossessed. Some of the lesser land-owners who entered the service of Normans as knights were able to keep their estates, but even this class gradually lost most of its possessions. Norman lords, between 1066 and 1100, found it advisable to settle their household troops on the land, usually at the expense of the English. As for the peasants, they continued cultivating the land for their new lords as they had for their old, but even they suffered in the long run by the introduction of precise Norman ideas of lordship and serfdom. Many men who would have been reckoned as free, though dependent on a lord, in the time of Edward the Confessor, were mere serfs by the thirteenth century. The towns suffered severely from William's military operations, but in the end they profited from increased trade with the continent. Many Norman and Flemish merchants settled in the boroughs, and the towns became steadily more important.

The changes in the Church were many and far-reaching. There was urgent need of reform, for the work of Dunstan had not endured, and many of the clergy could not be distinguished from laymen in education or morals. As we have seen, William favored reform when it did not interfere with his own prerogatives. He owed much to the pope, and he welcomed an excuse to strengthen his hold upon England by driving out the native prelates and substituting men who owed their position to him. Lanfranc, who was made archbishop of Canterbury in place of the "intruder" Stigand, was the chief agent in ecclesiastical matters and supported William's policy cordially. English bishops and abbots were gradually replaced by Frenchmen, and the powers of these new prelates were increased. Separate ecclesiastical courts were established, and cases "concerning the rule of souls," which had before been tried in the ordinary hundred courts, were now reserved to the Church alone. The residences of the bishops were moved from the villages in which they had been located and were fixed in important towns. The rule against clerical marriage, which had been a dead letter, was ordered to be enforced in the future. But while William was ready to reform the Church, he absolutely refused to give up his control over it. He would not do fealty to the pope for England, though the latter claimed it in return for his aid. William would not surrender his right to name bishops and abbots, and he even insisted that no papal letter could be published in England without his consent. The pope was too involved in other matters to protest at the time, and William used the Church for his purposes as completely as any German emperor had ever done.

Perhaps the most important political innovation made by William was the strengthening of the central government. The "great council" which he summoned to hear his will or to give advice, resembled in many ways the assembly of the *witan* which had existed under the Anglo-Saxon kings. It included the bishops, the more important abbots and the chief land-holders, and usually met at Christmas, Easter, and Whitsuntide. It was, however, more than an assembly of notables; it was the feudal court of the lord of England. As such, it could judge vassals who disobeyed the king, and it was usually responsive to William's wishes in such matters. Thus it was a useful means of keeping control over the great men. Even more important was the small council, which was always with the king and which aided him in all his administrative duties. This small council, composed of ecclesiastics, household officials, and vassals who had special aptitude for government, had all the powers of the large council. In fact, there was no very clear distinction between it and the large council; both were called *curia regis*—the king's court; both were competent to advise the king on any subject. The great lords of England would not have enjoyed spending most of their time at court helping William run the country; they were quite willing to let a few of their number perform their functions on all ordinary occasions. The king might have found it inadvisable to use the small council to judge a baron, but he could safely use it for all his routine work. Thus he possessed what the Anglo-Saxon kings had lacked—an institution which could check and supervise the work of local officials and local magnates. It would have been impossible to govern all England directly from London; a great deal of power had to be left in the hands of the lords and the sheriffs. Private courts continued to increase in numbers and jurisdiction, without opposition from the king, since he could not attend to details of purely local importance. The rest of the king's rights of government in the shires were concentrated in the hands of the sheriffs, who were usually vassals of considerable importance. But neither the great barons nor the sheriffs could become independent, for the king's council was always ready to remind them of the limits of their power and the duties they owed the king.

William, as a good Norman, knew the importance of a large and regular income. He had kept for himself many manors, and the sheriffs were responsible for a fixed sum from each manor each year. He received the usual feudal dues and a share in the fines of most courts. He levied Danegeld three times and made it a heavy assessment. In order to find out just how much he could secure from his kingdom, he ordered the famous Domesday Inquest to be made in 1086. Perhaps nothing shows his power and the perfection of his administrative machinery as clearly as this survey; no other ruler in western Europe had a government capable of making such an investigation, even if he could have forced his vassals to submit to it. Royal commissioners were sent to each shire to question representatives of each district. These representatives, who testified under oath, were usually the priest, the reeve and four villeins from each township. The questions ran like this: Who holds your manor now? Who held it under King Edward? How much land does it contain? How many plows? How many slaves, villeins, or freemen? How much woodland, meadow or pasture? How many mills and fishponds? What was its value under King Edward? What is its value now?

"So narrowly he had them investigate that there was not a single hide nor a rood of land, nor—it is a shame to tell though he thought it no shame to do—was there an ox or a cow or a pig that was not set down in the accounts." This survey was not only useful in increasing the king's revenue; it also informed him about his rights and settled many controversies among lords who, in the excitement of the Conquest, had established conflicting claims to estates and to rights of justice. For the historian it is a marvelous source of information about the changes wrought by the Conquest and about social conditions in eleventh century England. Unfortunately, the northern shires and the city of London are missing from the document as we have it; and since the survey was made for William's information and not for ours, it is often obscure.

Even with these limitations, it is the most important record in early English history.

The survey was very much disliked by William's subjects, but it was not as unpopular as his extension of forest reserves for hunting. His worst offense was the making of the New Forest, for which he condemned much land near Winchester, destroying many villages in the process. He allowed no one to hunt in the royal forests without special permission and had poachers blinded, "for he loved the tall deer as if he were their father." People soon told how the New Forest was accursed, and the hatred of the forest law is reflected in the legends of Robin Hood.

Yet after the Conquest was completed there was only one serious revolt, the rising of the earls in 1075, which was easily crushed. Through his barons and their castles William held the English in check, while he used the English *fyrd* or militia to check his vassals. In 1086 he took a new step by summoning "all the land-holders of any importance in England, no matter whose vassals they were" to Salisbury, where "they all submitted to him and became his men and swore oaths of allegiance to him that they would be faithful to him against all others." The exact significance of this Salisbury oath is still being contested, but it is clear that it would discourage blind obedience to a lord who was in revolt against the king.

The Conquest had important effects on English culture. Almost all important offices, lay and ecclesiastical, in England were held by Normans, and almost all the land was included in Norman fiefs. The towns were full of Normans and other foreigners; the mass of Englishmen were in villeinage; consequently there was a sharp division between natives and foreigners. The upper classes spoke French and kept records in Latin, and although English, the language of the bulk of the population, gradually triumphed, it became a very different language during the struggle. Most of its inflections perished, and thousands of French words were added to its vocabulary. In the same way the civilization changed; while English customs remained as the substratum, French fashions came in, in architecture, in literature, in education, in all that affected the life of the upper classes. In short, England had been forced from its connection with the Scandinavian North and had been brought into close contact with the centers of the new civilization, and especially with France.

This was the work of William. He died in France in 1087, leaving Normandy to his eldest son Robert, and England to his second son William Rufus. Even the English, who had suffered much from him, recognized his greatness. As one of the writers of the Anglo-Saxon Chronicle says:

King William was a very wise and a great man, and more honored and more powerful than any of his predecessors. He was mild to those good men who loved God, but severe beyond measure towards those who withstood his will. . . . Amongst other things the good order that William established is not to be forgotten; it was such that any man, who was himself aught, might travel over the kingdom with a bosomful of gold, unmolested; and no man durst kill another, however great the injury he might have received from him. . . . So also was he a very stern and a wrathful man, so that none durst do anything against his will. . . . Truly there was much trouble in these times, and a very great distress; he caused castles to be built and oppressed the poor. The king also was of great sternness, and he took from his subjects many marks of gold and many hundred pounds of silver, and this either with or without right and with little need. . . . The rich complained and the poor murmured, but he was so sturdy that he recked naught of them; they must will all that the king willed, if they would live, or would keep their lands.

William himself could hardly have objected to this portrayal of his character.

THE ECONOMIC REVIVAL

The religious revival gave Europe moral and intellectual leadership which had long been lacking. The political revival gave many parts of Europe greater security and better government. The economic revival gave Europe a higher standard of living and increased opportunities for specialization. During the eleventh and early twelfth centuries the production of the necessities of life greatly increased, the quality of manufactured goods was improved, and towns became more important in the economic life of the continent.

The basis of economic revival was agriculture. Until very recent times the great majority of the people in every European country depended on farming for their living, and no economic advance was possible until an increase in agricultural productivity had taken place. This was especially true in the early Middle Ages when Europe had to be self-sufficient, because it could not supply its deficiencies from other regions. Until the farming regions could yield a surplus of food over their own needs, there could be little growth of town life or of manufacturing. But while we know that there was an increase in the amount of food produced in Europe in this period, the exact reasons for this increase are still uncertain. Undoubtedly the greater security afforded by the Peace of God and by the government of the better feudal rulers saved the lives and the produce of many peasants. More children survived, so there were more hands available for farming. However, these extra hands (and mouths) might have been a burden rather than an aid, if improvements in agricultural technique had not been utilized at the same time. The history of these technical improvements is still very obscure. Many of them had been known for centuries in some districts, but seem not to have been generally used until the tenth or eleventh century. It is also true that several devices had to be combined before important results could occur.

The first important change was the general adoption in the North of the heavy, wheeled plow equipped with a mold-board. This type of plow not only digs a furrow but also turns the dirt over, and the heavy, wet soils of the northern valleys could not be efficiently cultivated until such a plow was used. Some elements of this plow have been found in excavations of settlements which antedate the Roman period by centuries, but the plow as a whole is probably not as old. Moreover, it was not used in all the regions for which it was suited until the early Middle Ages. For example, it was introduced into eastern Germany only in the period of colonization which followed the final victory over the Slavs.

This heavy plow, however, needed a great deal of animal power to make it move, and as we have seen, it was difficult for the medieval village to support many animals. Eight oxen were the usual plow team, and many teams were needed to cultivate a large extent of land, since the oxen moved so slowly. The more rapid horse team could not be used at first because it could not be harnessed so as to exert its full power. The traditional method, received from the Romans, was to place a band of leather around the animal's neck and let him pull on that. A heavy load, of course, strangled the horse, but the cost of using many horses to share the load, as was done with oxen, was prohibitive. During the Carolingian period, as nearly as we can now tell, Europeans learned, perhaps from the Eastern nomads, the use of the horse-collar. This transferred the pull to the horse's shoulders and let him throw his full weight into the work. This device made the horse more efficient than the ox, but it was a long time before the latter lost his place as the most important work-animal. The horse might be more efficient, but he was harder to feed, and as usual, the medieval village had to consider food before efficiency. However, horses were used more and more as time went on, and they made it possible to cultivate more land and to do it more rapidly.

The third device was the three-field system, which was discussed above.[3] Here again the idea was not new, but the general application of it was. The three-field system allowed crops to be produced on two-thirds of the arable land of a village instead of one-half, it gave the land almost as much rest, and involved no more plowing. By the twelfth century the system had spread through most, though not all, of the regions which had sufficient summer rainfall to permit the sowing of

[3] See pp. 125–126.

spring grains. Wherever it was adopted it meant an increase in the amount of food produced.

Improved methods of production, plus increased security, stimulated the growth of population. The old villages could no longer support their inhabitants; new settlements were necessary. In most regions it was not difficult to find land for the surplus populations. A very small proportion of the lands north of the Alps had been cleared in the early Middle Ages; forests and wastes abounded. Lords were glad to give this almost value-less land to groups of peasants on very easy terms, and new villages were founded all over Europe. The hundreds of towns in France named Villeneuve or Neuville show how extensive this movement of internal colonization could be, even in a country which had long been settled. In the newer countries of Europe the movement was even more important. The people of the Low Countries began their long fight against the sea, draining marshes and enclosing mud flats in order to gain more land. The Germans, after making the most of their western forests, began to flock into the countries beyond the Elbe from which they were driving the Slavs. The migration to this eastern frontier became increasingly important during the twelfth century; men moved hundreds of miles across Germany to reach the land of opportunity. The whole movement bears a curious resemblance to our own westward expansion in the nine-teenth century; emigration agents were sent through the older settle-ments to advertise the attractions of the new lands. But there was al-ways one important difference; there could be no individual pioneers in the eleven and twelfth centuries. Economic and political security could be obtained only in the village community protected by a lord, and the new settlements controlled the lives of their inhabitants almost as fully as the old.

The colonization of Europe by its own people had important results. Production was greatly increased, not only because there was more land under cultivation, but also because much of the new land was very fertile. Moreover, while the new villages had to have lords, the lord usually gave special privileges to the men who undertook the arduous work of clearing the land. Pioneering was as hard then as it was in the nineteenth century, and the chances of starvation or death from hostile neighbors were even greater. Only free men would take these chances, and serfdom was practically unknown in the new villages. Here again the names of the settlements witness the significance of the movement. France has its Villefranche, Germany its Freiburg. The lord usually granted a charter, which put definite restrictions on the sums which he could exact from his new tenants, and often freed them from vexatious tolls or excessive fines. Such charters made the new villages prosperous, and also weakened the old system of serfdom. Ambitious peasants fled from places where they were at the lord's mercy to the new villages where they were free, and the only way of stopping such movements was to give similar privileges to the older settlements. Thus the number of free men steadily increased, and the peasants became used to the idea that they could improve their conditions by changing their habitations. Both these conditions aided the growth of towns.

These changes in agricultural life did not, of course, occur all at once, or even within a period of one or two generations. The increase in population, the clearing of new land, the founding of new villages, the freeing of the serfs, were constant features of European civilization during the twelfth and thirteenth centuries. But even in their early stages they were exceedingly important, especially in connection with the rise of the towns. By 1100 Europe had a surplus of agricultural products, an increasing population, and a surplus of labor. The surplus of food made it possible to support large numbers of men who were not directly engaged in agriculture; the surplus of labor encouraged manufacturing and trade. As the towns grew they stimulated agriculture by affording markets which could absorb all the food produced for miles around. So more land was cleared, and more new villages were founded, and this in turn made possible a new increase in urban economic activities.

The history of commerce and towns in the ninth and tenth centuries is not easy to follow, and historians are still arguing about many of its phases. One school believes that there was little large-scale commerce and no real urban life at this time, while others see evidences of economic revival under Charlemagne and his successors. These disagreements, however, do not affect the fundamental points with which we are concerned. Both schools would agree that in the ninth century there was less trade, a smaller number of towns, and a much smaller urban population than under the Roman Empire. Both would agree that by the thirteenth century European commerce and manufacturing were far more important than they had ever been under Rome. This change is almost as startling as the one which occurred in the eighteenth and nineteenth centuries with the introduction of the factory system and steam power, and the causes are harder to understand. It is easy enough to say that Mediterranean trade routes became safer, that important manufacturing towns sprang up in the North, and that merchants, traveling all over Europe, made it easy for different regions to exchange their surplus commodities. But why did the Mediterranean become safer for commerce? Why did large-scale manufacturing become profitable for the first time since the second century A.D.? Why did merchants find it to their advantage to travel through a continent divided into petty, warring feudal states, when they had not been able to profit from the security and relative freedom of trade afforded by the Roman Empire?

Answers to these questions can only be tentative. The pressure of an increasing population probably explains many of the innovations. The old stability of village life was broken; Europe was full of men looking for opportunities to make a living. The decline of slavery and the change of the landlord class into a feudal nobility was also important. Both these shifts made it more difficult to preserve the estate as a self-sufficient unit. A serf, unlike a slave, could not be arbitrarily assigned to any task which pleased his lord, and the lords, as they became absorbed in warfare and politics, gave less and less thought to the administration of their estates. Moreover, as feudalism developed, many great estates were split into fragments, and no one lord could control all their economic activities. The number of artisans living on great estates declined markedly; they tended to congregate in trading centers where they could supply a whole region instead of just one lord. The growing importance of northern Europe stimulated trade by affording a new market for Mediterranean and oriental goods. As we have seen, under the Roman Empire the bulk of the population lived near the shores of the great sea; no one region had a monopoly of any important product of the area, and eastern goods could be distributed rapidly to all important cities from a few ports in the Levant. But when England, Scandinavia, and the northern parts of France and Germany became thickly settled they needed southern products, such as wine, and oriental luxuries, such as spices. New trade-routes had to be developed to serve these new customers. These southern and oriental goods at first came to the north through Russia and the Baltic, but nomad raids began to interfere with the Russian route in the twelfth century. Thus the Italians who used the Mediterranean route had a great opportunity to expand their commerce. Finally, the Church, with its insistence upon the dignity of labor, encouraged artisans to take pride in their work; a sentiment which was woefully lacking in the later Roman Empire. This certainly stimulated production and probably stimulated the advance in technology which is so typical of the Middle Ages.

Whatever the fundamental causes, the results are clear. In Italy, where urban life had never come as near vanishing as it had in the North, the seacoast towns showed their strength as early as the middle of the eleventh century. They had never been cut off entirely from trade with the East; their ships sailed regularly to Constantinople, and they frequently engaged in illegal but very profitable commerce with the Saracens. As a result they had a nucleus of ships and seamen which grew rapidly after 1000. At about the same time, the Moslem world was splitting up into petty states and was weakened by civil wars. Taking advantage of this weakness, Genoa and Pisa began to drive the Moslems from the western Mediterranean. Saracen fleets were defeated; the pirate town of Mehdia was sacked; Sardinia was recaptured by the Christians. By the time of the First Crusade (1095) Italian ships could sail safely all the way to Palestine. The Norman conquest of Sicily completed the work of giving Christians control of the Mediterranean. Roger II of Sicily was actually able to conquer and to hold for many years a long strip of the North African coast, and this feat practically put an end to Moslem piracy. Until the coming of the Turks, European commerce in the Mediterranean was subject to no serious interference.

The victories of the Italian towns and the Normans coincided with the growing prosperity of Western Europe. Eastern goods had been rare and expensive; now they were more plentiful and more men could afford to buy them. As a result, silks, fine cloth, spices, drugs, jewels and other luxury articles could enter Europe in as large quantities as they had in the days of the Roman Empire. To distribute them throughout the continent required the services of a number of men, both Italians and northerners. These men had to find safe places to lodge themselves and their goods as they traveled through Europe. They needed more or less permanent homes during the winter months when the roads were impassable. Old Roman cities with walls, or villages situated at cross-roads or fords and protected by castles or monasteries, acquired a population of merchants in a very brief period. The merchants attracted other people who came to satisfy their needs, and thus towns grew up all along the routes of trade. The first notable inland settlements were in the Po Valley, then they appeared in the Rhône and Rhine regions, and finally they emerged along all the secondary routes.

The revival of commerce was not the only reason for the rise of towns. Large-scale manufacturing began to play a part in European economic life, and this also encouraged urban settlement. The most conspicuous example of this development was to be found in the North, in Flanders. Here a tradition of fine cloth-making slowly developed. The marshy, low-lying coastal plain was not well adapted to agriculture, but was excellent for sheep-raising. The Flemings, concentrating on this activity, soon had more wool than they themselves could consume, and the only way to get rid of the surplus was to make it into cloth good enough to be desired by strangers. This was done as early as the Carolingian period, when the emperor sent the caliph a present of Flemish cloth. The development of an export trade in cloth was probably stimulated by the fact that Flemish seaports were the termini of routes which led to England, Scandinavia, and North Germany. Flanders suffered severely, perhaps more severely than any other European country, from the raids of the Northmen, but neither the tradition of cloth-making nor that of commerce with the northern peoples was forgotten. As soon as the counts of Flanders were able to give security to their people, Flemish cloth manufacturing grew with surprising rapidity. Soon every part of Europe was buying the products of Flemish looms. It may seem strange that a great export trade could be built up in a commodity that could be manufactured anywhere in Europe, but the Flemings had some clear advantages. Flanders was one of the regions where the population had grown most rapidly, and so there was a surplús of labor which could be hired very cheaply. Flemish wool was of excellent quality, and the country soon began to import English wool which was even better. Finally, it should be remembered that it is a long and tedious process to make cloth from wool, especially if the heavy, almost waterproof medieval product be desired. The wool has to be cleaned and carded, spun and woven, sheared, fulled and dyed. The medieval village was not equipped to do these tasks well; only in a large town could specialists in all these operations be found. The Flemings improved the technique of cloth-making; they produced fine cloth at a reasonable price before any other people. When other regions threatened to catch up with them, they made new improvements and so retained their superiority throughout the Middle Ages.

The existence of this great manufacturing center in the North aided the development of trade in districts which were too far removed from Italy to be greatly affected by the revival of Mediterranean commerce. Moreover, Flanders and Italy, the two regions in which economic activity was most highly developed, naturally sought contact with each other, and the passage of merchants through the intervening countries encouraged the growth of town life there. Flanders, however, was not the only manufacturing region. As we have seen, artisans were leaving the great estates and congregating in towns where they could supply a larger group of customers. By the twelfth century all but the most backward districts had their local manufacturing centers where cloth, leather goods, ironware, household utensils, and other common products could be purchased. Some of these towns were able to produce goods of such a high quality that they had a European market; thus the little town of Dinant was famous for copper and brass ware, Cordova for leather, Montpellier for dyes.

But even when the market was limited to a radius of twenty or thirty miles around the town the effects on economic life were important. There was an increasingly clear division between the functions of rural and urban settlements; the first raised food, the second supplied manufactured goods and imported luxuries for the wealthier classes. This division of functions seems so natural to us that it may appear foolish to insist upon it. But it was precisely this natural division of functions which had been lacking in Europe for centuries. Roman towns, in the Western Empire at least, had been parasites rather than producers; early medieval towns were too small to do much of the manufacturing which was necessary. There had always been a luxury trade, but this by itself could do little to develop an intelligent division of labor. The revival of trade and the concentration of manufacturing in the towns freed agricultural districts from the heavy task of trying to supply all the necessities of life and made it possible for each to produce the things for which it was most fitted. The luxury trade was still the most conspicuous and the most profitable branch of European commerce, but trade in articles of daily use was steadily growing. It was this latter trade which wrought a revolution in economic life. The towns of Italy might deal in the precious goods of the East, but the towns of the North were primarily interested in exchanging wine, salt, fish and grain with each other and in manufacturing cloth, leather and iron. Even in Italy the ordinary burgher was not a dealer in spices and pearls; he was a baker, a weaver, or a smith. The great increase in imports from the East was a stimulant which did much to revive town life in Europe, but the Eastern trade did not support the towns of Europe. Wandering merchants who dealt in Eastern wares often acted as catalytic agents; towns grew up around their halting places as crystals form on rods dipped into a supersaturated solution, but the towns were not inhabited exclusively by dealers in Oriental goods. Most medieval towns performed exactly the same function that a modern American town in the midst of an agricultural district performs; they were centers where the farmer could sell his goods and in return buy articles which were too much trouble for him to make himself.

The growth of towns speeded up the changes in agricultural organization which had already begun. They afforded an increasingly important market for food; therefore more land was cleared and the old estates were more carefully cultivated. They could supply most of the necessities of life; therefore rural districts no longer had to strain so hard for local self-sufficiency. The region around Bordeaux could specialize in wine-growing; the eastern part of England could specialize in sheep-raising. Townsmen preferred cash to payments in kind; therefore serfdom, which supplied food rather than money, received another blow. It was much easier for the lord to buy supplies in a town than to collect six bushels of wheat here and four bushels of rye there and store the whole lot for the winter. It was often more efficient for the lord to cultivate his own lands with hired labor rather than to depend on the slow, grudging service of his serfs. But if the lord wanted to buy supplies and hire labor, he needed more money, and the only way to get more money was to commute payments in kind and labor-services for cash. This left many peasants in the position of tenant-farmers; they paid a cash rent to the lord and disposed of their produce as they saw fit. Such men were not really serfs, and it was often possible for them to accumulate enough money to buy formal recognition of their freedom. This process went on slowly but steadily during the twelfth and thirteenth centuries. It was never complete, yet hundreds of thousands of serfs gained their freedom because the lord preferred ready cash to service and payments in kind. And even where the serfs remained, the old closed economy of the great estate was ended. Everywhere the land-owners wanted a cash crop which they could sell in the open market. The great estate was no longer a way of life; it had become an investment.

The revival of town life not only changed the economic system of Europe; it also introduced a new, disturbing element in the political and social life of the continent. A new class and a new kind of power had been created, and neither fitted into the old scheme of things. The inhabitants of the towns began to demand a social and political status for which there were no precedents. Conservative churchmen and nobles felt that these demands would destroy society, and yet they could not prevent the townsmen from slowly gaining most of their objectives. These objectives were of three sorts: the townsmen wanted personal freedom, they wanted relief from the financial exactions of their lords, and they wanted self-government.

The first demand was the easiest to satisfy. Many of the settlers who flocked to the towns were free in fact if not by law. They were peasants or homeless men who had wandered so far from their native land that no lord would ever think of reclaiming them. Settlers from near-by districts were not so fortunate; they were known to be serfs and were at first treated as such. But even the dullest lord was soon able to see that the duties of a serf and the life of a merchant or artisan were absolutely incompatible. No businessman could drop his work for two or three days to perform agricultural labor for a lord, and he was usually more valuable to his lord as a businessman than as a field-hand. A thriving town greatly increased the revenue which the lord drew from tolls and sales-taxes, and no town could thrive with a population of serfs. So a lord was usually quite willing to recognize the personal freedom of town-dwellers, especially if he were offered a lump sum for the grant. This in itself would not have been so upsetting, but the grant of freedom was usually worded so that it extended to all future settlers. In many regions a serf who lived a year and a day in a town without being claimed by a lord became automatically a free man. This naturally encouraged serfs to run away to the towns.

The second desire of the townsmen could also be satisfied without too much difficulty. Once the inhabitants were freed, the lord usually lost the right of arbitrary tallage which he had over serfs. Other dues could be commuted for yearly payments; a steady income was preferable to a multitude of petty payments which were difficult to remember or to collect. Frequently the lord was willing to fix maximum sums for fines. And some lords were enlightened enough to see that lower tolls, by increasing business, would increase their revenue. The exact degree of financial relief which a town obtained depended, of course, upon the necessities of the lord and the strength of the town. In practically all cases, however, the town gained a definite statement of the sums it owed to the lord each year, and in most cases the lord surrendered some of his claims in return for a regular income.

The third plank, the request for self-government, caused the most difficulty. Obviously, some new organs of government were necessary in the towns; feudal institutions were as incompatible with town life as was serfdom. To take one example, feudal courts were utterly incapable of handling commercial cases. They dealt chiefly with land; they thought in terms of possession rather than property; they permitted endless delays and required endless formalities. The merchant needed courts which would act quickly, before a reluctant debtor could run away; courts which would enforce a simple contract drawn up in a shop or a market. The towns also had a police problem which did not exist in the open country; they had to guard against professional criminals, and the riots which developed so easily from petty brawls. Finally, the town needed some sort of authority to take care of housing regulations, maintenance of streets and walls, and most important, the collection of the money which was promised the lord. Every ruler could see that his towns needed this new type of government; the real issue was over the question of control. The townsmen naturally wanted to handle their own affairs but the lords were afraid of a loss of authority and income if they surrendered political control.

Yet in most places the towns gained a limited degree of self-government without much difficulty. Petty lords often had neither the power nor the administrative resources necessary for keeping control of town governments. Other rulers found that they could avoid endless arguments and a wearisome burden of administrative routine by conceding some governmental powers to the burghers. By the end of the twelfth century most commercial towns in medieval Europe had gained the right to elect officials who could hold courts for commercial and petty criminal cases. These officials usually took care of local administration and were allowed to collect taxes to meet the expenses of the community. The lord might reserve the right to choose the mayor or to approve new taxes, but in all routine affairs the town was self-governing. To make a very rough comparison, such towns were in about the same position in regard to their lord as an American city is to the state in which it is situated.

Some lords granted personal freedom and commercial privileges to small towns and even to villages with no hesitation, hoping for increased revenues. On the other hand, there were lords who resented any demands for self-government, and there were towns which resented any assertion of the lord's rights. The king of France was very reluctant to make any concessions to the important cities of his domain; even Paris never had any real rights of self-government. Bishops and abbots who were bound to preserve all the rights of their churches were often unwilling to give up control of town governments. On the other hand, the real desire of most townsmen was not home rule; it was complete independence. Most medieval towns struggled ceaselessly to reduce the power of their lords; some of them were so successful that they became sovereign states. It is a great mistake to think that medieval towns favored the creation of large kingdoms. Their political ambitions were very like those of the nobles; they wanted complete control of a small district with no obligations to any superior. If they sometimes aided the growth of royal authority, it was simply because they needed the king's assistance in freeing themselves from local rulers.

The denial of self-government by the lords and the desires of the towns for greater independence occasionally led to uprisings in which the townsmen were successful. These rebellions were a shock to the old medieval social system. It was bad enough to have large groups of non-nobles becoming wealthy and influential, but it was infinitely worse when they rebelled against their superiors. Clergy and nobles, who disaagreed on so many other points, united in damning the upstart burghers. This opposition of the upper classes, very effective in individual cases, was not strong enough to stop the movement as a whole. Towns which had a large degree of self-government, if not complete independence, increased steadily in number during the twelfth and early thirteenth centuries. Such towns were usually called "communes" because the citizens formed a collective body, or community which had legal personality. "Commune" at first was a word which had all the sinister implications of "communism" today, but by the thirteenth century it was used freely by royal and ecclesiastical officials without any remembrance of its semi-revolutionary origins. Even the powerful kings of England recognized communes in their domains; even the conservative bishops of eastern France were forced to deal with communes established in their own cities.

One more result of the rise of the towns should be noted. It upset the balance of power in every European country. The towns were wealthy, they had great strategic value, and some of them had important military or naval forces. A ruler who could use the new wealth and new power of the towns could break any internal opposition; a ruler who could not control his towns had little authority. This is one of the most important keys to an understanding of the political events of the twelfth and thirteenth centuries. The kings of France and England, who gained control of their towns, were able to create powerful, unified monarchies. In the Low Countries, control of the towns went to the feudal lords, who became practically independent princes. In Italy the towns, aided by the pope, gained complete freedom and in doing so destroyed the power of the emperor. The political future of every European country was determined by the relations between its king and the towns.

VIII

-》》-》》-》》-》》《《-《《-《《-《《-

The Leadership of
the Church

THE STRUGGLE of the Church to reform itself and to free itself from secular influences was one of the most important factors in the great revival of civilization which began in the middle of the eleventh century. The fight, begun by the monks of Cluny and taken up by the papacy under Leo IX, was to last for over two centuries. As new wealth created new temptations, as the increasing power of secular rulers threatened the independence of the clergy, the Church had to tighten its discipline, improve its organization, and stand stubbornly for its rights. Europe was boiling with new energy; every class was seeking advantages for itself; the clergy had to work furiously merely to hold its own.

But the Church was not satisfied with merely holding its own. It wanted to lead society, to fit all activities into the framework of a Christian commonwealth. Influential as it had been in the early centuries of the Middle Ages, the Church had not enjoyed a position of unquestioned leadership. It had often been dominated by secular rulers; it had had comparatively little influence on the economic and political institutions which developed during the ninth and tenth centuries. General principles could hardly be imposed on a society which was suffering acutely from localism. But now that localism was receding, now that men were learning once more how to work together, the universal Church had a great opportunity. It was the one organization which reached everywhere; it was the one organization capable of conceiving a pattern for the new civilization. During the late eleventh and early twelfth centuries it gained the leadership of society; during the late twelfth and early thirteenth centuries it fought successfully to retain its leadership. This leadership was not absolute; secular interests continued to exist, and there were always men who were little influenced by religious ideals. Yet, until 1250 at least, the Church was the final judge of what was useful to society, and all other activities conformed, at least outwardly, to its standards.

THE INVESTITURE CONFLICT

The first task of the Church was to free itself from the control of the Empire. When Leo IX died in 1054 the emperor was still the strongest ruler in Europe, and the Empire was the one secular institution which could pretend to universal authority. If the Church could free itself from the emperor's authority, its prestige would become so great that it would have little trouble with other rulers. Conditions after 1054 were very favorable for the Church to begin such a struggle. As we have seen, Henry III had freed the pope from the Roman nobles, and Leo IX had greatly increased papal authority beyond the Alps. The new independence of the papacy was consolidated by a decree regulating papal elections which was drawn up in 1059 under Nicholas II. By this decree all secular influence in the choice of the pope was to be ended; neither the Roman mob, nor the local nobles, nor the German king were to intervene. The cardinals,[1] that is, the bishops of the dioceses surrounding Rome and the priests of the chief Roman churches, were to elect the pope. After their choice was announced, the Roman people were to give formal assent to the election, but no real power was left to the laity, and even the German king was given only a shadowy right of participation. This decree was somewhat modified in later years, but the basic principle was never shaken. From 1059 on, no German ruler was able to make a pope, and the cardinals' freedom of choice was interfered with only in the most exceptional circumstances. The new power given the cardinals made them an increasingly important factor in the government of the Church; they formed the papal council and headed the administrative services of the Church. Gradually, the pope began to select his cardinals from the leading clergy of all Christian countries instead of from the leading clergy of Rome, and so the College of Cardinals became a new link between the papacy and the transalpine churches.

While the papacy was thus strengthening its position, the German monarchy was suffering repeated blows. Henry III had died in 1056, leaving a six-year-old son, Henry IV, to succeed him. During the long minority the fundamental weakness of the German government became apparent. There were no institutions of central government, manned by trained officials, which could work automatically in the absence of a strong ruler. The dukes and count, who were still technically officials of the king

---

[1] "Cardinal" means "chief" or "important." The cardinals were the chief clergy of Rome.

had actually obtained hereditary rights of government. They had obeyed Henry III, but they would not obey his widow, who was acting as regent for the young king. Civil war broke out in Germany and Henry IV, kidnaped from his mother, was passed from one faction to another as the balance of power shifted. This unstable life made the boy erratic and passionate, but it also showed him what was needed if Germany was to have a really effective government. When he came of age Henry resolved to make himself independent of the magnates. He seems to have realized that this could be done only by the creation of a compact royal domain, which would be a sure source of wealth and military power, and by the creation of a royal bureaucracy, which would be devoted to his interests. For the domain he fixed his attention on the southern part of Saxony, which lay in the center of old Germany and contained important silver mines. For the bureaucracy he made increasing use of his *ministeriales,* a peculiar class of servile officials which existed only in Germany. They were definitely of unfree origin, yet they might be given very responsible positions in the administration of great estates. Henry's innovation was to use them for all sorts of public business, trusting that they could never adopt the viewpoint of the nobles from whom they were separated by a sharp class line.

Henry's plans for strengthening the monarchy were perfectly sound in principle, but he applied them rather tactlessly. He jailed the Saxon duke and confiscated Saxon lands on the slightest pretext in order to build up his domain. He filled his newly won lands with castles garrisoned with Swabian vassals who oppressed the natives. His use of the low-born *ministeriales* infuriated the nobles, who had had a monopoly of all governmental posts for centuries. Altogether, Henry had moved entirely too fast after a long period of weak government and had alienated some of his powerful subjects. As a result, when the Saxons rebelled, neither the lay nor the ecclesiastical magnates supported their king, and Henry was forced to surrender most of his acquisitions. Under these circumstances he turned to the pope for aid, a reversal of traditional positions which shows how the situation had changed in a brief twenty years.

Henry's letter asking assistance was very humble and shows his desire to keep the good will of the Church by accepting the ideas of the reforming party. It began:

> To the most watchful and best beloved Lord Pope Gregory endowed from heaven with the apostolic dignity, Henry, by the grace of God king of the Romans, renders most faithfully due submission. Alas! Sinful and in misery, partly owing to the impulse of youthful temptation, partly owing to the freedom of our unrestrained and mighty power, partly also owing to the seductive deception of those whose plans we, too easily led, have followed, we have sinned against heaven and in your sight and are no longer worthy to

be called your son. For not only have we seized ecclesiastical property, but also we have sold the churches themselves to unworthy men, although infected with the poison of simony . . . and now, because we alone without your aid cannot reform the churches, we earnestly seek your aid and advice concerning them and all our affairs; being most desirous to obey your commands in everything.

Humble as it was, this letter was sent in vain, since the reform leaders were not inclined to assist the German monarchy.

The pope to whom this letter was addressed was Gregory VII, one of the ablest leaders the Church has ever had. As the monk Hildebrand he had followed the reforming pope Gregory VI into exile. He returned to Rome with Leo IX and played an increasingly important rôle in the affairs of the papacy from that time on. He had spent some time at Cluny and had been impressed with the ideals of that center of reform, but his own program went far beyond a mere improvement in the morals of the clergy. There was to be a general moral reform; all Christians were to obey the decisions of the pope as to what was socially desirable; even kings and emperors could be judged and punished by the pope if they sinned. The Church, through its head, the pope, was to be the final authority in Christendom. In order to accomplish this mission the Church must be absolutely independent of any lay authority. Hildebrand aided Nicholas II to draw up the decree regulating papal elections in 1059 and he was the power behind the throne during the long pontificate of Alexander II (1061–1073). Curiously enough, his own election to the papacy in 1073 violated the law which he had helped to make, since he was chosen by acclamation, without the prescribed formalities. Yet there was no doubt that Gregory had the support of the cardinals and Henry IV had no hesitation, as we have seen, in recognizing his authority.

Once pope, Gregory carried on the work of reform with great energy. He first attacked the marriage of priests, a custom which involved the Church in all sorts of secular affairs. He ordered all married priests to separate from their wives and children under pain of forfeiting their parishes. This decree caused many protests, especially north of the Alps, where the marriage of priests had been accepted as a normal custom. On the whole, however, public opinion accepted this reform as necessary, and lay rulers made no great difficulties in allowing the decree to be enforced.

It was otherwise when Gregory struck at the second bond between the Church and worldly affairs. If the Church were to be really free it was necessary to liberate the clergy from the control of lay rulers. So, in 1075, Gregory forbade lay investiture under pain of excommunication. Technically, lay investiture meant the conferring of the insignia of ecclesiastical authority, such as the bishop's ring and staff, by secular rulers. But the slogan, "no lay investiture," meant much more; it meant

GERMANY AND ITALY AT THE TIME OF THE INVESTITURE CONFLICT

NORTH SEA

MARCH OF THE BILLUNGS

Hamburg

FRIESLAND

Bremen

NORTH MARCH

POMERANIA

SAXONY

Magdeburg
Goslar

Brandenburg

POLAND

Utrecht

Paderborn

SAXON EAST MARCH

ELBE

ODER

Bruges

Antwerp

LOWER

Ghent

LORRAINE

Cologne

THURINGIA

THURINGIAN MARCH

Prague

Aix-la-Chapelle

Fulda

BOHEMIA

MORAVIA

FRANCONIA

Laôn

UPPER

Frankfort
Oppenheim

Bamberg

Mainz

Nuremberg

Ratisbon

LORRAINE

Worms

Reims

Metz

Spires

Prague

Verdun

Toul

BAVARIAN EAST MARCH

Troyes

Strasburg

Augsburg

Vienna

ALSACE

SWABIA

BAVARIA

FRANCE

Basel

Constance

Salzburg

HUNGARY

CITEAUX

Zurich

ST. GALL

CLUNY

Besançon

CARINTHIA

Geneva

BURGUNDY

CARNIOLA

Lyons

VERONA

DANUBE

Vienne

Legnano

Milan

LOMBARDY

Verona

Venice

CROATIA

Turin

Pavia Mantua

Parma

PO

Genoa

Modena

Ravenna

Canossa

Bologna

NOMINALLY UNDER PAPAL RULE

Pisa

Florence

Arles

TUSCANY

Perugia

Marseilles

Siena

Assisi

HOLY ROMAN EMPIRE, c. 1100 A.D.

Spoleto

ADRIATIC SEA

CORSICA (PISA)

SPOLETO

PAPAL STATES

Rome

Bari

Benevento

Capua Benevento

ITALY

Naples Salerno

Bari

SALERNO

Capua
Aversa

Brindisi

Amalfi

Naples

Amalfi

Salerno

NORMAN
CONQUEST
OF SOUTH ITALY

NORMAN
PRINCIPALITIES

APULIA

CALABRIA

Palermo

Messina

1030 TO 1042
1057 " 1063
1071 " 1080
1090 " 1137

Palermo

Messina

SICILY (1060-1090)

Syracuse

SICILY

100 MILES

150 MILES

TRM

that kings and feudal lords were to have no voice in the selection of officials of the Church. This, of course, was absolutely necessary if the Church was to be an independent power, or if it was to force society to accept its standards. Yet it is easy to see the difficulties which the reform created for secular rulers. For bishops and abbots were not only ecclesiastical officials; they also held large estates, lordships, and even counties, and so had great secular responsibilities and powers. Every government was dependent, to a greater or lesser extent, on the resources and personnel of the Church. Ecclesiastical vassals often provided the military resources necessary to control rebellious lay nobles. All administrative and secretarial departments were staffed by churchmen; no one else was capable of doing the work. Churchmen were judges, ambassadors and royal councillors. It seemed hard that kings could not choose their own officials, and yet it was equally hard if the Church had to accept prelates selected for purely political reasons. The twofold duties of churchmen made a struggle inevitable, and at the same time almost insoluble, since neither pope nor king could afford to lose their services.

Of all rulers, the king of Germany had had the greatest power over the Church; of all governments his was most dependent on the aid of churchmen. Henry would have protested in any case, but Gregory's decree on lay investiture reached him just as his fortunes were taking a turn for the better. He was celebrating a great victory over the Saxons and for the moment the young king was supreme in Germany. He was not disposed to accept an attack on his authority. Henry's displeasure was increased by the tone of the letter which accompanied the papal decree. It began: "Bishop Gregory, servant of the servants of God, greeting and apostolic benediction:—that is, if he be obedient to the apostolic throne as beseems a Christian king. Considering . . . with what strict judgment we shall have to render account for the ministry entrusted to us by St. Peter, chief of the Apostles, it is with hesitation that we have sent unto thee the apostolic benediction." [2] The pope went on to describe Henry's sins, and to remind him that he was wholly under the authority of St. Peter and St. Peter's successor, the pope. Henry was warned not to imitate Saul in boasting of a victory won only by the grace of God.

Henry was intensely angry. Instead of negotiating and trying to win a reasonable compromise, he declared open war on the pope. In startling contrast to the humble letter of 1073 quoted above, the king's answer of January 1076 began: "Henry, king not through usurpation but through the holy ordination of God, to Hildebrand, at present not pope, but false monk." The king went on to assert that Gregory had tried to set himself up wrongfully over the whole Church and to exercise illegal authority over the German king.

---

[2] This and other passages are from translations in Henderson, *Historical Documents of the Middle Ages.* Some slight changes in wording have been made.

For the true pope Peter also exclaims: "Fear God, honor the king!" But thou dost not fear God, dost not honor in me his appointed one. Wherefore St. Peter, since he has not spared an angel of heaven if he shall have preached otherwise, has not excepted thee also who dost teach otherwise upon earth. For he says: "If anyone, either I or an angel of heaven, should preach a gospel other than that which has been preached to you, he shall be damned." Thou, therefore, damned by this curse and by the judgment of all our bishops and by our own, descend and relinquish the apostolic throne which thou has usurped. Let another ascend the throne of St. Peter, who shall not practise violence under the cloak of religion, but shall teach the sound doctrine of St. Peter. I, Henry, king by the grace of God, do say unto thee, together with all my bishops: Down, down, to be damned through all the ages.

As the letter indicates, Henry had forced the bishops present at his court to refuse to recognize Gregory as pope. Several of them were already under the papal ban, and all were so dependent on the king that they had to follow his policy. Thus the issues were clearly drawn. Could a German king nullify the Church's declaration of independence? Could the German bishops defy the orders of the Roman pope? Gregory was not the man to ignore an act which challenged everything in which he believed. As soon as the king's letters reached him, he excommunicated Henry and released his subjects from obedience. "Confident of my integrity and authority, I now declare in the name of the omnipotent God, Father, Son and Holy Spirit, that Henry, son of the emperor Henry, is deprived of his kingdom in Germany and Italy . . . because he has rebelled against the Church."

At the same time Gregory sought the support of the bishops and nobles of Germany. Many of them were glad to aid the pope. The power of the magnates had been slowly growing behind the façade of imperial authority, and they were now ready for an open contest with the king. Henry had alarmed them by his attempts to construct a government which would not need their support, and they were determined to end this threat to their position. Papal propaganda, spread through Germany by leaders of the reforming party, also had a profound effect. The value of the recent improvements in church organization was clearly demonstrated; Gregory VII was able to influence public opinion north of the Alps as none of his predecessors had done. The moral prestige of the reform movement was so great that many men turned against Henry, even though they had no personal grudge against him. As a result, the king was deserted by almost all his followers, and the victorious magnates held a meeting in October 1076 to discuss his deposition. Henry was unable to oppose them, and he was ready to agree to anything which would give him a chance to save his throne. The assembly finally decided that Henry should live as a private citizen under guard at Spires, and that he was to forfeit his throne unless the pope freed him from ex-communication within a year. He also had to promise complete submission and obedience to Gregory.

Henry's position was desperate. The pope had promised to take no action in his case until the German princes had been consulted, and it was fairly certain that they would insist on deposing him, or at least in depriving him of most of his power. But there was one weakness in this arrangement; the pope, as a Christian priest, could not refuse absolution to a sincerely penitent sinner who sought his presence. Henry, who was always clever if not wise, saw this weakness and took full advantage of it. He escaped from Spires and rushed to Italy to intercept Gregory, who was on his way to consult the German princes. Fearing a desperate attack, the pope retired to the castle of Canossa, but Henry soon showed that he was not going to add to his sins by an assault on the vicar of Christ. Instead he so humbled himself that Gregory was forced to forget his political plans and remember only his religious duties. The best description of the famous scene is the letter which Gregory himself wrote to the German princes to excuse his violation of his oath to them:

Finally he [Henry] came in person to Canossa, . . . bringing with him only a small retinue, and manifesting no hostile intentions. Once arrived, he presented himself at the gate of the castle barefoot and clad only in a wretched woolen garment, beseeching us with tears to grant him absolution and forgiveness. This he continued to do for three days, until all those about him were moved to compassion at his plight and interceded for him with tears and prayers. Indeed, they marveled at our hardheartedness, some even complaining that our action savored rather of heartless tyranny than of chastening severity. At length his persistent declarations of repentance, and the supplications of all who were there with us overcame our reluctance, and we removed the excommunication from him and received him again into the bosom of the holy mother church.

Henry had won a diplomatic victory at the price of great personal humiliation, but the moral victory won by the pope at Canossa was far more significant. The most powerful king of the West had been forced to bow before the successor of Peter. For the next two centuries no ruler was long able to withstand the opposition of the pope. For the Church, the establishment of this precedent was worth the loss of the alliance of the German princes. Later events were to show that even when the rebellious magnates remained on the pope's side long enough to place a new king on the German throne, the alliance was futile. The traditions of the office forced any king, however chosen, to oppose the papacy.

Gregory, however, wanted a political as well as a moral victory. He insisted that Henry's case was not settled, but once the excommunication had been lifted the opposition to the king was irrevocably weakened. The more stubborn princes elected an anti-king, who was pledged to respect their rights and who expressly renounced his descendants' claim to the throne. But this act, while it demonstrated the objectives of the king's opponents, was a failure politically. It merely started a devastating civil war in which Henry slowly gained the upper hand. Even a new excommunication by Gregory in 1080 had little effect; the magnates who were on the king's side felt that the pope had left them in the lurch once before and saw no reason for coming to his aid again. Henry, moreover, counterattacked by persuading his clergy to depose Gregory and elect an anti-pope. In this same year he won a significant victory: the anti-king fell on the field of battle, and many Germans felt that God had given judgment for the king. With this success Germany became obedient enough to make possible a direct attack on Gregory. Henry marched to Italy and, after a bitter struggle, succeeded in driving the pope from Rome. The anti-pope was installed in St. Peter's, and gave Henry the imperial crown on Easter Day, 1084. Gregory had to take refuge at Salerno where he died the next year. His last words were: "I have loved righteousness and hated iniquity, therefore I die in exile."

This victory seemed overwhelming, but the new prestige of the papacy could not be destroyed by mere brute force. Gregory's successors carried on opposition to Henry, and so gave the German magnates justification for renewed rebellion. The magnates could not long remain loyal to the emperor; they were bound to oppose him to protect their own interests. They had made an open bid for independence, and they could not stop fighting until they were sure that Henry could not weaken their power. So once again a great rebellion broke out; the duke of Bavaria and Henry's own wife and eldest son turned against him. Once again Henry succeeded in riding out the storm; the duke of Bavaria did not receive the reward he expected and deserted his papal allies, while the rebellious son died. But once again the emperor's victory did not end the struggle; Henry was still excommunicate, and the magnates were still disloyal. There could be no peace while Henry lived; he stood for everything which the Church and the princes hated. The emperor's surviving son and heir, young Henry, king of the Romans, recognized this, and apparently felt that his father must be removed before the prestige of the monarchy was irremediably lowered. He turned against his father, allied himself with hostile magnates, and in the last civil war of the reign forced the unfortunate emperor to abdicate. Henry IV died soon after, in 1106, but even his corpse had no peace. As he had died excommunicate, his body was transferred from one temporary tomb to another, until Henry V celebrated an ephemeral victory over the papacy by solemnly burying the father whom he had hounded to death.

The reign of Henry IV showed the weakness of the German monarchy. The ruler was dependent upon the good will of the great men, who might be technically royal officials, but who were actually hereditary princes. He was also dependent upon the resources of the Church. Henry IV alienated the magnates but failed to create a bureaucracy which would take their place. He alienated the Church but failed to create a royal domain which would make up for the loss of Church wealth. During his reign the revived Empire of the Ottos almost came to an end because it had lost its foundations. The magnates became independent rulers, the Church withdrew its support, and the emperor had to fight frantically to preserve even his title to the throne.

Henry V, who was cold-blooded, shrewd, and utterly unscrupulous, seems to have realized that a shift in policy was necessary. He would fight only one enemy at a time; he gave way to the magnates in order to concentrate on the pope. At first this policy seemed brilliantly successful. When pope Paschal II rebuked Henry for appointing bishops in Germany, the king promptly crossed the Alps with a large army (in 1111). The pope had few supporters at the time and was forced to propose a compromise. He suggested that the Church should give up all the possessions which it held of lay rulers in Germany, so that churchmen would no longer owe secular services. In return the king and lay lords would give up the right of investiture. Thus the Church would become independent, while the king would regain an immense domain. Agreement was reached on these terms and Paschal consented to crown Henry V as emperor. But when, on the coronation day, the pope's charter abandoning the Church's possessions was read in St. Peter's, scandalized churchmen began to riot. Henry, who had anticipated this, seized the pope and the cardinals and held them prisoners until the pope recognized his right of investiture. Then he returned triumphantly to Germany—emperor, and victor over the papacy.

The victory was worth no more than the triumph of Henry IV over Gregory VII. The clergy beseeched Paschal II to repudiate his agreement, which he did in 1112. The quarrel followed the usual course: Henry was excommunicated, a rebellion broke out in Germany, an anti-pope was elected, and the dispute dragged on until 1122. At this time Henry's system broke down. He had conciliated the princes, hoping to have their support in attacking the papacy, but by 1122 they were sick of the whole dispute. They used their new power to force a compromise on the emperor—the famous Concordat of Worms. By this treaty Henry gave up the custom of investing prelates with the ring and the staff, the insignia of ecclesiastical authority. Thus lay investiture, in the narrow sense, was definitely abolished. As for the real issue, control of Church offices, the emperor kept some of his powers. It was agreed that in Italy and Burgundy there was to be no imperial interference with elections, but in Germany all elections were to be held in the presence of the emperor or his representative. This, of course, gave the ruler an opportunity to exert great pressure on the electors. However, this system of influencing the choice of prelates was gradually abandoned in favor of a more indirect type of control. The twelfth century rulers of Germany for the first time emphasized feudal relationships, and tried to control both Church and magnates through feudal forms. By insisting that bishops take an oath of fidelity to them, by refusing to give fiefs of the Empire to men whom they disliked, they were able to determine many elections and to get a great deal of service from German bishops. Yet, after the Concordat of Worms the German monarchs never had the same unquestioned control of the resources and personnel of the Church which the Ottos had enjoyed. Even bishops who owed their position to the emperor need not be entirely subservient to him. The pope could now demand obedience as well as the king, and in the long run it was safer for the bishops to stay on the papal side. So the Concordat did not end the struggle between the papacy and the Empire, but merely transferred it to other fields. The question of lay investiture was settled, but the fundamental reasons for conflict still existed.

THE CHURCH AND THE EMPIRE

The growing independence of the princes was strikingly illustrated when Henry V died without male heirs in 1125. Otto III and Henry II had likewise died without male heirs, but in these cases the magnates had chosen rulers from collateral branches of the royal family. Their right of election had been merely the right to decide between the conflicting claims of relatives of the king. Henry V, while he had no sons, did have two nephews who seemed to have a good right to the throne. They were sons of Frederick of Büren, a faithful supporter of Henry IV, who had been rewarded with the hand of the emperor's daughter and the duchy of Swabia. These sons, who took their family name of Hohenstaufen from a favorite castle, were dukes of Swabia and Franconia and were closely allied to other powerful men. But the other princes still hated the old royal family for its attempts to curtail their power, and the supporters of the pope feared that a Hohenstaufen might try to continue the policies of the last two Henries. Consequently, the hereditary principle was set aside completely for the first time since 918, and Lothair, duke of Saxony, was chosen as king.

The Hohenstaufen brothers were naturally furious at this choice and waged a long, unsuccessful war against Lothair. This futile struggle was notable chiefly for the first appearance of the names Guelf and Ghibelline. Lothair, to gain support, had married his daughter and heiress to the Welf or Guelf duke of Bavaria, and hence his followers were called Guelfs. The adherents of the Hohenstaufen became known as Ghibellines, from the Italian form of one of their possessions, Waiblingen. Then, since Lothair and his heirs were generally friendly to the Church, while the Hohenstaufen became its chief opponents, Guelf came to be the name of the party which supported the papacy, and Ghibelline the name of the imperial party. Finally, like so many other party names, Guelf and Ghibelline became labels for factions in the Italian cities which contested for power without much regard for principles of any kind.

As might have been expected, Lothair was too troubled by the Hohenstaufen opposition to regain any power for the monarchy. When he died in 1137 the younger Hohenstaufen, Conrad III, was accepted as king. Many Germans had been disturbed by the abandonment of the hereditary principle in 1125, and Conrad's election was a vindication of the claims of his family. But it was also a new proof of the princes' fear of a powerful ruler. Lothair's heir was his son-in-law, Henry the Proud, duke of Bavaria in his own right and ruler of Saxony and Tuscany as successor to the late king. Henry might have seriously disturbed Conrad had he not died too soon—in 1139. However, his son Henry the Lion was to continue the family tradition of rivalry to the Hohenstaufen. This division of German leadership between the two rival families was a constant source of weakness to the kingdom, and Conrad III had almost as much trouble as Lothair.

Yet these two reigns were not entirely barren. Under Lothair the resistance of the Slavs was at last broken, and the eastward movement, checked since the days of Otto III, was resumed with tremendous energy. Before 1200 the area of German settlement was pushed up to the borders of Poland. The Baltic seacoast, long barred to German merchants, was opened, and many new trading cities, the most important of which was Lübeck, were founded. This conquest of the eastern territories started a great migration from the Rhine Valley to the lands about the Oder—a migration which, as we have seen, brought about profound changes in rural life. It also caused a shift in the balance of political power within Germany. The rulers of the East had larger territories and greater authority than the magnates of old Germany. They were not bothered by the overlapping rights and irrational boundaries which showed the antiquity of the political arrangements of the West. The king had taken little part in the expansion to the East and so had little authority there. The eastern princes could start with a clean slate, and amid the dangers of the conquest they could preserve a large degree of discipline among their followers. Thus as time went on the states of East Germany began to overshadow those of the West, a development which still further weakened the king, whose power was greatest in the old centers of German life along the Rhine. Even when the Polish frontier was reached, the eastward movement did not stop. Poland itself could not be conquered, but more of the Baltic seaboard could be acquired. During the later Middle Ages, under the leadership of military orders, the Germans settled East Prussia and gained temporary possession of the district of Courland farther north. Thus German influence became preponderant among the northern Slavs. Bohemia was already a vassal kingdom, full of German settlers. Poland, surrounded by Germans on two sides, accepted Western civilization in its German form. And even the Russian principalities, with their Byzantine inheritance, were influenced by the fact that almost all their contacts with the West were through Germans.

The quarrels between Guelf and Hohenstaufen had made many men pessimistic about the future of the German kingdom. Otto of Freising, a half-brother of Conrad III who was a Cistercian monk and later bishop of Freising, gives a very gloomy picture of conditions in Germany in his "Book of the Two States." He felt that the German kingdom was ruined and that the end of the world was near at hand. There was no hope except in the heavenly state, which was soon to come. Yet this same Otto was soon to write an historical work in a very optimistic mood. Conrad had not been as unsuccessful as he seemed; he had started to build up a royal domain which was to give the German ruler one last chance at power. And he had planted his family firmly on the throne; at his death his nephew Frederick "Barbarossa" was unanimously elected king.

Frederick was a Hohenstaufen, but his mother was a Guelf and there was some hope that he could conciliate the two parties. He was young, magnetic, and handsome. His accession was hailed with joy, especially by Otto, his uncle, who began his "Deeds of Frederick" with high hopes that civil strife would end and the Empire again be strong. These hopes seemed well on their way to fulfilment during the early years of the reign. Frederick was both energetic and tactful. He conciliated the Guelfs by allowing Henry the Lion, the Guelf duke of Saxony, to take over the equally Guelf duchy of Bavaria. He kept the lay and ecclesiastical magnates quiet by allowing them full control of their own territories, requiring only that they render him feudal service in time of need. At the same time he worked quietly and steadily to build up the royal domain along the Rhine. He traded outlying lands for rights of jurisdiction that cut into his own territories and so consolidated his power in one district after another. He gained the good will of the Rhine cities, which were already wealthy and powerful, and encouraged the growth of smaller places by grants of commercial rights. He obtained the "advocacies" of many monasteries, which meant that he administered their estates and exercised their governmental rights in return for his protection. He tried to unify these heterogeneous rights by establishing officials at key points (usually castles), who would exert all his powers in a given district. These officials were often *ministeriales,* men who at that time were still so inferior to the nobles that it seemed unlikely that they could ever gain independent power. In short, Frederick was trying to build up a state within Germany which would have made him independent of all other powers. It was rather late for such an effort; the magnates were creating similar competing organizations which hemmed in his territories, and his officials became more independent than he had expected. Nevertheless, by consolidating his domain and by enforcing his right as feudal lord he might have succeeded in creating a solid basis of power for his family had he not become involved in Italian affairs.

It is difficult to find any absolute necessity for Frederick's first expedition to Italy in 1154. He had effective control of the German church, and the pope was too involved in Italian difficulties to protest. Frederick's strength is shown by the fact that he made the bishop of Zeitz archbishop of Magdeburg and obtained the pope's consent to this illegal exercise of royal power. For whatever the king's rights in regard to elections, only the pope could transfer a bishop from one see to another. Yet Frederick was not satisfied with his power in Germany; he wanted to control Italy as well. He was young and proud; he undoubtedly dreamed of the glory to be won by a successful expedition. He was also annoyed by the slowness with which his projects were going in Germany. He may have felt that the wealth of the Italian cities would enable him to move faster, that a royal domain across the Alps would be richer and safer from the princes than anything which he could create in Germany. Finally, central and northern Italy were in such a state of disorder that they were bound to tempt an ambitious man. The Italian towns, which had profited more than those of any other region from the revival of commerce, were now the most powerful political organizations in the land. But within each town various factions were striving for leadership, and the weaker party was often ready to ask for outside aid. Each town was seeking a monopoly of economic and political power in its district, and so there was always friction and frequently open war between neighboring towns. The papacy itself was having serious difficulty with the people of Rome, who were trying to gain self-government under the leadership of Arnold of Brescia, and the pope was consequently favorable to German intervention.

The career of Arnold shows how difficult it was for the Church to keep control of the new forces which were emerging in the twelfth century. Arnold was a cleric who was born at Brescia about 1100. He had studied at Paris under a famous radical teacher, Peter Abelard,[3] and he soon became more radical than his master. He taught that the Church ought to give up its temporal power and wealth and return to apostolic poverty. He stirred up a revolution in his native Brescia and was banished from Italy as a dangerous character. He took refuge in France, but was soon expelled by abbot Bernard of Clairvaux, the most influential church-

[3] See below, pp. 263–265.

man of that kingdom. He finally found a haven in Zurich, where he lived until a revolution in Rome gave him an opportunity to return to Italy. This Roman revolution resembled those in other towns, though it had peculiar characteristics derived from the ancient traditions of the city. The pope, like many of the bishops of northern Europe, had allowed his subjects no self-government. The great feudal families—the Pierleoni, the Frangipani, the Colonna and the Orsini—who had actual control of the city, had oppressed both the lesser nobles and the people. This led to a revolt in 1143, in which the oppressed classes attempted to establish a self-governing commune. In memory of the old Roman forms, the people assembled on the Capitol hill and chose a patrician and fifty-six senators to rule them. When the pope attempted to seize the Capitol in 1145 he was fatally wounded by a stone. Arnold then went to Rome and soon became the real leader of the people. Thus the intellectual radicalism which grew out of the twelfth century Renaissance was united with the revolutionary spirit of the rising urban class, and the pope was temporarily helpless before the combination.

Arnold and the Romans had tried to ally themselves with Conrad III, and after the election of Frederick they renewed their attempt to get German support. They dreamed of a real Roman Empire, in which the city and people of Rome would have a predominant influence. But Frederick was not tempted by the offers of revolutionary fanatics; he had a surer basis of support in his alliances with the pope and cities of northern Italy. He set out for Rome in 1154 and met very little opposition from the Italians. He was crowned king of Italy at Pavia, and easily and cruelly crushed some cities in the North that opposed him. He then went to Rome, where he was crowned emperor by the pope in St. Peter's, but he was not able to occupy the city because of the opposition of the rebellious Roman people. However, the pope, now that he had the emperor's support, was able to get rid of his worst enemy. He had placed Rome under an interdict, which cut off a large part of the income of the Roman people, since pilgrims no longer frequented the city. Unlike other towns, which strove successfully for independence, Rome had little trade and manufacturing. It was a sort of medieval Washington, drawing its income from the papal court and the litigants and tourists who flocked to the capital of Christendom. The Romans could not bear the interdict, but the pope would not raise it until they agreed to expel Arnold, which they did early in 1155. He was captured in Tuscany and turned over to Frederick, who had him burned. His ashes were cast into the Tiber, lest the people, who were still attached to him, might worship his relics. But Frederick departed before the pope could crush the commune, and Rome remained independent for many years.

Thus far pope and emperor had worked together, but not entirely without friction. When they first met, Frederick had refused to hold the bridle of the pope's horse, and the latter consequently refused him the kiss of peace. It took a full day of negotiations to convince Frederick that it was customary for the emperor to hold the pope's horse and that it was no derogation of the imperial dignity. This inauspicious beginning of the relations between Frederick and Adrian IV, the only English pope, was followed by a serious quarrel as the result of a letter which the pope sent to Frederick while he was holding a diet at Besançon, in the kingdom of Burgundy, in 1157. In this letter the pope referred to the *beneficia* which he had given the emperor. The imperial chancellor translated *beneficia* as "fiefs," the usual meaning of the word at this time. This seemed to imply that the emperor was the pope's vassal, and the cardinal who brought the letter made matters worse by asking: "From whom, then, does the emperor hold his power, if not from the pope?" Frederick was thoroughly angry and ordered the legate to leave at once. He probably had heard the tale, recorded in the "Chronicle" of Otto of Freising, that the pope had had a painting made of the coronation of Lothair, with an inscription which read: "Then he became the man [vassal] of the pope, from whom he received the gift of the crown." Frederick wrote an open letter to his subjects declaring that he held his power from God alone, by the election of the princes. The pope, after sounding the opinion of the German nobles and bishops and finding it strongly on the emperor's side, wrote a conciliatory letter explaining that the chancellor had made a bad translation—that *beneficia* meant kindnesses, not fiefs. This closed the incident, but the pope and emperor remained suspicious of each other. Adrian began to feel that imperial intervention was a greater danger than any act of the Italian communes, while Frederick saw that he could never control Italy unless he could use, or at least neutralize, papal power.

The papacy gradually turned to a policy of alliance with the communes of North Italy. This was a disagreeable step to many churchmen, for the communes were hostile to the secular power of the bishops, and many townsmen were infected with heretical or anti-clerical ideas. Yet the military strength of the towns was too great to be ignored. They were well fortified, densely populated, and their citizens were accustomed to fighting. They were perfectly ready to attack any one who injured them; the great merchants who dominated their governments felt themselves as good as any noble. Otto of Freising could not restrain his indignation in writing about these men of low birth, who carried on despised trades and yet were armed like knights and held high offices in the cities. While the towns were ready to fight when necessary, they had not taken a very important part in the earlier strife between pope and emperor. During the investiture struggle both parties had vied with each other in according privileges to the northern or Lombard towns in order to secure their support, but neither had gained much assistance. Only after repeated aggression on Frederick's part was the rather unnatural alliance between pope and communes consummated.

As we have seen, each town was trying to crush or dominate its neighbors. Milan, the most important city on the Lombard plain, was especially active in extending its hegemony over other towns. In 1158 it was at the head of a league that included Brescia, Piacenza, Parma and Modena. To protect themselves from this group, Pavia, Cremona, Lodi and Como had formed another league; but as they were still too weak for safety, they sought the aid of Frederick Barbarossa. He was already exasperated against Milan on acount of its "arrogance," and on his first expedition he had destroyed one of its allies. Now he wished to turn "all the forces of the Empire against Milan in order to crush it."

Milan resisted vigorously at first, but had to yield and give hostages as pledges of its loyalty. It also had to promise that the consuls, the chief officials of the town, would seek confirmation by the emperor after election. Encouraged by this success, Frederick determined to restore imperial authority over the Lombard cities. He held a diet on the Roncaglian Plain at which professors of law from the famous school at Bologna helped him to define the imperial prerogatives or "regalia." These men were students of the old Roman law, and naturally had a very exalted idea of the emperor's rights. They ruled that he should control the appointment of the chief officials in each city, the levying of tolls and customs, coinage, mines, and most other sources of revenue. The emperor's forces were so great that the towns had to yield temporarily. Frederick at once placed a new official, the *podestà,* in each city, who was to be his immediate representative, and was to come from outside the place where he held office.

There was much to be said for this new office, and eventually many Italian towns adopted it of their own accord. Most Italian towns were ruled by consuls, who had judicial, administrative, and military powers, but who could take no important step without the advice of a council composed of the wealthier citizens. There might also be a general assembly, but even this seldom included all inhabitants; it was usually restricted to merchants and shop-owners. These governing oligarchies were not always fair to the poorer citizens, and they were usually divided by bitter feuds among themselves. Consequently, town governments were often more interested in promoting the interest of a class or a faction than in the welfare of the whole community. The *podestà,* an outsider with no local interests, was more apt to give even-handed justice. But the towns had been independent too long to allow such a reform to be imposed from the outside, especially as the new imperial officials were not neutral administrative experts, but active agents of a foreign power. Their attempt to revive feudal dues and other payments to the emperor was especially exasperating.

At Milan the attempt to introduce the *podestà* caused a rebellion. The emperor besieged the city, but Milan held out for three years before starvation compelled it to surrender. Frederick at first planned to kill all the citizens, but finally granted them their lives. He insisted that the town be destroyed, and people of neighboring cities hostile to Milan eagerly leveled the walls, filled the moats, and tore down the buildings. Frederick carried away the leading citizens as hostages and forbade all men to build again on the s.te of the rebellious city.

The awful fate of Milan ended all opposition for a time. But it was the final event necessary to convince the pope and the communes that an alliance was necessary. Adrian IV had already ordered the emperor to surrender many of his claims, especially the overlordship of Tuscany and all sovereign rights in Rome. As Frederick naturally refused, the pope allied himself with the king of Sicily, and with the Lombard cities. When Adrian died in 1159 he was succeeded by Alexander III, who as cardinal legate had made the rash speech at Besançon. Frederick knew that Alexander would be an implacable foe and supported an anti-pope elected by a minority of the cardinals, but only Germany recognized the intruder. So Frederick was forced to make a new invasion of Italy.

This expedition, in 1166, was unsuccessful. Frederick succeeded in taking Rome by assault, but an epidemic broke out in his army and compelled a rapid retreat. After great difficulties he regained Germany with only a small remnant of his host. Meanwhile, the cities of north Italy formed the Lombard League (1167) against the emperor. As a first act of defiance they rebuilt Milan, and the restored city recovered its old wealth and power with amazing rapidity. The news of Frederick's disastrous retreat added new members to the league—Venice, Bologna, and even old enemies of Milan such as Lodi and Cremona. Alexander III gave his blessing to the league, and the new city of Alessandria, built to control an important river junction, was named in his honor and made the headquarters of the confederation.

Frederick spent the next six years in Germany, continuing the work of building up his domain and striving to end serious quarrels which had arisen between the duke of Saxony and the rulers of the newly conquered eastern lands. Then, in 1174, feeling that Germany was safe, he set out again for Italy. Again he was unsuccessful. He failed to take Alessandria after an arduous siege, and found himself unable to break the Lombard League by force or diplomacy. Then in 1176 the despised town militias fell on the emperor's army at Legnano and inflicted a crushing defeat. The Lombard League, and its ally the pope, had triumphed completely.

Frederick was wise enough to know that he was beaten. He promptly reconciled himself with Alexander III and secured papal ratification of the appointments to important Church offices which he had made in

Germany during the schism. In 1183 he made the Peace of Constance with the Lombard League, in which he surrendered almost all the claims made at the Roncaglian diet. A vague imperial suzerainty was retained and the emperor received some payments from the towns in return for ceding his rights. But he had lost direct control, the towns were now virtually independent, with the right to elect their own officers and collect their own taxes. Yet Frederick's position was no worse than it had been at the beginning of the reign. Once the threat of imperial domination ended, the coalition against Frederick dissolved. The towns began to wage local wars, and Italy sank back into its state of disunion and weakness. Frederick gained some control over the towns of Tuscany, to replace his losses in Lombardy, and he remained influential in Italian politics.

When Frederick gave up his hopes of establishing a rich imperial domain in the Po Valley, it became more important than ever for him to build up his strength in Germany. But in Germany the princes also were creating compact, well-administered domains—"states" which were rivals of the one which was being formed by the Hohenstaufen. The most powerful of these rival states was that which Henry the Lion, duke of Saxony and Bavaria, had built up in northern Germany. Frederick apparently determined to make an example of this ruler; if Henry were defeated, lesser princes might yield without a fight. Henry had naturally made many enemies in building up his domain, and they carried their grievances to Frederick. The duke was summoned to answer their charges at the imperial diet of 1179. He refused to obey, confiding in his strength and his alliances with the kings of Denmark and England. He was cited to appear three times and on his failure to obey was condemned to forfeit his fiefs and to banishment. This was strictly in accordance with feudal usage, and shows what important results could follow from failure to fulfill the obligation of court service. Henry's attempts to resist were useless; in less than two years Frederick had conquered Saxony and forced the duke to submission. Saxony and Bavaria were taken from him and he was sent into exile. After a few years he was allowed to return, but of all his vast possessions he kept only Brunswick and Lüneberg, which were not fiefs of the Empire.

Frederick had not only broken the power of his most dangerous rival; he had also shown the way in which feudal obligations could be used to strengthen the monarchy. As we have seen, earlier German rulers had treated feudalism as a private arrangement which had no connection with the government. As a result, many of the nobles held lands and jurisdictions for which they owed no service to the king. They might have vassals of their own, but they were not vassals of the emperor. Thus there were many feudal groups, but no feudal system in which all power was derived directly or indirectly from one suzerain. Frederick had worked to change this, with a great deal of success. He insisted on the feudal obligations of the bishops; he tried to connect all the nobles to himself by feudal ties. As we shall see, in France and England the kings were able to increase central power greatly by the fact that they were universal suzerains, and Frederick's policy might have produced the same effects in Germany if it had continued for a century. But the centralization of German feudalism was begun too late, and Frederick could not complete the work in his own lifetime. Thus Brunswick, which was not a fief, could not be confiscated from Henry the Lion, and this territory was large enough to be a basis for future revolt. Even worse, the princes were able to insist that Frederick had no right to keep the forfeited duchies of Saxony and Bavaria. They had to be granted to members of the princely group, and thus a great opportunity to enlarge the royal domain was lost. Frederick's successors were unable to change this rule, and in the end German feudalism worked to strengthen the princes rather than the central government.

The last years of Frederick's reign were prosperous. His setback in Italy had not weakened him in Germany. There was still suspicion between emperor and pope, but the latter had been seriously weakened by the marriage of Frederick's son Henry to Constance, the heiress of the Norman kingdom of Sicily. The Normans had long been allies of the pope; now this support was lost. Yet Frederick, the great opponent of the papacy, was to die in a papal cause. The leadership of the Church was shown not only in its struggles with the Empire, but also in its organization of the crusades. And Frederick could not resist crusade propaganda any more than rulers who had always been obedient to the pope. He started on the Third Crusade and was drowned while bathing in a small stream in Asia Minor in 1190.

Frederick's death left the papacy in a very difficult position. The emperor left an heir who had already been crowned king, so that there was no hope of weakening the Hohenstaufen power by encouraging the princes to elect a representative of some other family to rule Germany. Worse, this heir, Henry VI, had a position in Italy which was far stronger than any his father enjoyed, since he had a claim through his wife to the Norman kingdom of Sicily. We have already seen how the Normans, especially the great king Roger II, had built up a powerful kingdom in the South. The kings who succeeded Roger had not been so able, but Sicily was still the most highly centralized state in Europe. Its kings could legislate for, and draw taxes from, the whole country at a time when other rulers were bound by local customs and limited to feudal revenues. Now this concentrated power was to pass into the hands of the natural opponent of the papacy; the papal states were to lie between the hammer of German invasion and the anvil of the Sicilian monarchy.

Henry's power seemed too great to many other men besides the pope, and his accession was greeted with a series of rebellions. The Norman nobles hated the idea of being ruled by a foreigner and set up a king of their own, Tancred. The party of Henry the Lion gave them support by a rebellion in Germany. The pope had reluctantly crowned Henry emperor, but refused to recognize his right to Sicily and supported Tancred. It was the old combination of a hostile papacy and rebellious nobles which had defeated so many emperors, but Henry was more fortunate and more skilful than his predecessors. He captured King Richard of England, who was crossing through his lands in disguise,[4] and extorted a tremendous ransom in return for freeing him. The German rebels, who were already hard pressed, realized that they could not hold out against a ruler with practically unlimited resources, and came to terms. As Henry moved south King Tancred of Sicily died and Norman resistance collapsed. The rest of the opposition was easily disposed of. Henry established his brother as ruler of Tuscany and built up a league of cities friendly to him to oppose the remnant of the Lombard League. Even Otto the Great had not had the power of Henry VI; he was feared and obeyed from the tip of Sicily to the German outposts on the Baltic.

Many German historians have speculated as to what might have happened if Henry VI had lived. Hard, cold, and intelligent, with no illusions and no scruples (witness his capture of the crusader, Richard), could he have unified Germany under his powerful rule? Or were the opponents of imperial authority already so strong that even Henry could not have restrained them more than a few years? There can be no answer to these questions, for Henry died in 1197 when he was only thirty-two. He was the last ruler who might have made something of the Empire. His death left the succession in dispute, and for more than eighteen years Germany had no real ruler. During this troubled time the papacy strengthened its position and prepared the way for the downfall of the medieval Empire.

THE FIRST CRUSADE

The crusades are much more than a romantic episode in the history of the Middle Ages. On the one hand, they show the terrific energy and the unbounded optimism of the new civilization which was rising in Europe. It took supreme confidence and sublime indifference to the realities of politics and geography to dream of establishing a Christian outpost in the heart of the Moslem world, at a time when Europe had barely recovered from the last invasions. On the other hand, the crusades show how the Church acted to turn the new energy and optimism of Europe to the service of its ideals. Even more than the investiture controversy, the crusades established the leadership of the Church.

The crusading ideal had been slowly growing during the tenth and

---

[4] See below, p. 243.

eleventh centuries. Popes had headed armies to drive the Saracens out of Italy; the German attack on the heathen Baltic Slavs was carried on in the name of religion; and the slow reconquest of Spain was aided by the Church. In Spain especially, many features of the later crusades may be found. Adventurous nobles, recruited in France, were sent to fight against the infidels, and the Cluniacs were especially active in encouraging this work. Thus there was a close connection between the reforming element in the Church and the nascent crusading movement—a connection which found expression when Gregory VII planned to send assistance to the hard-pressed Eastern Emperor. Gregory was never able to carry out his plan, but his successors, reformers like himself, did not forget the project.

There were many reasons why a pope at the end of the eleventh century should have desired to send an expedition against the Moslems. The Eastern Empire, while it had rallied from the defeat of Manzikert (1071), was still weak and the Turks had reached the shores of the Ægean. The papacy had no great love for the schismatic Greeks, but the schism was recent and it still seemed possible that it might be healed. And what better way to do it than to rescue the Byzantine Empire from its most dangerous enemies? Moreover, since the violence of feudal life could be atoned for only with equally harrowing penances, more and more men were undertaking the most severe penance of all, the pilgrimage to the Holy Land. This was especially true after the reform movement in the Church had begun to take effect. We know of six pilgrimages in the eighth century, twelve in the ninth, sixteen in the tenth, and one hundred and seventeen in the eleventh, before the First Crusade. Seven thousand Germans, under the leadership of their bishops, are said to have set out for Jerusalem in 1065. Great nobles made the journey; for example Fulk Nerra, count of Anjou, who visited the Holy City at least thrice, or Duke Robert of Normandy, the father of William the Conqueror. The difficulties of the journey were so great that it was at least an even chance that the pilgrim would die; when the rulers of the Holy Land added blackmail and violence to the hazards, it seemed most unfair. On the whole, the Abbasid caliphs had given adequate protection to pilgrims, but Palestine was now divided between a fanatical caliph of Cairo who hated Christians and a group of petty princes who could not protect them. The large number of pilgrims, and their difficulties, gave the pope at once an interest and a reason for interference in the affairs of the Near East.

There were also reasons nearer home. All the warlike nobles were not fighting Saracens and heathen; there was still plenty of violence and plundering among Christians. The investiture struggle was still dragging on; Henry IV had not yet met his final defeat. If the Church could remove some of the more belligerent nobles, it would have a better chance of carrying on its work of establishing peace and order in Europe. If it could create a European army under papal control, it would definitely assert its leadership and deprive the Emperor of his old position as the most important political figure on the continent.

The occasion for acting on these ideas came in 1095. The reigning pope, Urban II, had called a great council at Piacenza to consider reforms. At this council envoys of Alexius Comnenus, the Eastern emperor, appeared and asked for aid. Historians have long disputed as to what aid Alexius requested, and indeed, whether an official embassy was ever sent. It seems fairly certain that Alexius did ask for help, but apparently he wanted nothing more than a few thousand mercenaries. There were many laymen at the council and he may have hoped that the pope would encourage some of them to enlist in his army. Urban, however, saw the opportunity for a great stroke of diplomacy and began to make plans in which Alexius' needs played only a minor rôle. He consulted leaders in southern France, a region which had more than its share of turbulent nobles and also close contacts with Cluny and Spain. Encouraged by what he heard, he called a council to meet at Clermont in Auvergne in the late fall. Huge throngs gathered, brought together by the rumor of some great undertaking, and no building could hold the people who wanted to hear the pope. At Clermont, in the open air, on 25 November, 1095, Urban delivered the most effective oration recorded in history.

The pope began by praising the valor of the Franks and recalling to them the great deeds of their ancestors. Then he spoke of the necessity of aiding their brethren in the East, of the appeals for help that had come so frequently because of the victorious advance of the Turks. He dwelt at length on the sufferings that were inflicted on the Christians and on the desecration of the holy places. He gave examples of cruelty and aroused deep emotions in his hearers by pointing out the manner in which the places they held most sacred were being defiled. Then, emphasizing the special sanctity of Jerusalem, he declared that this was God's own work, that for all who participated the journey would take the place of all other penance. He urged them to engage in righteous warfare instead of wasting their strength and imperiling their souls by civil strife at home. Cruelty and greed were reducing many inhabitants of France to starvation. Here was an opportunity for acquiring homes in a land flowing with milk and honey and securing at the same time eternal rewards. He urged them not to let any ties prevent them from entering upon this holy undertaking in which Christ himself would be their leader.

This speech aroused the utmost enthusiasm and thousands pressed forward to take the cross. Urban seems to have been surprised at his own success; not only men of military age but cripples, women, and children clamored to take part in the great pilgrimage. The pope found it necessary to check the excessive enthusiasm by ordering that women should not go without the consent of their husbands, that priests and monks should not go without the consent of their superiors, and that old men and children should not go at all. But he was powerless to stay the flood that he had released. From beginning to end, the First Crusade was encumbered by hosts of non-combatants.

After Clermont, Urban preached the crusade in other places, but his task soon became one of organization rather than propaganda. He needed high-ranking nobles to command the divisions of the army, and knights to fight under their orders, not a motley crowd of pilgrims. His first great success came the day after the speech, when ambassadors of Count Raymond of Toulouse, the most powerful lord of the South, came to say that their lord had taken the cross. Gradually others joined in, Duke Robert of Normandy, Duke Godfrey of Lorraine, Hugh the Great, brother of the king of France, Count Robert of Flanders, the wealthy Count Stephen of Blois, and two Norman princes from southern Italy, Bohemond and Tancred. Fighting men slowly gathered around these leaders; it was said that some came from the uttermost islands of the sea and indicated by signs their desire to take part in the crusade. The work of organizing the armies and planning their lines of march took time, and Urban wanted to delay the departure of the crusaders until the late summer of 1096.

The crusade was more than a political and military project; it was a phase of the religious revival of the eleventh century. Men were no longer content with mere negative virtues; they wanted to make spectacular sacrifices for their faith. Even the pope could not control the tremendous emotional response to the idea of the crusade. Wandering preachers seized upon it and used it as a text for their revival meetings. They paid no attention to the practical problems which it involved; they looked upon it as an act of faith and piety. They assured their hearers that the infidels would flee without resistance from the banner of the cross and that walled towns would fall like Jericho before the pilgrim host. The most successful of these preachers was Peter the Hermit, who was formerly given credit for the whole movement. It is now perfectly clear that Peter had nothing to do with initiating the crusade, but he was very effective in popularizing it. He went through a large part of France, mounted upon a mule, preaching wherever he could find an audience. His arms and feet were bare, he ate very little, he preached repentance, and he soon came to be regarded as a saint. "Even the hairs were snatched from his mule to be preserved as relics." Throngs of people surrounded him, and when he reached Cologne in March, 1096, thousands had determined to follow him on his crusade.

Peter's followers were largely from the lower and middle classes, many peasants, some knights, and no great lords. They could not understand the pope's reasons for delay and insisted on an immediate start. Two bands, each numbering some thousands, set out in the spring of 1096 and marched across Germany, through Hungary and Bulgaria, and down to Constantinople. The first band had a remarkably successful march, but the second, which Peter led, was inclined to pillage instead of paying for its provisions. The Eastern peoples could not see that this was the will of God, and Peter's group was severely handled, especially by the Bulgarians. When the bands arrived at Constantinople the emperor was disagreeably surprised. Instead of the soldiers for whom he had asked, he was burdened with a poverty-stricken horde of untrained peasants. However, he tried to treat them decently, giving them a camp site near Constantinople and warning them not to advance into the enemies' territory. Unfortunately, some were unruly and fought with the Greeks, others could not pay for their provisions, and some were even accused of stealing lead from the roof of a church in order to sell it. Alexius soon felt that he had to get rid of them and shipped them across the straits, with one last warning to leave the Turks alone. They were too sure of their holy mission to pay much attention to this advice, and their chronic shortage of food practically forced them to pillage Turkish territory. The Turks immediately assembled an army, fell on the pilgrims, and almost exterminated them.

Other popular leaders had even worse luck. The people of the Danube route were thoroughly annoyed with these pious plunderers, and cut to pieces several bands which tried to march through their lands. As usual, there were demagogues and hypocrites who used a religious movement for their own purposes. Some of the Rhineland leaders turned the crusade against the Jews, with the plausible argument that they were just as much infidels as the Turks, and a great deal easier to attack. Conscientious churchmen tried to prevent this perversion of the crusading ideal, but the mobs could not be stopped. The Rhineland Jews were robbed and massacred, much to the profit of the leaders of the bands. These excesses, however, completed the work of discrediting the unorganized crusades, and they were never again such a problem.

Meanwhile, the real armies were getting under way. They left at different times in the summer and fall of 1096 and followed different routes, planning to meet at Constantinople. Godfrey took the Danube road, through Hungary and Bulgaria to the Greek Empire. Raymond of Toulouse chose the terribly difficult route across Italy, around the head of the Adriatic, and through the mountains to Greece. Robert of Normandy, Robert of Flanders, Hugh the Great and Bohemond all crossed over from Italy to Greece by ship, but at different times. All made their march with reasonable success, though they could not always keep their men from plundering and lost some stragglers as a result. Count Raymond had the greatest difficulty, since he passed through the wildest country, and he was finally compelled to terrify the mountaineers into submission. His chronicler also complains of the fog, which, he says, was so thick that it could be cut with a knife. Bohemond, who had had experience fighting in Greece, knew the country well and took his troops through with little trouble.

One by one the armies arrived at Constantinople. This was as far as their plans carried them, and serious difficulties now arose. To begin with, the attitude of the emperor was not entirely encouraging. He had asked for aid, but had not expected to have any such armies turned loose in his empire. He knew that the Westerners both despised and envied the Greeks. Bohemond and his father Robert Guiscard had almost succeeded in conquering his western provinces a few years before, and if the Normans alone could threaten the Empire, what would happen when they were reinforced by thousands of other barbarians? Gibbon has compared Alexius' plight to that of the "shepherd who was ruined by the accomplishment of his own wishes: he had prayed for water; the Ganges was turned into his grounds, and his cottage was swept away by the inundation." Yet, while the emperor feared the crusaders, he also wished to make use of them. Consequently, he endeavored by cunning, by violence, or by bribery, to win each leader over to his cause. He was aided by the fact that they arrived one by one and so could not present a united front against him. All the leaders were finally brought to take an oath that if they should conquer cities that had once belonged to the Greek Empire, they would restore them to Alexius. The emperor in turn promised that he would aid them in their crusade.

Another difficulty was that the leaders did not trust each other. Count Raymond of Toulouse was described as being "fanatical as a monk and land-greedy as a Norman." Bohemond and Tancred were shrewd and unscrupulous, and were dreaming of founding new Norman principalities in the East. Godfrey of Bouillon, duke of Lorraine, was honest and a hard fighter, but he was not able to dominate the other leaders. His brother Baldwin was an abler politician, but was also more selfish. Robert of Normandy was improvident and not very energetic; Hugh the Great seems to have been even weaker. The official head of the crusade was Bishop Adhemar of Le Puy, who had been the first to take the cross at Clermont and had been made the papal legate. He was a very able man, but it taxed even his gifts to keep peace among leaders of such different temperaments. He could not issue orders; he could only reason and persuade. Considering everything, it was a miracle that the crusaders worked together as well as they did.

They had one great advantage on their side. The Turkish Empire, created only a few years before, was already falling apart. Each local ruler was suspicious of his neighbors and unwilling to give them aid. Moreover, Syria was claimed by both the Turks and the Arab rulers of

Egypt, and neither party had a very solid footing there. Consequently, the crusaders never had to face the united opposition of the Moslems of the East and many petty rulers surrendered to them without a struggle.

Their first military undertaking was against the city of Nicæa, where all the army finally gathered in the summer of 1097. The crusaders besieged the city and brought it to the point of surrender. Just as they were rejoicing over the prospects of pillage, they saw the emperor's flag waving from a city tower. The inhabitants had preferred to surrender to him in order to avoid the horrors of a sack. Many of the crusaders were annoyed and all their old fear of Greek trickery was revived. The emperor tried to calm them by giving money freely to the leaders and, as one chronicler derisively described it, some brass coins to the common people. Consequently, they departed, "some with kindly feelings and others with different emotions." Stephen of Blois wrote home exultantly to his wife that the emperor had given him more money than he got with her dowry. Others, however, were sure that the emperor was merely trying to use them for his own purposes and that he had no interest in the recovery of the Holy Land.

After the fall of Nicæa, the emperor remained behind to complete the reconquest of western Asia Minor, while the crusaders pushed directly overland toward Antioch. The journey was exceedingly difficult, due to lack of water and provisions, and they eventually split their force into two divisions in order to make foraging easier. This was the opportunity for which the Turks had been waiting. On the 4th of July they swooped down on one division at Dorylæum and almost overwhelmed it. As usual in a medieval army, the crusaders had paid almost no attention to communications, and it was more or less by chance that the second division came up in time to rescue the first. The leaders fought so heroically that they redeemed their error in tactics; the Turks were completely defeated, and the road to Antioch was left wide open.

This victory, however, merely created new problems. As the crusaders approached the southern coast of Asia Minor, they found themselves far ahead of the emperor, in a friendly land full of Armenians and other Christians, where there was practically no government. The temptation was almost irresistible for men brought up in the feudal tradition. Leaders began to stake claims to various cities and quarreled bitterly with each other, with the emperor's representatives, and with the more pious crusaders who wanted to push straight on to Jerusalem. In the end most of these claims were abandoned, but one important territory was acquired at this time. Godfrey's brother Baldwin was called to Edessa by the Armenians of the town. He arrived there with a handful of knights, but was soon able to make himself ruler of the city and surrounding territories. The county of Edessa, which he created, was of great strategic value. Located right in the middle of the fertile crescent, it effectively blocked all Mohammedan reinforcements from the East as long as it was in Christian hands. Yet, valuable as Edessa was, Baldwin's example was a bad one. He had deserted the army without consulting his fellow-leaders, and if others had been successful in imitating him, the army would have dissolved in Asia Minor. As it was, the host reached Antioch, but not until late in the year 1098.

Antioch was the key to Syria, but the capture of the city was an arduous task. The crusading host was too small to blockade it effectively, so that there could be no question of starving it into surrender. Moreover, discipline was bad, and the army was improvident. In the first week of the siege they ate up most of their provisions and wasted their time in riotous living. Then, as food began to be scarce, they repented humbly for their sins, sent away evil women, and prayed for divine aid. There seemed little chance of success, but Bohemond found that an Armenian who commanded one of the towers of the city wall was willing to listen to financial arguments. After making sure of the traitor, Bohemond proposed to the other leaders that whoever found a way of capturing the city should be allowed to keep it as a principality. As soon as they agreed, Bohemond led his men to the Armenian's tower, a rope ladder was let down, and the crusaders were soon on the city walls. They opened the gates, and Antioch was captured.

The army found ample provisions in the city and once again devoted itself to feasting and other excesses. They did not even attempt to capture the citadel at the upper end of the town, which was still held by the Turks. Meanwhile a Turkish prince, named Kerbogha, came up with a large army and invested the city. Caught between the relieving army and the Turks in the citadel, the crusaders were in a desperate position. Their provisions were soon exhausted, and men fortunate enough to catch rats sold them for pieces of gold. Peter the Hermit, Stephen of Blois, and others attempted to escape by letting themselves down from the city walls by ropes. They were called contemptuously the "rope-dancers." Peter was captured and brought back, but Stephen of Blois made good his escape and, going northward, met the Greek emperor, who was hastening down with an army. Stephen, to justify his own flight, made the position of the crusaders seem absolutely hopeless, so Alexius retreated and left them to their fate. To the crusaders this was the final proof of his treachery, and their natural indignation led to a series of incidents which made further coöperation with the Eastern Empire almost impossible.

Meanwhile a certain peasant, Peter Bartholomew, had a series of visions, in which he learned that the Holy Lance was buried in a church in Antioch. This lance was the one which had pierced the Saviour's side as he hung upon the cross. The peasant went at first to Bishop Adhemar, who would not believe his story, and then went to Count Raymond, who was more credulous. Men dug all day in the designated place and as night was falling Peter jumped into the hole and came up with the Lance. Most of the leaders seem to have felt very doubtful about the authenticity of the relic, but after due deliberation they decided that it was worth using to arouse the army's enthusiasm. They also decided that it was better to sally out and fight while they were still strong enough to bear their weapons. Consequently, they marched out against the enemy with Bishop Adhemar bearing the Lance. Kerbogha was miraculously stupid. Instead of cutting them to pieces as they came out of the city, he allowed them to emerge safely and to secure an excellent defensive position where their flanks could not be turned by his larger force. His attack failed and the crusaders began to advance. The Turkish leaders, who were all political rivals, began to fear treachery, some of them started to run away, and when their line broke the battle was won. Kerbogha's army was practically annihilated, and no Moslem force was left in the North which could protect Jerusalem.

As usual, prosperity was bad for the crusaders. Bohemond took over Antioch, not without a good deal of back-biting. Other leaders began scurrying around looking for principalities which they could annex. Bishop Adhemar died, and no one was left with enough authority to keep peace. Disputes broke out as to the genuineness of the Holy Lance, and the crusaders were almost ready to fight about it. Count Raymond still believed in it, but the other leaders, after having used it in their hour of need, were now skeptical. Finally it was agreed to test Peter Bartholomew's honesty by the ordeal of fire. Raymond's chaplain, who believed in the Lance, describes the ceremony as follows:

The leaders and the people to the number of fifty thousand came together; the priests were there also with bare feet, clothed in ecclesiastical garments. The invocation was made: "If Omnipotent God has spoken to this man face to face, and the blessed Andrew has shown him our Lord's Lance while he was keeping his vigil, let him go through the fire unharmed. But if it is false, let him be burned, together with the Lance which he is to carry in his hand." And all responded on bended knees, "Amen." The fire was growing so hot that the flames shot up thirty cubits into the air, and scarcely anyone dared approach it. Then Peter Bartholomew, clothed only in his tunic, and kneeling before the bishop of Albar, called God to witness that he had seen him face to face on the cross, and that he had heard from him those words above written. . . . Then, when the bishop had placed the Lance in his hand, he kneeled and made the sign of the cross, and entered the fire with the Lance, firm and unterrified. For an instant's time he paused in the midst of the flames, and then by the grace of God passed through. . . . But when Peter emerged from the fire so that neither his tunic was burned nor even the thin cloth with which the Lance was wrapped up had shown any sign of damage, the whole people received him after he had made over them the sign of the cross with the Lance in his hand and cried

"God aid us!" All the people, I say, threw themselves upon him and dragged him to the ground, and trampled on him, each one wishing to get a piece of his garment, and each thinking him near some one else. And so he received three or four wounds in the legs where the flesh was torn away, his back was injured, and his side bruised. Peter had died on the spot, as we believe, had not Raymond Pelet, a brave and noble soldier, broken through the wild crowd with a band of friends and rescued him at the peril of their lives. . . . After this Peter died in peace at the hour appointed to him by God, and journeyed to the Lord; and he was buried in the place where he had carried the Lance of the Lord through the fire.

The test, however, did not convince Peter's opponents, who maintained that he had died of burns, and the quarrels continued. Finally the rank and file, more anxious to live up to their vows than the leaders, forced Raymond to promise to lead them to Jerusalem. Most of the other leaders accompanied him, but Bohemond remained in Antioch, and Baldwin in Edessa. The remnant of the army arrived before Jerusalem on 7 June, 1099. At first they hoped that the walls of Jerusalem would fall as those of Jericho, and they marched barefoot around the city, blowing their horns. Finally, by desperate valor, they succeeded in storming the walls, and the city fell into their hands on 15 July. Then followed one of the bloodiest and most pitiless massacres in history. The leaders wrote to the pope: "And if you desire to know what was done with the enemy who were found there, know that in Solomon's Porch and in his Temple our men rode in the blood of the Saracens up to the knees of their horses." And in the evening, weary of slaughter, covered with blood, the crusaders marched to the Church of the Holy Sepulchre where they thanked God for his infinite mercy.

THE KINGDOM OF JERUSALEM

The capture of the city raised a new set of problems. Was Jerusalem to be a secular kingdom or was it to become Church property like Rome? The clergy, of course, wanted the latter solution, but the papal legate was dead and no one else had sufficient authority to enforce their wishes. Then, if there was to be a lay ruler, which leader should obtain the coveted position? After a long period of secret negotiations, Godfrey of Bouillon was finally chosen "baron and defender of the Holy Sepulchre." This title was less annoying to the clergy than that of king and also gave Godfrey little authority over the other leaders. But it was only a provisional solution, and when Godfrey died in the summer of 1100 the whole question was reopened. The newly chosen patriarch of Jerusalem, leader of the clergy, tried to call in Bohemond, but he had just been taken prisoner by the Moslems. Meanwhile, Godfrey's party sent messengers to Baldwin of Edessa, who had been designated as heir by his

CRUSADING STATES

brother. Baldwin, "grieving somewhat at his brother's death, but re-joicing much more over the inheritance," set out for Jerusalem. He in-sisted on having the title and power of a king, and after some hesitation he was finally recognized by the patriarch. Thus Jerusalem became a feudal kingdom, with institutions copied from those of the West.

Setting up a kingdom was hard enough; holding it was even more difficult. Most of the crusaders rushed home as soon as they had com-pleted their pilgrimage, and Baldwin was left with only a handful of knights. The only thing that saved him was the extreme disunion of his enemies. Jerusalem was in the zone where the influence of the Egyptians neutralized that of the Turks; every petty Moslem ruler was striving for independence, and an able king could play one off against another and so preserve the Christian state. Baldwin realized that he would have to live in friendship with many of the natives and he set an example of tolerance in repopulating Jerusalem. As the original inhabi-tants had been massacred when the city was taken, outsiders had to be called in, and Baldwin offered privileges and freedom of trade to all, without distinction of race or creed. Thus the few Europeans were forced to live in close association with Greeks, Syrians, Armenians, Saracens, and others.

From the point of view of geography, the Christian holdings were almost indefensible. Their length, from the extreme north in Edessa to the extreme southern point of Palestine, was somewhat more than five hundred miles, but their breadth was in many places less than fifty miles. The Christians never conquered all the inhabited country between the sea and the desert; indeed it was only gradually that they took all the important coastal cities. Thus there were always Moslem forts in the back country, and there was always an easy line of communications between Moslems of the north and those of the south. There was no stronghold of the Christians that was not within a day's ride of the enemy; the two peoples were always face to face.

Close contact with the Moslems caused a great change in the feelings of the Christians. The preachers of the crusade had taught them con-tempt for the cowardly infidels, but in their first battles they learned to respect the bravery of their enemies, and this paved the way for more intimate relations. In their constant strife with each other, the Moslems welcomed assistance from the Christians, and the latter, who soon quarreled among themselves, were not slow to seek aid in turn from the infidels. Soon alliances between the Franks (the generic name for all Europeans in the Near East) and the Moslems became fre-quent. Both peoples were very fond of hunting, but this sport was im-possible if every chase was liable to lead into an ambush. So hunting agreements were made by antagonists who lived near each other, and hunting parties were freed from the danger of attack. The Franks had taken with them to the Holy Land their horses, hawks, and dogs. Very soon enthusiastic sportsmen among both peoples were comparing the merits of their animals and making trades. There was a good deal of visiting back and forth and some close friendships were formed between the adherents of rival religions.

There were never enough Franks to cultivate the land, or to build the necessary fortresses and churches. Native workmen had to be employed, and they had to be well treated, since it was always easy to escape from Frankish territory. Usually native overseers were given full authority over the workmen, and there was no interference with native customs or religions. In the second half of the twelfth century a Moslem traveler bemoaned the fact that his co-religionists preferred to work for the Franks because they received better treatment and more exact justice.

Close association with the natives led to adoption of new customs by men of the West. First of all, they began to wear the costumes of the country because they were more comfortable and frequently more handsome than their own. They acquired new tastes in food, and especially learned to need sugar and spices. They preferred Oriental houses, with their cool courts and running water, to anything they had known at home. As they became better acquainted with the natives, they recognized the superior knowledge of the Moslems in certain fields. In medicine, for example, they soon learned to prefer Moslem doctors, who had mastered the learning of the ancient world and added observations of their own, while Christian physicians were still struggling to acquire the rudiments of their profession. But the most striking illustration of the effect of the association between the different races is to be found in popular religious ideas. A wonder-working virgin was worshiped by Christians, Moslems, and Jews. Certain shrines were held holy by all races. Moslems said their prayers in Christian chapels. The intense feeling against heresy and schism, which was so strong in the West, was almost non-existent among the Franks in the East. Different sects worshiped in the same church, and once some bishops of the Roman Church actually consecrated a bishop of a schismatic church.

By adapting themselves to the country and by learning to get on with the natives, the crusaders who remained in the Near East were able to overcome many disadvantages. Their numbers were small, and their allegiance was divided among several overlords who were seldom friendly. The rivalries of the First Crusade persisted; the kings of Jerusalem descended from Baldwin, the counts of Tripoli of the house of Raymond of Toulouse, the Norman princes of Antioch, and the counts of Edessa quarreled just as their ancestors had done. Moreover, in each of these larger states there were feudal lords who, after the manner of their kind, resented all higher authority. But the Moslems were even more divided, and the first two kings of Jerusalem, Baldwin I (1100–1118) and Baldwin II (1118–1131), were able to conquer almost all the seaports and to extend the kingdom to the south and east. To secure the seaports, the aid of the Italian cities was necessary, since they were the only Christian states with fleets in the Mediterranean. Thus Arsuf and Cæsarea were conquered in 1101 by the aid of the Genoese, who had bargained for a third of the booty and for a section of the city to be under their administration. Similar terms were demanded and obtained by the Pisans and the Venetians when they aided in the capture of other towns. Thus a new Frankish element was added to the population of the kingdom, and the Mediterranean trade of the Italian cities was increased. The Italians, however, were not very helpful to the king after the coast was occupied. Their autonomy meant that he had no authority in parts of each coastal city, and their interest in trade led them to desire peace rather than further conquests. Additional territory in the interior could be gained only when the royal army was reinforced by bands of pilgrims who came for a few months. These men were often good fighters, but the king had no authority over them, and they never stayed in the Holy Land long enough for extensive campaigns. The two military orders, the Templars and the Hospitalers, whose rise will be discussed elsewhere, were helpful when they coöperated; but they were independent of the king, and in time came to be such bitter rivals that they could not be trusted to work together. Even with the enemy divided, it took great ability on the part of the kings to gain territory with such fluctuating and untrustworthy forces.

THE SECOND AND THIRD CRUSADES

Unfortunately for the Christians, the Moslems were not to remain divided. An able general, Imad-ed-din Zangi, began to conquer the petty states of Syria and the country to the northeast, and eventually gained enough power to attack the Franks. In 1144 he struck at their weakest point, the outlying county of Edessa. The city was strongly fortified but weakly defended, and was captured after a siege of only four weeks. All the northern Moslems could now unite, and every Christian state was exposed to sudden attacks from the rear.

The news of the fall of Edessa made a deep impression on the people of Europe. A new reform movement, under the leadership of St. Bernard of Clairvaux, was sweeping the continent, and once more a crusade seemed a logical means of carrying out many of the reforms. St. Bernard was ordered by the pope to preach the crusade, and he was fairly successful, though there was not the overwhelming response that there had been in 1095. Louis VII of France took the cross, and Bernard eventually succeeded in winning over Conrad III of Germany, much to the latter's surprise. In fact Conrad described his conversion to the crusading cause as "a miracle of miracles." The two armies started out in 1147, but during the difficult passage across Asia Minor most of Conrad's troops were killed and the French suffered a severe defeat. When the two kings reached Jerusalem they decided to attack Damascus. This was not a very wise decision; Damascus was on the whole friendly to the Franks and opposed to Zangi. Even if Damascus had fallen, the threat of the northern Moslems would have remained, and thanks to bad planning the siege was a complete failure. After lengthy recriminations, Conrad and Louis went home in disgust, and the crusading zeal of the West was chilled for a generation.

The failure of the Second Crusade meant that no effective obstacles could be placed in the way of the growing union of the Moslems. Zangi was succeeded by his son Nureddin, who added Damascus to the family possessions. When Nureddin died in 1174 an even greater danger arose. Saladin, who had already conquered Egypt, extended his power over the Moslems of the North, so that the Christian states were surrounded by his territories. He began to nibble at the possessions of the crusaders, and succeeded in taking some of their castles. The Christians were now more divided than the Moslems, and they were as usual short of men. Moreover, many of their leaders had been born in the East, and seemed to lack the vigor of the early adventurers from the West. This was especially true of the royal family, which was failing to produce male heirs. When only daughters were left, there was a mad scramble for their hands, and the disputes of rival claimants to the throne destroyed what unity was left.

The final catastrophe was caused by these quarrels among the Christians. Count Raymond of Tripoli, who advocated peace with the Moslems, made a truce with Saladin while acting as regent of the kingdom. Then a king was installed who was hostile to the peace party headed by Raymond, and the truce was promptly broken by the commander of a border castle. This made Saladin feel that he could not live in peace with his Christian neighbors, and he determined to make a great effort to break their power. All the Christians united to meet the danger, but quarrels broke out again in the army. Count Raymond was trusted neither by the king, whose accession to the throne he had tried to block, nor by the grand-master of the Templars. He was suspected of being unduly friendly with Saladin and as a result his sound advice was neglected. The Christians took up an unfavorable position and in the ensuing battle of Hattin they were completely defeated. The king and his leaders were captured, and so the kingdom was left without any real means of defense. One stronghold after another surrendered, and finally Saladin moved on Jerusalem itself. On 3 October, 1187, the Holy City fell to the Moslem leader, after the Christians had held it for eighty-eight years.

The fall of Jerusalem was a tremendous shock to Europe. The pope seized the opportunity to make peace among the warring monarchs of Europe, especially between the kings of France and England, who had been fighting during most of the twelfth century. Henry II of England and his son Richard, Philip Augustus of France, and Frederick Barbarossa of Germany all took the cross. It was realized that a long-continued effort would be necessary to defeat a ruler as powerful as Saladin, and the pope urged the crusading leaders to raise large sums of money to support their armies. As a result, the so-called Saladin tithe was imposed in France and England, a uniform tax on both income and real estate. Though levied for the benefit of Christendom rather than that of the kings, it encouraged the development of systems of national taxation, especially in England, where the government was strong enough to levy a tax for its own use within six years of the Saladin tithe.

The Third Crusade was well planned, well financed, and was led by the three most powerful rulers of the West. Richard was the best general of his day, Philip Augustus was the best diplomat, and Frederick Barbarossa had shown ability in both fields. Yet with so much in its favor the Third Crusade was cursed by an almost unbroken series of misfortunes. Henry II and Philip began to fight again in spite of their crusading vows. This war ended with the death of Henry in 1189, but meanwhile Frederick had set out alone for the East. He marched into Asia Minor without difficulty, but was drowned while bathing in a small brook. Perhaps the chill of the water gave the old emperor a heart attack; perhaps he was swept away by a sudden freshet. His death ended the crusading zeal of his followers. Most of them returned home to look after their interests, and only a small number continued the expedition.

Meanwhile Richard, now king of England, and Philip Augustus set out together by sea. Richard was really interested in the crusade, but he was even more interested in fighting every one he met. Philip hated the crusade into which he had been forced by public opinion; he was anxious to get back to his work of increasing the French royal domain. The two kings quarreled bitterly while they were resting in Sicily and Philip sailed at once for Palestine. Richard proceeded more leisurely, acquiring several new enemies on the way. He first quarreled with Tancred of Sicily and then promised to support him against the new emperor Henry VI, thus gaining the latter's ill will. He married a poverty-stricken Spanish princess who brought him no dowry and gave him no heirs. He conquered Cyprus from a relative of the Eastern Emperor and so turned the Greeks against him. Then he was ready to join the other crusaders at the siege of Acre.

This city was the most important port of Palestine, and the Christians had to take it before they could hope to regain other territories. Saladin was watching the Christian camp and attempting to rescue Acre, but the crusaders had sufficient strength to hold him off. Acre, however, was so well fortified that the siege dragged on for many weary months, and the crusaders came to hate each other almost as much as they did the Moslems. The enmity between Philip and Richard spread to their followers, and conditions became so bad that it was not safe to lead the English and French forces into action at the same time, lest they turn their weapons against each other. Richard also quarreled with the duke of Austria, and thus completed his work of alienating every important ruler from the Bosporus to the Bay of Biscay. The walls of Acre had to be torn down almost stone by stone; Richard offered a large sum for every stone dislodged, and so encouraged his followers to great deeds of valor. Finally the defenses of the city were so weakened that it surrendered on 12 July, 1191, after a siege of over twenty-one months.

During the progress of the siege some Germans had made awnings from sails and had turned their vessels into hospitals to care for the wounded. Their work was greatly admired, and from this humble beginning grew the great Teutonic Order. But this order, unlike those of the Temple and the Hospital, soon transferred its operations to Europe. It became the spear-head of the German drive to the East, and slowly conquered Baltic territories from the heathen Prussians. The former German province of East Prussia corresponds roughly to the territories which the Teutonic Order first occupied.

Another event of the siege throws some light on the ideals of the knights of the West. The Third Crusade is famous in romantic literature, and Richard is equally famous as the best knight of the late twelfth century. Richard did treat Saladin with respect; the two exchanged messages and presents, though they never met. But this same chivalrous Richard executed 2700 captives, taken at the surrender of Acre, because the ransom promised for them was not paid at the appointed time. The massacre was especially reprehensible since Saladin had released the prisoners captured in Jerusalem in 1187, even though the ransom demanded for them was not completely paid.

After the fall of Acre little was accomplished. Philip slipped away home and was soon making all the trouble he could for Richard, encouraging rebellions against him in England and attacking his French possessions. Richard remained and won some hard-fought battles, but he never had quite enough strength to risk a direct attack on Jerusalem. He did become a legendary figure in Moslem as well as Christian folk-lore; when an Arab horse shied without cause, his rider said that he had seen Richard in the bushes; when a babe cried the mother threatened him with King Richard. But these personal triumphs did not make the Third

Crusade a success, and Richard finally found it necessary to make peace, since his affairs at home were going very badly. Saladin was also anxious for peace and offered fairly good terms. By a truce made in September, 1192, it was agreed that pilgrims could enter Jerusalem freely, and the remnant of the Christian kingdom was secured for a time from attack. This truce and the capture of Acre prolonged the life of the kingdom of Jerusalem for another century, but it remained a mere strip of seacoast with no military strength.

The final episode of the crusade was the capture and ransoming of Richard. Instead of returning home by sea, which was safe but slow, Richard tried to rush across Europe in disguise. He was recognized and captured by the duke of Austria, whom he had offended at the siege of Acre. The emperor Henry VI, who had his own reasons for disliking Richard, compelled the duke to hand over the illustrious prisoner. Philip Augustus of France, who hated Richard even more than the German rulers, offered huge sums if Henry would prolong the king's captivity. Henry was not quite ready to do this, but he did demand an enormous ransom from Richard, even though every crusader was supposed to be safe from his enemies during his travels. Richard had to promise to pay £100,000—more than three times the normal annual revenue of England. To obtain this money new general taxes had to be imposed throughout England. Thus the ransom really aided the monarchy, in the long run, by giving it another precedent for taxation, however embarrassing it was for Richard. The ransom payment was also embarrassing for the papacy, since it showed that it could not enforce its rules giving immunity to crusaders. In fact, the whole Third Crusade demonstrated the limitations of the papal program. The crusading ideal gave the papacy an excuse for intervening in European politics, but it was not a strong enough ideal to enable the papacy to impose its settlement of political questions. The crusade had not stopped the enmity between France and England, nor had it produced a general peace in Europe. In fact, the crusade had failed because the leaders could not forget their old quarrels and because they had begun new disputes in the very face of the enemy. The papacy continued to use the crusade as an argument for European peace and as an excuse for intervening in European diplomacy—tactics which were occasionally very successful. But the hope that a united Christendom would place all its military forces at the disposal of the pope and fight only under his direction was definitely ended by the results of the Third Crusade.

THE REFORM MOVEMENT IN THE TWELFTH CENTURY

The religious revival which had begun in the eleventh century continued to be one of the most important features of twelfth century civilization. The monks were still the leaders, both in encouraging popular piety and in aiding the papacy to increase its control of the administration of the Church. The same impulse which sent thousands on the crusade sent thousands of other men and women into monasteries. In fact, after the first wave of crusading enthusiasm had spent itself, many felt that it was more salutary to enter a monastery than to go to the Holy Land, where worldly temptations were not lacking. As a result there was a striking increase in the number of monks and nuns, and many new orders were founded.

The influence of the Congregation of Cluny remained very great. Most of the new orders followed its policy of grouping many establishments under one head, in order to preserve discipline and increase their influence. Eventually even the Benedictine monasteries, which had had no common bond, were grouped into congregations which had general assemblies and regular inspection by "papal visitors." But while the organization of Cluny was copied, many of the reformers felt that its discipline was not sufficiently severe. The original Benedictine rule had made large allowance for human frailty, and Cluny had done little more than demand strict observance of the Benedictine rule. This was not enough to satisfy the desire for a life of extreme asceticism, and the more earnest monks of the period wanted higher standards which would demand greater sacrifices. The more prosperous Europe became, the greater were the fears caused by the new wealth. Asceticism was in some respects a reaction against the growth of a money economy.

This movement toward greater asceticism began in Italy in the eleventh century with the foundation of the order of Camaldoli. This order was composed of hermits living in detached cells, with as little social life as possible. It gave effective aid to the popes in their efforts toward reform. A little later, the order of Vallombrosa was established, which made an innovation in monastic practice by separating the monks into choir brothers and lay brothers. The latter were those who from lack of education were unable to chant the offices. To them was assigned the rougher work, so that the choir brethren might have more leisure for study, contemplation, and prayer. This division of duties was adopted by other orders, but it sometimes caused trouble. In the order of Grammont, the choir brothers complained that the lay brothers tried to dominate them, even in purely spiritual matters, and enforced their orders by cutting off supplies.

In France the order of Carthusians was established toward the close of the eleventh century in the mountains near Grenoble. It had the reputation of requiring a more austere mode of life than any other order; its monks were not allowed to speak except in case of necessity. Peter the Venerable, abbot of Cluny, described their life as follows:

Their dress is meaner and poorer than that of other monks, so short and scanty and so rough that the very sight affrights one. They wear coarse hair-shirts next their skin; fast almost perpetually; eat only bean-bread; whether sick or well never touch flesh; never buy fish but eat it if given them as an alms; eat eggs on Sundays and Thursdays; on Tuesdays and Saturdays their fare is pulse or herbs boiled; on Mondays, Wednesdays, and Fridays they take nothing but bread and water; and they have only two meals a day, except within the octaves of Christmas, Easter, Whitsuntide, Epiphany and other festivals. Their constant occupation is praying, reading, and manual labor, which consists chiefly in transcribing books.[5]

In spite of this severity—possibly because of it—the order won many converts, both men and women. It spread to Italy, Switzerland, and England. In the last, its convents were known as charter-houses, a corruption or misunderstanding of Chartreuse. Its members have boasted, if it is permissible to use such a term, that theirs is the only order that never had to be reformed: *Carthusia numquam reformata, quia numquam deformata.*

The most influential of the new orders was that of the Cistercians. This congregation, founded in 1092, soon became Cluny's greatest rival and played a rôle in the twelfth-century Church very like that of Cluny in the eleventh. This was due chiefly to two of its members—the Englishman Stephen Harding and Bernard of Clairvaux. The former, although not the founder of the order, was very influential in determining its organization and rules. Each daughter house was subordinated to the house that had founded it, and thus eventually to the abbot and convent of Cîteaux. Great care was taken to assure uniformity in practice throughout the order. The Cistercian rule was stricter than that of Cluny; in fact the Cistercians considered the Cluniacs rather worldly, especially in their fondness for fine churches and elaborate sculpture. Bernard was somewhat younger than Stephen Harding; he became a Cistercian only in 1113. The abbot of Cluny had many more monasteries under his direction, but Bernard soon came to have greater influence, and his order profited by his prestige. He is the best example of the power which the reforming monks enjoyed in the twelfth century.

Bernard was of noble birth and had received an excellent education. At twenty-two he became a Cistercian monk and two years later was made abbot of Clairvaux, one of the first off-shoots of Cîteaux.

Then [says a contemporary, who wrote before Bernard's death] the golden age reigned at Clairvaux. There were to be seen virtuous men, who had formerly been rich and honored by the world, now glorying in the poverty of Christ, building God's Church at the price of their blood, their sweat, and their fatigue, enduring hunger and thirst, cold, nakedness, persecutions,

[5] Translation by Abbot Gasquet in *English Monastic Life.*

outrages, and very great anguish, and thus preparing at Clairvaux the ease and peace which this house now enjoys. Believing that they were living not so much for themselves as for Christ and for the brethren who would come to serve God in this place, they thought what they themselves lacked was of no importance, provided they could leave behind them enough to satisfy their brethren and to provide for the necessities of a poverty embraced voluntarily for the love of Christ. When visitors descended from the mountain to Clairvaux and first caught sight of the house, God was manifest, while the silent valley revealed by the simplicity and humility of its buildings the simplicity and humility of the poor men of Christ who dwelt in them. In this valley full of men, where no one was permitted to be idle, where every one worked and was busy at the allotted tasks, visitors found in the daytime the silence of night, interrupted only by the noise of labor or at the holy hours when the brethren sang praises to God.

Bernard loved to live at Clairvaux in his narrow, comfortless cell. But there was another side to his nature, which drove him forth constantly into the world to right wrongs, to make peace, and to preach.

It has been truthfully said that, of all his miracles, the most surprising was his personality itself, the inconceivable union of two contradictory temperaments; on the one side the monk, according to the ideal of the age, contemplative, mystic, ascetic, who kept his body under almost to its destruction, and seemed to have lost the sense of things material, skirting Lake Geneva a whole day without seeing it, and drinking oil for water; on the other hand the man of action, the indefatigable preacher, the unofficial councillor of high barons, kings, and popes, the real chief of the Western Church.

Yet this remarkable activity of a reforming abbot demonstrates again the leadership of the Church and the way in which its ideals were imposed on the rest of society.

It is impossible to describe St. Bernard's work in detail. As Luchaire has written: "St. Bernard governed Christianity in the West from 1125 to 1153 by the mere prestige of his eloquence and holiness; recounting his life would be equivalent to writing the history of the monastic orders, of the reform movement, of orthodox theology and heretical doctrines, of the Second Crusade, and of the destinies of France, Germany and Italy during a period of almost forty years." A few illustrations of his activity must suffice. He ended the serious papal schism which broke out in 1130. The larger party among the cardinals had elected Anaclete II, while the rest had chosen Innocent II. The former took possession of Rome, and Innocent had to flee. He was fortunate enough to receive the support of Bernard, who declared that votes should be weighed, not counted. Bernard undertook to do the weighing, and found many reasons to prove that Innocent's side of the balance was heavier. When he succeeded in convincing the kings of France, England, Germany, Castile, and Aragon that his arithmetic was correct, Anaclete's cause was ruined and Innocent was universally recognized as pope. Bernard made peace between the emperor Lothair and the Hohenstaufen; he ended civil wars in several Italian and German cities; and, as we have seen, he was the chief promoter of the Second Crusade. In purely religious affairs, his influence was equally great. He saw the danger from the new heresies coming in from the East long before other churchmen and worked vigorously, though in vain, to convince the heretics of their errors. More than any other man, he found words and symbols to express the new piety which was developing in Europe. The old emphasis on the Last Judgment and Christ as the Supreme Judge was yielding to thoughts of God's infinite love and mercy and Christ as the Son of Man. Bernard's hymns express these ideas so perfectly that they are still sung in most Christian churches, Protestant as well as Catholic. His letters and sermons stressed the love of God and the hope of redemption for even the most miserable sinner. This fitted well with the mood of the twelfth century, which could not believe that most men would be damned and which loved stories of last-minute conversions. In emphasizing the human side of Christianity, Bernard was led to a deep devotion to the Virgin, and here again his example had great influence. The cult of the Virgin, heretofore unimportant in the West, became one of the most significant forms of religious expression during the latter part of the twelfth century.

It was this emphasis on divine love and the hope of salvation which gave St. Bernard his great influence. He could be unreasonable and even bad-tempered; he wrote some of the angriest letters which have ever been written by a holy man. But his anger was not mere violence; it was a desperate attempt to make men return to God, and it was often effective in causing a change of heart. And the multitudes who heard him preach found in his words a perfect expression of their religious ideals.

Such was the man who had the greatest influence in shaping the Cistercian order. He felt that the Cistercian monk should have the least possible contact with the world. Their abbeys were to be built in waste lands far from towns, and they were not to establish schools which might attract laymen to their dwellings. The rule of Cîteaux forbade the acquisition of parish churches, villages, mills, serfs, or any other thing which might bring with it worldly responsibilities. The monks were to do all the labor, but were not allowed to sell their products at retail. Their food was limited and usually poorly cooked, as there was no regular cook and each monk in turn prepared the food. No ornamentation was allowed in Cistercian churches; even towers were prohibited, unless they were of moderate height and made of wood.

The order grew rapidly during the twelfth century. Many men of great families, like Barbarossa's uncle, Otto of Freising, were attracted to it, and thousands of humbler persons entered the order. At the end of the thirteenth century there were at least seven hundred Cistercian

monasteries, not counting the ones for women. The order was very prosperous, due in part to the very restrictions which were designed to turn
it away from worldly affairs. The Cistercians were supposed to seek
waste land for their dwellings and the owners of such land were glad
to give away thousands of acres, gaining a reputation for charity at
very little cost. But just as the first Cistercian houses were receiving
their endowments, the economic revolution which was described in the
last chapter began to influence northern Europe. Many of these waste
lands were very fertile when they had been cleared or drained, and the
Cistercians became expert in this work. Other lands, especially in England, were well suited to sheep-raising, and with the growing demand of
Flemish weavers for wool, the Cistercians had a market for all they
could raise. Eventually the Cistercians became the greatest sheep-
raisers in England, and controlled a large part of the English wool trade.
The restriction which forbade the monks to have serfs, villages, and
mills prevented them from exploiting their property in the usual early
medieval fashion. This was also a blessing in disguise, since the old-
fashioned great estate, cultivated by servile labor, was not a very profitable property for its owner. The Cistercians had far more land than
they could cultivate themselves, and since they could not turn it over
to serfs they developed the practice of leasing it for a short period to
the highest bidder. This practice of leasing, or "farming" as it was then
called, proved profitable. The growing market for agricultural products
meant that there were many bidders, the price was usually high, and
the monks had almost no responsibility or expense. Many other landlords began to imitate this practice, especially in northern France
and England. The Cistercians were also very successful in breeding
cattle, horses, and sheep. In short, they were the leaders in the "scientific
agriculture" of the twelfth century. All this made them wealthy, and
wealth had the usual effects on monastic discipline. The Cistercians
began to live more comfortably, to build elaborate churches, and by
the thirteenth century they could no longer look down on the Cluniacs for
their lax discipline.

The Cistercians had been reluctant to admit women at first, but eventually allowed them to join the order and founded convents especially
for them. In contrast to this reluctance, the new order of Fontevrault,
founded by Robert of Arbrissel about 1096, was designed primarily for
women, and the male members had a subordinate position. Robert was
the son of a priest and of a priest's daughter, and was naturally interested
in the welfare of sinful women. He was a wandering preacher who made
so many converts that he had to establish a home at Fontevrault for the
repentant men and women who gathered about him. In the words of his
biographer, Baldric, bishop of Dol, "the poor were received, the feeble
were not refused, nor women of evil life, nor sinners, neither lepers nor

CHRIST WITH SYMBOLS OF THE FOUR EVANGELISTS
CHARTRES CATHEDRAL, WEST PORTAL, LATE 12th CENTURY

•

SAMSON AND THE LION, SOUTHERN FRANCE, EARLY 12th CENTURY

CHURCH OF THE NORMAN KINGS
MONREALE, SICILY, 12th CENTURY

The French Overseas

THE CRUSADERS' CASTLE, CRAC-DES-CHEVALIERS, 12th CENTURY

English Gothic

SALISBURY CATHEDRAL, 13th CENTURY

French Gothic at Its Height

THE NAVE OF AMIENS CATHEDRAL, 13th CENTURY

the helpless." Robert divided the men into classes, some for religious services, others for manual labor. The women were all to engage in labor. Robert placed the order under the patronage of the Virgin and made a woman the head. The order grew until it had about sixty convents in France. "Men of all conditions came; women came, the poor as well as those of gentle birth; widows and virgins; aged men and youths, women of dissolute life as well as those who held aloof from men."

The movement toward reform through monastic life affected even the secular clergy. The churchmen who officiated in a cathedral, or in the larger churches of a town, were called canons, and were very wealthy and influential. For the maintenance of these canons, a part of the property belonging to their churches had been divided into portions called prebends, of which each canon held one or more. These prebends were treated virtually as private property, and the canons of the wealthier churches had tended to live like feudal nobles. They were often married and lived very worldly lives, hiring vicars to perform their religious duties. To remedy the scandal caused by these degenerate canons, monks had sometimes been charged with their duties, but the work of a canon was hardly compatible with the life of a monk. Yet it was essential to reform the canons, for they often were able to delay or nullify the work of a reforming bishop. There were many attempts in the late eleventh century to make the canons lead a communal life under semi-monastic rules. St. Augustine of Hippo was supposed to have made such a rule for the clergy of his town, and many cathedral chapters adopted it during the twelfth century.

On the whole, however, the canons of the older foundations remained attached to their system of individual income and responsibility, and new orders were created which took over much of their work. The most successful of these was the order of Prémontré, founded in 1120 by the German Norbert. He was a noble who had been suddenly converted and had had a rather difficult time in Germany because he tried to make the clergy of the churches to which he was attached live up to their obligations. He finally went to France where, as a wandering preacher, he gathered many followers. For their abode he chose in 1120 a home in an unhealthy spot destitute of all natural advantages, which he called Prémontré, from the belief that the Virgin had pointed it out to him. His success was rapid. Crowds flocked to him and donations poured in. Women came as well as men, and double monasteries were established in which the women lived in one part of the property while the men occupied another part. This soon raised such problems that the monasteries for men and women had to be completely separated. But the Premonstratensians continued to increase in numbers and became the most influential of the canons regular (canons who followed a monastic rule). The orders of canons attracted many because their activities gave room for practical talents. Though they led a moderately ascetic life, they were not so much out of the world as the monks. Many took over the duties of pastors of small parish churches, others were missionaries, others engaged in philanthropic work. They founded hospitals and poor-houses, and were especially active among the growing city populations.

Finally, there were the military orders, which tried to combine monastic discipline with the duty of fighting the infidel. The first of these was the order of the Temple, which began when eight French knights formed an association to protect pilgrims on their journeys to the holy places. They took the three monastic vows of poverty, chastity, and obedience. The king of Jerusalem gave them part of his palace, which was near the site of the temple of Solomon, and from this they took their name of Poor Brothers of the Temple of Jerusalem. St. Bernard was much interested in their work and gave them his mighty support. Their rule, which he may have aided to draft, was approved at the Council of Troyes in 1128. There were three classes of members—clergy to perform the religious services; knights, who had to be of noble birth; and sergeants or squires, recruited from free-born men. Up to this time there had been only a few additions to the brotherhood; now it was flooded with recruits and showered with gifts. The Templars were given several castles in the Holy Land to guard and innumerable possessions in Palestine and Europe to support their activities. Kings and popes gave them privileges which freed them from all ordinary lay and ecclesiastical jurisdictions. The Templars were a disciplined force at a time when discipline was rare, and they performed great services to the Christian cause in the Near East. Yet their devotion to the order and their independence from all ordinary authority made it hard for the king of Jerusalem to control them, and they were sometimes accused of putting the interests of their order above those of the kingdom. Moreover, they soon became involved in business, and especially in banking. Their most important sources of income were in western Europe, but their greatest expenditures were in the Near East. They had to find ways of turning produce into money, and of transferring money or credits from one end of the Mediterranean to the other. In the effort to do this, they learned many tricks of banking, and soon other people were asking them to perform similar operations for their benefit. During most of the thirteenth century the Templars served as bankers and treasurers to the kings of France. But when the Temple became a great business organization, when there were more Templars living in Europe than in the East, the order lost much of its hold on public esteem.

The chief rivals of the Templars were the Hospitalers, the Knights of St. John of Jerusalem. They had developed from a small group which maintained a hospital at Jerusalem to care for sick pilgrims. In imitation of the Templars, the group took the monastic vows and devoted themselves to fighting the infidel, though they continued to maintain their original hospital. They became almost as wealthy as the Templars, and like the Templars provided stable, disciplined forces at a time when they were badly needed in the kingdom of Jerusalem. Yet each order was so anxious to build up its own resources and to gain a dominating position in the Near East that they frequently clashed. Their quarrels did much to weaken the crusading states at the end of the twelfth century. The Hospitalers were not as much involved in business as the Templars, and hence were not quite as unpopular, though they were severely criticized in the thirteenth century. Other military orders, founded in imitation of the Temple and the Hospital, had only local importance. The Teutonic Knights, as we have seen, did their chief work in the Baltic, while the various Spanish orders fought against the Moors of the peninsula.

The emphasis on service to the laity was stronger in many of the new orders than it had been in the early Benedictine monasteries. We have already seen the examples of the Premonstratensians, Templars, and Hospitalers. Other minor orders carried the idea even further—for example, the Bridge-Builders founded in 1189 to build bridges to make travel easier, or the Trinitarians founded in 1197 to redeem Christian captives from the Saracens. In fact, by the end of the twelfth century so many of these new orders had been established that leaders of the Church began to feel that there was a danger of dissipating the strength of the monastic ideal in too many specialized activities. The Fourth Lateran Council in 1215 prohibited the foundation of new orders, but this ruling could not be enforced. Just as it was made, the greatest social service orders of the Middle Ages, the Franciscans and Dominicans, were asking for the recognition which they soon obtained.

Contemporaries wondered at the rapid increase in the number of monks. Peter the Venerable of Cluny exclaimed that "the innumerable number of monks covers almost all the lands of France; it fills the cities, castles and fortified places. What a variety of garbs and customs in this army of the Lord, which has taken an oath to live according to the rule in the name of faith and charity!" It is impossible even to guess at the total number, but monks and nuns formed an appreciable part of the population of every European country. No part of Europe escaped their influence, no one from king to peasant could live long without coming into contact with monks of one order or another. This growth of monasticism was both a result of the religious revival and a means of spreading it further among the people. The deep, new piety, the desire for more intense religious experience, the revulsion against violence and sin, were all satisfied by entrance into a monastic order. Even those who were not ready to desert the world desired the presence and preaching of the reforming leaders. But while the movement was first and fundamentally religious, it had its practical side. The monks were very helpful in turning public opinion in favor of reforming measures desired by the papacy. During the twelfth century the popes continued to build up their control over the administration of the Church. Appeals to Rome were encouraged, and more and more cases were taken to the papal *curia*. Through appeals in cases of contested elections the pope gained more influence in the choice of bishops; he might choose one claimant instead of the other, or quash the election of both and impose his own candidate. The growth of papal jurisdiction also made it easier to discipline inefficient, worldly, or disobedient prelates. The clergy were made more and more independent of secular governments, while lay rulers were forced to acknowledge the pope's authority in matters of morals. In all these activities the monks were useful servants of the papacy and they were rewarded by being freed from all ordinary church authority. The number of exempt monasteries, subject only to the pope, increased steadily. Thus, if the bishops and other secular clergy proved lukewarm in the work of reform, the pope could always turn to the monks for support.

The monks, of course, were not always able to live up to their ideals. When their prestige and the services which they performed caused a flood of donations during the twelfth century, many houses acquired so many worldly possessions that their heads were completely occupied with administrative and political duties. This is very evident in the Chronicle of Jocelin of Brakelonde,[6] which describes the life of Abbot Samson of St. Edmondsbury. Samson found the revenues of the monastery dilapidated "so he caused inquests to be made in every manor belonging to the abbey" of all the annual dues, income and expenses. But knowing his rights was one thing, profiting by them was another. Although he had the presentation of more than sixty-five churches, some of them were claimed by other lords and it took repeated law-suits to establish his rights. He had to sell the wardship of a girl who was his vassal to the archbishop of Canterbury for £100 "because he could not obtain possession of her person save with the help of the archbishop." His vassals owed him the service of more than fifty knights, but he claimed an even greater number and quarreled bitterly with them throughout his abbacy. He was vassal of the king of England for certain holdings, and thus was forced to perform expensive and burdensome services. For example, in 1193 he took part in the siege of Windsor "where he appeared in arms with some other abbots of England and had his own standard. He had there also with him many knights of great expense." Samson was always engaged in disputes and litigation—with his own vassals and officials, with the kings of England, with the archbishops of Canterbury, with the earl of Clare, and even with the papal legates. It is quite evident, as Jocelin says, that Samson "appeared to prefer the ac-

[6] Translated by L. C. Jane in *The King's Classics.*

tive to the contemplative life, and praised good officials more than good monks."

Samson was perhaps too occupied with worldly things, but he was at least zealous for the interests of his monastery. Many monks had not even that virtue. A monastery which was well established and had large revenues attracted many men who had had difficulties in the outside world and sought only a comfortable life and a lessening of responsibility. Cæsar of Heisterbach, a Cistercian, describes such monks in the first section of his "Dialogue of Miracles." He says: "Innumerable are those who are brought to our order by necessity of many kinds, such as sickness, poverty, captivity, shame for some sin, deadly peril, fear or experience of hell's tortures, desire for heaven." A noble condemned to death was pardoned on condition that he enter the Cistercian order, and Cæsar adds: "I have frequently heard of such cases." A canon at Cologne was caught stealing and fled to the monastery; a man who had lost his property told Cæsar, "Certainly, if I had prospered in worldly affairs, I should never have entered the order." Cæsar quotes the Gospel, "Compel them to come in, that my house may be filled," as justification for these cases, though he confesses his fear that such conversions may not be lasting. But he adds that "the archbishop of Trier, who was a prudent man and knew well the secrets of our order, was wont to say that it was not usual for boys or youths who entered our order with no burden of sin on their conscience to be fervent."

Many of these monks who had no special interest in monastic life suffered from *accidia*, one of the "seven chief sins." There is no modern equivalent for the word; it was an acute form of boredom, a feeling that life was useless and dreary. It might result merely in laziness and distaste for monastic duties, or it might—and frequently did—lead to suicide. In its milder forms it caused monks to invent excuses for journeys and changes of occupation—some went to study at Paris, others to visit a shrine, others to visit sick kinsmen. Some of these wandering monks never returned, and their life became a scandal to the moralists.

Yet in the twelfth century the monastic ideal was still strong, and the monastic life was still honored by the people. The new vernacular literatures included many poems praising monastic virtues. One of the best is the *Life of St. Alexis,* written just as the new orders were beginning to rise. It is a reworking of a Latin life, done with much greater skill and charm than the original. The poet begins by lamenting the decline in faith and morals. Then he tells how Alexis' father, a wealthy Roman noble, bought as a bride for his son the daughter of a Frankish noble. But Alexis was a monk at heart and did not desire earthly pleasures. Immediately after the marriage ceremony he charged his bride to take Christ as her spouse and fled to the Orient. He gave all that he had to the poor and became a beggar at Edessa, while his parents sought for him

in vain. Finally Alexis returned home and lived for seventeen years un-
recognized in his parents' house, fed by scraps from their table, and insulted by their servants. On his death-bed, his identity was revealed by
a miracle and he received due honor as a saint. But his mother clung to
his dead body and cried: "My son, why have you had no pity for us?
My son, why haven't you spoken to me even once?" The moral is that
the monk must renounce all human ties and all worldly advantages.
Alexis had won heaven and sainthood by his humility and asceticism.
That these could be the virtues praised in a popular poem shows what a
deep impression the reformers had made on medieval society.

THE TWELFTH-CENTURY RENAISSANCE—LITERATURE

Our modern civilization has two roots. One stretches back into the
ancient world; the other reaches only to the Middle Ages. In many of our
activities we still follow the traditions and use the forms created in these
two periods. The two traditions have not yet coalesced, though they
have existed side by side for centuries. Often there has been active
competition between them. Thus most modern countries use either English (medieval) or Roman law; most modern churches are either Gothic
or classical (including derived styles); modern literature has seen a long
conflict between classical and romantic (medieval) styles.

In some activities we have never been able to use the classical tradition
and have merely perfected medieval forms. For example, no modern poet
has ever been very successful in using Græco-Roman meters and most of
them have preferred writing in the rhythmic, rhymed verse which was
first developed in the Middle Ages. Our educational systems, and especially our universities, in spite of centuries of emphasis on classical studies,
are still medieval in their plan and purpose. The influence of the classical
tradition has been greatly overrated; the influence of the medieval tradition has not been sufficiently recognized. This is especially true in intellectual and artistic activities. The energy and initiative of the twelfth
century, disciplined and controlled by the Church, were not exhausted
by the work of political and economic reconstruction. The twelfth century produced great work in literature, art and science; it created cultural
patterns which we are still following today. The twelfth century saw the
first masterpieces of the vernacular literatures, the culmination of Romanesque and the beginnings of Gothic art, the revival of legal studies,
the reception of Eastern science, the emergence of the first universities.
These things lie at the very foundations of our modern life; the age which
produced them can well claim that it witnessed the rebirth of European
civilization. In many ways the Renaissance of the twelfth century was
more original, more comprehensive and more influential than the better
known Renaissance of the fifteenth and sixteenth centuries.

Tradition insists that a revival of the Latin classics is the sign of a true Renaissance. The twelfth century can show its credentials here, even if the classics were not its chief concern. Practically all the Latin authors which we now possess were read and studied in the church schools of the period. Orleans and Chartres were famous as centers of classical studies. John of Salisbury, one of the most interesting of twelfth century writers, has left a detailed description of the teaching methods at the latter center. Passages of the classics were read and explained in class; the students had to reproduce the material in written and oral compositions, and special emphasis was placed on the development of a good Latin style. There were writers in twelfth century France who imitated the ancients as successfully as any fifteenth century Italian. Indeed, some of their work was confused by later scholars with that of Roman poets.

It is true, of course, that most twelfth century authors did not write—probably did not want to write—in a classical style. They usually studied the classics for utilitarian and not esthetic reasons. They wanted to increase their store of ideas and information; they wanted to enlarge their vocabularies; they wanted to improve their grammar. This effort is reflected in their works. No one can read John of Salisbury's treatise on politics without recognizing that he knew his classics far better than many modern professors of the subject. At the same time no one would ever confuse his work with that of Cicero. The medieval writer used words which were unknown in the first and second centuries, and his syntax was often that of a modern French author rather than that of a Roman of the classical age. This does not mean that he wrote bad Latin; rather it means that he was anxious to be understood. Latin was still a living language; it was the language of the Church, the schools, the governments of all European states. Christian theology, Arabic mathematics, feudal obligations could not be described in the language of the classical period. New words were needed and new words were created, as they always are in a language which has any vitality. In the same way the new rules of syntax made Latin much easier to understand. Relative clauses were clearly indicated; the horrors of indirect discourse were mitigated, and the word order was closer to that of a modern language. Classical Latin had often sacrificed precision to style; medieval Latin reversed this tendency. This made the language much more useful for governmental or scientific purposes, as a comparison of the writs of an English king with the rescripts of a Roman emperor will show. Yet it may be admitted that by purely literary standards medieval Latin prose did not equal that of the Augustan age. The ordinary writer was dull and monotonous or, when he tried to become eloquent, merely florid. Even the papal chancery, which at its best could produce sonorous and beautifully balanced passages, frequently betrayed these faults.

Something more may be said for medieval Latin poetry. It is here that we find for the first time that rhythmic, rhymed verse which has played such a rôle in all modern European literatures. Some of this verse was not much above the level of nursery jingles, but at its best it pointed the way to new and powerful effects. Moreover, medieval Latin poets dealt with emotions (such as religious fear and ecstacy) which classical authors had never known, and they usually expressed their emotions more intensely and directly than a Roman, with one eye on the rules of poetry and the other on the rules of good form, could do. There is a good deal of Latin poetry of the Middle Ages which is worth knowing, and most of it comes from the twelfth century. At one extreme are the great hymns of the medieval Church—the *Dies Irae,* the *De Contemptu Mundi,* the *Jesu dulcis memoriæ*—which shows the intensity of religious feeling. At the other extreme are the Goliardic poems, the songs of the wandering students, which show an equally intense delight in the joys of this world. The two extremes are both typical of the twelfth century. If thousands of men were singing with Bernard of Cluny (?) "The world is very evil, the hour is waxing late" thousands of others were singing with the students "In the public-house to die is my resolution." This poetry was not a scholastic exercise; it reflected the hopes and beliefs of the people and it had a great effect on vernacular literature.

All the serious writing of the twelfth century was in Latin. Theology, philosophy, science, history and political theory could not yet be discussed in a vulgar tongue. Even lighter works, such as the student songs, were often written in Latin. But French was already a literary language when the twelfth century began and Italian, Catalan, Spanish and German reached this stage before it ended. Twelfth century vernacular literature was composed primarily to amuse the wealthier classes, nobles and bourgeoisie; it was not until the thirteenth century that an effort was made to instruct them by translating large numbers of learned works. It is in these writings in the vernacular that we see most clearly the beginnings of the romantic tradition.

As in many other fields, France took the lead in this popular literature and authors in other countries were greatly influenced by French works. At the very beginning of the twelfth century wandering minstrels were already chanting the *chansons de geste*—long epic poems describing the life of legendary heroes. The earliest *chansons* are not rhymed, but something of the effect of rhyme is given by the use of assonance. That is, the first eight or ten lines will end in words with the same dominant vowel sound, then the next eight or ten lines will end in words with a different dominant vowel, and so on.[7] Later *chansons* were rhymed, as was most other poetry of the period. The verses are rough and sometimes

---

[7] "Queen—seen" is a rhyme, "queen—leaf" is an assonance.

monotonous and the poems are full of ready-made phrases and stock situations. Yet at their best the *chansons* have a straightforward simplicity which can be very moving. They praise the feudal virtues, bravery, justice, loyalty, generosity, unceasing war against the infidel. They have little to say about women and even less about romantic love. Religion does not fare much better; it is an excuse for fighting but hardly a guide to life. Kings and emperors are often treated rather rudely; in many *chansons* they are ridiculous figures whose chief function is to goad their vassals into deeds of desperate valor by acts of crude injustice. Yet the *chansons* are not mere descriptions of war and battle; they portray the emotions and thoughts of the military class with surprising skill. The earliest, and probably the greatest of these epics, the *Chanson de Roland*, tells not only of Roland's bravery, of the thousands of Saracens slain by his famous sword Durendal, but also of his foolhardy pride. Trapped by a Moslem army he will not call on Charlemagne for help for this would tarnish his reputation and cause men to say that Roland was afraid. The plot of another well-known *chanson, Raoul de Cambrai,* hangs on a question of feudal ethics that must have tormented countless knights. A vassal has been repeatedly insulted by his lord—is he justified in turning against him? After long hesitation the vassal decides to make war on his lord, and in the struggle kills him, but the deed haunts him for the rest of his life.

The early *chansons de geste* were often brutal, but seldom boring. As time went on, the authors began to run out of ideas, and to repeat themselves, and their audiences began to want stories that reflected more of the new interests of the twelfth century. So the *chanson de geste* died out, or merged with other literary forms to become the romance. At its best, the *chanson de geste* was very great poetry, but it was poetry too closely bound to a particular time and place. It had little influence on late medieval writers and even less on those of the modern world. A few characters and episodes of the *chansons* were used by Italian poets of the Renaissance and by romantic writers of the nineteenth century. But the form and spirit of the *chanson* died out very rapidly and were never revived. Almost all the epics of modern European literature have been based on the Graeco-Roman models, not on those of twelfth century France.

Other narrative poems of the twelfth century have had greater influence—the poems which tell the story of King Arthur and his knights, of Tristan and Isolde, of Percival and the Grail. The emergence of these Celtic legends is one of the most interesting phenomena in the literary history of medieval Europe. These stories, or at least the themes from which the stories were composed, must have been known for centuries before they were written down. France and the British Isles had been Celtic before they were Roman or Germanic, and Celtic traditions had persisted in Ireland, in Wales and in Brittany. But it was only in the twelfth century that professional writers and entertainers seized upon these legends and gave them prominent form. The Celtic stories, unlike the *chansons de geste*, emphasized magic and romantic love. There was fighting aplenty in them, but the fighting was in tournaments and jousts to impress a lady or to gain status among other knights. The love-story was often tragic; the typical hero was a married man who fell in love with a lady in a distant country, or a vassal who fell in love with his queen. Often he could not help himself, a spell or a love-potion made him forget earlier obligations. It is this theme of the overwhelming and tragic power of love that has impressed poets of all ages. The story of Tristan and Isolde has been told and retold; the guilty love of Lancelot and Guinevere is almost as well known.

In the hands of men of genius—Chrétien de Troyes in France, or, a generation later, Wolfram von Eschenbach in Germany—the Arthurian material could be used for striking portrayals of the characters of individual men and women. Lesser writers, however, could not resist the temptation to write mere adventure stories. Beautiful maidens and wicked magicians stocked every castle, and moonstruck knights ran all over Europe on idiotic errands. These romances were about as pure a form of escape literature as the world has ever known and they continued to delight readers for the next six centuries. Perhaps their lack of intellectual content made them impervious to criticism and protected them from changing literary fashions. Not even Cervantes' bitter satire could kill romances; even in the enlightened eighteenth century fashionable ladies were reading new versions of the old, marvelous stories.

There was little lyric poetry in northern France in the twelfth century, but in the South there was little else. This was the great period of Provençal civilization, and of the troubadours who were one of the glories of that civilization. Here in the South were flourishing towns, wealthy nobles, a refined—even artificial—social life, and an almost snobbish interest in literature. The northern minstrels who wrote down the first *chansons de geste* were anonymous. Not so the authors of the troubadour lyrics; they desired above all things to be known to men. They held poetical contests, they exchanged rhymed epistles, they wrote scurrilous lampoons on the morals, ancestry, and ability of their competitors. This Provençal poetry is French only by geography; it is based on Mediterranean rather than French culture. The people of South France were very close to those of Spain and Italy, and very remote from those of the North. Saracen Spain influenced them more than Christian Paris. The typical Provençal lyric, when it was not an advertisement or mere *vers de société*, was a love-song, addressed to a secluded and disdainful lady. It was a serenade, to be sung under her window in the evening, or an aubade, to wake her at dawn. The poet has seen the lady only once and he dies with longing for her; he has been rejected for no cause but he cannot forget his love. Close parallels to these themes may be found in Arabic literature, and it has been argued that the earliest Provençal lyrics are imitations of poems written by the Moors of Spain. Whatever their origin, they had a tremendous influence on European literature. The first Italian poets imitated the masters of Provence; the earliest French and German lyrics were based on the same source. Early medieval writing was impersonal and objective, but the Provençal lyric was intensely subjective. The feelings of the author, his reaction to the world about him were all-important; he was trying to express his own experiences in a way which would appeal to every one. This was a new and important addition to the field of medieval literature. It made it easier for writers to accomplish their great tasks of finding eternal values in the common experience of all men. Unfortunately, the range of the southern poets was very limited. Their love-poems were their best and most influential work; when they touched on other subjects they often became didactic and prosaic. They were also apt to pay too much attention to their verse-forms; they were as proud of an intricate rhyme-scheme as they were of a well-expressed thought. Within its limits Provençal poetry could be grace-ful and charming, but when it was imitated in other countries its virtues were soon lost and its faults were exaggerated. For generations European lyric poets wrote nothing but sonnets and *ballades* to imaginary ladies, and the results were appalling. Almost any one could write passable verse of this sort but only one or two geniuses could write great poetry while adhering to the old tradition. Provence had revived the lyric idea and had invented new forms in which it could be expressed. The Germans, and then the Italians picked up the idea and wrote great lyric poems in their turn. But after the thirteenth century had passed, Europe found very little to put into the new forms until the end of the Middle Ages.

THE TWELFTH-CENTURY RENAISSANCE—SCHOLARSHIP

The poets of the twelfth century created a new tradition in European literature. Their new forms, such as the use of rhymed verse, and their new themes, such as romantic love, were copied in every succeeding century. The scientists of the twelfth century were not as original; their task was not to invent, but to recover. They had the dull and uninspiring work of translating into Latin the Arabic and Greek books which contained the scientific knowledge of the ancient world. Yet while their work was not original, the idea that inspired them was. Neither the Romans of the late empire nor the men of the early Middle Ages had been interested in natural phenomena. The former had made little effort to preserve the Greek scientific tradition; the latter had made no effort to recover it. But the men of the twelfth century could no longer accept their world without question; they wanted a rational explanation for everything which they experienced. They were eager for knowledge, and they were willing to learn even from the infidel Moors and the schismatic Greeks. During the twelfth century, scholars from all parts of Europe flocked to the Spanish peninsula to acquire the wisdom of the Arabs, while a smaller group made the long journey to Constantinople in order to learn the secrets of the Greeks. Sicily was visited by fewer outside scholars, but the Norman kings encouraged their Mohammedan subjects to continue scientific work and their Christian subjects to translate or summarize Arabic books in Latin. Toledo in Spain, Palermo in Sicily, and Constantinople were the three ports of entry by which the Greek scientific tradition returned to western Europe. From these three points the new learning spread rapidly through Europe and, by the thirteenth century, it had a recognized place in the curricula of most educational institutions.

The men who translated Greek and Arabic works had no easy task. They were working without dictionaries, grammars, or any other linguistic aids. The greater number of them were trying to translate Arabic, which is a difficult tongue for Europeans to acquire. And when they mastered the foreign tongue their troubles were not ended, for there were no Latin equivalents for many of the scientific terms which they had to translate. It is not surprising that their translations are clumsy and that some passages are garbled; the amazing thing is that they were able to do as well as they did. Their errors seldom obscured fundamental points and the worst of the early translations were corrected by later scholars.

A more serious charge against the translators of the twelfth century is their lack of discrimination. Any Greek or Arabic book was viewed with veneration, and a great deal of time was wasted on works of little value. The translators were not always aware of each others' activities; the same book might be translated by several men in succession while more important but less available treatises were neglected. Yet this inefficiency in the division of labor was more than compensated by the energy of the translators. By the middle of the thirteenth century most of the important Greek and Arabic scientific works were available in Latin. It should also be remembered that many books which seem useless to us today were considered to have great practical value in the Middle Ages. Thus every one believed that astrology was an exact and very useful science. It was the applied form of astronomy, just as industrial chemistry is the applied form of the pure science. In the same way every one believed in the scientific character of alchemy, and twelfth century scholars would have hotly denied that they were wasting their time in translating works on this subject.

The translators are also accused of having no real understanding of scientific method and of imposing Aristotle's inadequate summaries as the final truth about natural phenomena. This is hardly fair. Like all scholars, the men of the twelfth century had to assimilate the knowledge of the past before they could criticize its methods and results. It is true that they concentrated on Aristotle and his Arabic commentators, and that they based most of their scientific theories on Aristotle's explanations. But it was not the fault of the twelfth century scholars that Aristotle loomed so large in the scientific tradition of the age; it was the fault of men of earlier periods who had neglected other writers and had preserved only Aristotle's works. Twelfth century scientists wanted the answers to a great many questions, and most of these answers could be found only in Aristotle. His answers were reasonable and consistent, and many of them were based upon accurate observations or acute inferences. We are apt to underestimate Aristotle's ability and knowledge today as badly as they were overestimated in the Middle Ages. Moreover, the dependence of medieval scholars upon Aristotle has been grossly exaggerated. Many other authors were translated—the great Greek and Arab doctors, the Arab astronomers and mathematicians—and Aristotle's teachings were not accepted blindly. In fact, by the thirteenth century, many people were trying to prove Aristotle wrong, and the first scientific experiments of the Middle Ages were made in an attempt to discredit Aristotle's authority. Not until Thomas Aquinas combined Aristotelian philosophy with Christian dogma in the late thirteenth century was there strong pressure to accept Aristotle as the sole possessor of scientific knowledge. And this pressure was far from silencing the opposition; both Aristotle and St. Thomas were frequently contradicted in the fourteenth and fifteenth centuries. The essential thing in science is to ask questions. The Greeks asked questions, and even if they often guessed at the answers, they were great scientists. The Romans never asked questions, and while they did less guessing than the Greeks no one would claim that they were better scientists. The men of the twelfth century asked the same questions which the Greeks had asked, and in so doing they revived the scientific tradition. Twelfth century method was not good, it was too bookish, too dependent on tradition, but it was important that the questions were being asked again. For if they were asked often enough the chances were that some one would become dissatisfied with the traditional answers and would try to find new solutions to the problems. The first great scientific discoveries of the modern period were made in testing the hypotheses which had been introduced into Europe by the scholars of the twelfth century.

The desire to fit all experience into a rational system was also apparent in the theology and philosophy of the twelfth century. Here again translations from the Greek and Arabic played a great part. Aristotle, after all, was primarily a philosopher and logician, and only incidentally a scientist. Before the twelfth century, Western Europe had possessed only the elementary logical treatises of Aristotle; by the end of the century practically all his logical and philosophical writings were available. With these writings came the great commentaries of the Arabs, which indicated some of the ways in which Aristotle could be used. It is hard to exaggerate the impact of this material on Western thought; it was like Newton's announcement of the law of gravitation, or Darwin's formulation of the theory of evolution. Like Newton and Darwin, Aristotle seemed to have found a way of reducing all the disorderly and confusing phenomena of the universe to a simple and comprehensible system. Moreover—and here he went beyond Newton and Darwin—he seemed to have discovered a method which could be applied to any body of knowledge and which would increase knowledge at a rapid rate wherever it was applied. If a few fundamental truths were known the use of Aristotelian logic would permit the deduction of a host of subsidiary truths.

In the twelfth century, men were sure that they possessed a great many fundamental truths, the basic doctrines of the Christian faith. Here was a beautiful new machine which would multiply these truths, which would explain everything in the world if operated with sufficient energy and perseverance. It is no wonder that they went a little crazy, that they became drunk with logic, that they applied Aristotle's method to completely unsuitable materials. We have seen the same thing happen to Darwin's hypotheses—the purely biological theory of survival of the fittest has been applied to politics, economics, and even to literature. The real wonder is that twelfth century scholars kept their heads as well as they did, that they did not lose touch completely with reality and tradition. They were saved by the pressure of competing interests and by the suspicions of the Church. There were too many activities in the intellectual world of the twelfth century for any one subject to become dominant. The students of the classics hated the emphasis on logic; the lawyers and doctors used it only as a tool in explaining their basic texts, and even the scientists, with all their reverence for Aristotle, were more interested in his facts than his method. Then the Church was very doubtful about the application of Aristotelian logic and philosophy to Christian doctrine. Many leaders agreed with Bernard of Clairvaux that it was unwise to reason too closely about matters of faith, that the application of logic to the creed would lead to heresy. This hostility of prominent churchmen forced the students of the new philosophy to be careful and to avoid extreme statements.

Nevertheless, it was clear by the middle of the twelfth century that logic, philosophy, and theology were becoming important studies. They were attracting more and more students and in France, at least, the ablest teachers were concentrating in these fields. Classicists, like John of Salisbury, sneered at the upstart logicians who pretended to give the key to all knowledge in ten easy lessons, but the classicists were fighting a losing battle. John of Salisbury was a wise and witty man, but he had little permanent influence on the course of medieval education. The man who expressed the strongest current of thought of his period, the man who helped lay the foundation for the educational system of the later Middle Ages was Peter Abelard—logician, philosopher and theologian.

Abelard was the eldest son of a minor vassal in Brittany. His father had had some education and wanted his children to have more, so he gave his son the best instruction available in the district. Abelard became inflamed with desire for knowledge and abandoned his birthright, preferring to spend the rest of his life in study rather than to take over the government of the family estates. This is remarkable testimony to the strength of the intellectual movement of the twelfth century. Brittany was one of the most disorderly and backward regions of France, and if minor Breton nobles were interested in education we can be sure that all Europe was feeling the impulse. Abelard, after he left home, wandered about France, studying logic under various masters, and finally reached Paris, which was already becoming famous as an intellectual center. Here Abelard finished his work in logic and here he first manifested the traits which made him both famous and infamous to the men of his age. He had a brilliant mind, he learned easily and taught well, but he must have been a very annoying person to have in a classroom. As soon as he had gained a smattering of a subject he began to contradict his teacher, and when he had finished a course he usually began to teach it in rivalry with his old professor. Since teachers at this time were largely supported by fees from their students, this unfair competition made Abelard rather unpopular with other members of his profession. He made matters no better by sarcastic references to their intellectual and moral shortcomings. Eventually his enemies succeeded in forcing him out of Paris, but this merely gave Abelard a chance to annoy them further. He studied a little theology, set himself up as an expert on the subject, and gradually edged his way into Paris again. This time he taught both logic and theology and attracted so many students that other professors were livid with jealousy.

At this point Abelard became too clever for his own good. He seduced a girl named Héloïse, who had been taking private lessons from him. Her uncle, who was a canon of Paris, eventually learned of the affair and forced Abelard to marry her. Abelard tried to keep the marriage secret and persuaded Héloïse to hide herself in a nunnery. This made the uncle fear that Abelard was planning to repudiate her and he determined to avenge the honor of his family. He hired some ruffians who broke into Abelard's house at night and castrated him. All Paris had heard the story by the next morning and Abelard could not stand the scorn which it aroused. He took refuge in monastic life, first as a monk of St. Denis, then as abbot of St. Gildas in Brittany. But Abelard was too much of an egoist to suppress his own personal desires and opinions, as a good monk should. He told the monks of St, Denis that they were too worldly and that some of the legends about their patron saint were false. He told his subordinates in Brittany that they were rude, uncultivated, and dishonest. It is not surprising that he found it impossible to live at either St. Denis or St. Gildas. Abelard was happy only when he was teaching and soon, in spite of his monastic vows, he was giving his old courses in a place as near Paris as he dared to come.

Abelard's teaching methods, however, had aroused deep suspicion among many churchmen. He was not a skeptic; he believed everything which the Church taught, but he wanted to justify and rationalize his beliefs. He felt that he could prove articles of the faith by reason, and, what was worse, he felt that he could reach many new conclusions about the faith by the use of logic. Moreover, while Abelard was undoubtedly sincere in saying that he wished to strengthen and clarify Christian doctrine, he did like to show off. He wanted to demonstrate his superior knowledge and ability by discussing very delicate subjects and in doing so he came very close to heresy. Two of his books, in particular, angered conservative churchmen. One was a treatise in which Abelard tried to define the attributes of each person of the Trinity. Now the Trinity was the central mystery of the Christian faith and it is hard to define a mystery without destroying it. Abelard's definition of the Trinity seemed to overemphasize the distinctness of the Three Persons and hence to destroy their essential unity. His other great fault was writing the *Sic et Non*—an exercise book in logic, with all the examples taken from theology. Here Abelard's love of reason and his conceit reached their height.

The prologue was bad enough, from the viewpoint of his enemies, for in it he said: "The first key to wisdom is this—constant and frequent interrogation. . . . For by doubting we are led to question, by questioning we arrive at the truth." But the body of the book was worse, for in it Abelard stated one hundred and fifty-eight propositions, collected authorities for (*sic*) and against (*non*) each, and left it to his readers to decide which was correct. This would have been harmless if the propositions had dealt merely with earthly phenomena, but most of them touched on theology. Typical problems were: "That God is threefold, and the contrary. That sin is pleasing to God, and the contrary. That nothing happens by chance, and the contrary. That it is lawful to lie, and the contrary." To find authority in the Church Fathers for both sides of these propositions was difficult. Abelard had to twist and distort quotations, and his cleverness in doing so made his enemies suspicious. Though he disclaimed any desire to raise doubts in the minds of his students, his method seemed beautifully calculated to produce this result. The fact that among Abelard's pupils were radicals like Arnold of Brescia made things worse. Bernard of Clairvaux, who believed that faith must be mystical and intuitive rather than rationalistic, led the attack against him. Abelard's treatise on the Trinity was condemned, and while he was not physically punished, he was practically debarred from teaching. He took refuge at Cluny, under the protection of a tolerant abbot, and there he died in 1142, at the age of sixty-three.

Abelard was a rationalist but not a free-thinker, an enthusiast who went too fast, but not an opponent of the Church's leadership. He relied on orthodox authorities and not on his own observation; he never denied the doctrines of the Church, though he loved to reason about them. The best proof of his essential orthodoxy is the fact that his methods and many of his results were adopted by later theologians who were never accused of heresy. The Church's fear of the new logic gradually dissolved and writers who were more cautious in using the new tool were able to reason about Christian doctrine with the full approval of ecclesiastical authorities. Abelard's method of collecting arguments on both sides of a question was followed by all the theologians of the twelfth and thirteenth centuries. For example, Peter Lombard, who wrote the first of the great theological encyclopedias, the *Book of Sentences*, cited authorities, pro and con, for every statement. Gratian did the same thing in the *Decretum*, a treatise on canon (ecclesiastical) law. But these men did one thing more than Abelard had done in his *Sic et Non*; after citing the authorities on both sides they indicated the preferred solution. Thus Gratian's book was called the *Concordantia discordantium canonum*—the reconciliation of discordant canons. This was safer than Abelard's system of leaving the question open for discussion, for it affirmed the orthodoxy of the writer. However, in oral discussion in the schools Abelard's method was followed—a proposition was stated, authorities were suggested, and the students argued until they reached a solution.

This emphasis on logic and *a priori* reasoning has been condemned by many writers, from the Renaissance to the present. It is true that it eventually degenerated into mere quibbling and sophistry—that men continued to argue about questions long after everything possible had been said on both sides. But it is hardly fair to accuse twelfth century scholars of wasting their time in displays of verbal ingenuity, of wrangling over words while they resolutely ignored facts. In the first place, this was a tendency which they shared both with the ancients and the men of the Renaissance. The Greeks, with all their intelligence, observed comparatively few facts, while they built up elaborate logical structures on the basis of these few observations. The greatest intellectual achievement of the Romans was their law, which again was based on logical deduction and definition rather than on observation. The men of the Renaissance, with all their scorn for the Middle Ages, were just as apt to mistake words for facts. They had changed their authorities, but they had not lost their veneration for the written word. Their discussions of antiquity are as unreal as any medieval discussion of the characteristics of angels. In the second place, it is not true that the study of words and their logical relationships was a waste of time in the twelfth century. It is impossible to think without words (try it if you doubt this statement) and until the meaning of words was defined and clarified, thinking was bound to be confused. It is almost impossible to study any subject seriously without using logical devices, and these devices are not inherent in the human mind. It may be true that primitive peoples have their own logic, but it is not the kind of logic on which science can be built. European thinkers had to learn logic before they could do much with the physical or even the social sciences. It was only when logical method had become embodied in the basic materials of all intellectual disciplines that the study of formal logic could be dropped from the curriculum.

Logic and theology flourished especially in northern France. In Italy, and in those regions of southern France which had close intellectual kinship with Italy, the great studies were law and medicine. Justinian's code, which had been almost forgotten during the Carolingian period, began to attract attention again during the latter part of the eleventh century. Italy and southern France still used Roman law, or rather the remnants of Roman law which had been preserved as local custom. These local customs dealt with only the simplest relationships, and as society became more orderly and social activity more complicated, men began to search the Roman law for principles which would supplement the deficiencies of customary law. The early stages of this process are still obscure, but by the twelfth century a very active group of professors of law at Bologna were studying and writing commentaries on the whole *Corpus Juris*. The most famous of these professors was Irnerius, who seems to have been largely responsible for organizing the systematic study of Roman law. His methods attracted many students and Roman law soon became one of the most popular subjects of the medieval curriculum. By the end of the twelfth century men who had studied Roman law could be found in every European country, though they were, of course, most numerous in Italy and southern France.

The rediscovery of Roman law was almost as stimulating to medieval thought as the rediscovery of Aristotle. No one had thought much about law in the tenth and early eleventh centuries. Men were born subject to a certain set of customs just as they were born subjects of a certain ruler and there was nothing to be done about either situation. If anything it was easier to change a ruler, who was human and therefore liable to err, than it was to change custom, which was sacred and infallible. But the study of Roman law revealed the imperfections and the barbarity of local customs. Roman law, as codified by Justinian, was a beautifully logical system which made the incoherence and incompleteness of customary law painfully apparent. All over Europe, in the twelfth and thirteenth centuries, customs were revised in the light of Roman law. In the North, where custom was too strong to be eradicated, it was organized and clarified so that it would bear comparison with the Roman model. Thus in English law the clear-cut Roman distinctions between civil and criminal cases, between possession and property, were introduced, though not without difficulty. In Mediterranean countries it seemed useless to waste time on degenerate Roman custom when pure Roman law was available. The courts were full of men who had been trained at Bologna, and gradually the scholarly version of Roman law took the place of the customs. Thus Roman law played an important part in the improvement of legal institutions which took place in the twelfth century. It was not the only factor; the greater power of rulers and the development of professional administrators were also important. Yet the discovery of a well-organized code which had an answer to every problem of human conduct certainly facilitated the work of kings and judges.

Closely allied with the study of Roman law was that of canon law. The Church had had its own laws (or canons) and its own courts since the fourth century, though they had remained in a rather rudimentary state during the early Middle Ages. But with the growth of papal power, the increased centralization of ecclesiastical administration and the greater influence of the Church over laymen, Church courts became very busy. Canon law, which had begun in the Roman Empire, was naturally similar to Roman law, but it had never had a Justinian. There were several compilations of canons, but they were incomplete and often contradictory. In the early years of the twelfth century, as papal and episcopal courts became more active, men began to study the law which they administered. They tried to organize it on the Roman model; they tried to find general principles comparable to those of Roman law, and finally the monk Gratian produced his *Decretum* in which canon law was reduced to a logical system. He discussed all important problems, cited authorities on both sides, and gave solutions which were as consistent with the general principles of canon law as possible. Like Irnerius, he founded a new science, and his pupils, like those of Irnerius, tended to congregate at Bologna.

The study of canon law soon became very popular. It was a sure road to ecclesiastical preferment, since the popes needed men who understood the principles on which the increasingly complicated administrative system of the Church was based. In fact, from Alexander III (1159–1181) to the end of the Middle Ages, almost every pope was a canon lawyer. Through canon law, ideas of Roman law were introduced into countries which clung stubbornly to their feudal or Germanic customs. Canon law was also important in its own right. The laws by which powerful and wealthy ecclesiastical units were administered could not fail to influence lay institutions. Moreover, canon law regulated all questions of marriage, legitimacy, and inheritance and shared the field of contract with secular laws. In these categories it has left its mark on the law of every European country.

The study of medicine was less important than the study of law, but it attracted many students in Mediterranean countries. In the late eleventh century the doctors of Salerno, a town on the bay of Naples, were famous for their knowledge of the traditional Greek texts. Here Constantine the African, a somewhat legendary figure, is supposed to have made some of the earliest translations of Arabic medical works. Later translators in Spain and Sicily completed the work of making Greek and Arabic medical books available in Latin. By the middle of the twelfth century there was an organized system of instruction in medicine at Salerno, and probably at other centers. This training was rather theoretical, since it was based on books rather than on clinical observation, but it was probably as good as that enjoyed by the Romans. The doctors knew enough to inspire confidence in their patients, which is at least half the secret of successful practice, and medicine was a respectable profession, though it did not rank with theology and law.

THE RISE OF UNIVERSITIES

The tremendous desire for knowledge which is such a marked feature of the twelfth century created a new problem for the Church. Students were wandering all over Europe seeking capable masters; books, which might or might not be orthodox, were being translated or written at a rapid rate; masters like Abelard were setting up schools which had little connection with either cathedrals or monasteries. The Church was at first very suspicious of the new knowledge, especially of Greek science and logic. It was equally suspicious of the wandering students, who were nominally clergymen, but were actually subject to no authority; and most of all it suspected the teachers who were neither monks nor cathedral canons, and hence could not be easily supervised by existing ecclesiastical organizations. Some of the more mystical or ascetic churchmen would gladly have suppressed all the new knowledge, which in their eyes was mere worldly vanity, but the leaders of the Church recognized that this was impracticable and probably undesirable. The new learning could not be suppressed, but it could be controlled. Control was made easy by the rise of universities. The Church did not create the first universities, but it rapidly realized that they were ideal institutions for regulating the conduct of students, the content of books, and the doctrine of teachers. Many later universities were founded by the Church, and they became the organs through which the Church controlled education and research.

The first universities were merely private associations, very much like the communes which governed the towns or the gilds which regulated commerce. In fact, throughout the Middle Ages the word "university" was regularly used to denote communes and gilds as well as educational institutions. These associations were formed because both masters and students were suffering from lack of regulation of education. Masters did not enjoy seeing untrained charlatans set themselves up as teachers, and the students were annoyed by professors who scamped their work. Moreover, the towns in which students congregated often fleeced them by charging high prices for rooms and food—even today a university town is apt to be an expensive place in which to live. By forming an association, teachers and students were able to keep prices down, since they could threaten to migrate in a body if they were mistreated.

The first university may well have been at Salerno, where, as we have seen, there had been a famous group of teachers of medicine at a very early date. Salerno certainly had a medical university before the end of the twelfth century, but we know very little about it. At Bologna, on the other hand, the organization of the twelfth century university is reasonably clear. Here the initiative was taken by the students of law, a group of relatively mature and influential men. The average student of liberal arts was a boy in his 'teens, but most of the law students had already had this elementary course, and hence were six or seven years older. Many of them occupied responsible positions in town and church governments and were studying in order to gain promotion. They were anxious not to waste their time, and as a result they made severe statutes regulating the activity of their professors. The teacher had to cover a fixed amount of ground during the year; he had to meet his class a certain number of times each week and keep his lectures above a minimum length; he could not even leave town without the consent of his students. Students of other subjects, who had been attracted to Bologna by its fame as an educational center, also organized associations. Finally the professors, in self-defense, formed a gild of their own. No one could enter this gild until he had proved his mastery of his subject by examination. Conversely, admittance to the gild of professors was conclusive proof that a subject had been mastered. Many men who had no idea of teaching took the examinations which qualified them as professors because it was the best way of demonstrating that they had successfully completed their work.

Thus all the essential features of a university existed at Bologna before the year 1200. Students attended regularly organized courses, they prepared for examinations, and if they passed they received a teaching license, or, as we would say, a degree. All this seems so natural that it is hard to imagine any other arrangement, yet it marked a great change from classical methods of education. The Greeks and Romans had concentrated more on individual instruction, and had never had anything like the teaching license. The individual instruction was often excellent, but it was far more expensive than the group instruction of the medieval university. And while professors of all ages have cursed the artificial nature of the standards for degrees, the existence of these standards does give the student a mark at which to aim and prevents, to some extent, the dilettantism which afflicted Roman education under the Empire.

Bologna, though it was the first fully organized university, was not entirely typical of such institutions. The lay element was strong there, as it was throughout Italy, and the Church never controlled Bologna as fully as it did northern institutions. Moreover, while the associations of professors and students were finally united in a sort of federation, the students remained the more powerful of the two groups. The University of Paris, which was supervised by the Church and administered by the professors, was the model followed by Oxford, Cambridge, and other universities north of the Alps. And in the late Middle Ages Paris was unquestionably the dominant educational institution of Europe. "The Italians have the Papacy, the Germans have the Empire, but the French have the University"—so ran a saying of the thirteenth century. In education, as in art and literature, France obtained an undisputed leadership.

The origins of the University of Paris are still very obscure. A school connected with the cathedral had long existed there, as at Chartres, Orleans, Laon and other ecclesiastical centers. It was not particularly eminent at first, but in the early years of the twelfth century the best teachers of the kingdom tended to congregate there, as is shown by the career of Abelard. The first teachers were probably attracted by purely material considerations. Paris was populous and wealthy and it lay at the intersection of important trade-routes which made it easily accessible to students. Once a group of eminent professors had settled there, other scholars were drawn to Paris by its reputation as an intellectual center. Soon the cathedral school became too small to hold all the teachers. They set up schools in other parts of the city, especially on the left bank, which eventually became the Latin, that is, the learned quarter. It is probable that all these men had to secure permission to teach from the chancellor of the cathedral, who was head of the cathedral school. During the latter half of the twelfth century the professors teaching at Paris began to organize, and to set up qualifications for admission to their gild. They did not, however, become independent of the Church. The chancellor retained the right to grant the teacher's license and he presided at the examinations which qualified students for the license. As Paris became the most important center of theological studies the pope began to take an interest in the affairs of the university. He granted Paris many privileges, but in return he influenced the curriculum and even the choice of professors. Once the leading European university had been brought under papal control, it was easier for the Church to make sure that the new learning would not harm the faith. Paris was fiercely orthodox and not apt to be seduced by heretical books or doctrines. At the same time the reputation of Paris was so great that ideas which were frowned on there were not easily accepted elsewhere.

Life at a twelfth century university was more strenuous than at one of its modern descendants. There were no university buildings and no endowments to make life comfortable and education relatively cheap. It is true that fees were not high, and that poor students were supposed to receive free tuition, but books were very expensive, even if the students only rented them instead of buying them. It took a long time to obtain even the lowest degree, and candidates for the doctorate in law or theology often had to study twelve or fifteen years. Begging was the recognized means of working one's way through college and many boys spent their vacations tramping through the country collecting what they could from charitable persons. Even if he had enough money the student suffered many hardships. The halls which the professors hired for their lectures were unheated and often had no benches, much less desks. The students burrowed in the straw spread on the floor and took notes as best they could on scraps of parchment. Few students possessed the necessary books, so the usual method of teaching was for the professor to read a sentence or two from the text, and then to give a long explanation of its meaning. All this material had to be memorized, and many students listened to the same course two or three times in succession to make sure that they had all the essential points. Examinations were always oral and were so difficult that at some institutions it was necessary to make rules against knifing the examiners. Yet the students seem to have had a good time. No regulations forced them to attend classes regularly or to present themselves for examination at the end of a fixed period. Their time was their own, to use or waste as they saw fit. There were serious students, who worked steadily year in and year out, but there were at least as many who engaged in the extra-curricular activities of drinking, gambling, love-making and fighting the police. If their rioting went too far—and it often ended in homicide—they were relatively safe from punishment, since most universities had secured the exemption of their students from the jurisdiction of secular courts. If a student fell into serious difficulties, or if he were bored with his work, he could always move to another university. This entailed no loss of time, since the basic courses and textbooks were the same everywhere. It was often advantageous, since it was cheaper to go from Oxford to Paris to hear a famous professor than it was to buy one of his books. The life of these wandering students is reflected in the Goliardic poems which are still one of the best expressions of the undergraduate mentality that we possess.

THE TWELFTH-CENTURY RENAISSANCE—ART

The same energy and skill which characterized other activities are evident in the architecture and the art of the twelfth century. The leadership of the Church is especially apparent in this field. All the important works of art of this period were ecclesiastical. The Church alone had the money and the organization necessary for completing large projects or for paying skilled workmen. Medieval art is one of the best examples of the way in which the Church stimulated the revival of civilization. It is also an excellent illustration of medieval originality. Beginning with degenerate Roman forms, then developing interesting adaptations of Roman models, medieval artists finally created a style which was almost the antithesis of the Roman and which has remained the great rival of classical styles down to the present day.

The typical Christian church of the late empire was an adaptation of the Roman basilica, or law-court. It was an oblong building, divided into three or more aisles by the rows of pillars which held up the roof. The roof over the center aisle was usually raised above the roof on each side, and light was admitted through windows in the clerestory wall which held up this center section. The roofs were flat and were supported by

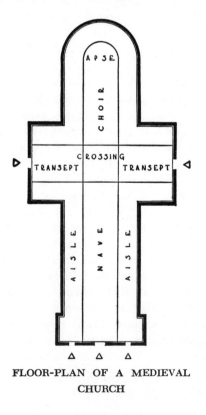

FLOOR-PLAN OF A MEDIEVAL
CHURCH

wooden beams. This type of building was only slightly modified by early Christian architects. Some of them rounded off the end opposite the door in order to give a better background for the altar. Others introduced a cross-aisle in front of the altar so that the whole church had the shape of a cross. These changes did not affect the general plan of construction, and the basilica remained the standard type of Christian church in the West throughout the early Middle Ages.

When the eleventh century revival encouraged churchmen to enlarge and rebuild their edifices, they found that the old pattern was not entirely satisfactory. The flat roof of Mediterranean countries was not practical in regions of heavy precipitation and the use of wooden beams encouraged disastrous fires. Both these difficulties could be avoided by the use of a vaulted stone roof, but this solution created new problems. It was hard to support the heavy roof over the center aisle, since the whole thrust had to be carried on the thin walls of the clerestory, which in turn were supported on a few scattered pillars. If the roof were lowered, or if the windows were made smaller, it was easier to support the weight, but these changes spoiled the proportions or the lighting of the church. Some architects, especially in Mediterranean countries, vaulted only the side aisles, and retained the wooden roof in the center, but north of the Alps there were persistent efforts to cover the entire building with stone.

Some small churches were covered with barrel-vaults,[8] without losing either their proportions or their strength, but this type of roof was not successful in large buildings. A solution was finally found by designing a roof on the basis of two barrel-vaults which intersected each other at

DEVELOPMENT OF THE CROSS-VAULT

right angles. As will be seen by the diagram, this concentrated the weight of the roof at a few points, which could be reinforced by buttresses. This invention made it possible to make the center aisle higher and broader, and to enlarge the rest of the church in proportion. It also made it possible to enlarge the windows and flood the interior of the church with light. These changes prepared the way for the new Gothic architecture of the late twelfth century.

[8] A barrel-vault looks like a vertical cross-section of a barrel. The weight is equally distributed along the entire supporting wall.

The churches built during the period of experimentation were often very beautiful. In the interior the eye was carried along by rows of pillars until it reached the altar, framed against the soft obscurity of the apse. The exterior was ornamented by bands of geometrical designs, and the west front, where the main entrance was placed, was often adorned with elaborate sculptures. The main lines of the building were horizontal, and the arches over the doors and between the pillars were broad semicircles. The general effect was one of restraint, moderation, and good taste. Perhaps the fact that the monasteries, and especially Cluny, were the leaders in developing this type of architecture, has something to do with this impression. This style of architecture is usually called Romanesque, since it was still based largely on the old Roman model. It flourished in all parts of Europe, and each region developed its own particular variety of the style. Generally speaking, Roman influences were strongest in Italy and southern France, while more originality was found in central and northern France.

By the middle of the twelfth century certain people in the region about Paris were no longer satisfied with Romanesque churches. One reason for their discontent was that technical difficulties made it hard to construct a large Romanesque church, and many churchmen were dreaming of edifices which should surpass anything yet built in size and magnificence. The change in religious attitudes may also have had something to do with the change in style. There was still something of the Roman spirit in the Romanesque church; it was practical, earthbound, and precise. It could not express the new piety which soared toward heaven, which veiled everything in tender mysticism, which thought in terms of the infinite. Architects and builders may not have been affected by these religious emotions, but they could not escape the general spirit of the age. Men of the twelfth century were enthusiastic, audacious, and romantic, and they found few of these qualities in the classical style or its derivatives. They may not have been entirely conscious of this fact, but in their experiments they always turned away from the classical tradition, instead of trying to restore it.

One of the first centers of the new style was the monastery of St. Denis, the burial place of the French kings. Here the great abbot, Suger, began to reconstruct the church in the first half of the twelfth century, and in his attempt to make it larger and more impressive employed many of the devices on which the Gothic style was based. Other neighboring monasteries also used the new technique. By the end of the century the bishops of the region had begun to rebuild their cathedrals and they, too, adopted the new style. Thus before 1200 the main principles of Gothic architecture had been laid down, though they had not yet been developed as fully as they were to be later.

Suger, in his account of the building of the new church at St. Denis, makes it clear that he was trying to get more light into the building. In doing this he developed a new style in which vertical lines were emphasized and window space was enlarged. These effects were secured by the use of rib-vaulting and the pointed arch. Cross-vaulting, or the use of two intersecting barrel-vaults, has already been described. In Gothic buildings it was improved in appearance (though not in strength) by supporting the lines of intersection by ribs of specially cut stone. This modified type of cross-vaulting is called rib-vaulting. Rib-vaulting concentrated all the weight of the roof at a few points on the clerestory wall. Instead of building heavy piers at these points, which would have extended into the interior of the church, Gothic architects preferred to use flying buttresses (see figure) which carried the thrust over the side aisle to a standing buttress on the exterior of the church. The result of these devices was that the walls of the church no longer had to carry the weight of the roof, which was supported entirely by columns and buttresses. Thus the walls between the buttresses could be knocked out and windows could take most of the space formerly occupied by walls. This last result was not achieved at once. Early Gothic architects left a good deal of blank wall space, and while their windows were large they were nothing like the size which was later attained. Notre Dame of Paris is a good example of this development. In the western end of the church, which was built first, the windows occupy only a small part of the wall; in the rest of the church they are greatly enlarged. The new system of vaulting made it possible to contruct churches which were much higher than any that had ever existed before. The pointed arch made them seem even higher than they were. A pointed arch, of course, stands somewhat higher than a semicircular one covering the same span, but it is more important to observe that it carries the eye upward and emphasizes the height rather than the breadth of the space it bridges. The pointed arch also gives somewhat more window-space than the round arch, and this may have been the first reason for its adoption. Here again development was very gradual. The first pointed arches were rather broad in proportion to their height; only in the late thirteenth century did the excessively narrow, extremely pointed arch become fashionable. Early Gothic churches still have some of the restraint and moderation of Romanesque; the new art has not yet been pushed to extremes.

Early Gothic churches are not as spectacular as those of the thirteenth century, but they have a special interest for the historian. Here we can see the men of the Middle Ages working out a difficult series of technical problems and follow them step by step in their work. They developed their new methods with amazing rapidity and displayed none of the conservatism which is popularly supposed to have been the dominant characteristic of the Middle Ages. Romanesque style was obsolete in Ile de France within less than a half-century after the first experiments.

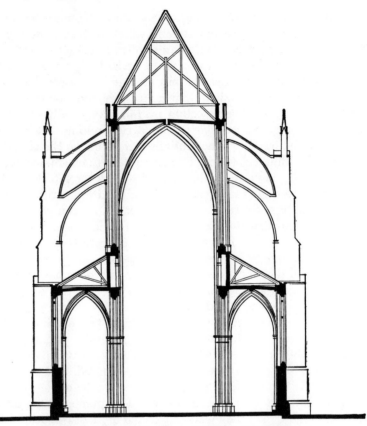

CROSS-SECTION OF A GOTHIC CHURCH

Within the next half-century some of the most perfect Gothic churches in existence had been built. Things do not move much more rapidly at present. The American sky-scraper, with its emphasis on height and lighting, is in many ways the modern counterpart of the Gothic cathedral. The technical device which makes the sky-scraper possible is the steel skeleton. This device was discovered in the 1880's but it was at least thirty years before architects began to emphasize vertical lines in steel buildings, and it was not until the late 1940's that they realized that the entire outside wall could be made of glass.

The development of Gothic architecture has been described at some length because it is the most striking and enduring example of medieval artistic work. It is impossible to discuss the other arts adequately in the limited space available. In general it may be said that the representational arts—sculpture, painting, and manuscript illumination—followed the same course. In the beginning, Christian art merely imitated the decadent realism of the late empire. Stumpy, doll-like figures were arranged in patterns which conveyed the essential elements of the Christian story. But this would-be realism was so unrealistic that it was soon abandoned. The essential thing was to tell the story, to convey the desired idea. Figures became symbols; there was no attempt to make them lifelike or to achieve the ideal beauty of the Greeks. Yet, by concentrating on the idea or the emotion which was to be portrayed, medieval artists attained a new type of beauty. It is a beauty based on faith and knowledge, it can be appreciated only after a little study, but the study is well worth while. Medieval sculpture, in particular, far surpasses that of the Romans, and is a worthy rival to the work of the Greeks.

IX

-》》-》》-》》-》》《《-《《-《《-《《

The Rise of
the Western Monarchies

A<small>T THE END</small> of the eleventh century the average inhabitant of Europe
was subject to many overlapping authorities. He had an immediate
lord, who controlled most of his ordinary activities. Besides this lord
there might be a higher authority, such as a count or a duke, who had
reserved certain rights of justice or of toll over him. Then there was the
king, who had ill-defined but not entirely forgotten claims to obedience.
Finally, the Church courts controlled many personal relationships and
the pope, as head of Christendom, could intervene in many political matters and could often overrule secular authorities. With so many claimants
to power, kings were neither especially dignified nor especially important.
In most regions of Europe they did not receive the primary allegiance of
their peoples and could not determine the political destinies of their countries. Primary allegiance went either to the local lord who controlled the
economic life of his district or to a duke or count who had military supremacy. And, as we have seen, the fate of Europe in the eleventh century
was determined by feudal lords rather than by kings. The revival of
civilization did not change this situation in central and eastern Europe;
in the long run kings became weaker there rather than stronger. In the
West, on the other hand, royal power increased during the twelfth and
thirteenth centuries. There were setbacks caused by weak reigns, but by
the end of the thirteenth century the kings of England, France, and Spain
had succeeded in gaining some degree of control over all their subjects
and in making their kingdoms effective political units. The first steps in
this development were taken during the twelfth century, first in England
and then in France.

ENGLAND—THE WORK OF HENRY I

When William the Conqueror died in 1087, the English monarchy was undoubtedly the most advanced in western Europe. Yet the power of the king was still very limited and England did not have a centralized government. Feudal lords had wide control of local government and the king could not raise an army nor run the central administration without their aid. There was a sharp division between the Norman ruling class and the subject Anglo-Saxons. Both king and barons had many interests across the channel and the welfare of England was often sacrificed in defending these interests. William had been very powerful, but his power was based to a large degree on his remarkable personality and on the unusual circumstance of the Conquest. It remained to be seen whether his successors could obtain the loyalty of the Anglo-Saxons and retain the loyalty of the Norman barons.

Upon the Conqueror's death, William II (Rufus) became king, but not without opposition. Many of the barons preferred his weak, good-natured elder brother Robert, who was duke of Normandy. Early in his reign, William had to put down a dangerous revolt of the barons. Robert, however, continued to make trouble until he joined the First Crusade and pawned his duchy to Rufus in order to obtain money for the expedition to the Holy Land. With the removal of this threat William began to treat his barons more harshly. He pushed his rights as lord to the limit, and made as much money as possible out of feudal incidents. Thus he demanded large sums of money as relief before he would allow the heirs of his barons to take over their fathers' lands. He also had a bitter quarrel with Anselm, the new archbishop of Canterbury. Anselm was imbued with the ideas of the reform party in the Church and in proclaiming the independence of prelates from lay control he naturally came into conflict with a Norman ruler who felt that his bishops were merely a more subservient type of baron. Anselm was forced into exile, and the leaders of the Church joined the barons in denouncing the Red King. Even the English seem to have disliked him and when he was shot while hunting in the New Forest there was a general feeling of relief. William Rufus had lost no power—in fact he had probably increased his authority over his vassals—but he certainly had not made the monarchy popular.

His younger brother Henry at once seized the royal treasure at Winchester and had himself crowned king. His right to the throne was very doubtful, as his eldest brother Robert was still alive. Therefore Henry sought support from all groups in England. He granted a charter of liberties to his barons, promising to refrain from his brother's abuses of feudal rights. Though Henry did not keep all his promises, the charter was an important precedent in later attempts to limit the royal power.

He married the English Edith, a descendant of Alfred the Great,[1] in order to secure the good will of the native population. He recalled Anselm and aided him in reforming the English church, though he was unable to avoid a new conflict on the question of investiture. Even this difficult problem was settled by a compromise in 1106. Henry gave up the right to invest prelates with ecclesiastical insignia but he retained his claim to fealty and service and the right to be consulted before ecclesiastical elections were held. In practice these reservations gave him almost complete control over the choice of bishops and abbots in his kingdom. This compromise was not unlike the one made at Worms in 1122 by the Emperor Henry V, and the German agreement may have been influenced by the English example.

By these moves Henry gained the support of most Englishmen, and the barons who, with Robert's aid, attempted to resist him were subdued. Henry then determined to end the Norman danger. After a long struggle he captured and imprisoned Robert and took over the government of Normandy. This was done in spite of the opposition of the French king, who would have preferred to keep the weak Robert as a neighbor. Henry was now so powerful that he could take up the task of strengthening the royal government and extending its authority without fear of opposition. All later kings built on his foundations and some of the institutions which he created survive today.

To understand his achievements we must again consider the nature of the *curia regis,* the king's court. The *curia* was composed of the men who happened to be with the king at a given moment, and it could assist the king in any of his work. Under the two Williams it had been more or less of an amateur body. Few members of the *curia* spent all their time in the service of the king, and any member of the *curia* was supposed to be capable of undertaking any sort of administrative work. The procedure of the *curia* was informal; its activity was intermittent and its records were incomplete. Under Henry I there was a beginning of specialization and professionalization. A separate financial department and a separate judicial system began to split off the main body of the *curia.* A group of trained administrators emerged, who devoted almost all their time to government service. The number of royal clerks was increased; more and better records were kept, and administrative traditions which were not dependent on the personality of the king were established.

The clearest example of these changes is the growth of the financial department known as the Exchequer. This name came from the table, marked off into squares like a checker-board, which the *curia* used when

---

[1] As the result of this marriage, all of Henry's successors on the English throne, with the single exception of Stephen, were descendants of both Alfred and William the Conqueror.

it audited sheriffs' accounts. The first column was reserved for pennies, the next for shillings, and the others for pounds and their multiples. The money and credits turned in by a sheriff were indicated by moving counters on the board. If the final figure equaled the sum which the records showed was due, the sheriff was dismissed in peace. If there was any deficiency, he was personally liable to the king. Obviously, this sort of work would not be attractive to an ordinary feudal lord, even if he were a frequent attendant at the *curia*. It required the the use of written records and of arithmetic, both of which were deep mysteries to the average baron. Thus the meetings of the *curia* at the Exchequer table were attended only by a handful of men who had an aptitude for this work and who were constantly with the king. This tended to separate the Exchequer from the rest of the *curia* and it gradually became a separate department with its own staff of clerks and its own records. The most important of these records was the pipe-roll, which gave all the details of the semi-annual accounting with the sheriffs. It derived its name from the fact that each sheet of parchment which contained the account of a county was known as a "pipe." Only one pipe-roll of the reign of Henry I has survived, but there is a continuous series from 1154 to the nineteenth century. No other country has such complete medieval financial records, and as a result we know much more about the English government than we do about those of the continent.

The importance of the Exchequer was very great. Royal political supremacy was based on royal wealth. The king mastered the barons because his financial resources were greater than theirs, and the organization of the Exchequer assured him a large and steady income at a very early date. The Exchequer also aided the king to free himself from dependence on the barons. It was a training-ground for professional administrators, a branch of the government which the barons could never control. It kept close check on the sheriffs, who were members of the feudal nobility, and kept them from quietly annexing royal rights and prerogatives. Finally, it gave the king detailed information about the state of the country and so enabled him to act swiftly and effectively.

Henry could not professionalize his judicial system as completely as his financial administration. Like most laymen of any period, the barons felt themselves much more able to decide law-suits than to audit accounts. The *curia*, when it acted as a judicial body, always included several feudal lords, and if it were trying a great baron it would include many men of his rank. Yet there was a small group of royal advisers who were almost always present and who were somewhat more expert in the law than the ordinary lord. In the local courts Henry was able to go much further. Cases reserved for royal justice had usually been tried by the sheriffs in the county courts. The sheriffs had so many other duties that they were not very efficient in administering justice, and this was bad both for the king's revenue and the peace of the land. Henry tried to remedy this by sending members of the *curia* to try pleas of the crown in local courts. These men, armed with the full authority of the *curia regis,* free from other responsibilities, were far more effective as judges than the sheriffs. By the end of the reign they were making circuits through groups of counties in England, dispensing royal justice and increasing royal prestige. Many of these judges served the king for several years, and they, too, began to develop professional traditions. They were the predecessors of the circuit judges who still exist in England and the United States.

Henry was obviously trying to free himself from complete dependence upon the great barons. One chronicler scornfully remarked that he surrounded himself with men whom he had "raised from the dust." His most trusted adviser was Bishop Roger of Salisbury, who had been a poor parish priest in Normandy. Roger had much to do with the organization of the Exchequer and he, with his nephews and grand-nephews, ran the finances of England for a half-century. Henry's sheriffs were usually minor vassals, not the great barons who had held the office under the Williams, and most of his judges were selected from the same class. These men owed everything to the king and were not dominated by feudal interests. They were powerful only as the king was powerful and they guarded his rights zealously.

Yet Henry did not end feudalism in England, though he prepared the way for its collapse during the next century. He could not ignore the great barons and never dreamed of depriving them of their legitimate authority. He consulted them on all important occasions and never interfered with their government of their own fiefs. His reforms prevented feudalism from growing any further; there were no large-scale usurpations of royal authority during his reign. His reforms also enabled him to use his reserved powers very effectively and to impress the people with the efficiency of his government. He was called the "Lion of Justice" and chroniclers praised the peace and security which he gave the land. As a result Henry was much more popular with the English than the two Williams had been, and during his reign the cleavage between the conquerors and the conquered began to disappear.

Henry's work was severely tested after his death. His son had been drowned in a shipwreck and his only other legitimate child was a daughter Matilda, who had married the count of Anjou. It was very doubtful whether a woman could inherit the throne, and Matilda was unpopular, both because of her arrogance and because she had married a hereditary enemy of the Normans. Henry's effort to secure the throne for his daughter was opposed by many barons, who favored the claims of Stephen of Blois, a son of the Conqueror's daughter. When Henry died, Stephen rushed to England, secured the royal treasure and the support of some bishops, and was crowned king. Matilda did not act promptly, so Stephen was accepted by the barons, though with no great enthusiasm. He had to grant a new charter of liberties and make many concessions to the Church. Then Matilda and her husband began the conquest of the Norman heritage. The count of Anjou invaded Normandy, while Matilda raised her banner in the west of England. This began a long and indecisive civil war, which was profitable only to the barons. By changing sides at the proper moment they were able to demand large rewards for their services, and some of them became virtually independent rulers of large territories. The peasants suffered severely, since they were plundered and tortured by both sides. The Church became much more independent of lay authority, yet its estates were devastated and some of its buildings burned. During the nineteen years of Stephen's reign England learned what uncontrolled feudalism could do.

Yet everything was not lost. Stephen remained king, in spite of temporary successes of his rival, and the central government did not collapse completely. The Exchequer continued to function, and some of Henry's administrators remained in the royal service. Most important of all, rear-vassals and knights could not forget the generation of peace which Henry had given them. As the war dragged on they became unwilling to fight for either side or to aid their baronial overlords to gain powers which made them local tyrants. England had had too long a period of stable government to lapse into feudal anarchy like that of the tenth century, and general disgust with the war eventually made a compromise settlement possible. When Stephen's heir died the old king agreed to recognize Matilda's son Henry as his successor. The weary ruler did not long survive this treaty. He died in 1154, and Henry of Anjou became king of England.

ENGLAND—THE WORK OF HENRY II

Henry II was only twenty-one when he ascended the throne but he had already had wide experience in war and in government. His father had conquered Normandy for him and he had been actual ruler of the duchy since 1150. In 1151 his father died, leaving him Anjou and Touraine, and in 1152 he married the greatest heiress of France, Eleanor of Aquitaine. With her he secured Poitou, Guienne, and Gascony, and claims to the lordship of the whole southwest corner of France. Henry was the greatest lord in France, with lands far wider than those of the Capetian king, before he became ruler of England. These French possessions explain many of his policies, for it was far more difficult to retain them than it was to hold England. As a result, Henry spent only about a third of his long reign in England and was frequently absent from the island for years at a time. Henry was French by birth, education, and speech and England was by no means the center of his empire.

Yet this Frenchman with predominantly continental interests was one of the great architects of the English constitution. This was partly due to enlightened selfishness. Henry needed the resources of England for his continental wars, and he could not get them unless the island were well governed. He could not leave England for long periods to its own devices unless he also left a smooth-running, bureaucratic administration which could function without him. But there was more to it than this. Henry had a passion for order and justice, and a real interest in the details of administration. He governed well, not only because it was profitable, but also because he enjoyed the work of government. He had no use for pomp and ceremony; he despised the new-fangled talk of chivalry; but he would spend hours on a difficult legal question and he audited his accounts down to the last penny. He was a man of tireless energy who exhausted his officials by his endless capacity for work and travel; he was determined to have order in his lands, even if he had to fight to get it, and he maintained his policies in the face of terrific opposition. He was harsh, and at times cruel, not a very lovable nor a very pious individual, but one who commanded, and still commands respect for the work he did. He was a genius in the art of government; his work was so well adapted to the needs of the period that neither his own severity nor the opposition of Church and baronage could make it unpopular.

His first task was to restore the good order of his grandfather's reign, who had "made peace for men and deer." The barons were compelled to surrender their castles or else to destroy them; armed bands of mercenary soldiers were driven from the country, and royal lands and rights which had been lost under Stephen were reclaimed. This work was made easier by the general war-weariness; no one would support the barons in their efforts to retain their spoils. Then the central administration was reinstituted and some of the old trained officials were recalled. The Exchequer was now able to work freely, without being hampered by semi-independent feudal lords, and the circuit judges went forth through all England again.

But Henry II went far beyond his grandfather. The elder Henry had made his courts efficient, but he had made no great effort to attract cases from baronial jurisdictions. Henry II did his best to bring all important lawsuits before his own justices. Thus he increased his revenues and at the same time restricted the power of the feudal barons. These results were obtained by a great extension of the use of the sworn inquest, or jury. Earlier kings, notably the Conqueror, had used the inquest primarily to obtain information for their own use. On rare occasions inquests had been used to settle disputes between prominent men. Henry had the brilliant idea of allowing any man the right to call an inquest in certain types of civil suits if he paid a small fee for the privilege. Since the king alone could authorize this procedure, any one wishing trial by inquest had to go to the royal courts. A great many people did want trial by inquest, since it was much more satisfactory than the older methods of compurgation or wager of battle. When the new procedure was used the judges called in a body of neighbors, usually twelve in number, and asked them specific questions about the property in dispute. The answer, or verdict, given by the group, might be based on firsthand knowledge, or on mere neighborhood gossip, but it was at least dependent upon some sort of evidence and not on superstition. Henry eventually allowed any freeman to demand an inquest if his title to a feudal holding were questioned. Since almost all civil suits between members of the upper classes involved questions of feudal tenure, this extension of procedure by inquest meant that the baronial courts lost most of their civil jurisdiction. In addition, since the tenure of rear-vassals was now protected by royal courts, the barons lost much of their authority over their followers. Knights and other petty vassals could no longer be dispossessed by their lords on flimsy excuses and they were much less ready to give blind obedience to their feudal superiors.

The inquest worked so well in civil cases that Henry determined to try it in criminal procedure. Before Henry's reforms, many crimes of violence went unpunished because it was the duty of the injured party or his friends to accuse the criminal. If the latter was a powerful man the injured often feared to bring charges against him, lest a worse fate befall them. By the assize of Clarendon, 1166, Henry made it the duty of the itinerant justices and sheriffs to call together twelve men from each hundred, and four from each vill, and to put them upon oath to say "whether there is in their hundred or in their vill any man who has been accused or publicly suspected of being a robber, or murderer, or thief, or of being a receiver of robbers, or murderers or thieves." A man accused by such an inquest had to undergo the ordeal of water. If he failed he was hanged or mutilated, but even if he came out successfully he might be banished if he were "of very bad reputation and publicly and disgracefully spoken ill of by the testimony of many reputable men." This assize not only brought many criminals to justice who would otherwise have escaped, but also weakened the criminal jurisdiction of the feudal lords. The king alone could call criminal inquests, and those accused by the jurors could be tried only in the king's courts. Thus all criminal cases of any importance were transferred to the king's jurisdiction.

Henry had created the civil jury much as we know it today. All that remained was to apply his principles to all types of civil suits and to allow witnesses to give testimony before the jurors. These steps were gradually taken during the next three centuries. He had not gone so far on the criminal side. The inquest there corresponded to the modern grand jury, but the men indicted were still tried by ordeal. In 1215, however, a church council forbade the use of ordeals, and it was necessary to find another means of determining the guilt of the accused. Since the jury was already there, English judges naturally turned to it for a solution to the problem. The accused was compelled to accept as final the verdict of the grand jury of his hundred or of the four neighboring vills. This was seen to be not entirely fair and eventually a second jury, the petit or trial jury, was selected to determine the guilt of men indicted by a grand jury.

Henry used the jury not only to settle other men's law-suits but to determine his own rights. The grand jury had to give information about all royal possessions and revenues in its district, and this information was very useful to the king and his ministers. It also reported on the behavior of local officials and so kept them from becoming too independent or corrupt. Henry did not object to severity and extortion as long as he profited by it, but he did not like to have his officials use their power to enrich themselves. The modern grand jury has inherited the right to investigate the acts of public officials, and this is probably its most useful function today.

The great increase in the use of the jury added to the powers of the circuit judges and still further decreased the importance of the sheriff. His judicial functions were now restricted to petty cases, and his work was constantly checked by the circuit judges and the grand juries. This gave the king much more control over local government. The circuit judges were absolutely in his power. They were given detailed instructions before they went out, and they had to render detailed reports when they returned. Because of their close personal relations with the king they carried out his orders far more carefully than the sheriffs had done, and they seem to have been much more honest. The Inquest of Sheriffs in 1170 showed how the new system could be used to improve local government. In that year Henry had juries all over the country give a special report on the behavior of the sheriffs, and as a result of this investigation fifteen out of twenty-two sheriffs were dismissed from office.

Henry's last judicial reform was the creation of a central court at the king's residence. Some cases were too important to be entrusted to the circuit judges, and many men were too impatient to wait for the royal judges to come to their neighborhood. Thus many law-suits were brought before the king and his followers. Yet English law was becoming too technical to be administered by the whole membership of the *curia regis*. Therefore Henry, toward the end of his reign, selected certain members of the *curia* who were well versed in law, and had them try most of the cases which were brought before his court. This was the beginning of a new split in the *curia*, since these judges eventually became members of an independent law-court. The old feudal *curia* continued to exist as an advisory body and it still tried cases of unusual importance, but the professional administrators had made another advance.

In his reforms of the courts Henry came into conflict with the Church. As we have seen, the bishops had become much more independent under Stephen, and the church courts had greatly increased their jurisdiction. Their right to try cases involving marriage and wills was universally recognized, but their claim to try all suits in which clerics or church property were involved was new in England. Even more extreme was their claim to try all suits involving breach of an oath—in other words all cases of contract. If pushed to a logical extreme, these categories would have included a large proportion of all suits, and this would have lessened the power and revenue which the king was deriving from his courts. The tribunals of the Church were popular, not only because the penalties imposed there were lighter, but also because they gave a very good brand of justice. The Church was improving its administrative system and legal procedure at least as rapidly as Henry II, and canon law was superior to that of the king's court in many respects. It is not surprising that many men sought to have their cases tried in ecclesiastical courts and that they devised many expedients to secure this privilege. The king was especially annoyed by the fact that many criminals were able to claim that they were members of the clergy, and hence to escape the severe punishments of the secular courts. Not only clergymen, as we understand the word, but also all students, all crusaders, all officials of the Church and all servants of churchmen could demand trial in church courts. In such a numerous and heterogeneous body there were bound to be some men of evil life, and Henry believed that many murderers and thieves were being protected by clerical privilege. He determined to check this abuse, and at the same time to limit the growth of the rival jurisdiction. This brought him into conflict with the Church, as represented by Thomas Becket, archbishop of Canterbury.

Thomas was the son of a Norman who had settled in London and become a wealthy merchant. He had received a good education and had entered the office of a London businessman who had many dealings with barons and prelates. This brought him to the notice of the archbishop of Canterbury, who took him into his household. There Thomas had an opportunity to learn much about the affairs of the realm as well as those of the Church. He proved an able subordinate and was sent by the archbishop to Bologna to study the new science of canon law. He also played a part in the diplomatic negotiations which enabled Henry II to succeed Stephen as king of England. He was then made archdeacon of Canterbury, which meant that he was responsible for all the secular business of the diocese. When Henry became king the archbishop recommended Thomas to him, and he was made chancellor. Thomas was sixteen years older than the young sovereign, but the two men had the same love of business and the same taste in amusements, so that they became inseparable companions. The chancellor received many gifts and rich benefices from the king and soon was leading a luxurious life. His household was one of the most splendid in Europe and in it the king's own son and many young nobles were trained in chivalry. At the same time Thomas was an able administrator and gave Henry loyal support, even against the Church.

Naturally, when the old archbishop died the king wished to make his faithful servant and friend the head of the English Church. By this appointment he hoped not only to avoid all conflict with ecclesiastical authority but also to gain the full support of the spiritual power in his work of rebuilding the government. Thomas is said to have hesitated and to have warned Henry that "an archbishop must give offense either to God or to the king." This story may have been invented later to explain the difficulties which eventually arose. In any case Thomas' reluctance was soon overcome and he was duly elected and consecrated. Shortly thereafter he resigned the chancellorship, much against the king's will, and renounced his luxurious life. He wore a hair shirt, visited the sick, and washed the feet of beggars. "As he had been accustomed to preëminence in worldly glory, he now determined to be first in holy living." Soon he was quarreling violently with Henry and denouncing his old master as a tyrant.

This sudden change in Thomas' life has been explained in many ways. Undoubtedly he was influenced by the traditions of his office. Thomas was always something of an actor and he tried to play every rôle assigned to him properly. He was also a proud man, and he may have wished to assert his independence of king and court after many years of subordination. But histrionic ability and pride are not the qualities which made him a saint and a martyr. Like so many leaders of the reforming movement, he had experienced a conversion which made religion a real force in his life instead of a mere form. Like other reforming leaders he felt that faith, personal morality, and the independence of the Church were inextricably bound together. Asceticism and opposition to the king were both necessary if he was to preserve his revivified belief.

The quarrel between king and archbishop came to a head in 1164, when relations between the secular and ecclesiastical courts were being discussed. Henry demanded that clerks found guilty of heinous crimes by the Church courts should be degraded and handed over to lay courts for punishment. Thomas refused, saying that clerks could not be judged by any secular power. Then Henry tried to solve the problem by making Thomas swear to observe the customs (that is, the past usages) of the land. Thomas at first would not agree, but the king became so angry at this refusal that the other bishops were frightened. They felt that this was no time for an open breach with Henry and finally persuaded Thomas to swear obedience to "the customs of the kingdom." Henry immediately summoned a council at Clarendon and asked "wise men" to write out the customs, so that there might be no question in the future as to what they were. The document produced by this inquest was known as the "Constitutions of Clarendon." When it was read to Thomas and he was asked to set his seal to it as he had promised, he replied: "Never, while there is breath left in my body." For these Constitutions settled many disputed issues in favor of the king and deprived the Church of almost everything which it had gained since 1100. Opportunities for the Church to draw civil suits into its courts were greatly restricted, appeals to the pope were forbidden, bishops were not to leave the realm without royal permission, vassals and officials of the king were not to be excommunicated until he had been notified, and finally, criminous clerks convicted in ecclesiastical courts were no longer to be protected by the Church but were to be punished by the royal justices.

While the Constitutions were hardly a fair statement of recent practice, they were reasonably close to the usages of Henry I's time. For this reason, and also because the pope was occupied with the struggle with Frederick Barbarossa, most of the English clergy were ready to accept them. Not so Thomas. Henry put more and more pressure on him and finally the archbishop, fearing for his life, fled to France to seek the support of the pope. But Alexander III, who had just been driven from Italy by the emperor, did not wish to antagonize the most powerful ruler of the West. He temporized, and finally a peace was patched up between Henry and Thomas which decided none of the disputed issues. Thomas returned to England full of bitterness against the king and against his fellow-bishops who had failed to support him.

As soon as he was reëstablished at Canterbury he determined to assert his archiepiscopal authority and to insist upon the freedom of the Church. He excommunicated the bishops who had sided with the king, and the laymen who had occupied the lands of Canterbury during his absence. This was in direct contravention of the Constitutions of Clarendon, which forbade excommunication of royal vassals, and meant that the whole struggle was beginning again. When the news reached Henry in France, he was seized by one of his typical and ungovernable fits of rage. He asked why he had no followers loyal enough to rid him of this "false priest," and the rhetorical question was taken seriously by four knights of the household. They crossed to England, hastened to Canterbury, and murdered the archbishop in his own cathedral.

Thomas secured a greater victory by his death as a martyr than he could have obtained if he had lived. Henry undoubtedly realized this and also was genuinely grieved at the result of his outburst of passion. For days he shut himself up, fasting and alone. He took oath that he was innocent of the murder and a year later did penance by receiving a public scourging at Canterbury which was so severe that he fell ill. He also had to yield some, though not all, of the claims made in the Constitutions. The royal courts retained the civil jurisdiction which they had asserted, but they surrendered their right to punish criminous clerks. Appeals to the pope and trips to the papal *curia* had to be allowed, and thus Henry's attempt to interfere with the development of the competing jurisdiction was defeated. He had been unable to regulate and limit the church courts as he had those of the barons, and ecclesiastical judges retained their power in England down to the time of the Reformation.

The murder of Thomas was also an excuse for a great rebellion against the king. The barons were annoyed by the inroads which Henry had made on their jurisdictions, by the rise of the professional element in the *curia,* and by a new military system which made feudal service less important. Early in the reign Henry had begun the practice of taking scutage (shield-money) instead of military service from most of his vassals. The vassal paid what the service would have cost him, and with the money the king hired mercenaries. Henry I had done the same thing in isolated cases, but, as usual, the generalization of the expedient by Henry II caused more of a shock than the first experiment. The mercenaries whom he hired with the proceeds of scutage made him less dependent on the barons and decreased their influence at court. The memories of the civil war of Stephen's day were growing dim and the assassination of Thomas weakened Henry's hold on his people. Thomas was soon canonized and his shrine at Canterbury became the goal of thousands who nourished feelings of bitter indignation against the king who had murdered a saint. The nobles took advantage of this feeling to organize a widespread revolt, but Henry's better-organized forces eventually succeeded in suppressing it. The king of Scots, who had aided the rebels, was captured and made to do homage for his kingdom. A little later Henry went to Ireland, where some of his vassals had already begun a conquest of the island, and received their homage as well as that of some Irish chieftains. Yet, in spite of these successes the rebellion marked a turning-point in Henry's reign. The king had been seriously threatened, and the steady growth of royal power was interrupted for a time. Even though the revolt failed, the tradition of rebellion had been revived and the great opponent of royal absolutism had been canonized. Henry moved cautiously for some years after 1173 and made fewer innovations in his government.

Increasing difficulties in his French fiefs also diverted Henry's attention from the problems of his English realm. His sons were greedy for power, anxious for a share of their father's lands, and willing to go to any extremes in order to obtain their desires. The astute French king, Philip Augustus, was eager to weaken the empire which Henry had created, and which overshadowed the French royal domain. Philip encouraged the ambitions of Henry's sons and supported them when they rebelled against their father. Henry held his own for a while, but was forced to make an unfavorable peace in 1189, and died brokenhearted, moaning, "Shame on a conquered king!"

JOHN AND MAGNA CARTA

Yet his work lived after him. During the last part of Henry's life and for the whole ten years of Richard's reign (1189–1199) the king was hardly ever in England. This would have been fatal to royal authority at an earlier period, but Henry had established his government so firmly that it could function even in the absence of a king. It not only preserved but even increased royal power by perfecting administrative and judicial techniques. The most notable example was the introduction of new general taxes into England during Richard's reign. A tithe for the Third Crusade, the money for Richard's ransom, and large sums for his wars in France were raised by taxes on real estate, personal property, and incomes. This was almost unprecedented, yet the government was so strong that there were only minor protests against the innovation. How remarkable this was may be seen by the fact that the tithe for the Third Crusade was so unpopular in France that it had to be abandoned; no new taxes could be introduced in that kingdom until 1295. The three kings who followed Henry II all had serious weaknesses, yet neither Richard's neglect, John's perversity, nor Henry III's lack of judgment weakened the institutions established by the great Angevin.

Richard made one hasty trip to England at the beginning of his reign to raise money for his Crusade. He made another equally hurried visit after the Crusade to secure funds to pay the ransom which he owed Henry VI. The rest of his reign he spent in France fighting his former ally, Philip Augustus. Richard cared little for England except as a source of revenue, but he was not unpopular in the country. He had gained a great reputation as a crusader, and he was the best general of his period. His brother John, who succeeded him in 1199, was just as greedy and had fewer redeeming traits. He was suspicious and erratic, unscrupulous and fearful. He trusted no one and, naturally, received no one's trust. He was always making clever and daring plans which were never fully executed, either because his own followers betrayed him, or because he lost his nerve. As a crowning misfortune, he had as his chief antagonists one of the greatest popes and one of the ablest French kings.

The defects in John's character first betrayed him to Philip Augustus of France. Philip had long sought to annex the Angevin fiefs, but had made little headway against Henry II and Richard. John gave Philip a perfect excuse for renewing the old quarrel by marrying Isabelle of

Angoulême, who was betrothed to one of John's own vassals. This was a clear breach of the feudal contract. John had dishonored his vassal, and the latter appealed to Philip Augustus who, as John's lord, had the right to judge such a case. Philip cited John to his court, but John refused to appear, thus breaking another feudal obligation. The French court then pronounced the forfeiture of John's fiefs and Philip went to war to enforce the sentence. He made further trouble for John by recognizing Arthur of Brittany as heir to most of the Angevin possessions. According to modern ideas Arthur had a better claim to Henry II's lands than John, since he was the son of John's early-lost elder brother Geoffrey. He already had some partisans, and Philip's act gave him increased support. John apparently solved this difficulty by capturing Arthur, but soon lost his advantage by allowing the boy to be secretly murdered. This new evidence of John's untrustworthiness, combined with his vacillating conduct of the war, alienated the nobles of Normandy and Anjou. Most of them swore allegiance to Philip, and the northern Angevin possessions were occupied without much difficulty. By 1204 John had lost all his French fiefs except Guienne, Gascony, and part of Poitou.

This defeat had many important consequences. It weakened John's prestige and strengthened the baronial opposition in England. Many English lords were deprived of lands in Normandy as a result of Philip's victory, and they blamed John for their losses. They were more than ever determined to preserve the rights and revenues which they still retained in England. At the same time the loss of Normandy stimulated the growth of English nationalism. From 1066 to 1200 England had been little more than an outlying province of France, and the ruling class had been French in speech and culture if not in blood. The loss of Normandy and the long war with France which followed broke the close connection with the continent and the great barons became more and more English during the thirteenth century. As they identified themselves with the country, suppressed English culture began to revive; it is no accident that English became a literary language again after the reign of John. This incipient English nationalism worked to the king's disadvantage, since both John and his son Henry III remained more interested in the continent than did their subjects. Thus the barons could pose as defenders of English interests against their foreign-minded kings.

The loss of Normandy was followed by a long struggle with the Church. The archbishop of Canterbury died in 1205 and a disputed election followed. Some of the monks of Christchurch (who had the right of election) secretly chose their subprior and sent him to Rome to seek confirmation. John was furious at this disregard of his interests and forced a new election. This time the chapter naturally chose a royal nominee. When the dispute came before him, Pope Innocent III refused to recognize either election as valid and ordered the monks to send a delegation to hold an election in his presence. Under strong papal influence the monks chose Stephen Langton, a very able Englishman who had been a professor at Paris and was, at the time, a cardinal attached to the papal *curia*. John could not object to his character, but he did object to the circumstances of the election. He was on weak ground even there, since the reforming popes had carefully built up precedents for imposing their candidates in cases of disputed elections. This, of course, eventually gave the papacy control of almost all episcopal appointments, since few medieval elections were undisputed, but no secular ruler ever found a means of blocking the process. In the end the kings discovered that they could gain many bishoprics for their favorites by direct negotiations with the pope, but John was not disposed to follow this plan. He wanted to preserve the old system in which elections were controlled by the king, and he was determined not to lose his influence over the primate of England. He refused to recognize Langton as archbishop and seized the lands of Canterbury for his own use. After repeated warnings the pope laid England under an interdict. John countered by confiscating all the lands of the Church and by threatening the clergy so that all but two bishops fled the realm.

Curiously enough, the interdict caused no immediate trouble for the king. Possibly this was due to the fact that it was not very rigorously enforced, possibly to the fact that it lessened financial burdens on the people for a time, since John obtained large sums from the estates of the Church. The interdict was followed by excommunication of the king in 1209. Even this did not shake John's position immediately. He was certainly not loved by his people, but they apparently did not feel impelled to fight the pope's battle for him. Finally, in desperation, Innocent summoned Philip Augustus to punish John and offered him England as a reward. This was serious. The English were not yet ready to fight against John, but it was quite evident that they would not fight for him. Heavy taxation and arbitrary punishments had alienated the feudal nobility, while the denunciations of the pope had weakened the loyalty of the common people. With no reliable forces on his side John had to yield, and in May, 1213, he made his peace with the pope. Stephen Langton was recognized as archbishop and John promised to return all the income he had received from church lands. He never completely fulfilled this promise but he did give up enough to involve him in financial difficulties. Finally, to obtain protection against his enemies, John surrendered England to the pope and received it back as a fief. This action annoyed the barons, not because they felt that England had been humiliated (several other kings were also papal vassals), but because it gave John a powerful ally.

By this submission John escaped a great danger, and if he had remained quiet for a few years he might have avoided further trouble.

Instead he immediately planned an elaborate campaign to recover his French fiefs. He allied himself with the emperor Otto IV and some rebellious French barons and agreed that they were to attack Philip Augustus from the north, while he marched up with an army from Aquitaine. The great weakness of this scheme was that John had to ask for money and military service from English barons who were prepared to give neither. John had already taxed the country at a high rate and had imposed many scutages for military expeditions which had been uniformly unsuccessful. Instead of giving him what he asked, the barons began to unite under the leadership of Stephen Langton, who proposed that they should ask for guarantees against royal exactions such as were contained in the charter of Henry I. John ignored this agitation and staked everything on a victory over France. His plan failed completely. He trusted his own army so little that he retreated hastily as soon as the French commander advanced toward him. A few days later his northern allies were decisively defeated at Bouvines (1214) by Philip Augustus.

This disaster destroyed the last fragments of John's prestige. The thing which never could happen, according to the theory of Norman feudalism, did happen; most of the great barons united against the king. They presented a statement of their grievances and of their demands to John, who angrily rejected it. The barons then marched against the king, and when London received their army, John's position was hopeless. He agreed to make the reforms which the rebels felt were necessary and in June, 1215, he set his seal to Magna Carta.

Magna Carta was a great landmark in the process of limiting the king's power, so great that later generations tried to read into it all the liberties which Englishmen gained only through centuries of struggle. It must be remembered that it was a feudal document, drawn up by feudal barons, and concerned primarily with the protection of feudal interests. It was not a constitution; the barons were chiefly interested in limiting the financial exactions of the crown. Magna Carta has much to say of wardship and relief, of aid and scutage, of amercement and purveyance; it has little to say of the liberties of all Englishmen. The serfs, who formed at least half the population, gained almost nothing by the charter; they were protected only as property of their lords. A few rather indefinite clauses benefited towns and merchants, while the Church gained the vague promise that it should be "free." The important provisions, in the eyes of the king and of all contemporaries, were those which regulated feudal rights.

Yet the Great Charter was exceedingly important in the development of the English government. Two basic ideas emerge from a study of its text. One is that the king is bound by the customs and laws of the realm; if he breaks them he may be punished. The other is that the English baronage, acting as a corporate body, has the duty of seeing that the king obeys the law. It was the union of these two ideas that made Magna Carta memorable and the development of English institutions unique. Every one in the Middle Ages believed that the king was bound by the law; the idea was implicit in the feudal contract. The real problem was to enforce the obligation. The great barons alone were strong enough to do this, and even they were powerless unless they united. In other countries they seldom went beyond provincial unions, and as a result they failed to impose lasting checks on the king. In France, for example, a feudal revolt in 1314–1315 resulted, not in a Magna Carta, but in a series of provincial charters which protected only local rights and which could be emasculated one by one. But in England, thanks to the centralization imposed by William I, Henry I, and Henry II, thanks also to the loss of Normandy by John, the English barons had been forced to unite. They had become conscious of their identity as the baronage of England, conscious of their interests as a group, conscious of the fact that only by acting as a group could they check the tremendous power of the king. Magna Carta was the first act of the united baronage and it created a new tradition in English government. From that time on organized groups, first of barons, then of all the upper classes, defended their privileges and the laws of England against the king. From that time on, summons to the king's council was considered a privilege, rather than an onerous duty. For if the baronage was to protect its rights through corporate rather than individual action, then it must check, and at times control, the actions of the central government.

The essential idea, then, of Magna Carta, was to prevent the king and the central administration from doing wrong. The royal government established by Henry II was not destroyed; it was not even seriously weakened. This moderation on the part of successful rebels may seem astonishing, but it was proof of great statesmanship. Extreme demands would have been wiped out by an inevitable royalist reaction; reasonable requests could survive all the strains of a rapidly changing social order. Archbishop Langton has usually been credited with restraining the more radical barons, but other influences also played a part. Many barons who joined the rebels were at heart loyal to the monarchy; they wished to bridle an evil king but not to substitute feudal anarchy for the good peace which Henry II had given. The few magnates who remained loyal to John succeeded in moderating some articles while discussing terms with the rebels. Finally, the army of the barons was made up of lesser men, of rear-vassals, knights, and petty tenants. These were the very men who had profited most from the judicial reforms of Henry II, whose fiefs had been secured from greedy lords and lawless neighbors by the spread of the jury system and the king's law. Far from desiring less royal justice they wanted more, and they succeeded in inserting in the Charter itself a provision that royal judges were to visit every county four times a year to hear cases about possession of feudal holdings.

As a result of all these forces the king lost few rights by the Charter. Only one important limitation was placed on the royal courts and the lawyers soon found a way to circumvent this prohibition. More significant were the limitations imposed on the king's financial powers. The amount which he could take from reliefs, wardships, and marriages was strictly defined and therefore limited. Any hope that he might meet his rapidly increasing financial needs by developing his purely feudal income was thereby blasted. He had to turn to taxation, and another article of the Charter forbade collection of aids and scutages without the consent of the baronage. Now scutage was not a tax but a commutation of the service owed for military fiefs, and the voluntary aid granted by vassals to their lord was not the only means by which the king could raise money from his subjects. Nevertheless, the most important taxes of the last few years had been based on the principle of the aid, and so the practical, if not the legal effect of this article was great. Even though the article was omitted from later issues of the Charter the principle was never forgotten. No king after John succeeded in collecting any important tax without the consent of the baronage.

This tendency to protect their pocketbooks rather than their governmental powers is another indication of the change which had come over the English baronage. They did not object to the king's taking over most of the work of government, but they did object to paying the bill. Even when they were completely victorious, even when the king was as unreliable as John, they did not seek to destroy the centralized royal government or to return to feudal localism. They accepted the new government, reserving to themselves the right to correct its abuses. The next two hundred years of English history are merely variations on this theme.

Neither John nor his barons could trust one another, and attempts to enforce the Charter led to new disputes which soon degenerated into civil war. John asked the pope to annul the Charter because it had been extorted by force and Innocent promptly did so. The barons then turned to John's ancient enemy, Philip Augustus, and persuaded him to send his son Louis with an army to aid them. The war was going against John when he suddenly died. The accession of his nine-year-old son, Henry III, weakened the rebellion. The boy was obviously not responsible for his father's acts, and the magnates could hope to gain much during a long minority. Though Innocent died shortly after John, the new pope was also interested in English affairs and sent a legate to aid Henry. Finally the regent, William Marshal, a baron with a great reputation for honesty, reissued Magna Carta. The reissue omitted a few clauses which restricted the king, but on the other hand it was now guaranteed by a man whom the barons could trust and was accepted by the papal legate. Louis' supporters dropped off one by one and in 1217 he was glad to make an honorable peace and to leave England. His intervention had made it impossible for the monarchy to annul Magna Carta.

FRANCE—THE FOUNDATIONS OF ROYAL POWER

At the beginning of the twelfth century the king of France had very little power. His direct authority was limited to the strip of territory connecting Paris and Orleans, and even in this restricted area his power was by no means undisputed. He had to build the Grand Châtelet to protect the plain of St. Denis, a few miles from Paris, from a petty baron of the Ile de France. Another minor vassal who held the castle of Montlhéry was, as we have seen, a constant thorn in the flesh. A third, Thomas de Marle, was so dangerous a tyrant that the papal legate organized a crusade against him, which checked him only for a moment. With such conditions existing in the royal domain, it is not surprising that the king had little influence over the great lords who had built up feudal states in the rest of the realm. They seldom attended the king's court, and their governments were absolutely independent of the royal administration.

Philip I had begun the work of consolidating the royal domain, but he had not carried it very far. After 1100, stupefied by his obesity and devotion to sensual pleasures, he turned the government over to his son Louis. Louis VI also suffered from the family disease of corpulence, but this did not keep him from being an energetic ruler. He is known in history as "Louis the Fat," but his other nickname, the "Wideawake," is a better summary of his character. Both as viceroy for his father and as sole king (1108–1137), he devoted himself to the task of pacifying the royal domain and chastising the more violent vassals of the Ile de France. Again and again he was called upon to protect a monastery or a town from the depredations of a petty tyrant, and he was never called upon in vain. He patrolled his lands as a policeman patrols his beat, and though it was a difficult task, he finally succeeded in becoming complete master of his own domain.

Louis was more of a policeman than a statesman, and he was not very successful in his attempts to exercise his authority outside the domain. He missed a great opportunity when he failed to intervene in the struggle between Robert of Normandy and Henry I of England, which led to the reunion of the duchy and the kingdom. His attempt to repair this mistake by supporting a pretender in Normandy against Henry I was not successful, and he gained nothing by a long war with the English king. A dispute over the succession to the county of Flanders enabled him to win a temporary advantage by installing his candidate as count, but the royal favorite proved so incompetent that he was soon expelled and Louis lost whatever prestige he had gained by his initial success. On just one occasion he was able to act as king of France, rather than as lord of Paris and Orleans. The emperor Henry V, in 1124, threatened to invade France to punish the king for the support which he had given the pope in the investiture struggle. The great lords of the North rallied to the defense of the realm and placed themselves temporarily under the king's orders. This was the first time in many a decade that the king's leadership had been so clearly recognized, and it is significant that this recognition of royal leadership was closely associated with an early manifestation of French nationalism. However, the episode led to no immediate increase in the king's power.

Louis' real achievement was to bring the government of the royal domain up to the level which prevailed in the better feudal states. His attempt to secure law and order gave him the support of the clergy and the common people, allies who were to prove very valuable to his successors. They felt, as Louis' biographer Suger said, "that he studied the peace and comfort of plowmen, laborers, and poor folk, a thing long unwonted." As a result the Church gave Louis its whole-hearted support, and supplied him with his ablest officials, chief of whom was this same Suger. Other officials, as in England, were drawn from the ranks of the petty vassals, and by the end of his reign Louis' court was beginning to function as a regular instrument of government. It even heard a few cases originating outside the royal domain, which was an indication that the king's prestige was increasing.

Another indication of increased prestige was the fact that duke William of Aquitaine chose Louis' son as the husband of his daughter and heiress Eleanor. This happened just before the king's death in 1137, so that he was unable to take advantage of the opportunities opened up by the marriage. For Aquitaine was almost one-fourth of the kingdom, and while the duke's authority was not very great in the interior of his fief, it was fairly well established in the plain which stretched from the Loire down to Bordeaux. If the new king, young Louis VII, had been able to annex this region permanently to the royal domain he would have saved France many weary wars and hastened the eventual unification of the country by three centuries.

The failure of Louis VII to retain Aquitaine has prejudiced historians against him. He has been represented as weak and over-pious, so that his reign was a long calamity for France. This is not entirely fair, for in his early years Louis was ambitious, energetic, rash, and not very respectful to the clergy. He was only sixteen when he became king, and was passionately in love with his young bride. She had been educated in the brilliant and sophisticated society of southern France, which put great emphasis on fine clothes, good manners, and elegant conversation, and very little on religion. Under her influence Louis fought his barons and defied the Church. An interdict forced him to make terms with the pope, but in all other respects the first eight years of his reign were reasonably successful.

Louis' misfortunes began with the Second Crusade. Bernard of Clairvaux had fired France with enthusiasm for the adventure and Louis placed himself at the head of the army. He took Eleanor with him, and at Antioch she compromised herself with her uncle, who was prince of the city. A divorce was suggested, but Louis was still so much in love with his wife that the pope was able to reconcile the pair temporarily. However, Louis remained very suspicious of the queen, and his jealousy prevented him from giving much attention to other affairs for some time.

Fortunately for France, the kingdom was well administered during Louis' absence by Suger. Suger was of peasant origin and had been educated at the monastery of St. Denis with Louis VI, where the two had become friends. He had risen by his ability to the position of abbot and, as St. Denis was one of the leading monasteries, he had become one of the most influential churchmen in France. He was an able administrator, fully conscious of the new economic situation, as is shown by the fact that he freed some of his serfs and founded a *ville neuve*. We have already seen his importance as a patron of art, for it was during his abbacy that the early Gothic church of St. Denis was begun. He accepted the Church's plan of reform, but he had little of the asceticism which was typical of other leading monks of the age. As his biographer said: "His food was neither coarse nor luxurious. . . . He ate a little of everything that was served to him. . . . His bed was neither too hard nor too soft." St. Bernard was a little suspicious of his interest in politics and of the love of magnificence which he showed in his church building. But Suger conciliated St. Bernard by giving him a free hand to reform the church just as he conciliated some of Louis VI's courtiers by making it apparent that he had no personal ambition. Suger's real ambition was for his church. But since, in his own words, St. Denis was the "crown of France," strengthening the monarchy aided St. Denis, just as beautifying St. Denis glorified France. Suger was one of the chief ministers in the last years of Louis VI and he retained this position under Louis VII. When the king left for the Holy Land he named Suger as regent. The abbot sternly suppressed all disorder and watched carefully over the royal finances. He is said to have paid the expenses of government out of his own income, saving all the royal revenue for the king. He had been opposed to the crusade, but after its failure proposed to finance a new one out of his own funds. For in spite of his vow of poverty as a monk, his remarkable business ability had secured to him as abbot an income which was almost incredible for that age. He died before he could begin the crusade, leaving no one capable of taking his place.

As long as Suger lived he prevented Louis from divorcing Eleanor, because he was determined that the king should not lose Aquitaine. "But," as his biographer wrote, "scarcely was this man taken from the midst of the living before France suffered grievously from his death. Thus we see it today, through the lack of such a councilor, despoiled of the duchy of Aquitaine, one of its most important provinces." Eleanor had caused her husband new pangs of jealousy by a flirtation with Henry of Anjou when the young prince visited the royal court. Louis apparently decided that he could endure no more and withdrew his garrisons from Aquitaine. Then in 1152 he persuaded a French council to dissolve his marriage on grounds of consanguinity. Two months later Eleanor married Henry of Anjou and Louis' efforts to prevent his supplanter from annexing Aquitaine were unsuccessful. After two years of war Henry was recognized as duke of Aquitaine and a few months later he became king of England.

Henry Plantagenet now ruled England, Normandy, Anjou and Aquitaine, and he threatened to add still more territory by enforcing vague claims to suzerainty over Toulouse and other fiefs in the South. For the next fifty years the kings of France had to struggle against this dangerous concentration of power in the hands of a rival dynasty. Louis VII had neither the resources nor the personal ability necessary to break up the solid block of Angevin possessions. However, he was fairly successful in a purely defensive policy, and Henry II made few important gains after 1154. Louis' most notable effort was his relief of Toulouse when the city was besieged by Henry II in 1159. This assertion of royal authority in a region which had almost forgotten the king strengthened the tenuous hold of the monarchy on the South and prepared the way for further intervention. On the other hand, Louis was unable to profit greatly from the quarrel over Thomas Becket, and the subsequent rebellion of 1173. As a matter of fact, neither antagonist was really trying for a decisive victory. Louis did not have the resources for a first-class war and Henry was not only restrained by his very real deference for his feudal superior, but also by his inability to coördinate the activities of his diverse and often unruly peoples. The net result of twenty-five years of fighting was small and the military position of the French king was certainly no worse at Louis' death than it was in 1154.

In other respects the French monarchy gained power. Louis gave asylum to Alexander III, when Frederick Barbarossa was supporting a rival pope, and thus strengthened the ancient alliance with the Church. Like his father, he defended bishops and abbots who were threatened by feudal lords, and these activities now extended far beyond the royal

ANGEVIN EMPIRE AND FEUDAL FRANCE

domain. Louis was not always able to give very effective aid to distant establishments, but the fact that outlying monasteries believed that he could help them is an important testimony to the growth of royal prestige. Petty feudal lords began to share the government of their fiefs with the king in order to gain protection against powerful neighbors. Many towns, especially those under episcopal rule, applied to him for charters, and this gave him a new chance to increase his influence. Most important of all, great men, dukes and counts and bishops, commenced bringing their disputes to the king's court, and it began to develop a professional personnel. As a result of these activities the influence of the monarchy became predominant in the cluster of petty fiefs which occupied the central part of the country. Even the larger fiefs along the frontiers could no longer be said to be entirely independent of the king.

This growth of royal power can hardly be ascribed to Louis' personal ability, even though he was less incompetent than some historians have believed. Rather it was a result of the great European revival which was, as we have seen, especially strong in France. The desire for better political organization, nourished by the teachings of the Church, by the growth of legal studies, by the revival of trade, could be satisfied in France only through an increase in royal authority. No feudal lord could claim the right to give law and order to all the realm; the king alone could act as supreme judge of the strong and defender of the weak. It was not the power of Louis VII which made great vassals submit their disputes to his court. Rather it was the fact that, if they accepted the new idea of settling their quarrels peacefully, there was nowhere else to go. It was not far-sighted royal policy which gained for Louis VII the support of the rising class of the bourgeoisie. He had no great love for urban liberties, and while he could see that by aiding towns outside the domain he was weakening his great vassals, he was not a consistent supporter of the communal movement. Towns in the royal domain received the bare minimum of privileges necessary for economic activity and the Church sometimes persuaded him to withdraw favors granted to rebellious episcopal cities. Yet the bourgeoisie on the whole remained loyal to the king because he was the only authority to whom they could appeal in their struggles against local lords. In short, the movement which strengthened the French monarchy was to a certain extent independent of the personality of the monarch. The king was a symbol; he stood for peace and security; and the men who wanted these blessings turned instinctively to him.

FRANCE—THE WORK OF PHILIP AUGUSTUS

Louis VII had not been entirely passive, but he had profited less from this revival of the monarchical ideal than he might have done. His great successor, Philip Augustus (Philip II, 1180–1223), exploited the movement to its limits. Cold-blooded, crafty, entirely without moral scruples, he spent his whole life in extending the royal domain and in perfecting the royal government. He was guilty of many acts of cruelty; he quarreled with the pope almost as vigorously as John; yet because his fundamental policy coincided with the desires of his people he retained the support of the clergy, the bourgeoisie, and even of most of the nobility throughout his reign.

Philip had been crowned during his father's lifetime, but was only fourteen when Louis' death left him as sole king. He was a nervous, sickly boy, full of ambition, but somewhat lacking in the political skill which he manifested later. One of his first acts was to marry the niece of the count of Flanders, who brought the rich region of Artois as her dowry. This extended Philip's power toward the channel and greatly increased his income. Philip then rejected the efforts of his wife's and mother's relatives to direct his policy and provoked them into rebellion. His position was dangerous for a time but he finally succeeded in defeating the coalition and in forcing the count of Flanders to surrender more territory in the North. Henry II had aided Philip by his benevolent neutrality during the struggle, but Philip could not afford to be grateful. He encouraged Henry's rebellious sons, and the old king's efforts to keep the peace by surrendering some border fortresses brought only a temporary respite. Philip soon resumed his intrigues and, in spite of a threatened interdict, supported Richard and John until they had defeated their father.

Henry's death and the Third Crusade interrupted the Angevin-Capetian feud, but only for an instant. We have already seen how Philip and Richard quarreled in Syria, how Philip hastened home to profit by Richard's absence, and how he sought to prolong Richard's captivity in Germany. Richard devoted the rest of his life to an attempt to crush Philip, and he had very nearly succeeded when his death freed the French ruler from his greatest danger. The erratic John could not take his brother's place and in five years Philip conquered the greater part of the Angevin holdings in France.

Meanwhile, he had begun a long struggle with the Church over the question of his marriage with Ingeborg of Denmark. Philip had married her in 1193, shortly after his first wife's death, primarily to obtain the use of the Danish fleet in his war with Richard. His nervous disorder was then at its height; he was unable to consummate the marriage and he soon took a great aversion to the queen. He forced his bishops to annul the marriage on a false claim of consanguinity, but Ingeborg refused to go back to Denmark and appealed to Rome. The pope at the time was a man of rather weak character. He protested feebly against the divorce but took no decided action, so Philip married Agnes of

Meran. Then Innocent III became pope and took up the case again. As Philip refused to send Agnes away and to take back Ingeborg, Innocent laid an interdict on France in 1200. It was severe enough to cause great hardship for the people, even though some of the bishops refused to observe it, and Philip had to make a show of yielding. He went through the form of a public reconciliation with Ingeborg, but she remained practically a prisoner while he continued to live with Agnes. The interdict was lifted, but Innocent soon found that he had been tricked and began to threaten Philip once more. The king played for time with remarkable diplomatic skill and submitted only in 1213. There was not much merit in this tardy repentance, for Agnes had been dead for many years and Philip wanted to qualify himself for the task of punishing the excommunicated king of England. John's submission to Innocent spoiled Philip's plans, but this time Ingeborg was not made to suffer for her husband's disappointments. She received due honor as queen for the rest of her life and survived Philip by many years.

Philip's last struggle was against the coalition which John organized in 1213–1214. The count of Flanders, and some other French barons, irritated by the steady growth of royal power, joined the English and German rulers in a pincers attack on the French king. In 1214, Philip met the Germans and Flemings coming down from the north at Bouvines. He decisively defeated them and captured most of the rebellious French barons, including the count of Flanders. John, who was coming up from the south to meet his allies, had been driven back by Philip's son a few days before, and this double victory assured the permanency of the recent conquests and the supremacy of the royal government over the great vassals. Philip had peace for the remaining nine years of his reign and was able to devote his time to the work of political reorganization.

He faced a very difficult task, for his conquests had more than tripled the size of the royal domain and had given the king direct control of regions that had laws and institutions very different from those of Paris. The rudimentary administrative system of his father was not working very well even in the old royal domain, and it would have been utterly inadequate as a means of governing the newly acquired territories. Philip had to find a system that would ensure royal control without offending subjects who were fiercely determined to preserve their old customs. He borrowed some ideas from his great adversaries, the Angevins, but the final solution was entirely his own, and it was so successful that it served as a basis for French government for centuries. Philip Augustus did even more for France than Henry II had done for England because he had less to build on. He was the real founder of the French bureaucracy and the French state.

Before Philip's reign the royal domain had been farmed out to *prévôts* who paid the king a lump sum annually for their districts and then collected all royal dues for their own profit. These men cheated the king, exploited the people and showed an alarming tendency to turn their offices into hereditary possessions. Even before his conquests, Philip sent out delegations from his court who investigated local administration, tried important local cases, and then reported back to the king. The resemblance to the English circuit judges is obvious. After the annexations, however, Philip came to feel that his agents should be sedentary rather than itinerant. He eventually adopted the plan of sending only one man to each district, giving him full judicial, financial, and military powers. These local governors, called *baillis* in the North and seneschals in the South, had to attend meetings of the king's court in Paris two or three times a year and seldom kept their posts for more than four or five years. There was thus no danger that they might become too independent of the king, since they were entirely dependent on him for their salaries —which were relatively high—and for their continuance in office. A *bailli* who had a good record might be sent to half a dozen provinces in turn; an inefficient *bailli* would lose his position after two or three years and would never be employed again. The *baillis* were assisted by lesser officials who were appointed directly by the king and who could rise to the position of *bailli* if they proved their ability.

Thus Philip had created something very like a modern civil service. At the same time, he had solved the problem of the diversity of laws and institutions in the newly acquired territories. Since the chief officials in each province were his men, Philip could allow his new subjects to retain their old customs, sure that those customs could never be interpreted in a way that would harm his interests. Normandy continued to be governed by Norman law, much to the satisfaction of the Normans, and much to the advantage of the king, who retained the large income and extensive rights of his Angevin predecessors. The fact that there were no serious revolts in the conquered provinces is evidence of the success of this arrangement. Philip was the first ruler of France since the Roman emperors to solve successfully the problem of delegating authority.

His other reforms were less striking. The king's court continued to gain in importance as the highest tribunal in France, but it was still not as advanced as the *curia regis* in England. The financial work of the court was given more attention and Philip seems to have insisted on more careful keeping of records. The oldest surviving account of royal expenses and income comes from his reign, and we know that the *baillis* had to send statements of their financial operations to the king. Philip favored towns and trade and was far more consistent in this policy than his predecessors had been. He employed burgesses as his officials, and entrusted the great seal and royal treasury to six Parisian merchants during his absence on the Third Crusade. He protected foreign traders even in time of war and gave many privileges to his own bourgeois subjects. As a result he gained not only the support of the bourgeoisie, but also important additions to his income. Towns paid liberally for grants of royal favors and the increase in trade made royal tolls and customs more productive.

At Philip's death in 1223 it could be said for the first time that the king was the wealthiest and most powerful ruler in France. The royal domain was now larger than the fief of any great vassal and the royal administration was efficient enough to enable the king to profit from his extensive territories. Philip had taken the French monarchy safely through a crucial period in its history. Before his reign the French king was struggling feverishly to keep up with the greater feudal princes; after his reign the French king was so far superior to his vassals that most of them gave up all hope of competing with him. The prestige which Philip had given the monarchy worked almost automatically to increase the territories and power of his successors. For the next century the kings of France did little more than continue and perfect his policies.

X

-›››-›››-›››-›››‹‹‹-‹‹‹-‹‹‹-‹‹‹-

The Church Struggles to Maintain
Its Leadership

D URING THE thirteenth century the Church found it increasingly difficult to maintain the leadership of European society. The great
revival of civilization, which it had done so much to promote, had
created competing interests and loyalties. Many secular governments had
become sufficiently strong and beneficent to secure the primary allegiance of their subjects and to convince them that the interests of the
individual state came before the interests of Christendom. Increased
prosperity made life more enjoyable for many people, and their absorption in worldly interests and material pleasures deafened them to religious
appeals. The Church suffered from its own success, for the creation of a
highly centralized papal government brought with it the dangers of
bureaucracy and legalism. Too many churchmen became immersed in
administrative routine and lost all interest in and influence over lay
society. But while the leadership of the Church was threatened, it was
not easily destroyed. A remarkable group of popes, scholars, and teachers
fought the rising tide of secular interests and loyalties and preserved the
Church's dominance over European society until almost the end of the
century. They found new ways of arousing religious fervor, new techniques for expressing religious emotion, new administrative and legal
devices for preserving the political position of the pope, new philosophical
formulæ for reconciling all knowledge with the faith. As a result the
thirteenth century continued and perfected the work of the twelfth;
there was no sharp break between the two. But tension was growing;
the Church had to make greater and greater efforts to preserve its leadership, and eventually the strain became too great. In the last quarter of
the thirteenth century the Church began to lose control of many ac-

tivities, and by 1300 it was much less powerful than it had been in 1200. In this chapter we shall discuss only the period in which the Church was fairly successful in its efforts to maintain its leadership; that is, the period from about 1200 to about 1275.

INNOCENT III

The dangers threatening the Church were already apparent at the end of the twelfth century. The kings of England and France were pursuing their own policies in defiance of papal mandates and the emperor Henry VI was dominating Italy and the Papal States. His sudden death removed an acute danger, but the pope was still threatened by Italian nobles and German adventurers who annexed portions of Henry's conquests. The growing class of the bourgeoisie was already showing disquieting signs of worldliness and heresy was rampant all along the shores of the Mediterranean. The clergy were being attacked for their avarice and worldliness and the monastic orders seemed to be losing their early zeal for reform. Celestine III (1191–1198) had done little to remedy these conditions and it was evident that a strong pope was needed.

He was found in the person of Lothario Conti, a member of one of the great noble families of Rome. Lothario had studied the liberal arts at Paris and law at Bologna and had been made a cardinal at the age of twenty-nine. While a cardinal he wrote a book which was long popular in Europe, *On the Contempt of the World*. This exhortation to asceticism and contemplation represents only one, and probably not the dominant, side of Lothario's nature. As he himself said later: "If the contemplative state is safer, the active is more fruitful; if the former is sweeter the latter is more profitable." While cardinal, he distinguished himself as an administrator and lawyer, and though he was only thirty-seven when Celestine III died, he was the logical choice as his successor. Elected pope in 1198, he took the name of Innocent III.

The pope had long been saluted at his coronation as "father of princes and kings, ruler of the world, vicar on earth of our Saviour," but the facts had not always corresponded to this formula. Innocent was determined to make good the claim of the pope to be the head of Christendom and the leader of European society. As he said in his letters: "No king can reign rightly unless he devoutly serves Christ's vicar. . . . The priesthood is the sun, and monarchy the moon. Kings rule over their respective kingdoms, but Peter rules over the whole earth. . . . The Lord gave Peter the rule not only over the universal Church, but also over the whole world." These expressions did not mean that Innocent wished to rule all Europe directly; he was quite ready to acknowledge that kings and princes had the primary duty of preserving order. But

Innocent believed that he could judge even kings when they sinned, and he hoped that he would be accepted as the final arbiter, the supreme judge in all important cases which could not otherwise be settled. If the unity of Christendom were a reality (as every one admitted, at least in theory), then some one must have the power to preserve that unity and to prevent quarrels among Christians. The only person with sufficient prestige to do this was the pope, and Innocent came very near making the papacy a World Court with a right to arbitrate every serious political dispute.

However, before the pope could intervene on a large scale in European politics he had to gain some sort of security in his own states. When he was first elected pope, Rome was ruled by a senator who represented the people of the city. Innocent succeeded in obtaining the right to nominate the senator and to receive an oath of fidelity from him. It is significant of conditions in Rome that the senator included in the oath a promise "to guarantee to the cardinals, to their following and to them, perfect security when they go to church, while they remain there, and on their return." In spite of Innocent's control of the senator the old dislike of papal government persisted and there was frequent strife in the city between his supporters and their opponents. Twice, at least, Innocent was forced to flee from Rome and he was not entirely secure there until he had been pope for ten years. Elsewhere in the Papal States he established his authority more rapidly. After two years of hard work he had control of most of the fortified places and had created a strong position in central Italy which could not be shaken either by his Roman or his transalpine enemies. His rule was never fully effective in some outlying districts, but Innocent was the real creator of the Papal States. He built a functioning government out of theoretical rights and by thus strengthening the papal position made the unification of Italy impossible for six centuries.

The next great problem was the question of the Empire. Henry VI had deepened the gulf between his family and the Guelfs by his severity, and they were not disposed to accept another Hohenstaufen ruler. Consequently, when the Ghibellines elected Henry's brother Philip as his successor, the Guelfs chose Otto, son of Henry the Lion. This disputed election gave Innocent an opportunity to play his favorite rôle of arbiter. For three years he weighed the merits of the two claims and finally decided in favor of Otto. The decision was almost inevitable, since the Guelfs had never threatened the papal position in Italy as their Hohenstaufen rivals had. Otto made his selection absolutely certain by renouncing all imperial rights in lands claimed by the pope. This renunciation practically fixed the boundaries of the Papal States for the next six hundred years. Innocent did all he could to aid Otto in Germany, but the German princes also intended to profit from the existence of rival kings. They extorted concessions from both claimants, hesitated and negotiated, and finally began to turn to Philip. Only Philip's assassination by a private enemy saved Otto. He married Philip's daughter in 1208, secured general recognition of his title in Germany, and received the imperial crown from the pope. The traditions of the office soon proved too much for him. He began to intervene in Italy and demanded territories which he had earlier conceded to the pope. Innocent turned from him in disgust and brought forward a new candidate—young Frederick of Hohenstaufen, son of Henry VI. In the end this proved to be a disastrous move, but at the time it seemed to be an excellent idea. Frederick, so young at his father's death that he had not even been considered for the Empire, had preserved his rights in Sicily only through the aid of the Church, and was apparently full of gratitude for the pope's assistance. He made elaborate promises to respect papal rights and never to unite Sicily and the Empire. Backed by the pope and by the Ghibellines of Germany, he soon had Otto on the defensive. In a desperate move to gain prestige and English support, Otto attacked France, but his defeat at Bouvines in 1214 ended his chances. His supporters deserted him one by one and in 1215 Frederick received the imperial crown. Innocent had attained his goal; he had secured the election of an emperor who seemed to be completely subservient to the papacy. But in securing his objective he had greatly weakened Germany by encouraging a long civil war.

Innocent lost no opportunity to extend his power over other European rulers. As we have seen, he forced Philip Augustus to accept a wife and John of England an archbishop whom they had repudiated.[1] Alfonso of Leon was compelled to break off a marriage with his cousin, and the pope's influence decided a disputed succession to the Hungarian crown. The kings of England, Aragon, and Portugal placed their realms under papal overlordship, while Sicily was already a papal fief. Innocent advised the rulers of Bohemia, Poland, and Denmark, and intervened in every great question of European politics. The ideal of a Christian federation of states presided over by the pope was never nearer realization. At the same time Innocent had involved the Church in politics to a dangerous degree. He had made the pope responsible for the choice of an emperor and for the maintenance of a papal state in Italy. He had been willing to use force to attain these political objectives. These precedents were to prove embarrassing to later popes.

Innocent's interest in European politics did not divert his attention from religious problems. His letters show his constant interest in preserving the independence of the Church, in choosing well-qualified bishops, and in disciplining immoral or disobedient clergymen. This work alone could have occupied most of his time, but he had many other projects. The Fourth Crusade, which took place under his pontificate, did not turn out exactly as he had hoped, but by the conquest of Constantinople the schism between the Eastern and Western churches was temporarily healed.[2] The heretics of southern France were crushed by a crusade organized by the pope.[3] Innocent encouraged Francis and Dominic to begin their work of reviving the piety of the townspeople and preserving the faith of scholars.[4] Finally, he called the Fourth Lateran Council, the greatest yet held in the West, to recover the Holy Land and to reform the Church.

The Council met in 1215 in the Lateran Palace at Rome. Seventy-one primates, including the patriarchs of Constantinople and Jerusalem, four hundred bishops, and eight hundred abbots and priors assembled at the pope's order. Envoys from the emperor, from the kings of France, England, Aragon, Hungary, Jerusalem and Cyprus, and from the Italian cities were present. A crusade was planned, but the real work of the Council dealt with the reform of the Church. The loss of influence over laymen, which was already apparent, was to be met by greater piety, better education, and better discipline of the clergy. The bishops were ordered to appoint competent men to preach and to provide free instruction for poor scholars. They were to make sure that candidates for the priesthood were properly instructed and that priests celebrated mass frequently and reverently. Priests were not to throw dice, to frequent taverns, or to spend too much time in worldly affairs. The Council also recognized the fact that the low standards of the priesthood were due to the greed of patrons who had appropriated the tithes which were supposed to support the parish clergy. These patrons were as often bishops and abbots as laymen, and some of the most poverty-stricken priests were to be found in churches dependent upon monasteries. As the Council said: "In some regions the priests are said to receive only one-quarter of one-quarter of the tithes. Because of this, scarcely an educated priest can be found in these localities." The Council therefore ordered that the priest receive a "fitting portion" of the tithes, so that he might be able to live decently.

The old type of simony, that is, the buying of church office from a layman, was much less prevalent than it had been in the time of Gregory VII. There were still bishops who owed their position entirely to lay influence, but they were becoming rare. Usually the pope was consulted, and while he did not bar all royal favorites from office, he was able to reject those of evil reputation. The character of the episcopate was fairly high at this time, although in the little-governed western provinces of the Empire bishops of the old, bad sort were still to be found. The real problem was farther down in the hierarchy, among the clerks who were administrative assistants to kings and feudal lords. These

[2] See pp. 339–340.
[3] See p. 317.
[4] See pp. 321–324.

men were not exactly immoral—they were honest financiers and just judges—but they wanted to make all they could out of the Church. They accumulated benefices—an archdeaconry here, a deanship there, and three or four prebends in other cathedral churches—and they were not very careful about performing the duties of their offices. The Council renewed the old prohibition against "pluralities," (that is, the holding of more than one office) but they continued to be a problem for centuries.

Another evil which was hurting the Church was the growth of bureaucracy, especially in the papal *curia*. Even Innocent could not secure prompt despatch of business. Members of the papal administration multiplied formalities, encouraged legal quibbling, and took years to decide cases pending before them. The *curia* had invented many excuses for taking fees which easily degenerated into bribes. Similar abuses were prevalent in episcopal courts. The Council legislated against all these evils—unfortunately without much effect.

The Council also forbade the sale of relics and ordered that no new relic should be venerated until it had been approved by the pope. There was need for this action, for the crusades had started a regular trade in relics imported from the East. As early as 1100 the pope had had to forbid clerks from carrying relics about the country for the sake of gain. A little later the French abbot Guibert wrote a remarkable treatise, questioning the genuineness of some objects. He remarked that there was one head of John the Baptist in the East and another in the West and said: "It is on the one hand certain that there has been only one John the Baptist, and on the other that no man can say without sin that one man had two heads." But Guibert's satire had little effect and the search for relics continued. It was enormously stimulated by the sack of Constantinople in 1204. Relics from all over the East had been deposited there to preserve them from the Moslems, and the Western conquerors carried them away in armloads. One abbot secured over sixty relics for his monastery and others did almost as well. This sudden influx made it easy for fraudulent relics to be introduced in the West, and the Council recognized the danger, though it must be said that its decree had little effect on the trade.

Two acts of the Council were especially important in the development of secular governments. The first, and most important, forbade priests to officiate at ordeals or judicial combats. These two methods of proof were thereby destroyed, since their efficacy depended upon the supernatural sanctions invoked by the Church. England alone obeyed the Council's ruling immediately, but other countries conformed during the thirteenth century and by 1300 rational methods of trial had almost entirely supplanted the older forms of proof. The other act reinforced the growing anti-Semitism of the West by placing various disabilities on Jews, such as the wearing of a distinctive badge.

Only a few of the Council's actions have been enumerated, but this hasty survey should have indicated the complexity and multiplicity of the problems which confronted the Church. The reader should not be misled by the long lists of abuses which were recited at the Council, nor by its failure to remedy all the evils which it discussed. The Church was still in a healthy condition, for it was still able to react vigorously against internal corruption. It realized the dangers which threatened it and took steps to counteract them. The real decadence of the Church came later, when it accepted many of these evils as inevitable and almost abandoned attempts at reform.

THE PROBLEM OF HERESY

The first canon of the Fourth Lateran Council contains a creed carefully formulated to express the differences between Christianity and the beliefs of the Waldensians and Albigensians. The Council went on to condemn these heresies and to order the punishment of all unrepentant heretics. This act shows the new importance of the problem of heresy at the beginning of the thirteenth century. For the first time since the suppression of Arianism the orthodox faith had a serious rival in the West. There had been minor heresies in the early Middle Ages, but they were usually the result of scholastic arguments and had little popular appeal. Even so well-known a teacher as Abelard had caused no real danger to the Church when he fell into heresy. Once his errors were exposed they were renounced by every one, including the offender himself. But the new heresies of the late twelfth century were popular, not academic; they enlisted the support of thousands of laymen, and they could not be wiped out by purely theological arguments. The Church had to find new methods of combating heresy and it took it some time to do so.

The chief force in weakening the hold of the orthodox faith on the people was disgust with the conduct of the clergy. It was not that churchmen of the late twelfth century were more immoral than their predecessors—on the contrary, their character had been greatly improved—but that laymen were setting a much higher standard for them. It was no longer enough for a cleric to refrain from open sin; he must also lead a life of active piety. Townspeople wanted more religious instruction; they were not satisfied with services without sermons, or with sermons recited from a book. Laymen refused to reverence prelates and priests who lived in luxury and who spent more time in administering their property than they did in performing religious duties. The Church was accused of worrying more about a decrease in its income than about an increase in sin, of squeezing tithes from the poor instead of giving them charity, of promoting extortionate lawyers to bishoprics and casting out saints. Let the clergy devote their time to preaching instead of to administration and their money to charity instead of soft living—then all would be well!

Obviously laymen were trying to relieve some of their own guilty feelings about greed and profit-taking by attacking the avarice of the clergy, but the attack was not without foundation. It was very hard to meet because the papacy itself had encouraged laymen to demand high moral standards from their pastors. When Gregory VII and Urban II forbade priests with wives or concubines to celebrate mass they relied on parish congregations to see that this order was enforced. Furthermore, as we have seen, these reforming popes supported the Italian cities in their efforts to drive out unreformed and imperialist prelates. Two very dangerous consequences flowed from these acts. First, by allowing laymen to reject their pastors for alleged moral lapses, a dangerous precedent was established. Heretical leaders always accused the orthodox clergy of immorality, and could always weaken their influence by this charge. Second, by forbidding priests living in sin to administer the sacraments, Gregory unwittingly revived the old Donatist heresy, which taught that the sacraments were of no avail in the hands of a sinful priest. Gregory protested that he meant no such thing, that the sacraments were efficacious to the faithful even when administered by a sinner and that his action had been purely disciplinary. Many people failed to grasp the distinction and continued to believe that a sinful priest was no priest at all. The danger of this belief is that it leads to an even more heretical conclusion. A sinful priest is useless; one can never be sure that the officiating priest is not a sinner; therefore all priests are useless.

Thus the reform movement, by emphasizing the importance of high moral standards for the clergy, made possible the growth of heresy. Every influential churchman of the twelfth century denounced the evil lives of some members of his order, and the heretical leaders attracted little attention when they began the same sort of attack. No heretic ever condemned worldly clerics in stronger language than did St. Bernard, and yet St. Bernard was the unofficial head of the Western Church. Only gradually did the leaders of the Church realize that some attacks on immorality concealed an attack on the faith, that some reformers had turned into revolutionaries. Donatist beliefs became more and more prevalent during the twelfth century and many leaders began to draw the final conclusion and to teach that the ordained clergymen of the Catholic Church were useless. Thousands of heretics who differed on other questions agreed in this belief, and they may all be lumped together as "anti-sacerdotalists."

The anti-sacerdotalists were especially strong in the towns. This was only natural, since the towns had played an important rôle in the reform movement and were quite ready to join in a new wave of moral indignation. Thus the North Italian towns, which had been so zealous for the Gregorian reforms, were hotbeds of heresy a century later. It is also true that townsmen were inclined to be more critical and less conservative than peasants, and were therefore more quickly seduced by new doctrines. They were not satisfied with the ordinary services of the Church; they wanted exciting sermons denouncing vice and corruption. If their parish priests failed to interest them, they were always ready to listen to street-corner revivalists of doubtful orthodoxy. The gregariousness of urban life gave townsmen frequent opportunities for discussion, and since religion was so important in their lives, they were bound to spend much of their time in talking about it. Anti-sacerdotalist theories were easily generated in this atmosphere, and they spread from one town to another through commercial contacts. As a result, by 1200 a large proportion of the urban population had accepted some form of heresy, and other townsmen, while nominally orthodox, were very critical of the clergy.

Arnold of Brescia, whom we have seen as the temporary leader of the Roman commune,[5] was also an early anti-sacerdotalist leader in the North Italian towns. He denounced the greed of the pope and cardinals, condemned the wealth of the Church, and seems to have taught the Donatist heresy. His influence survived his execution, and secret associations of Arnoldistas or "Poor Men" were formed to carry on his teachings. Other leaders preached similar doctrines in the cloth towns of Flanders and in the rich commercial region of South France. Both St. Norbert, the founder of the Premonstratensians, and St. Bernard of Clairvaux made great efforts to win these heretics back to the fold. They had some success, but they did not succeed in suppressing the movement.

The most important of all the anti-sacerdotal movements was founded by Peter Waldo, a rich merchant of Lyons. It is said that one day he stopped in the market-place to listen to a jongleur, who chanced to be telling the story of St. Alexis.[6] He was so moved by the tale that he determined to imitate Alexis and renounce the treasures of this world. After providing for his wife and daughters, he gave the remainder of his wealth to the poor. Like most townsmen he felt that the established clergy were not giving enough time to religious instruction, so he decided to devote himself to the preaching of the gospel. He had the New Testament translated into the vernacular and studied it eagerly. Soon he had a group of followers who wished to aid him in his work. They adopted a special costume and called themselves the "Poor Men of Lyons." So far the story is like that of any reforming order, but when Waldo tried

[5] See p. 219.
[6] See pp. 253–254.

to have his rule confirmed he was rebuffed by two successive popes. Apparently he had little respect for the hierarchy of the Church and made little distinction between laymen and clergymen. The Third Lateran Council, 1179, also refused to recognize the Waldensians and eventually they were forced into open opposition to the Church. They continued to insist that they were good Christians, which they certainly were, as far as their morals were concerned. They were generally known as the "good people" and even their opponents admitted their high character. However, they became more and more anti-sacerdotalist in doctrine. They refused obedience to popes and prelates and held that laymen, and even women, might preach. They taught that masses, prayers, and alms for the dead were of no avail and that prayer anywhere—in bed or in a stable—was as efficacious as in church. The Waldensians were active missionaries and their faith spread from Spain to Bohemia.

The anti-sacerdotalists accepted the Christian faith but rejected the organization of the Church. An even more dangerous group of heretics were those who rejected faith and organization alike. The old Manichean heresy, which St. Augustine had fought, had never been completely destroyed in the Orient. Some of its sectaries had been settled in the Balkans and there had come in contact with Western merchants. Spreading along the trade-routes, the heresy had been introduced into most of the commercial cities of the West. It was especially strong in Languedoc, where its adherents were known as Albigensians from the town of Albi where they were very numerous. These heretics were also known by many other names, such as Bulgars (from the country where they supposedly originated), Cathars (because they claimed to be purified) and so on. They were most dangerous to the Church in southern France, because they were tolerated there. The feudal lords of Languedoc were not very powerful and were much more interested in a gay and cultured social life than they were in defending the true faith. The population was very mixed and had been exposed to Jewish and Moslem influences which had made it receptive to new ideas. The clergy of Languedoc had had a rather bad record in the past and were looked down on by the laity. A favorite exclamation to express strong distaste was: "I'd rather be a priest than do that!"

The leaders of the heretics profited by the low level of education and morality among the Christian clergy. The heresiarchs were able men who led virtuous lives and practised extreme asceticism. Their prestige was so great that travelers sought their company in order to be protected by the reverence which they inspired. Orthodox Catholics begged to be buried in the cemeteries of the heretics, so that they might rest among the "good people." Many feudal lords protected the leaders of the heretics and allowed them to preach in public; some nobles openly accepted the new faith and many more practised it in secret. The success of the heresy was due not only to the virtue of its teachers, but also to the simplicity of its doctrine. The leaders, "the perfect," had to lead very ascetic lives, but few restrictions were placed on their followers. The latter, if they had faith, could attain salvation by receiving the last rite (the *consolamentum*) from the "perfect" on their death-bed. Since they believed that there was no hell and no purgatory they had few worries about the future life. They accepted the old Manichean dualism and believed that the power of evil had created the world and all material things, that the God of the Old Testament was really the god of evil, that Jesus had been killed by this evil god, and that the struggle between good and evil still went on. Extreme asceticism was the best way to free oneself from the power of evil because it freed one from the evil, material world, but if this were impossible much could be gained by hearing the teaching and receiving the blessing of the "perfect."

The orthodox clergy of Languedoc were either too weak or too indifferent to crush this heresy. Innocent III wrote in exasperation of the archbishop and clergy of Narbonne: "Blind men, dumb dogs, who are no longer able to bark, and simoniacs who sell justice, who absolve the rich and condemn the poor. They do not even observe the laws of the Church; they accumulate benefices and intrust sacerdotal functions to unworthy priests and illiterate children. That is the cause of the insolence of the heretics and the contempt felt by lords and people for God and his Church."

Since the local clergy were useless, Innocent sent legates and missionaries to convert the heretics. They had little success and Innocent, as he did on so many other occasions, turned to the use of force. He ordered a crusade against those who failed to see the light, offering the same indulgences as for a crusade to the Holy Land. There was little enthusiasm for this crusade at first, but in 1208 a papal legate was murdered by a follower of Count Raymond of Toulouse. Raymond was already suspected of heresy and this act seemed to prove the charge. This concrete example of the impiety of the greatest lord of the South was easier to exploit than abstract warnings about the dangers of heresy. The crusade became popular in North France and soon a large army, under the leadership of Count Simon de Montfort, advanced on Languedoc. The war which followed soon lost its religious character and became a struggle for the independence of the South. Catholics and heretics fought side by side against the invader and were aided in the end by the entirely orthodox king of Aragon. Montfort, on the other hand, massacred the inhabitants of captured towns indiscriminately, without inquiring about their faith. In the end the superior generalship of Montfort and the better fighting qualities of his men won the day. Most of the fiefs of Languedoc passed into the hands of northerners and Languedoc ceased to have a political and cultural life of its own. Close ties with the North ended the old autonomy of the region and little by little the upper classes began to use French instead of Provençal. Thus a brilliant, if somewhat artificial civilization came to an end.

The Albigensian Crusade was more of a political than a religious success. Heresy had been driven underground but it had not been wiped out, and in a few years the heretics seemed as numerous as ever in many places. Then even the political success was threatened by the death of Simon de Montfort. His son was incapable of defending the conquests of the northerners, and dispossessed southern lords began to regain their old holdings. A new crusade was necessary, and this time the king of France took the lead. Philip Augustus, fearing an attack by John of England, had taken no part in the first Albigensian war and even seems to have resented the diversion it caused. His successor, Louis VIII, had less to fear from England and seized the opportunity to strengthen the monarchy while showing his zeal for the faith. He received an assignment of all the Montfort claims and then ended southern resistance in a single well-planned campaign. The king annexed most of Languedoc directly to the royal domain and made sure that the holders of the remaining fiefs would be loyal to the Church and the crown. Protected by the king, the Church was at last able to make a direct attack on heresy.

This attack was directed by a new ecclesiastical tribunal, the Inquisition, which gradually took shape during the second quarter of the century. Bishops had long been intrusted with the duty of discovering and repressing heresy in their dioceses. Some had done the work well, but most of them had neither the time nor the knowledge necessary for the task. Heresy was not always manifested by overt acts and the bishops found it difficult to discover the secret thoughts of men. Heretics could be exposed only by experts in heresy, and few bishops could qualify in this category. Therefore the popes, beginning with Gregory IX, began to transfer the duty of investigating heresy to members of the new religious orders founded by Saints Francis and Dominic. As we shall see, one of the chief reasons for creating these orders was the desire to convert heretics and to prevent the orthodox from falling into heresy. Their interest in the problem of heresy made the Franciscans and Dominicans expert in discovering obscure manifestations of unorthodox thought and qualified them for the work assigned by the pope. Theoretically, the bishops always retained some supervisory powers over investigations of heresy, but in practice they interfered very little with the work. Under the pope's orders the Franciscans and Dominicans set up an elaborate organization for detecting and trying heretics. This organization, the Inquisition, was eminently successful. In less than a century it reduced the number of heretics to insignificant proportions and by the end of the next century it had practically annihilated itself by removing the cause for its existence.

The Inquisition took its name from the procedure which it employed. It is a name of evil reputation today, but we should realize that it was not particularly offensive to men of the Middle Ages. Inquisition simply means "investigation" or "inquest"; the early English grand jury shared the name of "inquisition" with the tribunal of the Church. Like Henry II's itinerant justices, the papal inquisitors collected accusations of crime; if they accepted rumor and neighborhood gossip, so did most secular courts. The great innovation in the procedure of the Inquisition was the development of very effective means for proving the guilt of the accused. As we have seen, it was difficult, even in England, to find a satisfactory way of testing the truth of accusations. How much more difficult it was, when the accusation dealt not with physical acts, such as theft or murder, but with a state of mind! An added hazard was the fact that in Languedoc the heretics had many friends, and witnesses against them were apt to suffer mysterious calamities after testifying. The Church succeeded in overcoming these difficulties, but only by adopting rules of evidence which were exceedingly unfair. In the first place, to protect the witnesses, they were examined secretly, one by one. The accused never saw his accusers, nor was he informed of the evidence against him. Then, since evidence on matters of belief is never very satisfactory, the inquisitors tried to secure corroboration from the accused himself. He was subjected to long interrogations, with questions skilfully designed to trap him into admissions of guilt. If this failed to produce the desired result the Inquisition, as a last resort, used torture to extort a confession. It was exceedingly difficult for a person accused of heresy to establish his innocence, for the Inquisition always assumed that he would not have been suspected if he had not been guilty of some error. On the other hand, the Inquisition sincerely desired the salvation, and not the death of a sinner. If he were guilty of only minor offenses, such as undue respect for heretical leaders, he might make atonement by a pilgrimage or an act of public humiliation. Those who confessed serious doctrinal errors were confined to prison. Only those who obstinately refused to recant, or who, having recanted, were caught again in heresy were "relaxed to the secular arm"—a euphemism for a sentence of death.

It may be difficult to understand how such an institution could have been accepted by the people of Europe. It must be remembered that, to the orthodox, heresy was a crime of unspeakable baseness. The heretic was a traitor to God and a murderer of his neighbor's soul. Those who suffered from other criminals lost merely the trivial goods of this earth, but those who listened to heretics were deprived of the inestimable treasures of heaven. Heretics destroyed the bonds of society by weakening the basic authority on which all institutions rested; their mere existence brought down the vengeance of heaven on the regions in which they lived. Heresy was a disease which had to be wiped out; the heretic must either be cured or be destroyed. Our own attitude to bearers of dangerous doctrines or diseases is not very different.

In addition the Inquisition received powerful support from lay rulers. This was not wholly disinterested, for they felt that their authority was threatened by heretical ideas, and they profited from the forfeitures of heretics' goods. Heresy was often associated with democratic or anarchical ideas; witness the case of Arnold of Brescia, who revived the Roman Republic after denying the spiritual power of the pope. Like all persecuted sects, the heretics thought of themselves as the elect and were apt to assert that no one outside their community could have any lawful authority. Therefore kings and emperors, whether supporters or opponents of the papacy, made laws against heresy, arrested suspects for the Inquisition, held condemned heretics in jail, and if necessary burned them at the stake. Pious kings felt that this was only doing their duty as Christian monarchs. More worldly rulers were glad to have a chance to confiscate heretical possessions and to pose as champions of the true faith while quarreling with the pope.

Backed, on the whole, by public opinion and the power of secular rulers, the Inquisition was able to work steadily and effectively. Its success was due more to careful investigation of all accusations than to mass executions. Only a small number of very stubborn heretics were burned; the great majority escaped with lighter sentences. But few men succeeded in keeping heretical tendencies a secret. The slightest manifestation of sympathy for heretical doctrines resulted in an immediate summons from the Inquisition; even the orthodox had to watch their tongues for fear of making some inadvertent remark that savored of heresy. By keeping constant pressure on the people the Inquisition succeeded in exterminating the Albigensian belief. The cities of northern France, Flanders, and Italy were also purified of unorthodox sects. Only in the remote Alpine valleys did a handful of Waldensians survive. There, in spite of repeated persecutions, they have endured to this day.

The Inquisition preserved the unity of the Christian faith for another three centuries. Against this achievement must be set two unfortunate results. In the first place, the people of Languedoc were demoralized by the work of the tribunal. Most inquisitors were honest, capable judges who tried to act fairly, but a few of them were insane fanatics who condemned every one brought before them. In addition, even honest judges were sometimes misled by blackmailers and backbiters who wished to ruin their neighbors. The resulting atmosphere of suspicion and fear did not promote the growth of candor, honesty, or courage in the people of Languedoc. The other consequence was more serious. As we have seen, the Fourth Lateran Council outlawed the old forms of trial. New procedures were needed just at the time that the Inquisition was beginning its work. Its methods were so wonderfully efficacious, at least from a prosecutor's point of view, that they were adopted by most European countries. Thus secret trials, failure to confront the accused with witnesses against him, torture, and complete reliance on the decision of the judge, came into European criminal procedure and remained to plague it for centuries. England alone escaped this baneful influence. This was due in part to the fact that England had already developed its own procedure of trial by jury, and in part to the fact that England was so orthodox that the pope never found it necessary to establish the Inquisition there.

THE MENDICANT ORDERS: ST. DOMINIC AND ST. FRANCIS

The purely negative work of the Inquisition was not enough to repel the danger which threatened the Church. Specific heresies might be exterminated, but as long as thousands of people felt dissatisfied with the behavior of the clergy and perplexed by the problems of a money economy, the state of mind which produced heresy would remain. Many zealous churchmen of the late twelfth century realized this and endeavored to regain the Church's lost influence by renouncing all wealth and living and preaching among the poor. An early attempt to establish an order based on these principles had been only moderately successful, due largely to the violence of the Albigensian Crusade and the opposition of conservative clergymen. But the idea did not die and was destined to bear fruit in the formation of the great mendicant orders.

Among the preachers who were active in Languedoc in the early years of the thirteenth century was a Spaniard named Dominic. He was born about 1170 and had studied for the priesthood at Palencia. He chanced to accompany his bishop in a journey to Languedoc and soon began to preach in an attempt to convert the heretics. We know very little of his early work, but he must have distinguished himself as a leader, since a small group of able men soon gathered around him and assisted him in his labors. Eventually he was able to found a monastery for women at Prouille, where converted heretics might find shelter and "poor girls of gentle blood" might receive an education. This establishment was soon richly endowed. Dominic then began to think of establishing his group of preachers as a regular religious order. He attended the Fourth Lateran Council and in 1216 obtained recognition from Honorius III. At that time there were only sixteen members in his order, but they were picked men from many different regions. Six were from Spain, but Toulouse, Provence, Lorraine, North France and England were also represented.

Dominic and his associates adopted the rule of the canons regular of St. Augustine. They took the name of "Preaching Friars," which Innocent had used in speaking of them. This name denotes their ideals. They were to preach, and in order to do this effectively, they were to devote themselves to study. They were to be friars, not monks; they were to live in the busy haunts of men instead of secluded in a convent; the world was to be their cloister. By preaching and by example they were to spread Christian doctrines and ideals among the people. In 1217 Dominic sent his followers out on their mission. He said: "You are still a little flock, but already I have formed in my heart the project of dispersing you abroad. You will no longer abide in the sanctuary of Prouille. The world henceforth is your home, and the work God has created for you is teaching and preaching. Go you, therefore, into the whole world and teach all nations. Preach to them the glad tidings of their redemption. Have confidence in God, for the field of your labors will one day widen to the uttermost ends of the earth." Accordingly, some went to Spain, some to Paris and some to Bologna. Their success was very rapid. At Dominic's death, four years later, the order already had sixty convents scattered through Spain, France, England, Italy, Germany and Hungary. Its influence was increased by the adoption of a vow of absolute poverty. The friars could have no property and no regular income. They could attack the problems created by the new wealth without being accused of profiting from the new wealth. Instead they supported themselves by begging and the Dominicans thus became a "mendicant" order.

The emphasis which Dominic had placed on learning made his followers especially active in university towns. Some of them became noted scholars, and they soon obtained professorships at Paris, Oxford, Montpellier, Bologna and Toulouse. The secular clergy were jealous of this success and tried to bar the Dominicans from the higher faculties, but with papal support they overrode all opposition. Eventually the Dominicans established their right to a certain number of chairs in the theological faculty at Paris, and since Paris was the leading university, this brought them recognition everywhere. Some of the most influential scholars of the thirteenth century were Dominicans—for example Thomas Aquinas, the greatest philosopher of the Church, and Vincent of Beauvais, who summed up medieval knowledge in a huge encyclopedia. Because of their learning and their early interest in heresy, the Dominicans were especially interested in the Inquisition, and its most active branches were under their control.

The other great mendicant order was founded by Francis of Assisi. He was born in Italy in 1182 and was thus some twelve years younger than Dominic. He was the son of a rich merchant of Assisi and as a youth led a joyous life. Francis was greatly interested in stories of chivalry and longed to distinguish himself as a knight. His one military adventure, however, proved disastrous and he returned home desperately ill. The collapse of his hopes turned his thoughts to religion, and he went through a long internal struggle, trying to discover what he should do to be saved. When he was about twenty he finally became convinced that he must renounce wealth and family ties and serve God in poverty through charity. He did not withdraw from the world but instead began to preach and to do good works among his neighbors.

Other men of like mind gathered about him until there were twelve in all. They then sought the pope at the Lateran Council in 1215 to have their undertaking confirmed. The pope hesitated at first, for there were obvious resemblances between Francis' plan, and that of Peter Waldo. Francis, however, was willing to accept suggestions from the leaders of the Church, which Waldo had never done, and the need for a new type of religious order was more obvious in 1215 than it had been in 1179. So Francis' followers, the "Minorites" or "Friars Minor," as they called themselves in their humility, were allowed to begin their work. From the first, Francis insisted on absolute poverty. The brethren were to labor with their hands, but they were not to receive wages in money, though they might accept gifts of food or clothing. They were to take no thought for the morrow and were to give to the poor all that was not absolutely necessary for the day. The rule ordered:

> The brethren shall appropriate to themselves nothing, neither house, nor place, nor other thing, but shall live in the world as strangers and pilgrims, and shall go confidently after alms. In this they shall feel no shame, since the Lord for our sake made himself poor in the world. It is this perfection of poverty which has made you, dearest brethren, heirs and kings of the kingdom of heaven. Having this, you should wish to have nought else under heaven.

The success of the order was due to the spirit of Francis, which many of his early followers imbibed. He tried to apply the precepts of Christ literally, and to imitate His life in all things. He delighted in sacrifice for the poor and especially for the lepers, who were the outcasts of society. He renounced worldly pleasures without becoming bitter and sad. He loved all created things; he chanted the praises of the sun and preached sermons to the birds. He was always gay and at times even playful. He named one of his followers "the plaything of Jesus Christ" and called the brethren "the Lord's clowns." [7]

"Is it not in fact true," he said, "that the servants of God are really like clowns, intended to revive the hearts of men, and to lead them to spiritual joy?" Francis also succeeded in spiritualizing his early chivalric ideals. He sang the praises of "My Lady Poverty" as a troubadour would sing the praises of his mistress, and he sought spiritual adventures as a wandering knight would seek temporal combats. He was patient and humble, yet "he possessed an original and well-balanced mind, ex-

---

[7] *Joculatores*, here and elsewhere translated as "clowns," is an inclusive term for entertainers, players, acrobats, and gleemen.

traordinary common sense, an iron will, and indomitable courage."
He was a remarkable speaker and his sermons swayed thousands of men
to do his will. Under such leadership it is not surprising that the order
grew rapidly and soon included thousands of members.

The two mendicant orders were founded by men of very different
temperaments, for reasons which were not altogether the same, and
the lapse of time did not efface all these differences. The Dominicans
were somewhat more interested in scholarship and theology, while the
Franciscans concentrated on missionary work among the masses. Yet
the two orders influenced each other and much of their work overlapped.
It is possible (though the Dominicans deny it) that the Preaching
Friars borrowed the idea of absolute poverty from the rule of St. Francis.
The Franciscans, on the other hand, were not content to allow the
Dominicans to possess a monopoly of scholarship. Franciscans began
to seek chairs of theology at Paris, and their great doctor, St. Bonaventura, is hardly less important in the history of medieval philosophy than
St. Thomas Aquinas himself. In their work among the people both
orders drew from the same source of strength. Their poverty freed them
from the reproach of worldliness and luxury which had been thrown
at other clergymen. Their training and their zeal kept them from holding
the perfunctory services by which many priests had killed the interest
of intelligent laymen. Their active charity contrasted favorably with the
routine distribution of alms practised by older orders. In these respects
Franciscans and Dominicans were much alike and the people made few
distinctions between them.

The great achievement of the mendicant orders was to revive the influence of the Church on lay society. They were honored by kings for
their wisdom, by nobles for their disinterestedness, and by peasants for
their holiness. They were especially successful in dealing with townsmen, who had become so scornful of ordinary clergymen. The friars
gained the confidence of the bourgeoisie by vigorous denunciations of
worldly churchmen, and secured their respect by living Christianity as
well as preaching it. They reminded townsmen that they were not entirely free from responsibility for the decline of morality, and that they
manifested the same excessive love of riches which seemed so odious
in priests and prelates. Even in Italy the bourgeoisie were somewhat uneasy about their concentration on worldly interests, and the uncompromising attack of the friars drove them into agonies of penitence. As
a result the friars acquired an influence even greater than that of the
reformers of the eleventh and twelfth centuries. Thousands of men joined
their ranks, and both orders found it necessary to create monasteries
for women who wished to aid in their work. In addition, they established lay organizations for men and women who had to continue their
activities in the world, but wished the support and protection of the

order in their attempts to lead Christian lives. The Franciscan association was known as the "Tertiary Order of Minorites," the Dominican as the "Militia of Jesus Christ." Thousands of pious laymen enrolled themselves in these groups; Louis IX of France was a tertiary of St. Francis.

The popes soon realized the value of the new orders and gave them many privileges. In 1217 the friars were permitted to preach, to hear confessions, and to grant absolution in any parish. A few years later they were freed from the control of the regular hierarchy and were placed directly under the pope. These privileges enabled the friars to take over much of the work of the parish clergy, for laymen who disliked their own priests could secure almost all necessary spiritual services from wandering Franciscans or Dominicans. This situation naturally brought violent protests from bishops and priests who saw their authority, their prestige, and their revenues diminish from day to day. They pointed out that the privileges of the mendicant orders injured ecclesiastical discipline, and that many a layman preferred to confess to a wandering friar, whom he would never see again, rather than to his own priest, who would make sure that appropriate penance was performed. There was just enough truth in these charges to make some popes consider limiting the rights of the two orders, but they could not adopt this as a permanent policy. The friars were too useful to the papacy to be restrained; they served it as the monks of the reformed orders had served it in the investiture struggle. They were the most effective propagandists in the service of the Church and they exercised tremendous influence over the thoughts and beliefs of laymen. Therefore, in spite of some hesitations, the popes continued to load them with privileges and honors. Many friars were made bishops, in order to leaven the whole Church with the spirit of Francis and Dominic. Some were made cardinals and, by the end of the thirteenth century, there had been several mendicant popes. The exalted position of the mendicant orders caused much jealousy in other churchmen, but it was justified by the results it produced. More than any other group, the friars were responsible for the fact that in the thirteenth century Europe made a new effort to put Christian ideals into practice.

The early zeal and idealism of the mendicant orders declined, of course, after the death of the first generation of friars. It soon proved impossible to enforce the rule of absolute poverty. The great popularity of the orders caused a flow of donations, and pious laymen sought to provide the friars with houses and land as well as with food and clothing. Eventually a distinction was made between the poverty of the individual friar and the property which could be used by the order as a whole. This property was held for the use of the order by self-perpetuating groups of trustees, and thus was created a legal device which has had great importance in our own time. Whether this distinction saved the letter of the rule is doubtful, and it certainly injured its spirit. Wealth for the order meant more comfortable lives for the members, and this in turn meant that many men became friars because their entry into the order promised them an interesting and not too strenuous career. A minority of the Franciscans were shocked by these changes, but their protests were suppressed. The majority in both orders were ready to relax and to accept an easier life. Yet the friars never became entirely like the monks of the older orders. They still went out among the people, they still brought the teachings of Christ to the masses instead of waiting for the masses to come to them. Until the very end of the middle ages the influence of the friars remained greater than that of any other group among the clergy.

THE PAPACY AND FREDERICK II

From the death of Innocent III in 1216 to the death of the last male Hohenstaufen in 1268 the history of Italy and Germany was dominated by the struggle between the popes and the imperial family. Innocent III had prepared the way for this struggle by aiding Frederick II of Hohenstaufen to replace Otto IV as ruler of Germany and the Empire, but Innocent did not live to see the consequences of his act. He thought that Frederick was bound to the papal cause by gratitude and solemn promises. He failed to realize that the character and hereditary claims of the young emperor were to make him an irreconcilable foe of the papacy.

Frederick was not quite three when his father, the Emperor Henry VI, died. His mother's death a year later made him king of Sicily and ward of the papacy, since Sicily was a papal fief. Innocent III was not able to perform his duties as guardian very effectively, though he did intervene occasionally to preserve the young ruler's rights. He failed, however, to give Frederick the one thing which was most necessary for the growing boy, a secure and stable environment. There was no regularly organized regency in Sicily, and the central government almost collapsed during the long minority. Norman nobles and Germans brought in by Henry VI quarreled for the possession of the child king, and he was handed about from one faction to the other as the result of palace plots and petty wars. No one showed him any loyalty; he was merely a symbol of power to be secured by the strongest or cleverest faction. "Without a relative or friend, without ever feeling a ray of love, the child grew up in the midst of intrigues of the worst kind, among men whose empty greed he saw through only too quickly." He learned to use craft and deceit very early in life. He was precocious, brilliant, fascinating, versatile, passionate, restless. When Frederick was nearly thirteen years old, one of his attendants described him as follows:

The king's stature is not only small, but also not large for his age. Nature has, however, endowed him with strong limbs and a vigorous body, with the ability to persist in every undertaking. He is never quiet, but is in motion all day long. In order to increase his strength by exercise he trains his supple body in the use of arms; and when he is practising he seizes his sword, which he trusts especially, and falls into a wild rage as if he wanted to slash his antagonist's face. He is skilful in the use of the bow, and practises shooting industriously. He delights in fine swift horses; you may well believe that no one knows better than he how to drive them or to spur them to a gallop. Thus practising the use of arms in every fashion he spends the entire day in constant and varied activity, and even continues his exercises through the first watch of the night. Moreover, he possesses royal dignity; he has the appearance and the commanding majesty of a ruler. His face is of gracious beauty, with a godlike forehead, and his eyes are so full of joy that it is a pleasure to look at him. He is wide awake, full of sagacity and docility. But his bearing is impertinent and unbecoming; . . . he is completely unwilling to take advice, and follows only the dictates of his own free will. As far as one can see, he considers it degrading to be under guardianship and to be regarded as a boy and not as a king. . . . His talents so far surpass his age that now, before he is a man, he is well equipped with knowledge and has the shrewdness that he would naturally have acquired only in the course of years.

Frederick retained the energy and self-confidence which he manifested at this early age throughout most of his life. He made his own decisions, not only because he believed that he was wiser than his councillors, but also because he trusted no one. He was sure that every man had his price, and the events of his reign seemed to justify this belief. Frederick's most engaging characteristic was his genuine love of learning. Somehow, during the troubled years of his boyhood, he had acquired an excellent education, and his court was always full of learned men. He was especially devoted to science and delighted in posing difficult questions to his scholars. He was also interested in poetry, and Dante speaks highly of his compositions in verse. Such was the boy who, at the age of seventeen, was called by Innocent III to be emperor.

Frederick gained the imperial crown only through the support of the pope, and he paid for this support with two promises which were to plague him for many years. In the first place, he swore to relinquish his Sicilian kingdom as soon as he was firmly established in Germany, and thus to free the Papal States from the threat of encirclement. Frederick, however, had no intention of giving up either realm. His imperial title gave him prestige, but little financial or military power. Only by retaining Sicily could Frederick secure the men and money he needed to play the rôle of a great emperor. In the second place, Frederick took the crusader's vow when he was crowned at Rome. This promise was probably sincere; the boy was elated by his recent success in Germany and he may have felt that the East could be conquered as easily as the North. But the vow was to hamper him for a dozen years; it gave the pope a weapon to use against him if he did not start for the Holy Land within a reasonable time. Frederick soon discovered that all his energy was needed to establish his authority in Italy and that he had no time for a crusade. Fortunately for him, Innocent III died before he could insist on the fulfilment of either promise. The new pope was Honorius III, a mild and kindly old man who once had been Frederick's guardian. He did not insist upon the immediate abandonment of Sicily and was very willing to accept Frederick's repeated excuses for postponing the crusade.

Honorius was succeeded in 1227 by Gregory IX, an old man who was anything but mild and kindly. Gregory was alarmed by the way in which Frederick was strengthening himself in Italy. He had made himself practically absolute in Sicily and was reviving the old imperial claims to authority in the Po Valley. The independence of the Papal States was threatened and Gregory feared that he might be reduced to the position of an Eastern patriarch, entirely subservient to the emperor. A crusade would remove Frederick from Italy, and Gregory insisted that the emperor fulfil his vow. Frederick was very unwilling to start, since he was trying to regain Jerusalem by negotiations rather than by fighting. The sultan of Egypt, who held the Holy City, was threatened by the prince of Damascus and was ready to make great concessions in return for peace with the Christians. Frederick had acquired the title of king of Jerusalem by marrying Isabelle of Brienne, the heiress, in 1225, and so he was in a position to give the sultan the guarantees he desired. However, under pressure from Gregory, Frederick proclaimed his crusade and set sail with great pomp in September, 1227. A few days later he crept back into port, saying that he and most of his army had been smitten with a mysterious disease. That there had been sickness on board is unquestionably true; how serious it was is another matter. Gregory took no stock at all in the story and excommunicated the emperor for not fulfilling his vow. A few months later Frederick set out again for Palestine, without troubling to secure absolution. The pope excommunicated him once more, this time for going on a crusade while excommunicate. Gregory also forbade any one in the Holy Land to assist the emperor, but Frederick still had no intention of fighting a real war with the Saracens. Though the sultan had been freed from his worst difficulties, he was still willing to negotiate, and Frederick made an advantageous treaty with him. Jerusalem, Bethlehem, Nazareth and a corridor to the sea were surrendered to the Christians. In return Frederick allowed the Moslems to retain the mosque of Omar and to worship freely in Jerusalem. He also promised to keep the princes of the West from attacking Egypt for a term of ten years. The pope promptly denounced these clauses as evidence of Frederick's lukewarmness toward the true faith.

He was even more angered by the fact that Frederick, still excommunicate, went to Jerusalem and crowned himself king there. Gregory was not quite ready to proclaim a crusade against a crusading king, but he sent an army, led by two cardinals, to attack the kingdom of Sicily. Frederick hastened home and easily defeated the papal forces, which had little popular support. The Italians seemed to feel that, if Frederick had been careless about his religious obligations, Gregory had been unreasonable in enforcing the strict letter of the law, and that neither contestant deserved much sympathy. Frederick tried to gain public favor by offering very generous terms to the pope when peace was made in 1230, but few people were impressed by this maneuver. As soon as he was absolved Frederick renewed his attempts to dominate Italy, and the peace of 1230 was only a truce.

If Frederick was to dominate Italy, his first task was to restore royal power in Sicily, where the institutions of the Norman kings had been almost overthrown during the troubled years of the minority. This task had almost been completed before the crusade of 1228, and soon after his return Frederick was able to take the last step toward absolutism. The "Constitutions for the Kingdom of Sicily," promulgated in 1231, deprived the privileged classes of most of their power and centralized all authority in the emperor. Nobles were forbidden to make private war and only servants of the king were allowed to carry weapons. Criminal jurisdiction was taken away from feudal lords and they were forbidden to marry their children off without the emperor's consent. Clerical courts were deprived of jurisdiction over laymen, except in cases of adultery. The clergy were forbidden to hold public office and were compelled to pay taxes. Towns were not allowed to elect their own *podestàs* or consuls, but were ruled by royal officials. There were to be no independent local authorities; everything was to be controlled by the court.

This centralization went far beyond that of England, where local governments were weakened but not annihilated. Frederick also went further than any English king in depriving the magnates of influence. His elaborate central government was run by professional bureaucrats who used Byzantine and Arabic rather than feudal procedures. The nobles naturally took no part in this work and they also had little voice in determining major questions of policy. Frederick, as ruler of Sicily, was freer from restraint than any other monarch of western Europe.

His financial policy in Sicily is especially interesting. He taxed the kingdom heavily, but he realized that commerce must thrive if taxation was to continue. He eliminated many interior customs barriers and tolls, and stabilized the currency. He encouraged foreign traders to break their voyages to and from the East in Sicilian ports, and thus increased the revenue from customs and harbor dues. He made Sicilian waters safe by maintaining a large and efficient navy, and his friendly

GERMANY AND ITALY UNDER THE HOHENSTAUFEN

NORTH SEA

Danzig
POMERELIA
PRUSSIA
POMERANIA

Lübeck
Hamburg

Bremen

SAXONY

BRANDENBURG
Brandenburg

Magdeburg
Goslar

LUSATIA

SILESIA (ADDED TO H.R.E. IN 14TH CENT.)

KINGDOM OF
POLAND

Utrecht

Paderborn

MEISSEN

Bruges
Antwerp
Ghent
Cologne
LOWER
LORRAINE
Aix-la-
Chapelle

THURINGIA

HESSE
Fulda

Prague

BOHEMIA

MORAVIA

Laôn

Reims

Verdun
Metz
UPPER
Toul
LORRAINE

Mainz
Oppenheim
Worms
FRANCONIA
Spires

Frankfort

Bamberg
Nuremberg
Ratisbon

Troyes
CLAIRVAUX

Strasburg
ALSACE

Waiblingen

DANUBE
Augsburg

AUSTRIA

Vienna

DANUBE

FRANCE

CITEAUX

SWABIA

Basel

Constance
Zurich
ST. GALL

BAVARIA

Salzburg

STYRIA

CLUNY

C. OF
BURGUNDY
Besançon

Geneva

CARINTHIA

TIROL

FRIULI

CARNIOLA

DRAVE

SAVE

Lyons
Vienne

SAVOY

Turin

Legnano
Corte-
nuova
Milan
LOMBARDY
Pavia
Roncaglia
Alessandria
Genoa

Mantua
Verona
RONA
Padua
Venice

PO

Parma
Modena
Bologna
ROMAGNA
Ravenna

KINGDOM OF HUNGARY

BOSNIA

RHONE

PROVENCE

Arles
Marseilles

KINGDOM OF
ARLES
(BURGUNDY)

Pisa
TUSCIA
Florence
Siena

Perugia
Assisi
Spoleto

PATRIMONY
OF ROME
CLAIMED BY
THE POPE

ADRIATIC SEA

CORSICA
(PISA)

HOLY ROMAN
EMPIRE,
1138

ADDED UNDER THE
HOHENSTAUFEN,
1138-1254

SARDINIA
(PISA & GENOA)

Tagliacozzo

Rome
Anagni

ITALY

Capua
Aversa
Amalfi

Benevento
(A PAPAL CITY)
Naples
Salerno

Bari

Brindisi

APULIA

(HOHENSTAUFEN, 1194
ANJOU, 1266)

UNDERLINED NAMES
WERE TOWNS
BELONGING TO THE
LOMBARD LEAGUE

150 MILES

MEDITERRANEAN SEA

KINGDOM OF
SICILY

Palermo

Messina

SICILY
(HOHENSTAUFEN, 1194
ANJOU, 1266
ARAGON, 1282)

TRM

relations with Moslem rulers still further decreased the risks of Mediterranean trade. At the same time, Frederick regulated commerce in great detail and created royal monopolies in many commodities. Typical of his methods is the way in which he cornered the grain market. He forbade the export of grain from his kingdom in a year when there was a surplus. This depressed the price to a point where royal officials could buy grain very cheaply. Then he loaded his navy with grain and sent it to the Moslems of North Africa, who were suffering from famine. The grain sold at many times its original cost and Frederick made a tremendous profit from the transaction.

Backed by the resources of Sicily, Frederick was able to intervene effectively in central and northern Italy. Towns which feared their neighbors and factions which feared their fellow-citizens allied themselves with the emperor. Frederick found a new source of support in the tyrants, who were just beginning to appear in some regions in the North. These men, profiting by the endless civil wars of the Italian towns, had substituted their own autocratic rule for the ineffectual republican governments of certain communes. They agreed with Frederick that municipal freedom was "a poisonous weed which must be rooted out," and like Frederick, they were frequently on bad terms with the Church. Local intrigues sometimes made them waver, but they were usually on the emperor's side. With this support, Frederick gained power steadily in Tuscany, Lombardy, and even in some parts of the Papal States. Gregory was alarmed by his success and started a vigorous diplomatic campaign against him, while the Lombard cities revived their old League, which had been inactive for some time. This opposition, however, was not at first effective.

While increasing his power in Italy, Frederick paid little attention to his German territories. He may have felt that he could easily re-establish his authority north of the Alps, once he had full use of Italian resources, or he may actually have believed that Germany was unimportant. At any rate, he spent little time in Germany and contented himself with leaving his young son Henry there to represent him. The boy received the title of King of the Romans, but he had no real power, and his advisers did nothing to strengthen the monarchy. Germany was actually ruled by the great lay and ecclesiastical princes, and Frederick accepted this situation with equanimity. In fact, he surrendered the last remnants of imperial authority by grants to the ecclesiastical princes in 1220 and to the lay princes in 1232. These grants made the princes practically independent rulers in their lands; even the towns, which had been strongholds of Hohenstaufen power were subordinated to the princes. The kingdom of Germany had long been declining and these acts deprived it of any importance as a political unit. Henceforth it was to be a very loose confederation of princes who occasionally consented to work together under the emperor, but who usually pursued their own independent and selfish policies.

German historians have blamed Frederick severely for abandoning his rights in the northern kingdom, but it is doubtful whether the opposite policy would have been more successful. The princes had been gaining power steadily for over a century and an attempt to arrest this development would have meant a long and hazardous fight. The rights which Frederick surrendered had little more than a nuisance value; they allowed him to interfere, but not to govern. The emperor had never developed adequate legal and administrative systems; many of the princes had more advanced governments. The potential royal domain which the Hohenstaufen had created in Swabia had been frittered away during the war between Philip and Otto. Barbarossa's attempt to strengthen royal power in Germany through a systematic, centralized feudalism had also proved a failure, partly because the princes would not allow the emperor to add confiscated or escheated fiefs to the royal domain. (Compare this to the situation in France, where Philip Augustus gave the French monarchy its first real impetus by annexing fiefs confiscated from John.) In short, there was no solid basis for imperial authority north of the Alps and the task of creating a strong, centralized government in Germany seemed almost hopeless. Frederick had some reason to concentrate on Italy, where he had inherited more power.

Frederick asked little of Germany, but he did expect not to be troubled by German problems. This hope was disappointed when his son Henry, who disagreed with his father's do-nothing policy in Germany, rebelled. The uprising was not very dangerous and was eventually suppressed, but the cities of the Lombard League thought that it offered them an opportunity to strike at the emperor. They assisted Henry, and this angered Frederick much more than the original rebellion had done. He was willing to forgive the German magnates, but, in spite of the pope's pleas, he would not forgive the Lombard cities. They were his most dangerous opponents and he determined to make the most of his grievance against them. He declared war on the League and won a brilliant victory at Cortenuova in 1237. If Frederick had not pushed too hard this battle might have given him a preponderant position in Italy. The Lombards were ready to make large concessions to him and the pope was for the moment helpless. But Frederick insisted on absolute surrender by the Lombard cities and at the same time threatened the Papal States. His enemies were driven to desperate resistance and the pope excommunicated him in 1239.

This started a conflict which was to continue until the emperor's death. Both Frederick and Gregory appealed to the public opinion of Europe through letters and pamphlets. Neither side, of course, discussed the real issue, which was the control of Italy. Gregory laid stress on the emperor's impiety and misdeeds. Frederick spoke of his high prerogatives and warned other rulers that if the pope could crush an emperor he would have no difficulty in dominating lesser monarchs. Gregory called a council, in order to give the widest possible publicity to his denunciation of Frederick. Since the emperor knew that the council would act against him, he sent his navy to attack the Genoese fleet which was carrying the northern bishops to Rome. His admiral drowned or captured so many prelates that the council could not be held. This was perhaps Frederick's greatest mistake. It transformed a personal quarrel with Gregory IX into a war with the Church. It cost Frederick the sympathy of non-Italian rulers who were annoyed by the fact that bishops from their countries suffered from the attack. It made it easy for the pope to mobilize public opinion against the emperor; almost any aspersion on Frederick would now be believed.

Gregory IX died a few months later and it took the cardinals almost two years to agree on a successor. The new pope, Innocent IV, had not been unfriendly to Frederick before his election, but the emperor's hopes that he would reverse Gregory's policy were in vain. Frederick's Italian ambitions were so dangerous to the papacy that no agreement between the two rulers was possible. After negotiating for a time, Innocent withdrew to Lyons in order to hold a council in safety. There Frederick was declared guilty of perjury, heresy and sacrilege and was once more excommunicated. He was deprived of all his thrones, Germany, Sicily, and Jerusalem. Innocent preached a crusade against him and papal partisans elected an anti-king in Germany. The war which followed was waged as much with propaganda and bribery as it was with arms. There were savage fights within Italian towns, a few prolonged sieges, and only one or two battles on a large scale. On the whole, the war was indecisive. Frederick had no trouble with Sicily, held his own in North Italy and lost ground in Germany. Innocent did not succeed in crushing the emperor, but he did make the formation of a united Italian kingdom impossible. Neither party gained much moral support in other European countries. The pope's use of religious weapons in a struggle which was largely political alienated many good Christians, including the pious Louis IX of France. On the other hand, Frederick's undisguised hostility to the papacy and his imperial ambitions shocked rulers who might otherwise have been friendly to him. An emperor who aspired to be real, as well as nominal head of Christendom was worse than a politically minded pope, for he could not be restrained by any theory of the separation of the two powers. So Europe preserved an attitude of watchful waiting until Frederick's death in 1250.

It is easier to describe the tangled events of Frederick's reign than it is to form an estimate of his character and achievements. His own contemporaries, even those who were his enemies, admitted that he possessed amazing talents. Chroniclers described him as "Stupor mundi," and the Germans would not admit that such a man could die. They said that he was sleeping in a cave, surrounded by his warriors, waiting for a summons to save Germany.[8] In our own age historians have admired the great and varied abilities of the emperor. He was an excellent diplomat, a careful administrator, and a capable general. These qualities enabled him to hold his own in a twenty years' struggle with the papacy, even though it was at the height of its power. He was interested in new ideas and men of all religions were welcome at his court if they had skill in any branch of knowledge. Important scientific works were written or translated at his request, and Frederick himself composed a notable treatise on falconry. This book is much more than a tract on hunting; it is really a manual of ornithology. Different species of birds are described and compared, the training and care of hawks are discussed, and their diseases are explained. Remarkably accurate illustrations add to the value of the work. Frederick knew a great deal about birds and was rather scornful of earlier writers on the subject. He checked all their statements against his own observations and frequently pointed out their mistakes. Besides being a patron of science, Frederick was also, as Dante says, "the father of Italian poetry." Provençal lyrics were imitated at his court, and the emperor seems to have encouraged his followers to write Italian verses. Frederick himself was a poet, and the works of his school are among the earliest monuments of Italian poetry.

Yet this brilliant and versatile ruler, who seemed so well fitted to begin a new age, blighted everything he touched. His reign marked the end of the medieval empire and the beginning of the rapid decline of the kingdom of Sicily. His long wars in North Italy left the region more disunited than ever, and even his successful crusade proved useless in the end, since the Moslems regained Jerusalem in 1244. Within a few years of his death Tuscany had replaced Sicily as the center of Italian poetry and by the end of the century Sicily had lost its importance in scientific work. Frederick created nothing permanent; he is significant for what he ended, not what he began.

Frederick's failure was apparently caused by his peculiar emotional defects. He suspected every one; toward the end of his reign his most faithful minister was accused of treason and tortured until he committed suicide. He did not inspire loyalty or affection; he ruled chiefly through fear. Even worse was Frederick's failure to understand his own age. As we have seen, the remarkable feature of the twelfth and thirteenth centuries was that new ideas and activities were harmonized with old beliefs; that the new energy of the great revival was made to serve Christian ideals. Frederick understood and used the new ideas, but he did not

---

[8] This legend was later transferred to Barbarossa; quite rightly, for he was much more of a German hero than his brilliant, Italianate grandson.

understand or sympathize with the old beliefs. He seems to have been a complete religious sceptic. The pope denounced him for writing a book on "The Three Impostors, Moses, Christ and Mohammed," and while the accusation was probably unfounded, the fact that it could be made and believed tells much of Frederick's character. His mode of life was not Christian, or even European; he has been aptly styled a "baptized sultan." An account of one of his journeys reminds us of the Arabian Nights' Tales. He traveled with a harem guarded by eunuchs, and with a menagerie which included camels, lions, panthers, white bears, monkeys, and other animals. He had an enormous elephant, a gift from the sultan of Egypt, which was guarded by Saracen attendants. His bodyguard was composed of Sicilian Moslems, and he was accompanied by Ethiopian trumpeters and Moorish dancers and jongleurs. Thus Frederick stood for everything which was strange and different and dangerous; he represented the new ideas acting without restraint or connection with the past. He could not secure the wholehearted support of his subjects or the friendship of other Christian rulers because he had little in common with them. He did not speak the same language or think the same thoughts. Even when he tried to give the appearance of orthodoxy he deceived no one. He persecuted heretics cruelly and energetically, partly to gain favor with the pope; even more because he feared their radical political ideas. He founded a university at Naples, less to advance Christian knowledge than to keep his southern subjects from going to the anti-imperial university at Bologna. He gained about as much credit from these moves as he did from his crusade. Even when he acted as an orthodox Christian ruler, no one believed that he was one.

Another difficulty was the fact that Frederick took his position as *Roman* emperor too seriously. He used the language of the old Roman law to describe the sanctity of his position. He spoke of his birthplace, Jesi, as the "noble city where our divine mother brought us into the world, . . . this Bethlehem where Cæsar was born." In a letter to his prime minister, Peter de Vineis, Frederick applied to him the Biblical text, "Thou art Peter, and on this rock I will build my church." He had no reverence for the pope and little respect for other European monarchs. These pretensions angered many people who were not supporters of the papacy. They did not like the idea of a Europe dominated by the pope, but they liked the idea of a Europe dominated by Frederick even less.

Rulers who moved less rapidly, who respected old forms, who kept on reasonably good terms with the Church, accomplished much more than Frederick. His contemporaries, Louis IX of France and Henry III of England, were less intelligent and less capable than the emperor, but they left behind them states which had a future and not merely a past. Their governments corresponded to the needs and beliefs of their peoples.

Neither Frederick's scepticism nor his absolutism had a place in the thirteenth century. People were awed by his ability, his daring, and his wickedness; they were never convinced that he was right.

THE CRUSHING OF THE HOHENSTAUFEN DYNASTY

Frederick's great ability had preserved him from the full consequences of his mistakes, but his descendants were to reap the whirlwind which he had sowed. Innocent IV had been too frightened by his struggle with Frederick to forgive the "viper breed of the Hohenstaufen," and he and his successors determined to end the power of the hated family. It took them eighteen years to achieve their purpose, and the long, vindictive struggle injured the prestige of the Church. Not every one had approved the use of spiritual weapons against Frederick, but at least there was some sort of case against him. Frederick was a strange, dangerous person, quite probably an unbeliever and certainly an enemy of the papacy. His successors were more conventional and less dangerous; to proclaim excommunications and crusades against them smacked of personal vengeance. It annoyed many people to see the popes use their spiritual power to obtain a satisfactory political settlement in Italy. The popes could answer, of course, that they would have no spiritual power if they were at the mercy of unfriendly Italian rulers, but this answer did not entirely allay dissatisfaction. Gregory VII and Alexander III had gained sympathy by going into exile when threatened by an emperor. Innocent IV and his successors stirred up suspicion when they tried to protect themselves from the Hohenstaufen by attempts to conquer Sicily. However noble their end, they had used rather questionable means to achieve it, and the influence of the Church declined steadily after the extermination of the Hohenstaufen.

Frederick's successor in Germany was his son, Conrad IV (1250–1254). In spite of papal opposition, backed by a crusade against him, Conrad retained both Germany and Sicily. But he did little to strengthen his family's position during his short reign, and when he died the princes were unable to agree on a successor. Eventually the rival factions each elected a king, but these claimants were both foreigners who had no real power. One, the brother of the English king, did visit Germany and issue a few charters; the other, Alfonso of Castile, did not even take the trouble to enter his new realm. The first ruler who was accepted by all the princes was Rudolph of Habsburg, elected in 1273, and he did not even dream of reviving imperial authority.

During the Great Interregnum, from 1254 to 1273, the German princes continued their work of building up small, independent states. Some were successful and created principalities which could bear comparison with the Western monarchies; others could not hold their lands together and allowed lesser lords to become independent in their turn. One may say that feudalism had at last triumphed in Germany if one remembers that the feudalism of the thirteenth century was very different from that of the tenth. Feudalism still meant localism and the confusion of public office with private property, but it no longer meant a semipermanent state of war with government reduced to bare essentials. Thirteenth century feudalism was compatible with written laws, well-developed legal and administrative systems, and considerable respect for peace and security. Germany had failed to secure unity, but it was not therefore in a state of anarchy. Rather, all the political energy and ability of the Germans was devoted to the development of their local governments. The old Germany of the Rhine was so badly split up by ecclesiastical principalities that no strong government could arise there, but in Bavaria and the new Germany of the East powerful, well-organized states were created. The western cities took advantage of the weakness of their lords to gain independence and to organize leagues which frequently held the balance of power in that region. The Teutonic Knights carried on the old tradition of expansion to the East by conquering and colonizing Prussia. Germany was not to play a heroic rôle again in European history until the sixteenth century, but it suffered no more from war than did France or England during the fourteenth and fifteenth centuries and it was probably as well governed.

In Italy Frederick's illegitimate son Manfred seized the throne of Sicily after the death of his half-brother Conrad. He was very like Frederick in many ways and was therefore especially detested by the popes. They tried one scheme after another to get rid of him, but he defended himself skilfully, and even gained a foothold in North Italy. Finally, the pope offered Sicily to Charles of Anjou, brother of the king of France. Charles was given full crusading privileges and the proceeds of a tax on the French clergy. In a well-planned and swiftly executed campaign he defeated and killed Manfred in 1266 and became king of Sicily. Two years later, Conradin, the young son of Conrad IV, entered Italy with a small army to claim his heritage. The boy gained some support in the peninsula, but was decisively defeated by Charles of Anjou after a hard battle. Captured while fleeing from the field, he was condemned to death and perished on the scaffold at Naples. The execution seemed unnecessarily cruel to many people at the time, and the pope was blamed for not preventing it. Whatever the effect on public opinion, the papacy had gained its political objectives. The last male Hohenstaufen was dead; the union of Sicily and the Empire was dissolved; no future emperor could threaten a pope. The papacy was at last free from the danger which had been threatening it since the time of Gregory VII. It remained to be seen what it could do with its victory.

THE FOURTH CRUSADE

The failure of the Third Crusade had dampened Europe's enthusiasm for Eastern adventure, but the Church was not ready to abandon the idea of rescuing Jerusalem for a second time from the hands of the infidel. Innocent III, with his usual energy, began planning a crusade almost as soon as he became pope, even though conditions were unfavorable for the venture. France and England were absorbed in the struggle for the Angevin fiefs, while the Guelf-Hohenstaufen feud meant that there was no generally recognized emperor in Germany. Thus none of the great monarchs of Europe was available for a crusade and most of their subjects were too interested in local diplomatic and military conflicts to pay much attention to the Holy Land. However, in 1201 some powerful French lords and one Italian marquis were persuaded to take the cross. They decided to avoid the dangerous land route and travel by sea, so they sent messengers to the Italian cities to make terms for transportation. The messengers finally made a bargain with Venice on fairly reasonable terms. Venice was to supply the necessary vessels and provisions for a year, on the payment of four marks for each horse and two marks for each man.[9] In addition, the Venetians were to furnish ships and troops of their own and they were to receive one half of all conquests made. All this was fair enough, but the messengers had displayed the usual medieval optimism about figures and had grossly overestimated the size of the crusading army. The Venetians prepared their fleet on the basis of this estimate, and as a result, when the crusading leaders reached the city in 1202, they were faced with a staggering bill for accommodations which they could not use. The crusaders who had come to Venice could not supply enough money to pay the bill and it was evident that the crusade was dead unless some new bargain could be made.

As it happened, the Venetians saw a possibility of using the expedition for their own purposes. There was a convenient ambiguity in the terms of the contract, since Venice had merely promised to carry the crusaders *outre-mer*—beyond the sea. The host of pilgrims undoubtedly thought that this meant Palestine; the leaders had probably intended an attack on the ruler of Egypt, who held the Holy Land at this time; but other destinations were equally possible. One contemporary chronicler states that the Venetians had made a treaty with the sultan of Egypt and had promised, in return for commercial privileges, that they would not carry crusaders to his land. There is not much evidence to prove the truth of

---

[9] A French scholar estimated the value of the mark at about fifty-two francs, at a time when the franc was worth nineteen cents. This would mean that each man was to be provided with transportation and food for a year for about twenty dollars. Of course this is entirely misleading, and is an example of the difficulty of reducing any medieval sum to a modern equivalent.

this story but the crusade was diverted from Moslem lands. The Venetians first proposed that the crusaders should cancel their debt by capturing the Christian city of Zara. This seaport, situated across the Adriatic from Venice, was a thriving commercial center, and the Venetians wanted to end its competition. The leaders agreed to the proposal, but kept the matter secret from the mass of the army. The latter, thinking they were at last starting for the Holy Land, made great bonfires and were very joyful.

After some weeks of indecisive movements [10] the crusaders reached Zara. The army was shocked when it learned that it was to attack a Christian city, and many soldiers refused to fight. Innocent III, warned of the diversion, ordered the crusaders not to war against Christians. In spite of these obstacles the leaders succeeded in inducing a sufficient number of their men to act with the Venetians, and the city was captured without much difficulty. Since it was then late in the fall the Venetians refused to proceed further during the stormy season, and the crusaders wintered at Zara.

When spring came there were fresh plots on the part of the leaders and the Venetians. Apparently the mass of the army did not know the exact terms of the contract and thought that the Venetians had agreed to supply food for only nine months. Since this period was virtually over it was easy to argue that new arrangements must be made. The Venetians suggested that Byzantium would be a wonderful base for a crusade, if they could find an excuse for occupying it. Then the Italian marquis of Montferrat proposed that the crusaders make an alliance with the Byzantine Prince Alexius who was seeking help for his deposed father. Alexius was close at hand and an agreement was soon made. The crusaders were to aid him and his father to recover the throne of the Eastern Empire. In return he promised to bring the Greek Church under the obedience of the pope, to give the crusaders money, provisions, and men for the conquest of Egypt, and to maintain five hundred knights in Palestine as long as he lived. These terms were enticing, not only to the leaders, but also to many in the army. Since the time of the First Crusade the Westerners had suffered from the indifference, and at times the hostility of Constantinople. To change this for active support would greatly improve their chances for success. As for the Venetians, it was clear that an emperor whom they had made would give them a practical monopoly of the commerce of Constantinople. Therefore most of the crusaders accepted the new arrangement, though a few who wanted to fulfil the letter of their vows separated from the army and went directly to Palestine.

[10] The reason for the long delay in reaching Zara has never been fully explained. It is possible that the attack on Constantinople was already being planned, and that the time was spent in negotiations with young Alexius, son of a deposed emperor.

The crusaders set sail for Constantinople and found the population so divided by factional struggles that the city was captured without much trouble. Alexius and his father were placed on the throne, but their position was not very secure and they did not dare press their people for money. This made it impossible for them to fulfil their promises to the crusaders and bad feeling soon arose between the former allies. When repeated requests failed to produce any money, the crusaders laid siege to Constantinople, and after great hardships finally succeeded in getting a foothold on the supposedly impregnable walls. This ended the resistance of the city and the crusaders sacked it pitilessly. Parts of the town were burned; priceless treasures of art were broken in pieces; gold and silver and relics were stolen and divided among the hosts. Indescribable orgies accompanied the sack, and the scene of the worst was the great church of Santa Sophia.

Innocent III had repeatedly commanded the crusaders not to attack Constantinople and had placed the Venetians under excommunication for their misdeeds. Some men had left the army because of his exhortations, but he had not been able to influence the leaders. He was also indignant over the sack of Constantinople and denounced the conduct of the crusaders in scathing terms. Nevertheless, once the city had been captured, he acquiesced in the accomplished fact and ordered the crusaders to stay at Constantinople for a year in order to consolidate their conquest. Innocent seems to have been affected by the same arguments which had moved the crusaders earlier, the advantage of a base in the East and the hope of ending the schism with the Greeks.

With their position thus regularized, the crusaders were able to carry out the arrangements for dividing the spoils which they had made before the city fell. An emperor, elected by a commission of the army, was to receive one-fourth of the empire, three-eighths was to go to Venice, and the rest was to be divided among the other leaders of the crusade. Count Baldwin of Flanders was elected emperor, and a Venetian became patriarch of Constantinople. A subordinate kingdom was created for the Marquis Boniface, and other leaders received duchies and counties of varying extent.

The Latin Empire of Constantinople, created by the Fourth Crusade, was always weak. The Greeks succeeded in establishing independent states in Asia Minor and on the Adriatic, while the Bulgars seized territories to the north of Constantinople. The Empire lasted only a little more than half a century, collapsing in 1261, when the ruler of one of the rival Greek states succeeded in capturing Constantinople. The whole episode did great damage to the Christian cause in the East. The revived Byzantine Empire never recovered its strength after 1261 and was unable to hold back the Moslems as it had once done. Adventurous westerners were attracted to Constantinople for a half century and few went to fight in the Holy Land. The Greeks became even more bitter toward the Roman Church, which had sanctioned the conquest, and the hope of ending the schism proved vain. Only Venice profited in the long run. She received, as her share of the Empire, islands and coastal towns and thanks to her sea-power she was able to retain these for many years.

THE LATER CRUSADES

Innocent III was always eager for a new crusade. His preachers went through the West urging people to take the cross, but had little success. Finally, in 1212, a curious movement began which is indicative of the state of feeling at that time. A large number of children gathered together both in Germany and France, under the leadership of mere boys, saying that they were going to Jerusalem. They took as their motto, "Out of the mouths of babes and sucklings hast thou ordained strength, O Lord," and declared that they would recover the Holy Land without fighting. The band of French children wandered about in northern France and received a good deal of popular support. The king, however, was worried and consulted the doctors of the University of Paris. They told him that the movement was unwise and he commanded the children to return home. They did so, and the Children's Crusade in France came to an end.

In Germany, however, some twenty thousand children gathered under the leadership of a boy named Nicholas and set out on their march. The band was composed of boys and girls of every rank in society, with some evil men and women who joined the host in order to prey on the children. They marched up the Rhine, across the Alps, and down into Italy. On their way they suffered severely from the heat but were well treated by the people. They believed that the heat and drought were a sign that the Lord would dry up the Mediterranean so that they could pass it dry-shod, as the children of Israel had crossed the Red Sea. When they reached Genoa the band was estimated at about seven thousand, and the local authorities at first refused to let them enter the town. Finally permission was granted them to remain a single night. As the sea did not open before them the children separated to seek a passage elsewhere. Some went through Italy as far as Brindisi, and there the bishop persuaded them to return home. Others went to Marseilles and were sold into slavery by some merchants of the city. Many were unable to return home and were forced to stay in Italy. The episode shows that faith in the crusading cause was still strong among the people, even if rulers were becoming a little sceptical.

It would have been comparatively easy for the Christians to recover Jerusalem during the early years of the thirteenth century. Saladin died soon after the Third Crusade, and civil war ensued among his numerous heirs. The sultans of Egypt, who were the nominal rulers of the Holy Land, were threatened not only by rival rulers, but by plots of their own generals. However, the Christians who remained in the Holy Land were mainly of the merchant class and were more interested in commerce than in fighting. They lived on fairly good terms with the Moslems and preferred not to have their trade disturbed by war. Expeditions from the West during this period were either badly led or had insufficient manpower to take advantage of Moslem weakness. The Fifth Crusade succeeded in capturing the important Egyptian port of Damietta, which could have been traded for Jerusalem. However, quarrels among the leaders caused an ill-advised attack on Egyptian forces which turned out so badly that Damietta had to be surrendered without compensation. Frederick II recovered the Holy City by treaty, but the nobles of the kingdom of Jerusalem resented his attempt to strengthen the monarchy and wasted their strength in a rebellion against him instead of consolidating their position against the Moslems. As a result, the Moslems reoccupied Jerusalem without difficulty in 1244 and began to push against the strip of seacoast which the Christians still held.

The Sixth Crusade, led by Louis IX of France, was the last expedition which had any chance of success. Egypt was still weak, and Louis took Damietta easily. He planned an attack on Cairo, but showed remarkably bad judgment in his choice of a route and soon had his army hopelessly entangled in the streams and canals of the Nile delta. The Egyptians halted the Christian army in a severe battle at Mansourah, and cut off its supplies by gaining control of the Nile. Starvation and disease so weakened the crusaders that they were forced to surrender. The prisoners were freed in return for a large ransom and the surrender of Damietta, and Louis courageously proceeded to Palestine instead of returning home. He strengthened the coastal fortifications and regained a little land for the kingdom of Jerusalem, but he was unable to recapture the Holy City.

By the time of the Seventh Crusade (1270) Mongol conquests had forced the Moslems of the Near East to unite and the Christian position was almost hopeless. What chance was left was thrown away by Louis IX, who again led a French army into disaster. He was persuaded to make a futile attack on Tunis by his brother Charles, who had just conquered the kingdom of Sicily. Charles had obvious reasons for wanting to attack Tunis—for one thing, it had sheltered refugees from Conradin's army—but it is hard to see how even a successful attack would have aided the Holy Land. As it was, the host was stricken by disease, King Louis died, and the army returned home. Meanwhile Prince Edward of England had led a force to Palestine, which was too small to do anything but postpone the loss of the seacoast for a few years. The Moslems pressed in steadily after his departure, and the last Christian possession in Palestine was lost in 1291.

It is evident that the crusades of the thirteenth century were less under papal control than the earlier ones had been. Yet the leadership of the papacy was still strengthened by the preaching of a crusade. It enabled the popes to stress their position as heads of Christendom and to consolidate their authority over the Church. They could intervene in wars and diplomatic negotiations in order to secure the coöperation of European rulers. They could tax the clergy heavily for a crusade and in collecting the taxes they built up an efficient and highly centralized financial administration. There was evidence, however, that crusading propaganda was losing its effectiveness. Rulers became less and less willing to drop their private quarrels in the interest of Christendom, and the clergy protested bitterly against crusading taxes and against the papal bureaucracy which had been created to collect them. This growing lukewarmness to the old ideal may be explained by several factors. The ill-success of all the thirteenth century expeditions to the East discouraged many men. Respect for the crusading ideal was lessened when it was used as a political weapon against European opponents of the papacy such as Frederick II. Most important of all was the fact that the people of Europe were reacting less and less vigorously to religious stimuli. They were losing interest in the concept of a united Christendom and were becoming absorbed in local, secular activities.

There had been no great enthusiasm for the Seventh Crusade, even in France, the old center of crusading zeal. The pious lord of Joinville, who had fought bravely in the Sixth Crusade, refused to take part in the new expedition and wrote that it was a sin for the king to neglect his duties as ruler of France by engaging in such a foolish enterprise. This feeling was widespread in Europe and the Seventh Crusade proved to be the last great military expedition to the East.

The popes still urged the recovery of the Holy Land, and the Western monarchs still talked of taking the cross, but something always turned up to keep them from leaving their own countries. Small parties of nobles occasionally went off to fight the Turks, but these expeditions had little importance and less success. The crusading ideal no longer moved the people of Europe as a whole. The idea of an army of Christendom, fighting under papal leadership, was dead. The interests of the separate states were now more important than the interests of the whole Christian community. The decline of the crusading movement is an indication of the decline of the influence of the Church.

While the later crusades were uniformly unsuccessful, they aided in multiplying contacts with the East during the thirteenth century. The Christians retained ports in Syria until 1291, and the Italian cities drew many of their commodities from the kingdom of Jerusalem. Thousands of men took part in Eastern expeditions, and on their return they continued the process of familiarizing Europe with the products of the Orient. The crusades stimulated the development of Mediterranean commerce in many ways. Almost all thirteenth-century crusaders took the sea-route to Palestine and larger vessels had to be constructed to carry them, their horses, and their provisions. A regular tourist trade developed and vessels made two trips a year with pilgrims, one for those who desired to keep Easter at Jerusalem and a second for people who wished to celebrate Christmas in the Holy Land. The vessels which carried the pilgrims returned with cargoes of Eastern products, and since the passengers paid a large part of the cost of the voyage, the charges for transporting freight were considerably reduced. At the same time the need for sending money to crusaders in the East hastened the development of primitive banking methods. Instead of shipping specie, a deposit would be made with a banker in the West and he would instruct his agent in the East to pay an equivalent sum to the crusader who had asked for money. Rulers who went on crusades often borrowed large sums in anticipation of taxes and nobles mortgaged their lands to raise money for a crusade. The Templars engaged in all these operations but there was so much business that societies of Italian merchants also became important as bankers for the crusades.

Other specific results of the crusades are less important. The demand for Eastern textiles was so great that some European cities began to make Saracen rugs and other imitation Oriental products. Sicily became important as a silk manufacturing center, and from Sicily the industry spread to other regions in Italy. The Italian cities borrowed the crossbow from the East and it soon became the most important infantry weapon in Western armies. The terms and techniques of heraldry were worked out in the crusading states and the Western nobles seem to have acquired the habit of wearing beards from contact with Greeks and Moslems. In general, however, the crusaders merely stimulated activities which had already begun, and it is impossible to say that their influence was decisive in any important development. They were part of the pattern of European life in the thirteenth century, but they were not the dominant factor in determining that pattern.

THE EXPANSION OF CHRISTIAN EUROPE—SPAIN

The crusades were only one form of the reaction of Europe against the non-Christian peoples who ringed it. During the twelfth and thirteenth centuries the Moslems lost most of their possessions in the Spanish peninsula, most of the heathen peoples in Europe proper were converted or exterminated, and Christian missionaries penetrated the Middle and Far East. The number of Christian kingdoms was increased and the political system of Europe was correspondingly complicated.

The most important of these activities was the reconquest of Spain. The Ommiad caliphate in the peninsula [11] had never been very strong, and the Moslem rulers had been troubled by struggles of different factions among their subjects. The Arab aristocracy and the Berber army were usually at odds with each other; the "Slav" bodyguard, which included Slavs, Franks, Lombards and others, engaged in frequent palace revolutions; and the conquered Christians were always a possible source of danger. During the tenth century there had been a period of good government, but when Almansor, the able prime minister, died in 1002, the Ommiads soon lost their power. In place of one caliphate a score of independent governments were set up in Moslem Spain, and this facilitated the expansion of the Christian states.

At the time of the Arab conquest the whole peninsula had been subdued, except for a small, mountainous tract in the northwest. According to an Arab legend, nothing remained unconquered except a steep mountain on which "Old Pelayo" had taken refuge with thirty men and ten women. "Would to God that the Moslems had then extinguished the sparks of fire which were fated to consume all the dominions of Islam in those lands." Gradually the hardy mountaineers were reinforced and began to make raids, occasionally capturing a town or village. The kingdoms of Leon and Navarre were formed in the mountains of the north. Castile was at first merely the frontier county of Leon, defended by the castles from which it took its name. As the conquests extended southward the name Castile marched with them. In the northeast was the county of Barcelona, an outgrowth of Charlemagne's Spanish March, which had become independent because the later Carolingians were too weak to protect it. At the beginning of the eleventh century these states were confined to a narrow strip of territory in the North, and the Moslems held all the rest of Spain.

At first Navarre was the strongest of the Christian states, but its able ruler, Sancho the Great (970–1035), used his position to annex the other Christian territories rather than to wage war on the Moslems. At his death he divided his empire among his sons, one receiving Navarre, a second Castile which was now made into a kingdom, and a third the territory which was later to be Aragon. For a time the Christians carried on Sancho's tradition of fighting each other, but Alfonso VI (1073–1109), king of Leon and Castile, realized the opportunities afforded by the break-up of the Ommiad caliphate. He took advantage of disputes among the enemy and frequently allied himself with Moslem rulers. These tactics enabled the Christians to make rapid conquests and they soon held Madrid and Toledo. Toledo was the religious center of the

[11] See p. 142.

Spanish Moslems, and they were so moved by its loss in 1055 that they decided to call to their aid their fellows in Africa.

There a fanatical sect controlled by Berbers from the Sahara had set up a new dynasty, generally known as the Almoravides. Their leader, Yusuf, landed in Spain in 1086 and routed the Castilians in a single battle. He was hailed as "Emir of Andalous"—ruler of Moslem Spain. Fortunately for the Christian cause, he was soon engaged in strife with other Moslem rulers, who considered Yusuf and his followers half-savage religious bigots. The Spanish Moslems had never allowed the precepts of the Prophet to interfere with their enjoyment of life, and they were shocked by the puritanical zeal of the Almoravides. The Christians profited by these divisions among their enemies to make further conquests, including Lisbon, but their success was only temporary. Yusuf succeeded in overcoming his Moslem opponents and then won back many of the strongholds which the Christians had taken. He secured the support of the common people by remitting most of the taxes. Moslem power in Spain seemed fully restored during his reign.

After Yusuf's death in 1106 his followers became demoralized. They oppressed the people in order to obtain money for luxurious living and lost much of their fighting ability. They retained enough of their religious zeal to anger their Christian subjects by their intolerance, but they were not sufficiently puritanical to retain the support of the Berbers of Africa. A new reforming sect, led by mountaineers from the Atlas, threatened their possessions across the straits and cut off their supply of troops from Africa. Under these conditions the Christians found it easy to resume their raids. They penetrated far into Moslem territories, destroying crops and fruit trees, burning villages, and carrying the people away to be sold as slaves. The lands (Castile and Andalusia) over which they fought for generations became impoverished and much of Spain never recovered from these raids.

The most noted of all the Christian warriors was a Castilian noble, Rodrigo Diaz of Bivar. By his exploits while still a youth he won the title of *campeador* or challenger; that is, one who at the beginning of a battle challenges an opponent to single combat. Exiled, he became the leader of a band of freebooters, fighting indiscriminately in the service of Christian or infidel, and plundering mosques or churches with equal indifference in order to obtain booty to satisfy his mixed band of Christian and Moslem warriors. The name by which he is best known, the Cid or master, is one which his Moorish followers gave him. The Spaniards have made him their national hero, and some have suggested his canonization as a saint. He has been represented as the champion of the Christian faith and as an exemplar of all the Christian virtues. The real Cid was a brave, ruthless leader, who fought for his own advantage and only incidentally aided the Christians to acquire new territory. His

SPAIN
c. 1212

MOSLEM
POSSESSIONS
ABOUT 1212

RECONQUEST OF SPAIN

greatest exploit was the capture of Valencia, which was accompanied by much brutality. His lady was a worthy mate for such a warrior. She defended Valencia for two years after the death of the Cid in 1099, and departed in triumph with the body of her lord. Their deeds are told in the *Chronicle of the Cid,* which was translated into English by Southey.

It has been said that the Spaniards lived in a perpetual crusade. This is true in a certain sense, but the career of the Cid shows that it should not be taken too literally. Christian nobles and even Christian kings made alliances with the Moslems and fought each other as cheerfully as they did the infidel. However, when there was a war with the Moors, it had all the prestige of a crusade, and many foreigners, especially Frenchmen, came to fight in Spain. The frontier county of Portugal, which became a kingdom in 1143, profited especially from the aid of crusaders. Many northerners stopped there on the way to the Holy Land, and Lisbon was reconquered with the aid of the English in 1147. The other Christian kingdoms received less help from crusaders during the twelfth century.

A new threat from the Moslems came when the sect of the Almohades began to gain power. These hardy mountaineers from the Atlas conquered the Almoravides, first in Africa, and then, in the middle of the twelfth century, in Spain. They defeated the Christians and checked their advance. For sixty years they ruled Moslem Spain from their headquarters in Africa. Then Innocent III succeeded in uniting all the Christian monarchs of Spain, with the exception of the king of Leon. He also induced many crusaders from other lands to join the Spaniards. In 1212 the united Christian forces met the Almohades at Las Navas de Tolosa and won a victory that decided the fate of the Moors. "After that fatal day the empire of the Saracens in Spain weakened constantly, and they no longer had any success." The Christians pushed on, and a half-century later the Moors held only the little kingdom of Granada in the extreme South.

Granada became very thickly populated, wealthy, and prosperous, as the Moors flocked thither from lands conquered by the Christians. The king of Castile forced the ruler of Granada to pay tribute, but the Christians were too busy at home to attempt to conquer the last Moorish stronghold. The great tracts of lands seized from the Moors had to be settled, governments had to be reorganized to deal with the problems of larger territories, and the civilization of the rest of Europe had to be absorbed. Gothic cathedrals were built, universities were founded, and a vernacular literature was developed. Barcelona became a great Mediterranean port, rivaling the Italian cities, and the growth of trade had its usual upsetting influence on old traditions.

The most difficult problem was that of creating strong governments. The nobles were proud and independent, holding allegiance to their kings very lightly. They could disown a king at any time by a simple notice and transfer their services to a rival monarch. The clergy were probably more powerful than in any other country. During the reconquest they had received enormous estates and many privileges. Many cities had been founded as military colonies on the frontier and had been given extensive privileges, or *fueros,* which conferred an unusual degree of independence. The growth of trade made the towns even more powerful, and they formed leagues, or *hermandadas,* which defended their rights against all aggressors, even their kings. The growth of royal power in each realm was slow and was not completed in the thirteenth century. It was hindered by the ambition of some of the monarchs to play a rôle in European politics. As we have seen, Alfonso X of Castile, called the "Wise," had himself elected emperor of the Holy Roman Empire during the Great Interregnum. The rulers of Aragon had inherited the county of Barcelona, and this led them to seek territories to the eastward, along the routes of trade. They conquered the Balearic Islands, and Peter III of Aragon married the daughter of Manfred of Sicily, thus securing a claim to his realm. When the inhabitants of the island revolted against the stern rule of Charles of Anjou in 1282, they turned for aid to Aragon, and an Aragonese prince eventually became ruler of Sicily. These diversions, however, were not as fatal to the Spanish kingdoms as interest in Italy had been to the German realm. Royal power increased, in spite of temporary set-backs, and by 1300 the position of a king of Aragon or Castile was not greatly inferior to that of a king of France.

THE EXPANSION OF CHRISTIAN EUROPE—THE EAST

Outside of Spain, the only non-Christian inhabitants of Europe were to be found in the extreme North and Northeast. The Danes, because of their close association with the Germans, had been partially Christianized before the eleventh century, but as late as the reign of Canute the Great, half of the people were still pagan. The complete conversion of Denmark was accomplished only in the latter half of the eleventh century. The Christianizing of Norway was due mainly to King Olaf (1015–1028) who, killed in 1030 in an attempt to win back his kingdom from Canute, became the national saint. The faith was introduced at the same time in Sweden, but was not fully established there until the middle of the twelfth century.

The introduction of Christianity among the Scandinavians was not accomplished easily because it upset the customs of the people. It interfered with their freedom of marriage; it condemned the eating of horse-flesh, their favorite food. The Northmen objected to fasting, doing penance, and paying tithes, and a strong pagan party existed in Sweden and

Norway which opposed the kings and the Church. The pagan opposition reinforced the old dislike of monarchical authority and civil wars were frequent in both countries. Pagan customs gradually disappeared, but neither Sweden nor Norway was a strong kingdom in the twelfth and thirteenth centuries. Denmark had been more powerful during the twelfth century and had conquered much Slavic land along the Baltic, often in association with the Germans. Philip Augustus' marriage to a Danish princess shows the prestige which Denmark and her fleet enjoyed at this time. In the thirteenth century, however, the Germans seized most of the Slavic lands which Denmark had subdued, and Denmark ceased to be a powerful state.

The more important Slavic peoples had been Christianized before 1100. The Russians had accepted the Greek Orthodox faith, while the Poles, Czechs, and Slovaks had become Roman Catholics. The pagan tribes in the Elbe and Oder valleys and along the Baltic coast were subdued by the Germans in the twelfth and thirteenth centuries. Those who were not massacred accepted Christianity, but they soon lost their national identity. The Teutonic Knights and the Knights of the Sword finished the work of conversion by conquering the Prussians and the Letts, while the Lithuanians accepted Christianity in the fourteenth century. Thus all of eastern Europe became Christian. It lagged far behind the West, however, in civilization, and especially in political organization. There was no strong state to the east of the German frontier, and the boundaries between the different peoples shifted with amazing rapidity.

Poland had been at one time the most powerful Slavic state. It accepted Christianity in 965 and, during the next half-century, conquered Bohemia, Silesia, Pomerania and part of Russia. Its political institutions were too weak, however, to hold such an empire. There was no fixed rule of succession, and disappointed claimants to the throne could always count on German aid in starting rebellions. The lay nobles were very independent and worked only for themselves. The clergy had won great wealth and authority and strove to free the Church entirely from royal control. Poland gradually lost most of its conquests and was left shut off from the seacoast, without any natural boundaries to protect the country. By the thirteenth century the country had become divided, and the conflicting ambitions of the rulers of the several parts made good government impossible. Even the growth of trade and industry helped the Poles very little, for all commerce was in the hands of foreigners, who were granted special privileges without any compensating duties. German artisans entered the country in great numbers and formed important colonies. An even stronger German influence was introduced when Polish rulers invited the Teutonic Knights to protect them from the heathen Prussians. The order was given wide territories and a practically independent status and occupied most of the Baltic coast. It has been well said that in the thirteenth century there was a Polish people, but no Polish nation.

Bohemia was converted to Christianity early in the tenth century. After throwing off Polish domination in the eleventh century it became, in turn, the leading Slav power in the West. German influence was even stronger in Bohemia than in Poland, since the first king of Bohemia obtained his title from Henry IV in 1086, and his successors usually acknowledged the overlordship of the emperor. If the Czech ruler became too independent, the Germans could always bring him to terms by supporting a rival candidate to the throne. In the twelfth century Bohemia welcomed German colonists, and began to copy the more advanced German civilization. By the thirteenth century Bohemia was an advanced and powerful state. The right of primogeniture was established and dangerous disputes over the succession were thus avoided. The kings invited a new and larger group of German immigrants who developed the mineral resources of the country and built up its commerce. At the same time the native monarchs very shrewdly exploited the troubled conditions in Germany. They aided the popes against the Hohenstaufen and during the interregnum annexed large territories to the south. In 1273 Bohemia's territory extended to the Adriatic and all eastern Germany looked to her for protection. This marked the height of Bohemian power. Five years later she was crushed by a combined attack from the Magyars and the newly elected emperor Rudolph of Habsburg. All the conquests were lost, and while the original kingdom remained intact, it soon came under foreign domination. The native dynasty died out and was replaced by the house of Luxemburg, from the western frontier of Germany. Under its rule Bohemia became even more Germanized and was deeply involved in the troubled politics of the Empire.

The Hungarians accepted Christianity about the year 1000, under the leadership of King Stephen. He laid the foundations for a strong monarchy, but his immediate successors were not able to continue his work. The emperor Henry III forced the ruler of Hungary to acknowledge his overlordship, but the investiture struggle freed the country for a time from German interference. Two strong kings, ruling from 1077 to 1114, greatly increased Hungarian power. They annexed Croatia, Dalmatia, and part of Galicia, and gained complete control over Transylvania, which had been only partially subject to their predecessors. The Magyar government of the twelfth century was remarkably strong for the period and gained the admiration of the Germans. Otto of Freising has a remarkable passage in which he describes the country as a paradise, even though the people were short, ugly. barbarous, and ferocious in manners and speech.

All obey the prince so well [he says] that in all the seventy or more counties two-thirds of all judicial fines are paid into his treasury. . . . The king's will alone is held by all to be right. . . . When he summons them to war, no one dares to remain at home unless absolutely obliged to.

Otto was evidently contrasting conditions in Hungary and Germany—not to the advantage of the latter country.

Even while Otto was writing, the situation in Hungary was changing. After 1114 the kings were less able and wasted the resources of the country in unsuccessful wars. They allowed the great lay and ecclesiastical nobles to usurp royal power and finally agreed that all offices held from the crown should be hereditary. This aroused the lesser nobles, who suffered from the tyranny of the magnates, and in 1222 they compelled the king to grant the Golden Bull. This has often been compared to Magna Carta which, in two of its clauses, it resembles very closely. Like Magna Carta, it attempted to define the rights of the privileged classes and limit the power of the king, but it was never as fully enforced as the English document. The breach between the magnates and the petty nobles was not healed, and the kings, accused of favoring foreigners unduly, lost much of their power. Disputed successions and civil wars were frequent, and by the middle of the thirteenth century Hungary was no longer a strong kingdom.

RUSSIA AND THE MONGOL INVASION

Thus all along the eastern frontier of Germany stretched a band of weak states. They were advancing in civilization, thanks to German immigration and the influence of the Church, but they had not yet reached the level of the Western peoples. The agricultural populations were oppressed, the nobles were powerful and unruly, and the town populations, composed largely of foreigners, were interested only in their own special privileges. The Germans looked down on their eastern neighbors and thought of them as proper subjects for economic and political exploitation. Obviously neither Poland, Bohemia, nor Hungary was strong enough to stop an invasion from the East.

This would not have been serious had Russia been strong, but Russia in the twelfth and thirteenth centuries presented an amazing spectacle of political disorganization. The Scandinavian rulers had gradually been assimilated by their Slavic subjects and had adopted the Slavic principle of dividing the realm among their sons. They tried to guard against the evil results of this practice by establishing an elaborate and unworkable federal system. The chief city of Kiev was to be held by the head of the family, and the other towns were to be divided among the remaining princes in order of seniority. When the prince of Kiev died he was to be replaced by another one of the elder princes, and the remaining towns were to be redistributed. This system, which postponed the rights of sons to those of distant relatives, was admirably calculated to produce civil war. The suzerainty of Kiev became weaker and weaker, no principle of succession was recognized, and every prince seized all the lands he could. During the hundred and seventy years which elapsed between the death of Yaroslav, the last powerful prince of Kiev, and the first appearance of the Mongols, it has been calculated that there were sixty-four different principalities, two hundred and ninety-three princes or pretenders, and eighty-three civil wars.

In 1169, eleven of the other princes joined in attacking Kiev, which they sacked thoroughly, not sparing even the churches. This ended whatever unity was left in the Russian federation; for no other principality secured the supremacy. Kiev never recovered from the blow, and two thirteenth century raids by the nomads almost put an end to its existence. The most important Russian town after the fall of Kiev was Novgorod in the North, which ruled over wide, but ill-defined territories. The town was a republic, and called itself "My Lord Novgorod the Great." The people elected a prince to rule over them and, when they wished to, expelled him, but they were too divided by factional strife to profit from their independence. They controlled the regions which produced most of the furs used in Europe, but they allowed the Germans of the Hanseatic League to dominate this important trade. They permitted the Knights of the Sword to conquer Livonia, their natural outlet to the sea. Yet Novgorod was the strongest and most prosperous Russian state. Evidently the Russians were in no position to defend themselves against a new and powerful enemy.

Civil war had not been the only cause of Russia's weakness. The nomads of central Asia repeatedly crossed the steppes and occupied the shores of the Black Sea, thus cutting off the profitable trade between the Russian towns and Constantinople. The Russians succeeded in reopening the route several times, but a great invasion in the twelfth century closed it permanently. Loss of contact with Constantinople was one reason for the fall of Kiev and the increased importance of Novgorod, which traded with Germany instead of with the Byzantine Empire. These earlier attacks had injured Russia, but had not destroyed its independence. A new invasion in the thirteenth century placed Russia under Oriental domination and changed the whole history of eastern Europe.

This new invasion was the result of the formation of the Mongol Empire, far in the east of Asia. The growth of Mongol power followed the same pattern which we have seen in the growth of other nomad empires. The Mongols were neither a very large nor a very powerful people, but at the close of the twelfth century they produced a great leader. A contemporary Chinese author says that he was "a man of gigantic stature, with broad forehead and long beard, and remarkable

MEDIEVAL RUSSIA

500 MILES

TRM

for his bravery." He fought his way to the leadership of all the Mongol tribes, and this concentration of military power forced other nomad peoples to accept his authority. In 1206 he assumed the title of Genghis Khan, "inflexible emperor," and soon afterwards he turned his forces against the Chinese Empire. He took Peking in 1216 and then started westward to subdue other peoples, leaving his subordinates to complete the conquest of China.

At that time the Charismian Turks had control of all central Asia, but they were overcome by Genghis Khan in a single campaign. By 1225 central Asia, and parts of Afghanistan, Persia, and Caucasia had been conquered. In the meantime a detachment of twenty-five thousand men, led by two sons of the Great Khan, had made one of the largest raids in nomad history. Their original assignment was to pursue the remnants of the Turkish army, but they kept on to the westward long after they had accomplished this mission, probably in order to spy out the land. In three years they traversed Persia and Armenia, crossed the Caucasus, defeated a Russian army in the battle of Kalka (1223) near the Sea of Azov, went on to the Dnieper, and then retraced their course. Genghis Khan now ruled over an enormous empire, which extended from China to the Caucasus and from the Far North to the Himalayas. Even more remarkable than his conquests is the fact that he was able to administer these territories effectively and that his authority was unquestioned even on the remotest frontier. After his death in 1227 the Mongol princes elected one of his descendants to succeed him as Great Khan, while the others were given whole countries to rule as subordinate princes. This system eventually caused the disintegration of the Mongol Empire, but until 1300 it remained a fairly effective political unit.

For a time the successors of Genghis Khan were busy in Asia, but in 1236 his grandson Batu began a new invasion of Europe. The Russian princes did not unite against the Mongols, and one after another was captured. City after city was sacked and the inhabitants were killed or carried away into slavery. If a fortified town resisted, the Mongols carried out a policy of frightfulness, torturing the inhabitants cruelly before they put them to death. When they defeated an army they cut off an ear from each dead foeman and filled bags with these trophies. The savage and irresistible advance of the Mongols caused almost unbelievable terror among the people of Europe. Large villages surrendered to a single nomad horseman, and unbound prisoners did not even dare flee from the executioner's axe. After Russia had been completely overrun the turn of Poland and Hungary came. No effective resistance was made in either country and the invaders advanced as far as the Adriatic. Only when news of the death of the Great Khan reached Batu did he turn back to the East, in order to take part in the election of a new ruler.

The Mongols abandoned Poland and Hungary after plundering them thoroughly, but they retained control of Russia. They settled on the steppes and in the lower valley of the Volga and dominated the rest of the country from this base. Novgorod was the only important city that had not been conquered and even Novgorod paid tribute. The Mongols remained in southern Russia and did not attempt to administer northern Russia directly. They allowed the Russians to keep their land, religion and laws, but they insisted on the payment of a heavy tribute. Mongol officials were sent through the various principalities to number the inhabitants so that they could collect the largest possible sums. Russian princes had to visit the court of the Mongol khan from time to time; they were often put to death because they had been slow in paying tribute or because they were suspected of disloyalty. Actual rebellions were treated with great severity; towns were burned and their inhabitants were massacred.

This Mongol domination lasted for two centuries and separated Russia, to a large extent, from the peoples of the West. Contact with western Europe was difficult; it was confined almost entirely to dealings with German traders who came to Novgorod. Contact with the East was at first easy, but gradually dwindled as the Mongol Empire broke up. By the fourteenth century the Russians seldom had any reason to go to Mongolia or to China; they dealt almost entirely with the Mongols who lived north of the Black and Caspian Seas. These were the least civilized of the Mongol groups; the Russians learned little from them and did not trade extensively with them.

Thus Russia was thrown back on itself. It clung desperately to its old traditions—its Orthodox faith and its semi-Byzantine culture. It looked with deep suspicion on all outsiders. Differences between Russia and western Europe, which had already existed in the twelfth century, became even greater because Russia did not share the experiences of western Europe. It had no feudalism, no Investiture Conflict, no universities, no Renaissance, no Reformation. All the energetic efforts of modern rulers, from Peter the Great to Stalin, have not succeeded in wiping out the results of this long separation from the West.

The Mongol conquests did not diminish the extent of Christianity as the earlier Arab conquests had done. The Mongols had no highly developed religion of their own and were rather tolerant of other faiths. Their most dangerous enemies were the Moslems, not the Christians, and they suffered their first serious defeat at the hands of an Egyptian sultan in the 1260's. Consequently, they were at first rather favorably inclined to the Christians and welcomed envoys and missionaries from western Europe. The unification of the vast territories stretching from the borders of Hungary to the Yellow Sea gave missionaries a remarkable opportunity to spread the faith, and medieval Christianity reached its widest extent while the Mongol Empire was at its height.

As might have been expected, the mendicant orders were the most active in missionary work. Our first good description of the Mongol Empire comes from two Franciscan friars, John of Planocarpini and William of Rubriquis, who, in 1245 and 1252, traveled to the court of the Great Khan. Others followed them to China and a flourishing Christian church was formed there in the fourteenth century, with an archbishop at Peking. Missionaries who took the sea-route to the Far East stopped off in India, and established a church there, while the friars were so active in Persia that it seemed at one time as if the Mongol rulers of that country might accept the Christian faith. Early in the fourteenth century there was an almost continuous chain of Christian missions stretching from Persia to Peking. This promising beginning, however, led to no permanent results. The western Mongols accepted Islam and blocked missionary work in their territories. Travel became more dangerous as the Mongol Empire broke up into a mass of quarreling principalities. Western Europe suffered from wars, plague, and misgovernment during the fourteenth century, and had neither the energy nor the faith necessary to support distant missions. Like many other activities, the expansion of Christianity was arrested during the later middle ages.

UNIVERSITIES AND SCHOLARS
OF THE THIRTEENTH CENTURY

During the thirteenth century the Church continued to be the most important, and often the only patron of scholars and artists. Lay rulers were beginning to show some interest in art and science, but their support of these activities was limited and spasmodic. Frederick II, who was probably more interested in scholarship than any other ruler of his age, maintained a group of learned men at his court, but he was unable to assure the uninterrupted existence of the University of Naples, which he founded. Frederick's son Manfred and some of the Spanish kings were also supporters of scientists and universities, but the rulers of France, England, and Germany did relatively little for the cause of learning. Universities and schools, as a whole, remained under the control of the Church, and all the leading scholars of the thirteenth century were churchmen. Lay support of artists was more widespread than lay support of scholars. Almost all the great churches of the thirteenth century depended heavily on contributions from laymen. At Chartres, for example, many of the finest stained glass windows were given by laymen of all classes, ranging from the gild of shoemakers to members of the royal family. The great kings of the West were now wealthy enough to engage in extensive building operations; thus Henry III of England paid most of the cost of constructing Westminster Abbey while Louis IX of France spent large sums for the Sainte-Chapelle in Paris. Kings had always needed castles, but by the end of the century castles were becoming palaces, as can be seen in the remnants of the building that Philip the Fair of France erected on the Ile de la Cité in Paris.

Frederick II encouraged a revival of classical style in sculpture, and most kings were interested in jewelry and goldsmiths' work. Nobles, town governments, and even a few wealthy merchants imitated these activities as far as they could, and artists were not entirely dependent upon the Church for their commissions. It was still true, however, that the finest buildings were those erected for the Church, that sculptors and painters did very little work for laymen, and that religious art set the style for all other work. The Church maintained its leadership in intellectual and artistic activity with less difficulty than in most other fields.

The way in which the Church supported, and at the same time controlled, scholarship is well illustrated by the growth of universities during the thirteenth century. There had been many important centers of learning in the twelfth century, but only three, Salerno, Bologna, and Paris, had any claim to be universities, and of these Bologna was the only one with more than a rudimentary organization. By 1300 there were at least fourteen universities, scattered through Italy, Spain, France and England, all possessing highly developed institutions and wide privileges. The popes encouraged this growth in every possible way. They aided the foundation of new universities; they freed universities from the control of ordinary church officials; they gave high offices to university professors; they assisted poor students to obtain an education. In return they secured almost complete orthodoxy among learned men. The scholars who taught in the universities succeeded in reconciling the new knowledge, derived from the Greeks and Arabs, with the doctrines of the Church. The faculties of theology watched zealously for signs of heresy in books and lectures, and nipped unorthodox speculations in the bud. They were often more rigorous than the popes, for their logical training enabled them to scent danger in apparently harmless hypotheses. The few teachers who failed to heed their warnings were suppressed before they attracted large followings, and no academic heresy of the thirteenth century had any widespread success. At the same time Christian theology and philosophy were perfected and many obscure points of doctrine were settled.

The history of the University of Paris offers a good example of the development of institutions of higher learning during the century. Paris had had a gild of masters in the late twelfth century, but this gild, while it had considerable influence on the granting of licenses, was still subject in many ways to the chancellor of the cathedral. Shortly after 1200 the masters began a vigorous drive to obtain complete control of instruction at Paris. Innocent III, who had studied at Paris, showed his usual good judgment in recognizing that an autonomous organization was necessary and favored the masters in several decisions. He acknowledged that they formed a corporation and recognized their right to make statutes. The bishop and chancellor tried to preserve their supremacy by a series of law-suits, but the long struggle was definitely settled in favor of the masters by Gregory IX. In 1231 he published a bull which has been well called the Magna Carta of the university. The masters were granted the right of making "constitutions and ordinances regulating the manner and time of lectures and disputations, the costume to be worn, the burial of the dead; and also concerning the bachelors, who are to lecture, and at what hours, and on what they are to lecture; and concerning the prices of lodgings or the interdiction of the same; and concerning a fit punishment for those who violate your constitutions or ordinances, by exclusion from your society. . . . If the assessment of lodgings is taken from you, or anything else is lacking, or an injury or outrageous damage, such as death or the mutilation of a limb, is inflicted on one of you, unless through a suitable admonition satisfaction is rendered within fifteen days, you may suspend your lectures until you have received full satisfaction. And if it happens that any one of you is unlawfully imprisoned, unless the injury ceases at a remonstrance from you, you may, if you judge it expedient, suspend your lectures immediately."

This last point deserves emphasis. By it the right of migration was recognized; that is, if the members of the university felt aggrieved they could leave the city and establish themselves elsewhere. It was very easy for them to move, since the university owned no buildings, and all classes were held in hired rooms. Many new universities were founded as the result of migrations. Troubles at Paris in 1229 sent many students to Oxford and greatly stimulated the development of a university there. Later Oxford, in turn, was to suffer from a similar migration to Cambridge. Several Italian universities were founded by withdrawals of students from Bologna during the thirteenth century.

The autonomy of the University of Paris was recognized by Gregory's decree, but its organization was still rudimentary. It had no head, and no permanent officials. These defects were remedied by the growth of the curious units known as "nations." Scholars from the same region naturally came together for mutual protection and social pleasures. These groups gradually amalgamated until they formed four large associations, "the honorable nation of the Gauls, the venerable nation of the Normans, the very faithful nation of the Picards, the very constant nation of the English." These "nations" had little connection with existing political units. For example, the nation of the English included the Germans and other northern Europeans, while the nation of the Gauls included men from all the Mediterranean countries, and even distant Persia and Armenia. There is some dispute as to whether the nations admitted students as well as masters. Certainly the students in the higher faculties of theology, medicine, and law were members, since they were already masters of arts, and they, with the masters of arts who were actually teaching, dominated the activities of the nations. The nations chose a common head, the rector, and contributed to a common treasury, administered by delegates from each group. Technically, the rector represented only the masters of arts, but since the other masters were few in number they allowed him to represent them as well. Thus the rector became recognized as head of the whole university. His powers were limited by a short term of office, and by the necessity of consulting the masters in all important questions. Other universities had similar institutions. At Bologna there were more nations than at Paris, and they corresponded more closely to actual political divisions. The rector at Bologna was always a student, since the students controlled the university, but he had usually had at least as much education as a Parisian master of arts.

As we have seen, Paris had the three higher faculties of theology, medicine, and law, as well as the faculty of arts. This was not true of all advanced schools, but it was generally admitted that to rank as a university a school must possess at least one of the higher faculties. At Paris each faculty had a considerable degree of freedom in regulating its own affairs, but in matters of general concern the faculty of arts was dominant. At first this was merely a result of the greater number of masters of arts, but after the middle of the century the faculty tried to find a legal basis for its *de facto* supremacy. All students who received the degree of master of arts had to take an oath to obey the decrees of the faculty of arts, no matter what position they might eventually secure. Since a man had to be a master of arts before he could become a student or teacher of theology, law or medicine, this gave the faculty of arts control over most members of the university. Most other universities were dominated by their faculties of arts. Bologna, with its great law school, was an exception.

A final development in university organization was the foundation of colleges. Thoughtful people had long been shocked by the lack of discipline and application among some scholars and by the abject poverty of others. Thirteenth century students were just as riotous as their predecessors, and there were more of them to riot. Each student was supposed to have a master who supervised his studies, but this supervision amounted to little in practice and most students did as they pleased. The great increase in university enrollment made it increasingly difficult for poor scholars to support themselves by begging. All these difficulties could be met by endowing colleges which would regulate discipline, supervise studies, and provide decent food and lodgings. In the latter half of the thirteenth century many pious people made large gifts to such foundations. The most noted college was the Sorbonne at Paris, founded by Robert de Sorbon about 1257 for students in theology. The students had a building where they lived and dined, and were under the supervision of a master, to whom they recited their lessons. Other colleges were soon established at Paris and at the leading universities of Europe. They have disappeared on the continent, but they are still the basic units at Oxford and Cambridge, where students live and receive most of their instruction in the colleges.

By far the largest number of students were enrolled in the faculties of arts. In the higher faculties the lucrative studies of law and medicine were most popular. The study of Roman law was forbidden at Paris during most of the thirteenth century, in part because the popes feared that its popularity would interfere with the teaching of theology, in part because the upper classes of northern France feared the influence of Roman law on their customs. Canon law, however, was taught at Paris, and students of canon law could easily acquire wide, if unofficial knowledge of Roman law. The thirteenth century was a great age for lawyers, and legal training of any sort led to high positions in church and state. Some students aspired to the mastery of both Roman and canon law, so that they might be qualified for any sort of administrative post; it is significant that the most common honorary degree today is LL.D. or J.U.D.—Doctor of Laws or Doctor of Both Laws. Orleans and Montpellier were more important than Paris as centers of legal studies, but they in turn were overshadowed by the famous school of Bologna.

The thousands of students who took courses in law did not all aspire to the doctorate. Legal studies were difficult and time-consuming, since the bulky codes and even more bulky commentaries had to be learned by heart from lectures. Many law students were satisfied with a preliminary degree that allowed them to practice in the courts. Others engaged in the less exacting, but lucrative study of the *ars dictaminis* or *ars notaria*. This was a branch of the art of rhetoric that trained students to write well-worded and persuasive letters. At first all kinds of letters were used as models, but gradually the subject-matter became restricted to the study of business and legal documents. Men who had had this training could act as notaries, and there was a great demand for their services in regions that used Roman law, such as Italy and southern France.

The course in medicine usually took about six years. Galen was the basic authority, but other textbooks of Greek or Arabic origin were the most important books. The training was far too theoretical (there were few opportunities to observe actual patients) and the theory was bad. It was based on the idea that there were four "humors" in the human body corresponding to the four elements of earth, air, fire and water, and that good health depended on keeping the four humors in balance. Thus a man in a high fever was bled in order to reduce the fiery element in the blood. Dissection of the human body was rarely practiced in the thirteenth century; the first good records of human dissections begin about 1300. Most students gained their knowledge of human anatomy from textbooks or from the study of the anatomy of animals, especially of pigs.

Salerno, the old center of medical studies, continued to be important after Frederick II incorporated it with the University of Naples, which he founded in 1224. A few years later Frederick issued a decree regulating the practice of medicine in his kingdom of Sicily. The law stated that no student could obtain a license to practise medicine unless he had spent three years in general training, and three years in specialized study of medicine and surgery. This academic training had to be followed by practice under the guidance of an experienced physician. Finally, the candidate had to present a certificate proving that he had studied the anatomy of the human body. Montpellier was the most noted medical school north of the Alps, but medicine was popular at many other universities because its practitioners could amass large fortunes. An advocate of the study of the liberal arts, who disliked the attention paid to medicine, wrote: "With the copper and silver which they receive for their poisons they build them fine houses in Paris." "She (chirurgy) has such bold hands that she spares no one from whom she may be able to get money." This comment is obviously prejudiced, but it is true that there was little advance in medicine during the century. The basic doctrine was already established and was not altered by some acute clinical observations made by Moslem doctors. While there were some common-sense treatments there was also far too much bloodletting and use of medicines that were distinguished only by their high cost or bad taste.

The study of science was inextricably mixed up with that of other subjects. Aristotle, the chief authority on science, had also written on logic, metaphysics, politics and ethics and most students thought of his scientific works as merely illustrating his logic or philosophy. Nevertheless, there were men who were interested primarily in Aristotle's scientific treatises, and they played a significant role in the development of western thought. They did little original work, but they kept interest in science alive in Europe at a time when it was dying out in the rest of the world.

The Church was at first suspicious of men who took an excessive interest in the sciences, because scientific knowledge was often used in unlawful or at least dubious ways. Astronomy merged with astrology; chemistry was devoted to the research for the elixir of life or formulae to turn lead into gold, and mathematics was often used for conjuring (e.g., magic squares). Pope Innocent III condemned mathematicians because they practiced black magic. When Frederick II attracted the famous scholar, Michael Scot, to his court, he was at least as interested in Michael's fame as an astrologer as in his ability to translate Aristotle's work on zoology. Moreover, Aristotle was a pagan and the most popular commentary on Aristotle, at least for western scholars, was written by the Moslem Averroës. Dangerous ideas, implicit in the work of Aristotle, such as the eternity of the world, were quite explicit in the commentary of Averroës.

Nevertheless, the Church never seriously interferred with the translation and the study of Aristotle's scientific works. It is true that the teaching of those works was forbidden at Paris early in the thirteenth century, but this may have been because the authorities wanted advanced students to concentrate on philosophy and theology. The leaders of the Church could hardly believe that the scientific works as such were very dangerous, since they allowed them to be taught at the newly founded University of Toulouse in the heart of the area affected by the Albigensian heresy. Toulouse made the most of its opportunity and tried to attract students from Paris by advertising its courses in "natural philosophy." Scholars of the mendicant orders, the pillars of orthodoxy, wrote commentaries on all of Aristotle's works, and showed how they could be used as a basis for a Christian philosophy. It was soon evident that a thorough knowledge of Aristotle was necessary as a preliminary to advanced work in many fields and by 1254 even the University of Paris prescribed study of Aristotle's chief works for candidates for the degree of master of arts.

Since most of the men who wrote on science were also interested in other subjects, it is not surprising that they did little more than assimilate and clarify the materials that they had received from Greek and Arabic sources. Their chief accomplishment was to complete the work of translating Greek and Arabic treatises that had been begun in the twelfth century. Thus the work of Archimedes, almost unknown before, began to exercise an influence in the thirteenth century. Bad translations from Arabic were replaced with better translations from Greek. One of the few good results of the conquest of Constantinople was that some western scholars settled in Greek-speaking regions and were able to work directly with Greek manuscripts. But on the whole, even the ablest scholars made little effort to add to the knowledge that they had received from the East. The believed that science was an interesting, but on the whole inferior kind of learning. At best, it offered some useful analogies and some rather dubious generalizations, reached from casual observations of transitory phenomena. Philosophy and theology provided much better ways of arriving at essential truths; they were based on the eternal verities and the unerring rules of logic.

The few exceptions to this attitude usually occurred among men who were out of sympathy with the dominant philosophy of the period. Frederick II was interested in astrology, but he also enjoyed scientific knowledge for its own sake. He wrote a treatise on falconry in which he made some rather acute observations on the behavior and illnesses of birds. He is also said to have performed some crude experiments. For example, he gave two condemned criminals a hearty dinner, allowed one to sleep, made the other exercise, and then had them killed and cut open to see which one had digested his food better. The mathematicians, who had the advantage of using the generally accepted rules of logic, also made some progress during the thirteenth century. The ablest of them, Leonardo of Pisa, introduced Arabic numerals into Europe, though few scholars used this notation until the sixteenth century.

European scholars were fascinated by the study of optics, as the Moslems had been before them. The basic rules were mathematically demonstrable and therefore acceptable to men who preferred deductive reasoning. Light itself was, at least allegorically, a direct emanation from God—an idea that appealed to men with an inclination to mysticism. Many writers worked on the problem of the rainbow, and the first completely satisfactory explanation of the phenomenon was reached by the German Dietrich of Freiburg. There was also some experimentation with lenses that went far enough so that spectacles could be invented in the next century.

The most interesting group of scientists were the English Franciscans led by Robert Grosseteste, bishop of Lincoln. These men disliked the dominant school of philosophy which had been worked out by their Dominican rivals. They felt that it was too rationalistic and based too much on Aristotelian texts. Grosseteste himself worked on the problem of the rainbow and talked a good deal about experimentation, although when he used the word he usually meant merely a conclusion drawn from ordinary experience. The famous and much overrated Roger Bacon was one of his followers, and was equally confused about the difference between experiments and experience. Bacon appealed to nineteenth-century scholars because, unlike most men of his time, he believed that science could have practical value by teaching men to construct self-moving vehicles and other marvelous machines. But Bacon had no idea of how his prophecies could be fulfilled and he had little influence on medieval scholarship. He was always quarreling with his superiors; he was closely confined for many years and his books were not widely read. The really significant successors of Grosseteste were the Oxford scholars of the fourteenth century. They accepted the idea that Aristotle might be wrong and that his errors could be demonstrated by careful mathematical reasoning. They challenged especially his theories of motion and so laid the foundation for the investigations that culminated in the work of Galileo.

Theology and philosophy were closely associated and may be discussed together. It was impossible to study one subject without learning the other, and while the philosophical speculations of the theologians were not articles of faith, they were based solidly on Christian dogma. The few philosophers who accepted principles contradicting Christian doctrine were driven from the schools, and the dangerous proposition that a statement might be true in philosophy though false in theology was not tolerated during the thirteenth century. Theology was the most honored study in the curriculum; it was the "queen of the sciences" and all other subjects were its handmaidens. At the same time it was a very difficult subject, and even at Paris only a small proportion of the student body was enrolled in the faculty of theology. The course at Paris in the thirteenth century lasted for eight years, and early in the fourteenth century it was extended to fourteen years. Few men received their degrees at the end of the minimum period and a candidate for the doctorate had to be at least thirty-five years old. The law degree was somewhat easier to acquire, and a reputation as a canon lawyer was more apt to lead to advancement in the Church than proficiency in theology. But while the number of theologians was small, their influence was great. They reconciled reason and faith and prevented the feverish intellectual activity of the thirteenth century from being dangerous to the Church. They organized all knowledge into a harmonious system based on Christian principles. This is the great intellectual achievement of the Middle Ages, and one of the greatest achievements of all time. Scholars have always sought a simple, unified explanation of the universe. Few have ever found one as complete, as consistent, and (accepting their premises) as satisfactory as that developed by the theologians of the thirteenth century.

The method used in the study of theology was that of Abelard, as perfected by Peter Lombard. A question was stated, authorities pro and con were collected, and then a solution was given. Important improvements were made, however, in organization of the material during the thirteenth century. Early theological treatises were poorly planned; the connection between topics was not always clear, and it was difficult to obtain an idea of the author's basic positions. The great thirteenth century books, on the contrary, are masterpieces of organization. The subject is broken up into a few large parts, each part is divided into chapters, each chapter is divided into topics, and each topic may be still further subdivided if necessary. Though thousands of problems are discussed, the authors seldom contradict themselves, and their essential ideas are not concealed by the mass of details. This ability to classify and organize a great body of knowledge is necessary for any significant intellectual activity, and it is doubtful if any group of scholars ever possessed it in a higher degree than did the thirteenth century theologians.

The work of two Dominicans (both eventually canonized) was especially important in this field. Albertus Magnus, a German, during his long life (1193–1280) commented on all the works of Aristotle and also added material drawn from other writers, especially in the fields where Aristotle failed him, such as botany. The Italian Thomas Aquinas (1225–1274) studied with Albert, and built the material prepared by his teacher into a great system of philosophy and theology. Thomas, more than any other scholar of his age, gave a rational, consistent and detailed explanation of the visible and invisible worlds. Both men taught for a while at Paris and their ideas were spread throughout the western world by the great French university. Europe still formed a single intellectual unit, though the political unity of Europe had long since disappeared.

Perhaps the outstanding characteristic of Thomas Aquinas was his belief that everything made sense, that there was order and logic in the universe. Therefore there could be no conflict between faith and reason. God had placed man in a physical world and given him the gift of reason so that he could be enlightened by observing God's work. Sense impressions could be trusted; honest reasoning could be trusted; the work of the great scholars of the ancient world could be used without fear. Faith, of course, went far beyond reason, but they could travel part of the same road together. Thus the existence of God could be proved by natural reason, while the existence of the Trinity could be known only by faith. Man fulfilled God's plan for him by using his reason to the utmost, and by allowing his reason to be illuminated by faith. In this way man might arrive at true knowledge which would enable him to build a better society on earth and achieve salvation in heaven. Man's highest end was knowledge of God, a phrase which meant very much the same thing as salvation to Thomas but which his critics naturally attacked as placing too much emphasis on the intellect.

Thomas Aquinas wrote many volumes; his two most important works were the *Summa contra Gentiles* and the *Summa Theologica*. The first, written for the unbeliever, shows how reason can demonstrate some truths of religion, can show that others are probable, and can never prove that any article of the faith is impossible. His second book, though never completed, is the greatest work of medieval scholasticism. In it Thomas proceeded steadily from one problem to another, listing all possible solutions and objections, and then gave a final answer. He dealt with secular as well as with religious problems; for example he wrote a long section on the sources and authority of law. He also showed how all human activities, properly conducted, fulfill God's purpose. Thus the state is a positive good, not a mere negative remedy against sin, because without the state, men could not demonstrate civic virtue. God gave man the potential for exhibiting this virtue; therefore it should be fulfilled; therefore, even among the infidels the state is divinely instituted.

In the long run, a very long run, the system developed by Albert and Thomas was accepted as the official philosophy of the Church. There was no such agreement in the thirteenth century. It would be a great mistake to think of medieval scholars as a docile, harmonious group who merely elaborated the statements of their predecessors. Like modern scientists, they had certain fundamental premises and methods in common, but like modern scientists they disagreed violently about the results that they had obtained. In fact, their disagreements make the disputes of modern scientists seem mild. Thomas, as we have seen, stressed the importance of knowledge for salvation; a man must *know* the truth before he can achieve his highest end. St. Bonaventura, a theologian whom many would consider the equal of Thomas, emphasized the importance of the *will* and taught that knowledge was of secondary importance. A man's will must be purified and in harmony with that of God before he can be saved. Two sentences sum up the difference between the two scholars. "There is nothing in the intellect," said Thomas, "that has not come to it through the senses," and by using his intellect man may aspire to salvation. "In everything that is perceived by the senses," said Bonaventura, "God lies concealed." God will reveal himself in his own way through divine grace, not through human reason. Since Thomas was a Dominican while Bonaventura was a Franciscan, the two Orders took up this dispute enthusiastically and their doctors quarreled over reason and will for years.

On the other hand, the two mendicant groups had to work together to protect themselves against the hostility of the University of Paris. Dominican and Franciscan scholars were seeking places in the Parisian faculty of theology. The masters of Paris naturally opposed this, since they could not hope to control the friars who obtained professorships. The popes backed the claims of the mendicants, but the university used every available legal device to put off the evil day, and Dominican and Franciscan theologians were admitted only after a long, bitter struggle. During the controversy each side naturally attacked the doctrines of its opponents. Even the supremely orthodox Thomas Aquinas was accused of holding dangerous beliefs and after his death his adversaries made a determined effort to have some of his opinions condemned as heretical.

Most intellectual activity of the thirteenth century was merely a continuation of that of the twelfth, but in one respect there was an important innovation. An attempt was made to popularize knowledge by writing books which could be understood by the educated layman. These books were usually written in French, the language of the upper classes throughout Europe, and they dealt with most of the subjects taught in the universities. Parts of the Bible and Aristotle were translated or paraphrased, some of the classics were imitated in French verse, and real encyclopedias, such as the *Livre dou Trésor* of Brunetto Latini, were compiled. Innumerable little tracts on theology and morals were written for princes and barons. A few histories and works on customary law were also composed in the vernacular. Undoubtedly romances, short stories, and love songs were more popular with noble and bourgeois than these more sober productions, but there is plenty of evidence to show that some laymen read scholarly works. With very few exceptions, the learned literature produced for laymen was writen by churchmen, and contained only the simplest and most orthodox ideas. Nevertheless, the emergence of a group of educated laymen was an important phenomenon. In the later Middle Ages they began to write their own books and thus weakened the leadership of the Church in intellectual activities.

THIRTEENTH-CENTURY ART

In art the thirteenth century played its familiar rôle of carrying to their logical conclusion principles which had already been established in the twelfth century. It was the great age of cathedral building, especially in France, and Gothic architecture reached its highest point in the churches of Chartres, Paris, Amiens, Rheims and Bourges. During the century the French realized the full possibilities of Gothic style. They emphasized height and light more and more; roofs were raised, windows were enlarged, and walls were reduced to a mere skeleton. The Sainte-Chapelle at Paris is an extreme example of this tendency; its walls are all glass, except for the thin pillars that sustain the roof. The English and the Germans, while they adopted Gothic vaulting and Gothic decoration, never went this far, but preserved something of the solidity and sobriety of Romanesque architecture. In most English and German churches of the thirteenth century a window is still an opening in a wall, not a substitute for a wall, and horizontal lines have not been entirely concealed by vertical lines.

Fully developed Gothic architecture was an almost perfect style for church building, as our own architects discovered during the nineteenth century. It was so perfect that by the end of the thirteenth century architects could do nothing but imitate it or elaborate it. Both courses were followed in France, and neither was very satisfactory. There is always something lacking in an imitation; the cold perfection of St. Ouen of Rouen is much less moving than the first halting experiments in Gothic in the Ile de France. The alternate course at least gave the architect a chance to be original; he could elaborate the system of vaulting, divide and subdivide the windows, and cover the outside of his church with spikes and buttresses. The only trouble was that this originality was often in bad taste; it eventually led to the wedding-cake style of the late Middle Ages, of which the classic example is St. Maclou (also at Rouen).

As churches became higher and lighter they also became more richly adorned. Here, too, France set a standard which was seldom equaled elsewhere. It had long been customary to ornament the portals of a church with sculptures representing the Last Judgment, the life of Christ, scenes from the Old Testament or the lives of the saints. During the thirteenth century these sculptures became more elaborate and many new themes were introduced. There are literally hundreds of figures on the portals of the cathedrals of Chartres or Amiens, each telling some part of the Christian story, illustrating some point of doctrine, or showing the connection between secular knowledge and religious belief. Thus the Seven Liberal Arts are represented at Chartres as a tribute to the Virgin, who possessed all knowledge. The signs of the zodiac and the labors of the months may be seen on the portals of the cathedrals of Paris and Amiens. The cult of the Virgin, which had become so important during the twelfth century, continued to flourish during the thirteenth, and every cathedral gave a great deal of space to scenes from her life. Medieval love of allegory was not forgotten and the Old Testament characters who prefigured Christ, the Seven Wise and Seven Foolish Virgins, the triumphant Church and the blindfolded Synagogue were to be found on most of the great cathedrals. Within, the story was taken up again in the great, stained-glass windows which occupied most of the wall-space. Usually the lower windows were filled with scenes from the lives of the saints, while the higher windows portrayed the ancestors of Christ, the Crucifixion, the Virgin in glory and the prophets and evangelists. It has been well said that a great cathedral summed up all Christian doctrine in pictorial form just as the great treatise of Thomas Aquinas summed it up in intellectual form.

In the thirteenth century, as in the twelfth, the primary concern of the sculptor was to represent abstract ideas. His figures were symbols devised to recall articles of the faith or to stimulate religious emotion. They had to be recognizable to fulfil these functions, but they could not be realistic. A realistic work of art can say only one thing, and it must say that in words of one syllable, while a symbol must express many ideas and overtones of emotion which can hardly be put into concrete form. Thirteenth century sculpture has a power and a beauty which is neither classical nor modern. However, as the century went on, a tendency toward realism became apparent, first in details of ornament and then in the main figures themselves. Some scholars argue that this indicates a growing interest in worldly phenomena and a decreasing interest in religious symbols, while others hold that it was merely one of those experiments in a new style which artists are constantly trying. Whatever the cause, the results are evident. While the apostles on the west front of Chartres represent merely the abstract idea of saintly leaders, the apostles at Amiens are individual men, obviously copied from living models. This tendency to realism was not altogether to the advantage of either religion or art. Figures which were too realistic lost their spiritual beauty, while they failed to recapture the earthly beauty of the classical period. The result may be seen in the famous Virgin of Amiens. She is no longer the majestic Queen of Heaven, inspiring awe and reverence. She has become a simpering, earthly princess, who is pretty, stylish, but scarcely beautiful. Germany suffered less from this uninspired realism than did France, for in Germany there was a strong tendency to idealize the human face, if not the human form. Some of the finest individual figures in thirteenth century sculpture may be found in Germany, and during the later Middle Ages sculptors from Germany or the old Middle Kingdom far surpassed those of France.

Stained glass was the one new artistic medium developed in the Middle Ages. It had first been used in the twelfth century, but few windows from this period have survived. Twelfth century artists seem to have discovered the effective color combinations and the basic window patterns, but the full possibilities of the medium were first worked out in the thirteenth century. There could be, of course, no question of realism in stained-glass work. Light must pass through the figures, obscuring details, and the colors must be unnaturally brilliant to secure the desired effect. The jewel-like colors of thirteenth century glass were just what was needed to form a contrast to the monotonous gray of the stonework; a cathedral which has lost its windows has lost half of its life. This art, too, fell on evil days in the fourteenth century. In an effort to obtain more light the upper halves of the windows were filled with canopies done in white and yellow glass, and other colors were made less intense. The windows ceased to form a contrast with the rest of the cathedral; they whispered instead of shouting the glory of God. Modern stained glass has gone back to thirteenth century products; very wisely, for it was this century which brought the new art to perfection.

XI

The Growth of
Secular Institutions and Interests

THE CHURCH was still the most important single influence on society in the thirteenth century. But, as we have seen, the Church found it increasingly difficult to maintain its leadership. New interests and loyalties were arising which were eventually to reduce the influence of the Church to a much lower level. On the one hand secular princes, especially the rulers of France and England, were building states which could command the allegiance of their subjects even when they directly opposed the Church. On the other hand, all classes in lay society were developing interests and activities which were entirely outside the sphere of influence of the Church. These developments paved the way for the collapse of the leadership of the Church at the end of the century.

THE GROWTH OF THE STATE IN FRANCE

It might have seemed that neither Louis VIII (1223–1226) nor Louis IX (1226–1270) of France would do anything which would weaken the Church. Both were pious rulers, both continued the old French policy of supporting the papacy, both died on crusades. Louis IX was recognized in his own lifetime as a model of what a Christian king should be and was canonized within a generation of his death. Yet under these two devout monarchs the primary loyalty of Frenchmen shifted from the Church to the state, and the political influence of the pope was greatly decreased. Neither Louis VIII nor Louis IX consciously planned this; they merely did their work as well and honestly as they could. The efficiency of their government created respect for the state; the virtues of St. Louis inspired devotion to the monarchy.

Louis VIII's brief reign of three years was remarkable for two things. On his accession to the throne he preserved the new system of government which Philip Augustus had created but he discharged and punished many of Philip's functionaries. These men had served the king and oppressed the people with almost equal zeal. Strong-arm methods were no longer needed and Louis' purge made the government more respectable without weakening its authority. His other important achievement was the establishment of royal power in the heart of Languedoc. By taking part in a new crusade against the Albigensians he gained important territories in the South and secured an assignment of the Montfort claims to other lands in the district. He died before he could enforce these rights, but it was his work which made possible the treaty of 1229, by which Raymond of Toulouse surrendered part of his territories to the king and married his daughter and heiress to a younger brother of Louis IX. This greatly increased the royal domain and the king's power and revenues, and it gave the French ruler for the first time an outlet on the Mediterranean.

The premature death of Louis VIII threatened the accomplishments of the last fifty years. His son, Louis IX, who succeeded him, was a boy of twelve, and a regency was necessary. The queen-mother, Blanche of Castile, who became regent, was an able woman, but she was disliked both because she was a foreigner and because of her rigid and rather haughty character. The great feudal nobles naturally thought that this was a heaven-sent opportunity to regain the power and independence which they had lost under Philip Augustus. They secured English aid and formed coalition after coalition against the royal government. Dangerous as these plots seemed, they were all repressed without much difficulty. The king of England was anxious enough to recover his lost provinces, but he was having troubles at home and could not afford to give the French lords sustained support. Without large subsidies from England, the rebellious nobles could not hope to overcome the king's superiority in men and money. He could raise a larger army and keep it longer in the field than any coalition. Most important of all, the nobles did not really want to fight the king. They talked largely about their rights, but they regularly refused to attack royal armies. Whether this was caused by respect for the royal person, genuine distaste for the horrors of civil war, or well-founded fear of treachery in their own ranks, is immaterial. The fact remains that even the nobles no longer desired complete independence and had some scruples about destroying the central government. Nothing shows more clearly the growth of royal power than the ineffectiveness of these feudal rebellions.

When Louis began to govern personally, the monarchy was in a stronger position than ever before, thanks to the demonstrated weakness of its opponents. Other rulers—men like John of England or Louis' own grandson, Philip the Fair—might have been intoxicated with this power and have gone too fast, increasing royal possessions and prerogatives at the expense of royal popularity. But Louis had been greatly influenced by his pious and upright mother, and there was something in his own character which made him want to live up to the highest ideals of his age. He sought the reputation of a devout Christian, a just ruler, and a true knight. He would preserve his own rights and respect those of others. This attitude was just what was needed to consolidate the gains which had been made by his father and grandfather. The loyalty of the conquered provinces was gained completely; even the rebellious Poitevin nobles ceased to plot with the English. The moderation and equity with which Louis used his power justified the great increase in royal authority. Devotion to the monarchy became a French tradition, which endured in spite of the blunders and crimes of Louis' successors.

The churchmen who wrote biographies of St. Louis naturally stressed his almost monkish piety. They tell how assiduously he attended the services of the Church, how thoroughly he mortified the flesh, how humbly he washed the feet of the poor and the sores of lepers. All this is true, but it does not explain his greatness as a king. Fortunately Louis had another biographer, the lord of Joinville, his friend and companion during the long years of the Sixth Crusade. Joinville's biography is the masterpiece of early French prose and it permits us to see that Louis was a human being as well as a crowned saint. He gives a wonderfully lifelike picture of the king: as a lover, stealing interviews with his bride while attendants watched to warn the young couple of the approach of the jealous queen-mother; as a judge, seated under the great oak at Vincennes, hearing any cases that might be brought before him; as a soldier, impetuously leaping into the sea in order to be first in the attack on Damietta. He never forgets that Louis was a saint, but he remembers that the king also wanted to be known as a gentleman and good knight, and that he protected his rights against the bishops as firmly as against the barons. Joinville's very evident love and admiration for the king give us some idea of the way in which Louis' personality captured the hearts of his subjects. Louis was not only the strongest monarch of his age; he was also the best-loved.

During the reign of St. Louis the government developed along the lines laid down by Philip Augustus. Local administration remained in the hands of the seneschals and *baillis,* and they gradually acquired a large number of subordinates who assisted them in their work. As in Philip's reign, local officials were frequently shifted from one district to another, and Louis devised a new method to keep them from abusing their power. He sent *enquêteurs,* delegates from the central court, throughout the land, with full power to hear and to investigate all complaints of his subjects. Some of these complaints have survived, and they throw an interesting light on conditions in France at the time. As might be expected, they expose some graft and oppression in local government. Even a saintly king could not have a completely honest police force. The complaints also show that many men still failed to realize the new power of the monarchy. They were indignant when they were punished for acts which would have been ignored a century before, such as dealing with the king's enemies. Taken as a whole, the complaints give the impression that Louis' government was remarkably just, as governments go, and that the king had the confidence of his people, whatever his officials did.

Changes in the central government were more important than changes in the system of local administration. Under St. Louis the *curia regis* began to split into specialized departments, as had the English *curia* a century before. Thus the judicial functions of the royal court were gradually segregated and given to a body known as the Parlement. At first the Parlement was merely the *curia* meeting to give justice, but it gradually acquired a separate staff of judges, expert in the law, and a body of clerks who kept its own records. In the same way a separate financial administration began to emerge from the *curia*. Final accounts were still rendered to the king in the presence of the magnates, but the actual work of supervising the king's finances was performed by a group of expert clerks, who had remarkably full records of royal rights and revenues. Other departments were also taking definite form. For example, the royal household was no longer completely confused with the general administration, and a rudimentary forest service was established. All these changes increased the importance of the bureaucracy and decreased the influence of the magnates. They were still called in to discuss questions of general policy, but they had little to do with the daily routine of government. As in England, the actual work of administration was performed by professional civil servants.

Thus St. Louis completed the work of organizing a strong and efficient royal government, a government which was so strong and efficient that it rapidly reduced competing jurisdictions to impotence. Louis, of course, had no idea that this was to be the result of his policies. He wanted to preserve the *status quo* and he ordered his officials again and again to respect the rights of others. How sincere these injunctions were may be seen from his dealings with Henry III of England. Henry had attacked France again and again in an effort to regain some of the territories which John had lost, and Louis had every excuse for annexing the remnant of the old Angevin holdings. Yet he never took advantage of the repeated rebellions of the English barons to seize Henry's French fiefs. On the contrary, in 1259 he ended the long quarrel with a treaty which not only confirmed Henry's right to Guienne and Gascony but also surrendered to him certain border districts long occupied by the French.

But while Louis scrupulously respected the rights of others he expected, and could enforce, equal respect for his own rights. This was fair enough, but it immediately raised the problem as to just what rights the king had. Here is where the existence of a professional bureaucracy was decisive. Obviously, a group of men thoroughly imbued with new ideas of government, dependent upon the king for office and income, would have a very different concept of royal rights from that of a council of feudal nobles. It was the plain duty of royal officials to recover all lands and revenues of which the king had wrongfully been deprived. It was their duty to prevent barons and Church from usurping the jurisdiction of the royal courts. It was to their advantage to increase royal power by any means, since their own delegated authority was thereby increased. Like most men, they wanted as much power as they could get, and they sincerely believed that the more they had, the better for the country. Naturally enough, they interpreted every doubtful question in favor of the king.

Even if royal officials had not had this conscious bias, the mere definition of royal rights would have shaken the old order. The essence of feudalism was confusion, confusion between theory and practice, between public and private rights, between royal and baronial powers. Feudal law avoided definitions as far as possible; faced with Solomon's dilemma it would have awarded the baby to both mothers. It drew no precise boundaries between rival fiefs and jurisdictions; the same land might be subject to two different lords, the same case might be triable in two competing courts. Loss of early records, rapid changes in custom, transfer of rights by marriage had increased this fundamental confusion until it is no exaggeration to say that there were at least two claimants to every piece of land and every right of government in France. Obviously, in these circumstances the power to define was the power to destroy. If the king's rights were made clear and certain, all the counter-claims, all the reservations, all the exceptions which limited his rights would be wiped out. All the infinitely varied compromises, whereby wealth and power were shared between king and barons, were threatened by definition of royal rights.

A few examples will make this clearer. The great lords of the South recognized the king's overlordship, but had never given him any real service. When royal officials asked these lords to send soldiers to the royal army and when they punished them for default, they were destroying the *de facto* independence of the South. Yet these officials argued, often with complete sincerity, that they were only enforcing the king's rights as suzerain. Again, the right of the king to remedy defects of justice had long been admitted in theory, while in practice the decisions of the courts of the great barons had been accepted as final. Then, in the second half of the thirteenth century, royal officials began to encourage

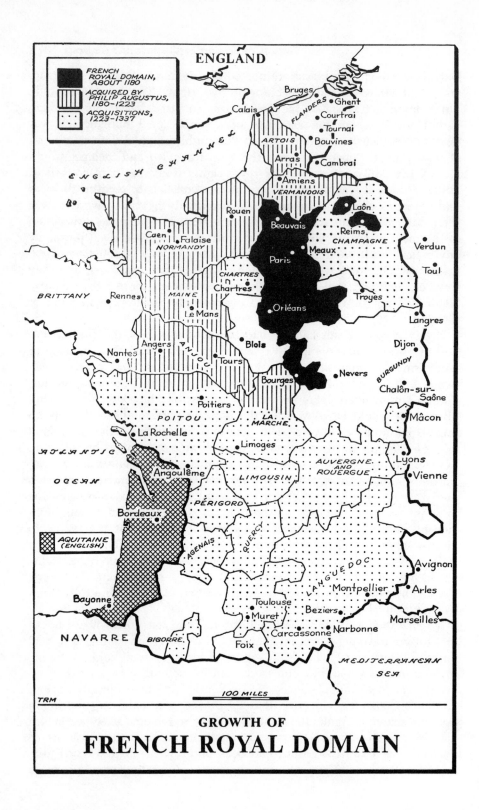

ENGLAND

FRENCH
ROYAL DOMAIN,
ABOUT 1180
ACQUIRED BY
PHILIP AUGUSTUS,
1180-1223
ACQUISITIONS,
1223-1337

Bruges
Calais
FLANDERS
Ghent
Courtrai
Tournai
Bouvines
ARTOIS
Arras
Cambrai
Amiens
VERMANDOIS
Laôn
Rouen
Beauvais
Reims
CHAMPAGNE
Verdun
Caen
Falaise
Meaux
Toul
NORMANDY
Paris
CHARTRES
Troyes
BRITTANY
Rennes
Chartres
Langres
MAINE
Orléans
Le Mans
Dijon
Angers
Blois
BURGUNDY
Nantes
ANJOU
Nevers
Chalôn-sur-
Tours
Saône
Bourges
Mâcon
Poitiers
POITOU
LA.
MARCHE
La Rochelle
ATLANTIC
Limoges
Lyons
AUVERGNE.
AND
ROUERGUE
Vienne
OCEAN
Angoulême
LIMOUSIN
PÉRIGORD
AQUITAINE
(ENGLISH)
Bordeaux
AGENAIS
QUERCY
Avignon
LANGUEDOC
Montpellier
Arles
Bayonne
Toulouse
Beziers
NAVARRE
BIGORRE.
Muret
Marseilles
Foix
Carcassonne
Narbonne
MEDITERRANEAN
SEA

TRM

100 MILES

GROWTH OF
FRENCH ROYAL DOMAIN

men to appeal from baronial courts to the Parlement. Such appeals seriously weakened the authority of the lords, yet no one could deny the right of the king to act as supreme judge. In the same way the growth of ecclesiastical jurisdiction was halted by defining the power of royal courts and by insisting that certain cases could be heard only by lay judges.

In major issues, such as those just mentioned, Louis undoubtedly knew and approved of the actions of his officials. He had a high idea of the responsibilities and powers of a monarch. He knew that he must answer to God for the welfare of his people and he believed that it was his duty to supervise all subordinate governments in his realm. But there were other cases in which the bureaucracy seems to have proceeded without consulting the king. For example, royal officials interfered repeatedly with other jurisdictions and forced cases into the royal courts on the flimsiest excuses. Louis was not pleased by such excessive zeal and he regularly ordered amends to be made to the injured parties. However, he probably did not hear of all these cases, and his orders for restitution were not always promptly obeyed. As has so often happened, the bureaucrats were more royalist than the king, and Louis had to exert all his authority and prestige to keep them within reasonable limits. His weaker successors were unable to do this, and for the next half-century royal officials were almost unrestrained in their efforts to magnify monarchical authority.

When Louis died in 1270, royal prestige and power had greatly increased and French government was more centralized than it had ever been before. The barons retained some powers of local government but they were definitely subordinate to the king and their actions could be reviewed and if necessary reversed by Parlement. The *baillis* and seneschals protected royal rights in every section of the realm, and their work was checked by an increasingly efficient central government. No one in the kingdom could avoid having some contact with the royal government, and every one was impressed by its power. Respect for the power of the government and respect for Louis' virtues bred loyalty to the monarchy. By the end of the thirteenth century the primary allegiance of the people of France had been transferred from the feudal princes and the Church to king.

THE GROWTH OF THE STATE IN ENGLAND

Henry III of England, like Louis IX of France, came to the throne as a child and had to face a serious baronial revolt at the very beginning of his reign. The English aristocracy, outraged by John's repudiation of Magna Carta, had called in a French pretender, and half the realm was in his power when the old king died. Henry's mother was unable to play the rôle of Blanche of Castile, but the English regent, William Marshal, was at least as able as the French queen. He gained the support of many barons by reissuing Magna Carta and then ended the revolt by a combination of effective military action and skilful diplomacy. William's early death might have endangered the peace he had just won, but the papal legate, acting as representative of the suzerain of England, succeeded in keeping the great men on reasonably good terms with each other. The papacy did not repeat its mistake of denouncing Magna Carta, and the barons, once they felt that their great privilege was safe, allowed the central government to carry on as it had under Henry II and Richard.

Thus when Henry III began his personal rule he possessed both extensive rights and an efficient bureaucracy through which his rights could be enforced. In many ways he was better off than Louis IX; England was more united than France, and the English lords as individuals had much less power than those of France. Yet with all his advantages Henry III was a less successful ruler than Louis IX. This was due in part to his own defects of character. Henry was one of those men who have every good quality except that of statesmanship, whose very virtues lead them into political difficulties. He was well educated, a patron of the arts, generous to his family and loyal to his friends. But most of his relatives were Frenchmen or Savoyards and he found few Englishmen who were sufficiently cultivated to meet his exacting standards and become his friends. As a result his court was filled with foreigners, and the English aristocracy, just becoming conscious of the fact that it was English, was profoundly irritated. Henry was deeply religious and rivaled Louis in saintliness. He was also grateful to the Church for the aid it had given him during his minority and he believed whole-heartedly in the ideal of a united Christendom directed by the pope. Therefore he allowed large sums to be collected in his realm for papal enterprises and he supported the popes in their savage attack on the Hohenstaufen. This policy also annoyed the barons, who did not share in the king's idealism and gratitude. They were losing interest in the welfare of Christendom and were becoming more and more concerned with the the welfare of the realm and of their class in the realm. Henry represented the old international, or rather pre-national order; the barons stood for the new nationalistic order which was just beginning to emerge. This difference in attitude between the king and subjects caused a strain, which was made worse by Henry's lack of political sense. There was a similar tension in France, where St. Louis shared many of Henry's ideals, but the French king knew how to gain the loyalty even of those who thought he was mistaken. Henry could not do this; he was a poor judge of men and situations and he failed to secure the personal devotion of the baronage and the people. As a result, during his reign the English developed a tendency to be loyal to their law and institutions rather than to the king in person.

Henry's personal defects were important, but it is also true that no king would have found it entirely easy to rule over England after Magna Carta. The barons had learned how to unite, how to act as a group, how to limit the king without throwing the country into feudal anarchy. They were willing to accept the centralized government which Henry II had created, but they insisted on having a voice in running that government. They claimed that they represented all England, that they spoke for the "community of the realm," that they were the natural defenders of English rights and English customs. The king could no longer pose as the sole defender of law and order, for the united baronage could argue that they were just as interested in the welfare of the realm as their sovereign. The government was not as dependent on the personal supervision of the king as it had been; it could carry on without him, or even against him if necessary. The highly trained officials of the Exchequer and the learned judges of the central and itinerant courts had their own traditions and were not mere agents of the king. They could and did serve a baronial government just as faithfully and efficiently as they had served the king. Thus, in a contest between king and barons for control of the government, the king was far from having all the advantages.

Henry made such a contest inevitable by his ambitious foreign policy. Thrice he attempted to regain the French fiefs which John had lost, and he repeatedly gave financial support to rebellions against Louis IX. He consistently supported the papacy and allowed it to collect large sums from the English clergy. In return for a promise of the crown of Sicily for his second son, Edmund, he made large contributions to the papal crusade against the descendants of Frederick II. Like all his predecessors, he had difficulties with the Welsh and had to lead expeditions into that dangerous country. Henry's foreign policy was not only expensive; it was also a complete failure. He gained not an inch of territory by his wars, and his one diplomatic success—the election of his brother Richard as King of the Romans—gave the royal family only an empty title without any additional power.

Henry could not carry on such an ambitious foreign policy without the aid of the barons. He needed their military service and even more he needed their money. His ordinary revenues were probably insufficient for the normal expenses of government and were certainly inadequate for his policy of expansion. Therefore he had to ask the great council repeatedly for grants of taxes. The great council—now coming to be known as the parliament—was far less under royal control than it had been. It spoke for the united baronage, it had its own leaders and policy and it frequently criticized or rejected Henry's plans. In the first half of the reign it granted taxes grudgingly and only in return for such concessions as the reissue of Magna Carta. In the second half of the reign, as Henry's personal defects and the failure of his foreign policy became more evident, it refused to grant taxes at all. Each refusal was usually accompanied by a denunciation of Henry's favorites and a demand for reform of the government. Henry's lack of money made it possible for the barons to oppose the king by peaceful means, and their perfectly legal refusal to grant aids was a far more effective check on royal power than feudal rebellion had ever been.

The quarrel between the king and the baronage came to a head in 1258. A famine and an unsuccessful war against the Welsh had caused general dissatisfaction. Just at that moment the pope told Henry that he must make a new contribution for the war against the Hohenstaufen or forfeit his son's claim to Sicily. Henry's request for money to pursue this will-o'-the-wisp infuriated the barons. They demanded that he exile his foreign advisers and that he appoint a committee to reform his government. Henry was in such financial difficulties that he could not refuse. The committee drew up the Provisions of Oxford, which gave the barons complete control of the government. A permanent council dominated by the king's opponents was set up, which was to name all high officials and determine all important questions of policy. Royal officials were to be responsible to this council rather than to the king, and the council, in turn, was to answer to the barons in parliament. For the next few years this council governed England.

The most influential member of the council was Simon de Montfort, the son of the leader of the Albigensian Crusade and the grandson of an English heiress. Like so many other foreigners, he had gone to England to seek his fortune and had won the favor of the king. He was given the earldom of Leicester, to which he had a claim through his grandmother, and he married the king's sister, much to the indignation of the English nobles. Then he quarreled with the king and went on a crusade. On his return he and the king were reconciled and he was made governor of Gascony. There he was accused of bad government and, though he was acquitted at a formal trial, Henry eventually removed him from office. This reward for twenty-five years of faithful service made him so indignant that he joined the barons who were opposing the king. His great ability soon made him their leader, even though some of the magnates retained their dislike of the upstart foreigner.

Simon and his friends realized that the barons must give England better government than the king had done if they were to remain in power. They also saw clearly that the great lords could have no real power unless they were supported by the lesser landholders. Therefore they sent out itinerant justices to collect complaints and redress grievances, while they drew up rules to protect petty vassals against unjustified demands of their lords. Unfortunately, this wise policy was not understood by all the barons and the old jealousy of Simon became stronger as his power increased. The barons were united in their dislike of Henry's policies but they differed widely as to what was to be done, once they had control of the government. Many of them refused to take any responsibility for national affairs; they knew how to criticize, but not how to rule. Others were shocked by Simon's plans for reform and still others were annoyed because they failed to secure lucrative offices for themselves or their friends. These weaknesses remained characteristic of the English baronage for the next two centuries. They were frequently able to gain control of the government but they never succeeded in running the government. They were too lazy to attend to the dull routine of official business; they were too selfish to subordinate their separate interests to the common welfare; they were too jealous to follow leaders who arose from their own ranks.

As a result of the split in the baronial party, Henry was able to regain power slowly and to dismiss officials appointed by the council. He then became confident enough to persuade the pope to annul the Provisions of Oxford. This stirred up a new storm, but Henry succeeded in inducing the barons to submit the dispute to the arbitration of Louis IX of France. Louis naturally felt that feudal lords had no right to control a royal government and ruled that the limitations on Henry's power were illegal. Simon at once took up arms, and though many barons were lukewarm to his cause few of them liked Henry well enough to aid the royal army. In 1264, at Lewes, Simon defeated and captured the king. A new council was promptly set up, which carried on the government in Henry's name for about a year.

This new council was even more under Simon's control than the old one had been, and only a few barons gave it real support. In order to make his position more secure and more legitimate, the earl summoned a parliament in 1265. Since it was evident that many barons would fail to attend the meeting, Simon attempted to gain the support of other groups. Each shire was asked to send two knights and each borough (town) was asked to send two burgesses. The knights represented the class of lesser landholders, whose interests were not precisely the same as those of the great lords, and who were already well disposed toward Simon because he had favored them during his first period of power. It was no great innovation to summon these men, since Henry had asked them to attend meetings of the great council at least twice in the years just before the revolt. It was, however, a new idea to summon representatives of the boroughs to parliament. Though English towns were becoming wealthy and populous they were still rigorously controlled by the king, and Henry had never felt it necessary to consult them about national policies. Simon, however, was well acquainted with the assemblies of southern France which included representatives of the bourgeoisie, and he seems to have believed that summoning burgesses would strengthen his hold on public opinion. The significance of his act should not be exaggerated. Knights and burgesses had little power, either in his parliament or in those of the next half-century. They were summoned to hear explanations of policy rather than to determine policy and they were expected to bind their constituents to courses of action which had already been determined by the great men. Nevertheless, the summoning of knights and burgesses in 1265 marked an important change in English political ideas. It meant that the barons were no longer the only class with opinions about national affairs, that it was no longer enough to conciliate the barons to ensure the success of a governmental policy. It meant that the barons no longer controlled their subjects, that the government must deal directly with the lesser landholders and the townsmen and explain and justify its policies to them. Simon's fall did not alter these facts and both Henry III and his successor found it advisable to summon knights and burgesses to many of the parliaments which met after 1265.

Simon's parliament set an important precedent, but it did not unite the upper classes in support of the earl. Edward, the eldest son of Henry III, succeeded in raising an army which defeated Simon's forces at Evesham in 1265. Simon was slain in battle and his death ended the opposition to the king. Henry, however, had learned his lesson, and pursued an intelligent and conciliatory policy during the remaining years of his reign. He was greatly influenced by Edward, who had at one time been a friend of Simon's and seems to have absorbed some of the earl's ideas. The men who had fought against the king were allowed to redeem their lands with moderate fines, and many of the reforms of the baronial period were retained. For example, Henry summoned representatives of shires and boroughs to a parliament in 1268. The king engaged in no more foreign adventures and the barons at last agreed to grant him a tax. England became so peaceful that the heir to the throne, Edward, felt that it was safe to go on a crusade. Henry died in 1272, while his son was still abroad, but the absence of the new ruler caused no difficulty. The government was running so smoothly that Edward saw no reason to hasten his return, and it was more than two years after his father's death before he appeared in England. The quarrel between king and barons had been ended by a tacit compromise which endured for the rest of the century. The barons had established their right to be consulted on all important questions of policy and especially in matters of taxation. The king had maintained his right to appoint all officials and his control of the administration.

The most striking events of Henry's reign were connected with the struggle between king and baronage, but the long quarrel did not stop the development of the royal government. As in France, the number of professional civil servants increased steadily, and a bureaucratic tradition which had little respect for older feudal ideals was created. The English bureaucrats were less dependent upon the king than their fellows in France, since the structure of the central government was too firmly established to be shaken by baronial opposition, but they were just as anxious to increase the authority and prestige of their offices. They insisted that primary allegiance was due to the central government and that its commands overrode those of other authorities.

The most important institutional change during Henry's reign was the development of the English common law. Opposition to the extension of royal justice practically ceased, and by 1272 almost all secular cases above the police-court level were tried in the king's courts. New writs were devised which made possible the use of juries in most civil suits, and the abolition of the ordeal by the Lateran Council in 1215 made it necessary to devise a new type of jury for criminal cases. The grand jury, as devised by Henry II, was simply a machine for collecting accusations; actual guilt or innocence of the accused was determined by ordeal. Now that the ordeal was abolished, Henry III's judges had the unpleasant choice of punishing men merely because they had been indicted, or of setting men free who were probably guilty of serious crimes. After a long period of hesitation and experiment the justices finally hit on the device of calling a petit jury to decide the fate of persons accused by the grand jury, and so our present criminal procedure was created. While these changes were going on, the justices began to study records of earlier decisions and to derive from these precedents general rules of law which would fit almost any case. Thus the law administered in the king's courts was ceasing to be a special law which covered only particular cases; it was becoming the common law of the realm, a law which had an answer for almost every problem of human relationships. All of this activity was summed up in the great treatise on the laws of England, written by Henry of Bracton. Bracton was trained by one of the ablest judges in England and served both Henry and the barons faithfully as itinerant justice. He had studied the decisions of his predecessors and he knew something of the revived Roman law which was so influential on the continent. This background made it possible for him to discuss English law as a coherent, logical system and to put it on a par with the law of Rome. His treatise remained the standard work on English law for over a century.

During Henry's reign there were also important changes in English society. As we have seen, the lesser landholders were becoming more and more independent of the barons. The feudal bonds between them and the barons were weakening, while their connection with the royal government became steadily closer. The lesser landholders dominated local government; they were the men who sat on the grand juries, who collected the king's taxes, who served as sheriffs, coroners, and keepers of royal estates. They gave the king most of his information about local affairs and were responsible for the local enforcement of his orders. Such men could not be ignored or dealt with only through the magnates, and their inclusion in parliament is only one indication of their increasing importance. At the same time the class of burgesses was increasing in numbers and wealth. Commerce and industry were becoming important and taxes on these activities were beginning to furnish a large part of the king's revenues. The government, therefore, found it necessary to consult leading burgesses, not only in parliament, but also when it wished to carry out its economic or financial policies in the towns. But the most significant change in English society has yet to be described. This was the beginning of English nationalism. Nationalism is a dangerous word to use in describing medieval beliefs and we should not assume that it existed in its intense modern form under Henry III. Nevertheless, during his reign it is evident that his subjects were beginning to feel that they were English, and English alone. The old distinctions between districts and between Saxon and Norman were becoming effaced. No political unit smaller than the realm could command men's loyalty. At the same time the old interest in the continent was dying, and there was little loyalty to the larger unit of Christendom. Few people cared whether Henry could recover his French fiefs or succeed in placing his son on the throne of Sicily. Few people cared whether the pope could defeat the Hohenstaufen or reconquer the Holy Land. The Norman kings had used Italian churchmen and French nobles freely in their government, but Henry III could not give offices to Poitevins and Savoyards without raising a storm of protest. Even the pope was criticized for ignoring these new nationalistic interests. Agents collecting papal taxes were mobbed because they were "impoverishing the realm," and there were violent objections when the pope gave English benefices to foreign and especially to Italian clerics. There was nothing anti-religious about this; many of the prelates, many of the most pious men in England attacked papal taxation and Italian intruders. But it was evident that the people of England felt that English interests were paramount, that they were not concerned with what happened elsewhere. It was evident that a ruler who concentrated on the defense of English interests would be able to defy many of the strongest traditions of the Middle Ages.

In 1272 England was the most unified and best governed country in the West. Every one in the country was subject to royal government and royal law; there were no isolated provinces clinging with stubborn loyalty to their old institutions. The barons had abandoned their attempt to retain individual power and had recognized that their influence depended on their ability to work with and through the central government. The English clergy, like the baronage, had formed itself into a compact pressure-group, and the lesser landholders were beginning to imitate these examples. Even the towns, in spite of their overwhelmingly local interests, were commencing to take some interest in national affairs. But this very unity of England made it impossible for the king to be absolute. He could not deal with individuals or local districts one by one; he had to face groups organized on a nation-wide basis. He could ignore the protests of an individual baron and even of an individual bishop; he could not ignore the demands of the baronage and clergy of England. He had to consult the magnates on all important questions; he had to conciliate public opinion. The king was still unquestionably the head of the government, but the government was no longer his private property. England was becoming a national state, but both the English state and the English nation were something more than the English monarchy.

LAY SOCIETY IN THE THIRTEENTH CENTURY— THE NOBLES

Everywhere in thirteenth-century Europe, lay governments were becoming more efficient and more influential. They were performing their duties better; they kept the peace and gave justice more effectively than they had done before. They were imposing heavier obligations on their subjects; by the end of the century most of the people of Europe were bound to pay taxes, to give military service, and to assist in the work of local administration. Government officials were becoming a professional class and the number of officials was increasing everywhere. The old overlapping of jurisdictions and powers was coming to an end; in most districts of Europe one single lay government was obtaining a practical monopoly of political power. The dominant government was not always a monarchy—the towns in Italy and the princes in Germany had all real political power—but whether king, count, or commune came out on top the result was the same. Europeans now had to deal with governments which did their work well enough to inspire respect and which were strong enough to secure obedience. These governments were not yet absolute, for they were restrained by general customs and special privileges. In Spain and Hungary, as well as in England, the privileged classes had organized to check the monarch, and even the powerful king of France could not set himself above the law. But lay governments, while not absolute, were so busy and so powerful that every one in Europe was affected by their activities. Interest in lay politics increased; respect for lay government increased; loyalty to the dominant lay ruler increased. These changing attitudes had profound effects on the structure of society.

At the same time the economic revolution, which had begun in the late eleventh century, continued to be a disturbing factor. The cumulative results of earlier changes were felt in their full force only in the thirteenth century. Towns increased in number, in population, and in political importance. Both industrial production and the volume of commerce increased. The Italian cities, thanks to their early start, had accumulated large amounts of capital and were able to begin large-scale banking operations. More luxuries were available for the rich and there was some improvement in the standard of living of the poor. At the same time the importance of status and tenure decreased, while the importance of money increased. In the early Middle Ages the individual's standard of living depended upon the class to which he belonged, the amount of land which he held, and the terms by which he held it. Now his standard of living tended more and more to depend upon his ability to acquire money. It was not easy to adjust to this new situation and all classes in society were affected by the change.

The nobility, more than any other group, was disturbed by the political and economic developments of the thirteenth century. They were more class-conscious than they had been in earlier periods, more aware of who was and who was not a noble. Of course, counts and other great lords had always been considered noble, but petty vassals did not necessarily possess this status. Some knights in Germany and eastern France were clearly of servile origin. Free but poor knights would not have been reckoned as nobles in most European countries before 1200. But during the thirteenth century definitions shifted and class distinctions sharpened. Most knights were considered nobles (or, in England, gentlemen, which socially meant much the same). The basic tests were ancestry and the ability to "live nobly," that is, to live on the income from landed estates and dignified offices without having to engage in business or perform manual labor.

Unfortunately, just as the nobility was becoming conscious of itself as a class, it was losing many of its old functions. The nobility represented the tradition of amateurism and localism in government, a tradition that was being weakened by the tendency toward centralization and professionalism. In the western monarchies the nobles lost much of their power as local governors and judges to agents of the central authority. They retained a sort of police-court jurisdiction over their peasants—no central government had the time or the manpower to settle every village squabble—but in England and in parts of northern France this was all they retained. Elsewhere the greater lords kept high justice and some degree of administrative control, but they could exercise these rights only under the supervision of their suzerains and in accordance with the new principles of government. In these circumstances the nobles usually found it expedient to hire professional bureaucrats to perform their administrative and judicial functions. For example, most of the great French lords imitated the king by creating *baillis* to administer their lands, and they often gave the office to men who had been trained in the royal administration. The princes of the Low Countries and Germany escaped the interference of central governments only by setting up professional governments of their own. Princes who depended upon the old system of amateur government were overwhelmed by neighbors who adopted the more efficient methods of the Western monarchies. The lord who wished to retain his independence had to hire bureaucrats and soldiers and develop at least the rudiments of a centralized state. This was, of course, both difficult and expensive for the ruler of a small district. Some of these men either could not afford or did not wish to make the necessary effort and sold their rights of government in return for pensions which enabled them to live in comfort. For example, the counts of Mâcon and Burgundy sold their counties to the French king during the thirteenth century.

Loss of rights of local government did not mean that the nobles lost all political importance. They still had social prestige and wealth and could exert great influence on the central government, especially if they combined their strength. They did this quite successfully in England and some other countries, but in France, where provincial feeling was still strong, they combined only at the local level and as a class had relatively little influence on national politics. And even in England there were many nobles who took no interest in politics or who exerted themselves politically only in moments of crisis. Some nobles entered the service of powerful rulers and became more or less professional administrators themselves, but these men were a minority of their class. In all European countries there were many nobles who no longer had any important political functions and who tended to devote themselves to courtly pleasures.

The military importance of the nobility did not decline as rapidly as its political importance. The nobility still provided the best armed and best trained cavalry, and cavalry was still the dominant arm in European armies. The substitution of paid soldiers for unpaid feudal vassals did not greatly alter the situation. A common practice was to summon all the men who owed military service and then to offer wages to the best trained knights in order to induce them to remain for a long campaign. Even the purely mercenary companies were often commanded by nobles and might include many poor knights in their ranks. It is true that there were cavalry units composed of non-noble men-at-arms, but these soldiers were never considered the military equals of knights. Generally speaking, no ruler north of the Alps could hope to wage a successful war without securing the military service of many nobles. But while the nobility remained *the* military class, it did less fighting during the thirteenth century than it had done before. Feudal warfare was dying out, while international warfare was just beginning, and Europe enjoyed a period of relative peace while the shift was being made. Private war was frowned upon by the great western monarchs, and in any case the ordinary feudal lord could not afford to make war very frequently because he could not often afford to hire an army. More powerful rulers, who could afford to hire armies, were absorbed in domestic affairs. There were no great wars north of the Alps between 1214 and 1285, and even the most bellicose nobles had no opportunity to devote all their time to fighting.

Thus the nobles had lost many of their political functions and were by no means absorbed in their military duties. They remained a class with assured social position, large unearned income, and considerable leisure. Like all classes in this situation they had to invent artificial standards and social activities in order to justify their privileges and occupy their time. These standards and activities are usually summed up in the word "chivalry." [1] As a moral code, chivalry taught the rule of "noblesse oblige"—the true knight was the defender of religion, the protector of the weak and the oppressed, the exemplar of loyalty, courage, and generosity. As a pattern of aristocratic life, chivalry emphasized the accomplishments of the courtier—the true knight distinguished himself in jousts and tournaments, composed love-songs, recited romances and stories, played chess and backgammon, and devoted himself to the service of his lady. Needless to say, few men in real life either lived up to the code or possessed all the accomplishments of the ideal knight. Nevertheless, the ideals of chivalry had some influence on most of the nobility, and every feudal court was to some degree a training ground for gentlemanly behavior.

It is evident that chivalry was based on several distinct traditions. In its military aspect it was derived directly from feudalism. As a specialized military class, knights had always been expected to possess the virtues of loyalty and courage and the physical strength necessary for fighting. The need for keeping this specialized class in training produced tournaments at a very early date. The first tournaments, however, were artificial private wars rather than sporting events. Nobles who were anxious to get some practice in fighting assembled and charged each other in a confused mêlée. The chief object of the contestants was to capture as many knights as possible and force them to ransom their horses and armor. There were no single combats, no lists, and practically no rules. It was not improper for several knights to attack a single opponent, and serious, even mortal wounds were often inflicted. Only under the influence of other traditions did the tournament become an athletic spectacle suitable for the eyes of ladies.

[1] The best brief description of chivalric ideas and practices may be found in Sidney Painter's *French Chivalry* (Baltimore, 1940).

It is more difficult to discover the origin of the courtly tradition in chivalry. Certainly it does not come from feudalism. The military class of the tenth and eleventh centuries had neither time for, nor interest in, social accomplishments. It was not distinguished for courtesy or a sense of fair play. It had no special regard for women; they were treated very much like other inferiors. It is also certain that the beginnings of courtliness, courtesy, and respect for women are first evident in southern France in the twelfth century. Some scholars argue that this development was indigenous, a natural result of the greater wealth and leisure possessed by the nobles of the region. But other aristocracies, medieval and ancient, with as much or more wealth and leisure never produced the peculiar pattern of aristocratic life to be found in Languedoc. This has led students of the period to seek a special influence and many of them believe that they have discovered it in the proximity of Moslem Spain. The Moslem aristocracy for centuries had emphasized the courtly accomplishments which were characteristic of chivalry. They composed poems and love-songs; they enjoyed chess and backgammon; they had an elaborate code of etiquette; they made romantic love the dominant interest in their lives. Even such a debased product of Moslem civilization as the Arabian Nights' Tales reveals these characteristics. Again and again we find the story of the young prince who falls desperately in love with a beauteous maiden, writes her elaborate poems, and performs amazing adventures in order to secure her favor. The parallel is striking and it is difficult to reject completely the hypothesis of Moslem influence.

Whatever its origin, the courtly tradition had profound influence on aristocratic society as it spread from Languedoc throughout Europe. The wealthier nobles spent an increasing amount of their time at the great castles where the new ideas had taken root, and their violent manners were softened by the demand for social graces. The poorer knights might not attend the courts of the great lords, but they felt it necessary to imitate their superiors as far as possible. Even more important was the influence of the idea of romantic love. Most of the ancients, as well as the men of the early Middle Ages, thought of love as a sort of contagious disease. It was difficult to avoid this sickness, but a sensible man would cure it as soon as possible. The idea of glorifying love, of making it the central interest in life and in literature, was new and disturbing. It conflicted with the customs and morality of the age. There could be, at first, no idea of romantic love as a prelude to marriage, for marriage was a matter of business, not sentiment. Marriages were arranged to ally two families, to unite two fiefs, to cement a coalition, to thwart a plot. The personal preferences of the individuals concerned were unimportant compared to these economic and political considerations. Romantic love had to come after marriage, and it usually took the form of adoring some other man's wife. This was often a perfectly harmless social game, but it sometimes led to serious consequences, and adultery might be condoned in the name of chivalry. Only gradually was romantic love recognized as a means of bringing about marriages rather than as a means of breaking them up, and even then it was to have a long struggle with the older idea of marriage of convenience. The conflict between romantic love and family interests has been a commonplace in European literature from the end of the Middle Ages to the present, and in this case literature has faithfully reflected life.

Finally, there was a religious tradition in chivalry, though this was less effective than the military and courtly traditions. The Church was worried by the growing worldliness of the nobility and, in conformity with its principle of guiding and controlling the new forces in European life, it tried to spiritualize chivalry. The true knight was supposed to possess not only the military virtues of bravery and loyalty, but also the Christian virtues of faith, charity, and humility. Renouncing the pleasures of courtly life, he was to combat the enemies of the faith and give aid to the weak and helpless. Ecclesiastical rites were introduced in the ceremony of making a knight, and many knights took a vow to assist the Church in its work. Thus chivalry absorbed a religious flavor which justified its existence in the eyes of medieval society. How effective the religious element in chivalry was, is another matter. It may have prevented the nobles of the thirteenth century from becoming completely absorbed in worldly pleasures, but it certainly did not make them act as if they were members of a lay religious order. During the century they showed increasing reluctance to make any sacrifices for the Church and increasing preoccupation with secular interests and amusements.

The centers of chivalric life until the end of the thirteenth century were the courts of the greater French nobles. The kings of France and England, with the single exception of Richard Lionheart, were either too busy or too pious for such elaborate triflings. The nobles of Germany lacked the wealth and the leisure necessary for a fully developed court life, while the nobles of Italy had become urbanized and were less interested in the military aspects of chivalry. But in France the greater barons were civilized enough to enjoy social life, wealthy enough to afford expensive festivities, and active enough to engage in warlike sports. Chivalry began, as we have seen, in the courts of southern France in the twelfth century. In this region there was special emphasis on the courtly side of the movement and on the cult of romantic love. Many of the southern nobles became famous as poets: a petty vassal like Bertran de Born and a great king like Richard Lionheart (who was educated in Aquitaine) are both reckoned among the troubadours. The court of Eleanor of Aquitaine was a center of this cultural activity, and was also a focal point from which chivalry spread to the North. By the end of the twelfth century the new ideas had taken root in the provinces beyond the Loire, and the court of Champagne was rivaling the older centers of the South. Thus the destruction of the civilization of the Midi by the Albigensian Crusade did not stop the development of chivalry, since it was already acclimated in the North. The northern barons emphasized the military and religious aspects of chivalry. They preferred tournaments to love-making, and seldom centered their lives around devotion to a lady. But, while they changed the proportions, the essential ingredients of the mixture remained the same. The northern nobles did not make a cult of romantic love, but they were anxious to impress the ladies and to gain a reputation for good manners. As a result, tournaments were better regulated and less bloody, and more attention was given to social accomplishments. Northern nobles played the proper parlor games, told stories, sang songs, and even composed verses, though this last activity was less common than it had been in Languedoc. In Champagne, as in Aquitaine, chivalry was the code of the gentleman: it taught him to do his duty to God and his lord, to deal courteously with members of his class, and to be a good companion and an entertaining lover. English and German lords sent their sons to French courts to learn this code, and by the fourteenth century it was well established in all countries north of the Alps. Thus a common European tradition of the proper behavior for a gentleman was created, and this tradition has persisted, with some modifications, to our own day.

The development of chivalry naturally influenced the vernacular literature of the period. Stories and poems written for the nobles reflected their new interests, and at the same time spread propaganda for chivalry among sections of the aristocracy which had not yet been affected by the movement. This influence was not always for the best, since it tended to introduce conventional sentiments and stereotyped situations into the older literary forms. The Provençal love-lyrics, which at first had expressed real feeling, rapidly became formal and artificial, and by the end of the thirteenth century they had lost all vitality. Almost any one could grind out these verses; every one knew the conventional rhymes and epithets. This practice in versifying had a certain mechanical value in perfecting the new techniques of European poetry, but otherwise there is little to be said for it. The Provençal poets were more interesting when they turned their attention to current religious and political problems, and it might be noted that they were less influenced by chivalric conventions when they wrote on these topics. They were naturally outraged by the Albigensian Crusade, and they expressed their feelings in a long series of attacks on the Church. The greed and ambition of the clergy were satirized, the policies of the papacy were criticized, and enemies of the Church, such as Frederick II, were praised. A few troubadours urged participation in the crusades as a knightly duty, but most of them believed that any movement led by the Church was *ipso facto* suspect. They pointed out that the pope used the crusades for his own political purposes, and suggested that most of the money contributed for the crusades was misappropriated. These angry verses are important as reflecting the opinions of a certain section of the aristocracy, but they are not, on the whole, great poetry.

The longer narrative poems of northern France were also contaminated by contact with chivalric ideas. In the early years of the century some poets were still able to compose *chansons de geste* which had the old sincerity and simplicity, but in general both *chanson* and Arthurian lay tended to become mere stories of adventure. Some of these stories were very well told and are still amusing reading, but as literature they rank no higher than an adventure story does today. The characters are pasteboard and the plot moves only through the stimuli of unbelievable coincidences and fantastic displays of magic. Pious writers tried to redeem the *genre* by introducing religious motives for adventure, such as the search for the Holy Grail, but these stories in turn became conventionalized. One unknown French writer tried to counteract the drift to adventure stories by writing the delicate satire of *Aucassin et Nicolette*. In this story the lover is less of a hero than his lady, and his foreign adventures culminate in a battle in which the opponents assail each other with pieces of cheese, but this skilful attack on conventional romances was never popular in the Middle Ages. On the whole, we must admit that French vernacular poetry declined steadily during the latter part of the thirteenth century.

To some extent the decline of French poetry was balanced by the rise of German and Italian verse. Writers in these languages borrowed some of their forms and themes from French sources, but they were less influenced by the conventional ideas of chivalry and still had something to say. The German Walter von de Vogelweide expressed himself freely and vigorously and his love-lyrics described real emotions instead of a conventional pose. Wolfram von Eschenbach told the story of the search for the Grail with deep sincerity and great effectiveness. In Italy the first vernacular poetry was a mere imitation of Provençal works, but by the end of the century the Tuscan poets were showing that it was possible to achieve new and striking effects with the old forms. These experiments culminated in the work of Dante,[2] in which the structure and rhyme-scheme of a love-lyric was used to convey the most profound religious and philosophical ideas. Yet Italy and Germany did not escape the influences which were crippling French poetry. By the end of the century the tendency to emphasize elaborate rhyme-schemes instead of content in lyric poetry, and adventure instead of depiction of character in narrative poems was evident in both countries.

[2] For a fuller discussion of Dante's work see below, p. 537.

A more fortunate consequence of the new interests of the nobility was the rise of French prose. A knight living in a great court could no longer be completely uncultured; there were certain things which every gentleman had to know. Hence the flood of elementary treatises on everything from theology to table manners, and the one-volume encyclopedias such as the *Livre dou Trésor* of Brunetto Latini. Hence also the translations of important Latin works which we have already considered. Every gentleman might not know Latin, but every gentleman was supposed to know French, since French was the language of chivalry. The Italian Brunetto Latini wrote his encyclopedia in French *"parceque c'est la plus noble langue dou temps."* One might almost say that the aristocracy was trying to atone for the increasing triviality of its favorite verse by devoting itself to these very solid and often very dull prose treatises. French didactic works of the thirteenth century have little to recommend them from a literary point of view, yet they had an important influence on the development of French literature. In their struggles to make Latin learning available in the vernacular, French writers increased their vocabulary and improved their syntax. As a result French prose was much more highly developed than that of any other country in the Middle Ages and gradually gained those qualities of clarity and precision which gave it a preëminent position in the modern period. Even more important than these didactic works were the narratives written, or rather dictated, by members of the French aristocracy. In keeping with chivalric principles, these men wished to record the heroic exploits which they had witnessed. The most famous of these narratives are Villehardouin's *Conquête de Constantinople* and Joinville's *Vie de St. Louis*. The first describes the Fourth Crusade; the second is primarily an account of Louis' adventures in Egypt and Syria during the Sixth Crusade. Both are written in a simple, direct style and reveal the character of the aristocracy as no other records do. They are masterpieces of prose, and French is the only European language which can make such a claim for a work of the thirteenth century.

Certain poems of the thirteenth century must be classified with didactic works in prose. They were written primarily to convey information and they covered the same subjects as the prose works. The versification was a mere sugar-coating, added to make it easier to swallow and retain the facts. At its worst it was pure doggerel; at its best it was technically perfect but uninspired. Nothing was safe from these earnest versifiers; the Bible, Ovid, theological works, medical treatises and moral tracts were all translated into French verse. Some of the original compositions are more interesting, especially the rhymed chronicles and biographies. A good example of this last class is the *Histoire de Guillaume le Maréchal* —the life of that fortunate knight who eventually became Regent of England and saved the throne for Henry III in the troubled years following Magna Carta. There are also the elaborate allegories, which seem dull to modern readers but which fascinated the aristocracy of the thirteenth century. Medieval men had always found it easier to understand abstract ideas when they were personified and had always enjoyed discovering hidden meanings in concrete facts. These tendencies were evident at the very beginning of the period in the work of Martianus Capella and Gregory the Great, but they reached a new height in the thirteenth century. Amusing examples of this love of allegory may be found in the bestiaries, where marvelous tales about animals are used to illustrate points of the Christian faith. Thus the pelican which feeds its young with its own blood portrays the Crucifixion, while the lion-cub, born dead but revived after three days by its father's voice, signifies the Resurrection.

The most famous allegory of the thirteenth century is the *Roman de la Rose,* a long poem which begins as an idealization of courtly love.and ends as an encyclopedia. The first part, written by Guillaume de Lorris, is an attempt to describe the psychology of falling in love. But instead of reproducing the thoughts of the lover and his lady, the Rose, as a modern novelist would do, Guillaume personifies all their ideas and emotions. The element of adventure is furnished by the struggle which goes on among these abstractions; for example, Reason opposes Love and Fair-Welcome is imprisoned by Jealousy. Guillaume shows us courtly love at its best; the lover must shun everything foul in order to be worthy of his lady. There are many charming passages in this part of the poem, but as a whole it is always conventional and often tedious. Guillaume never finished his work, but the story was continued, some years later, by Jean de Meung. Jean carried on the allegory and eventually allowed the lover to possess his lady, but he was not greatly impressed by the conventions of courtly love. He was a bourgeois, and, like most members of his class, he was suspicious of high-flown idealism and very much interested in hard facts. He aired his prejudices and displayed his knowledge in interminable lectures which he placed in the mouths of his allegorical characters. He repeated all the old stories about the fickleness of women and all the satires about the greed and hypocrisy of the clergy; he summarized what he knew of science, medicine, theology, and etiquette. Some of Jean's criticism of contemporary society is very amusing, but his work is unoriginal, badly organized, and much too long. It may seem surprising that a poem as inconsistent, as pedantic and as long as the *Roman de la Rose* should ever have been popular, but the evidence of the manuscripts cannot be contradicted. Hundreds of copies still exist; every well-educated gentleman or bourgeois knew the work. It contained everything which interested men of the thirteenth century—chivalry, allegory, idealism, satire, and popular science. It summed up the lay culture of the age, and in doing so it illustrated some of the dangers which threatened the Church. It idealized worldly love and criticized the clergy; even more important, it testified to the existence of a large class of educated laymen. The Church was losing its monopoly of scholarship and this was an important factor in undermining its leadership.

Chivalry affected the material as well as the intellectual standards of the aristocracy. It demanded a higher standard of living, more splendor on great occasions, more comfort in everyday life. Even the nobles who paid little attention to social conventions were anxious to possess the new luxuries, and luxuries, as usual, soon became necessities. Every one wanted more comfortable living quarters, and the old stone towers, half-fort and half-storeroom, were generally abandoned. The great barons constructed elaborate buildings protected by a surrounding ring-wall, lesser men built stone houses which gave them more space and greater privacy. Clothing became more elaborate and more expensive, as every moralist pointed out, while the new, improved plate-armor cost much more than the old chain-mail. Tournaments, banquets, and other entertainments absorbed the greater part of the income of some nobles. Besides these social expenses there were other new demands on the income of the nobles. Even though they were a privileged class they did not entirely escape the increased costs of better government. As we have seen, the barons who tried to maintain their political independence were forced to spend large sums in building fortifications and hiring bureaucrats and soldiers. Those who left the burden of government to their superiors found that they were often called on for financial aid. The substitution of litigation for private wars was not an unmixed blessing, for many law-suits were more bitterly contested than any battle and a stubborn litigant could be ruined by court expenses and lawyers' fees. All these new expenses were made more burdensome by the fact that prices increased, slowly but steadily, during the thirteenth century, while the income of many nobles was fixed by custom or charter. It was difficult to increase peasant dues that had been officially recorded; it was almost impossible to break long-term leases of land that had been made at prices far below the current value of the property. Commutation to money of labor services and payments in kind could sometimes be reversed, but if it could not the lord was bound to suffer. A lord who had agreed in 1200 to accept a shilling for each measure of grain owed him had lost about 20 percent in real income by 1280.

In these circumstances it is not surprising that the financial position of the nobility became precarious during the thirteenth century. Matters were made worse by the fact that most members of the aristocracy felt it beneath their dignity to worry about money. They believed that their rank entitled them to a high standard of living, and chivalry reinforced this tendency toward extravagance with its emphasis on conspicuous waste. Largesse—that is, open-handed spending and giving—was one of the great chivalric virtues, and the wandering minstrels never let their patrons forget that the generous knight would be praised in their songs, while the thrifty soul would be damned as a mean-spirited miser. Some nobles resisted this social pressure and succeeded, in spite of many difficulties, in increasing their incomes. They leased their lands for short terms and so profited from the rising value of real estate; they collected everything due, and some things which were not due, from their peasants; they kept careful records of income and expense. These business-like nobles seem to have been especially common in England, where several books on estate-management were written during the thirteenth century. But even in England these men were in a minority and the average noble, faced with rising prices and increasing expenses, often solved his problem by borrowing. Since the money was used for current expenses instead of productive purposes, this could be a fatal step. The nobles were such poor financial risks that interest rates were fantastically high, and if a loan ran for a few years the interest would amount to many times the principal. There was little opportunity for the average noble to save enough from his regular income to pay such a debt, and only the greatest lords could flatly repudiate their obligations. Kings and princes of the thirteenth century had developed the lucrative, if somewhat oppressive practice of taking over all the credits of the money-lenders in their countries from time to time, and this naturally made them uphold the sanctity of contracts. Men who had influence at court might succeed in persuading the ruler to reduce the amount of their debt, but others had to resort to more humiliating expedients. They might sell part of their land to meet their obligations and so lose income and status. They might become mercenary soldiers in the hope that their employer would reward them with a pension or grant of land. Worst of all, they might marry the daughters of wealthy burgess families and so redeem their lands at the cost of social humiliation. Unfortunately for the nobles, even these desperate expedients were not always successful in averting disaster. Many families were utterly unable to secure enough money to preserve their social position; they ceased to "live nobly," as the chroniclers put it. They lost their lands; they had to work for their living, and they soon became absorbed in the great mass of common people. There was a striking decrease in the number of knightly families in certain parts of Europe during the thirteenth century, and this decrease was almost certainly caused by financial difficulties.

The difficult economic position of the nobility during the thirteenth century explains much of their behavior. They could not oppose the growing administrative and judicial power of kings and princes, but they fought taxation bitterly because it reduced their income. Opposition to taxation, in turn, often stimulated the nobles to use parliamentary assemblies as a means of restraining their kings. The nobles gradually lost interest in the crusades because they could not afford the voyage overseas. They became suspicious of Rome and hostile to foreigners because they felt that these outsiders were making off with money which might have gone to them. They talked longingly of the good old days, yet they were in no position to act as a real conservative force in medieval society. They were too fond of their luxuries to upset the new economic order which made those luxuries possible. They were too devoted to worldly pleasures and too harassed by worldly cares to wish to protect or restore the leadership of the Church. But they had no real desire to assume the burden of leadership themselves; they thought mainly in terms of preserving their class interests. They wanted to keep their old privileges, which they could no longer justify by their political services, and at the same time they demanded a share of the new wealth, which they had done little to create. Frustrated and trapped by forces which they could neither understand nor control, by the fourteenth century they were ready for any reckless adventure which promised to increase their influence and their income.

LAY SOCIETY IN THE THIRTEENTH CENTURY— THE BOURGEOISIE

The thirteenth century was a golden age for the inhabitants of the towns. The nobility and clergy might suffer, but the bourgeoisie profited from the new economic organization of Europe. Commerce and manufacturing increased, urban populations became larger, and new forms of business activity began to appear. The growing wealth of the towns was reflected in their increased political importance. In the western monarchies, representatives of the towns were summoned to national assemblies, while in Italy and Germany the leagues of independent city-states often had a decisive influence in the struggles between rival rulers. The attitudes and beliefs of the bourgeoisie became important because of its wealth and political power. Its behavior affected that of other classes and by the end of the thirteenth century European civilization had acquired, for the first time, certain bourgeois characteristics. There was more interest in practical knowledge, more desire for immediate worldly gains, more use of business methods by ecclesiastical and secular governments, more scepticism about the value of ideals and distant, future rewards. Other forces, of course, played a part in this shift of attitudes, but the influence and example of the bourgeoisie were among the chief causes.

All these phenomena were especially evident in Italy, the region in

NORWAY

SCOTLAND
St. Andrews
Edinburgh

NORTH SEA

DENMARK

Armagh
IRELAND

ENGLAND

Dublin

York

Lincoln

Oxford
Cambridge
Bury St. Edmunds
St. Albans
London

Southampton
Canterbury

Bruges
Ghent

RHINE

Hamburg

Bremen

Goslar

Magdeburg

HOLY

Cologne

Fulda

Lei

ATLANTIC

Rouen

SEINE
St. Denis
Paris
Lagny
Chartres
Provins
Troyes
Bar-sur-Aube
Orléans
Tours

Reims

Trier

Mainz

Spires

Worms

Bamberg

Nurem

Strasburg

ROMAN

Clairvaux

Augsburg

Freis

OCEAN

Dijon

CITEAUX

ST. GALL

FRANCE

CLUNY

EMPIRE

Bordeaux

GARONNE

Geneva
Lyons

Milan

Pavia

Padua

Ven

Parma

Santiago de
Compostella

(THE PORTUGUESE UNIVERSITY
WAS SOMETIMES IN LISBON
AND SOMETIMES IN COIMBRA)

Albi
Toulouse
Nîmes
Montpellier
Avignon
Marseilles

Genoa

Bologna

Rav

LOIRE

RHONE

Pisa

Florence

Coimbra

EBRO

Siena

A

Salamanca

CASTILE AND LEON

CORSICA

ITALY

Lisbon

PORTUGAL

TAGUS

Toledo

ARAGON

Ro

Monte Cassi

Barcelona

Cordova

Valencia

Na

Seville

GRANADA

SARDINIA

Cadiz

M   E

A

F

P

Tunis

S

R

Tripo

I

UNDERLINED NAMES ARE
THOSE TOWNS WHICH HAD
A UNIVERSITY BEFORE 1300.

MEDIEVAL TOWNS

TRM

500 MILES

which the towns had the greatest wealth, the most complete independence, and the most fully developed bourgeois culture. Mediterranean trade was still the most profitable branch of European commerce, and the Italian towns still dominated this trade. They had some competition from western ports such as Marseilles and Barcelona, but these towns had neither the shipping nor the overseas establishments necessary to secure a really important share of the trade. Prosperity increased the population of the Italian towns and these two factors, in turn, ensured their political independence. We have already seen how Frederick II was defeated in his attempts to subdue the Italian communes, and no later king dared renew the plan. Charles of Anjou, the French conqueror of Naples and Sicily, did succeed in controlling some Lombard and Tuscan towns, thanks to local party conflicts, but this led to no permanent results. By the end of the century the towns of Lombardy and Tuscany were, in fact, independent city-states, controlling the whole northern half of the peninsula. In these circumstances it is not surprising that townsmen dominated the intellectual and artistic life of Italy. Nowhere else were educated laymen so numerous and nowhere else could the towns support so many artists and writers. The earliest Italian writers, sculptors, and painters were drawn from the bourgeoisie and their work was produced primarily for members of their own class.

The towns of the North could not compare with those of Italy in wealth and influence. In England and France the kings were careful to keep control over their municipalities. They granted them rights of local self-government, but the desires of the towns were never allowed to interfere with the interests of the central government. French and English townsmen were prosperous, but their trade did not approach that of the Italians in value. Moreover, the Italian towns dominated the surrounding rural districts and exploited the peasants, while in England and France the nobles still controlled this source of wealth. This economic division naturally caused a cultural division in the northern countries. In Italy the nobles lived in the towns and shared the intellectual and artistic tastes of the bourgeoisie, while in the North they lived in the country and set their own standards. As we have seen, the northern nobles had a romantic, idealistic literature of their own, and while it was influenced to some extent by the realistic and satirical literature of the bourgeoisie, the two types did not blend completely.

The towns of Germany and the Low Countries had greater political freedom than those of England and France, but they were far from having the position of the Italian communes. The counts and dukes of the Netherlands never lost complete control of their towns, though they had to grant them many privileges. Even Ghent and Bruges, the wealthiest communities in the region, could not ignore the wishes of the count of Flanders, and their repeated revolts never gave them complete independence. Some German towns remained in a similar position, but others gained practical independence as imperial free cities. These German towns, however, were not very wealthy; they dealt largely in bulky commodities, such as salt, timber, fish and furs, which yielded small profits for each voyage. They seldom controlled the agricultural lands in their immediate neighborhood and were often ringed around by the castles of hostile and greedy nobles. Hence no German town became a territorial power like Venice or Florence, though leagues of German cities did have some political influence. The division between rural regions controlled by the nobles and urban centers dominated by the bourgeoisie had the same results in the Low Countries and Germany that it did in England and France. In Flanders, the most thickly settled region of the North, the nobles were influenced, to some extent, by bourgeois attitudes and beliefs. Yet even in Flanders the two cultures were not completely amalgamated, and elsewhere they remained fairly distinct.

The century-old preëminence of the Italian cities explains why most of the new forms of economic organization originated south of the Alps. The most important innovation in the thirteenth century was the development of commercial banking. Italian merchants had to transact business in dozens of different currencies and they frequently received or made payments in foreign coins. They naturally wanted expert assistance in determining the relationships between different currencies, and they were glad to find specialists who would buy or sell foreign exchange as needed. The money-changers who performed these operations were not, at first, very wealthy. They came largely from the inland towns, such as Florence and Milan, which had only the crumbs of Mediterranean trade. But if they had the necessary knowledge they were almost certain to profit on every transaction; there was much less risk in changing money than in sending a ship to Acre or Alexandria. Thus they gradually built up a surplus of liquid capital, and by the thirteenth century they were ready to engage in real banking functions. At the same time, many merchants began to use their surplus capital in banking operations. During the century they established agents in the principal commercial centers of the European world, and this in turn made it possible to perform financial transactions through simple bookkeeping operations. If, for example, a papal agent had collected five hundred pounds of a crusading tithe in England and the pope wished the money transferred to a French noble, the merchant could accomplish the transfer without the risk and expense of shipping actual coins. His English agent would receive the money and add it to the firm's working capital in England, while his French agent would pay out five hundred pounds from his French resources. It is evident that this type of transaction, in which credit was extended only while the books were being balanced, would soon lead to real loans, for several months, or even several years. These loans were often secured by assignments of future revenues, especially revenue from taxation, and so the money-lenders were often obliged to act as tax-collectors for kings and popes. Thus by the end of the thirteenth century many Italian businessmen had become commercial bankers. They received deposits, paid out money on order of their depositors, made short-term loans and acted as financial agents for governments. The pope, the king of England, and the king of France all had their favorite bankers and these men often exercised great influence in political affairs.

The Italians did not have an actual monopoly of the banking business, but they took the cream and left their competitors the skim milk. They alone had the capital to make large-scale loans and the organization to finance wide-ranging operations. They were often able to disguise their interest charges by various devices, such as underestimating the value of revenues assigned them, or collecting penalties for delayed payments. Even when they openly charged interest they were usually able to keep the rate lower than that of their competitors. The Templars were their only real rivals, and the Templars usually restricted themselves to the respectable, but relatively unprofitable business of receiving deposits and transferring funds. Even in France, where the Temple functioned as a royal treasury, the king found that he needed the assistance of the Italians whenever he was faced with unusual expenses and wanted to anticipate his revenues. Other bankers and money-lenders were less important. The Jews were reduced to making small personal loans at high rates of interest. Such loans were usually for unproductive purposes and attempts to collect them made the Jews very unpopular. They had been treated fairly decently in the twelfth century, but the thirteenth century was an age of growing anti-Semitism, which culminated in the expulsion of the Jews from England in 1290 and from France in 1306. The local Christian money-lenders who began to appear in various northern countries toward the end of the century, engaged in much the same sort of business as the Jews. The South French, or Caorsins [3] as they were called, had an especially evil reputation. Some Flemish money-lenders had enough money to rise above the loan-shark level, but there were not enough of them to take over the international banking operations of the Italians. The great financiers of the thirteenth century were all Lombards or Tuscans, and Lombard was practically a synonym for banker in France and England.

The rise of banking was merely the most striking aspect of a more general phenomenon, the rise of the capitalist. Of course, every medieval merchant was to some extent a capitalist, since every purchase of goods was a capital investment. But the early merchant invested his labor, his knowledge, and sometimes even his life, as well as his money, and these

[3] From Cahors, a small town of Languedoc.

intangible investments were largely responsible for his profits. By the thirteenth century, however, it was possible to invest money alone, and let other men furnish labor and expert knowledge and run the physical risks. For example, a wealthy Italian might assist in financing a voyage to the Levant, and receive a share of the profits in return for his money. He would not make the voyage, nor assist in buying and selling the cargo; his one function was to supply some of the capital. This is an extreme case; in other fields the capitalist usually contributed his organizing ability as well as his money. The cloth industry, with its numerous specialized operations, offered an attractive field for this sort of work, and by the end of the thirteenth century many Italians and Flemings had grasped the opportunity. The basic idea was simple enough; the merchant would buy raw materials and pay wages to the different craftsmen who worked on them, instead of buying semi-finished or finished goods from independent artisans. But it required considerable skill to carry it out. A balance had to be kept between the three main stages of production—cleaning and spinning, weaving, and finishing and dyeing—and different tactics had to be used with the laborers in each stage. The spinners were unorganized home workers, while the dyers were highly skilled, very class-conscious craftsmen. In between were the weavers, weaker than the dyers because their trade could be learned more easily, but still a turbulent, self-assertive group. In these conditions it is not surprising that none of the capitalists who tried to organize the cloth industry was able to operate on a very large scale.

Banking and capitalistic organization of industry were new in the thirteenth century, and for that very reason they were not typical of the age. They were eventually to destroy the medieval economic system, but they had done nothing more than strain it before 1300. Capitalism is essentially individualistic, and the ordinary townsman of the Middle Ages was not yet ready to abandon his belief in the advantages, and indeed the necessity of strong communal organization. Capitalism is based openly on the profit motive, and the bourgeoisie was not yet ready to admit that it was better to seek a maximum profit than a smaller, but more assured income. The Church still had influence in the towns and the Church taught that the profit motive should be restrained by ethical considerations. The seller should be content with a just price that would repay him for the cost of his materials and his labors; he should not try to profit from the necessity or the ignorance of the buyer. Conversely, the buyer should not try to deprive the seller of his just return for his efforts. The Church admitted that the principle of supply and demand would usually determine the just price, but it wanted to guard against excessive and unwarranted gains. Profit-seeking could easily become avarice. Interest-taking was legitimate when a man risked his money (e.g., by investing in an overseas voyage) or when he lost the use of his money because repayment of a loan was delayed, but interest could easily become usury. The sins of avarice and usury, which showed a corrupt use of the intelligence, were much worse than purely physical offenses which arose from momentary yielding to lust or anger. Bankers and international merchants might not have agreed, but the average small businessman or artisan had no trouble in accepting these principles. They wanted security, not unrestricted opportunity to rise and fall. They wanted moderate profits for a whole group, not large profits for one man and a bare living for the rest. They joined the clergy and the nobility in denouncing money-lenders, and they created institutions which hampered, for a time, the rise of the capitalist.

The most important of these institutions were the gilds. Gilds existed in northern Europe in the twelfth century, and in Italy even earlier, but they were neither as well organized nor as specialized as they became in the thirteenth century. By 1300 a gild usually included only the men who did one particular kind of work; thus the pastry-cooks did not belong to the same gild as the bakers, and the tanners, saddle-makers, shoe-makers and shoe-repairers all had separate organizations. The gilds usually included only artisans or local retailers; they were not very effective in controlling international merchants and bankers. Not all towns had gilds, but the lord or the municipal government of a non-gild town usually imposed regulations on artisans or tradesmen which had some of the same effects as gild regulations.

The chief purpose of a gild was to obtain a monopoly for its members; in return it guaranteed fair prices and good workmanship. In towns in which the gilds were strong no one could engage in any trade without joining the appropriate organization. Each gild was restricted to the use of certain materials; substitutes could not be used to cheapen the product and expensive materials could not be added to make it more attractive to the purchaser. Gild members were not supposed to take advantage of their fellows by cutting prices, or by working at night or on holidays. Thus, in theory, every member of the gild produced about the same amount of finished goods, which were of uniform quality and sold at a uniform price. In practice, of course, skill and industry enabled some gildsmen to make more money than others, but the difference could never be very great. The poorest gild member was bound to get a certain amount of business; the richest could never hope to dominate the market. The gilds also acted as religious and charitable associations. They contributed to the building and upkeep of churches and organized special religious services. They aided sick members and took care of the widows and children of those who died. In this, as in some of their other activities, they resembled modern trade-unions. It should always be remembered, however, that the gilds were dominated by the masters, that is, the employers, rather than by the journeymen wage-earners, and that their chief interests were those of an association of small retailers.

In later centuries the gilds were denounced as selfish and reactionary organizations which throttled initiative and protected incompetence. By the end of the Middle Ages they were doubtless guilty of many oppressive practices, though the motives of the men who attacked them were not always as unselfish as they seemed. But in the thirteenth century the gilds seem to have performed many real services and to have done comparatively little harm. They did not make it difficult for a man to enter a trade, nor did they unduly prolong the period of training. Boys taken on as apprentices became journeymen, that is, fully paid employees, in a relatively short time. The seven-year apprenticeship, common in later years, was at first rare. Journeymen did not find it impossible to save money and open shops of their own; the elaborate rules which restricted the number of masters and set up family monopolies of certain crafts were made, for the most part, in the fourteenth and fifteenth centuries. Even the rules regulating manufacturing methods were not unduly restrictive in the thirteenth century. They were not, as yet, very specific, and they do not seem to have prevented important technological changes in such operations as weaving. Finally, it should be remembered that many towns had no gilds and that there were unorganized occupations even in the gild towns, so that individuals who could not enter a gild still had a chance to find urban employment. It does not appear that these unorganized workers were any more prosperous, or any more progressive, than the gild-brethren. The tendency to stabilize prices, production, and employment was very strong in the thirteenth century, and if there were no gild regulations, custom or municipal ordinances usually took their place. Only the great international merchants and bankers could escape these influences, and even these men had to accept some limits on their individual initiative.

All the forces of thirteenth century business and commerce can be seen at work in the four little towns of eastern France where the famous fairs of Champagne were held. During most of the year these towns, Provins, Lagny, Bar-sur-Seine and Bar-sur-Aube resembled all the other small municipalities of the neighborhood. They had their gilds, which produced goods for local consumption, and their bourgeois courts and councils, which had limited rights of government. But at certain times each of these towns, in turn, was overrun by a horde of merchants, money-lenders, brokers, carriers, peddlers, minstrels, and vagabonds who came from the four corners of Europe. Thanks to the fact that they lay on one of the great North-South trade-routes, thanks also to the wise policy of the counts of Champagne who granted safe-conduct and free passage to merchants, these towns had become focal points of European commerce. There the cloth of Flanders was exchanged for the Oriental goods imported through Italy; there the bankers settled their dealings in foreign exchange and arranged their credits. Important loans were regularly paid at the fairs of Champagne, wherever they had been contracted, for the borrower was sure to find both a market for his goods and a banker who could arrange for the transfer of the money. Yet, even in the midst of this individualistic and capitalistic activity, the older medieval principles of coöperation and group responsibility could not be forgotten. Foreign merchants were often made to answer for the debts and misdemeanors of their compatriots, whether or not they had any business relationships with them. The French government often regulated the Lombards as a group, in spite of the intense municipal and personal rivalries which divided them. Therefore the foreign merchants found it wise to organize under "captains," to accept some responsibility for one another's actions, and to negotiate with public authorities as a group and not as individuals. Even the men of Languedoc did not feel entirely safe in northern France and accepted the leadership of the captain of Montpellier. The fact that international traders and bankers found corporate organization necessary on some occasions explains the strength of the gilds of the thirteenth century. If the wealthiest and most powerful members of the bourgeoisie did not feel secure when they stood alone, it is not surprising that the ordinary retailer or artisan felt it necessary to submerge himself in his gild.

The increase in wealth and business activity was on the whole favorable to the development of municipal institutions. The old hostility to self-governing towns had almost disappeared, and most thirteenth century rulers were quite willing to let urban communities regulate their own affairs. The kings of France and England were careful to reserve their rights to tax, to hear appeals from town courts, and to confirm local officials and ordinances, but they were generous in granting charters to any place which had the slightest semblance of commercial activity. Paris was the one great exception to this rule; the King of France governed it directly, and allowed only limited power to make economic regulations to merchant and artisan groups. But on the whole the older towns of England and France improved their administrative systems and often gained additional privileges, while the municipalities of Germany and Italy became practically independent. Yet, by the end of the thirteenth century there were definite indications that municipal institutions were not functioning properly and some towns had already surrendered their rights of government to outside authorities. Internal dissensions, suppressed as long as the towns had to face the hostility of the clergy and nobility, emerged when security was achieved. All the inhabitants of the towns did not share equally in the new prosperity, and a sharp class division between the rich and the poor appeared. The old families who had grown up with the towns and owned the most valuable building sites, the great merchants who engaged in international trade, the bankers and dealers in luxury goods merged to form an urban patriciate. Legally or otherwise, the patriciate gained control of town governments. Many municipal constitutions were based on the principle of a self-perpetuating board of directors, and in such places the oligarchs merely rotated the offices among the members of the ruling families. In other towns the assembly of all citizens was supposed to have full power, but the patriciate found it easy to dominate these assemblies by persuasion, bribery, or threats.

The government of an urban aristocracy was almost always selfish and shortsighted and not infrequently corrupt. Financial administration was especially bad; money was borrowed at ruinous rates of interest, unnecessary expenses were incurred, and taxes were unfairly apportioned. It is only fair to say that this situation was aggravated in France and England by the constant demands of the kings for money, but royal taxation alone does not explain the financial difficulties of the towns. In the second half of the thirteenth century conditions were already so bad in many towns that the poorer inhabitants rebelled against the oppressive government of the rich. When such rebellions took place in a country with a strong central government, the ruler was naturally inclined to intervene and to restore order at the expense of municipal liberty. Louis IX of France, in spite of his respect for established rights, found it necessary to put several towns in receivership and to administer them through his own officials. His less scrupulous successors used every disturbance as an excuse to revoke or modify town charters. In Italy, where there was no king to intervene, conflicting class interests caused almost continuous civil war in some towns. These conflicts, in turn, cleared the way for the dictators, the Italian tyrants of the fourteenth and fifteenth centuries. After 1300 the self-governing towns were on the defensive all over Europe. Few new charters were issued, and existing privileges were threatened by internal revolt, royal pressure, and the rise of despots.

Life in a thirteenth century town was exciting, if not very comfortable. Most activities were carried on in the streets or public places. Markets and public assemblies were held in the open air, and the most famous revivalists preached their sermons in the squares in front of the churches or in the fields just outside the city. Peddlers wandered through the streets, calling their wares—fish, meat, honey, onions, cheese, old clothes, charcoal—and the town criers periodically announced important news. Most shops had no front walls or windows, and were separated from the street only by a counter, so that passers-by could see all that was being done within. On holidays the young people danced in the open places and even in the cemeteries, much to the indignation of the clergy, while the men attended their gild-meetings or engaged in cock-fighting, bull-baiting, wrestling and other sports. There was always something interesting to see, something new to know, and this intensely social life attracted men in the thirteenth century just as it does now. Unfortunately, it had its usual results—overcrowding, dirt, and disease. To guard against raids by hostile forces, it was essential that the town be enclosed by a wall, and there was often not space enough within the wall for people to live decently. During the thirteenth century most towns enlarged their walls—some of them two or three times—but this gave only temporary relief. It has been calculated that the density of population in London in 1379 was about that of Manhattan Island in 1905, and the overcrowding was certainly greater in London because the average house was only two or three stories high. Whole families slept in one room and houses were built on bridges, town walls, and even in the moats to ease the strain. Town buildings before 1200 were generally made of wood, but during the thirteenth century many municipal governments tried to increase the use of brick or stone. They often ruled that party-walls could not be made of wood, but these ordinances were not well enforced and disastrous fires frequently occurred. Most streets were very narrow; only the main thoroughfares leading from the gates to church and market-place were wide enough for a cart. In Paris the most important streets were not more than twenty feet wide, and the others ranged from five to ten feet in width. There was not much light or air in these narrow lanes, especially since the upper stories of the houses often projected several feet beyond the building line. Each householder was supposed to keep the street in front of his house clean, and it was absolutely forbidden to throw garbage and other refuse into the public ways, but it was difficult to enforce these rules. Street-cleaning usually depended on the rain, which washed rubbish down the gutters in the middle, or on scavenging birds and pigs. By the end of the thirteenth century some cities were advancing beyond the pig-cleaning stage of sanitation, and London passed the first of a long series of ordinances restricting the right of its citizens to keep live stock in their homes, but not all towns were so advanced. It is not surprising that the mortality rate in the towns was high. They survived only by replenishing their population with immigrants from rural areas.

Town-dwellers were separated from the rest of the population, not only by their wall, but also by their way of life. They were businessmen in an agricultural world and traders in a society which suspected the basic motives for trade. They understood the mysterious ways of money; they engaged in operations which endangered the welfare of their souls; they were not ruled by hereditary or divinely appointed officials. Noble, cleric, and peasant looked upon the townsman with suspicion, and their suspicion was repaid with mocking scorn. The bourgeoisie had its own literature, and in that literature the whole medieval system was ridiculed. The most typical products of the bourgeois spirit were the *fabliaux* —short, humorous stories told in verse. They were realistic and quite often indecent, since the funniest thing in the world, to most men of the Middle Ages, was a deceived husband. The heroes and heroines of the *fabliaux* were the clever, unscrupulous people who knew how to get what they wanted by flattery, trickery, and deceit—the poor clerks who stole clothes, dinners, and mistresses from rich priests, or the wives who concealed their lovers from their husbands by taking advantage of their credulity or superstitions. The victims of the jokes were the stupid and idealistic—two qualities which were almost synonymous to a writer of *fabliaux*—and the representatives of established authority. There was no respect for women or reverence for the clergy—it is hard to find a good woman or an honest priest in the whole collection of stories. Even the saints were ridiculed, as in the story of the villein who got into heaven by matching every one of his sins with a worse one committed by St. Peter. The spirit of the *fabliaux* appears again in the longer story of Reynard the Fox. This was a favorite tale with the merchant class and exists in English, French, and German versions, the last being the most complete. It is a direct satire on chivalry and feudalism, both in form and content. It apes the style and structure of a romance, with long descriptions of court life, war, and battles. But the hero is Reynard, the sly, hypocritical, deceitful, revengeful fox, who makes a complete fool of the Lion King and his vassals. Reynard takes care of himself and his family, but he has no compassion for others and no respect for law or religion. His two basic principles are that good people will believe any vigorously told lie and that, while it is helpful to have a reputation for piety, it is foolish to be restrained by any religious or ethical principles.

It would be unfair, of course, to assume that all the bourgeoisie resembled the characters of the *fabliaux* or Reynard. In our own country the cycle of gangster stories and films did not mean that the entire middle class had joined the rackets. In both periods the average member of the middle class was a conventional, law-abiding citizen who might envy the criminal's freedom from restraint without being ready to imitate him. In every medieval city there were hundreds of pious and honest men who may have laughed occasionally at the *fabliaux,* but who read by preference serious and edifying books. It must not be forgotten that the bourgeoisie played a great part in stimulating the production of those works of popular science and theology which have already been discussed. But while the *fabliaux* represented an extreme rather than the average, it is significant that they pointed toward an extreme of worldliness rather than its opposite. They exaggerated certain bourgeois characteristics—shrewdness, scepticism, greed—but there is no doubt that the bourgeoisie had these characteristics.

The bourgeoisie had a code of ethics, but it was the code of the good businessman, and the Church had not yet sanctified it, as it was to do in the sixteenth century. The code of morality taught by the thirteenth-century Church did not fit the new economic system very well. The Church had been successful in adapting the chivalric code to meet its standards; it was not nearly so successful in dealing with the businessman's code. This failure meant that while the ordinary thirteenth-century bourgeois was not yet ready to give up his belief in the teachings of the Church, he was less and less ready to apply those teachings in his daily life. Christianity was becoming an external force rather than an internal stimulus, and even the new energy of the mendicant orders could not reverse this trend. It was easier to deal with heresy than with apathy, and the friars who crushed the Albigensians were eventually infected with the worldliness of quite orthodox members of the bourgeoisie. The friars were not the only ones to be affected, by the end of the century other clergymen and some nobles had a bourgeois outlook on life. Members of the bourgeoisie served popes and kings as administrators and as financial and legal experts. They were bureaucrats rather than policy-makers, but they had some influence on their superiors. The kings who ruled England and France in 1300 resembled Reynard the Fox more closely than Noble the Lion, and some of their advisers could probably have given Reynard lessons in realpolitik.

Nevertheless, the bourgeoisie in 1300 was not yet ready to assume the leadership of Europe. Like the nobility, it sought chiefly the preservation of local rights and privileges. Individual members of the bourgeoisie might serve centralized governments, but the bourgeoisie as a class had neither the desire nor the ability to play a major role in the administration of large states. The typical bourgeois sought independence or a wide degree of autonomy for his own town; he was reluctant to risk his gains by combining with leaders of other towns, either to form a tight-knit confederation or to influence the policy of a king or a prince. In short, the bourgeoisie had added a new and disturbing element to the structure and concepts of western European society, but it was in no position to relieve the tensions that it had helped to create.

LAY SOCIETY IN THE THIRTEENTH
CENTURY—THE PEASANTS

Like the bourgeoisie, many peasants found the early thirteenth century a golden age. They had gained security from the devastations of petty feudal wars and they were yet to experience the wider devastations caused by international wars. They had freed themselves from some of the worse abuses of the manorial system and they had not yet become subject to the new tyrannies of the tax-collector and the banker. The number of serfs was diminishing and many labor services had been commuted for money payments. By the middle of the century the more fortunate peasants were practically in the position of small free farmers. They owed only a fixed money rent for their land, and rising prices for agricultural products made this rent easy to pay. Peasants of this class actually accumulated a little capital; they rented or bought additional lands and so raised their standard of living still higher.

Even the peasants who still owed labor services had a tolerable existence, provided that they held enough land. Their crops sold for good prices and the ordinary feudal lord was too careless about financial matters to find ways of depriving them of their increased income. The heavy taxes that ruined many peasant households in the fourteenth and fifteenth centuries did not yet exist. Even in England taxation was still infrequent, and many of the middling and poorer peasants were exempt from taxation because they did not own enough chattels. They were more secure than they had been for centuries and yet they paid very little for this increased security.

There were, of course, groups of peasants who were unhappy and depressed. On the whole the peasants of England and Italy were less well off than the peasants of France and Germany. In England the land-lords were very reluctant to surrender any profitable rights over their peasants. Their loss of political power made them anxious to preserve their economic privileges, and, as we have seen, they paid more attention to the management of their estates than aristocrats in other countries. They could not do much about the free peasants who owed only a fixed rent, but they made some effort to prevent the growth of this class. There was less freeing of serfs in England than across the Channel, and where the status of a peasant was doubtful, the courts were more apt to rule that he was a serf than that he was free. Some English landlords tried to reverse previous trends by substituting short-term for long-term leases of land and by demanding labor-services instead of the cash pay-ments that they had previously accepted. Some of them even succeeded in increasing the amount of rent and services owed by peasants on their estates. In Italy serfdom decayed rapidly, but there was less security in rural areas than in France and England. The papal-Hohenstaufen wars and the feuds among the towns caused a great deal of hardship for the peasants. Moreover, the Italian towns were extending their control over the countryside and showed some inclination to tax peasants more severely than dwellers within the city walls. Italian merchants who in-vested some of their surplus capital in land were just as careful as Eng-lish lords to extract the largest possible income from their estates.

Another depressed group was composed of men with very small holdings. These men were not necessarily serfs; some of them were free men from families that had lost their property or had divided it among many children. Legal status was often less important than a man's economic position; a serf who farmed large amounts of land was better off and might be more respected in his village than a poor free cottager. Some of these poor peasants had four or five acres; some of them had only a garden-patch, but none of them could raise enough food to live on, and very few of them possessed work-animals. They had only the labor of their arms to sell and wages were rising less rapidly than prices. As a result, they could not profit from the opportunities that were open to the peasant who held thirty or forty acres. They could not sell their surplus production in the town markets because they had no surplus. They seldom could save enough money to rent extra land and so rise above the subsistence level. If they migrated to the towns, as many did, they had to take the worst-paid jobs because they lacked the skills of men who had served as apprentices to artisans. Thus the rural proletariat was often a source of the urban proletariat, and both groups lived on the edge of starvation.

Toward the end of the thirteenth century, the condition of peasants of all classes began to decline. They had made their greatest gains when land was plentiful and labor scarce, when lords were willing to lease waste land for a few pennies an acre in order to get it cleared, when lords tried to steal each other's peasants by offering them freedom from serfdom and labor-services. But by 1300 almost all the good land (and some that was not so good) was under cultivation. Population had grown to a point where there was, in many regions, a surplus of labor. Some districts in Normandy and England had as many inhabitants in 1300 as they did in 1930—this in a period when agricultural techniques were still so primitive that a fourfold yield from the seed sown was considered good and five- or sixfold yield was exceptional. Industrial production had also come very close to reaching its limits and so there were fewer opportunities for peasants to find work in the towns, though some replacements were needed to make up for the high urban death rate. Thus the labor surplus made it even more difficult for the poorer peasants to survive and the scarcity of land made it more difficult for the richer peasants to increase their holdings. It was only when the Black Death of the mid-fourteenth century reduced the population sharply and thus again created a situation where land was plentiful and labor scarce, that the peasants had the sort of opportunities that they had enjoyed in the twelfth and early thirteenth centuries. And it may be that the Black Death struck Europe with special severity because the pressure of population on resources had caused widespread physical deterioration.

We know very little about the life and beliefs of the peasants. Manorial "extents" are not rare in the fourteenth century, but they give only descriptions of the amount of land held by each peasant and the rents and services that he owed. For example, an English document tells us that:

> Hugh Miller holds one virgate of land (25 acres in this case; more commonly 30) in villenage by paying thence to the abbot (of Peterborough) 3s. 1d. Likewise the same Hugh works throughout the whole year except one week at Christmas, one week at Easter, and one at Whitsuntide; that is, in each week three days, each day with one man, and in autumn each day with two men, performing the said works at the will of the said abbot as in plowing and other work. Likewise he gives one bushel of wheat for benseed and eighteen sheaves of oats for fodder corn. Likewise he gives three hens and one cock yearly and five eggs at Easter. Likewise he does carrying to Peterborough and to Jakele and nowhere else, at the will of the said abbot. Likewise, if he sells a brood mare in his courtyard for ten shillings or more, he shall give to the said abbot 4d., and if for less he shall give nothing. He gives also merchet [a payment owed if a villein's daughter married outside the manor] and heriot [a sum due when a villein tenant died] and is tallaged at the feast of St. Michael at the will of the said abbot.[4]

We can see that these are onerous terms of tenure, and they illustrate the fact that the English peasant was worse off than his fellows on the continent. But just how onerous were they? What did Hugh have left after he had made his payment? How much of a crop could he make on his own land when he worked three days a week for his lord? What did he have in the way of work-animals, barnyard fowls, sheep and pigs? Did he have a garden and a strip of meadow? What sort of house did he live in? How many children did he have? All these things would determine his standard of living, and no extent gives all this information. Another example is furnished by a survey of the possessions of the king of France in the region around Rouen, which was made about 1260. A typical entry reads:

> At Petit Couronne are seven villein holdings, each worth 35s. 8d. Each villein owes one load of oats and 5s. for every acre of arable land. He reaps one day, and must cut and carry hay from 21 acres of meadow. He pays 16d. in cash, 5 hens, 20 sheaves of barley and as many of rye, 20 eggs and a penny for every pig. These villeins have bought off all their services (exclusive of the land-rent), each for 43s.

Obviously, these men are better off than the English peasant whose services were described above. They owe very little labor to their lord and have succeeded in commuting what they do owe for a money payment. While they pay a much higher rent for their land (1s. an acre [5] as opposed to 1½d.) this is more than made up for by the absence of week-work. Good farmland in Normandy was usually reckoned as worth 2 to 4s. sterling an acre, so it should not have been difficult for them to

---

[4] Edited by E. P. Cheyney, in *Translations and Reprints*, Vol. III, no. 5.
[5] The Norman shilling was worth only ⅕ the English, so 5s. an acre in Normandy would equal 1s. sterling.

pay the rent and still have something left over. But once again, how much did they have left over after paying for their land and services? How much grain could they raise on their land, and what price did they get for it in the market? No one was interested in answering these questions; the lord wanted a list of his dues, not a description of the life of a peasant household.

Literary productions of the thirteenth century give little more information than the manorial extents. Most writers took the peasants for granted; they were mentioned briefly as one of the essential orders of society, but they were not worth detailed study. Some of the sermon-writers seemed to be annoyed by the increasing independence of the peasant class. They criticized their impudence, their reluctance to pay the dues which they owed, and their grumbling against persons in authority. They were especially irritated by the peasants' unwillingness to pay the full amount of the tithes claimed by the Church, and by their ignorance and superstitious practices. One French preacher claimed that men living in isolated forest and mountain districts did not even know the Lord's Prayer, while they had preserved all sorts of idolatrous festivities and ceremonies. But, on the whole, the peasants received little attention in the sermon-literature of the period. A few general remarks usually sufficed for them; they were told to beware the sin of avarice and to serve God in the station to which he had pleased to call them, and then the preacher passed to the more spectacular offenses of the bourgeoisie and nobility. The peasants also appear in the *fabliaux*, often in no very favorable light. The townsmen of the thirteenth century had the usual contempt of city-dwellers for their country cousins, and the simple, stupid victims of their humorous stories were frequently peasants. On the other hand, they disliked the peasants less than they did the clergy and petty government officials, and they sometimes gave the peasants their revenge by telling how they tricked the village priest and the lord's bailiff. Yet the best that the writers of *fabliaux* could say of the peasants was that they had a sort of shrewd naïveté which might disconcert their superiors. They admired a clever peasant as we might admire a clever dog, but they hardly thought of him as being the same type of being as themselves.

Sympathetic and understanding descriptions of peasant life are rare in thirteenth century literature. One famous passage occurs in *Aucassin and Nicolette*, where the unconventional author of that disconcerting story contrasts the real troubles of a peasant with the sentimental agonies of the love-sick hero. Aucassin is searching for his lost lady and meets a young peasant on the road.

> Tall he was, and marvellously ugly and hideous. His head was bigger and blacker than smoked meat; he had very large cheeks and a monstrous flat nose with great nostrils; lips redder than uncooked meat and teeth yellow

and foul. He wore leggings and shoes of ox-hide, wrapped around with coarse string to well above the knee. Upon his back was a rough cloak, and he stood leaning on a huge club. He asked Aucassin why he was weeping, and the young man, ashamed to confess his love, said he had lost his favorite greyhound. "Hear him!" cried the peasant scornfully, "you make all this lamentation for a filthy dog. Sorrow be his who thinks you are worth more. I am the one who has real reason for weeping. I was hired by a rich farmer to drive his plough, with a yoke of four oxen. Three days ago, by great mischance, I lost the best of my bullocks, Roget. I have been looking for him ever since, and have neither eaten nor drunk for three days, since I dare not go back to the town, because men would put me into prison, as I have no money to pay for my loss. Of all the riches of the world I have nought but the rags on my back. My poor old mother, too, who had nothing but one worn-out mattress, why, they have taken that out from under her and left her lying on the naked straw. That hurts me more than my own trouble. For money comes and money goes; if I have lost today, why, I may win tomorrow, and I will pay for the ox when pay I can. And you— you weep aloud for a filthy cur!" [6]

Certain South German poets were also less scornful of the peasants than most writers of the period. The story of *Meier Helmbrecht*, written by a Bavarian about the middle of the thirteenth century, illustrates their point of view. It describes the life of a peasant boy who was anxious to escape from the drudgery and dull routine of farm life. His father was a wealthy peasant, who leased a farm as his father had done before him. The boy, encouraged by his mother and sister, was determined to seek his fortune as a knight. He persuaded them to make him fine linen clothes, not homespun, ornamented with fur of lambs and goats. He had a "fine jacket, to make which his mother cut up one of her own skirts, and also bought some blue cloth." His shoes were of real Cordova leather. But his greatest glory was in the multitude of buttons which adorned his coat—gilded buttons down the back, silver buttons down the front. "His whole chest is covered with small buttons, yellow, blue, green, red, black and white. Whenever he dances, these buttons glisten, so that matron and maid follow him with loving glances." His hair fell down on his shoulders in heavy curls, and his cap was a wonderful piece of work, embroidered in silk with scenes from history and romance.

His father's house was hardly in keeping with his fine clothes. It contained only a living-room, with a cellar below, and an attic above. There was a large stove, on which some of the family slept, a table, a bench, and a bed, but no sheets. The food was simple—porridge and bread made of rye and oats seem to have been the staples; beer was sometimes to be had.

Young Helmbrecht finally had his way and left home to become a

[6] From *Aucassin and Nicolette and Other Mediæval Romances,* translated by Eugene Mason.

knight, much against the will of his father, who feared that his son would learn vicious habits. The degeneracy of the knights, their poverty and crimes, are insisted upon throughout the poem. They made their living by robbery and were noted for their brutality. The whole account is notable for the contempt in which the sturdy old peasant held the nobles of his day. Also, he had little respect for the clergy. He "paid the Church his exact tithes, and nothing more; he would not even give a priest a night's lodging."

The old man's fears were more than realized. The son became a robber knight and plundered and oppressed the peasants of his own community. The law finally caught up with him, and he suffered the savage penalties of the day. Blind, mutilated, and bankrupt, he sought refuge in his old home, but his indignant father refused to receive him. As he made his way off across the fields some of the peasants recognized their oppressor and beat him to death.

The author of this story may have exaggerated the independence of the peasants of his neighborhood, but many of his statements are corroborated by the poems of Neidhart von Reuenthal. Neidhart was a poor noble who lived among the peasants, largely at their expense, until he had gathered together enough money to spend some time at court. Then he made fun of his former hosts, boasting how the girls preferred to dance with him and how jealous the young peasants were. Both the fallen prestige of his own class and the relatively advanced position of the peasants of South Germany are evident in his work. There were few other regions in Europe in which a knight could have lived on such familiar terms with villeins, or in which he would have found himself so comfortable in a peasant household.

If we try to summarize the impressions of peasant life which we gather from the scanty sources, we should conclude that this class changed less than any other in the thirteenth century. The ordinary peasant still lived in a poorly constructed one-room hut, and his clothing was rough and simple. He had more food, and probably a greater variety of food, than in previous centuries, but his diet was still very monotonous by our standards. Even the more prosperous peasants, who increased their income by renting additional land, did not reach the level of the well-to-do businessmen of the towns. The peasant had greater security, both economic and political, than he had had before, but he was still harassed by a host of daily cares. There was still no great margin between him and disaster; bad weather, sickness, a temporary drop in the price of grain, a local war might reduce him to abject poverty. It is no wonder that the preachers found that avarice was his besetting sin. The pennies had to be counted, and the demands of the lord and the Church ate into his slender store of ready money. Like his modern descendant, the thirteenth century villein haggled over prices, was economical of the truth in selling his products, and was sometimes guilty of moving boundary stones to acquire a few feet of his neighbor's land. He was usually very conservative, for he still lacked the surpluses which make experiment possible, and he still needed the support of a closely organized village community which could be kept going only through rigid observance of custom. He had been little affected by the new ideas and new luxuries which were weakening the faith of the upper classes. He might grumble about tithes and wax sarcastic at the expense of well-fed, lazy clerics, but he still accepted the teachings and the leadership of the Church. The peasants would gladly have preserved the precarious equilibrium between the new forces and the old forms which was established in the thirteenth century. Their ignorance and lack of economic and political power restricted their influence, and they were unable to play a significant part in the crisis which was slowly developing in Europe as the thirteenth century neared its end.

XII

-»»-»»-»»-»»-«««-«««-«««-«««-

The Church Loses
Its Leadership

THE PONTIFICATE OF BONIFACE VIII

FOR THE FIRST THREE-QUARTERS of the thirteenth century the papacy had an almost unbroken record of success. In the political field it ended once and for all the claim of the Empire to share in the leadership of Christendom. The Hohenstaufen, last of the great imperial families, were exterminated; Germany and northern Italy were left to the mercies of local rulers, and Sicily was given to a papal protégé. No other king aspired to take the place left vacant by the fall of the Hohenstaufen. France was ruled by the saintly Louis, England by the equally pious though uncanonized Henry III, while the monarchs of the peripheral kingdoms were faithful sons of the Church. The papacy had been equally successful in controlling the new ideas and economic forces of the century. The universities and the great scholastic theologians had reconciled science and revelation. The Inquisition had ended the danger of heresy and the Franciscans and Dominicans seemed to be dealing successfully with the worldly minded bourgeoisie. The one dark spot was the failure of the papal crusading policy, and even there the leaders of the Church still had hopes of ultimate success. The influence of the Church had never seemed greater than in the third quarter of the thirteenth century, and some modern historians have claimed that the pontificate of Gregory X (1271–1276) marked the peak of papal power.

Yet the young men who witnessed the execution of Conradin, who studied under Thomas Aquinas, who accompanied St. Louis on his last crusade, were hardly more than middle-aged when the medieval papacy received a blow from which it never fully recovered. In an open conflict between the head of the Church and the kings of France and England, the secular rulers carried off the victory. As a result of this victory the popes deserted Rome and established themselves on the borders of the kingdom of France. The prestige of the papacy was tarnished and the leadership of the Church was shaken. The popes of the fourteenth century could no longer make all important social activities serve the cause of Christianity. They were placed on the defensive and had to devote most of their energy to the task of preserving the machinery of ecclesiastical government.

This reversal of fortune was not as sudden as it appears. As we have seen, during the thirteenth century it had been increasingly difficult to keep the new forces within the old religious framework. Loyalty to successful secular rulers had become stronger; interest in worldly pleasures and worldly profits had become greater. The tension between the officially accepted ideals of society and its actual practices had reached such a pitch that something was bound to give way. The Church had been fighting on many fronts to preserve its leadership and it is small wonder that it showed signs of exhaustion by 1300.

Constant strains revealed weaknesses which were inherent in the position of the papacy and the organization of the Church. The successors of Innocent III were not only the spiritual heads of Western Christendom; they were also bishops of Rome and temporal rulers of an Italian state. All too frequently, the first of these positions was sacrificed to the other two. The population of Rome was turbulent and rebellious, and it took much of the pope's time merely to keep order in the streets of the city. The great families, led by the Colonna and the Orsini, were constantly warring for the spoils of office, particularly of the papal office. Each faction had its fortresses and its bands of armed retainers; each faction bid for the support of the debauched and fickle mob which called itself the Roman people. A petty quarrel between two great families could throw Rome into a state of anarchy in a day. Most of the other towns in the Papal States were the scenes of similar struggles and only the greatest popes were obeyed in districts remote from Rome. The popes could not govern the States of the Church, but they were determined that no secular ruler should take their place. The independence of the papacy seemed to be inextricably involved with the independence of the Papal States, and this belief was a chief cause of the long struggle with Hohenstaufen. That struggle, in turn, lowered the prestige of the papacy throughout Europe. The popes may have been convinced that they were seeking purely spiritual objectives, but few men in Europe shared their belief. Catholic opinion was disgusted and temporal rulers were alarmed by the use of spiritual weapons in a secular quarrel.

The indirect consequences of the war with the Hohenstaufen were equally dangerous to the papacy. The people of Sicily were not pleased with their new French king, Charles of Anjou, who owed his position to papal support. Heavy taxes and the harsh rule of French officials led them to revolt in 1282. They massacred the French garrisons and called in the king of Aragon, who had married a granddaughter of Frederick II. Charles of Anjou succeeded in keeping Naples and the mainland, but the island of Sicily passed to the house of Aragon. The indignant pope preached a crusade against the Spanish ruler, and succeeded in persuading Philip III of France to invade Aragon. This was an even more flagrant abuse of spiritual weapons than the war against the Hohenstaufen, since the king of Aragon posed no threat to the Papal States. The moral was pointed by the failure of the crusade. The French army advanced along the coast, but its sea-borne line of supply was cut by an Aragonese naval victory. The French were forced to withdraw, and Philip III died during the retreat. The French, who had been consistent supporters of the papacy for centuries, were disgusted, and their confidence in the political leadership of the Church was shaken. The new king, Philip IV, soon became an open opponent of the pope. Even more important, because it touched more men directly, was the indignation caused by papal demands for money to carry on these wars. The pope levied extraordinary taxes on the clergy and insisted that men whom he appointed to ecclesiastical offices pay him a large part of their first year's income. Crusaders were allowed to commute their vows for a money payment and indulgences were sold. All through northern Europe, clergy and laity alike complained of the avarice of the papal court and accused the popes of selling offices, justice, and even spiritual benefits.

The complications created by their Italian policy were not the only factors which made it difficult for the popes to concentrate on their spiritual duties. Centralization of ecclesiastical government forced them to devote an increasing amount of time to supervising the administrative and judicial work of the papal *curia*. This emphasis on administration rather than salvation spread through the whole hierarchy and lawyers, tax-collectors, and practical men of affairs filled the highest offices of the Church. The resulting preoccupation with worldly matters caused a split within the Franciscan Order. A noisy and popular minority, the Spiritual Franciscans, created consternation in the ranks of right-thinking churchmen by demanding that the clergy as a whole adopt the life of apostolic poverty preached by St. Francis. Apocalyptic sects proclaiming the impending overthrow of the worldly Church by the Holy Spirit recruited followers all over Europe.

From this complex of forces resulted the tragicomedy of Celestine V. From 1292 to 1294 there was no pope. Within the college of cardinals the factions were so evenly balanced than an election was impossible. At length Europe was astounded and delighted by the choice of Pietro di Morroni, a famous ascetic and hermit. By this move the cardinals hoped to quiet the murmurings of the pious and at the same time to secure a pliable tool who would let them control the government of the Church. They were soon disillusioned. While multitudes followed the holy man, beseeching his blessing, the business of a papacy was in chaos. Celestine was completely bewildered by the worldly forces surrounding him and was appalled by his responsibilities. After a brief rule of five months he took the unprecedented step of resigning his office and retreating to his hermitage. The cardinals, in great relief, hastened to elect a member of their own college who had all the practical qualities which Celestine had lacked. Benedetto Gaetano was an able canon lawyer, a man of affairs who had grown rich in the service of the *curia*, but not exactly a saint. As Pope Boniface VIII he worked earnestly and stubbornly, according to his lights, for the welfare of the Church. He failed, however, to understand that the papacy was in a dangerous position, that men were ready to criticize acts which they would have applauded fifty years before, that the Church had become so involved in worldly affairs that it could be injured by worldly weapons. Worst of all, he failed to realize that his own election had shocked the conscience of Europe. Few papal elections were free from political maneuvering, but the intrigues of 1294 were particularly shocking because the election of Celestine had raised such high hopes. Boniface was suspected of having been one of the cardinals who persuaded Celestine to abdicate, and when the old hermit died shortly after his resignation, scandal-mongers added the charge that the new pope had found a quick way to get rid of his inconvenient predecessor. That such a story could be believed shows how papal prestige had been injured by the election. Boniface VIII assumed office under a shadow of suspicion and disillusionment resulting from the "great refusal" of Celestine V.

The conscience of Europe was a nebulous thing, and it might have been safe to disregard it as long as there were no political organs through which it could find expression. Unfortunately for the papacy, there were rulers in the early fourteenth century who were ready and able to exploit religious discontent for their own ends. As we have seen, secular as well as ecclesiastical governments had been strengthened and centralized during the thirteenth century. The kings of France, England, and Spain were gaining control over all inhabitants of their realms while the pope was gaining control over all the clergy. Since many of the clergy were subjects of the Western monarchs there was an inherent danger of conflict in the parallel drives for power. Conflict was avoided by tact and compromise throughout most of the thirteenth century. Both kings and popes refrained from extreme claims and made a tacit alliance for exploiting the resources of the Church. The popes wanted to tax the clergy to obtain money for their crusades and their increasingly expensive government; the kings expected to be paid by the clergy when they took up arms in behalf of the Church. Popes and kings alike wanted to control the choice of bishops and abbots in order to place their supporters in important positions. It would have been difficult for the popes to tax the clergy or to control ecclesiastical appointments without the good will of the kings; it would have been impossible for the kings to do these things without the consent of the popes. United, they could override all opposition. Under Louis IX of France and Henry III of England there had been a sort of gentlemen's agreement which gave the kings a share of ecclesiastical taxes and appointments in return for their general support of papal policy. The arrangement had worked satisfactorily, and the protests of exploited churchmen and pious or patriotic laymen went unheeded. Boniface VIII not only broke this alliance; he pushed relentlessly into the foreground theories of papal supremacy which were bound to irritate temporal rulers who were just becoming conscious of their own power. Boniface made no new claims; every point in his program may be found in the writings of earlier canonists, theologians, or popes. But to insist on official recognition of claims which had been only tacitly admitted under his greatest predecessors, and to make this demand at a time when papal financial exactions and papal political activities had raised a host of enemies, was to invite the catastrophe which followed.

Boniface entered the lists against formidable opponents. In England the troubled days of Henry III were over, leaving a strong desire for peace and good government and an equally strong dislike of foreign influence on English politics. Edward I was able to take full advantage of this reaction. Tall, handsome and determined, he impressed his subjects with the majesty of royal authority. His angry outbursts terrified his opponents and stimulated his officials, while his reputation for chivalry gave him a hold on his barons. He could be both violent and deceitful, yet he was sensitive to public opinion and seldom put himself in a position where he did not have the support of the upper classes. His experiences during the Barons' War had given him an understanding of his people and a skill in political maneuvers which few other English kings have possessed. He was determined to make himself supreme on the island of Great Britain, and he shared his subjects' hatred of foreign influence. His suspicion of the international Church was shown by the Statute of Mortmain (1279), which prohibited the acquisition of land by ecclesiastical bodies without royal consent, and by his efforts to narrow the jurisdiction of ecclesiastical courts. When Boniface began his campaign, Edward stood at the height of his power, after twenty years of successful and, on the whole, popular rule.

Even in the unimaginative writings of medieval chroniclers, Edward stands out as a strong, vigorous, impressive figure. Philip IV of France, on the other hand, is so elusive a personality that historians have never yet been able to separate the king from his advisers. He was so hand-some that his subjects called him Philip the Fair, but some of them de-clared that his good looks were his only royal characteristics. Discon-tented inhabitants of Languedoc nicknamed him King Owl, and said that he looked wise and majestic "but could do nothing but stare fixedly at people without saying a word." An Aragonese writer, on the other hand, describes him as a masterful personality who was "pope, emperor, and king all in one."

If contemporaries could not decide whether Philip was master or tool of his ministers, it is almost impossible for a modern writer to determine the question. It is true that Philip usually let his ministers speak for him and that the actual behavior of his officials was often at variance with the pious language of royal letters. But it might be argued that a clever ruler would make his subordinates assume responsibility for unpopular or hazardous actions, and that many kings have preached virtue and prac-tised oppression. In any case, all historians will agree that the French bureaucracy was seeking to increase royal power in every possible way and that Philip was quite willing to accept anything they could give him. Moreover, Philip took an active part in the work of government and it is hard to believe that he did not approve policies which were steadily followed for over a quarter of a century.

It is this unrestrained drive to increase royal power which makes the reign of Philip the Fair one of the less attractive periods in French history. All rules of morality and fair play were thrown overboard in the process of making the king strong and wealthy. Blackmail filled the royal treas-ury; dubious evidence and far-fetched arguments determined law-suits in favor of the king; slander settled political disputes. The king's ministers were masters of the art of propaganda and covered their basest acts with words of unctuous hypocrisy. The Church was attacked in the name of religion and the people were robbed in the name of reform. This propagan-da undoubtedly allayed the misgivings of many men, and it was swallowed more easily because St. Louis had taught the French to give the monarchy the benefit of the doubt in any dispute. All through the thirteenth century the people had favored the extension of royal government because they believed it was better government, and no amount of oppression could immediately shake this belief. There were individual and local protests against specific acts of the royal agents, but there was no organized oppo-sition until the very end of the reign. France was united only in her king and his bureaucracy. Outside the royal court, provincial and class lines were so sharp that it was difficult for discontented groups to combine. The men of Languedoc could not coöperate with those of Normandy, and the nobility and the bourgeoisie had little interest in protecting each others' rights. Each of the privileged classes was weakened by the fact that many of its members were in the royal service. Most of the higher clergy, many of the nobility, some of the bourgeoisie were grateful to the king for gifts, pensions, and lucrative offices. The natural leaders of the opposition had been won over and the papacy was to find few allies in France in its hour of need.

Taxation of the clergy caused the first clash between Boniface and the kings of France and England. Earlier popes had frequently imposed taxes on the clergy for the benefit of rulers who had taken the cross. These crusades were not always for purely spiritual purposes and the kings of France and England had come to feel that they could tax their clergy for any important war. Boniface refused to allow this when he became pope, a step which caused great embarrassment to both Philip and Edward, since they had just declared war on each other and were in need of money. They determined to secure grants from their clergy without consulting the pope and put pressure on the prelates to obtain their consent. Philip's demands were not unreasonable and he was able to preserve the form of an amicable agreement, but Edward used open threats. In 1294 he confiscated all the ready money to be found in monastic establishments and in addition demanded half of all clerical incomes. When a council of the English clergy ventured a protest, Edward flew into such a rage that the Dean of St. Paul's dropped dead of fright. To end these abuses, Boniface issued the bull *Clericis Laicos* in 1296, which began by stating that "the laity have been from the most ancient times hostile to the clergy," proceeded to remind temporal rulers that "all power over clergymen and over the bodies and property of clerical persons is forbidden to them," and concluded that all persons taxing the clergy without papal consent "shall incur the sentence of excommunication by their very act." The response to this papal declaration of independence was prompt and effective. Philip persuaded his archbishops to protest to the pope that clergy who did not pay taxes for national defense were looked on by the people as traitors. In addition, he prohibited the export of gold and silver from France, thus cutting off a substantial part of the papal revenues. In England, Edward's chief justice declared: "Henceforth there shall be no justice meted out to a clerk in the court of the lord king; however atrocious be the injury which he may have suffered. But sentence against a clerk shall be given at the instance of all who have a complaint against him." These drastic measures seem to have had the support of public opinion in both France and England, and Boniface, hampered by rebellion in Italy and opposition in Germany, was forced to back down. In 1297 he admitted that a king might tax his clergy without papal consent in a great emergency for the defense of the realm.

During the next three years Boniface strengthened his position in Italy and Germany. The papal jubilee of 1300 was a complete success; thousands of northern pilgrims flocked to Rome, and Boniface was greatly encouraged by this evidence of popular attachment to the See of Peter.

When Philip IV defied the Church anew by arresting a French bishop on a rather flimsy charge of treason, Boniface was determined not to yield again. Philip was also ready for a test of strength; he refused all compromise and neither negotiation nor threats could persuade him to release his prisoner. His ministers began to stir up public opinion against Boniface; inaccurate summaries of papal bulls were prepared which made it appear that the pope was claiming temporal sovereignty in France. In June, 1302, the prelates, barons, and representatives of the towns were summoned to Paris where they endorsed a protest against the pope's supposed attack on the liberties of the realm. Undaunted by the success of this propaganda, Boniface issued the bull *Unam Sanctam*, a strongly worded statement of the papal claim to supreme power. In it, Boniface asserted his right to overthrow disobedient kings, and concluded with the famous sentence: "We declare, proclaim and define that subjection to the Roman pontiff is absolutely necessary to salvation for every human creature."

Philip, who in his private life was a very pious man, was sure that his faith was as good as the pope's. He met *Unam Sanctam* by calling a great council in Paris and laying formal charges against Boniface before it. This document was drafted by Guillaume de Nogaret, the king's chief agent in ecclesiastical affairs, and is worth describing in some detail, since it is a typical example of the government propaganda of the period. It raked up all the old scandals about Celestine's abdication; it asserted that Boniface denied the immortality of the soul and the miracle of the Eucharist; it accused him of leading a foul and vicious life; it charged that he consulted his personal demon before making any decision, and ended with the statement that he hated Philip because the king was the glorious defender of the Catholic faith which the pope was trying to destroy. In short, Nogaret was using the pope's own weapons against himself; he was making the same kind of charges against Boniface which had destroyed Frederick II.

There was "evidence" to support all these charges, some of it based on depositions of Boniface's personal enemies, some of it built up from careless remarks made by the pope himself. For example, Boniface was said to have shouted in a fit of anger that he would rather be a dog than a Frenchman. This, of course, proved that he did not believe in the immortality of the soul, since a dog has no soul, while even the most miserable Frenchman has one. How far the council was convinced by such reasoning is hard to say. The lay members seem honestly to have believed that the pope was an enemy of France and that he wished to injure the kingdom in every possible way. The clerical members were less influenced by these semi-nationalistic arguments and were desperately anxious to avoid a scandal in the Church, but they were unable to resist the king's will. The combination of propaganda, patriotism, and royal pressure was effective, and the assembly demanded that a church council be called to try the pope. Such a request was not entirely unprecedented, but never before had it been anything but a formal move in the game of influencing public opinion. Nogaret was not content with mere words; he set out for Italy to arrest Boniface and bring him to France for trial. He gained the support of some of the pope's Italian enemies and surprised Boniface in his palace at Anagni. The attack was successful and Nogaret held the pope a prisoner for several days, while he pondered the insoluble problem of moving the most distinguished personage in Christendom halfway across Europe guarded only by a handful of mercenaries. Nogaret was rescued from his embarrassment by an uprising of the people of Anagni who freed the pope and expelled the Frenchman and his followers. For a moment it seemed that Boniface had succeeded in placing both Nogaret and Philip in a terribly compromising position, but the pope was in no condition to use his opportunity. The shock had been too great for a man of eighty-five, and he died shortly afterward, broken in body and spirit.

The fate of the medieval papacy depended upon the actions of Boniface's successor. Though respect for the papacy had decreased it had not vanished, and the outrage at Anagni provoked expressions of horror and disgust all over Europe. Dante, who detested the political ambitions of the papacy and longed for a revival of the Empire—Dante, who had been so outraged by the conduct of Boniface that he placed him in one of the lower circles of Hell, nevertheless compared the events at Anagni to the Passion. "Christ is made captive in the person of his Vicar . . . I see him once more derided; I see the vinegar and the gall renewed, and himself done to death between living robbers. I see the new Pilate so merciless. . . ." A vigorous pope might have taken advantage of this reaction and saved the independence of the papacy. The cardinals, however, could see no chance of securing secular allies strong enough to defeat Philip and were unwilling to run the risks of independent action. They elected a man of compromise, Benedict XI, who absolved Philip while refusing forgiveness to Philip's agent, Nogaret. Benedict lived less than a year after his election, and his death was followed by another deadlock in the college of cardinals. After eleven months a French archbishop, Clement V, was elected. Though we have no direct evidence, Clement's conduct as pope indicates that he owed his office to French influence. The first great decision of his pontificate demonstrated his weakness. Though he had started for Rome on hearing of his election, he interrupted his journey at Lyons and soon made it plain that he had no intention of crossing the Alps. Pressure from Philip, fear of the hazards of Roman political life, and natural attachment to his native land all played a part in this decision, and the fact that he could be influenced by such considerations showed that Clement was not the man to rescue the papacy from its dangerous position.

Clement soon discovered that he had purchased physical safety at the price of spiritual servitude. Nogaret continued to manufacture evidence against Boniface and to demand a public investigation of the life and beliefs of the dead pope. Determined to avoid scandal at all costs, Clement retreated step by step. He explained away the obnoxious sections of Boniface's bulls; he let Philip tax the clergy year after year, and finally, in 1311, he exonerated the king and freed his agents from excommunication. He even declared that Philip had shown "praiseworthy" zeal in accusing Boniface and had fulfilled the duties of a Christian ruler. This act marked the end of the medieval papacy. "The extraordinary thing about the episode at Anagni," as Renan says, "is not the fact that the pope was successfully ambushed. It is rather that the attack produced durable results, that the papacy collapsed at one blow, that the papacy apologized to the sacrilegious king." The Church had lost its political leadership; it could argue and protest, but it could no longer command the powerful kings of the West.

As soon as he saw that Clement was yielding on the question of Boniface VIII, Philip began to push his advantage. Nogaret trumped up charges of heresy against the Templars and forced the pope to take them seriously by threatening independent action. The order had lost its excuse for existence with the collapse of the kingdom of Jerusalem, and its members were deeply immersed in worldly affairs, but its real crime was that of possessing wealth which the king coveted. Once again Clement acted to avoid scandal and suppressed the order, though its guilt was not completely proved. At the same time he made certain that the papal exile from Rome would be prolonged by filling the college of cardinals with Frenchmen and by choosing a permanent residence at Avignon. This city, technically in the Empire, was separated from France only by the river Rhône, and was thoroughly French in culture. It was a much more comfortable and secure place to live than Rome, but comfort and security did not make up for loss of prestige. With the establishment of the papal court at Avignon the "Babylonian Captivity" of the Church began, to last until 1377.

THE GROWTH OF SECULAR LEADERSHIP
IN FRANCE

The struggle of Philip the Fair and Edward I with Boniface VIII has been discussed at length, both because of its significance in the history of the papacy and because it illustrates the policies and methods of the more powerful secular rulers of the period. The kings of France and

England were determined to have no rivals in the political leadership of their own countries. They would allow subordinate powers to exist, as long as they conformed to the general policy of the central government, but they would not tolerate coördinate powers, which might oppose the royal will. The nobles and burgesses might retain limited rights of local government, if they admitted that they held those rights subject to royal supervision and guidance. The clergy might administer their own affairs, punish sinners, and deal with matters of marriage and wills in their own courts, if they would admit that the king could determine the limits of their jurisdiction. But bishop, baron, and commune must realize that the interests of the king were paramount and that all their rights were subordinate to the welfare of the realm. A general law, made for the common good, overrode all local customs; a general tax, levied for defense, overrode all privileges. From the point of view of the royal governments, the struggle with Boniface was merely an episode in the long campaign to give the king a monopoly of political leadership in his realm. They could not have defeated Boniface if they had not already subdued most of their lesser rivals for leadership, and they could not have profited from the victory if they had not been prepared to continue their drive for political power.

The purposes of Philip IV and Edward I were almost identical, but they could not use the same means and they did not achieve the same results. France was less united than England; it was a country in which royal government had been superimposed on fully developed provincial institutions and customs. Most laymen had not yet realized the significance of this change and were still more interested in provincial laws and privileges than in the work of the central government. In one respect this made the work of centralization easier, since even the nobles were not apt to combine on a nationwide scale to oppose the king. In many other ways it made the task more difficult. No common formula could be used in applying an administrative decision or in collecting a tax, since each province had its own institutions and customs. No one central assembly could speak for all France, or even for all Frenchmen of a given class. Local communities could not be trusted to perform routine acts of administration, since the methods of the central government were foreign to them. Work which could be done in England by the county courts and the local juries had to be done in France by royal officials. As a result, the French government was much more complicated and much more bureaucratic than the English. General policies were determined by the king, in consultation with a small group of professional administrators. The application of these policies was left to the thousands of officials scattered about the country—bailiffs, seneschals, revenue collectors, attorneys, special commissioners, and policemen. These men were drawn from both the nobility and the middle class and some of them had been trained in Roman or canon law. They combined the force-fulness of a military class with the practicality of a bourgeois and the shrewdness of a lawyer. They adhered to the strict letter of the law when it favored the king, and invoked general principles of royal sovereignty when legal precedents were unsatisfactory. They magnified royal power in every possible way so that they themselves could become powerful and wealthy. Their strong *esprit de corps* made them justify each other's actions and enabled officials drawn from the lesser nobility to work smoothly with officials of bourgeois origin. Even a St. Louis might have had trouble in controlling this formidable instrument, and Philip IV seems to have been content to let it work without restraint for his own aggrandizement.

It was not too difficult to assert royal authority in the interior of the kingdom. Bishops, barons, and communes were too weak to resist the king as individuals, and they never succeeded in combining against him. Local rulers learned that they must make their acts conform to the wishes of royal officials, that they must allow a wider field to royal justice, and that they must pay large sums of money to the royal treasury. Those who refused to learn this lesson were so harassed by investigations and law-suits that they often found it necessary to sell or surrender their rights. On the frontiers this policy was not quite so successful. Philip's agents tried to break down the authority of the English king in Aquitaine and to weaken the count of Flanders by encouraging appeals from local courts to Paris, by taking enemies of the king or count under their pro-tection, and by inflicting heavy fines on English or Flemish officials for supposed breaches of the law. This led to ten years of war, first with England and then with Flanders, and put a heavy strain on Philip's resources. He was unable to win a decisive victory against either oppo-nent, though he gained some border towns in Aquitaine and a strip of Flanders which included the wealthy town of Lille. On the eastern fron-tier the legalistic technique of aggression worked better. The Empire could not defend its subjects and the petty princes who held fiefs along the French border dared not resist their powerful neighbor. Philip an-nexed Franche-Comté and Lyons, and even established his suzerainty over parts of Lorraine.

This policy of expansion imposed an enormous burden on the royal treasury and many of Philip's policies were dictated by his need for money. His struggle with the Church began because he wanted to tax the clergy. He forced the pope to suppress the order of the Temple be-cause he wanted to confiscate its property. He expelled the Jews in 1306 in order to seize their credits and personal possessions. He repeatedly altered the value of the currency in order to increase his profits from coinage; the chroniclers considered this the greatest catastrophe of the reign. The royal courts were used to extort money from wealthy subjects;

again and again we read of men who swear that they are innocent but who offer the king a few hundred or a few thousand pounds in order to have peace.

These expedients were ingenious and profitable, but they did not furnish enough money to pay for the great wars of the reign. Philip had to impose general taxes throughout the crucial years of the struggle with England and Flanders. Taxation was no more popular in France than in England, and Philip, like an English king, had to bargain with his subjects in order to collect his money. Unlike an English king, he could not conduct his negotiations through a central assembly, and this fact is a striking illustration of the difference between the governments of the two countries. Philip always consulted his council before imposing a tax, but the council was so subservient to the king that its consent to taxation did not impress the country. As a result, Philip had to send agents all through France to negotiate with powerful individuals and with local assemblies of clerics, nobles, and burgesses, before he could collect a tax. These negotiations took a great deal of time, and frequently reduced the tax-rate below the level which the king desired. Philip must have envied the English government, which could obtain a general tax from a single central assembly, but in the end the inefficient French system proved more favorable to the development of royal power. The local assemblies which granted taxes were much weaker than Parliament, and opposition to taxation was ineffective because it was divided.

It may seem strange that Philip did not use the Estates-General, which originated in his reign, as a means of securing consent to taxation. The lack of unity in France, and the circumstances in which the Estates-General were first called explain this omission. No central assembly could speak for all France, or override the privileges of provinces and classes. Moreover, the Estates-General had a purely passive position in the structure of the French government. They were not associated with the executive council and the highest law-court, as was the English parliament; they were merely a sounding-board for royal propaganda. The first session of the Estates-General was held in 1302, to hear the charges brought against Boniface VIII; the next meeting was held in 1308 to hear the charges against the Templars. In neither case did the delegates have any freedom of action; they were "to do what the king and council shall ordain," or "see the justice of the king." By summoning them, Philip gained the appearance of public support and spread his ideas throughout the country, but he did not expect them to criticize or modify his policy. In 1314 he summoned delegates of the towns to Paris to hear his reasons for a new tax, but all the evidence shows that he did not attach much importance to their consent. The tax was decreed in council before the assembly met, and the collectors were told to negotiate with local assemblies, even though the central assembly had approved the king's request.

Apparently the government hoped to influence public opinion by impressing leading citizens with the king's need for money, but realized that actual consent had to be secured from local groups. Given these precedents, it is not surprising that the Estates-General never obtained full power over taxation. Not until the middle of the fourteenth century did it become customary to seek consent to taxation in meetings of the Estates, and it was always possible to replace them with provincial assemblies if they proved recalcitrant.

Philip and his advisers had succeeded in strengthening the central government without creating a united opposition which might seek to control that government. They had carried the policy of Philip Augustus and St. Louis to a triumphant conclusion; the king, through his bureaucracy, ruled directly over France. This tradition of powerful monarchy and bureaucratic administration was so strongly established that it survived all the disasters of the later Middle Ages. For the next five hundred years every powerful French ruler followed the system of government perfected under Philip IV. But the king and his ministers had paid a high price for their success. To rule France they had created a bureaucracy that rapidly became inbred, self-seeking, and inefficient. They had forfeited the monarchy's old reputation for justice and they had established dangerous precedents in their haste to reach their goal. They hoodwinked public opinion instead of enlightening it; they had found it easier to pay lip-service to old ideals than to justify the new type of political organization. The government had gained its ends through chicanery, slander, blackmail and brute force, and its subjects were not slow to follow this example. The old devotion to the monarchy had been seriously weakened, and there was a noticeable decline in the prestige of the royal government during the fourteenth century. Philip himself died just in time to avoid a dangerous reaction against his policies. Discontented nobles formed provincial leagues to regain their old privileges, and in 1315 they forced the new king, Louis X, to issue a series of charters confirming their rights. Because the charters were issued to provincial groups, instead of to the baronage as a whole, they never gained the importance of Magna Carta, and the government was able to evade most of the restrictions which they imposed. Yet, while the movement was a failure in the long run, it had important consequences for Philip's immediate successors. The discontented nobles had to be conciliated and their influence on both the central and the local governments increased. A new feudalism arose in France, which would not have been tolerated if the people had not lost much of their faith in royal government. This feudal reaction, in turn, was responsible for many of the disasters of the Hundred Years' War. Only when the nobles had demonstrated their political incompetence was France ready to return to the principle of strong monarchy. Philip and his advisers had gained little by their haste to complete the structure of royal authority; it was a century and a half before another French king could wield the power which Philip had claimed.

THE GROWTH OF SECULAR LEADERSHIP IN ENGLAND

With the experience of six centuries as a guide, it is easy for us to see that England in 1300 was very different from France. Foreign observers at the end of the thirteenth century were more impressed by the resemblances between the two countries. Both kingdoms were united under strong central governments which ruled through a bureaucracy of lawyers and clerks. It is true that the English bureaucrats were somewhat less numerous and powerful than those of France, but under Edward I this distinction was rapidly being effaced. In both countries the kings were interfering with the rights of the clergy, attacking feudal privileges, and seeking to annex the weak states on their frontiers. Edward employed dubious interpretations of the law to increase his power just as readily as did Philip—witness his attempt to use a very shaky claim of overlordship to subdue Scotland. Like Philip, he resorted to force when legal quibbling failed. The existence of Parliament seems to us an important difference between the two countries, but it did not impress men of the thirteenth century. The English Parliament and the French Parlement resembled each other in functions as well as in spelling. Both were primarily high courts of justice. It is true that Edward used his Parliament for other purposes, but that was a matter of convenience rather than necessity and did not affect the main structure of his government. Philip the Fair and Edward I differed greatly in character and personality, but since they were seeking the same ends and using very much the same means, there were naturally certain similarities in their governments.

The great difference between England and France lay in the history rather than in the aspirations of the two monarchies. England had been united long before France; provincial loyalties hardly existed and provincial customs had been overridden by the common law. The privileged classes had been forced to deal directly with the central government and had gradually learned that they must unite if they were to save any of their privileges. On the other hand, the kings had created a centralized government before it was possible to create a bureaucracy and therefore had relied on the unpaid services of the landholding class for much of the work of local administration. Even a strong king might have found it hard to deal with a united aristocracy which had great influence in local government, and for almost a century there were no strong kings in England. While Philip Augustus and St. Louis were carrying the prestige of the French monarchy to new heights, Richard, John, and Henry III were losing the confidence of the English upper classes. The privileged groups found it easy to unite and to impose limitations on the king. Repeated rebellions established the supremacy of law and the right of the baronage to be consulted on important changes in policy.

The reign of Edward I can be understood only in the light of this tradition of successful resistance to royal authority. Edward was surpassed by no ruler of his age in energy, intelligence, and desire for power, but he could not ride roughshod over the rights of his subjects. He was no more scrupulous than Philip the Fair, but he had to be more careful about observing the law and had to pay more attention to public opinion. To his contemporaries, Edward was great because he perfected English law, reformed the English administrative system, and conquered Wales and Scotland. To most modern historians Edward is great because he developed Parliament as an agency for expressing and influencing public opinion.

As a legal reformer Edward has often been called the "English Justinian." The comparison is apt, for Edward, like Justinian, was a codifier rather than an innovator. English law had developed rapidly in the thirteenth century; the chancery had created many new writs and the judges, through their decisions, had worked out many new principles of law. As is usual in a period of rapid change, development had been uneven and uncoördinated. Some problems had never been settled, and others were obscured by contradictory decisions. Edward, in the first half of his reign, tried to make the law reasonably complete and self-consistent through a series of great codifying statutes. In the words of the Canon of Oseney: "Edward revived the ancient laws which had slumbered through the disturbance of the realm; some corrupted by abuse he restored to their proper form; some less evident and apparent he declared; some new ones, useful and honorable, he added." These codes had two important effects. Since they were almost the first English statutes, they set a precedent for changing the law by formal legislative enactment rather than by judicial and administrative decisions. The chancellor and the judges continued to interpret, and thus to modify, the law but they never again possessed the freedom to make law which they had enjoyed in the thirteenth century. This limitation on the power of the judges in turn put a stop to the intrusion of principles of Roman law into the English legal system. The great English judges of the thirteenth century were churchmen who knew a good deal of canon and civil law, and who used this knowledge in determining cases which came before them. Judges of the fourteenth century, limited by statutes and precedents, studied only the English law and paid little attention to foreign systems.

One idea runs through all of Edward's statutes: the determination to extend the royal power and to give the king direct control over all the men in the realm. For example, the Statute of *Quia Emptores* forbade subinfeudation in the future, and so, through a slow process of sale and exchange, practically all land in England came to be held directly of the king. Ignoring existing feudal relationships, Edward ordered all men with a certain income to become knights and to serve him in emergencies. Religious houses were forbidden to acquire land without license, or to send money to foreign superiors. The powers of church courts were defined and limited, and Edward attempted to do the same thing for feudal courts through the Statute of Gloucester or *Quo Warranto*. This act required feudal lords to show documentary evidence for every right of jurisdiction which they claimed, but it stirred up such opposition that it was not wholly effective. When questioned by the royal commissioners Earl Warenne unsheathed his sword and said: "Here is my warrant. My ancestors won their lands with the sword and with my sword I will defend them against all usurpers." Edward realized that he had gone too fast and allowed the lords to keep their ancient privileges, contenting himself with recovering a few of the more recent usurpations. *Quo Warranto*, however, proved useful in preventing any reform of baronial courts which might have made them more popular. The nobles were restricted to the rights which they had claimed under Edward and this definition made future development impossible. Edward could safely leave the rest to time. Feudal courts, restricted to obsolete procedures, could not compete with royal courts, which could adapt themselves to new situations.

Edward's desire to increase royal power is demonstrated not only by his statutes, but also by the administrative system which he perfected. As we have seen, the older departments of government, such as the Exchequer and Chancery, had become more or less autonomous during the thirteenth century. They had their own traditions and routine; they were always slow and often inefficient. A king who wanted to act rapidly and secretly, who wanted to impress his own personal policy on the government, needed other instruments. Edward found these instuments in various branches of the Royal Household. The Household was composed of the personal servants and companions of the king and it had always had certain financial and secretarial duties. It paid for the king's food and traveling expenses; it handled his private correspondence; it supplied him with messengers and envoys. Since the line between private and public business was never very sharply drawn in the Middle Ages, it was easy for Edward to expand the functions of the Household until it performed the greater part of the work of government. The Wardrobe, which was the financial branch of the household, became the principal royal treasury. Most of the king's income went to the Wardrobe instead of to the Exchequer and most payments, especially in time of war, were made by the Wardrobe. The Privy Seal, which was kept in the Wardrobe, replaced the Great Seal, which was controlled by the chancellor, as the means of authenticating the king's personal commands. At the same time Household clerks were used to carry verbal orders from the king to his officials and subjects. Thus Edward could control the entire administration through his friends and dependents, while the great public bureaus were left with only routine work to perform.

Edward found this new administrative system especially useful in time of war. His own aggressive foreign policy in the British Isles, and the equally aggressive policy of Philip IV toward Aquitaine, kept England involved in hostilities during more than half the reign. On the continent Edward usually remained on the defensive. He did as little fighting as possible with his own troops and tried to divert Philip's attention from Aquitaine by encouraging the count of Flanders and the princes of western Germany to attack the northeastern frontier of France. Philip IV defeated both the English and their allies but lacked the resources necessary to exploit his victory, and Edward retained most of Aquitaine. This struggle settled none of the real issues between the two countries and was little more than a dress rehearsal for the Hundred Years' War. In Great Britain, on the other hand, Edward's wars left a lasting impression. He was determined to be master of the whole island, and so turned his attention first to the Welsh, who had become practically independent during the reigns of his weak predecessors. Llewelyn, Prince of Wales, had gained the support of most of his countrymen, and on Edward's accession felt strong enough to evade his feudal obligations to the English king. In 1277 Edward lost patience and began a struggle which lasted intermittently for over five years. Finally the country was subdued, and in 1284 the Statute of Wales imposed English law and the English administrative system on the Celtic province. In 1301 the title of Prince of Wales was conferred on Edward's heir, establishing a precedent which has endured to this day.

Wales was permanently subdued, but Scotland proved a more formidable problem. English kings claimed feudal suzerainty over their northern neighbors but this claim had no practical results until 1290, when Scotland was left without a direct heir to the throne. Edward insisted that his position as overlord gave him the right to decide among the rival claimants to the crown, and the Scots, to avoid a civil war, accepted his intervention. Edward selected John Balliol as king and attempted to dictate the new ruler's policies. Balliol soon tired of this interference, and in 1296 renounced his allegiance to the English king. Edward immediately marched on Scotland with a large army, deposed Balliol with little difficulty, and put his own officials in charge of the country. As a token of his conquest he carried back to England the famous Stone of Scone, on which the Scots kings had sat at their coronation. No sooner had Edward turned his back than the Scots rose under William Wallace and trounced the English soundly at Stirling Bridge.

Six years of strenuous effort passed before Wallace was captured and executed (1304), and two years later Robert Bruce began the struggle anew. Edward, now over seventy, spurred himself to the ordeal of another campaign, but died before he reached the border. With him passed all hope of subduing Scotland. Little survived of his efforts except the implacable hatred of Scot for Englishman which produced border raids and border ballads, and the alliance of Scotland with France, which was to be a thorn in the side of English kings for over two centuries.

THE DEVELOPMENT OF THE ENGLISH PARLIAMENT

The people of England admired Edward's vigorous leadership but there were times when his ambitions put a considerable strain on their loyalty. Frequent taxation was still considered a sign of avarice or extravagance, yet Edward's energetic foreign policy forced him to ask repeatedly for grants of taxes. Edward, as a good politician, realized that if his plans were to succeed he must make a special effort to conciliate the propertied classes, and his attempts to secure their support form one of the most interesting chapters of his reign. Like Philip the Fair, he found that he could swing public opinion to his side by calling large assemblies of influential men, but unlike Philip he combined these assemblies with meetings of the Parliament, the highest judicial and executive authority under the crown. The combination was unique in medieval Europe, and historians have long been puzzled by the peculiar nature of English representative institutions. They have not yet agreed on the causes of the remarkable development of Parliament under Edward I, and the account which follows represents merely a balancing of probabilities and not absolute certainty.

Parliament was first of all a very full meeting of the king's council. It was the direct descendant of the old *curia regis* and, as such, it could assist the king in any of his functions. Edward used his Parliament primarily to assist him in his judicial work. Difficult legal cases were sent to Parliament by other courts and hundreds of petitions asking the king to punish or admonish his officials, to pay his debts, to alter or enforce administrative rulings were brought up to Parliament every year. Most of this legal and administrative work was handled by the trained officials of the central government, though the magnates occasionally assisted them in hearing and determining petitions. Parliament also had the duty of giving the king advice on any problems which he laid before it. This was the work in which the prelates and barons showed the greatest interest. The development of the professional administrative services had removed the magnates from direct contact with the daily routine of government, but they had made it very plain under Henry III that they expected to be consulted when important decisions were reached. Edward, on the whole, followed the precedents of his father's reign and consulted the barons whenever he thought that their interests were involved. Laws dealing with technical legal questions or the regulation of coinage and commerce might be made by the king and his officials alone, but the magnates were usually given a chance to discuss statutes which touched such important matters as tenure and inheritance. Edward was also careful to consult the magnates on questions of war, peace, and alliances. It is difficult to determine how much influence the prelates and barons had on the decisions of the strong-willed king, but at least they were given an opportunity to ask for explanations and voice objections. By meeting the magnates in Parliament Edward was usually able to secure their support for his policies.

The development of Parliament up to this point was perfectly normal, and almost inevitable, considering the precedents which the aristocracy had established in the reigns of John and Henry III. But there were no equally compelling reasons for summoning the knights and burgesses to Parliament. There were only two precedents for this step, one in the revolutionary year of 1265 and one in the period of reconstruction in 1268 when the government was trying to heal the wounds left by the civil war. Edward's behavior during the first part of his reign shows that he did not feel himself bound by these abnormal actions. Both knights and burgesses were summoned in 1275, but during the next twenty years the burgesses never appeared in Parliament and the knights came only infrequently. These groups were not ignored—the merchants were consulted about commercial legislation and both knights and burgesses were summoned to provincial assemblies in 1283 to grant a tax—but they were not definitely associated with Parliament. Then, in 1295, Edward returned to the precedents of 1265, 1268, and 1275 and summoned town and shire representatives to a very full meeting of Parliament. This famous assembly has been given the name of the Model Parliament, an appellation which should not be taken too literally, but which contains an element of truth. Though many Parliaments of the latter part of the reign contained no knights or burgesses, these representatives were summoned much more frequently after 1295 than before, and their presence became customary rather than exceptional.

The reasons which led Edward to adopt this policy may be inferred from a study of the position of the knights and burgesses in Parliament. They took no part at all in the judicial work of the assembly and had almost as little to do with the determination of policy. Most of the important political decisions were made before they arrived or after they went home, and there are only two occasions when the preamble to a statute suggests that they were present when it was passed. On the other hand the knights and, after 1295, the burgesses were usually asked to consent to grants of taxes. Many scholars have argued that this was the chief, if not the only reason for summoning them to Parliament. There are, however, certain objections to this theory. On some occasions the knights and burgesses were not asked to grant taxes when they came to Parliament. As far as we can tell they did nothing in these sessions but listen to a few speeches and then go home. Moreover, while it was undoubtedly necessary for the king to discuss taxation with members of the upper classes, no rigid rule determined how this consultation should take place. It was evident that the consent of the magnates alone was not enough, but consent of the lesser landholders did not have to be obtained in Parliament. It could be secured through negotiations with local communities or provincial assemblies and Edward actually followed these methods in 1282 and 1283. The burgesses had no right to be consulted at all, since even the men of London could be tallaged at will. If the king consulted the knights and burgesses in Parliament, convenience and not necessity determined his policy. It was easier to meet the representatives of the lesser landholders all at once, instead of conducting tedious negotiations with each community. It was more efficient to tax the towns with their consent than to tallage them against their will. Since the number of royal officials was small, every tax-assessment had to be made with the assistance of the local communities, and obviously the assessment would be more honest if the people were convinced of the necessity of the tax. A meeting of Parliament offered a unique opportunity to instill this conviction. Overawed by the presence of the magnates, impressed by speeches of the king or his ministers, it was seldom that the knights and burgesses refused a tax or even haggled over the rate. Edward's method of obtaining consent to taxation in Parliament was far more efficient than the French system of negotiations with local communities, as is shown by the fact that his taxes were granted more frequently and at higher rates than those of Philip the Fair.

It seems quite possible that Edward's chief reason for summoning the knights and burgesses to Parliament was his desire to influence public opinion, or at least the opinion of the upper classes. This would explain why representatives were summoned to sessions in which no taxes were voted, and why the burgesses were called in, even though it was not legally necessary to obtain their consent to taxation. According to this theory Parliament, except for its judicial activities, was primarily an agency for royal propaganda. The most important objective of this propaganda was to make people willing to pay taxes, but other royal policies, such as the attack on ecclesiastical privileges, also needed popular support. In short, Edward used his Parliaments as a means of strengthening his position, and had no idea of sharing or limiting his power.

This attitude appears clearly in the crisis of 1297. In that year Edward had built up a powerful coalition of continental princes against Philip the Fair and was anxious to strike his enemy before treachery or bribery dissolved the alliance. Most of his barons disliked his plan of sending an English army to the Low Countries, but Edward was so anxious to press his advantage that he made one of his rare mistakes in gauging the strength of public opinion. He needed money for this expedition and, after a hasty consultation with his council and a few barons, he imposed a heavy tax on his subjects. This violation of recent precedent caused a violent protest, culminating in a threat of armed baronial revolt. After arguing as long as he dared, Edward yielded and agreed to seek confirmation of the tax in a full meeting of Parliament. But when his opponents tried to obtain a promise that he would ask the consent of the magnates, knights, and burgesses to all future taxes Edward balked. He did promise to ask the consent of the magnates and the "community of the realm," but this left him free to decide who spoke for the "community" and how they should be consulted. The promise, coupled with the precedents of the last half-century, established the principle that something more than the consent of the council was necessary, but it did not bind the king to ask for taxes only in Parliament. While most general taxes after 1297 were granted by the knights and burgesses in Parliaments, Edward's successors were still free to negotiate with separate classes, such as the merchants, or with special assemblies which were not Parliaments.

Yet, while Edward surrendered no power to Parliament and continued to use it for his own purposes, he had created a situation which his weaker succesors found hard to control. He had made Parliament the key to the English government. It was the highest court in the land, the center of the executive power, the meeting-place of the magnates, the usual tax-granting body and the chief agency for influencing public opinion. This concentration of functions was very convenient for Edward, but it could be very dangerous to a ruler who lost control of the great central assembly. If the magnates could gain control of Parliament and secure the support of the knights and burgesses, they could influence all the other branches of government and arouse public opinion against the king. This is exactly what happened during the century after Edward's death. The magnates slowly weakened the hold of the king's servants on Parliament and learned how to use the assembly for their own purposes. The knights and burgesses frequently supported the barons against the king and, in return, were allowed to initiate legislation favoring their interests. All the opponents of royal authority and royal policies could unite in Parliament, and thus the institution which Edward developed to increase his power became a means of restricting the power of his successors.

Edward left his son other problems besides that of controlling Parliament. In spite of heavy taxes, he had never succeeded in paying for his wars, and the country was practically bankrupt at his death in 1307.

Invasions and executions had not subdued the Scots, and the northern kingdom was in open rebellion against English domination. The English barons were not reconciled to government by the king's Household, and the ·whole country had been irritated by repeated taxation. Edward's ministers had not been as unscrupulous as those of Philip the Fair in increasing royal power, but there had been many petty tyrants and grafters in the royal administration. The death of Edward, like the death of his great rival Philip, was the signal for an aristocratic reaction. The kings of France and England had destroyed the leadership of the Church, but they had not succeeded in establishing their own leadership on a firm basis.

THE BABYLONIAN CAPTIVITY

The feudal reaction which followed the deaths of Philip the Fair and Edward I did not aid the Church to regain its lost leadership. The national monarchs had profited from a general loss of faith in ecclesiastical institutions to give a death-blow to the medieval papacy, but they were not responsible for the growing worldliness of European society, and the secular spirit was not dependent upon strong, centralized monarchies for its existence. No matter what their government, the people of Europe were suspicious of the international character of the Church, resentful of its interference in temporal affairs, and critical of its organization and personnel. It was natural enough that men who were feeling the first impulses of nationalism should lose faith in the old Christian commonwealth and that men absorbed in worldly interests should lose interest in the institution which led them to the other world. Much more dangerous was the fact that the Church failed to satisfy the intellectual and spiritual needs of people who were neither nationalists nor capitalists. Scholars had increasing difficulty in reconciling faith and reason and many of them gave up the task in despair. Thousands of pious men and women found the formal services of the Church inadequate and sought closer contact with God through the meditations and ecstasies of mysticism. Ordinary people, who could be neither scholars nor mystics, still felt vaguely that there was something lacking in their religious experiences and tried to stimulate their dwindling faith by artificial means. They flocked to revivals; they multiplied forms and ceremonies and frequently took refuge in grossly superstitious practices.

These conditions put the papacy on the defensive throughout the fourteenth century. The people felt that the organized Church was somehow to blame for their own mental and spiritual discomfort and greeted every attack on the hierarchy with ferocious joy. Even a line of saintly and statesmanlike pontiffs would have had trouble in meeting this situation, and the popes of the fourteenth century were not distinguished for

PALACE OF THE POPES, AVIGNON, 14th CENTURY

SIEGE OF A TOWN, 15th-CENTURY FRENCH MANUSCRIPT

MADONNA OF CHANCELLOR ROLIN, VAN EYCK, 15th CENTURY

MEDICI-RICCARDI PALACE, FLORENCE

•

PIERO DEI MEDICI
BY GOZZOLI

either quality. They were not bad men, compared with the popes of the early Middle Ages or of the Renaissance, but they were not the men whom the Church needed in a critical period. Skilful lawyers and able financiers, they perfected the judicial and fiscal organization of the Church, but they did little to restore the shaken faith of the people of Europe. In fact, they weakened the position of the Church still further by acts which were entirely justifiable from the point of view of worldly wisdom, and completely inexcusable from a religious point of view.

The most dangerous of these acts was the decision to remain at Avignon. There were many good reasons for this decision. Avignon and southern France were peaceful and prosperous, while Rome and central Italy were in a state of anarchy; at Avignon the pope was relatively free from political pressure, while in Italy he was forced to take part in a never-ending series of alliances, betrayals, and wars; France and not Italy was the center of European civilization and the chief source of papal revenues. But these arguments were more than counterbalanced by two simple facts. From the very beginning, papal prestige and authority had been connected with the great tradition of Rome. A pope who did not perform his most important functions in Rome had lost much of his spiritual dignity; an exile could hardly speak with authority. In the second place, ever since the surrender of Clement V to Philip the Fair, the people of Europe were convinced that a pope living at Avignon was little more than a functionary of the French king. This opinion was strengthened by the fact that the pope and a majority of the college of cardinals were French throughout the period of the Babylonian Cap-- tivity. It was useless to point out that Avignon was in the Empire and not in France, or that the fourteenth-century popes were less dependent on the French king than many of their predecessors. The charge of French influence was too valuable a weapon to be relinquished by the politicians who wanted to exalt national interests at the expense of Christian internationalism, and it was used repeatedly by enemies of the papacy.

In their attempts to meet the danger caused by the rise of powerful secular governments, the Avignonese popes strengthened the administrative system of the Church and weakened its spiritual authority. Since individual bishops and abbots were often dominated by lay rulers, the popes of the fourteenth century tried to centralize all important ecclesiastical business in their own court. Tribunals and bureaus were multiplied, and churchmen from all parts of Europe had to go to Avignon to settle their legal and administrative problems. This was an expensive and time-consuming practice, and reformers soon began to complain of the inefficiency and venality of the papal bureaucracy. Moreover, this elaborate administrative system created new expenses just as the old papal revenues were declining. Neither the Italians of the Papal States nor the people of England and the other vassal kingdoms were anxious to pay taxes or tribute to a pope who, they believed, was under French domination. Few pilgrims came to the unholy city of Avignon and there were consequently few voluntary contributions to the expenses of the papal court. The only sources of revenue which remained were taxation of ecclesiastics and sale of indulgences, and neither of these could be developed very far without causing scandal. Yet the Avignonese popes felt that they had to have money in order to preserve the independence of the Church and as a result they adopted financial expedients which proved disastrous in the long run.

Both the good and the bad side of the Avignonese period are epitomized in the pontificate of John XXII (1316–1334). He perfected the financial system which kept the Church solvent but undermined popular respect for the papacy. By the fourteenth century the pope had gained the right to appoint most of the higher officers of the Church and John found in this right an unending source of profits. "Expectancies" were sold which gave the buyer the right to expect appointment to an office when it became vacant—unless some one else should offer a higher sum. "Annates," the first year's income less expenses, had to be paid by ecclesiastics appointed to new offices by the pope. Heavy income taxes were imposed on all but the poorest of the clergy. The churchmen who paid these sums to the pope naturally tried to indemnify themselves by squeezing their subordinates, and in the end the parish clergy and the laity bore most of the burden of papal taxation. Heavy fines were imposed in ecclesiastical courts, full payment of tithes was demanded, and great pressure was put on laymen to make contributions when they were receiving the ministrations of the Church. In addition, the popes continued to make war on their Christian enemies while talking of crusades against the infidel, and they raised large sums of money for both their real and their imaginary expeditions. As the possibility of a real crusade diminished, the evils of indulgence-selling grew. Fantastic claims were made by ignorant agents and many religiously illiterate people came to believe that salvation, like everything else, could be bought for money.

It is not surprising that all the old attacks on the greed and dishonesty of the clergy were renewed and multiplied during the fourteenth century. "Whenever I entered the chambers of the ecclesiastics of the Papal Court, I found brokers and clergy engaged in weighing and reckoning the money which lay in heaps before them"—this from a zealous defender of the popes. Petrarch went further. Avignon, to him, was "the fountain of anguish, the dwelling-place of wrath, the school of errors, the temple of heresy, once Rome, now the false guilt-laden Babylon, the forge of lies, the horrible prison, the hell on earth." Parliament tried to keep the pope from making appointments to English benefices and spoke scornfully of the "sinful city of Avignon." The clergy of Cologne drew up a formal protest:

> In consequence of the exactions with which the Papal Court burdens the clergy, the Apostolic See has fallen into such contempt, that the Catholic faith in these parts seems to be seriously imperilled. The laity speaks slightingly of the Church, because, departing from the customs of former days, she hardly ever sends forth preachers or reformers, but rather ostentatious men, cunning, selfish and greedy. Things have come to such a pass, that few are Christian more than in name.

Discontent with the government of the Church was intensified by the protests of the Spiritual Franciscans and by the quarrels of John XXII with the Emperor Lewis the Bavarian. The Spiritual Franciscans disliked the compromise through which their order enjoyed the use, though not the technical ownership, of large amounts of property. They wished to return to the real poverty of their founder, and said that all ecclesiastics should do likewise, since Christ and his apostles had had no possessions. This idea horrified John, who felt that temporal possessions were absolutely necessary to the welfare of the Church, and he tried to cut it off at the root by declaring it heresy to teach that Christ owned no property. A long struggle followed, in which the Spiritual Franciscans, though defeated in the end, made many effective attacks on the papacy. Their General appealed to a future council "which in faith and morals is superior to the pope, since a pope can err . . . but the Universal Church cannot err, and a council representing the Universal Church is likewise free from error." This idea, elaborated by later writers, resulted in a vigorous attack on the papal monarchy in the early years of the fifteenth century. Other Franciscans took refuge with Lewis the Bavarian and helped to compose the anti-papal pamphlets which streamed from his court.

The political significance of the struggle between John XXII and the Emperor Lewis was very slight, since both the papacy and the Empire were mere shadows of their former selves. The two antagonists went through the time-honored forms; Lewis invaded Italy and set up an anti-pope in Rome, while John declared that Lewis had forfeited his throne and supported anti-kings in Germany. This shadow-boxing had little effect on the princes and cities who held the real power in Germany and Italy, but it was accompanied by a war of pamphlets which still further disturbed the already troubled minds of men of the fourteenth century. John's adherents made the most extreme claims for the temporal authority of the pope which were ever composed, but few people were impressed by their arguments. The political independence of secular rulers was an established fact and the events of the pontificates of Boniface VIII and Clement V could not be reversed by mere words. Far more important were the works of the anti-papal writers. These men justified a process which was already taking place; they gave Europeans good, logical excuses for rejecting clerical influence in temporal affairs. They completed the task of destroying the leadership of the Church and of wrecking the thirteenth century balance between reason and revelation.

The most important of these writers were William Ockham, Jean of Jandun, and Marsiglio of Padua. Ockham was an English philosopher who was not satisfied with the synthesis of secular learning and Catholic doctrine which had been constructed by Thomas Aquinas. In criticizing the work of his great predecessor, he became very sceptical about the possibility of discovering religious truth through the use of human reason. He did not deny the truth of the Christian faith, but asserted that men knew that faith only because God had willed it, and not because it was consonant with natural human reason. This emphasis on the importance of will rather than reason marked a profound change in European thinking and showed how completely the medieval system had disintegrated. Translated into politics, it meant that action rather than reflection, success rather than abstract justice were the qualities which were going to be honored for the next two centuries. Ockham was also a strong nominalist, that is, he denied that abstract ideas had any real existence and asserted that our only sure knowledge is of specific facts. According to this reasoning, the individual Christian is far more important than the artificial and unreal idea of Christendom. Thus one could conclude from Ockham's work that councils as well as popes might err, since truth was to be found only in Scripture and not in the abstraction called the Church.

Ockham's ideas were revolutionary, but they were expressed in the form of philosophical hypotheses which appealed only to scholars. Jean of Jandun and Marsiglio of Padua were as radical as Ockham and were more anxious to demonstrate the practical implications of their beliefs. The *Defensor Pacis*, which they completed in 1324, is the most important political writing of the later Middle Ages. Both Jean and Marsiglio had taught at the University of Paris and had been influenced by Ockham's nominalist philosophy. Jean had also studied Aristotle's *Politics* carefully, while Marsiglio seems to have drawn some of his ideas from his practical experience in Italian politics. Their book is a searching examination of the nature of government, spiritual as well as temporal. In politics they favored a limited monarchy, guided by the laws and customs chosen by the better element [1] among the citizens. A king who defied the basic laws of his country could be displaced by this group of leading citizens. This is an interesting theoretical expression of the tendency toward aristocratic parliamentary government which was evident in

[1] The Latin phrase here translated as "better element" is *valentior pars*.

every fourteenth century country. In religion they asserted that the Church was the whole body of the faithful and denied that the clergy had any coercive authority. Churchmen were physicians of the soul, as doctors were physicians of the body, but neither group of healers could claim the right to make law, to judge or to defy secular authority. The Church was merely one form of social activity, and, like all other activities, was to be subordinate to the state. Even questions of internal organization and discipline were to be determined by the prince, or by a council representing the whole body of the faithful. This was the first clear assertion of the supremacy of secular rulers over the Church, and it was studied diligently by all opponents of papal power for the next two centuries. Wycliffe, Huss, Luther and Calvin were all directly or indirectly indebted to the *Defensor Pacis.* The pope was naturally shocked by the book and damned Marsiglio and his followers as "monsters from the deeps of Satan and the sulphur pools of Hell."

The ideas brought forth by this last struggle between the papacy and the Empire were too extreme to be completely accepted in the fourteenth century. Secular rulers were having troubles of their own and were unwilling to take radical steps against the Church, while John's successors were anxious to restore the old working compromise between lay and ecclesiastical authority. So the storm gradually subsided, but the writings remained to torment the papacy in its next great crisis. Meanwhile, the popes of Avignon reaped the benefits of the fiscal system which John XXII had perfected. The centralization of Church government was completed, the administrative system was perfected, and a real effort was made to reconquer the lands of the Church in Italy. With all these expenses, there was still enough money left to establish a splendid court, and Avignon became a center of European art and literature. The Palace of the Popes, which was built at this time, is a testimony to the wealth, the artistic taste, and the worldly outlook of the Avignonese pontiffs. To the great Catholic scholar, Pastor, it symbolized the history of the Captivity:

> This gigantic pile stands on the rock of the Doms, and with its huge, heavy square towers, its naked yellowish-brown colossal walls, five yards in thickness and broken irregularly by a few pointed windows, is one of the most imposing creations of medieval architecture. In its strange combination of castle and cloister, prison and palace, this temporary residence of the popes reflects both the deterioration and the fate of the papacy in France. . . . The Palace of the Popes, in comparison with which the neighboring cathedral has an insignificant appearance, also manifests the decline of the ecclesiastical, and the predominance of the worldly, warlike, and princely element, which marked the Avignon period.[2]

[2] *History of the Popes* (London, 1891), Vol. I, p. 84.

While the popes were establishing themselves in luxury and seeming permanence at Avignon, the Patrimony of Saint Peter was sinking into misery and lawlessness. Some conception of the condition of the country-side may be gathered from one of Boccaccio's stories, in which he casually describes the depredations wrought by packs of wolves, the omnipresent bands of robbers, and the incessant wars of the barons as events so common as to need no special comment. Rome itself was reduced to poverty by the removal of the papal court and the cessation of pilgrimages. Buildings fell in ruins and cattle grazed in front of Saint Peter's and the Lateran. The miserable inhabitants of the decaying city consoled themselves with memories of their past greatness and insisted that the Roman people would yet again rule the world. Since the pope had moved the spiritual capital of Christendom to Avignon, they began to talk of making Rome a political capital by reviving the Republic. Soon a leader appeared who promised to fulfill all their aspirations. Cola di Rienzi was a strange mixture of prophet and charlatan, statesman and visionary. His eloquence and beauty enthralled the mob, while his plans for restoring order by ending the interminable feuds among the nobility gained him some support from the papal representatives. He was made Tribune and virtual dictator of Rome in 1347 and for a few months he seemed to have succeeded in reviving the prestige of the ancient Republic. But he soon disgusted every one by his exaggerated claims to authority both in Rome and in Europe, and before the year was out the people drove him from the city. Life in the Papal States became more violent than ever, until six years later, Cardinal Albornoz made a new effort to restore order. Albornoz was a skilful diplomat and an able soldier, but it took years of hard fighting to win even a partial victory. He forced the people to be obedient to the pope, but he could not build up real loyalty to an absentee ruler.

Fear that a sudden uprising might undo Albornoz' work forced the pope to consider the advisability of a return to Rome. This inclination was strengthened by the fact that Avignon was no longer the quiet refuge it had seemed earlier in the century. The Hundred Years' War had filled France with mercenary soldiers who soon found that organized pillage was more profitable than formal warfare. Their raids extended to the walls of Avignon, and the pope himself was forced to pay them tribute. Finally, Urban V (1362–1370) was a sincerely pious man who felt keenly the need of reform in the Church and the decline of papal prestige. By returning to Rome he hoped to gain the moral strength necessary for his two favorite projects—ecclesiastical reform and a crusade against the Turks. Despite the protests of his cardinals and of the French king, he set out in 1367 and was received with jubilation in Rome. For three years he battled manfully with the intricacies of Roman politics, but in the end, defeated and disillusioned, he returned to Avignon, where he died disconsolate. His successor, Gregory XI, though pious and quite conscious of the need for reform, naturally hesitated to make a second attempt, but he finally decided to risk the move to Rome. A few months in the Eternal City convinced him that he had made a mistake and he was preparing to flee when he died in 1378.

THE GREAT SCHISM

The papal conclave of 1378 is one of the most important in the history of the Church. Out of this election grew the Schism, and from the Schism came a host of evils from which the Church never entirely recovered. The details of the election are confused and the evidence we possess is full of contradictions, so there is still no certainty as to what actually happened. Only sixteen cardinals took part in the election; six others remained at Avignon and one was absent on papal business. The French had an overwhelming majority in the college, but they were divided by provincial jealousies, so that every one realized that it would be necessary to choose a compromise candidate. The situation was further complicated by the fact that most of the cardinals wished to return to Avignon, while the Roman populace was determined to put an end to the Captivity. All through the conclave a mob milled around the Vatican howling "a Roman, a Roman, we want a Roman for a pope or at least an Italian." Before the formal voting began a majority composed of the North French and Italian cardinals had agreed on the archbishop of Bari as the logical candidate, since he was an Italian and at the same time was thought to be a lover of Avignon. His election seemed certain when the conclave was disrupted by an invasion of the populace. The cardinals fled, but later in the day met secretly and formally ratified the choice of the archbishop, who took the title of Urban VI. The violence of the mob does not seem to have been a decisive factor in the election. Creighton, a modern Protestant scholar, says: "It would seem that there was some sense of popular pressure, but not enough to influence the conduct of the cardinals." The cardinals recognized Urban as a lawful pope after the mob had dissolved and reported to their colleagues at Avignon that they had voted "freely and unanimously."

Doubts began to appear only when Urban proved to be anything but the pliable tool they had anticipated. The cardinals had known him as a faithful and obedient subordinate, without initiative or program of his own—just the person to obey them in all things. They were soon undeceived. Urban's character was transformed or liberated by his elevation to power, and he became both a brutal autocrat and a fanatical reformer. Urban not only silenced harshly all suggestion of a return to Avignon but lectured the cardinals on their private lives, reduced their incomes, and humiliated them in public. The task of reforming the behavior of the cardinals would probably have exhausted the patience of a St. Francis, but Urban's irritability and violence made even St. Catherine of Siena cry out: "For the love of Christ, moderate a little the violent actions to which your nature drives you!" Under the circumstances, it was not difficult for the cardinals to convince themselves that Urban's election had been uncanonical and, after submitting to his tirades for a few months, they fled to Anagni, declared Urban no pope, and elected a Frenchman, Clement VII, who took up his residence at Avignon.

The action of the cardinals created an unparalleled situation. There had been schisms in the past, but it had always been easy to decide which of the rival claimants was the real pope. Never before had the college of cardinals declared that an election was illegal, and never before had Europe been so divided that neither candidate could gain the allegiance of a majority of the faithful. Politics dominated the decisions of rulers, and the division between the two obediences might have been predicted in advance from the alliances of the states of Europe. The French naturally supported the pope of Avignon, as did the Spanish kingdoms and Portugal. Scotland, the ancient ally of France, also accepted Clement, while England and Germany, as enemies of France, backed Urban. Most of Italy also supported the Roman pope, though some princes whom Urban had offended turned to Clement. The faithful were dismayed by a scandalous situation which provoked the mirth of Jews and Mohammedans, and soon the best minds of Europe began to search for a solution of the problem. The suggestions which were first made were of a frankly opportunist nature. It was proposed that both popes agree to appoint no more cardinals, so that in time one line would die out, but neither Urban nor Clement would consent to this. The rivals were also equally reluctant to resign, as such an action would impugn the legality of the election of the one who gave way. Each professed his willingness to resign simultaneously with his opponent, but this could be done only at a meeting of the two popes, and, whether from accident or design, projected meetings never took place.

As years went on and the Schism continued, the condition of the Church became increasingly desperate. Urban died in 1389 and Clement in 1394, but the cardinals of each camp promptly elected new popes, instead of profiting by these opportunities to heal the breach in the Church. It seemed as if Europe were to be divided forever between the two allegiances and gloomy prophecies were rampant. "They say that the world must be renewed," exclaimed a devout Catholic. "I say it must be destroyed." Many of the common people began to wonder whether the sacraments administered by either group of clergymen were valid, and some declared that no soul had entered heaven since the beginning of the Schism. The rival popes, engaged in a bitter political struggle, could spare little thought for reform. More than ever it was necessary to raise money by every possible means and to appoint prelates who were shrewd politicians and good businessmen rather than spiritual leaders. Conditions were worst in the unhappy dioceses of doubtful obedience where rival appointees fought for the possession of office, but even in the regions which were unquestionably loyal to Rome or to Avignon, there was a decline in ecclesiastical discipline and morality. Even the orthodox began to denounce both popes indiscriminately, because they were refusing to make any sacrifice for the good of Christendom. "The pope today is Anti-Christ!" declared an English knight. "Your bishops and prelates are the members of the beast, and the friars are his tail." Other men were so disgusted with the situation that they broke with the Church entirely, and heresy became a problem for the first time since the suppression of the Albigensians.

The intellectual father of the most dangerous heresies of the late fourteenth century was an English professor, John Wycliffe.[3] Like Ockham, Wycliffe insisted on the importance of the Scriptures and denounced traditions and authorities which seemed to him to contradict the clear meaning of the Bible. Like Marsiglio, he denied the superiority and special sanctity of the clergy and taught that lay rulers had the right to correct the Church when it erred. Like the Spiritual Franciscans, he denounced the wealth of the Church and suggested that secular authorities would do well to confiscate it. In defending these positions he fell into some doctrinal heresies—for example, he denied the orthodox view about transubstantiation—but his chief attack was on the government and privileges of the Church. As the Schism developed, he rejected the authority of the pope and claimed that Christ was the only Head of the Church. He denounced the sale of indulgences and asserted that the whole system of penance and absolution had become a mechanical performance which had no spiritual validity. There was nothing very new in what he taught, but the troubled conditions of Europe gave him greater influence than his predecessors.

The English aristocracy, already resentful of papal financial demands, supported him even before the Schism began, and the breach in the Church gave him a chance to spread his doctrine among the people. "Poor priests" went through the country, teaching a radical version of his beliefs, and made many converts. His insistence on the importance of the Scriptures led to English translations of the Bible which were widely read. The pope made several efforts to have him condemned, but he was supported by so many powerful Englishmen that he was never seriously disturbed, and died in peace in his rectory of Lutterworth. His followers, the Lollards, were severely persecuted after the change of

---

[3] His name has also been spelled "Wyclif," "Wiclif," or "Wyclyf." The last form is most common in contemporary documents, but the spelling used in the text is found in most modern books and it seems unnecessary to insist on an unfamiliar form.

dynasty in 1399, but while the movement was driven underground it was never entirely extinguished. Scholars disagree as to the influence of the Lollards on the English Reformation, but there is no doubt that they still existed in the sixteenth century and that they took part in the next great attack on Rome.

Wycliffe's influence was even greater in the distant kingdom of Bohemia than it had been in his own land. The Czechs were naturally inclined toward heresy, since Catholicism had been brought in by German overlords and seemed to many of them a symbol of the domination of Teuton over Slav. The fourteenth century kings of Bohemia, though foreigners, had encouraged the growth of nationalism in their efforts to build up a strong state. Charles IV, the ablest of the Luxemburg dynasty, had encouraged popular preachers who attacked the morals of the clergy and the administration of the Church. Charles had also founded the University of Prague, and this institution, originally dominated by Germans, soon became a center of Czech nationalism and a breeding-place of religious reformers. The Bohemians were already criticizing the Church when Wycliffe's writings were brought to Prague by scholars who had studied at Oxford. They rapidly became popular, for they supported ideas which the Czechs had been working out by themselves. John Huss, rector of the university and already a leader of the movement for clerical reform, was especially stimulated by Wycliffe's work and soon found himself in open conflict with the Church. Like Wycliffe, he began with attacks on the abuses of clerical power and was led on until he was forced to deny the authority on which the power was based. Against the tradition and doctrine of the Church, he asserted the right of the individual to work out his own belief from a study of the Bible. Huss was supported at first by the king and many of the clergy, but as he passed from reform to heresy, he lost their support. His opponents denounced him to the pope, who condemned the doctrines of Wycliffe and excommunicated Huss. This action had very little effect. Huss always thought of himself as a good Catholic and failed to see that his insistence on the rights of the individual conscience must be branded as heresy by the Church. As for the Czechs, they were ready to follow Huss whether he were a heretic or a saint. He was attacking intolerable abuses among the clergy, he was giving them a religion which stirred their hearts, and he was opposing the hated foreigners. Most of Bohemia was Hussite in the early years of the fifteenth century, and the orthodox Catholics who remained were unable to turn the tide.

THE COUNCILS AND THE PAPAL RESTORATION

The situation of the Church about 1400 seemed hopeless. The Schism had lasted for twenty-two years and showed no signs of healing; England was full of heretics; Bohemia was almost ready to break away; and even the orthodox were denouncing the Church with unparalleled vigor. Some historians have claimed that the Church was far weaker, far more corrupt in 1400 than in 1500, and have wondered why the Reformation was delayed for a century. The only answer that can be given to this question is that the Middle Ages were dying but were not yet dead. The rulers of Europe were not quite ready to stand alone or to assert openly that religion was merely a branch of politics. The people of Europe were not quite ready to abandon their old belief in the unity of Christendom. It was possible to make one last effort to save the Church. That effort resulted in the Conciliar Movement.

The idea of rescuing the Church by calling a council which would be independent of both popes originated in the University of Paris. That fact alone shows how desperate the situation was. Paris, for generations, had been the stronghold of orthodox theology, the supporter of papal monarchy. But the papal monarchy had failed, and the scholars of the university began to examine the history of the Church to see if they could find any other basis for its government. First tentatively, then with more vigor and courage as the Schism wore on, theologians like Gerson and Pierre d'Ailly argued that the Church needed something like parliamentary government. History and natural law, they said, proved that general councils of prelates and scholars, representing the Universal Church, had final authority to determine the articles of the faith and the forms of ecclesiastical government. Since the popes could not heal the Schism, a council composed of the better elements of the Church should take up the task. The council should also reform the Church, both morally and politically, so that a catastrophe such as the Schism could not recur. These beliefs slowly gained ground, but one great difficulty blocked the acceptance of the theologians' solution. Who had the right to call a council, and who should preside over it in the absence of a universally recognized pope? Scholars wrestled with this problem in closely reasoned volumes, but produced no generally acceptable solution. At last the cardinals became alarmed by the growing radicalism of the discussion. An attack on the papal monarchy was an attack on them, since practically all their power came from delegations of papal authority. To save the situation, most of the cardinals of both obediences abandoned their masters and issued a call for a council to meet at Pisa. This action met with wide approval and, in 1409, an imposing assemblage set about the task of healing the Schism. The rival popes were deposed and after long argument it was decided that a new pope should be elected by a two-thirds majority of each college of cardinals who were to elect "in place of the council." This evasive phrase showed that the council was not quite sure of its own power but was still unwilling to abandon the idea of conciliar supremacy. The cardinals elected the archbishop of Milan, who was acceptable to both sides because he was a Greek and therefore not strongly committed to either of the deposed popes.

The jubilation aroused by the election of Alexander V was short-lived. Neither of the deposed pontiffs recognized the legality of the Council of Pisa, and both excommunicated the adherents of Alexander. The attempt to heal the Schism had created a new breach in the Church; there were now three popes instead of two. The prestige of the Pisan party was further impaired when, on the death of Alexander V in 1410, the cardinals elected John XXIII, a famous Italian warrior, an excellent general, but scarcely an edifying Vicar of Christ. John did his best to gain support by appointing some of the ablest theologians of Europe to the college of cardinals, but scandalous stories of his private life continued to circulate. Moreover, the Council of Pisa had been unsuccessful in dealing with the problems of ecclesiastical reform and the suppression of heresy, and John was too busy fighting in Italy to devote much time to his spiritual functions. The cry for a council recommenced, with more vigor than ever. The avowed determination of the conciliar party to impose permanent checks on papal power naturally made John reluctant to assemble the fathers of the Church again, but in 1411 the reform party secured the aid of the Emperor Sigismund. The advocates of conciliar supremacy had been troubled because the traditional way of summoning a council was through a papal proclamation, which in itself was a recognition of the pope's power over the Church. The expedient of letting the cardinals call a council had not proved too successful, and it was evident that the support of secular rulers was necessary if the reform movement was to continue. Sigismund saw in this situation an opportunity to revive the power and prestige of the Empire and may even have hoped to put the ideas of Marsiglio of Padua into practice. Accordingly, after recognizing John as the true pope, he demanded the calling of a council. John resisted until his position in Italy became so weak that he could not risk the displeasure of the emperor. In 1413 he met Sigismund at Lodi, and there the pope and emperor issued a call for a council to meet in the following year at Constance. The choice of an imperial city showed Sigismund's strength and John's weakness; it meant that it would be very difficult for the pope and his officials to dominate the assembly.

For four years the little Swiss town was the capital of Christendom. The Council of Constance was no mere assembly of prelates, but a European Congress in which representatives of kings and princes had as much influence as bishops and learned doctors of the universities. The spiritual, intellectual, and political leaders of Europe had united in one last effort to preserve the medieval Church. They were agreed that three things were needed: the healing of the Schism, the reformation of the Church "in head and members," and the elimination of heresy. Most of them believed that this program could not be achieved without imposing severe limitations on papal power, and John was aware of the danger even before he reached Constance. The fierce old warrior punctuated his passage over the Alps by gusts of anger, in which the language of the guard-room took on a heightened vividness by contrast with his pontifical robes. At his first glimpse of Constance, lying between its lake and the protecting wall of mountains, he exclaimed, between terror and cynical amusement, "A trap for foxes!"

The problem first attacked by the council was the one on which there was the least divergence of opinion: the suppression of heresy as represented by John Huss of Bohemia. Prelates and scholars were agreed that the Hussite movement must be broken, and the Czechs had no political influence to use against the representatives of orthodox theology. The Emperor Sigismund, as heir to the Bohemian crown, was naturally worried by the turmoil in his future dominions, while the German princes were annoyed by the anti-Teutonic character of the heresy. However, at first neither party thought that extreme measures would be necessary. Sigismund asked Huss to appear at Constance to answer the charge of heresy and sent him an imperial safe-conduct for the journey. Huss consented gladly, confident that he could convince the council of the reasonableness and orthodoxy of his position. To his surprise, he no sooner appeared at Constance than he was placed under surveillance and shortly afterward imprisoned. Sigismund protested this violation of the imperial safe-conduct, but the council stood fast on the ancient contention that "neither by natural, divine nor human law was any promise to be observed to the prejudice of the Catholic faith." The emperor's attitude changed when Huss stated that if he had not wished to come to Constance no human power could have forced him to appear. This challenge to royal power so irritated Sigismund that he washed his hands of the whole affair. The council itself was not anxious to execute Huss, and for many months every effort was made to induce him to admit his errors and recant. With full knowledge of the consequences of a refusal he stood fast. "I stand before the judgment seat of God," he cried, "who will judge both you and me after our deserts." Finally, when all persuasion failed to move him, he was condemned and burned. The council, representing medieval Catholicism, could have done nothing else, since it was still generally believed that a heretic was the most dangerous of all criminals. But the fifteenth century was not the thirteenth, and the people of Bohemia were not ready to accept the sacrifice of a national leader for the sake of Christian unity. Neither the execution of Huss nor that of his chief lieutenant, Jerome of Prague, a year later, put an end to the Bohemian heresy. The Czechs rebelled against their German king as well as against the Catholic Church, and for over a generation maintained their political and religious independence. Though Bohemian resistance collapsed in the second half of the fifteenth century, Hussite beliefs were not blotted out of existence. In Bohemia, as in England, embers of revolt remained which were fanned into flame by the storm of the Reformation.

On the question of the extirpation of heresy there was little division in the council. There remained the thorny questions of the Schism and reform. John XXIII wished to have his own title confirmed and his two rivals deposed anew, but he realized that many leaders of the council felt that reform should begin with a careful examination of his own actions. To prevent hostile moves he had brought a host of Italian prelates in his train, confident that their votes would enable him to dominate the council. To his dismay, the non-Italian members, led by Sigismund, insisted on the revolutionary idea of voting by nations rather than by head. This innovation represented more than mere distrust of John; it was an indication of the growing national feeling which was dividing Europe into political units suspicious of one another and hostile to the supra-national position of the Church. The division by nations gave powerful rulers an excellent opportunity to influence the voting, and embassies from the kings of France and England frequently determined the decisions of the council. John's alarm was heightened by pointed remarks about his fitness for office, and in 1415 he sought to wreck the council by fleeing from Constance. He almost succeeded; only the cool-headedness of Sigismund calmed the panic-stricken delegates. Once reassured, the council took the offensive and voted that "this Synod, lawfully assembled in the Holy Ghost, forming a general council representing the Catholic Church Militant, has its power immediately from Christ, and all men, of every rank and dignity, even the pope, are bound to obey it in matters pertaining to the faith and the extirpation of the present schism and general reformation of the Church of God in head and members." The cardinals protested against this assertion of conciliar supremacy but, when threatened with exclusion from the conferences, they gave way and accepted the decree. For a time the flight of the pope encouraged the council to take prompt and vigorous action. A long list of charges against John was prepared, and the council voted to depose him. Shortly afterward he was frightened into resigning. Then Gregory XII, pope in the line descended from Urban VI, resigned, after convoking the council anew. Both his actions had great significance in the subsequent history of the Church. Had he waited to be deposed, as did the representative of the Avignon line, there could have been no doubt of the council's control of the papacy, since all three claimants would have been deprived of office by conciliar action. By his resignation he preserved the tradition that no power could depose a true pope. Moreover, by calling the council anew, he maintained the tradition that the pope alone could call a council.

From 1415 to 1417 there was no pope. During this period the council set up committees to examine problems of Church reform. The nature and extent of the abuses to be corrected may be judged by the following account, written by a doctor of the University of Paris who was a papal secretary.

Nowadays in undertaking a cure of souls no mention is made of divine services, of the salvation or edification of those entrusted to the priest's care; the only question is about the revenue. . . . The popes in their desire for money have drawn all manner of elections into their own hands, and appoint ignorant and useless men, provided they are rich and can afford to pay large sums. The rights of bishops and patrons are set at naught, grants of benefices in expectancy are given to men who come from the plow and do not know A from B. Papal collectors devastate the land, and excommunicate or suspend those who do not satisfy their demands; hence churches fall into ruins and the church plate is sold; priests leave their benefices and take to secular occupations. Ecclesiastical cases are drawn into the papal court on every kind of pretext, and judgment is given in favor of those who pay the most. The papal curia alone is rich, and benefices are heaped on cardinals who devour their revenues in luxury and neglect their duties. [The clergy] strive, scold, litigate, and would endure with greater calmness the loss of ten thousand souls than of ten thousand shillings. If by chance there arises a pastor who does not walk in this way, who despises money or condemns avarice, or does not wring gold justly or unjustly from his people, but who strives by wholesome exhortation to benefit their souls and meditates on the law of God more than on the laws of men, forthwith the teeth of all are whetted against him. . . . Ecclesiastical jurisdiction is useless. Priests condemned for theft, homicide, rape, sacrilege, or any other serious offense, are only condemned to imprisonment on a diet of bread and water, and are imprisoned only until they have paid enough money, when they walk away scot free. On the other hand, the episcopal jurisdiction is eagerly extended over harmless rustics, and summoners scour the land to pry out offenses against canon law, for which the luckless victims are harassed by protracted law-suits and are driven to pay heavy fines to escape. Bishops do not hesitate to sell to priests licenses to keep concubines. No care is taken to ordain proper persons to the priesthood. Men who are lazy and do not choose to work, but who wish to live in idleness, fly to the priesthood. As priests, they frequent brothels and taverns and spend their time in drinking, revelling and gambling, fight and brawl in their cups, and with their polluted lips blaspheme the name of God and the saints, and from the embraces of prostitutes hurry to the altar.

Like most medieval diatribes this statement is exaggerated, but all the abuses it describes did exist and some of them were so common that they had become a regular part of the administrative system of the Church.

The council was well aware of the need for reform, but the decrees which it passed were utterly inadequate to remedy the situation. The tendency toward centralization of Church government could not safely be reversed, and no one seemed able to find a way of halting the abuses which went with centralization. Practically nothing was done to improve the financial system, though the pope was forbidden to transfer prelates against their will from one post to another, or to demand money from the bishops without just cause. The council placed most of its hopes for reform in the famous decree, *Frequens*, which prescribed that councils were to meet at regular intervals, even if the pope were unwilling to call them. These periodic assemblies were to continue the work of reform and were gradually to purge the Church of its abuses. Thus the pope would be assisted by a sort of ecclesiastical parliament and the dangers of the Schism could never recur.

This was an inadequate program, but the failure of the council to reform the Church was as natural as it was complete. The council produced no great leader, like St. Bernard or Gregory VII, to unite the wavering fathers into a crusade for the purification of the Church. Instead of unity there were three conflicting elements—cardinals, prelates, and representatives of the secular rulers. From the cardinals little could be expected, because any change would lessen not only their wealth, but also their power. Among the other ecclesiastics, most desired reform, but where should the process begin? Any worthwhile reform would injure the interests of some group and might weaken the government of the Church at a time when it needed all its strength to meet the increasing danger of secular control. No one possessed the imagination, the knowledge, or the courage to formulate a plan which would demand equal sacrifices from all groups and which would eradicate financial abuses while leaving the Church the income necessary to preserve its independence. Many prelates reasoned, like the heads of colleges which have become dependent upon the revenue produced by football, that if the abuses were eliminated the institution would cease to exist. Nor could much aid be expected from temporal rulers. They had found that talk of reform was an effective way of putting pressure on the clergy, but they were not anxious to end a system which enabled them to share ecclesiastical appointments and revenues with the pope. Even Sigismund's zeal for reform dwindled as the council continued, and toward the end he spent most of his time in securing his own rights. With no political or religious leadership, the council began to flounder, and by 1417 most people were rather tired of the whole business. The members of the council realized that their work was only half done, but they had been in session for over two years and were anxious to go home. They comforted themselves by the thought that the papacy was no longer autocratic and that subsequent councils could complete the work of reform. Even this hope was soon to be destroyed.

In 1417 the council decided to elect a pope, in spite of the protests of a few members who realized that this action would threaten the whole reform movement. Most prelates were anxious to establish the government of the Church on a normal basis; they felt that recovery should precede complete reform. As a final concession to the conciliar idea, delegates from each nation were added to the college which was to elect the new pope. Martin V, who was chosen by this unusual procedure, soon showed that he was going to maintain all the old traditions of papal absolutism. His first action was to confirm the rules of the papal chancery as issued by John XXIII. This dismayed the council, for these rules sanctioned all the financial abuses which had grown up in the last century. Martin was undeterred by criticism, for he judged correctly that the council had exhausted its strength and that Europe would not tolerate a new civil war in the Church. He proceeded to defy the whole theory of conciliar supremacy by announcing that "no one may appeal from the supreme judge, that is, the Apostolic see or the Roman Pontiff, Vicar on earth of Jesus Christ, or may decline his authority in matters of faith." Individual members demanded the withdrawal of this statement, but most of the fathers were unwilling to quarrel with a pope whom they had just made, and refused to protest. In 1418 the council was formally adjourned and Martin was left in full control of the government of the Church.

The Council of Constance had healed the Schism, and the importance of this achievement should not be underestimated. The history of Europe would have been very different if the Church had broken up into national units in the fifteenth century. But while the council preserved religious unity, it failed in its other tasks, and the Church did not regain its lost power and prestige. The effort to reform the Church "in head and members" had produced no result of importance. The attempt to limit papal power had been challenged by the pope chosen by the council itself. The burning of Huss and of Jerome of Prague failed to end the danger from heresy because the council did little to remove the real causes of heresy. Many earnest Christians still found the clergy too worldly and the services of the Church too mechanical to satisfy their religious aspirations. As a result, the criticism of ecclesiastical institutions and Catholic dogma, begun during the Captivity and the Schism, continued throughout the fifteenth century. The Council of Constance succeeded in postponing the Protestant Reformation, but it had not killed the seeds from which it was to grow.

The crisis through which the Church had just passed and the criticism to which it had been subjected, made imperative a strengthening of its spiritual foundations, but there was little recognition of this fact by the popes of the fifteenth century. The architectural monuments left to us by these pontiffs express perfectly the ideals of the age. Here is no sense of mystery and aspiring faith such as one finds embodied in the cathedrals of the twelfth and thirteenth centuries, but only a sense of worldly, pagan power. This secularization of the papacy is evident in the policy of Martin V. His great work was the subjugation of the States of the Church and the restoration of the prosperity of Rome. These were legitimate objectives, but they entailed the expenditure of large sums of money, and these funds could be secured only through the perpetuation of the financial abuses which had already weakened the Church. A year before Martin's death, an envoy of the Teutonic Knights wrote: "Greed reigns supreme in the Roman Court, and day by day finds new devices and artifices for extorting money from Germany under pretext of ecclesiastical fees. Many questions in regard to the papacy will arise, or else obedience will be entirely renounced to escape from these outrageous exactions of the Italians; and the latter course would be, as I perceive, acceptable to many countries." Martin's financial needs were increased by his desire to enrich his family. Nepotism was not a new thing in the papacy, but in the fifteenth century it mounted to unheard-of proportions. It became a public scandal when popes began to shower not only money, but also high offices in the Church, on their relatives and even on their illegitimate children.

Protests against papal exactions naturally took the form of renewed demands for conciliar supremacy. Martin did not dare violate his promise to summon councils at stated intervals, but he was successful in preventing the one assembly held during his pontificate, that of Pavia-Siena, from accomplishing anything of value. This check angered the reformers, and they arranged for the next council to meet across the Alps at Basel, where it could not be so easily dominated by the pope and his Italian supporters. Eugenius IV, who had succeeded Martin, saw that the reformers were going to make a great effort to realize their program and when the council met in 1431, he tried to dissolve it before it began its deliberations. This caused such a storm of protest that he was forced to hold his hand while the council issued bulls asserting its supremacy in the Church and its intention to effect a thorough reformation of all abuses. As at Constance, however, the members were unable to take prompt, effective action because they could not agree on specific remedies, and the sessions dragged on year after year. Eugenius still controlled the government of the Church and was able to bring some prelates to his side by offers of high office, while others deserted the council because they were weary of its ineffectual radicalism. In 1438 Eugenius felt strong enough to summon a council of his own, ostensibly to effect a union with the Greek Church. The reform party protested, but it found few supporters, and most of these became disgusted when the council threatened a new schism by electing an anti-pope. By 1440 Eugenius had triumphed and the conciliar movement had collapsed.

The failure of the movement to change the government of the Church may be attributed to several factors—to the feeling that papal power was ordained by God, to the skilful maneuvering of Martin and Eugenius, to the protracted meetings which wearied public opinion and dulled the zeal of the reformers. More important than these was the attitude of the temporal rulers, who instinctively feared popular movements like the councils and felt that the Church would be easier to control if the pope were theoretically supreme. The attitude of the French monarchs is typical. Charles VII and his advisers wished to subjugate the Church, like everything else, to the royal will. In order to secure support from the clergy and the reform party, as well as to frighten the pope into submission, Charles at first encouraged the Council of Basel to attack reservations, annates, and other devices which ensured papal control of the Church. Then the king withdrew support from the council and in 1438 issued the Pragmatic Sanction of Bourges. This document, under the pretense of reform, made the French church practically independent of Rome and gave the king almost complete control over appointments of prelates. Most of the clergy supported the edict in the hope of securing relief from papal extortion, but they soon found that they had gained little by the change of masters. Both Charles, and his successor, Louis XI, used the Pragmatic Sanction as a weapon by which concessions could be secured from Rome, now enforcing, now relaxing or even revoking the edict. They were quite willing to recognize the absolute power of the pope within the Church, if he would give them a share of the appointments of French prelates and revenues of the French clergy. In other countries much the same situation prevailed. Many rulers made concordats with the pope—formal treaties dividing the spoils of the Church in proportion to the relative strength of pontiff and monarch. In England, the acts of Parliament which forbade papal interference in the affairs of the Anglican church were used very much as the French used the Pragmatic Sanction of Bourges. They were never fully enforced, but their existence made the pope more willing to grant concessions to the English king. Thus, by one device or another, secular rulers gained a large degree of control over the clergy of their lands and were disinclined to support reforms which might have made that control less valuable. This situation led directly to the Reformation. On the one hand the reform movement, blocked within the Church, was forced into unorthodox channels. On the other, the princes who had obtained some control over the Church began to desire full power in ecclesiastical affairs. The Reformation, from this point of view, merely completed the work of nationalizing the Church which was begun in the fifteenth century.

The popes disliked the interference of secular rulers in ecclesiastical affairs, but their opposition was based on political and financial considerations rather than on religious principles. They were willing to compromise on almost any issue if their ecclesiastical supremacy was formally recognized and their revenues were not reduced. They paid little attention to the religious condition of the northern countries and concentrated their energies more and more within Italy. Some popes were wily politicians, seeking to increase their temporal possessions; others were humanists, endeavoring to make Rome the center of art and learning; others were absorbed by family interests, attempting to create fortunes and principalities for their sons and nephews. Occasionally a fitful effort was made to commence reforms, and two successive popes sought vainly to unite Christendom against the Turk, but on the whole the Vicar of Christ was lost in the Italian prince. It would be interesting to follow the careers of these fifteenth century pontiffs, who were almost without exception extraordinarily vivid personalities—Nicholas V, prince of humanists and founder of the Vatican library; Pius II, who reveled in the joys of this world until his elevation to the papal throne, and then turned ascetic reformer and crusader, dying of grief at the failure of his plans; Sixtus IV, who embroiled all Italy in war to further his political ambitions and who earned the epitaph "No force could extinguish the savage Sixtus; At the great name of peace, he died"—all fascinating figures, not one capable of bringing the Church into harmony with the needs of the modern world. Our period ends with the election of Rodrigo Borgia as Alexander VI in 1492. Alexander was no worse than his immediate predecessor, Innocent VIII—both secured the papal office through bribery and both used their position to advance the fortunes of their illegitimate children—but he was a much abler man and was therefore more dangerous to the Church. Only his premature death prevented his son Cæsar from establishing a central Italian kingdom in the Papal States and Tuscany, and it is doubtful if the papacy could have maintained its independence if this effort had succeeded. Stories about the crimes of the Borgias circulated through Europe and completed the work of discrediting the papacy. As a result the Church was in a desperate position at the beginning of the sixteenth century. The conciliar movement had failed, the papal restoration had failed, and no new solution of its problems was in sight. Bankrupt in leadership, false to its ideals, the great medieval Church was moving toward the ordeal of the Protestant Reformation.

XIII

-»»-»»-»»-»»《《-《《-《《-《《-

The Failure
of Secular Leadership

THE DISINTEGRATION OF MEDIEVAL SOCIETY

THE DECLINE of the medieval Church imposed a serious strain on the structure of European society. No civilization can endure unless its members are occasionally willing to sacrifice immediate personal advantages for ultimate social gains. Obviously, this willingness to coöperate for the good of the group requires general agreement on values and objectives. Medieval society, on the whole, had accepted the values and objectives which had been defined and upheld by the Church. This does not mean that all the dictates of ecclesiastical authorities were accepted without question, or that there was complete correspondence between the teachings of the Church and the actual life of the ordinary layman. Most men, however, accepted Christian ideals as a desirable standard and were sufficiently affected by those ideals to ensure the minimum of coöperation necessary to keep their civilization going. But as the Church became weaker the influence of its ideals declined, and the new ideals that were emerging were not yet strong enough to take the place of those that were dying.

The secular rulers who had weakened the leadership of the Church had won their struggle by appealing to the ideals of loyalty to the sovereign state and loyalty to the ruler who was head of the state. But these were still uncertain and relatively weak forces. They were strong enough to justify the rejection of outside interference and to preserve the identity of the state and the continuity of its administrative apparatus. The Church did not regain its political power and most of the sovereign states of 1300 still existed in 1500. But for some decades mere existence was the most that a state could achieve. Rulers could not inspire their sub-jects with that wholehearted, unquestioning spirit of coöperation that enables a state to achieve its full potential as a means of organizing human activities. Even in time of war and foreign invasion there was reluctance to serve the state either by paying taxes or by joining the army. In time of peace, regional and class interests usually prevailed over appeals to act for the common welfare.

Kings and princes had only limited means of influencing public opin-ion, or rather the opinion of the propertied classes, who were the only groups that were politically significant. They patronized writers who extolled the virtues of monarchy; they founded orders of chivalry (e.g., the Order of the Garter) to reward nobles for their loyalty; they tried to impress lesser folk by the pomp and ceremony of their courts. But the device that had proved most useful at the end of the thirteenth century—the calling of a large assembly of representatives to hear ex-planations of royal policy—lost some of its effectiveness in the fourteenth century. It was not that the assemblies opposed royal policy, even though they might be a little grudging in granting it financial support; it was rather that they acted as focal points for all the grievances of the groups they represented. They complained about bad administration, financial mismanagement, and infringement of privileges. A representative was apt to come home from one of these meetings with the feeling that many agents of the government were grasping, inefficient and corrupt—senti-ments that scarcely inspired undying loyalty.

The assemblies reflected the opinion of most members of the privileged classes. The nobles and the bourgeoisie knew that they could not live without a central government to protect their property and their priv-ileges, but they wanted the government to interfere as little as possible in local affairs. The government knew that it had to leave many details of local administration to country gentlemen and urban patricians, but it wanted to supervise the activities of these local notables and make them conform to the interests of the state. The resulting tension meant that the propertied classes gave only lukewarm support to central govern-ments. They did not strengthen royal leadership and their preoccupation with local and class interests made them incapable of providing an al-ternative leadership.

Finally, secular governments were weakened by a split between bu-reaucrats and policy-makers. Some divergence between these groups exists in any state, but it was particularly acute in the fourteenth century. The judges and the financial officers, the household officials and the clerks who were responsible for the administration of the country tended to form tight, closed professional corporations. They adhered rigidly to their well-established routines; they quarreled with each other over their areas of competence; they defended their privileges against all outsiders, even against the king. There was certainly some merit in their insistence on following regular procedures and in establishing clear-cut divisions of responsibility among departments. The strength of the bureaucratic tradition helped preserve the state in times of trouble and speeded recovery after periods of disorder. But devotion to tradition and emphasis on the acquisition of specialized skills made the average bureaucrat a poor adviser on policy. The semi-professional bureaucrats of the thirteenth century had had a more varied experience and a wider point of view; they could play an important role in policy-making as well as in judicial and financial administration. But by the fourteenth century only the heads of the great departments sat in the Council, the chief policy-making body, and they were often less influential in making important decisions than the princes of the blood and the leaders of factions of the nobility who also sat in the Council. The aristocracy had long been jealous of the bureaucrats and no fourteenth-century king could rule without the coöperation of at least some members of the aristocracy. Ordinary affairs could be handled by the bureaucrats, but the great questions of war and peace, of preventing or suppressing civil war and rebellion, had to be referred to men who had higher status and more influence in the country. It was politically necessary to involve princes and nobles in the decision-making process; the only trouble was that they were not very good or reliable advisers. They were ill-informed; they shirked their work; they often used their position to advance their own interests, to reward their favorites or to punish their enemies. Only very able kings could control these noble policy-makers and unfortunately there were few able rulers in western Europe between 1300 and 1460.

The fourteenth century would have been a difficult period in any case; lack of effective leadership only made a bad situation worse. The economic boom that had supported the great achievements of the twelfth and early thirteenth centuries came to an end about 1300. Given existing techniques, western Europe had reached its limits in production and trade. There were no new lands to clear, no new products to sell, no new trade-routes to exploit. Until new types of industry, new markets, and new agricultural methods could be found, the European economy could do no more than stagnate, which meant that in many regions it was bound to decline. Except in Italy, most cities lost population and wealth. Many governments were unable to pay their debts, and their failure to do so led to the bankruptcy of merchants and bankers. A series of natural and man-made disasters reduced the amount of land in cultivation. Everyone realized that there were economic problems, or, to put it more simply, everyone realized that there was not enough money to do everything that was desirable or even everything that was necessary. No one had the slightest idea of what should be done to improve economic conditions. There were advocates of inflation and deflation, of monopoly and free trade, but no government could follow a consistent policy, both because of ignorance and because of the pressures of special interest groups. Modern governments, with much greater resources and powers, have found it difficult to deal with depressions. It is not surprising that the weak governments of the later Middle Ages could not cope with one of the greatest depressions in history.

The confusion caused by economic problems was made worse by the great plague that devastated Europe in the second half of the fourteenth century. The Black Death, or bubonic plague, seems to have entered the Mediterranean from the East about 1347. Carried along the routes of trade by merchants and sailors, it swept through the continent in a great arc, from the south through France and England into Germany. The medical profession understood neither the causes nor the treatment of the disease, and few of those who were infected survived. Since no European country kept any record of vital statistics, it is impossible to estimate the mortality caused by the plague. We do have figures for some monasteries, towns, and rural districts where the death rate ran from thirty to fifty percent. The overall average may have been thirty to forty percent, but, whatever the incidence, the Black Death killed more people than any war has ever done. The very old and the very young suffered most, but the impact on men of working age was severe enough to cause serious economic dislocations. Moreover, there were secondary epidemics during the rest of the century which killed many of those who had escaped the original onslaught.

The economic and moral effects of the plague are as hard to evaluate as the mortality. The only certain fact is that during the half century after the plague there was a decrease in the number of agricultural workers. Many peasants went to the towns to fill up the gaps caused by the heavy loss of life among the urban population. Those who remained on the land took advantage of the shortage of manpower to demand increased wages or more favorable terms for leases of land. The upper classes tried to check this movement through legislation that fixed wage-scales for agricultural work. Unlike much late medieval legislation, these laws were enforced, but only the poorest peasants were much affected by ceilings on wages. The real problem, for the landed classes, was to find farmers to lease their estates and in this situation the peasants had a clear advantage. They could select the best land; they could bargain for minimum payments, and for a century after the Black Death their real income increased. Serfdom disappeared in England, and in many parts of France. Perhaps its survival in central and eastern Europe was due to the fact that the plague had had less effect there.

The Black Death caused a sharp decrease in the population of Europe, and it was over a century before this loss was made up. Population was stabilizing even before the epidemic; it seems fairly certain that by 1300 Europe was already supporting about as many people as its resources allowed. A long period of stable and then decreasing population intensified the effects of the economic depression. Markets contracted instead of expanding; the townsmen paid more for their food (thanks to the improved position of the peasants) but had fewer people to whom to sell their goods. Much of the bad feeling among different economic groups can be traced to this economic squeeze. With no new business, producers had to fight bitterly for a share of the existing market.

The Black Death also contributed to the moral disintegration of European society. There were, of course, other causes—loss of confidence in ecclesiastical and secular governments, loss of respect for law, and bewilderment over economic problems had already made many men selfish and cynical. Europe, disillusioned and pessimistic, was in no condition to stand the sudden shock of the plague. We have been accustomed to blame many of our ills on the strain caused by the World Wars, and the Black Death was more terrible than any war. It killed more people than a hostile army and it gave its victims no chance to fight back. There was none of the enthusiasm which accompanies a war, none of the feeling that through pain and death a noble cause might be served. Instead men waited hopelessly for the approach of a foul and agonizing disease, knowing that when they were stricken they might be abandoned by family and friends and left to die in misery. Some took refuge in sensual pleasures and ate, drank, and were merry until they died. Others became fanatically religious and tried to ease their consciences through exaggerated penances. The Order of the Flagellants, who marched through the streets of European towns beating each other with chains and knotted whips, recruited many new members at this time. The sect soon turned its violence against the Jews and accused them of causing the plague. Riots and massacres followed, until ecclesiastical and secular authorities combined to outlaw the movement. Even when the immediate disorder caused by the Black Death had passed, Europe seemed to be suffering from a case of collective shell-shock. Emotional and moral instability, violent swings between religious idealism and brutal realism were typical of the age. People thronged to revivals; they multiplied their devotions; they meditated on the Sorrows of Mary and the sufferings of Christ until their hearts were filled with unbearable anguish. Yet these same people flocked joyously to executions and tore each other to pieces during the frequent civil wars. This was also the period in which the witchcraft delusion first became prominent in Europe—a delusion which had a certain basis in fact. It is true that many old men and women were put to death for no better reason than that they had cursed their neighbors in fits of anger, or that they babbled nonsense in their fits of senile dementia. But in the general breakdown of European morality there were people who believed that they could ally themselves with the powers of evil and who committed the foulest crimes in order to secure the aid of Satan. When a Marshal of France, a companion of Joan of Arc, could be found guilty of sacrificing children to the devil, the extent and danger of these beliefs are evident. Diabolism was extreme manifestation of the discontent with organized religion and the search for stronger emotional experiences. The devotees of Satan were usually convinced that they were headed for eternal damnation, but they were willing to run this risk in return for earthly power and pleasure. Nothing shows more clearly the extent to which the old ideals were losing their hold on society.

The effects of economic depression and plague were intensified by civil and foreign wars. In a contracting economy each economic group tried to make sure that it would receive its old income, whatever effects this might have on other classes. In the towns the old families that had made their fortunes early fought with the new rich; the international merchants fought with the artisans; the wealthy gilds fought with the poorer gilds. In the countryside there was constant antagonism between landlords and tenants, antagonism that occasionally broke out into peasant rebellions. There were jealousies within the landlord class itself; families that benefitted from royal grants of estates were hated by those which did not receive gifts. A number of civil wars were simply attempts to redistribute landed property. And even when there was a reasonable degree of internal tranquillity, rulers and their friends among the nobility were tempted to engage in foreign war. In a stagnant economy, this seemed to be the only way to increase one's income. The ruler could profit from new revenues and new taxes from conquered lands; the nobles could sell their military service to the government and hope to profit from booty, ransoms, and gifts of confiscated land. The thirteenth century had been a peaceful century; the fourteenth saw an almost uninterrupted series of wars and rebellions.

No one was any happier about the political situation than they were about the economic situation, and no one had any better solution for political than for economic problems. As human beings always do, men of the fourteenth century reaffirmed, with the energy of despair, the ideals that they had betrayed. As we have seen, the most extreme claims for papal power were made in the fourteenth century, when the political power of the papacy had been irremediably shattered. The most elaborate plans for crusades were prepared at a time when all hope for a successful crusade had vanished. The English kept on confirming Magna Carta; the French continued to talk of a return to the good days of St.

Louis, but neither people could recapture the equilibrium that had existed in the thirteenth century. The most popular word in the fourteenth century was "reform," but while some very intelligent plans for reform were drawn up, they were seldom implemented. For example, in most states the tax structure was inequitable and inefficient. The privileged classes paid too little; the poor paid too much, and techniques of collection were so bad that the final yield was often only about half of what it should have been. These facts were generally known, but in an age of recurrent crises no one could afford to give up short-term profits for long-term advantages. For pope and king, prince and city-state, it was better to have fifty thousand pounds at once, whatever the cost in graft and oppression, than one hundred thousand pounds collected two years later after a careful campaign against corruption. Governments staggered from emergency to emergency with scarcely a chance to review their administrative organization or to consider long-range policies. It says much for the work of the thirteenth century that under these circumstances European states did not altogether collapse. Everyone was convinced that the state was necessary and that eventually it could be made to work properly. Meanwhile its basic apparatus could be kept going by the bureaucracy.

It also says much for the work of the earlier period that European society did not disintegrate under the strains of the fourteenth century. Certainly conditions in many parts of Europe were as bad as they had been in the period just before the collapse of the Roman Empire. But recovery from the collapse of the Empire took six or seven centuries; recovery from the crisis of the fourteenth century took at most only a century and a half. The difference was that the Romans were apathetic; they did not care enough about their state and their civilization to make an effort to save it. Europeans of the fourteenth century did care, and they expressed their concern with a vehemence that was at times frightening. They retained their faith in Christianity, if not their respect for the Church; they retained their belief in the value of their political institutions, even if they despised individual rulers, and they hoped passionately that Christianity and monarchy could some day work together to bring back peace and prosperity. In the long run this faith and this belief brought about a realization of their hopes.

LITERATURE, ART, AND SCHOLARSHIP IN THE LATER MIDDLE AGES

The literature and the art of the later middle ages reflected some of the weaknesses and problems of the period. Many writers and artists adhered to the old forms of|expression because they could find nothing in the confusion around them that inspired them to create new ones. But the old forms had become lifeless and sterile from over-use. Literature especially suffered from conventional imitations of past masterpieces. Writers understood their age no better than kings and parliaments, and like their rulers they took refuge in elaborations of ancient ideas. They rewrote the old romances; they composed endless series of love-songs; they combined and expounded the didactic works of their predecessors. Even when they were writing about current events they could not analyze causes and effects, but contented themselves with lengthy descriptions of surface incidents. The historians of the Burgundian court offer a notable example of this tendency. For three-quarters of a century the dukes of Burgundy played an amazingly skilful diplomatic game which enabled them at times to control the fate of France and England. But there is little of this in the writings of the Burgundian chroniclers; instead there are elaborate accounts of festivals and ceremonies. The famous historian Froissart hardly rises above this level. There is a vividness in his descriptions of battles and skirmishes which still enchants the reader, but his ideas about the causes and strategy of the Hundred Years' War are childishly naïve. In his pages the bitter struggle becomes a series of splendid tournaments, and he is more interested in the feats of a few knights than in the fate of a people.

There are, of course, exceptions to these generalizations. Leaving out the Italian writers, who will be considered in a later chapter, there were men in France, England, and Germany who rose above the general level of respectable mediocrity. The mystics, who deliberately withdrew from contact with their own generation in order to contemplate the eternal verities, produced some of the most powerful religious literature that has ever been written. The *Theologica Germanica* had great influence on Luther, and the *Imitation of Christ,* ascribed to Thomas à Kempis, has been read for centuries by devout men. *The Vision of Piers Plowman,* by William Langland, is more practical than the German works; much of it is a satire on the hypocrisy and immorality of fourteenth-century English society. But the mysticism is there too; man is to be saved by inner faith and not by external reforms.

Most of the great mystics were Germans; the leading French writers were more interested in secular subjects. Charles of Orleans, a prince of the royal house, succeeded in breathing a little personal feeling into the old forms of courtly poetry. François Villon also adhered to the old forms, but his somber and violent personality transformed them into bitter expressions of the pessimism and cynicism of his age. An associate of prostitutes and thieves, himself a convicted criminal, Villon described his ruined life and the underworld of Paris with savage humor. Like many men of his generation, he was superstitious and irreverent, scornful of the smugly respectable bourgeois and terribly afraid of the pains of hell, morbidly interested in death and violently determined to enjoy life. Villon was driven to degradation and despair by the unresolved conflicts of his age; the great English poet, Geoffrey Chaucer, took things as he found them and lived tranquilly in the midst of corruption. He held a series of profitable governmental positions, thanks to the patronage of the duke of Lancaster, and he died a country gentleman. He knew the evils of English political life from the inside; Lancaster was a leader of a faction of the nobility and many of Chaucer's own colleagues were convicted of misconduct in office. He had no illusions about the society of his own day, but he liked people and he described them with a friendly realism which has made his work endure. Chaucer borrowed his stories from Latin, French, and Italian sources, but his characters were real men and women, drawn from his own observation of English life. The famous company of the *Canterbury Tales* is a good cross-section of medieval society, ranging from the priest and the knight, who are attempting to follow the ideals of their callings, to the rascally friar and summoner who make a good living out of their connection with the Church. Most of Chaucer's people are neither very good nor very bad; they would not wilfully harm others, but they would not mind committing a few sins in order to satisfy their fleshly desires.

In architecture as in literature, northern Europeans repeated and elaborated old forms during the fourteenth and fifteenth centuries. They carried the principles of Gothic art to their logical conclusions, but most of their work lacks the serenity and the sense of proportion that made Gothic art of the thirteenth century great. They tried to incorporate exterior space into their churches by covering their buildings with pinnacles and buttresses until it was impossible to tell where the real framework of the structure began. They divided and subdivided the great windows into intricately related panels; they developed the simple rib-vaulting of the earlier period into elaborate patterns resembling the interlacing branches of a forest. This style was most effective in England, where thirteenth-century churches had retained something of the simplicity and solidity of the Romanesque, and where an increase in lightness and decorativeness emphasized rather than concealed the basic structure. But even in England the very perfection of the detailed work sometimes distracted attention from the overall pattern, and elsewhere detail tended to degenerate into fussiness. Like later medieval poetry, later medieval architecture was often too clever to be beautiful.

Sculpture suffered from the same defects as architecture, as long as it was treated merely as a form of church decoration. But by the end of the fourteenth century northern sculptors began to produce works that could stand alone, without any necessary relationship to the building in which they were placed. There was still a close association between religion and sculpture, but the sculptors worked to please a private, rather than a public audience. Their most striking productions were the tombs of the great nobles and kings of the West. Here we see the same tendency toward a realistic portrayal of their subjects that we have already observed in Villon and Chaucer, and that we will see again in the painting of the period. The figures of the dead rulers were made as lifelike as possible, and around the base of the tombs were carved Biblical and allegorical figures and processions of mourners. The finest work of this kind was done at the court of the dukes of Burgundy by Claus Sluter, but some of the French and German productions of the period are almost as impressive.

Painting, like sculpture, became an independent art only in the later Middle Ages. Before the fourteenth century, churches had been adorned with frescoes and manuscripts had been illuminated, but in each case the painting was an integral part of the building or the book. By the fifteenth century a new style of manuscript illumination had been developed in which the pictures were separated from the text and occupied whole pages by themselves. At about the same time we find the first easel paintings, paintings that could be carried from place to place and were not inseparably attached to a building. And, even more than in the case of the sculptors, the painters worked chiefly for private patrons. This tendency of the arts to become independent of each other, less controlled by the Church and more responsive to the wishes of laymen is another indication of changing attitudes. Men could no longer encompass all experience in a single unit, such as a thirteenth-century cathedral, and while they were still strongly moved by religion, religion was becoming more of a private and individual concern.

The tendency toward realism, that we have already noted in literature and sculpture, appeared also in painting, even in depicting religious scenes. Abstract symbols of the faith no longer moved the more worldly men of the fifteenth century, and the northern artists never had much of the tendency to idealize the human figure which became so strong in Italy. Like the great poets and great sculptors of the same period, they portrayed men as they saw them, with their scars and warts and swollen knuckle-bones. Most manuscript illumination hardly rises above the level of *genre* painting, with its interesting glimpses of daily life, but some of the easel painters can be ranked among the greatest artists whom Europe has ever produced. They had the same love of detail as the architects, and occasionally their meticulous reproductions of embroidered robes and richly carved interiors cluttered up a picture, but their realism went far beyond careful copying of outward appearances. They could seize on the essential elements of a man's character and their portraits of nobles, government officials, and wealthy burghers give us a vivid impression of the men and women of the fifteenth century. As was the case with the sculptors, the greatest of these artists were Flemings, attached to the brilliant court of the dukes of Burgundy. Jan van Eyck, who served the dukes as a diplomat as well as a painter, was perhaps the most skilful of the group, but some of the work of Rogier van der Weyden would rank almost as high. Hans Memling diverged somewhat from the realistic school of Flemish painting, and his pictures have a deeper religious content than those of most of his contemporaries. Yet while Memling tended to idealize his figures, he was interested in spiritual rather than physical beauty, and he never showed any of the Italian desire to glorify the human body. The Flemish school had great influence on northern European art for the next two centuries, and in one of its technical developments it influenced painting everywhere. The Flemings were apparently the first to perfect the technique of painting in oil and this method, which made possible a whole new range of effects, was borrowed from them by the Italians. As this example shows, painting was less bound by tradition than the other arts, and for this reason it was the most successful of the arts in expressing the interests and attitudes of the people of northern Europe during the later Middle Ages.

The scholarship of the fourteenth and fifteenth centuries has often been dismissed as useless pedantry. Some of it was undoubtedly pedantic, but dull books often preserved useful knowledge. For example, Columbus acquired some of his most important ideas about geography from manuals written by scholars of the fifteenth century. More important than the preservation of old knowledge, however, was the active intellectual controversy that went on throughout the later Middle Ages and that opened up new lines of inquiry. We are just beginning to understand the significance of this controversy because it centered on problems and was conducted in a language that are hard for modern readers to understand. There is this much truth in the old charge of pedantry—technical terms were multiplied beyond all reason; distinctions were drawn so finely that it was often difficult to follow the argument, and many writers merely repeated the ideas of a few first-rate minds. But the first-rate men were debating real problems and they had more influence on the early modern world than we once thought.

The disputes centered about the philosophy, and especially about the theory of knowledge of St. Thomas Aquinas. Thomas had taught that divine revelation and the truths acquired by the use of the human reason meshed together perfectly. It was possible to prove universal truths, such as the existence of God, through human reason; it was possible through human reason to understand more completely the mysteries of the faith. Conversely, it was impossible for a truth discovered by human reason to be contrary to the faith, if reason had been rightly used.

This rationalistic approach had worried the contemporaries of St. Thomas and it worried his successors even more. It had been easier to be optimistic about the unity of faith and knowledge in the calm of the mid-thirteenth century than it was during the stormy period that followed. First Duns Scotus demonstrated that the distinction between faith and reason was not quite as clear as Thomas had claimed and that reason was used in many different ways to arrive at truths of varying degrees of validity. Then, as we have seen, William Ockham went even further and denied that reason could ever discover anything that was necessarily true about the faith. All that reason could do was to draw conclusions about the physical world from observations of natural phenomena. These conclusions might be true in philosophy—that is, they might offer a satisfactory explanation of the events they described—but they were not necessarily true in theology. Revelation and reason did not reinforce each other; they might even conflict.

Both Duns Scotus and Ockham were Franciscans and their arguments encouraged the Franciscan-founded group of mathematicians and scientists at Oxford to continue their investigations. Since reason could not help with the problems of faith, a philosopher might as well devote himself to the study of earthly objects and leave theology to the theologians. So the Oxford group continued to work on problems of physics. They found a formula for accelerated motion that was very nearly the correct one and they refined some of the early work on optics. These interests spread to Paris where Bishop Oresme was even willing to speculate about the possibility that the earth moved about the sun instead of remaining fixed in the center of the universe. He rejected the idea on religious grounds, but admitted that it was perfectly possible according to the laws of physics—a nice example of the idea that a proposition might be true in philosophy but false in theology.

From Paris the scientific-mathematical tradition moved to Italy, where it was to influence Copernicus and other scientists of the early modern period. It was never a very strong tradition, but the fact that it survived at all owed something to the philosophical controversies of the period. And, as we have seen, the survival of the scientific tradition in the West at a time when it was dying out everywhere else was to be of inestimable value to Europe.

From a broader point of view, the attack on Thomism led to a prolonged split in the theological faculties of Europe. The followers of Duns Scotus and Ockham did not have everything their own way; there were ardent supporters of St. Thomas everywhere. The result was often a double faculty of theology, one group of professors to teach the *via antiqua* or Thomistic doctrine, and the other to teach the *via moderna* or new philosophy of Ockham and his followers. This division allowed, and even encouraged, fairly free discussion of problems touching the faith. A writer on theology could go very far before he would be charged with heresy, as Wycliffe's career illustrates. And open discussion stimulated the kind of speculation that was one of the sources of the Reformation.

Finally, it should be remembered that laymen supported and were interested in the work of the scholars. Bishop Oresme was in high favor in the French court. Charles V of France, probably the ablest and certainly the wisest of fourteenth century rulers, supported dozens of scholars in assembling his remarkable library. He wanted everything translated into French—histories, the Bible, Justinian's Codes, St. Augustine, the works of Aristotle, and medieval treatises on politics. Two generations later Duke Humphry of Gloucester, uncle of the king of England, also built up a first-rate library. As we have said before, the number of learned laymen was increasing steadily everywhere, in the North as well as in Italy. And the scholarly tradition was strengthened by the fact that laymen were reading works on theology, law, political theory and science.

ENGLAND AND FRANCE IN THE FOURTEENTH CENTURY

The disintegration of medieval society created a difficult problem for rulers of all European states. The great mass of the people, bewildered by economic depression, stunned by plagues, wars, and famines, uncertain of their standards and their goals, merely sought to exist with as little discomfort as possible. They pursued limited and selfish objectives and were apathetic to all appeals for general coöperation. The tough-minded minority saw a chance to gain power and wealth in the general confusion and was ready to wreck all existing institutions to gain its ends. Conditions were worst in Central Europe, where no strong states had developed during the great centuries of the Middle Ages, but even the powerful monarchies of the West came close to collapse during the troubles of the fourteenth and fifteenth centuries. The kings of France, England, and Spain were far weaker in 1400 than in 1300 and the nobles in all three countries regained much of their old power as the authority of the monarchs declined. In the end, however, the institutions of central government established in the earlier period proved their value. They were weakened but not destroyed during the years of trouble, and they minimized, if they did not prevent, some of the most dangerous manifestations of the spirit of violence. Class struggles in the towns never reached the peak of violence in France and England that they did in Italy, and the robber baron was less of a problem west of the Rhine than in Germany. Recovery was more rapid in the countries which had once had strong, centralized government. By 1500 England, France, and Spain were once more united under powerful rulers, while Italy and Germany, and the Slavic states were floundering in a morass of political difficulties.

The extent of the political crisis of the later Middle Ages is most evident in studying the history of France and England. Here were two countries which had been advancing steadily toward powerful, centralized monarchy during the twelfth and thirteenth centuries. Edward I and Philip the Fair seemed to have put an end to feudalism and provincialism and to have established themselves as the supreme political authorities in all their lands. The people were attached to the ruling dynasties and the first signs of national feeling were already appearing in both countries. Yet this apparently inevitable progress toward strong, national monarchy was halted early in the fourteenth century, and for the rest of the Middle Ages the kings of France and England had to fight for mere existence. The most orderly and best governed parts of Europe were not immune from the contagion of unrest and rebellion.

Besides the general difficulties which beset all Europe, England and France had problems of their own. As we have seen, both Philip the Fair and Edward I had gone too fast in their efforts to increase royal power. Unscrupulous methods had discredited both governments and had given subjects a bad example. The kings of both countries tended to overestimate the extent of their victory over feudalism. Political feudalism had been killed in England and seriously weakened in France, but the nobles still had great power and influence. They owned most of the land, which was the chief source of wealth; they were indispensable as organizers and leaders of armies, and they were still accepted by men of all classes as the natural advisers and aids of the king. Philip and Edward had tried to minimize the influence of the aristocracy on their governments, and this attempt produced a violent reaction. Able kings might have been able to check this reaction before it reached dangerous proportions, but the successors of Philip and Edward were, with two or three exceptions, utterly unfit for their positions. Some wasted their slender resources on futile wars; others were incipiently or actually insane. The few able kings who ruled in the fourteenth and early fifteenth centuries succeeded in restoring some degree of order, but they were invariably succeeded by incompetent sons who let their work fall to ruin. Finally, influencing and complicating all other problems, there was the series of devastating conflicts between France and England known as the Hundred Years' War.

The reign of Edward II of England offers a good example of all these difficulties. Edward inherited from his father a bankrupt government, a discontented nobility, and a losing war with Scotland. He made everything worse by his own defects of character. He had neither capacity nor taste for the strenuous business of governing, but amused himself with vulgar pastimes while his favorites ruled for him. Under such a ruler, the aristocracy felt it safe to make an effort to regain their power, and in 1311 they seized control of the government. They forced Edward to accept a series of reforming ordinances which diminished the political importance of the Household and threw all important political decisions into Parliament. Since the magnates always attended Parliament in full force, they were able to use it for their own purposes, and they found it very convenient for thwarting the king's attempts to keep personal control of the government. Unfortunately, the barons were more successful in thwarting the king than in ruling the country themselves, and they soon displayed the same weaknesses which had ruined the aristocratic government of 1258. Their pride prevented them from giving wholehearted support to any leader, and their laziness made it impossible for them to supervise the daily activities of the government. Disunity in England enabled the Scots to regain their independence in the decisive battle of Bannockburn (1314), but even this disaster did not put an end to the quarrels of the magnates. Some of their disputes turned into private wars, and the country became so disgusted with baronial misgovernment that Edward received wide support when he made a bid to regain his power. He defeated the barons decisively in 1322, repealed the reforming ordinances of 1311, and for the next four years reigned without restrictions on his authority. He was still incapable of attending to business himself, but his favorites, the Despensers, to whom he trusted the government, were able and energetic men. They restored the influence of the Household, with modifications which made it less distasteful to the upper classes, and they brought Parliament once more under control of royal officials. Their very success made them unpopular, and when they began to use their power to build up great lordships for themselves in the Marches of Wales, the magnates were ready again for revolt. The signal was given by the queen herself, who eloped with one of the aggrieved barons. Edward was unable to make any resistance to the united opposition of the aristocracy. He was captured and imprisoned, while the barons took charge of the government. They formed a committee to ask Edward to abdicate and drew up a long list of his misdeeds, which they submitted to a Parliament held early in 1328. Since Parliament was controlled by the magnates, it could do nothing but accept the charges. Edward yielded the throne to his eldest son, Edward III, and soon afterward was quietly murdered in prison.

The immediate result of the revolution of 1327 was no more satisfactory than that of the *coup d'état* of 1311. Since Edward III was a minor, his mother ruled in his name, and it soon became evident that she was using her power to increase the possessions of her lover, Mortimer. The discontented magnates grouped themselves around the young king, and in 1330 Edward III declared himself of age, drove his mother from court, and executed her paramour.

All England rejoiced at the prospect of another period of strong leadership, and for a time Edward justified the hopes of his people. In appearance and manner he was a worthy successor to the first Edward— tall, handsome, affable and generous. He shared the aristocracy's fondness for the chase and tournaments, and this community of interests made it easy for king and barons to work together. Like his grandfather, too, Edward had a more practical side. During the first ten years of his reign he ran the government effectively and without any serious opposition. The magnates were kept quiet by grants of land and jobs. The leaders of the towns were conciliated in the same way. They received profitable government jobs and contracts, including a near monopoly of the key positions in the customs service. In spite of the renewal of the futile attempt to conquer Scotland, England was relatively prosperous and contented during the first part of Edward's reign.

Edward, however, had certain weaknesses which slowly overrode his good qualities. He not only enjoyed the same sports as the aristocracy; he tended to adopt their view of life. He was deeply imbued with chivalric ideals and was inclined to engage in useless wars and battles in order to display his knightly prowess. While he began his reign with an effort to restore royal authority, he lacked the determination necessary to fulfil his program. He met his first real opposition in 1340 when he tried to punish Archbishop Stratford of Canterbury for some of his own failures in policy. The nobles supported the archbishop and Edward backed down, though he tried to revoke some of his concessions when the danger was over. This remained the pattern for the rest of the reign; in spite of backing and filling Edward in the long run yielded more and more to the barons. He may have realized that the reign of Edward II had made it impossible to restore the conditions of the reign of Edward I, or he may have feared that a serious conflict with the aristocracy would keep him from waging the wars in which he so delighted. Whatever the reasons, his internal policy became purely opportunistic; he merely postponed difficulties instead of solving them. At his death the conflict between king and barons for control of the government was to break out with renewed force.

Edward's first adventure in foreign policy was the attempted reconquest of Scotland but this objective was soon forgotten in the great struggle with France. The two countries had so many reasons for quarreling that war was inevitable as soon as Edward developed belligerent tendencies. The basic difficulty was English possession of Aquitaine. Every French king was bound to make an effort to increase his authority in the duchy, while English rulers naturally resented the persistent interference with their government and the repeated annexations of fiefs on the frontiers. The French supported the Scots in their resistance to English domination in order to divert attention from Aquitaine, while the English retaliated by encouraging the Flemings to rebel against France. Flanders was the chief outlet for English wool, and no English king could tolerate the thought of having this important market dominated by a deadly rival. Another minor but persistent source of friction was the continual raiding and piracy of English and French sailors, who could never resist the temptation of seizing each other's ships to satisfy uncollected debts and ancient feuds.

The fuel of war was thus piled high when the question of the succession to the French throne set off a conflagration which was to last for over a century. Between 1314 and 1328 the three sons of Philip the Fair— Louis X, Philip V, and Charles IV—reigned in succession and died without male heirs. All three had daughters, but the French lawyers declared that "custom prohibited the succession of a woman, and consequently also of her son, to the throne of France." Accordingly, Philip of Valois, cousin of these last Capetians of the direct line, became king as Philip VI. The decision of the lawyers was actually based on expediency, not on law, although in the next generation an obscure clause regulating private successions in the law of the Salian Franks was dug up to strengthen their case. The real basis for the decision was the fact that the princesses had all married into French feudal houses, and the barons preferred to keep the throne in the old royal line rather than to raise one of their fellows to a position of supremacy. There was also the danger of an English claim to the throne, since Edward II had married a daughter of Philip the Fair, but this peril was at first remote. However, when Edward III commenced his personal rule he began to urge his rights as grandson of Philip, and he refused to recognize the Valois ruler until he was threatened with the loss of his French lands. His claim was very flimsy, since by strict feudal principles the princesses and their heirs were closer to the throne, but he possessed the one thing which the princesses had lacked—independent military power. As a result Edward became the chief opponent of the new principle of succession through male heirs only, and the claims of other descendants of Philip the Fair were forgotten.

Edward had recognized Philip of Valois as king because he did not want war at the time of his accession. A few years later the situation in Flanders gave him an opportunity to reopen the question under more favorable circumstances. The Flemings had long been practically independent under their count, and they bitterly resented the effort of the French kings to tax them and to interfere with their courts and government. The political grievance was sharpened by a bitter class struggle in the Flemish towns between the urban aristocracies and the workers in the cloth industry. Since Flanders imported its wool from England and exported its cloth to all parts of Europe, men with large amounts of capital and widespread business connections found it easy to dominate the trade. By the end of the thirteenth century the great merchants and bankers had reduced the weavers and other artisans to the status of day-laborers and had gained full control of the governments of the larger towns. During the fourteenth century the exploited cloth-workers tried to free themselves from the domination of their wealthy fellow-citizens, and the oligarchs, fearing for their lives and property, invoked the aid of the French king. Thus resistance to the urban patriciate implied resistance to France, and Edward saw that the workers of the Flemish cloth towns were his natural allies. His agents soon proposed that the Flemings should renounce French suzerainty and place themselves under English protection. When the leaders of the proletariat hesitated at this radical proposal, Edward gave them a convincing demonstration of the need for an agreement with England by forbidding the export of wool from his realm. With their looms idle and unemployment rife, the Flemings were forced to accept an English alliance. The workers had already gained control of most of the county through a series of uprisings, and in 1337 their leader, Jacques van Artevelde, agreed to recognize Edward as suzerain if he would declare himself king of France. Edward accepted the proposal, and in the following year Philip VI made the rupture complete by declaring that the English fiefs in France were forfeited. These acts marked the beginning of the Hundred Years' War.

"To the end that the honourable and noble adventures of feats of arms, done and achieved by the wars of France and England, should notably be enregistered and put in perpetual memory, whereby the brave and hardy may have ensample to encourage them in their well-doing, I, Sir John Froissart, will treat and record an history of great louage and praise." This begins the most famous chronicle of the great war, and thus for centuries the tale was told as a school of chivalry, "all noble hearts to encourage and to shew them ensample and matter of honour." But the modern eye looks past the pageantry of knightly combat to see a record of horror, atrocity, and devastation surpassing that of the barbarian raids of the ninth century. As was usual in medieval wars, noncombatants suffered more severely than soldiers. Crops were destroyed, villages were burned, peasants and townsmen were tortured and killed by greedy soldiers seeking their hidden treasures. Some districts in France lost all their inhabitants and reverted to a state of wilderness; others were so harassed that both religious and secular officials abandoned their posts, while the people became little better than savages. Never was the contrast between the chivalric ideals of the aristocracy and their actual behavior more acute.

Early in the war the strengths and weaknesses of the two countries became evident. The English, trained in the long struggle with the Scots, had by far the better army. They had developed tactics which ensured victory whenever they were properly applied. Foot-soldiers, equipped with the long-bow, were supported by heavy-armed knights and men-at-arms. A cavalry charge, the favorite French tactic, would be disrupted by flights of arrows which struck down the horses. The few knights who reached the English line could be dealt with by the men-at-arms. The French could not stand off and exchange volleys of arrows, not only because they used the cross-bow which shot less rapidly than the long-bow, but also because their noble commanders thought it unknightly to rely on bowmen. Thus the English won most of the battles, but they found it impossible to win the war. England had neither the men nor the money necessary to conquer and garrison all France. Whenever the French contented themselves with holding their cities and forts, and re-fused to risk pitched battles, English expeditionary forces could do noth-ing but engage in futile raids. These facts explain both the length and the destructiveness of the war. The English, encouraged by repeated vic-tories, could not believe that they were unable to conquer France and were unwilling to abandon the attempt. The French could not prevent English raids, but they could profit from English exhaustion, and every English victory was followed by a French reoccupation of lost territory. Neither country could win a final victory by purely military means, and in the end economic difficulties and political unrest proved more decisive than maneuvers of the armies.

All this was abundantly illustrated by the first campaigns of the war. Edward began with a naval victory at Sluys in 1340, which gave him control of the Channel. Northern France was now open to English raids, but no important action took place until Edward came over with a large army in 1346. He pillaged France from La Hogue to the gates of Paris, and then, loaded down with plunder, began a retreat to the coast. A much larger French army overtook him at Crécy, and his position would have been serious if the French nobles had not made every conceivable mistake in their attack. They refused to give the army time to rest and re-form itself; they refused to wait for the Genoese cross-bowmen to soften the English line with a few volleys of arrows, and they insisted on trying to carry a strong position by direct cavalry charges. The Eng-lish slaughtered their foolhardy opponents like driven game, and only darkness enabled a remnant of the French army to escape. After a brief rest, Edward moved on to Calais and sat down before that great com-mercial center for a siege which lasted almost two years. Philip VI at-tempted to relieve the town, but he was afraid to attack Edward in his entrenchments, and when the English king refused a summons to come out and fight like a gentleman, the discouraged French marched away. The starving burghers soon surrendered, giving England an entry port to

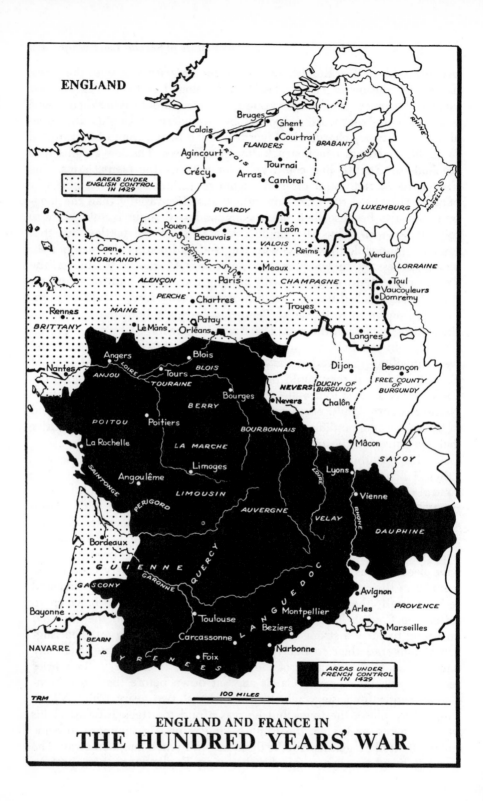

ENGLAND AND FRANCE IN
THE HUNDRED YEARS' WAR

the continent which she was to hold for the next two centuries. So ended the glorious campaign of Crécy. Edward had exhausted his treasury, wearied his own country with taxes, devastated northern France—and conquered one town. This might have suggested the futility of trying to acquire and hold all France.

The first great outbreak of the Black Death occurred soon after the surrender of Calais, and for a time neither France nor England was capable of putting an army in the field. During the lull in the fighting Philip VI died, but his successor, John the Good, had learned nothing from his father's misfortunes and was even more enamored of the outworn chivalric ideas which had cost France so dear at Crécy. In 1356 Edward's eldest son, the Black Prince, sallied forth from Aquitaine on another great plundering raid, and John went to meet him with the old feudal array. The armies met at Poitiers, and again the French tried to storm a strong defensive position without using bowmen. This time the knights were dismounted so that the French lines would not be thrown into confusion by the mad plunges of wounded and dying horses, but men who charged up a hill in heavy armor were in no condition to fight when they reached the top. The French became so absorbed in the struggle that they forgot to guard their rear, and they were completely routed when a Gascon detachment circled the field of battle and struck them from behind. Hundreds of Frenchmen were slaughtered, while King John and many of his court were taken prisoner. Yet the English gained little territory by this overwhelming victory and did nothing but make sporadic raids until the Peace of Calais [1] in 1360 brought the war to a temporary halt. By this treaty Edward tacitly surrendered his claim to the French throne and was granted in return full sovereignty over southwestern France—the ancient Aquitaine—and Calais and Ponthieu in the north. In addition, the French were to pay an almost unbearably large sum as ransom for John the Good.

Peace had been made only because both sides were exhausted and neither country intended to observe the terms of the treaty. John's ransom was never paid, and, like a gallant knight, he surrendered himself to the English. He remained in captivity until his death in 1364. His absence was a blessing for France. His son Charles who acted as regent, was a poor knight—he had fled from the field at Poitiers—but he was an excellent statesman. In civil affairs he relied on bourgeois advisers, who succeeded in restoring order and even a certain degree of prosperity. The army was entrusted to a rough Breton gentleman, Du Guesclin, who raised an efficient fighting force from the bands of freebooters who had settled on the French country-side. Charles himself bewildered the

[1] This was formerly known as the Treaty of Brétigny, but it now seems established that, while preliminary negotiations took place at Brétigny, peace was actually made at Calais.

English with skilful and unscrupulous diplomatic maneuvers and stirred up rebellions throughout Aquitaine. When the English in desperation renewed the war in 1369, Du Guesclin refused to meet them in open battle, but contented himself with besieging isolated garrisons and cutting off small detachments of their army. The old trick of sending a large raiding force through the heart of France was tried, but Du Guesclin refused to take the bait, and in 1375 the exhausted English consented to a truce. Of their French possessions, only Calais and a small area around Bordeaux remained. Before the truce expired Edward III and the Black Prince were dead, and a child was on the English throne. The war continued in theory, but for the next generation the fighters were merely pirates and robbers.

The reign of Edward III, which had begun so auspiciously, was to end most dismally. At first the French war had been very popular in England and the people rejoiced in the easy victories and the rich plunder. Repeated taxes soon cooled the martial ardor of the middle class, and in the years after the Treaty of Calais, disillusionment and anger became general. The conquests were melting away, while French pirates hampered trade and inflicted on English coast towns the horrors which had become a commonplace in the devastated areas of France. Returned soldiers, unwilling or unable to find legitimate employment, harried the rural districts, either as bandits or as the hired retainers of some unscrupulous magnate. And over every one hung the terror of the Black Death, which struck again and again in the latter part of Edward's reign.

The increased participation of the privileged classes in the work of the central government did nothing to allay rising discontent. Barons, knights, and burgesses had no plan for solving economic or social problems, except the hopeless policy of trying to preserve the *status quo*. Only in political matters did they have a positive program, and in that field they made notable gains in their efforts to limit royal power. Edward was too anxious to secure support for the war to resist the demands of powerful groups of subjects, and while he broke his promises again and again, steady pressure from below gradually forced him to change his methods of government. The Household slowly ceased to have much influence on public affairs; the Council was filled with magnates, and Parliament became almost independent of the king. All these changes lessened royal power and gave the upper classes, and especially the barons, greater influence on the government. The decline of the Household and the presence of large numbers of magnates on the Council meant that royal officials no longer had complete control of policy and appointments to office. The increased independence of Parliament changed its character completely and made it a real check on the king. Now that it was no longer dominated by royal officials, it could not be used primarily as a law-court. It gradually lost its function of hearing and answering petitions and almost lost its function of deciding difficult legal cases. On the other hand, its legislative work greatly increased in importance. Edward occasionally raised taxes after consulting other bodies, but he ran into so many difficulties when he did this that he finally came to rely almost entirely on parliamentary grants. When he needed money in a hurry, as he usually did, Parliament was the best place to get it.

Early in the reign the knights and burgesses combined to form the House of Commons, and this body gained considerable importance during the middle years of the century. Both king and magnates realized that the Commons represented the tax-paying communities of the country and that therefore the requests of the Commons deserved careful consideration. Thus the petitions of the Commons became the basis for the greater part of the legislation of Edward's reign. This did not mean that the Commons were running the government, since most of their petitions dealt with trivial or local matters. Their chief influence on general policy was in economic legislation, for example, regulations affecting the wool trade and statutes fixing the wages of laborers. In political crises, however, the Commons usually followed the wishes of the dominant group of barons, since the knights, who controlled the House, were closely connected with the lords. They were landlords, even if lesser landlords; their economic interests were much the same as those of the magnates. Many knights were relatives or retainers of barons; many others feared to arouse the hostility of magnates who dominated their counties.

On the surface, England seemed to be developing a form of limited monarchy in which the king was controlled by an aristocratic Parliament, but appearances were deceiving. In the first place, the magnates, who were the strongest group in Parliament, wanted to influence the government without taking the responsibility for running it. They intervened only when their pride or their interests were touched; they were perfectly content to let the king and his officials handle ordinary affairs. One could never be sure what kind of action would offend the magnates —a situation that made some bureaucrats rather timid—but one could be sure that the magnates would lose interest in almost any problem after a year or two. Such continuity in policy as there was had to be assured by professional civil servants. In the second place the magnates were seldom in complete agreement with each other, and their factional disputes weakened their ability to influence policy.

These points are illustrated by the intrigues that marred the last years of the reign of Edward III. As the king became older and less capable of ruling, the aristocracy split into two loosely knit factions. One group, headed by one of Edward's younger sons, John of Gaunt, duke of Lancaster, had considerable influence on policy in the 1370's. But the war in

France was going badly and John and his adherents were accused of incompetence and corruption. The opposing group, led by the Black Prince, gained control of Parliament in 1376, and invented the process of impeachment in order to punish some of John's friends. But the Black Prince died; John of Gaunt used his influence to secure a new Parliament that was favorable to him, and he was the dominant political figure in England when the old king died in 1377.

The premature death of the Black Prince had made his ten-year-old son, Richard II, heir to the throne. Since the boy was not yet of age, control of the government rested with the Council, and the magnates strove to gain places for themselves or their friends in this important body. Naturally, the Council did not govern very effectively, but worse than its inefficiency was its failure to realize that England was on the verge of rebellion. The evil advisers of the king were blamed not only for political fecklessness and corruption, but also for all the other ills of the time. Wycliffe's radical religious ideas had unsettled many minds and had made it easy for radical economic and social ideas to spread. England was full of wandering priests and agitators who denounced the exactions of the upper classes, and who preached on that disconcerting text:

> When Adam delved and Eve span
> Who was then the gentleman?

Resentment was strongest among the lower classes of the towns and among the poorer peasants. Both groups felt that they were being exploited by the rich and that they were being deprived of all opportunity for advancement. They were especially aggrieved by the Statute of Laborers (1351) which fixed prices and wages at pre-plague figures and kept them from profiting from the great demand for labor caused by the Black Death. As the author of *Piers Plowman* says:

> Then laborers landless, that lived by their hands,
> Would not deign to dine upon worts a day old;
> No penny ale pleased them, no piece of good bacon,
> Only fresh flesh or fish, well fried or well baked . . .
> He must highly be hired, or else he will chide.
> Bewailing his woe, as a workman to live . . .
> He grumbles 'gainst God, and grieves without reason,
> And curses the king, and his counsel after,
> Who license the laws that the laborers grieve.

The actual outbreak came in 1381, when the government bungled the assessment and collection of a poll-tax. The tax was unpopular anyway, and when royal commissioners were sent out to see if more money could be raised they were driven from the towns of the southeast. Soon Kent and Essex were in arms and Canterbury was taken. Then a motley army of peasants and artisans started for London, while the rising spread through the rest of England. In most places there was surprisingly little violence. Old charters and manor records were burned and the peasants demanded new leases which abolished labor services and granted them their lands at moderate rents. Many of the rebels, showing pathetic confidence in written promises, went home as soon as they had received their charters, but enough remained united to spread panic in London. The incompetent government, which had been unable to foresee a rising which had been brewing for years, showed no more skill in defending the chief city of the realm. The Council ordered the gates closed and took refuge with the king in the Tower, but the rebels had adherents in London who admitted them as soon as they arrived in force. For several days the mob held the city and took vengeance on those whom it blamed for misgovernment and depression. Records were burned; the palace of John of Gaunt was destroyed; merchants, lawyers, and foreign tradesmen were massacred. When the king left the Tower for a conference with one group of rebels, another band invaded the royal stronghold and put to death Sudbury, archbishop of Canterbury, Hales, the treasurer, and other unpopular members of the Council. In spite of this violent action, the king himself was respected; the rebels wished to put an end to evil customs and evil counsellors, not to overthrow the monarchy. The importance of this distinction was shown on the following day, when Richard went out to parley anew with the insurgents. During a heated discussion, the rebel leader, Wat Tyler, was struck down by the king's escort, and Richard and his followers stood helpless before the angry mob. With superb courage the boy rode into their midst, saying "Sirs, will you shoot your king? I will be your chief and captain; you shall have from me all that you seek." The rebels took him at his word, and when a loyal force came out from London to protect him they meekly dispersed.

Reaction now commenced. The aristocracy recovered from its amazement and remembered that it was still the dominant military force in the country. Rebels were hunted down and killed in the disaffected counties. No one paid any attention to the charters which had been granted during the period of danger. When a deputation of peasants dared remind Richard of his promises he retorted: "Villeins ye are and villeins ye shall remain." Before the vengeance of the nobles the violence of the rebels in London pales to insignificance. All the fury of a frightened class was vented on the helpless peasants and for some years their lot was worse than before the rebellion. Serfdom was to disappear almost completely in England during the next century, but only because economic change made it an unprofitable anachronism.

The intrigues for control of the Council and the clumsy handling of the Peasants' Rebellion had given Richard every reason to be disgusted with government by the magnates. When he came of age he made a determined effort to diminish the political power of the aristocracy and to withdraw the concessions which had weakened royal authority. His plans were thwarted by a violent protest of the barons in 1388, but Richard waited patiently for the storm to subside and began his work anew. By 1397 he had succeeded in executing or exiling his principal opponents, in placing his supporters in all the key positions of the government, and in making Parliament once more subservient to the crown. He had shown great political skill in achieving these results, but he seriously overestimated the extent of his success. He had irritated the aristocracy by attacking its leaders, by confiscating the lands of men he distrusted, and by removing most of the great lords from his Council. But he had not deprived the aristocracy of military power, nor had he built up an army of his own to counterbalance the forces of the barons. Thinking that England was completely under his control, Richard led an expedition to Ireland to put an end to the chronic state of anarchy that prevailed in that island. Henry of Lancaster, son of John of Gaunt, whom Richard had exiled in 1397, seized this opportunity to return and to start a rebellion. The barons rushed to his support, and when Richard returned to England he found himself helpless and friendless. He was seized, imprisoned, and forced to abdicate, while Henry called a great assembly [2] to sanction his assumption of power. Since Henry had already won a decisive military victory and had received the support of the magnates, the assembly could scarcely refuse its assent. It approved a long list of charges against Richard II and accepted Henry of Lancaster as King Henry IV.

Like Edward II, Richard II had found that he could not govern England without allowing the barons to participate in the government. Richard was probably right in thinking that baronial influence on appointments and policy caused confusion and instability, but he was wrong in thinking that he could eliminate that influence with the resources at his disposal. The fact that Richard II was more intelligent and more skillful in political maneuvering than Edward II only made his failure more striking. His Lancastrian successors profited from his example. They had come to power through an aristocratic revolution and they knew that they could keep power only by ruling with the assistance of the aristocracy.

Intrigue and revolution did not solve the problems of fourteenth

---

[2] There has been a long controversy as to whether this assembly was a Parliament or not. Technically, it probably was not a Parliament, but it was composed of the usual groups of the lords, and the representatives of the counties and boroughs, and most of these representatives were men who had been elected to the House of Commons before the revolution.

century England but at least they established certain constitutional rules that were to be useful in the age of absolute monarchy. No tax could be imposed without the consent of Parliament; no statute could be made without going through the forms of parliamentary approval. The propertied classes, divided on so many other questions, remained united in these two points. They would not give the king a free hand in taxation or legislation.

Intrigue and rebellion in France accomplished even less than they did in England because they did not lead to the creation of institutions which could later be used to restrain the king. The French aristocracy increased its influence on the king and on central and local government, but the French aristocracy was even less united than the English. The vast majority of French nobles were mainly concerned with preserving personal and provincial privileges; only a handful sought power in Paris. Moreover, the French aristocracy seldom gave any support to the demands of the bourgeoisie. Perhaps this was due to the fact that the knights in France were definitely members of the nobility while the knights in England occupied a sort of middle position between the nobility and the burgesses and hence could act as a link between the two groups. Finally, it should not be forgotten that the Hundred Years' War was waged almost entirely in France. It was France that suffered from English raids and from the looting of the "free companies" of unpaid or mutinous soldiers. The essential thing, for the French, was to gain some degree of security, not to make constitutional reforms.

War and pestilence, conspiracies and misgovernment almost ruined France during the reigns of Philip VI and John the Good ("good" only in the sense of being a "good fellow"). Neither king showed any ability in meeting the crises, and the national and local estates, though frequently called together to vote taxes, developed no programs for recovery. The final disaster of Poitiers was the signal for a widespread revolt. The Estates-General met in Paris and, under the leadership of Etienne Marcel, head of the Paris merchants, demanded a reform of the government's financial procedures and a change in the composition of the royal council. When Charles, Duke of Normandy, who was ruling in place of his captured father, King John, procrastinated, Marcel and his followers murdered the unpopular councillors. Charles fled, leaving Marcel in control of Paris. At the same time a rebellion began in the rural areas. In 1358 armed bands of peasants burned country houses and destroyed records much as English peasants were to do in 1381. But the French rising, the Jacquerie as it was called,[3] was more bloody and more revolutionary than the English Peasant's Rebellion. The French rebels

---

[3] The upper classes thought of "Jacques" as a typical peasant name, hence a "Jacquerie" was a peasant movement.

massacred many members of the aristocracy and showed little faith in promises of reduced rents and services.

The royal government seemed for a while to be in a hopeless position, but the rebels were too divided to form a rival political organization. Marcel was supported chiefly by the bourgeoisie of Paris; other towns were unwilling to accept Parisian leadership. Many members of the nobility were disgruntled, but they had no desire to join with middle-class radicals. The Parisians had little sympathy for the despised peasants; in fact many Parisians were owners and exploiters of rural estates. Cooperation between Paris and the leaders of the Jacquerie was almost impossible, and Marcel lost much of his popularity when he tried to arrange such an alliance. The nobles soon rallied and suppressed the peasant rising with atrocious cruelty. When Charles moved on Paris, Marcel committed the final mistake of seeking the support of English sympathizers and was murdered by his own followers. Once more it had been shown that unity and order in France depended on a strong monarchy.

Charles of Normandy, who became king as Charles V in 1364, had united with the nobles to resist Marcel and the peasants, but he had little sympathy with the narrow and selfish views of the nobility. During the twenty years between the Treaty of Calais and his death in 1380, Charles labored to restore royal authority and to rebuild his country. He suppressed, to a large degree, aristocratic factionalism, and while he employed nobles as his officials, he gave them little opportunity to influence his policies. He made few innovations; he merely revived and perfected the bureaucratic government that had been created by St. Louis and Philip the Fair, but this was enough to restore order and some degree of prosperity. The extent of his success may be measured by the fact that during the regency of eight years that followed his death France remained relatively calm. His heir, Charles VI, came of age in 1388 and carried on his father's work until he was suddenly stricken with insanity in 1392. The importance of the king as a bulwark of law and order almost immediately received a new proof. The princes of the royal family and their supporters began quarreling for control of the government and France slowly declined into a miserable period of civil war.

ENGLAND AND FRANCE TO THE END OF THE HUNDRED YEARS' WAR

With the accession of Henry IV in 1399 England began an experiment with aristocratic, parliamentary government which was to last for sixty years. Henry's position was none too secure, even after Richard II had been secretly murdered, since there were other descendants of Edward III who had a better claim to the throne. He had to make every effort to gain the support of the upper classes, and early in his reign he promised that "he would not be guided by his own will nor by his own desire or individual opinion, but by common advice, counsel and assent." This meant, in practice, that the Council was filled with magnates and that important decisions were referred to Parliament for approval. As usual, the barons preferred to have as much work done in Parliament as possible in order to prevent the king from acting rapidly and secretly while they were absent from court. They continued to coöperate with the Commons, in order to secure the support of the lesser land-owners and the middle class, and the lower house gained two important privileges during the reign. It was agreed that all money bills must originate in the House of Commons, since it represented the classes which paid most in taxes. Henry also promised to make no important changes in the wording of the petitions of the Commons if he decided to enact them into law. Before this time the king had been free, not only to accept or reject petitions, but also to amend them until they bore little resemblance to the original proposal. The new rule left the veto power with the king, but seriously limited his right of amendment and marked a new and important step in parliamentary control of legislation.

The propertied classes not only had a strong position in the central government, they also had a large degree of control of local government. Most local officials—sheriffs and tax-collectors, mayors and collectors of customs duties—were unpaid local notables. During the late fourteenth and early fifteenth centuries an even more important figure began to emerge in the counties and the boroughs—the Justice of the Peace. Neither the sheriffs nor the handful of royal circuit judges could cope with the growing wave of crime, and disobedience to the commands of the central government. Therefore leading men in each county were commissioned to arrest and to try lawbreakers. Serious offenses, such as murder and highway robbery, were left to circuit judges, but misdemeanors and violations of administrative regulation were handled by the Justices of the Peace. For example, the Justices enforced the rules that limited the wages received by laborers. Like earlier local officials, the Justices of the Peace were unpaid. They were well-to-do men; they came from the same class as sheriffs and members of Parliament. Often they were closely allied to the barons of their region and in periods of weak government they followed the wishes of the local strong man rather than those of the king. Even when the king was stronger than the barons, the Justices of the Peace protected their local and class interests. They made no great effort to enforce laws or ordinances that might injure their fellow property owners or stir up trouble in their districts. In the long run, most governmental policies had to be enforced by the Justices of the Peace, and thus the propertied classes were in a position to modify, delay, or even to thwart the wishes of the ruler.

Though he was willing to share his power with the aristocracy, Henry IV had difficulty in finding a stable basis for his government. Factionalism and intrigues continued, and so the personnel of the Council had to be altered frequently. The barons of the Marches of Wales and the North were not content with mere intrigue. They wanted virtual autonomy in their own regions as well as influence in the central government, and they broke into open rebellion when Henry refused to meet their demands. The king was not really secure until he had fought two bloody wars and had almost exterminated the powerful Percy family, which had led the risings from its strongholds in the North. Great political skill, judgment and energy were required to guide England through this difficult period. Henry not only possessed these merits; he also knew how to make the most of his limited financial resources and so avoided the resentment that arose whenever taxation was too frequent or too heavy. When he died in 1413, exhausted by his endless difficulties, England was relatively peaceful and prosperous, blessings that the country rarely enjoyed in the fourteenth and fifteenth centuries.

His son Henry V was viewed askance by many, because in his youth he "had served Venus no less fervently than Mars," and because he appeared to lack the sober virtues of his father. Responsibility changed his character, and during his brief reign (1413–1422) he attended strictly to the business of government. Strong-willed, persistent, and intelligent, he might have been able to build a strong state in England if he had devoted his energies to internal affairs. But no pressing problems demanded solution at home, and his own love of combat combined with the opportunities offered by French weakness led him to renew the attempt to conquer France.

For over twenty years the princes of the French royal family had been engaged in increasingly bitter quarrels. An ancient royal policy made these quarrels especially dangerous to the kingdom. Since the time of St. Louis it had been customary to grant whole provinces to younger sons of the royal house, on the theory that relatives of the king would be loyal to the head of the family and would aid him in governing his large and imperfectly united realm. Following old precedents, Philip the Hardy, a son of King John the Good, had been invested with Burgundy. He then acquired Flanders through a marriage arranged by Charles V. Later Charles VI gave his younger brother Louis the duchy of Orleans. When Charles VI became insane in 1392 the houses of Burgundy and Orleans began a long struggle for control of the government. Until the death of Philip the Hardy in 1404, the contestants had limited themselves to intrigue and bribery, but Philip's successor, John the Fearless, precipitated civil war by compassing the murder of Louis of Orleans in 1407. Leadership of the Orleanist faction was assumed by the count of Armagnac, father-in-law of the young duke of Orleans, and from this circumstance the ensuing disorder has taken the name of the Burgundian-Armagnac feud. Both sides, in their efforts to gain power, intrigued with Henry IV of England, who encouraged each in turn, but wisely refused to intervene. The burgesses of Paris, supported by the university, sought to end the strife in 1413 by the *Ordonnance Cabochienne,* which aimed at strengthening the bureaucracy and increasing bourgeois influence in the bureaucracy. This new attempt to end the evils of aristocratic influence on the government was no more successful than that of Étienne Marcel, and the Orleanists soon suppressed the movement.

Such was the situation when, in 1414, Henry V revived the English claim to the throne of France. Legally his position was absurd, for even if the tacit surrender of the claim by Edward III were ignored, the usurping Lancastrians were not his nearest heirs. This fact did not deter Henry, who invaded France in 1415 and won a spectacular victory at Agincourt. Far more important than the battle, which, as usual, settled nothing, was an English alliance with John of Burgundy. With the most powerful noble in France on Henry's side, effective resistance to English aggression became almost impossible. Henry returned to France in 1417 and began a systematic conquest of Normandy. Three things distinguished this campaign from earlier English invasions. First of all, Henry prohibited, and severely punished, plundering. He realized that he could not hold France without the good will of the inhabitants, and he wanted the people to feel that English rule gave them security and order. In the second place, the French showed an intensity of national feeling hitherto unknown. Though Henry offered to respect their laws and privileges, the cities of Normandy held out tenaciously and yielded only when their walls were destroyed and their people were starving. Finally, in this campaign, artillery began to play a conspicuous part. The guns were still crude, and blew up so easily that they were often more dangerous to their own crews than to the enemy, but they proved valuable in siege operations. The slow pounding of the heavy stone balls could make a breach in the strongest fortifications, and Henry's conquest of Normandy was greatly accelerated by his use of artillery. The days of the heavy-walled castle with its bristling turrets were almost over, and with the castle went one of the last bulwarks of feudalism.

While Henry was taking town after town in Normandy, desperate efforts were being made to end the paralyzing strife of Burgundians and Armagnacs. The Dauphin Charles, heir to the throne, who had allied himself with the Orleanists, at last consented to meet John of Burgundy at Montereau. It is likely that Charles or his friends had planned in advance to assassinate John. In any case the conference ended in a scuffle during which John was murdered. The new duke of Burgundy, Philip, miscalled the "Good," was eager for vengeance and gave Henry his full support. He secured possession of the mad Charles VI and in 1420 sold France to the English king at the Peace of Troyes. By this treaty the Dauphin was declared a rebel and Henry was recognized as heir to the French throne. Henry was to marry Charles' daughter Catherine and to take over the government of France at once. With his claims thus fortified, Henry began the conquest of the rest of France and had obtained possession of all the lands north of the Loire, when he died in 1422, worn out with incessant campaigning. A few months later Charles VI followed him to the grave and a year-old baby inherited the crowns of England and France.

The patriotic resistance which the cities of northern France had offered to the advance of Henry V made the chances of a permanent occupation seem small. The accession of the infant Henry VI and the quarrels which inevitably accompanied a regency further weakened the position of the invaders. Hostility to the English was general, showing itself in sporadic risings of nobles, burghers, and peasants alike. Even in Burgundy the alliance with the foreigner became unpopular as soon as the English showed that they were not mere tools of the duke but were working to build up their own power. The English themselves were somewhat worried by their success and gave only lukewarm support to their expeditionary force. They were beginning to grudge the cost of the war and to fear that their king might eventually subordinate the interests of his small island kingdom to those of his larger French realm. Despite these disadvantages, the fortunes of the English rose steadily higher during the years immediately following the death of Henry V. This surprising result was due largely to the great political skill of the duke of Bedford, the English regent at Paris. He gave the half of France which was under his control firm but just rule, preserving local customs and using French officials wherever he could. The duke of Burgundy was kept in line by soft words and bribes. Finance was Bedford's greatest problem, but with the meager grants reluctantly conceded by Parliament and such taxes as his impoverished French provinces yielded, he managed to maintain a small but efficient army. Slowly but steadily the territory of the *Roi de Paris,* as Henry VI was called, was enlarged, until in 1428 English troops reached Orleans, the gateway to southern France. Bedford had not enough men to surround the city, but he succeeded in cutting off most of its supply of food, and the defenders soon began to feel the pinch of hunger.

Bedford could not have been so successful if the French had had a leader capable of uniting the country against the invader. The exiled Dauphin, Charles VII, was the logical person to undertake this task. Almost half of France was in his possession and even in the North the people were only waiting for the signal to rise. But Charles was a sorry leader for such a movement. Weak and cowardly, he surrounded himself with flatterers, most of whom were Armagnacs who had been involved in the murder of John the Fearless and were therefore anxious to prevent a reconciliation between Charles and Philip of Burgundy. The taxes which were voted by the Estates of the South were appropriated by court favorites for their own uses. The Constable Richemont, a Breton warrior of the school of Du Guesclin, was exiled from court when he endeavored to stir Charles to action. The nobles of the South were still warlike, but their belligerent spirit manifested itself only in private wars and family feuds.

In 1429, with the English before Orleans and Charles cowering miserably at Chinon, the leadership which the Dauphin had failed to provide was assumed by one of his humblest subjects. Under the pressure of English invasion, national feeling had ceased to be intermittent and sporadic; it had spread through all classes and regions. Jeanne d'Arc was a woman and a peasant; she lived in a remote border province; but in spite of these handicaps she was to lead the armies of France because she embodied the spirit of French patriotism. She was born in Domrémy near the northeastern frontier, at some time between 1410 and 1412. Her childhood was passed in the midst of the turmoil of the Burgundian-Armagnac feud and the disasters of the English invasion. Brooding over "the pity that was in the Kingdom of France" she took refuge, as did many women of her time, in an intense inner life. At an early age she began to hear "voices," messages from her favorite saints, and in time the voices designated her as the one chosen by God to save her suffering country. At first she resisted the suggestion, but repeated messages forced her to yield.

Her visions gave Jeanne confidence in her mission, but they would not in themselves have been sufficient to inspire a generation which had seen rather too many prophets. But Jeanne was not only absolutely convinced that she was guided by God; she also had the gift of leadership. Though she knew "neither A nor B," she possessed shrewd common sense, a quick and witty tongue, and remarkable powers of persuasion. Thus armed, she set forth in 1429 from Domrémy. Surmounting the barriers of her youth and sex, and the inertia, scepticism, and hopelessness of the Dauphin and his favorites, Jeanne soon found herself at the head of a force to relieve Orleans. She slipped through the loose English cordon and entered the city with little trouble. The effect of her presence was almost magical. The people of Orleans "felt comforted, as if the siege were already lifted, by the divine virtue which was felt to dwell in this simple maid whom all—men, women and children—love with a passionate affection."

The enthusiasm of the French was equaled by the discomfiture of the English. Bedford reported that "there felle by the hand of God, as it semeth, a greet stroke upon youre peuple . . . caused in greete partye, as I trowe, by . . . a disciple and leme of the fende called the Pucelle, that used fals enchantments and sorcerie, the which stroke and discomfiture not oonly lessed in greet partie the nombre of youre peuple ther, but as wel withdrawe the courage of the remnant in marvaillous wise, and courage your adverse partie and enemyes."

With enthusiasm and confidence transferred to the French side, the pressure on Orleans was soon relieved by a series of daring attacks on the English positions around the city. On the news of the victory there was a great stirring all over France. The Dauphin was still the greatest handicap to his own cause, and it required all Jeanne's persuasive powers to goad him to the second step in her program, the coronation at Rheims. Spurred on by the voices which cried unceasingly "Fille de Dieu, va, va, va! Je serai à ton aide!" she persisted and won again. Through the heart of the English possessions her little army moved to Rheims, where Charles was crowned according to the ancient ritual. Jeanne had realized what the Dauphin's sophisticated advisers had forgotten, that the ceremony at Rheims gave divine sanction to kingship in the eyes of all good Frenchmen, and that loyalty to Charles would be greatly increased by the coronation. As she had predicted, the journey to Rheims aroused a new wave of enthusiasm, and it seems probable that a vigorous campaign might have freed France from the invaders within a few months. But Charles was weary of action and weary of Jeanne's harangues. The favorable moment was allowed to slip by, leaving France to suffer for twenty long years. The Maid was captured while leading a raiding party near Paris, and Charles did not lift a finger to save her. The English took their revenge at Rouen. A servile ecclesiastical court condemned Jeanne as a heretic, and two years after her departure from Domrémy she was burned at the stake.

The cowardice and folly of the king she had saved enabled the English to kill the Maid, but nothing could kill the impression made on France by the events of 1429. Despite Charles and his favorites, despite the valiant efforts of Bedford, the tide had definitely turned. In 1433 the faction led by Richemont drove Charles' evil advisers from court. The English now began to suffer from divided counsels, and an uncle of Henry VI committed the supreme folly of alienating Philip of Burgundy by trying to secure a fief which the duke coveted. Philip deserted the English in 1435, and in the same year the death of Bedford left the invaders without a leader. Paris was taken in 1436 and town after town opened its gates to the French. Charles, under the tutelage of energetic and patriotic counsellors, began to emerge from his apathy and to take some interest in military affairs. From 1444 to 1449 there was a truce, during which the French army and finances were reformed. When the war was renewed, the English posts fell rapidly, and by 1453 only Calais remained in their possession. The Hundred Years' War was over.

During the second half of his reign, from the truce of 1444 to his death in 1461, Charles VII earned the title of "The Well-Served." Once more, as under Charles V, the Council was dominated by men chosen for their ability and not for their rank, men who wanted to build up the king's power instead of their own. Charles VII never became a great leader, but he loyally supported his councillors and suppressed the efforts of the disaffected princes and nobles to regain control of the government. The problems confronting the king and his Council were stupendous. To expel the English was only a beginning; there remained the task of repairing the damage wrought by a century of misgovernment and war. Large tracts of arable land had gone out of cultivation, even in the region of Paris wolves prowled around the city. "The English," it was said, "brought forests to France." Commerce was stagnant because roads had disappeared, and rivers and harbors had become unfit for use. Elements of the population had become thoroughly demoralized; this was the period when the witchcraft delusion reached its height and when a companion of Joan of Arc sacrificed children to the devil. Bands of unpaid soldiers and outlaws, the "flayers," wandered through the countryside, stealing, maiming and killing.

By the end of Charles' reign the more obvious ravages of the war had been repaired. The "flayers" were hunted down and killed, or driven out of the country. Commerce was encouraged, and fairly large sums were spent for repair of roads and harbors. Waste land was brought back under cultivation, and many peasants found it easy to acquire small holdings on favorable terms. The Estates grumbled at the high taxes entailed by the royal reforms, but Charles' success in driving out the English and in suppressing internal disorder gave him an almost impregnable position. Few men were ready to resist a victorious king, and in the end the Estates surrendered most of their powers, including control of taxation. They accepted the king's ruling that almost all taxes, including the famous *taille* (paid mostly by peasants) and sales-taxes (paid mostly by the bourgeoisie) could be levied without consent, since they were needed for the welfare of the realm. The aristocracy had never been greatly interested in the work of the estates, and did not object to this decision (especially since nobles were exempt from many taxes). Princes and nobles did become annoyed, however, when they found that Charles was not as generous with gifts of pensions and money as his father had been. The king was successful in preventing the formation of a united front of princes and nobles against him, but during the latter part of his reign he did have to worry about growing disaffection among many members of the aristocracy. His difficulties increased when his eldest son Louis developed political ambitions and allied himself with the more rebellious nobles because Charles would not give him a share in the government. When Louis fled to the court of the duke of Burgundy, Charles was urged to disinherit his undutiful son. Age had taught the old monarch wisdom, and he contented himself with the cynical—and accurate—prophecy that "my cousin of Burgundy is nourishing the fox that will eat his chickens." But in spite of these troubles, Charles could well rejoice in the accomplishments of his reign. France had made a wonderful recovery since the dark year of 1422, when the disinherited Dauphin wandered listlessly about the South while an English regent issued orders from Paris.

LOUIS XI OF FRANCE

Charles' successor, Louis XI (1461-1483) is one of the less attractive figures in French history, yet he is one of the men who made France. He completed the task, begun centuries before, of uniting all the great fiefs to the royal domain, and he broke the power of the house of Burgundy, which had threatened France for almost a century. Jeanne d'Arc had shown the power of profound religious faith and selfless love of country; Louis derived his strength from other and less admirable characteristics. He was an able and utterly unscrupulous politician, and while he was outwardly a pious Catholic, his religious beliefs did not deter him from lying, cheating, and plotting. He believed that money could buy any man, or any saint, and his relations with supernatural powers were marked by the same corrupt diplomacy that distinguished his relations with secular potentates. He made lavish offerings to the patron saints of his enemies just as he bribed the advisers of his enemies; he bought relics of his favorite martyrs just as he bought the services of able diplomats. On his deathbed he had the pope send him a saintly hermit to pray for his recovery—and had spies test the holy man to make sure that he was not a charlatan.

Nevertheless, Louis' malevolence and eccentricities should not obscure the fact that he was a very significant figure. He was no worse than most other rulers of his day; he was simply more intelligent and persevering. He belongs in the select company of the founders of the "new monarchies," the men who took the steps that were to lead to the absolute states of the sixteenth and seventeenth centuries. And like the other founders of the "new monarchies," Louis achieved surprising results with very little institutional change. He worked hard at his job; he saw to it that he and his advisers were well-informed; he depended largely on men who had no independent power base and who could be destroyed in a moment if they displeased the king. Commines, one of the diplomats whom Louis succeeded in recruiting from the ranks of his enemies, has left an unforgettable portrait of the king in his *Memoirs*. He praises Louis' shrewdness, his ability to manipulate men, his tenacity in pursuing his objectives, his skill in avoiding open confrontations with his opponents while steadily undermining their position. Commines deserted his old master, the duke of Burgundy and came over to Louis' side because he felt that Louis was playing the political game better than any of his enemies. Commines' estimate was correct. Through good judgment, hard work, and complete lack of scruples, Louis drew new strength from old institutions and in the end he dominated France as none of his predecessors had ever done.

Louis acquired political wisdom at some cost to himself and his people. During the first years of his reign he allied himself with the nobles and banished the advisers of his father. Then he endeavored to emancipate himself from the nobles by stirring up strife between rival families and by encouraging malcontents in the great fiefs, especially Burgundy, to revolt. His plans miscarried, and in 1465 he was confronted by a league of magnates, led by Charles the Rash, who had taken over the rule of Burgundy from the aged Philip the Good. The nobles dignified their rising with the name of the "War of the Commonweal," but in reality they were making a last stand for provincial independence against royal centralization. Louis' foolish policy had alienated all classes and he was unable to make any effective resistance to the league. Realizing that he was beaten, he bought peace by promising to cede large portions of the royal domain to the rebels. He never entirely fulfilled these promises, but the nobles, as usual, could not remain united long enough to insist on receiving all the fruits of their victory. Louis worked strenuously to widen the rifts in the hostile coalition, and during the next decade he slowly regained a position of supremacy. He avoided war, since intelligent planning might be upset by the chance results of a battle, but he became a master of diplomacy and intrigue. He had spies in every court and the advisers of many lords were in his pay. Members of the League of the Commonweal were detached from their allies by enormous bribes. Those who could not be convinced by golden arguments found themselves deserted and confronted with the alternatives of unconditional surrender or imprisonment in the dungeons of a royal castle.

One opponent, however, could neither be bribed nor threatened.

Thanks to the efforts of his father and grandfather, Charles the Rash of Burgundy was one of the most powerful rulers in Europe. In the southeastern corner of France he held the duchy and county of Burgundy, rich agricultural provinces which supplied him with hosts of fighting men. In the Northeast, the well-planned marriages of the Burgundian house had added province after province to their original county of Flanders, until almost all the Low Countries were in their possession. The inhabitants of the rich northern towns, exhausted by a century of class struggles, had allowed the dukes to withdraw their old privileges and to burden them with heavy taxes. The wealth of the Netherlands not only made the Burgundian court the center of northern art, it also enabled the dukes to pay for the armies which they raised in their southern holdings. There was only one weakness in Charles' position; his possessions in the Netherlands were separated from Burgundy by the imperial duchy of Lorraine. If he could acquire this territory, Charles would possess an unbroken domain stretching from the Alps to the North Sea and be in a position to revive the ninth century middle kingdom of Lotharingia. This plan Louis was determined to frustrate. A strong state on the eastern frontier was a menace to French security, and no victory over the nobles could be permanent as long as they could hope for Burgundian support.

The contest between Louis and Charles was merely one phase of the long struggle for possession of the middle kingdom, a struggle which began with the grandchildren of Charlemagne and is not yet ended. In the fifteenth century the result was determined largely by personal temperament. Alike in ambition, Louis and Charles differed in almost every other respect. To the patience, craft, and diplomacy of the French king, the Burgundian opposed a fiery temper and a stubborn and short-sighted reliance on military power. While the League of the Commonweal remained united, Charles was able to extort many concessions from Louis, but as internal opposition subsided, the French king slowly gained the upper hand. Without committing himself in any overt way, Louis sent agents to incite the Rhine princes and the Swiss against Charles. They were already uneasy about Burgundian aggression in Lorraine and Alsace, and when they were secretly promised French subsidies, they joined forces against the duke. After suffering several defeats from the Swiss, Charles finally was killed in an attack on Nancy in 1476. Louis made a rapid pilgrimage of thanksgiving to his favorite shrines and then plunged eagerly into the task of seizing as much of the Burgundian inheritance as possible. Since Charles had left a daughter, and since many Burgundian territories were fiefs of the empire rather than of France, it was difficult to find a good excuse for wholesale annexations. Louis' first thought was to settle the whole problem by marrying Mary of Burgundy to his eldest son, but this plan was frustrated when Mary espoused Maximilian of Habsburg, son of the Emperor Frederick III. Then as many Burgundian fiefs as possible were declared forfeited to the French crown under the Salic law, which barred female succession. The Habsburgs resisted, but a compromise was finally effected in 1482 by the Treaty of Arras, by which Louis received the duchy and county of Burgundy, and Artois and Picardy in northern France. Flanders and the other provinces of the Netherlands remained in the hands of the Habsburgs, to trouble sorely the rulers of France in the next three centuries. Nevertheless, Louis had notably enlarged the royal domain and had eliminated the Burgundian menace. At almost the same time, the counties of Anjou, Maine, and Provence escheated to the crown, leaving Brittany as the only large, semi-independent feudal state. This last great fief was acquired shortly after Louis' death, when his successor married the heiress to the duchy. Now that they no longer ruled whole provinces, the nobles were less of a menace to the monarchy. They still made trouble in the sixteenth century, but they could no longer threaten to set up independent states, as the duke of Burgundy had done.

The "War of the Commonweal" had revealed to Louis the need for securing the support of the middle class. Many of his ministers were commoners, and he did his best to encourage the growth of commerce and industry. His economic policy was not always very wise, but at least he showed a real interest in business. Peace, and a more orderly government, restored prosperity and France became again one of the wealthiest countries in Europe. In return, the middle classes loyally supported his attacks on the nobles and gave without complaint the money required for his diplomacy of corruption. More surprising, they accepted with equanimity a policy of centralization which struck down civic liberties as well as feudal privileges. The great majority of townsmen had lost faith in their old policy of autonomy and self-government. Autonomy had encouraged foreigners and feudal brigands to attack the isolated towns; self-government had meant either domination by the wealthy or endless class war. They now prized security more highly than liberty and were willing to surrender local privileges in return for greater opportunities to trade.

Sure of the support of the bourgeoisie, Louis also controlled the clergy, thanks to the Pragmatic Sanction of Bourges (1438) and subsequent deals with the papacy. The peasants had little political influence, but they were grateful for the restoration of order and no longer troubled the country with their desperate rebellions. Even some of the nobles, tired of futile private wars, became supporters of the monarchy. With increasing support from all classes, Louis became more autocratic as the years went by. Even his ministers were not allowed to criticize his policies, and insubordinate officials were ruthlessly crushed. Louis was no easy master—he was suspicious, jealous of his prerogatives, and frequently unjust—but the French people felt that it was better to have a hard master than none at all. The story of France in the later Middle Ages ends as it began: Louis XI completed the structure of royal absolutism begun by Philip Augustus, St. Louis, and Philip the Fair.

THE WARS OF THE ROSES

The ease with which Charles VII had completed the task of rescuing his realm from the foreign invader was due in large part to the distracted condition of England. In spite of his victories, Henry V had left a legacy of trouble to his heir. Even in the lifetime of the victory of Agincourt there had been gloomy foreboding—

> Woe is me [mused an ancient chronicler] mighty men and treasure of the realm will most miserably disappear about this business. And in truth the grievous taxation of the people to this end being unbearable, accompanied with murmurs and smothered curses among them from hatred of the burden, I pray that my supreme master become not in the end a partaker of the sword of the wrath of the Lord.

In undertaking the conquest of France, Henry had not only committed his country to a task far beyond its strength, he had also brought about his own early death, leaving England to face the dangers of a long royal minority. Even his final triumph, the Treaty of Troyes, was marred by his marriage to Catherine, daughter of the insane Charles VI. Henry VI, the one child of this union, was to have enough trouble to drive a normal man to madness, but his mental stability was not improved by his unfortunate ancestry. His forty-year reign was to see the complete breakdown of aristocratic government and the beginnings of the Wars of the Roses, the last great feudal struggle for power.

During the minority the nobles intrigued and quarreled for control of the government, but actual fighting was prevented by the conciliatory efforts of the king's uncle, the duke of Bedford. After Bedford's death in 1435 the situation became worse. Henry was a "good, simple and innocent man," more fitted for the monastic cell than the throne. His rigid morality, his sublime trust in his friends and ministers, his hatred of violence were all admirable qualities, but they did not fit him to deal with the corrupt and turbulent barons who filled his court. The king's chief advisers were accused of profiteering, misappropriation of funds, and treason, and were usually too busy defending themselves to pay much attention to the war in France. The Commons were weary of endless unsuccessful campaigns and were naturally reluctant to vote taxes which they believed would be either stolen or wasted. In these circumstances it is not surprising that the English lost ground rapidly in France and that they were forced to accept the "shameful truce" of 1444, by which Henry admitted the loss of most of his French inheritance and agreed to marry the niece of Charles VII. The truce made the government more unpopular than ever. Though the English had been reluctant to give money for the war, their pride was hurt by French success, and they cursed the men responsible for their humiliation. Henry's marriage with Margaret of Anjou was a further insult to their patriotic feelings, and their anger was not lessened when the queen began to exercise a dominating influence over her husband. Loyalty to the Lancastrian dynasty had been shaken, and the king could no longer count on the support of most of his subjects when threatened by revolt.

The barons were stronger than they had been for centuries. The profits of sheep-raising, pensions, lands granted by kings who needed their support, and plunder from France had given great wealth to a few score families. With this wealth they bought the services of bands of returned soldiers and of other unemployed or adventurous men. These retainers not only wore the livery of their master and fought his battles, they also "maintained" the cause of their lord in all legal disputes and were in turn protected from punishment for their own misdeeds. They terrorized witnesses, threatened jurors, and not infrequently persuaded corrupt officials to place them on juries which were trying cases in which they were interested. Since many justices of the peace and some judges of the central courts were relatives or dependents of great lords, it was almost impossible to stop these practices. There was repeated legislation against "livery and maintenance," but by the middle of the fifteenth century there was little chance of convicting a powerful lord or his followers in the royal courts.

Public order began to disintegrate with the return of English troops from France, and the progress toward anarchy was greatly accelerated when in 1453 Henry VI suddenly went insane. The old struggle for control of the government was greatly intensified and private feuds ripened into civil war. One party was headed by the queen and her favorites, the other by Richard, duke of York. Richard was descended, in the female line, from the third son of Edward III, while Henry VI was the heir of the fourth son, John of Gaunt. Thus Richard had an excellent claim to the throne, and his appearance as leader of the opposition was an ominous sign. At first he asked only for the regency, and since the alternative to his rule was the domination of the foreign-born queen, Parliament allowed him to govern the country during 1453 and 1454. Then Henry recovered his senses and removed Richard and his followers from power. The disappointed Yorkists began armed resistance and in 1455 fought their first battle with the adherents of the Lancastrian king. Thus began the Wars of the Roses,[4] a struggle which brought out the worst side of the English aristocracy. No great moral or constitutional principles were at stake, and neither party had a definite political program. Personal interests dictated the behavior of the barons; they fought to gain lands, to kill their rivals, and above all to be on the winning side. Few men remained consistently loyal to one party, and the Wars of the Roses are one long record of betrayals, ambushes, and assassinations. In one important respect they fell short of the horrors which France had experienced; there was comparatively little pillaging of cities or devastation of the country-side. The great majority of Englishmen took no interest in the fighting; the cities threw open their gates to any victorious army and Parliament ratified the acts of whichever faction was in power. The barons apparently did not want to disturb this neutrality and refrained from acts which might have driven the middle and lower classes into the ranks of their opponents.

In 1460 Richard of York was slain at Wakefield, but the leadership of his faction was promptly assumed by the earl of Warwick. The "Kingmaker," as he was called, controlled such an enormous body of retainers that he could almost determine the result of the civil war through his own forces. In 1461 he entered London and proclaimed Edward, the young duke of York, as rightful king of England. Henry VI, after a feeble resistance, fled. For four years he wandered about, a miserable exile, and then was captured and imprisoned in the Tower.

The reign of Edward IV is of interest because in many particulars it foreshadows the policy later followed by the Tudors. No sooner was he placed on the throne than he commenced to build up a party of his own in order to emancipate himself from Warwick. The Kingmaker was angered by this ingratitude and began to intrigue with Louis XI to gain support for a Lancastrian restoration. In 1470 he staged a well-planned revolution which replaced Henry VI on the throne, but the English had little confidence in Henry and no desire to be ruled by Warwick. A year later Edward returned from exile and defeated and killed the Kingmaker. To avoid further trouble Henry was quietly murdered, though according to the official report the saintly king died "of pure displeasure and melancholy."

For the next twelve years Edward's rule was practically absolute. "He appeared to be dreaded by all his subjects, while he himself feared no man." The Council was dominated by the king and lost much of the independence it had possessed under the Lancastrians. The justices of the peace, on the whole, supported royal policies. Edward was thrifty and showed great ingenuity in developing non-parliamentary sources of revenue. He forced his wealthy subjects to give him "benevolences"—

[4] The white rose was the badge of York and popular fancy soon invented the story that the red rose was the badge of Lancaster.

supposedly free gifts; he had shares in private trading ventures; he received a large pension from Louis XI as payment for neutrality in the Franco-Burgundian struggle. His financial independence made it easy for him to restore royal control over legislation. Most of the statutes of his reign were drafted by royal advisers and few petitions of the Commons became law. Yet he could not dispense with Parliament entirely, for it was sometimes necessary to ask for grants of taxes, and royal laws needed the stamp of parliamentary approval. Edward had no trouble on these occasions; the nobles were cowed and the middle class gave whole-hearted support to the king. As in France, they had learned that strong royal government was the only alternative to aristocratic anarchy, and they were ready to surrender some of their privileges in return for peace and order. Moreover, Edward was encouraging English industry and commerce and increasing prosperity made it easier for every one to pay taxes.

Edward might have established his house firmly on the throne if, like so many English kings, he had not made an unfortunate marriage. He fell in love with Elizabeth Woodville, widow of a minor Lancastrian baron, and married her in spite of the protests of his supporters. The Yorkists might have forgotten the queen's antecedents if they had not been exasperated by the greed of her relatives, who were never weary of seeking titles and high offices from the king. Edward's own brother, Richard of Gloucester, was an enemy of the queen, and led a faction of the Yorkist party which opposed her influence. When Edward died in 1483 his thirteen-year-old son, Edward V, inherited his mother's unpopularity with his father's crown. After a few months, Richard of Gloucester found it easy to usurp his nephew's throne. Edward V and his little brother were secretly murdered, while relatives and supporters of the queen were executed as rebels and traitors. These crimes outraged the country, and Richard III, in spite of his attempts to give England good government, never secured widespread support. Respect for the rights of the legitimate heir had been the strong point of the Yorkist position, and Richard, by violating this principle, had ruined the hold of his family on the country.

As a result, many barons began to show interest in the fantastic claims of Henry Tudor, earl of Richmond, to the throne. Henry was descended in the female line from an illegitimate son of John of Gaunt and thus had a shadowy connection with the Lancastrian family, but there were many people in England who were more closely related to the royal house. However, he was the only man who had both the courage and the ability to oppose Richard, and when he landed in Wales in 1485 some of the discontented barons gave him their support. Richard could raise only a feeble and untrustworthy force to oppose the rebels, and when the armies met at Bosworth Field he was defeated and killed. The victor was proclaimed king as Henry VII and the country accepted the sudden change without protest. Not more than ten thousand men had fought in the decisive battle, but those few thousands had determined the destiny of England. With the advent of Henry VII and the Tudor dynasty, England left behind the confusion and violence of the later Middle Ages and began a period of prosperity and expansion which was to make her one of the great European powers.

The fifteenth century often seems a peculiarly futile period in English history. The war with France was a disaster and the attempts of the aristocracy to govern the country ended in the turmoil of the Wars of the Roses. Yet even the failures were to influence English character and policy in the next hundred years. In England, as in France, the Hundred Years' War intensified national feeling and prepared the way for the great burst of patriotism which was to distinguish the Tudor period. In England, as in France, selfishness and violence had discredited the aristocracy and had made the country eager for strong royal government. Moreover, there were solid accomplishments in the fifteenth century as well as failures. The long struggle of the English barons for power had not been completely futile. Unlike the French nobles, they had succeeded in making a permanent change in the institutions of their country. By insisting for two centuries that all important acts be done in Parliament, the barons had made Parliament an essential part of the machinery of government. It was not the motor—the driving force behind political decisions always came from the king or the great lords—but it was the transmission belt which conveyed political decisions to the country. No law was valid until it had been approved by Parliament, and while it was usually easy enough to secure this approval, it would have been dangerous to try to dispense with it. The country had become accustomed to the formality, and would have suspected the genuineness of laws which were not stamped "Made in Parliament." The Tudor rulers, with all their power, never attempted to legislate without Parliament and were even willing to listen to some of the suggestions of the Commons. Thus the traditions established in the fourteenth and fifteenth centuries carried English representative institutions safely through the sixteenth century reaction toward absolutism. Parliament was weakened, but it never ceased to meet, and in the seventeenth century it used the old medieval precedents to impose new limitations on royal authority.

Besides modifying her government, England improved her economic position during the later Middle Ages. Relatively few Englishmen took part in the political struggles of the fifteenth century, and the country suffered less from violence and war than did the states of the continent. Even the weak and inefficient governments of the period had encouraged the growth of manufacturing and shipping. The much stronger governments of Edward IV and Henry Tudor carried on an active commercial policy. They sought markets for English goods abroad and insisted on

CENTRAL AND EASTERN EUROPE c. 1360

the use of English ships. By 1500 the country had an important cloth industry and a flourishing merchant marine. Thus England was prepared to take part in the great expansion of commerce which was to open the sixteenth century.

THE EMPIRE AND THE HABSBURGS

France and England, the two most successful monarchies of the Middle Ages, had barely preserved their unity during the troubled years of the fourteenth and fifteenth centuries. It is not surprising that the loosely knit German kingdom disintegrated completely during the later Middle Ages. It is impossible to find any one theme around which the story of Germany may be centered in this period. Instead, several threads must be followed. There is, first of all, the growth of the power of the princely houses, which keeps pace with the decline of the central power. The house of Habsburg is the greatest of these, and the story of this family takes us beyond the limits of Germany, into the Netherlands and Spain. Next, there is the development of the Swiss Confederation, the first democratic state of modern times. In the third place, we must trace the history of the municipal leagues, which played a great rôle in the political and economic life of western and northern Germany. Finally, we must glance briefly at the history of those lands to the east which have so often influenced the fate of central Europe.

The medieval empire might well have been permitted to die with the Hohenstaufen; its great days were over, not only in international affairs, but even in Germany. The force of tradition was strong, however, and the confusion and "fist law" of the Great Interregnum (1256–1273) convinced many Germans that an emperor was necessary to keep central Europe from drifting into complete chaos. The pope supported the movement, since disorder in Germany hindered the organization of a crusade, and in 1273 the princes chose Rudolph, count of Habsburg, to head the Empire. The rule of this first Habsburg emperor [5] shows clearly the tendencies which were to be apparent in the future development of his family and his office. Rudolph was no genius, but the success which marked his policy shows how correctly he analyzed the situation which confronted him. As far as the Empire was concerned, he completely abandoned the Hohenstaufen tradition. He surrendered all claims to dominion in central and southern Italy in return for papal support, and even in the North he contented himself with purely verbal recognitions of his theoretical suzerainty. Within Germany he showed the same respect for established power. He proclaimed an imperial peace pro-

---

[5] For convenience and brevity the rulers of Germany during the fourteenth and fifteenth centuries are referred to as "emperors," though few of them were actually crowned by the pope.

hibiting all private war, but the imperial knights were the only class of
trouble-makers whom he dared attack directly. Many of these petty
tyrants had imposed unauthorized tolls upon commerce or had endeavored to supplement their incomes by robberies, and Rudoph's attempts to punish them were generally popular. He had to be much more
cautious in dealing with the feuds of the princes. He sometimes succeeded in patching up a peace by diplomatic means, but if negotiation
failed he had no other way of ending a quarrel. The result of all his
efforts was almost negligible; the depredations of the knights were
checked, but the princes continued to wage devastating wars.

As emperor, Rudolph was a mere figure-head; as founder of a great
royal house he was much more successful. The Habsburgs at his accession
controlled lands extending from modern Switzerland into Alsace, a substantial, though not a princely heritage. Rudolph used his position as
emperor to acquire other territories for his family; in this, as in his imperial policy, he set an example followed by most of his successors. He
succeeded by playing on the jealousy felt by the princes toward Ottokar,
king of Bohemia. During the Interregnum, Ottokar, like every one else,
had seized as much land as possible and had completely upset the balance
of power among the princely houses by acquiring the inheritance of the
last Babenberg duke of Austria. Ottokar's lands now stretched from the
Polish frontier to the Adriatic; none of his rivals controlled such wide
territories. His legal position was weak, however, since Austria was a
fief of the Empire and should have returned to the crown when the old
dynasty died out. In 1274, at the Diet of Nürnberg, Rudolph was instructed to occupy the escheated lands. Ottokar resisted bravely, but two
years later he fell at the battle of Marchfeld, near Vienna, and all
Austrian territory except Carinthia was turned over to Rudolph. Thus
the Habsburgs acquired their first important province and gained the
strategic position from which they were eventually to dominate central
Europe.

The princes were alarmed by Rudolph's success and, upon his death in
1291, endeavored to check the Habsburgs by electing Adolf of Nassau
as emperor. Adolf possessed all his predecessor's greed and none of his
tact, so that Albert of Austria had little difficulty in overthrowing him
in 1298. This second Habsburg was a stronger ruler than either of his
predecessors and gave the princes a bad fright before his career was
ended by an assassin's dagger. He regularly annexed fiefs of lords who died
without heirs and thus acquired lands all over the Empire. He supported
the Rhine cities against neighboring lords and defeated the most powerful
princes of western Germany when they protested against this policy. The
nobles were greatly relieved when Albert was murdered in 1308, and they
did their best to guard against any repetition of his energetic rule. Subsequent emperors were restrained by preëlection promises and were closely

watched lest they overstep the feeble authority left them. The Habsburgs were systematically excluded from the imperial office, and for over a century other families occupied the throne.

Between 1273 and 1308 the Habsburgs had risen from obscurity to the position of the most feared house in Germany; during the succeeding century and a quarter the house of Luxemburg was to gain even greater power. The first Luxemburg emperor, Henry VII, was a curious mixture of the new and the old. By adroit political maneuvers, he secured the throne of Bohemia for his son John, and thus raised a second-rate princely family to a position of great power and prestige. At the same time he was fascinated by the old traditions of the Empire. Led on by his romantic imagination and the pleadings of Italian imperialists like Dante, he allowed himself to be drawn across the Alps into the land which had brought ruin to the great Henrys and Fredericks. He was crowned in Rome by representatives of the pope (who refused to budge from the peace and security of Avignon). Henry hoped to reëstablish imperial power in Italy by ending the feuds which set city against city and faction against faction. He had at first some success, but soon all the quarreling groups agreed on one thing—that imperial interference was intolerable. Harassed at every turn, Henry fell ill and died in 1313. His love of adventure passed to his son, John of Bohemia, whose chivalrous exploits have been sung and written ever since his own day—how for years he maintained a precarious hold on northern Italy with no power but his fascinating personality, how he fought and plotted all over Europe and how, old and blind, the last of the great knights errant, he appeared at Crécy to fall fighting on the French side.

Between the death of Henry VII in 1313 and the accession of his grandson Charles IV, in 1346, confusion reigned in Germany. The princes had learned that a family might greatly increase its power through possession of the imperial office and competition for the succession was keen. Lewis of Bavaria and Frederick of Austria were the leading candidates, but in spite of bribery and intrigue, neither prince was able to secure the unanimous support of the electors. The votes were counted on the battlefield, but Lewis had no sooner defeated his rival than he was confronted by a new foe. The popes at Avignon were annoyed because they had had little influence on recent elections, and in 1323 John XXII announced that no imperial election was valid until the successful candidate received papal recognition. This contention precipitated the last great struggle between pope and emperor, a quarrel over empty forms rather than real power. National feeling at first drew most of Germany to Lewis' side, and in 1328 the Diet, composed of the greater and lesser princes, passed the decree *Licet Juris*, which stated that the electors and Diet determined the choice of an emperor to the exclusion of papal claims. Lewis' triumph was brief; he was a clumsy politician and his ambitions far outran his powers. By 1346 he had alienated most of his supporters and in that year he was formally deposed by the electors. His reign had little importance for Germany, but his struggle with John XXII had stimulated anti-papal feeling all over Europe. As we have seen, some of the most radical political works of the later Middle Ages were written by supporters of Lewis.

With Lewis' successor, the Luxemburger, Charles IV, we return to the tradition of Rudolph of Habsburg, which had been interrupted by Italian dreams of Henry VII and the fruitless quarrel of the Bavarian with the pope. Charles' patrimony was Bohemia and "to Bohemia he was a father, but a stepfather to Germany." In character he resembled Louis XI of France—superstitious rather than devout, an intriguer rather than a warrior, clear-sighted, cold-blooded and perfectly unscrupulous in seeking his ends. His ambition was to create a strong state centering about Bohemia, which might in time dominate Germany. He annexed principalities lying to the north of the Bohemian mountain-wall and prepared the way for further acquisitions by the carefully arranged marriages of his children. Within Bohemia he encouraged trade and industry, reorganized and strengthened the government, and founded the first German university at Prague. In imperial affairs his great work was the Golden Bull of 1356, an attempt to stabilize the political situation in Germany by defining the powers of the greater princes. Since the Interregnum the number of men taking part in the election of the emperor had steadily declined, but while there was general agreement that only a few of the most powerful princes had the right to vote, it was not entirely certain who those princes were. The problem was still further complicated by the fact that some electors had divided their territories among their children. Charles attempted to end all disputes by fixing the number of electors at seven and by forbidding them to divide their lands. The choice of electors represented a nice balancing of conflicting interests in Germany—three ecclesiastics (the archbishops of Mainz, Trier, and Cologne) against four laymen (the count Palatine of the Rhine, the duke of Saxony, the margrave of Brandenburg and the king of Bohemia)— four princes from the old Germany of the Rhine (the archbishops and the count Palatine) against three from the new Germany of the eastern frontier. The electors were given practically sovereign authority within their principalities, and their towns and vassals were forbidden to seek assistance from outside powers. Bryce scornfully remarked that the Golden Bull "legalized anarchy and called it a constitution," but this is hardly a fair description of a very sensible political move. Charles could not abolish the electoral system, but by defining the powers of the electors he decreased the excuses for contested elections and civil wars. He could not unite Germany, but by making the electors strong he encouraged the development of compact, well-governed principalities within the

Empire. Most important of all, from Charles' point of view, the Golden Bull made the electors well disposed toward the house of Luxemburg and protected it against the jealousies which had cost the Habsburgs the throne.

The Golden Bull was promulgated in 1356; in 1492 Maximilian I ascended the throne. Between these two dates there is scarcely an event worth chronicling in imperial affairs. Charles died in 1378, and his two sons, first Wenceslas, one of the most astounding drunkards in all history, then Sigismund, ruled the Empire for all but ten years of the period to 1437. With the acquisition of Hungary through Sigismund's marriage, the house of Luxemburg reached its greatest territorial extent, only to become extinct with Sigismund's death.

By a curious reversal of fortune, the Luxemburg lands fell by inheritance to a second Albert of Austria and made him so strong that the electors were practically forced to choose him emperor. From his accession to the extinction of the Empire by Napoleon, the Habsburgs retained the throne, except for a short interval in the eighteenth century. Sigismund had added some prestige to the imperial title by his part in the Council of Constance, but the fifteenth century Habsburgs lost all that he had gained. Albert II was an able ruler, but he died in 1439, the year after his election, and his successor, Frederick III, was a remarkably worthless man. Year after year he refused to show himself outside his dominions, refused even to attend the meetings of the imperial Diet. His lands were invaded repeatedly by hostile armies; he was insulted and browbeaten by the nobles; his financial resources dwindled to the point where he was forced to wander about aimlessly, an uninvited and unwelcome guest of monasteries and cities. Throughout, his confidence in the destiny of his house remained unimpaired. Stamped on his personal belongings, engraved on his seal ring, scrawled over countless bits of papers, was his cryptic device, made up of the five vowels and signifying *Austriæ est imperare orbi universo,* or *Alles Erdreich ist Oesterreich unterthan.* In Germany princes and people murmured, but political disintegration had gone so far that the electors did not depose Frederick because they could not agree on any one to take his place.

The condition of Germany in the fourteenth and fifteenth centuries defies description. The political map shifted with bewildering rapidity; territories changed hands again and again by marriage, war, or purchase; family fortunes rose and then collapsed, as had those of the house of Luxemburg. The possessions of a single family might be scattered over hundreds of miles, with other states intervening, as in the case of Luxemburg and Bohemia, which lay on the western and eastern borders of the Empire. The full title of even a mediocre prince would take up several lines of print. No map of ordinary size could represent the innumerable political divisions; no historical work could describe all the wars, alliances, and conquests. Cities, whose very existence depended upon some security and order, formed leagues for mutual protection, but particularism was so strong that even the cities could not remain permanently united. As the city leagues fell to pieces, the princes tried to create alliances to enforce peace, but they had little more success. In some states secret tribunals, the Fehmic or Vehmic courts, meted out summary justice and developed an organization very similar to the Ku Klux Klan of Reconstruction days in the United States. The fact that the Emperor Sigismund felt it wise to encourage this society and even to become a member shows how little reliance could be placed on the regular courts. The peasants found that the quarrels and wars among their masters made their burden heavier, and Germany, like France and England, had its peasant rebellions in the later Middle Ages. These blind and hopeless uprisings were easily crushed, and the rural population did not even have the satisfaction of seeing serfdom wither away from economic causes, as it did in England. The political disintegration of Germany went so far in this period that the powerful Habsburg emperors of the sixteenth century found it impossible to reunite the country. Strong local patriotisms had developed which bound each German to the tiny area of his "homeland," and not until the nineteenth century could these provincial loyalties be even partially overcome.

Yet through all the confusion and war, certain trends remained fairly constant. The balance of political power slowly shifted from the old Germany of the West to the new Germany of the East. The duchies along the Rhine had been shattered into fragments by grants to ecclesiastical princes, by interdynastic wars, and division of territories among several heirs. The largest principalities in the region were those of the bishops and archbishops, and these states suffered from the same weaknesses which were evident in the papal possessions in Italy. A bishop could not increase his holdings by marriage, he was not supposed to strengthen his position by conquest, and he had to rule through secular officials who were often disloyal and almost always dishonest. No lay ruler of the Rhine region had enough power to dominate his neighbors, and all the wars, treaties, and marriage alliances of the later Middle Ages failed to produce a strong state in western Germany. In the East, on the other hand, the principalities were larger and less cut up by ecclesiastical holdings, and the ruling houses were either abler or more fortunate. The fourteenth and fifteenth centuries saw the rise of four great families who were to dominate Germany in the early modern period, and all of these families derived their power from the possession of eastern territory. The Wettins had long held a margravate on the upper Elbe; in 1423 they were invested with the electoral duchy of Saxony, the nucleus of the future kingdom. The Wittelsbachs were given a fragment of the old Bavarian duchy at the end of the twelfth century, and to this they added neighboring lands bit by bit until they had a strong, compact state in a very strategic location. The Palatinate was held by another branch of the family, but their attempts to acquire other territories, such as Brandenburg and the Tyrol, were only temporarily successful. This was to be typical of Bavarian history; the duchy was again and again on the verge of becoming the most powerful state in Germany, but it never quite made the grade. It was always important, but never supreme. The history of the third great eastern family is in some ways the most typical of all. The Hohenzollerns had ruled a little territory in southwest Germany for generations, but they had had no importance until they were granted the electorate of Brandenburg in 1417. Transplanted to the East, the family flourished and eventually created the great Prussian kingdom.

The Habsburgs, like the Hohenzollerns, owed their importance to a shift to the East. We have already seen how Rudolph of Habsburg increased the family possessions by the acquisition of Austria. In the fourteenth century control of the main routes to Italy was secured when Carinthia and the Tyrol fell to the Habsburgs as a result of the complicated web of intrigue woven about that unfortunate and superlatively hideous heiress, Margaret Maultasch. The extinction of the Luxemburg line in 1437 brought Bohemia and Hungary to Albert of Austria, but this stroke of fortune seemed more than counterbalanced by Albert's premature death in 1439. Leadership of the Habsburg house then passed to the incompetent Frederick III and both Bohemia and Hungary soon asserted their independence. Frederick's weakness made his mystical confidence in the future greatness of his family seem ridiculous, but his hopes were justified by the career of his son Maximilian. Maximilian has been called the second founder of the house of Habsburg and this title he richly deserves, for by an amazing combination of shrewdness and luck he raised his family to the foremost position in Europe. His political career began in 1477, when at the age of eighteen he foiled the astute Louis XI by marrying Mary of Burgundy. By this move he secured the Netherlands and, as a result of subsequent negotiations, the Free County of Burgundy. In 1491 he paved the way for a second great increase in territory by a treaty with Ladislas, king of Bohemia and Hungary, who agreed that his states were to pass to the Habsburgs, should he have no male heir. Two years later the death of Frederick III gave the imperial throne to Maximilian and in 1494 he made his final and most profitable alliance. His son Philip was married to Joanna, heiress of Spain, Sicily, Naples, and the scarcely known lands of the New World. Frederick's boast no longer seemed an empty one; by the end of the fifteenth century the Habsburgs were well on the road to world domination.

THE SWISS CONFEDERATION AND THE HANSEATIC LEAGUE

In spite of reversals and misfortunes, the Habsburgs greatly increased their eastern holdings during the later Middle Ages; their one permanent loss of territory occurred in the West. The oldest possessions of the family lay in the forests and valleys of what is now Switzerland, but then was a patchwork of feudal holdings owing allegiance to at least a score of lords. Within the mountain fastnesses of the western Alps a constant struggle with nature had helped to produce a sturdy, self-reliant race, more shrewd and independent by far than the peasants of the lowlands. For the most part they were farmers and herdsmen, but along the trade-routes which led from Italy to the Rhine small towns developed, such as Zurich, Lucerne, Berne, and Basel. Many romantic legends of the origin of the Swiss Confederation have been told, most of them centering about William Tell. There is little truth in any of these tales, but their loss is not to be regretted, for the actual story is as heroic as the melodramatic inventions of misguided patriots.

Swiss history begins in the thirteenth century with the resistance offered to the Habsburgs by the three Forest Cantons—Uri, Schweiz, and Unterwalden—which cluster around the Lake of Lucerne. The cantons claimed that Frederick II had recognized them as imperial rather than Habsburg fiefs. This was a virtual declaration of independence, since no one had any real control over fiefs of the Empire. When Rudolph of Habsburg became emperor, they feared that he might use his new position to strengthen his family claims, so in 1291 they united in a "Perpetual Compact" to resist any encroachment. Rudolph had too many other troubles to attack the Swiss, but under his heirs a bitter guerilla war began, with forays, burnings, and outrages on both sides. The troubles came to a head in 1314, when the Swiss sacked the abbey of Einsiedeln, which was under Habsburg protection. The nobles of the Rhine region were alarmed by this violent manifestation of the strength and boldness of the peasant communities and feared that their own subjects might follow the example of the Forest Cantons. They joined forces with the Habsburgs, and in 1315 a large feudal army attacked the presumptuous peasants. The Swiss concealed themselves above the pass at Morgarten and, as the Habsburg army advanced, threw the array into confusion by rolling down large boulders and tree trunks. Then the peasants charged into the mass of men and horses and wielded their battle-axes to such good effect that the Austrians lost more men than the total number in the Swiss forces. The Habsburgs, after this rout, abandoned the struggle and concluded a truce which practically recognized the independence of the cantons.

The victory at Morgarten made other mountain communities which were striving for independence anxious to ally themselves with the Forest Cantons. During the next half-century Lucerne, Zurich, Zug, Glarus and Berne joined the confederation, each retaining its own government and peculiar institutions but surrendering some of its independence in foreign affairs. Self-confidence grew with size, and one feudal lord after another found his rights infringed without compensation. Then the cantons began to extend their alliances to include many Rhine cities and the princes of the region became really alarmed. Twice—in 1386 at Sempach, and in 1388 at Näfels—the Habsburgs and their allies tried to crush the Swiss, and twice they failed. As at Crécy and Poitiers, feudal cavalry found that it could not ride down well-disciplined infantry occupying a strong defensive position. In the year after Näfels the Habsburgs agreed to a truce which proved a definite surrender, for the struggle was never renewed.

For the sake of brevity the allied cantons have been called the Swiss. This name came into use in the fourteenth century, but not until the nineteenth century was the name "Switzerland" officially adopted; in the later Middle Ages the confederation called itself the "League of Upper Germany." There was no Swiss state or Swiss government, but only a group of self-governing cantons, held together by military alliances. A few common rules were imposed on all members of the confederation, but they were essentially negative and did nothing to create central institutions. In 1370 the jurisdiction of church courts was restricted and appeals to tribunals outside the confederation were practically eliminated. Later, war between members of the League was prohibited and an effort was made to define the military obligations of each canton. However, there was no federal government to enforce these regulations, and there were bitter arguments among the cantons over foreign policy and contributions of men and money in time of war. The small, rural cantons were suspicious of their urban allies and only the fear of foreign foes held the confederates together.

Yet, with all their political weaknesses, the Swiss greatly influenced the history of Europe in the later medieval and early modern periods. They furnished an almost unique example of republican governments which were able not only to preserve their independence but even to increase their territory. They also contributed largely to the revolution in military technique which resulted from success of infantry armies in the fifteenth century. The Swiss had at first fought purely defensive battles, but they soon learned that a compact mass of well-disciplined infantry could successfully attack loosely organized feudal armies. Armed with their twenty-foot pikes, Swiss forces could hold off any cavalry charge and could push ordinary infantry out of the way. Their reputation was greatly increased by their victories over Charles the Rash of Burgundy. The rulers of Italy, France, and Germany soon began to bid for the services of Swiss contingents. A few patriots opposed the idea of turning the armies of the cantons into mercenary forces, but the Swiss were poor and could not resist the temptation of high wages. They fought in almost every battle of the Italian wars which began at the end of the fifteenth century, and the Swiss Guard which still serves the pope is a reminder of the days when the Swiss were the backbone of the armies of Europe.

The "League of Upper Germany" was the most successful of the federations which were formed in the Empire during the later Middle Ages, but it was far from being unique. The Rhine towns combined again and again to end the depredations caused by warrior and robber barons, but they failed to form a permanent confederation. They were even more suspicious of each other than the Swiss cantons and lacked the military strength which was the chief reason for Swiss success. The best Swiss soldiers came from the rural cantons and self-governing peasant communities were rare outside of the mountains. Switzerland could not be invaded or blockaded, while most German towns could easily be besieged by the feudal lords in their neighborhood.

Along the North Sea and the Baltic, however, a league of German towns was formed which for a time was more powerful than many kingdoms. As early as the twelfth century, German merchants trading in the North— in England, Flanders, Sweden and Russia—had banded together for mutual protection. Association abroad naturally led to alliance at home and by the middle of the thirteenth century the towns of northern Germany often worked together to defend their interests or to secure economic privileges. Temporary alliances became permanent and by the middle of the fourteenth century a federation of North German towns, called the Hanseatic League, was well established. German trade in the Baltic had greatly expanded, following the work of the missionaries and the conquests of the Teutonic Knights, and the League included the string of trading-posts and towns which extended from Lübeck at the base of the Danish peninsula, through Stettin, Danzig, Königsberg, Memel and Revel to Novgorod in Russia. In addition the Hanseatic merchants had a large settlement at Wisby, on the island of Gothland off the Swedish coast and important "factories" in London and Bruges. The chief objective of the League was a monopoly of trade in northern products— fish, fur, wax, ship-stores and salt—and for most of the fourteenth and fifteenth centuries it succeeded in suppressing all competition. German merchants traded freely in England, Flanders, and the Scandinavian kingdoms, but natives of these countries were rigorously barred from the Baltic trade. The success of the League's economic policy is surprising in view of its political weakness. The federation's only organ of government was an assembly of delegates from each town which met infrequently and was usually poorly attended. It is impossible to say how many cities felt themselves bound by the obligations of membership; estimates of the number of allied towns at the height of Hanseatic power vary between seventy and eighty. There was friction between members and groups of members; Cologne and the cities of the lower Rhine were often opposed to Lübeck and the Baltic towns. A member which refused to coöperate could be punished by being excluded from the privileges and protection of the League, but it was difficult to secure unanimous support for such a step. Only in times of great peril could unity of action be secured, as in the struggle with Denmark between 1361 and 1370, when the League was threatened with the loss of its Baltic monopoly. This conflict marked the height of the League's power; it not only defeated the king of Denmark after two costly naval wars, but also gained such privileges in the Scandinavian countries that it was practically independent of the local governments.

Such successes, however, were due as much to the weakness of opponents as to the League's own strength. The volume of Baltic trade was as large, or even larger, than that of the Mediterranean, but pound for pound it was far less valuable. Fur and fish could not create fortunes to equal those based on silk and spice, and while the towns of northern Germany were wealthy, they did not possess the concentrated economic power which enabled the Italian cities to hire armies and bribe kings. As soon as the states of northern Europe emerged from the troubles of the fourteenth and fifteenth centuries, they began to attack the privileges and monopolies of the Hanseatic League. English merchants received protection against German competitors; the Grand Duke of Moscow seized Novgorod; interlopers from every country forced their way into the Baltic in spite of the opposition of the League. An accident of nature added to the woes of the Hanseatic merchants; the herring suddenly abandoned their old spawning beds in the Baltic and migrated to the North Sea. This enabled the Dutch to take over the trade in salt fish, which had been one of the most lucrative occupations of the League. At the same time the cities of southern Germany found ways of trading directly with England and Flanders without using the Hanseatic merchants as intermediaries, and so another important source of profits was lost. The southern towns became the leaders in German economic activity; they had learned much about banking from the Italians and they adapted themselves to the new, individualistic, capitalistic economy better than the Hanseatic cities. At the end of the fifteenth century the Fuggers of Augsburg and the Welsers of Nürnberg were engaged in financial operations of astonishing proportions. They carried on commerce all over Europe, operated mines, and even helped finance exploration and settlement in the New World. They were bankers of the Habsburgs and in turn received the support of that powerful family. The Hanseatic towns had little part in this new economic activity, and their old principles of coöperation and monopoly were no longer successful. As a result, the League slowly decayed during the fifteenth and sixteenth centuries, and its members either fell under the domination of German princes or became completely independent city-states.

SPAIN

The lack of political unity in Germany explains why the Habsburgs were so delighted to acquire Spain and why the heads of the family made it their chief place of residence in the sixteenth century. Spain was far from being a unified national state, but compared to Germany, it was a model of centralization. The rulers of the different Spanish kingdoms had had an extraordinarily difficult task in building up and holding together their realms. First they had had to drive out the Moors, and then they had had to deal with conquered peoples who clung stubbornly to their old customs and privileges. Each kingdom was made up of provinces which had been acquired at different times and under different circumstances, and each province had its own laws and institutions. The nobles felt themselves as good as the king, the towns had extraordinary privileges, and even the peasants in some districts were free to choose and abandon their lords. The peninsula was full of Moors and Jews, some converted and some not, but all of them difficult to fit into the framework of medieval Christian society. Spaniards had a bad reputation in medieval Europe; they were thought a restless, unpredictable people, full of radical ideas about government, education, and religion. In spite of all these handicaps, the kings of the twelfth and thirteenth centuries had increased royal authority and had imposed some unifying institutions on their realms. The petty kingdoms of the early Middle Ages had gradually been consolidated into four states with more or less permanent boundaries— the little kingdom of Navarre, hanging like a pair of saddle-bags over the Pyrenees; Portugal, which occupied its present position on the map; Aragon, which held the Mediterranean coast with its hinterland, and Castile, which included all the central and northwestern lands and occupied more than half of the peninsula. The Moors still held Granada in the extreme South, but this petty kingdom was so weak that it seemed only a matter of years before it would fall. Then came the collapse of the fourteenth century and Spain suffered all the misfortunes which afflicted France and England. Feudal rebellions, disputed successions, and minorities kept Castile involved in almost endless civil war, while the kings of Aragon spent their strength in foreign adventure, meddling in the affairs of France and Italy and even sniffing hopefully for scraps of territory in the wreckage of the Eastern Empire. Monarchy survived in Spain only because it had struck deep roots in the earlier period, and because the heads of the various factions needed kings to legalize their actions. The Church fared somewhat better; the people became more orthodox and at the same time more intolerant of Moors and Jews.

For two centuries these conditions went unchanged, until the two largest kingdoms were united by the marriage of Isabella, who became ruler of Castile in 1474, to Ferdinand, who succeeded to the throne of Aragon in 1479. Both monarchs were fired with the ideal of absolutism, which Louis XI was realizing across the Pyrenees, and both used methods which resembled those of the French ruler. They knew how to profit from the general desire for orderly, peaceful government, a desire which was so strong that it led men to condone all the misdeeds of successful rulers. In an age of unscrupulous despots, Ferdinand was preëminent for the fervor with which he made promises and the ease with which he broke them. Slowly, but inexorably, all classes were subjected to the crown, and feudal, provincial, and municipal privileges were curtailed. The nobles, who were most likely to offer resistance, were placated by leaving them exempt from taxation. The distinction between Castile and Aragon could not be effaced, and some of the more powerful provinces retained a certain degree of autonomy, but Spain took a long step toward unification during the reign of the Catholic Kings.

Unfortunately, Ferdinand and Isabella did not always wield their power wisely, and some of their policies eventually proved disastrous to Spain. Like many other rulers, they were attracted by the ease with which sales-taxes may be collected, and based their financial system on a ruinous tax on purchases. The rate was high, and no rebates were granted on finished products which had already been taxed as raw materials. Thus commerce and industry were discouraged in Spain at a time when they were rapidly expanding in northern countries. In their attempts to unify the country, Ferdinand and Isabella persuaded the pope to revive the Inquisition and to subject it to their control. They used it to stifle all unorthodox opinion and to harass, and eventually to expel, the Moors and the Jews, whether converted or not. A high degree of uniformity was thus obtained, but it was hardly worth the price. The Moors and Jews were the best artisans and businessmen in the kingdom and their expulsion accentuated the economic weakness of Spain. Finally, the Catholic Kings inaugurated an ambitious foreign policy far beyond the resources of their states.

The conquest of Granada in 1492 was a logical and not too expensive move, and support of the great explorations which began in the same year proved a wise investment. Isabella had hoped only for a few unknown islands and a share of the East Indian trade; instead she received vast kingdoms which could be conquered and held by a few thousand soldiers and officials. But the conquest of Naples and ensuing wars with France brought only deficits and heavy taxes. The need for allies against France was one reason for the marriage of the heiress of Spain to Philip of Habsburg and this alliance involved Spain in the wars which resulted from Habsburg ambition.

EASTERN EUROPE

While the Habsburgs, from Rudolph to Maximilian, were laying the foundation for their power on the ruins of the Holy Roman Empire, and dreaming of the time when their might should dominate the world, there was growing up in the East a rival empire with which the fortunes of the Habsburgs were to be inextricably entwined down to our own century. The Ottoman Turks emerged from the great reservoir of nomadic peoples in central Asia early in the thirteenth century. At first they served as loyal allies of the Seljuk sultan of Konia, but when their master's empire fell to pieces in 1307, the Ottomans asserted their independence under Othman or Osman, from whom they take their name. Under Othman and his son, Orkhan, extensive conquests were made in northern Asia Minor at the expense of the Eastern Empire, so that by 1340 they controlled the southern shore of the Sea of Marmora and a short stretch on the Black Sea. The ease with which these conquests were made is attributable in part to the strong military organization of the Turks and especially to the excellent discipline of the Janissaries. The corps of Janissaries was the creation of Orkhan, who levied a tribute of young boys from the subject Christians, gave them an excellent education and military training, and then selected some for the army and some for the civil service. By this Spartan method he secured a group of men trained from earliest youth to the one idea of service to the state. A more important reason for Turkish success was the weakness of the Eastern Empire, which had never recovered from the setback given it by the Franks in the Fourth Crusade. After the recovery of Constantinople by the Greeks in 1261, the Empire did, to be sure, embrace Thrace, most of Macedonia, and western Asia Minor, but even in these provinces its authority was slight. The population of Constantinople was fickle and easily excited; the imperial armies were turbulent and disloyal; the imperial office was the prize of intrigue, and many of its occupants were powerless and incompetent. In struggles for the throne, rival claimants even sought the support of the Turks, who first entered the European provinces as allies of an imperial pretender. The empire was still further distracted by inroads from the West, where the Serbians, under Stephen Dushan, and the Bulgarians were carving out large states for themselves.

Encouraged by this chaotic situation, the Turks crossed the Straits in 1354 and captured Gallipoli. From this base they expanded west and north. Thrace, Bulgaria, and most of Serbia were conquered; a crusading army was crushed at Nicopolis in 1399, and the Eastern emperor was forced to pay tribute. Constantinople itself was saved only because of the defeat of the Turks in 1402 at Angora by Tamerlaine, who was trying to revive the Mongol Empire. While Tamerlaine lived, the Ottoman advance was checked, but he died shortly after his victory and the Turkish conquests began anew. Finally, in 1453, Constantinople was taken after a siege of over a year, and the Byzantine Empire was wiped out of existence. The fall of Constantinople sent a thrill of horror through western Europe and demonstrated the reality of the Turkish peril. Except as a symbol, however, the event does not merit the attention it has received. The Fourth Crusade had so weakened the Eastern Empire that, during the last two centuries of its existence, it had been unable to perform its old function of guarding Europe against Eastern invaders. The Byzantines had been unable to keep the Turks from advancing to the Danube, or even to assist the Balkan peoples in resisting them. As for the old story that the fall of Constantinople sent a flock of refugee scholars to Italy, where they started a revival of classical studies, the facts will not support the conclusion. Italian interest in the classics began long before the fall of the Eastern Empire; Greek scholars were teaching in Italy in the late fourteenth century, and all the important works of the Greek classical period were known in the West before 1453. The loss of Constantinople did show the peoples of the Danube basin their danger, and in 1456 a large crusading army under the Hungarian János Hunyadi met and defeated the Turks in Belgrade. This reversal slowed down the Moslem advance. For the rest of the fifteenth century the Turks did no more than conquer the fragments of territory in the Near East which had escaped them during their first advance.

The coming of the Turks marks the beginning of the "Near Eastern Question." In this same period another of our modern problems, the relation between the Germans and the Slavs, appeared in acute form. Ever since the days of Charlemagne the Germans had been pushing back the Slavs, sometimes by force, sometimes by peaceful settlement. The territories which were first conquered were completely Germanized and no mixed populations were left to create trouble in later days. But in Poland, Bohemia, and along the Baltic coast the Germans were never able to absorb or exterminate the Slavs. German settlements remained isolated in the midst of Slavic populations, and German rulers never gained the complete loyalty of their Slavic subjects. Even in Bohemia, where Germans were numerous and where the ruling house of Luxemburg had done much for the welfare of the kingdom, resentment against German domination grew during the fourteenth century. The Bohemians supported Huss as much for nationalistic as for religious reasons. When the Luxemburg line became extinct they rejected Habsburg claims and remained independent under their own kings for the rest of the fifteenth century.

Farther north, the situation was even worse. The Teutonic Knights had conquered the Baltic coast as far as the Gulf of Finland. The Poles and

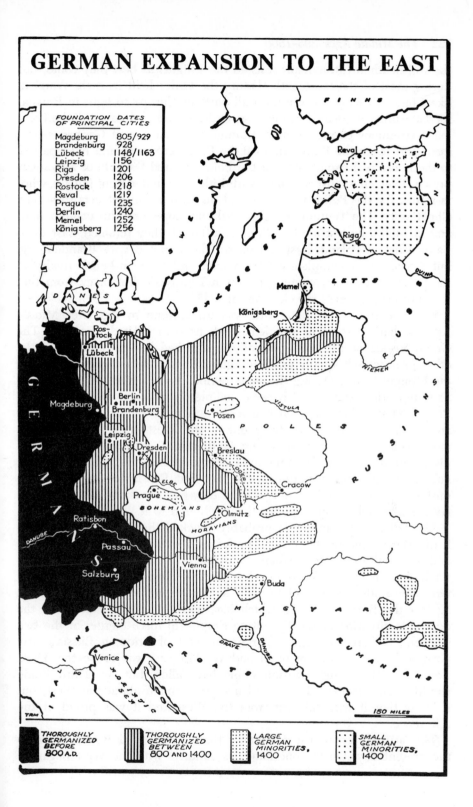

GERMAN EXPANSION TO THE EAST

FOUNDATION DATES
OF PRINCIPAL CITIES

Magdeburg	805/929
Brandenburg	928
Lübeck	1148/1163
Leipzig	1156
Riga	1201
Dresden	1206
Rostock	1218
Reval	1219
Prague	1235
Berlin	1240
Memel	1252
Königsberg	1256

150 MILES

THOROUGHLY GERMANIZED BEFORE 800 A.D.	THOROUGHLY GERMANIZED BETWEEN 800 AND 1400	LARGE GERMAN MINORITIES, 1400	SMALL GERMAN MINORITIES, 1400

the still-heathen Lithuanians resisted the Knights as best they could, but during most of the fourteenth century the Order held its own. Warriors like Chaucer's Knight came from all parts of Europe to fight in Prussia. As the century wore on, however, the Order began to decay, and the Poles made strenuous efforts to break through the thin line of German settlement and reach the Baltic. In 1386 the Polish crown should have passed to the house of Luxemburg, but the Poles rejected the rule of a German prince. They chose instead union with Lithuania under King Jagello, who, in return for the Polish throne, forced his Lithuanian subjects to accept Christianity. The Teutonic Knights could not cope with this combination, and in 1466 they lost most of Prussia, although they retained East Prussia as a fief of Poland. East Prussia was later united with Brandenburg, but it was never completely Germanized and German-Polish rivalry in the province was a disturbing factor in European diplomacy from that time until expulsion of the Germans in 1945.

Russia had few contacts with western Europe in the later Middle Ages. It had to solve its problems with its own limited resources. The Grand Prince of Moscow gradually established his authority over the other princes and equally gradually gained complete independence from the Mongol khans. During the same period the old Russian nobility lost its independent status and became completely subservient to the Grand Prince. They gained in exchange more and more power over the peasants. Just as serfdom was dying out in the West, it began to become more widespread and more severe in Russia. Free peasants practically disappeared; they all became serfs of the prince, the Church, or the nobles. Perhaps this was due to the fact that Russia had almost no industry or commerce. The only source of wealth was the land, and the land was valueless unless peasants were bound to it.

The fall of Constantinople probably shocked the Russians more than it did the people of the West. The Byzantines had given their religion and their culture to the Russians; most of the leading clergymen in Russia had been of Greek origin. Now Russia stood alone to defend the Orthodox faith and way of life. There was strong resentment in Russia against the Roman Church, which had tried to take advantage of the desperate situation of the Byzantine Empire to force merger of the two Churches. There was also a certain amount of pride in Russia's new position as the champion of orthodoxy. Moscow was to be the Third Rome; old Rome and Constantinople had fallen, but the Third Rome would endure forever. Russia did not know much about the West, but it knew that it was different from the West and it was proud of the difference.

This attitude created a dichotomy that has plagued Russia down to the present day. On the one hand, as contacts with the West began to increase in the fifteenth and sixteenth centuries, the Russians realized that they could profit from using western administrative institutions and western technology. On the other hand, there was always the danger that imitation of the West would destroy Russia's cultural and spiritual identity. No one has yet found a satisfactory and generally acceptable solution to this problem.

XIV

->>>->>>->>>->>>(<<-(<<-(<<-(<<-

The End of the Middle Ages

MEDIEVAL SOCIETY and medieval institutions were changing during the fourteenth and fifteenth centuries, but the change was so gradual that, over most of Europe, men were unaware that it was taking place. They knew that there was a growing gap between the ideals they professed and the way in which they actually behaved. They knew that they had lost the feeling of security and stability that had existed in the thirteenth century. They knew that it was hard to make a living, that there were few opportunities to improve their economic status and many hazards that might reduce them to poverty. In some minds this knowledge produced profound pessimism and emotional instability. All reactions were exaggerated; the age was marked by an almost morbid piety and an utterly cynical worldliness, by quixotic displays of loyalty and extreme examples of treachery; by pity for the unfortunate and callous cruelty towards the poor, the vanquished and the unsuccessful. Yet underneath the tension and the violence there was a strong desire for political stability and moral certainty. The people of Europe had been battered, but they had not given up hope. Everywhere men were seeking a solution to the problems of their society, and in their search for a solution they produced, more or less unconsciously, a new type of European civilization. This new pattern began to appear in Italy in the fourteenth century and in the North towards the end of the fifteenth century; it was a way of life that was no longer medieval, though it owed much to the Middle Ages.

The change came most rapidly in Italy, and therefore the Italians were more aware than the northerners that their society was being transformed.

They made a deliberate effort to break with the medieval past and to seek guidance either in their own current experience or in the examples of the Greek and Roman worlds. In the North there was more continuity, more of an effort to reform rather than to discard old institutions and ways of thinking. These two attitudes remained quite distinct until the sixteenth century, although there were reciprocal borrowings that foreshadowed the eventual amalgamation of the northern and southern cultures. For this reason it will be necessary to discuss Italy and the North in separate sections.

THE ITALIAN CITY-STATES

Italy found it easier to break with medieval traditions than the North, because Italy had never fully accepted some of the essential elements of medieval civilization. For example, Italian towns had never decayed as had the towns of the North in the early Middle Ages; the Italian economy was based on commerce and industry, not on agriculture. Feudalism did not grow up spontaneously in Italy; it was brought in by northern conquerors and it never flourished in the peninsula. The Italian states that developed in the Middle Ages were based on control of towns, not on control of feudal duchies and counties. Most important of all, northern forms of art and expression came to Italy very late and were always in conflict with Italian traditions. The Italians experimented only briefly with the Gothic style of architecture, and, as we shall see, they never fully understood that style. In spite of the fact that the two greatest theologians of the thirteenth century, St. Thomas Aquinas and St. Bonaventura, were Italians, the Italian universities were at first not greatly interested in theology or philosophy; they specialized in law and in medicine. St. Thomas made his reputation at Paris, not at Bologna. It was only in the fourteenth century that scholasticism (that is to say, the Paris curriculum based on logic, philosophy, and theology) became fashionable in the Italian universities. In short, one might say that the strongest impact of medieval culture on Italy came at a time when that culture had already passed its peak in the North. It was easy to react against it, both because it was weakening and because it was a foreign importation.

The Italian way of life developed in the Italian towns. As we have seen in earlier chapters the Italian towns had been deeply involved in the conflict between Church and Empire. During that struggle almost all other sources of political authority had been destroyed or greatly weakened. The emperor, the landed nobility, and the bishops had lost whatever power they had once had in the towns. Even the pope had only nominal control over most of the urban centers in the Papal States. The towns, on the other hand, had become the masters of the rural areas that surrounded them. By 1300 all of Italy north of Rome was divided among independent, self-governing city-states.

Because they were independent, each Italian town had its own history, and few generalizations will apply to every community. It is possible to say that the strains caused by new methods of economic organization were especially acute in Italy, and that the problems created by the rise of capitalism and the depression of the small artisan dominated the political life of most towns. It is also safe to say that the incessant conflict between rich and poor, and between old rich and new rich families, expressed in revolutions, persecutions, and new constitutions, so wearied the ordinary town-dwellers that in the end most of them were ready to accept the arbitrary rule of a despot in return for the boon of internal peace. But the forms which class-warfare took were innumerable and the results also showed endless variation. Some towns received their tyrants early, others late, and a few never found tyranny necessary to preserve order. Some tyrants were mere brigands; others, while just as unscrupulous, tried to save their reputations by acting as patrons of art and literature; a few were really interested in the welfare of their subjects. It is impossible to tell the story of all the Italian towns in a few pages, but an account of three of the most important centers—Venice, Florence, and Milan—will illustrate the common problems and the divergent solutions of the Italian municipalities.

The long connection of Venice with the Eastern Empire had given her a favored position in Mediterranean commerce, and by the end of the thirteenth century the Venetians formed one of the most prosperous communities in Europe. During the next century Venetian galleys and traders pushed beyond their old Mediterranean routes into new waters. The coast of the Black Sea was dotted with their trading-posts, or "factories," and at regular intervals a great fleet was sent through the Straits of Gibraltar up the French coast to England and Flanders. To the Venetian factories were brought the Eastern wares which had once seemed luxuries, but were now almost necessities. Brocades, jewels, and silks were no longer worn only by prelates, and lords and their ladies on great occasions; masters, in their gild hall ceremonies, and many a burgher's wife and daughter now wore rich stuffs and jewels. The demand for spices, sugar, perfumes and rare woods increased steadily, and most of this trade fell to Venice, due largely to the paternalistic activities of her government. From earliest times commercial leaders had dominated political affairs. In this island city there was no landed nobility to be subdued, Guelfs and Ghibellines were unknown, and even the Church was viewed with a cold realism which seems foreign to the Middle Ages. In 1297 the commercial aristocracy ensured its continued predominance by preparing the "Golden Book." Membership in the Great Council, the chief governing body of the city, was restricted to families whose names were inscribed in the book, and new men found it increasingly difficult to obtain recognition. A few years later the establishment of a Council of Ten, elected annually by and from the Great Council, provided a small executive body with absolute powers. The doge, or duke, was reduced to the position of a picturesque figurehead, a master of ceremonies. The lower classes were cut off from all participation in the government. But economic welfare meant more than democracy to the sailor or dock-worker; plots against the Ten were usually the work of impoverished and disgruntled aristocrats, who were easily subdued.

The power of this commercial oligarchy was absolute—the actions of every citizen were closely regulated—but it was exercised with intelligence. The great aim of the government was to secure a monopoly of the Eastern trade on which the prosperity of Venice rested. Galleys were built, owned, and controlled by the state, which rented space in the ships to merchants. The route to be taken by commercial fleets was determined by the Great Council, and expeditions were regularly convoyed by warships. Eastern produce had to be unloaded and examined at Venice, where a duty was collected before it was sent on to the West. Foreign merchants, chiefly South Germans, were allowed to engage only in the land trade over the Alps and were forced to pay dearly for the privilege. They had to live in their own quarter, the *Fondaco dei Tedeschi,* submit to close regulation of every daily action, and pay very high export and import duties. Venetian foreign policy was merely a militant expression of her commercial policy. In order to secure her food supply and her control of the Alpine trade-routes, Venice began to covet the territory of her neighbors on the mainland early in the fourteenth century. By taking advantage of civil and intermunicipal wars, she succeeded in annexing most of the little towns in her hinterland and in gaining a dominant position in the northeast corner of Italy. Desire for a monopoly of the Eastern trade precipitated a war to the death with Genoa, which almost exhausted both cities. From this struggle Venice emerged victorious in 1380 at Chioggia. During the next half-century Venetian conquests proceeded apace. By the middle of the fifteenth century the Venetian Empire included a large block of territory on the Italian mainland, most of the Dalmatian coast, part of Albania, Corfu, part of southern Greece, Crete and many Ægean islands, in addition to trading-posts in the East. Commerce had given Venice this high position, for Venetian power expanded as surplus capital derived from trade accumulated. The aristocrats who deliberated in the Great Council, the ambassadors who resided at foreign courts and developed the traditions of modern diplomacy, the builders of the jewel-like palaces along the Great Canal, the captains of the galleys—all were capitalists, either investing their money in commercial ventures or letting out funds at interest to traders. Venice was the first modern state to be run by and for "big business."

By contrast with the smoothly functioning absolutism of Venice, the political history of Florence seems absolutely chaotic. Dante in exile castigated his native city which made "ordinances of so fine a texture, that the threads thou spinnest in October last not till mid-November. How many times within my memory hast thou changed thy laws, thy currency, thine officers and customs and renewed thy members! . . . Thou art like the sickly dame, who finds no rest on her bed of down, but shifts her posture to alleviate her pain." It is, in truth, impossible to follow the kaleidoscopic changes which preceded the establishment of Medici rule in the fifteenth century. Guelfs and Ghibellines, nobles and burghers, capitalists and workers—all these elements fought and intrigued within the tiny wall-enclosed area along the Arno. Every faction had its own strongholds and the few "towers" which survive to our own day bear witness to the time when Florence was a collection of bristling fortresses. Riots, insurrections, and rebellions were so common that the expression "go down to the public square" came to mean a street brawl. And yet through all this turmoil the city prospered, and Florentine bankers rivaled Venetian merchants in their wealth.

The unifying thread of Florentine history is economic rather than political. Florence, like Venice, had accumulated a surplus of capital by the end of the thirteenth century, but Florentine wealth came from industry rather than commerce. Textiles—first wool and then silk—formed the foundation for the prosperity of the city. Rough cloth made from English wool was bought in Flanders or France, brought to Florence to be dyed and finished, and then exported to all parts of Europe. This sort of work required the labor of a great number of poorly paid artisans, and the existence of this large urban proletariat certainly contributed to the political instability of the city. Some historians would add that the relatively small number of artisans in Venice explains the immunity of that city from revolution, and that in general, commercial communities are less exposed to social upheavals than industrial ones. It may be doubted whether this proposition would always hold good, but it is certainly true that the poorer classes in Florence were much more discontented than the corresponding groups in Venice. The ordinary cloth-worker had neither the capital nor the experience necessary to purchase rough cloth or to market the finished product, and by the end of the thirteenth century control of the woolen trades had fallen into the hands of the capitalists. Gild organization was retained, but the large working population was at the mercy of the moneyed men. Ordinary textile workers became wage-earners, and even the highly skilled artisans, such as the dyers, were dependent upon the great merchants from whom they obtained their materials and to whom they sold their finished products. Antagonism developed between the two classes, and feeling was made worse by the intervention of the landed nobility, who were being harassed by the prosperous burghers and who often sided with the poorer citizens in order to strengthen their political position. By the end of the thirteenth century the men who controlled the textile industries, with their allies from other prosperous trades, had subdued the nobles and gained control over the government. The lot of the lower classes became increasingly hard as the employers lowered wages in order to meet foreign competition.

In 1378 the workers rose against their masters in the Ciompi revolt, but the rising eventually failed, and after that the artisans had little influence on politics. They depended entirely on favors granted them by the ruling class and profited only slightly from the increasing prosperity of the city. Peasants and neighboring cities as well as the poorer citizens of Florence felt the heavy hand of the business oligarchy. In order to secure a stable food supply and access to the sea, Florence fought all her neighbors until the fall of Pisa in 1410 gave her domination over Tuscany. The conquered territory was exploited without scruple for the benefit of the capital. The commerce of Pisa and other subject towns was diverted to Florence, and the peasants found that bourgeois masters were far more efficient than the nobles in collecting rents and dues. In addition, the prices of agricultural products were kept low, and the peasants were so miserable that one wonders why Florentine policy did not defeat its own ends by depopulating the country-side. Florence was really practising mercantilism on a small scale; it treated Tuscany very much as Spain and England were to treat their colonies in the eighteenth century.

Florence was as active in finance as in industry. In an age of fluctuating currencies, the Florentines were careful to keep their money up to a rigid standard, and this gave their businessmen an advantage over those of other Italian towns. By the end of the thirteenth century the bankers of Florence had outdistanced most of their rivals and were lending money to Edward I, Philip the Fair, and Boniface VIII. The canonical prohibition against interest was evaded even by churchmen, either by setting an impossibly short term for repayment and giving "damages" for delay, or by granting valuable privileges to the lender in return for the loan. The banker might be given the monopoly of the sale of some commodity, he might exploit a mine, or he might farm a tax. The profits from these transactions were great, but the risks were even greater. The pope usually compelled ecclesiastics to repay their loans, but there was no power capable of compelling repayment from monarchs. Edward III went bankrupt after the campaign of Crécy (1346), bringing ruin to many famous Florentine houses and poverty to the whole city. After this experience the bankers became more cautious, and put most of their money into industry and commerce. Loans to monarchs and nobles were still made, but only when ample security was offered.

The power of the Florentine bankers is illustrated by the history of the Medici. This family began its rise after the great panic caused by the bankruptcy of Edward III and reached its zenith a century later. Branches of the house were established in many of the cities of western Europe, and from those centers political events were closely watched and often influenced by the refusal or the granting of loans. The Medici galleys competed with the Venetians in the East, and many members of the family were active in the textile industry. Within Florence the wealth of the Medici gave them ever-increasing influence in politics. Cosimo dei Medici became head of a popular party in 1429 and, after a close escape from the plots of rival families, made himself "boss" of Florence in 1434. All the machinery of republican government was preserved, but Cosimo manipulated the choice of officials so that his supporters monopolized all important positions. He seldom held office himself, but he dominated Florence until his death in 1464 and made his family so popular that his son Piero and his grandson Lorenzo the Magnificent (1469–1492) inherited his power without opposition. Through his political skill, Cosimo ended the revolutions which had filled the preceding century and gave Florence an orderly, stable government. He secured a balance of power among the larger Italian states which enabled his city to avoid serious wars for almost half a century. Order at home and peace abroad increased the prosperity of the city and, while the working classes were still poorly paid, they were protected to some extent from violent economic fluctuations. They were not entirely satisfied, but revolutions in the past had gained them little but suffering, and Cosimo was careful to exile all men who seemed to be capable of leading an opposition party. Florence acquiesced in Medici rule, and there was little protest when in 1480 Lorenzo changed the constitution to give himself and his friends almost despotic power. When Lorenzo died there was a brief return to republican rule, but this movement failed, and the Medici were soon reëstablished, first as lords of Florence and then as grand dukes of Tuscany. In the sixteenth century two Medici popes and several cardinals, two Medici queens of France, and marriage alliances with other royal lines gave proof of the international prestige of this famous banking family.

Venice was the leading commercial city and Florence was the most important banking and industrial center in Italy. Milan, which occupied only a secondary position in both fields, was perhaps a more typical

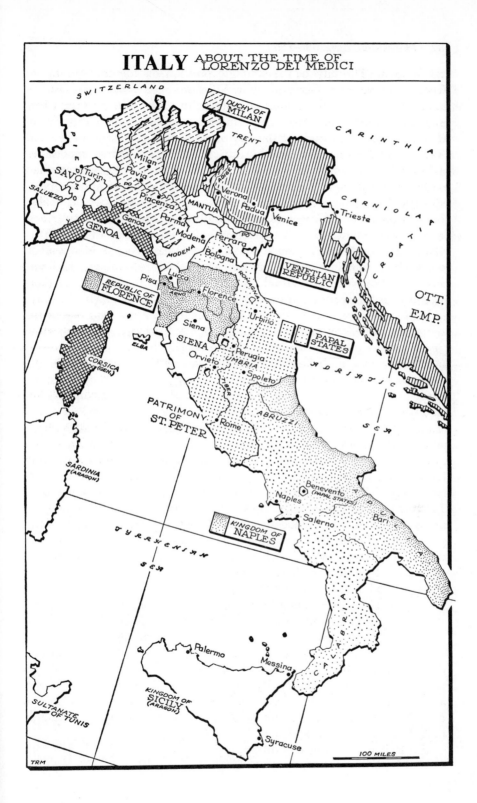

ITALY ABOUT THE TIME OF LORENZO DEI MEDICI

SWITZERLAND

DUCHY OF MILAN

CARINTHIA

TRENT

PIEDMONT

SAVOY

Turin

Milan

Pavia

Piacenza

Parma

MANTUA

Verona

Padua

Venice

CARNIOLA

Trieste

SALUZZO

Genoa

GENOA

Modena

Ferrara

CROATIA

MODENA

Bologna

Pisa

Lucca

ARNO

Florence

ROMAGNA

VENETIAN REPUBLIC

REPUBLIC OF FLORENCE

OTT. EMP.

Siena

SIENA

Urbino

PAPAL STATES

CORSICA (GEN.)

ELBA

Orvieto

UMBRIA

Perugia

Spoleto

ADRIATIC

SARDINIA (ARAGON)

PATRIMONY OF ST. PETER

Rome

ABRUZZI

SEA

Benevento (PAPAL STATES)

Naples

Salerno

Bari

KINGDOM OF NAPLES

TYRRHENIAN SEA

CALABRIA

SULTANATE OF TUNIS

Palermo

Messina

KINGDOM OF SICILY (ARAGON)

Syracuse

100 MILES

TRM

Italian town. The city had a strategic position on the trade-routes to France and western Germany, but Milanese merchants were usually middlemen. They had no trading-posts in the East and possessed few establishments beyond the Alps. There were flourishing industries in Milan, but the cloth trade of the city never rivaled that of Florence and the armor-makers had a relatively restricted market. The real importance of Milan lies in its turbulent political career. History and geography had made it the leading city of the Po Valley, and the rulers of Milan repeatedly tried to create a great state in northern Italy which would enable them to dominate the peninsula. Internally, the struggle of classes and factions was conducted with a violence which would have astonished the citizens of Venice and Florence. Venice, as we have seen, seldom had to worry about uprisings, and Florence, with all its revolutions, shed surprisingly little blood. The usual punishment for political dissent in Florence was financial ruin and exile, but factional disputes in Milan always ended in massacres, executions, and assassinations. Milan was one of the first Italian towns to accept a tyrant and the Visconti family ruled the city, with few interruptions, from 1317 to 1447. They were an ambitious and prolific race and their attempts to conquer the other towns of the North were frequently interrupted by family quarrels. They ruled by terror and torture; one Visconti was accused of feeding his dogs on human flesh and none of them hesitated to execute men on mere suspicion of treason. The great man of the family was Gian Galeazzo (1385–1402), who gained control of Milanese territories by ambushing his uncle and two of his cousins, and who enlarged his possessions until every other Italian ruler felt himself threatened. Gian Galeazzo not only held Lombardy up to the Venetian frontier but also gained control of towns in Tuscany and the Papal States. He secured the title of duke of Milan from the worthless emperor Wenceslas, and was said to be aiming at the kingship of Italy when he died in 1402. His heirs were as unscrupulous as their father, but they lacked his great diplomatic and political ability, and Milan lost many of her territories under their rule. When the last Visconti died in 1447, the city tried to revive republican forms of government, but it was surrounded by enemies and it was soon evident that a strong ruler was needed. Francesco Sforza, who had served the Visconti as leader of a mercenary army, took advantage of the situation and soon secured recognition as duke of Milan. The new ruling house developed the same ambitions and the same vices as the Visconti tyrants, but it was not to have so long a history. By the end of the fifteenth century France and Spain, reorganized under strong kings, were contending for control of Italy, and the Sforza, caught between two great powers, were unable to maintain themselves in Milan.

The Italian towns seemed to have solved many of the problems which were harassing northern Europe. They were outwardly prosperous; they had developed strong and efficient governments; they had worked out a whole new science of politics and diplomacy. The people of the North imitated many of their achievements. Italian bankers and merchants taught businessmen all over Europe their advanced financial and commercial techniques. The rulers of the sixteenth century learned much from the mercantilistic practices of Venice and Florence. The basic ideas of mercantilism were not new—every medieval town sought trade monopolies and regulated commerce for the benefit of the community—but they had never been applied on as wide a scale as they were in the Venetian empire or in Florentine-dominated Tuscany.

Even more did the rulers of the North profit from the example of the Italian despots. To maintain themselves in power, the rulers of the Italian towns had invented all the machinery of absolute government—concentration of power in the hands of the prince, division of delegated authority among subordinate ministers, creation of a political police force, and establishment of secret tribunals. They had developed the practices of modern diplomacy; the Italian princes were the first to maintain ambassadors in more or less permanent residence at foreign courts, and the reports of these ambassadors gave them political information such as no northern ruler possessed. Most important of all, the Italian despots worked out two principles which were to guide European politics for the next three centuries. The first was the idea of balance of power—the chief states of the peninsula were to conduct their foreign policy in such a way that they would all remain approximately equal in strength. If one state showed signs of becoming too strong, the others were to combine to pull it down. Cosimo dei Medici had applied this principle with notable success during his principate in Florence and the wiser rulers of other Italian states, including several popes, found it profitable to follow his example. The other principle of Italian politics was the "reason of state"—the idea that the chief duty of every government is to perpetuate itself and that it is justified in doing anything which will strengthen its own position or weaken its enemies. Perjury, treachery, murder are no crimes when done for the good of the state; right and wrong, justice and injustice do not exist in the sphere of politics. This was not an entirely new idea; Philip the Fair had used the same techniques and justified himself in the same way in his struggle with Boniface VIII, and some medieval political theorists had argued that an individual was justified in sinning if by sinning he could save his community. But the Italians pressed the principle of "reason of state" to its extreme limits and talked about it more frankly than had their predecessors. They did not try to hide behind such phrases as the "common welfare"; they simply admitted the fact that rulers want to stay in power and will take any steps necessary to retain power. When Machiavelli wrote *The Prince* he was merely summing up generations of Italian political experience. His book was denounced, but all Italian rulers of his day followed his principles—and for that matter, so did the kings of France, Spain and England.

Yet while the Italians led Europe in economic and political organization in the fifteenth century, they had only partially solved their problems. Their greatest defect was their failure to obtain political unity, or, if that were impossible, to create a North Italian state large enough to hold its own with the transalpine powers. The result of this failure was economic and political collapse in the sixteenth century. As strong monarchy was revived in England, France, and Spain the Italians found that their financial and commercial markets were curtailed. The Western kings began to apply mercantilism on a national scale and the little Italian states could not retaliate effectively when restrictions were placed on their trade. The great discoveries of Portugal and Spain hurt Italian trade even more. When the Portuguese found an all-sea route to the Indies, they were able to break the Italian monopoly of Eastern goods, since their transportation costs were lower. When Spain found new sources of the precious metals in America, the Italian monopoly of banking was broken, since the Italians no longer controlled the largest part of the European stock of gold and silver. Given its geographical position, Italy could hardly have played an important rôle in Atlantic exploration, but a strong Italian state might have been able to secure a share in the new trade. The fall of Constantinople in 1453 and the establishment of a Turkish Empire across the main land-routes to the East did much less harm than the explorations of the Western powers. There was a momentary dislocation of trade during the actual conquests, but the Italians soon renewed commercial relations with the new masters of the eastern Mediterranean and imported as much from the Turks as they had from their predecessors. The real economic weakness of Italy was that it could merely maintain its old volume of trade in an age when other countries were expanding their commerce ten, twenty, and a hundred fold.

Politically, the situation was much the same. Absolute government was far more effective on a national than on a municipal scale. The kings of France and Spain were far more powerful than any Italian ruler, and they soon found that they could invade Italy with impunity. The Italian despots could make no effective resistance, not only because they lacked resources, but also because they could not make the most of the resources which they did possess. Their people were unwilling to fight to the death to save them, because they had never been able to secure the loyalty of their people. They had gained power by force and had ruled by terror; they had been tolerated because tyranny was less evil than civil war, but they had not been loved. They lacked the two great supports of the northern monarchs—legitimacy and national feeling. Many kings of

France were incompetent or tyrannical, but they belonged to a family which had held the throne for centuries, a family which had produced saints and heroes, a family which was part of the tradition of the French people. No Italian prince could claim an ancient origin and a divine sanction for his power; no Italian prince could identify himself with the traditions of the Italian people. This was the great weakness of the Italian political system, for no government is really strong unless it is based on an ideal as well as on the fact of brute power. People will not make sacrifices for a government which gives them nothing in which to believe, and for this reason the political skill of the Italian princes proved useless when their system met the test of foreign invasion. The political collapse of Italy was even more complete than the economic collapse, and for three hundred years foreigners dominated the peninsula.

THE ITALIAN RENAISSANCE

Not many years ago students of history spoke, with the assurance that they would be understood, of two distinct periods, the "Middle Ages" and the "Renaissance." The former was likened to a "Dead Sea," a period when Europe lay in "ignorant prostration before the idols of the Church in dogma and authority and scholasticism." The Renaissance was "the liberation of the reason from a dungeon, the double discovery of the outer and inner world. . . . The intellect, after lying spell-bound during a long night, when thoughts were as dreams and movements as somnambulism, renewed its activity, interrogated nature, and enjoyed the pleasures of unimpeded energy." During the fourteenth and fifteenth centuries the Italians "bridged the gap between the medieval and modern world" and diffused a new spirit, "the foe of obscurantism, the ally of all the forces that make for light, for the advancement of knowledge, and for reasonable freedom." Few would make such dithyrambic statements today. The twelfth and thirteenth centuries, far from seeming a "long night," are now known to have been years of intense and lasting activity. In Gothic architecture we see a beauty which makes us forget that the name "Gothic" was invented as a term of contempt by admirers of the Italian Renaissance. The creation of the Western monarchies, the development of English law and Parliament, the establishment of universities, the beginnings of the great vernacular literatures, the revival of commerce— these are hardly fruits of the "Dead Sea." Appreciation of medieval achievement has gone so far that some writers would "abolish the name, and perhaps even the fact, of a Renaissance" and would consider Italian civilization of the fourteenth and fifteenth centuries as merely a minor variant of the declining culture of the later Middle Ages. This extreme view is almost as misleading as the original legend, for many Italians of the fourteenth and fifteenth centuries did make a conscious effort to break with the medieval tradition and to substitute new forms of thought and artistic expression. The Renaissance was an attempt to glorify the new way of life which had developed in Italy and to solve the conflict between the ideal and the actual, which so disturbed the later Middle Ages, by creating new ideals which were closer to actual life.

It will be remembered that in economics and politics Italy had almost entirely discarded the medieval tradition. Nowhere else in Europe were there such concentrations of capital and nowhere else in Europe were the men who controlled these concentrations of capital so free from religious and political restraint. The leaders of Italian business competed openly for profits and by the end of the fourteenth century had discarded even the pretense of coöperation for the good of the community. In politics the same rule of individual self-aggrandizement held good; Italy was governed by men who had seized power without any legitimate title and who retained it by bribery and terror. These tendencies had been evident in Italy from the beginning of the thirteenth century, and it was only natural that they should have affected literature and art as they became dominant in the peninsula. The great merchants and princes had forsaken everything else in order to enjoy the rewards which power and wealth can give in this world. They did not entirely discard their old beliefs, but they wanted something new as well—books which would glorify the life of an urban, sophisticated society, paintings and statues which would glorify the human body. Like wealthy men in all periods, they were able to find writers and artists who gave them what they wanted.

And yet the Renaissance in Italy was not wholly a product of the political and economic forces which have just been mentioned. In art and literature, as in social organization, Italy had never been entirely happy with medieval forms. The Roman tradition persisted, and modified or distorted the concepts imported from the North. For example, the Italians never fully accepted the Gothic emphasis on the vertical line; they were never able to forget the Roman principle of making the most important lines in a building horizontal. The classic example of this tendency is the cathedral of Siena, where the builders used Gothic detail consistently, and then spoiled the whole effect by constructing the walls with alternating bands of light and dark stone, which emphasized horizontal lines. In the middle of the thirteenth century the greatest Italian sculptors were imitating Roman models, and, though there was a swing over to the Gothic style a little later, Roman influence never disappeared. Italy was full of intellectual and material relics of the classical age; almost every town had its Roman ruins and its version of Roman law. Thus it was easy for Italians to turn away from medieval forms and to use ancient models in creating new styles in art and in literature.

It is also true that there was a strong emphasis on individualism among members of the upper classes in fourteenth-century Italy. This individualism, expressed in the rise of great capitalists and political bosses, affected artists and writers as well. It conflicted in many ways with the medieval tradition which put more, though not exclusive emphasis on group welfare and activities. The Italian Renaissance was not exclusively individualistic any more than the Middle Ages were exclusively collectivistic, but the balance had definitely shifted.

The transition from medieval to Renaissance attitudes may be seen especially clearly in three great Italian writers of the fourteenth century, Dante, Petrarch, and Boccaccio. Though Dante lived at a time when the merchant oligarchies had already destroyed the old political and economic system in Italy, he steadfastly adhered to the ideals which expressed the highest aspirations of the Middle Ages. He believed that society would never have peace until it was organized under the ægis of the Empire and that the individual would never have peace until he accepted the teachings of the Church. Church and Empire had been willed by God and existed from eternity as ideas in His mind, though they might be held in abeyance through the wickedness of man. Learning served to give knowledge of God and his workings; human love led to love of God; true knowledge and love of God led to right action and eventually to salvation. Man could strive for both felicity in this life and happiness in eternity; there was no contradiction between the two objectives if he were rightly taught and rightly governed. Dante held these beliefs so strongly that his convictions remained unshaken through one disaster after another—exile from the Florence he passionately loved, poverty, and the failure of all attempts to revive the Empire. There was confusion without, but in Dante's mind all was clear. It was this certainty which ennobled his life and work, which enabled him to sum up the medieval view of life in a great epic and to endure the bitterness of exile when a slight compromising of his ideals would have permitted him to return to Florence.

Dante died in 1321 in his fifty-seventh year; Petrarch was born in 1304, and Boccaccio nine years later, so that their lives overlapped that of their great fellow-Florentine. This fact makes more remarkable the gulf which separates the author of the *Divine Comedy*, who brings one epoch to a close, from his younger contemporaries, who usher in the new era of the Renaissance. In Petrarch we find no trace of the unity of character which lent strength and dignity to Dante in adversity and exile. Depth and tenacity of conviction brought Dante unshaken through the most bitter disappointments. Petrarch's writings are filled with lamentations about "the dangers and apprehensions I have suffered. . . . I was born among perils and among perils have grown old—if old I am, and there are not worse trials ahead." When his catalogue of woes is examined, we find the events enumerated took place before his birth or in his early childhood, while we know that all through his life he was petted and courted by the great of his day. Indeed, as he himself assures us in his complacent *Letter to Posterity:* "The greatest kings of this age have loved and courted me. They may know why, I certainly do not. With some of them I was on such terms that they seemed in a certain sense my guests rather than I theirs." His unhappiness came from within, from his inability to unite his conflicting aspirations and interests into a workable scheme of existence. He longed for solitude and quiet, yet he was constantly on the move. At times he was strongly attracted by the monastic ideal and berated the pomp and show of this world, but he fawned after the poet's crown and gloried in his celebrity. Author of passionate love sonnets and not above amorous adventures, he could describe love as a most foul sin. His best remembered work was his Italian verse, and yet he was never sure, as Dante was, that real poetry could be written in the vernacular.

With all his vanity and inconsistency, Petrarch had a real love of learning, and it was in this field that the "Father of Humanism" was to leave the greatest impress on subsequent thought. His interests were on the whole much narrower than Dante's. From the whole field of medieval philosophy he recoiled in disgust, as many scholars of the Italian Renaissance were to do. He declared that Aristotle, Dante's "Master of them who know," erred "in the most weighty questions," and rejected him vehemently as a guide. Although Aristotle "has said much of happiness both at the beginning and end of his *Ethics,* I dare assert, let my critics exclaim as they may, that he was so completely ignorant of true happiness that the opinions upon this matter of any pious old woman, or devout fisherman, shepherd or farmer, would, if not so fine-spun, be more to the point than his." At science he scoffed for the same reason, as "helping in no way toward a happy life." Lack of interest in these fields he atoned for by devotion to classical literature and Roman antiquities. When in Rome, his imagination was fired by the majestic ruins, and he was one of the first to start collecting Roman inscriptions and coins. That Dante had reverenced the poets and philosophers of Greece and Rome is shown by his choice of Virgil as a guide in the *Divine Comedy* and by his description of the sages in Limbo. In Petrarch, however, we find a new spirit: reverence for the classical past becomes worship and slavish imitation. He was a little ashamed of his writings in the vernacular and he feared that his Latin style might seem barbarous because it did not fully conform to the usage of Cicero. "O great father of Roman eloquence!" he wrote. "Not I alone but all who deck themselves with the flowers of Latin speech render thanks unto you, . . . In a word, it is under your auspices that we have attained to such little skill in this art of writing as we may possess." Each of Petrarch's letters was, so far as he could make it, a polished Ciceronian essay obviously intended for publication, with all intimate or routine details which would mar the symmetry of the production, or which could not be described in classical language, relegated to a separate sheet, written in Italian or medieval Latin. His enthusiasm for classical studies led him to ferret out and copy previously unknown letters and speeches of Cicero and to attempt unsuccessfully to learn Greek, which was then little studied. There is something at once amusing and pathetic in the way that he hugged to his breast a Greek manuscript of Homer, which he could not read and knew only through received opinion and a translation so bad as to discourage even his invincible conviction that Homer, together with Virgil, was more than human and of a stature which rose above the clouds. From his infatuation with the past came the *Africa,* a dull epic of the Second Punic War written in Latin; it was on this work that he fondly believed his fame with posterity would rest. For him there was no impassable gulf separating his age from that of Augustus or his work from that of Roman poets of the first century.

Yet Petrarch the classical scholar remained completely medieval in his religious outlook. His preoccupation with learning and literature gave him qualms of conscience. "I closed the book, angry with myself that I should still be admiring earthly things who might have learned from even the pagan philosophers that nothing is wonderful but the soul, which, when great itself, finds nothing great outside itself." For him the reconciliation between the good of this world and that of the next which Dante made was impossible. Petrarch had rejected the intellectual tradition of the Middle Ages while adhering to its moral code; he passionately desired human knowledge and worldly fame, though he believed that they were snares set to keep him from the path of salvation. As a result, there was a constant struggle between Petrarch the lover of Laura, Petrarch the dictator of learning, and Petrarch the trembling Christian.

It would be difficult to discover a parallel for the extraordinary popularity and influence of Petrach; even Voltaire could not boast of such universal adulation. His letters and poems were awaited as great events; his style and his veneration for the classics were imitated all over Italy. The most famous, and one of the most devout worshipers of Petrarch, was Boccaccio, who to the end of his life preserved the attitude of a respectful pupil toward the older scholar. He had the same interest in classical literature and joined eagerly in the search for manuscripts, but fate and a hard-headed father had prevented him from acquiring a thorough knowledge of Latin.

However [he writes] when I had well nigh reached maturity, and was become my own master, then at no man's bidding and through no man's teaching, against the opposition of my father who condemned such studies violently, I resorted spontaneously to the little I knew of the poetic art, and this work I have since pursued with the greatest eagerness, studying the works of its professors with incredible delight and straining all my ability to understand them . . . I doubt not that if my father had been indulgent to my wishes while my mind was pliable in youngest years, I should have turned out one of the world's famous poets. The fact, however, is that through bending my abilities first to a lucrative business, and next to a lucrative branch of study, I failed to become either a merchant or a canonist, and missed the chance of being an illustrious poet.

One may be permitted to believe that his mercantile travels, which took him through most of Italy and through France as far as Paris, strengthened his interest in, and knowledge of, humanity, while the discipline of legal studies was probably no more cramping than imitation of classical forms would have been. Certainly, he never attained to a Petrarchian absorption in the past. Recognition of his inadequate knowledge of Latin may account for the fact that Boccaccio turned to Italian. From earliest youth he was experimenting with varied forms of composition in the vernacular—the prose romance, idyll, epic, allegory, even the psychological novel. From these efforts came new verse forms and modes of expression, but little of great importance. In this youthful period we find nothing of Dante's metaphysical and political passions, or of Petrarch's preoccupation with his soul. Boccaccio's ideals are those of the scholar devoting himself to the study of literature, of the artist using old literary forms or inventing new ones in the search for appropriate means of expression, and of the courtier, rejoicing in the favor of the Neopolitan court. It was at Naples, with the encouragement of Queen Joanna, whose unsavory career he sought to rehabilitate by his rhetoric, that he is said to have begun his great work, the *Decameron*, in which his genius at last found expression.

The *Decameron* is not only a literary masterpiece, it is also a precious historical document, since from its pages we may glean a knowledge of the standards and ideals of the fourteenth- and fifteenth-century Italian. The *Decameron* took Italy by storm and was read and copied as was no other work of the period. It was not a work for scholars, and in the epilogue Boccaccio felt it necessary to admit that there were many "who will say that the said stories are too full of jests and merry conceits, and that it ill becomes a man of weight and gravity to have written in such wise." Scholars might raise their eyebrows, but we are no less grateful than his contemporaries, though possibly for different reasons, to this poet who forsook the epic and the idyll long enough to catch and transmute into a work of art the life of his age.

Boccaccio, of course, did not break away entirely from medieval tradition. His stories were not new; they had circulated for centuries in all parts of Europe and even Asia, before they were given a home in fourteenth-century Florence. The company of young men and women of the *Decameron* accepted the external observances of medieval Christianity. They sang allegorical songs, observed perfect propriety of conduct, and told no stories on Friday so that they might have time for prayers. Chivalry was held up to admiration in tales of extraordinary deeds of magnificence and magnanimity performed by kings and knights. The morals of the clergy were criticized, but the validity of the Christian faith was never questioned.

But amid these old ideas and situations one feels a new and distinctive point of view toward life. Story after story shows the conviction that the true motive power of this world is not God but Fate. The heroes of Boccaccio's world are those who know how to take advantage of opportunities as they offer themselves. The unforgivable sin is stupidity, and unsuspecting husbands, innocents, or simple souls deserve no quarter. Those who have keen wits live by them at the expense of others; the brazen liar and the plausible cheat can expect to satisfy all their desires. The most cruel practical jokes find justification in the demonstration of wit. All this is the antithesis of the Christian virtues, which in many places are held up to contempt. A violent attack on the immorality of the friars is used to prove the sinfulness of a woman who, threatened with damnation by a friar, had given up her lover. God enters on the side of love and the story ends; in other words, the God of the *Decameron* is a deity who helps those who help themselves. Such exaltation of shrewdness, sharpness of wit, and keenness of eye for the main chance can be found only in one field of medieval literature—the *fabliaux* of the northern merchants, and with these crude burghers of France the commercial Italian of the Renaissance was closely allied in feeling, though he might have regarded the northerner as a barbarian.

The gulf which separates the world of Boccaccio and the world of Dante may also be seen from the lack of understanding apparent in the attitude of the author of the *Decameron* toward his older contemporary. Boccaccio admired and reverenced the work of Dante; he wrote a life of the great Florentine exile, and his last work was a ponderous commentary on the *Divine Comedy*, which in fifty-nine lectures had covered only half of the *Inferno!* Despite this love and study, Dante remained completely incomprehensible to him, except as a writer of beautiful Italian poetry. Two examples will suffice to demonstrate this incapacity to understand the medieval writer. For Dante, Beatrice was the "youngest of the angels," a personification of the divine beauty, and through love of her the poet aspired to attain love of God. But Boccaccio cannot understand spiritual love and exhausts his ingenuity in finding physical causes for Dante's state of mind. In his description of Beatrice "there is less of the angelic than the carnal nature visible. Beatrice becomes one of the beauties of his own prose fictions." Of more serious import, possibly, for the future of Italy, was his inability to explain Dante's participation in politics, which Boccaccio could attribute only to vanity. Boccaccio had an acute mind, and such an interpretation indicates how far the Italians had already moved from the fierce patriotism of earlier centuries.

Boccaccio in his youth earned the nickname of "Giovanni della Tranquillità." His world seemed to contain its ideals within itself; the next world was not present, either as the culmination of life or as an uncomfortable preoccupation. Never denied, it merely ceased to have enough validity to affect his life. The instability and inadequacy of this happy acquiescence in the exclusive claims of this world were shown by his panic when, in 1361, a dying monk warned him of impending damnation unless he changed his mode of life. Under the influence of this message, Boccaccio immediately decided to sell his library, give up study, and take orders. Although he abandoned all these resolutions when the first shock had passed, he did forsake light literature. He never regained his old carefree spirit, and thoughts of the next world and the condition of his own soul obtruded uncomfortably from time to time.

In contrasting Dante with Petrarch and Boccaccio we have taken three unusually vivid personalities, and in doing so have run the risk of exaggerating the shift of interest which took place during the fourteenth century. If we remember that few people in the Middle Ages attained to the complete moral and intellectual unity of a Dante, and that few in the fourteenth century felt as keenly the impossibility of reconciling the demands of this life and that of the next as did Petrarch, or with Boccaccio made first a complete surrender to the joys of the world, and then recoiled in terror at the thought of the yawning jaws of Hell—in short, if we remember that these are the great, in whom alone we can expect to find acute sensitiveness to current modes of thought—we may hope to minimize this distortion. The ordinary citizen of an Italian town was slow to realize that there was any conflict between his ideals and his actual life. He would have been shocked if any one had told him that he was not a good Christian, or that worldly pleasure was becoming more important in his mind than salvation. He would have answered that heresy was less common in Renaissance Italy than it had been in the greatest period of the Middle Ages, that the friars could still bring thousands of people together for revival meetings, that the men who read Petrarch also read ponderous theological treatises, that the wealthiest merchants and princes spent huge sums in building and decorating churches. Even in Florence, the city which led the Renaissance, few men abandoned their faith in the Christian religion. The Medici were on intimate terms with the heads of the Franciscan and Dominican convents; Cosimo dei Medici had a cell in the monastery of San Marco to which he retired at times, and Lorenzo the Magnificent summoned the puritanical friar Savonarola to hear his last confession. The career of Savonarola himself shows the persistence of medieval ideals. Preaching in the last decades of the fifteenth century, he filled the Florentines with loathing for their worldly lives and sinful luxuries. Great bonfires were built in the streets in which the "vanities" were burned—ornaments, fashionable clothes, secular books and games. Savonarola also inspired the citizens of Florence to drive out the Medici and reëstablish their ancient republican government. All this is true, and yet these manifestations of religious feelings were largely on the surface; they were neither deep nor persistent. The Christian drama of salvation and damnation had become formalized and few felt its import, save at the approach of death or in times of crisis. The claims of religion were not rejected; they were simply pushed aside by new interests. The temporary enthusiasm stirred up by revivals soon evaporated, leaving no permanent results. The fate of Savonarola is instructive; when he fell into disfavor with the pope the Florentines made little effort to save him. He was burned at the stake for denying papal authority; the people returned to their "vanities," and the Medici were soon restored. Within a decade of Savonarola's death, no one could have told that he had ever had any influence on Florence.

The old ideals had not been denied, but they had lost their force; they were no longer effective guides to conduct. There remained only the determination to enjoy life, to make the most of every opportunity and every talent which the individual possessed. In some men the search for worldly satisfactions led to complete bestiality, but most Italians of the upper classes were saved from this fate by their sense of beauty. It was not enough merely to accumulate wealth and power; wealth and power had to be expressed in forms which struck the imagination and produced an esthetic response. The table service and the decorations were more important than the food at a banquet; the style of a palace was more important than its size. Even the tyrants tried to conceal the naked fact of military dictatorship by festivals and ceremonies which gave dignity and splendor to their usurped authority. This love of beauty made the life of the upper-class Italian extraordinarily rich. Every humble utensil became a work of art; every ordinary action became a pageant. At the same time, it tended to concentrate attention on external appearances, for the Italians were often contented merely with beauty of form. The magnificence of a court might bear no relation to the actual power of the ruler; the polished style of an author might conceal an utter lack of ideas. Even the marvelous technique of the artists was sometimes used only to represent the outward splendor of Italian life.

Interest in beauty of form reinforced the tendency to concentrate on the study of the classics. The Italians were not entirely wrong in criticizing the style of medieval scholars; it was based on a rigid application of the rules of logic and it was full of highly technical terms. One can admire the work of the great medieval philosophers, but one seldom enjoys reading it, any more than one would enjoy reading the equations of a modern mathematician. The Italians believed that an idea was useless unless it was attractively presented; rhetoric, to them, was more important than a series of logical proofs. The Romans had known how to say things well, how to put their ideas in striking and memorable phrases. Therefore classical Latin was the model for all writers who wished to influence their contemporaries. The study of Greek had less impact on style (though perhaps more on ideas), but in both Greek and Latin the Italians found precedents for their love of the beauty of this world.

We speak of the "Italians," but we must not infer from this that the whole population of Italy devoted itself entirely to classical studies. Educated men continued to read medieval treatises and the classicists, or "humanists" as they were called, never dominated the universities. In fact, it required some effort for them to obtain university positions, just as it requires an effort to establish a new department in a university today. Law, medicine and scholastic philosophy still attracted the attention of many students, and these subjects were at first barely touched by the classical revival. As for the mass of the Italian people, few of them even knew that there was a classical revival. Throughout the Renaissance the peasant tilled his fields, oppressed by heavy taxes and made miserable by the petty wars, but on the whole ignorant of the fact that this was a different age from that his forefathers had known. In the cities, the populace reveled in the carnivals and gloried in the artistic adornment of churches. Except for the rare youth who attracted the eye of a patron, however, life for the artisan was a matter of dire poverty, relieved at intervals by feast days and festivals. The Renaissance was aristocratic to a degree that few intellectual movements have been, the concern of rich burghers, princes, and popes. The emphasis on the study of Greek and Latin by itself shows that only the educated—the well educated—could participate, but in Boccaccio and elsewhere we can easily discern the contempt and aversion felt by the gentleman for the peasant and the artisan, even for the new rich. The Italian verses of Dante were sung in the field and the workshop; the learned translated Dante into Latin and debated over his allegory. A few hymns, a few gay carnival songs, lovely buildings, and pictures—these were the property of high and low alike. Learning and cultivation were the property of the few.

Bearing in mind, then, that we are dealing with an aristocratic and imitative movement, let us trace briefly the rise of humanism and the result of the worship of antiquity on Italian life and thought. In Petrarch the medieval Christian and the Renaissance classicist were combined, to the torment of his soul; a few years after his death, by the beginning of the fifteenth century, the classical cult had captured the upper classes of Italy. Petrarch's tremendous popularity was at once an indication of the trend of the times and a means of spreading the love of Greek and Roman literature. A year after Petrarch's death we find Salutato, a politician as well as a scholar, lecturing to an eager audience in Florence on the classics, particularly on the necessity of an improved Latin style. Like Petrarch, he took Cicero as his model and imitated his style as closely as possible. Salutato and his pupils and friends also searched diligently for manuscripts, and each discovery provoked an outburst of ecstatic applause and enthusiasm. When Poggio, a protégé of Salutato, discovered a manuscript of Quintilian, a rhetorician of the Latin "silver" age, in a monastery near Constance, a friend wrote:

> Through you we now possess Quintilian entire; before we only boasted of the half of him, and that defective and corrupt in text. O precious acquisition! O unexpected joy! And shall I, then, in truth be able to read the whole of that Quintilian which, mutilated and deformed as it has hitherto been, has formed my solace? I conjure you to send it me at once, that at least I may set eyes on it before I die.

Bankers and merchants joined in the hunt; branch banks of the Medici were instructed to find manuscripts and pay for the copying. Many humanists made their living as agents for collectors, visiting monastic libraries and buying, copying, or stealing new finds. A well-stocked library became a mark of distinction, and although most collectors generously permitted others to use or copy books at will, others guarded their treasures jealously, rejoicing in the possession of unique or rare manuscripts. In 1396 there was a new wave of enthusiasm when a distinguished Greek scholar, Manuel Chrysoloras, came to lecture in Florence at the invitation of the government. With his arrival began the serious study of Greek. Petrarch had attacked the language without success; Boccaccio had picked up some scraps from an almost illiterate teacher; Chrysoloras offered his eager hearers the best Byzantine scholarship. Students and agents ransacked Constantinople for manuscripts, which descended on Italy singly or by hundreds. Translations into Latin were made for those unable to read Greek. Bruni tells us how at the coming of Chrysoloras he deserted the study of law for Greek so that he might converse with Homer, Plato, and Demosthenes "concerning whom so great and so wonderful things are said. . . . I delivered myself to Chrysoloras with such passion that what I had received from him by day in hours of waking occupied my mind at night in hours of sleep."

He was far from unique in this enthusiasm; conversion to scholarly pursuits became as popular as religious conversions had earlier been. We read of a young nobleman "born with thy face and throat, Lyric Apollo!" who won acclaim by deserting a life of pleasure—to spend the rest of his days memorizing Livy and the *Æneid!*

From Florence the movement spread in a great wave over all Italy. Tyrants, princes, popes, the king of Naples—all bid for the services of scholars, who spent their lives wandering from city to city as teachers or paid companions and civil servants. With printing unknown, manuscripts expensive, and, until the end of the fifteenth century, few mechanical aids to classical studies available, teaching was almost inevitably a combination of lecturing and dictation. A good memory was essential, and many developed this faculty to the point where they could repeat from memory a poem heard only once—one infant prodigy, we learn, could recite a poem backward after a single hearing. Others could do no more than work up a set of lectures on a single author which they delivered in one city after another. In addition to teaching, government service was open to the humanists. Meticulous purity of Latin in public documents came in the fifteenth century to be an object of special care, and the scholar with a good Ciceronian style was always sure of a lucrative post. The Renaissance came to Rome with the scribes in the papal chancery. Everywhere the humanist was courted, loved, and feared. It is difficult today to conceive of the power wielded by the learnèd in the fifteenth century; only the press can now compare with their influence. Tyrants who ruthlessly suppressed their own subjects quailed before a barbed Latin epigram. The humanist claimed the power to confer immortal praise, ridicule, or opprobrium on all of whom he wrote, and so great was the reverence for learning that his claim was generally admitted.

Until the middle of the fifteenth century the classical revival had been concerned largely with the search for manuscripts, the founding of libraries, learning and teaching, and translating. With the labor of acquisition and assimilation completed, the Italians turned their learning to more urbane uses. In almost every city academies were formed, more or less formal organizations of cultivated people who assembled to hear poems, orations, and scholarly dissertations, or to discuss literary or philosophical questions. The Platonic Academy at Florence was founded by Cosimo dei Medici, who set the tone for the organization by training Ficino for the express task of translating and explaining Plato. The Academy reached the peak of its fame under Lorenzo the Magnificent, when, around a bust of Plato, before which a light always burned, the Florentine aristocracy of learning discussed the teachings of the Greek master or tried to decipher the supposed allegory of Virgil's poetry. The characteristic approach of the humanist to philosophy, as well as to literature, was stylistic. Bruni was at first a Platonist, but after reading Aristotle in the original he became an Aristotelian, because he believed Aristotle to have a better style. The leaders of the Platonic Academy, however, were not so enthralled by mere beauty of form; unlike the lesser humanists, they were interested in content as well as style. They felt that no product of the human reason should be scorned, and embarked on the ambitious project of making a synthesis of all known philosophical systems. In 1486, Pico della Mirandola arrived in Rome and published his *Conclusiones*. On the "annexed nine hundred theses, relating to dialectics, ethics, physics, magic, mathematics, and the cabala, partly his own, partly collected from the works of Chaldaic, Arabic, Hebrew, Grecian, Egyptian, and Latin sages, Joannes Picus of Mirandola, Count of Concordia, will dispute publicly." This material he confidently expected to work into a coördinated whole, which would lay bare the secrets of nature and lead men through the various branches of learning to ultimate repose in the contemplation of God. He was then twenty-three years old. The same ideal haunted Ficino, the translator of Plato, who in his youth sang the Orphic hymns to the accompaniment of his lyre and dreamed of founding a new mystical and all-embracing religion. Against these reconcilers of Christianity and ancient philosophy, St. Antonino, bishop of Florence, raised the protest of common sense. If the pagan philosophers and the Fathers really said the same thing, he argued, it would be unnecessary to study the pagans, "but only the most superficial consideration is needed to persuade us that what the partisans of conciliation see there was not in the least intended by those philosophers themselves, and that their words must be distorted to adapt them to Christian truth."

At Rome, humanism ascended the papal throne in the person of Nicholas V. Nicholas was himself no mean scholar, and he attracted many others to Rome by lucrative posts in the papal *curia*. Here, too, an academy grew up, composed of enthusiasts for the past who collected archælogical remains and tried to live, dress, and talk like Romans. Pomponius Lætus, the leading figure in this academy, "had a small plot of land which he tilled in accordance with the precepts of Varro and Columella, and he was himself regarded as a second Cato. His vineyard on the Quirinal was frequented by his enthusiastic pupils. Before daybreak that 'insignificant little figure, with small, quick eyes, and quaint dress' might be seen descending, lantern in hand, from his home on the Esquiline to the scene of his lectures, where an eager crowd awaited him." [1] The Neapolitan academy, composed of scholars drawn to Naples by the hope of royal patronage, was chiefly occupied with problems of

[1] Sandys, *History of Classical Scholarship*, II, 92.

literary style. Here grew to fame many of the purists who prided themselves on the fact that their every word and every grammatical construction—every idea, they might have added—had an impeccable classical ancestry. At the other extreme was Venice, where in 1493 Aldus Manutius began his great project of printing the Greek classics, and, a few years later formed the "New Academy," to which belonged the scholars who aided him in preparing texts for the press. The beautiful and inexpensive little books that poured from the Aldine press had a double significance for Italian learning. They spelled the doom of the second-rate humanists, whose only stock-in-trade had been their knowledge of works not generally available to the public. Only the better scholars could flourish in an age when every educated man could possess his own copies of Cicero and Horace. At the same time, printing strengthened the hold of the classics on the minds of the upper classes of Italy. Now that classical works were easily available, everyone with any pretensions to culture was expected to have read at least some of the Latin authors.

Humanism created several problems for the Church. Many humanists took orders, and their reputation was so great that they gained high positions at Rome, as heads of administrative departments or as members of the College of Cardinals. They were not irreligious, but there was nothing in their training that enabled them to understand the yearning of ordinary men for a more intense, a more personal religious experience. These unfulfilled longings were especially strong north of the Alps, a region about which the humanists knew little and cared less. And, for the greater misfortune of the Church, the influence of the humanists at Rome reached its peak in the years immediately preceding the Protestant Reformation.

Another problem was created by one of the most useful accomplishments of the humanists, their skill in textual criticism. Since style was so important, it was necessary to be sure that one possessed the exact words of the ancient authors who served as models. This led to the comparison of manuscripts and to the correction of the received version of many texts, and works concerning the Church were not exempt from this sort of criticism. For example, the humanist Lorenzo Valla found it easy to demonstrate that the Donation of Constantine was a forgery. Even more upsetting was the discovery that the Vulgate— the official Latin version of the Bible—did not always give a completely accurate translation of the original biblical texts. In the long run, intensive study of the various versions of the books of the Bible strengthened rather than weakened the authority of the Church, but in the short run it led to a certain amount of discussion of the meaning of key passages and a reliance on individual rather than official interpretations of these passages.

Humanism—the study of the Greek and Latin classics—is the most striking aspect of the Italian Renaissance. It is the activity of which the Italians themselves were proudest; the field in which they were surest that they had surpassed the Middle Ages. Yet humanism was far from absorbing all the energies of Italy during the fourteenth and fifteenth centuries. Artistic activity was equally intense, and while the Italians talked less about their artists than their scholars, later generations have found the work of the artists more interesting. Renaissance art shows some of the same characteristics as Renaissance scholarship—emphasis on the work of the individual, interest in worldly beauty (especially the beauty of the human body), and reliance on classical models. There are, however, important differences between the artists and the scholars. Many artists had first of all been artisans; they often came from the lower classes and had received little or no education. They were more aware of the realities of Italian life than the scholars, more willing to develop already existing traditions, less apt to be slavish imitators of Greece and Rome. Even the architects, who had acres of Roman ruins to study and who often read the classical authorities on their subject, never reproduced their ancient models exactly. Renaissance architecture was based on classical principles, and it used classical ornament, but it adapted this material to the needs of its own age. A Florentine palace, seen from the street, is still very much of a medieval fortress, even if it has lost the towers and crenelations of the earlier age. A Renaissance church is still a church; it has not yet become a Greek temple. Neo-classical architecture is a product of the eighteenth and not of the fifteenth century. The same thing is true of the sculptors; they learned from the ancients but they seldom copied them. They worked out technical problems without much assistance from classical models and with few exceptions their figures were much more human and much less impersonal than those of their Greek and Roman predecessors. Michelangelo, the greatest Italian sculptor and one of the greatest Italian painters, perhaps came closest to the classical spirit, but he did it by developing his own ideas and forms, and not through copying.

Renaissance painting was even less dependent on the past than Renaissance architecture and sculpture. No ancient paintings were then known, and the only things which Italian artists could borrow from Greece and Rome were mythological or historical subjects and a few decorative details. Italian painters were free to solve their problems in their own way. They could develop the techniques of the later Middle Ages and they could respond to the life around them without breaking rules laid down by the ancients. Italian painting is the best expression of the spirit of Renaissance Italy because it was the least imitative of the arts of that period. And the fact that it is a completely honest, and at times almost naïve, expression of the ideals and aspirations of its age explains why it may still be enjoyed today. Even scholars can read the works of the humanists only with difficulty, but any one can feel the joy in living and the love of beauty in the works of the great Italian painters.

The Italian painters set themselves the difficult task of representing the human figure accurately. Giotto, the first great Italian painter, tried to portray real men and women rather than abstractions. He was not entirely successful in this effort, since he knew little of anatomy and tended to make all his people resemble each other. He does, however, give the impression that his figures are alive, that they exist in a real world, and that they are filled with personal emotions. Following Giotto, there was a period of intensive experimentation, in which painters struggled with the problems of anatomy, perspective, and light and shade. The most important work of this sort was done at Florence, where Masaccio (1401–1428) summed up all the experiments of his predecessors and added many discoveries of his own. Generation after generation of ambitious young artists learned the techniques of painting from Masaccio's work. Realism was now possible, but most of the Italian painters wanted something more than a mere reproduction of external appearances. Even the most uninspired artists tended to idealize their subjects—to make the women more beautiful, the men more handsome, and the background more luxurious than in real life. Ghirlandaio's prosperous Florentine burghers and Veronese's gorgeous Venetian festivals are good examples of this sort of work. The greatest painters were not content to draw merely beautiful figures and luxurious backgrounds; they wanted to represent the glory and the tragedy of human aspirations. Botticelli deliberately turned aside from the slick illustrations admired by his fellow-citizens of Florence to paint religious and mythological subjects which had a profound allegorical significance. His figures seem to have the gloomy knowledge that man must always strive, and strive in vain, that all human activity is carried on under sentence of death. Medieval in his beliefs, though not in his technique, Botticelli has never been a popular artist, though he was one of the finest painters of the Renaissance. Michelangelo has gained a greater reputation, though, like Botticelli, he was one of the few deeply religious Italians of his age. His super-human figures, bursting with energy, show the strength of human aspirations, but they also know that, under the sun, all things are mortal. Leonardo da Vinci and Raphael were more conventional in their attitudes. They mastered all the techniques of their trade and added new discoveries of their own, especially the art of arranging and balancing their figures to make a perfect composition. They were interested especially in character, and their portraits of real and imaginary personages pierce through the surface to the inner soul.

The cult of the classics and the love of beauty were the most striking characteristics of the Italian Renaissance. The upper classes in Italy were content with these adornments of life and looked no farther, but the ethical and social problems left by the Middle Ages could not be solved by humanists and artists. The classics might have provided a new set of standards, as they did for many men in seventeenth century France and England, but few Italians ever understood the spirit of the classical age. Classicism stands for restraint, order, respect for eternal truths—all qualities which were conspicuously lacking in Renaissance Italy. The humanists, who should have been imbued with the classical spirit, were as violent and as unprincipled as the tyrants. Poggio and Lorenzo Valla, two of the greatest scholars of the fifteenth century, illustrate these weaknesses. They engaged in a long controversy over the relative merits of Scipio Africanus and Cæsar, and the writings growing out of this quarrel have been called "the most infamous libels ever to see the light." When Poggio described the trial of Huss's disciple, Jerome of Prague, he seemed completely incapable of understanding why any one of learning and intelligence should persist in holding an opinion which endangered his life. When Valla was accused of heresy because he had demonstrated that the Donation of Constantine was a forgery, he recanted, saying "he believed as Mother Church believed; it was quite true that she *knew* nothing, yet he believed as she believed." The only conviction left to most scholars was their reverence for beauty of style and this led to disregard of other standards. Politian, the most famous Florentine poet of the fifteenth century, was an acute scholar and critic of classical texts. Yet we find him writing to the king of Portugal, offering his services as an historian and asking for some annals as a basis for his work "composed in any language and without regard for style or accuracy." Politian would supply the style, and accuracy was of small importance. It is not surprising that the great mass of writing, from which hundreds of humanists hoped to reap eternal fame, lies buried in oblivion.

Humanism could not create new standards of conduct, nor did it succeed in discovering ideals which would unite the Italians for a common effort. Only at the very end, when it was already too late, did a few writers such as Machiavelli begin to preach the values of patriotism and Italian nationalism. If the scholars and philosophers failed, it would hardly be fair to expect the artists to do better. The artist may express the ideals of his age or react against them; he does not create them. Renaissance writers and artists did nothing to modify the excessive individualism which was the greatest weakness of Italy in the fourteenth and fifteenth centuries; instead they often emphasized and glorified it. *Virtú*—manliness—was the real ideal of the upper classes in Italy, and *virtú* meant making the most of yourself, expressing all your possibilities, without regard for others. This release of individual energy produced some amazing figures—men who would attempt anything, always with confidence, and often with success. It also produced social chaos.

When the foreign invasions enslaved the Italian cities, when the shift in trade-routes lessened the importance of Italian trade, when the Reformation focused attention on a real intellectual problem, the Renaissance rapidly collapsed. The first threats to Italian security came at the end of the fifteenth century, with French and Spanish armies marching almost unopposed through the peninsula. Quarrels between the invading powers gave Italy a generation of respite and then, in 1527, came the sack of Rome. Charles V, emperor of Germany and king of Spain, concentrated a mercenary army in northern Italy to force the pope to favor Spanish policy. When the soldiers failed to receive their pay, they persuaded their commanders, without much difficulty, to lead them in a march on Rome. Burning, pillaging, and murdering, the army moved southward, plundered Rome, and blockaded the pope in the Castel Sant' Angelo until he agreed to pay a huge ransom. Italy was too weak to recover from such a shock, though, for a few years longer, artists and writers pretended that nothing had changed. Men continued to imitate the old forms from which the spirit had fled, but the ideals of the Renaissance were of no avail in a period of adversity. The center of art and learning moved across the Alps, and Italy was left with a handful of second-rate painters and pseudo-classical poets to console her for the revival of the Inquisition and the imposition of foreign rule.

What was the result of all the efforts of the Italians of the fourteenth and fifteenth centuries? In some respects the Renaissance bore its full fruit only after it had merged with the culture of the North. For centuries northern art and classical scholarship were based on work done by the Italians of the Renaissance, though the northerners developed some ideas more fully than had the Italians. In science Italian influence was less pervasive. There were able scientists in Italy in the fifteenth century, and it should never be forgotten that Copernicus was educated at Padua, a university that had preserved the scientific tradition of fourteenth-century Oxford and Paris. But the Italians did not give the same adulation to their scientists that they did to their humanists and their artists. The case of Leonardo da Vinci is instructive. What he wrote on painting was eagerly discussed, while his speculations on science and technology remained buried in manuscripts that were scarcely known until our own century. Nor did the Italians have much influence on the great revolution in communications that made ocean routes instead of land routes the principal means of intercontinental trade. All the basic notions about geography and all the techniques of navigation that made possible the voyages of Vasco da Gama and of Columbus were available early in the fourteenth century. Both the Spaniards and the Portuguese had discovered islands lying far out in the Atlantic in the thirteenth and four-teenth centuries. The discovery of America was a logical result of this earlier activity and owed little to the work of Italian geographers of the Renaissance.

The Italians had a considerable influence on philosophy, because they were fascinated by Plato. There had always been a strong current of Platonic thought running under the surface of medieval Aristotelianism. But very few Platonic texts were available in the Middle Ages; Plato had been neglected in the great wave of translations from the Arabic or Greek that poured over Europe in the twelfth and thirteenth centuries. During the Renaissance all of Plato became available, both in the original Greek, and in translation. Italian Platonism was distorted, just as earlier work on Plato had been, by the mystical interpretations of the Neo-Platonists, whose ideas could be reconciled fairly easily with orthodox Christian doctrine. As in other cases, the full impact of Plato's thought was felt only after the Italian contribution had been restudied in the North.

Italian literature had a profound influence throughout Europe, partly because Italian writers used familiar themes and forms. As we have seen, many of the stories of the *Decameron* were akin to the French *fabliaux*, and Chaucer borrowed some of Boccaccio's plots for the *Canterbury Tales*. Ariosto wrote an epic on Roland, and Tasso one on the First Crusade; both themes were familiar in the North, and both works influenced northern writers, such as Spenser. Of all the medieval verse forms, the Italians preferred the sonnet, and their preference had much to do with making the sonnet the dominant form for short, lyric poems in sixteenth-century Europe. Michelangelo's sonnets express his powerful personality almost as fully as do his works of art, and his example im-pressed writers everywhere. The Italians also gave fresh life to biography and to history. Their interest in the character of the individual made their biographies interesting, if not always accurate, and their auto-biographical writings were more striking than anything that had been written since the time of St. Augustine. The masterpiece of this genre is the *Memoirs* of Benvenuto Cellini, a work that reveals better than any-thing else the self-confidence, the terrific energy, and the complete amorality of an Italian artist. Cellini knew that he was an uncommon man, and he therefore felt that he did not have to be bound by the rules that restrained ordinary mortals. History was for a time tortured by humanists who persisted in fitting events and persons of their own age into classical molds. But it emerged, with a new depth of understanding of human character, in the work of Machiavelli and Guicciardini. Both men were influenced, but not dominated, by Livy and Tacitus; both of them were trying to interpret their own times in the light of past experience. Even the *Prince,* in one sense, is simply a commentary on recent Italian history.

In the long run, it may be that the chief importance of the Italian Renaissance lay in the revival of the classics and in the formation of a system of education based on the classics. It was in the schools of Italy that the ideal of the "cultured gentleman" first appeared, an ideal which has had great influence, for good and ill, on all modern countries. The most famous teacher of the Renaissance was Vittorino da Feltre, who in 1425 opened a school for the children of the Gonzaga princes of Mantua. He was so successful that students from all Italy and even from Germany were sent to him for instruction, some sons of princes, some dependent upon the charity which Vittorino dispensed so freely that he was frequently in debt. The classics formed the foundation of Vittorino's course of study, but religion, physical exercise, personal cleanliness, and manners all had a place in his scheme of education. "His house was a sanctuary of manners, deeds, and words." In an age of grasping selfishness, immorality, and cruelty such as was the fifteenth century, Vittorino's self-sacrifice, devotion to learning for its own sake, and purity of ideals and action, seem the more conspicuous, as indeed they did to his contemporaries. His school represents Renaissance education at its best; his fame, and that of two or three other schoolmasters, greatly influenced the spread of classical instruction into other countries, with all the advantages and disadvantages which have followed from the classical curriculum down to our own day. One of Vittorino's pupils was Frederic, duke of Urbino. This tiny Umbrian principality received in the later fifteenth century the unusual blessing of peace, and peace, aided by Frederic's charm and generosity, led to the formation of a brilliant court society made famous by Castiglione's *Book of the Courtier.* This work is the most celebrated of several Renaissance "books of etiquette" which received wide currency in the sixteenth century and laid the basis for modern concepts of gentility. Castiglione's gentleman must be a courtier from the nature of things, for, as we have already seen, the Renaissance was an affair of courts, but the standards of the court soon became those of European society. A list of the courtier's virtues will show the modernity of Castiglione's ideas. The courtier must be of gentle birth. His aim should be to fit himself for social intercourse. To this end his clothes, his speech, his manners, and his accomplishments should be directed. He should be proficient in sports and arms, possess "polite culture in letters and sound scholarship," and acquire some knowledge of dancing, music, and the arts. In all these things he should strive to acquire "a certain carelessness, to hide his art, and show that what he says or does comes from him without effort or deliberation." The ruling classes of Europe have followed this pattern for centuries and it is not unknown in America. The modern historian may decide whether or not it has been an adequate guide to life.

THE NORTHERN SOLUTION

Italians who traveled beyond the Alps in the fourteenth and fifteenth centuries were filled with horror by the "barbarism" of the northern countries. Poggio, who wandered as far as London in a vain search for lucrative employment, felt isolated in a wilderness of coarseness and ignorance. Petrarch left a vivid description of the desolation of France during the Hundred Years' War. Æneas Silvius Piccolomini, later Pius II, who spent much time in Germany as papal legate, was nauseated by the "swinish" Germans. A cursory survey would seem to confirm the Italian verdict; a heavy atmosphere of decay hung over northern Europe during these two centuries. Old ideas, customs, and practices lingered on, many of them to outward appearances more vigorous than ever. Among the aristocracy, the forms of chivalry were never made more of than in this age when the plebeian infantryman and gunpowder were making the knight obsolete. All the great orders of chivalry date from this period. The Order of the Garter was founded by Edward III about the time of Crécy and the Order of the Golden Fleece by the dukes of Burgundy a little later. A few years before Poitiers, John the Good, that paragon of knightly stupidity, established the Order of the Star, "for the honor of God and Our Lady, and the exaltation of chivalry and the strengthening of honor"; even Louis XI founded an order. Lengthy chronicles, such as that of Froissart, were written to perpetuate the praiseworthy deeds of chivalry in the memory of man. Royal and feudal courts took on a tone of ostentatious display hitherto unknown. The court of the Valois dukes of Burgundy was the most splendid in Christendom; in Burgundy were developed those meticulous rules of courtly etiquette which were to reach their climax in the time of Louis XIV. Among the wealthy burghers the extravagant manners, speech, dress, and style of living of the nobles were assiduously aped.

The splendor and gaiety of the nobles and the rich formed a thin and transparent veneer over the general pessimism of the period. Even at the courts there were indications of weariness; pastoral poetry abounded, filled with praise of the simple life. Disillusionment and a sense of the futility of existence breathe through even mediocre writings and obtain classical expression in François Villon's ballads on the fleeting life of the lovely, the valiant, the renowned, and the pious: "But where are the snows of yesteryear?" As we pass to the mass of the people, the tone changes from one of fashionable cynicism or ironical laughter to horror and despair. These were terrible times for the poor and the simple; it was an age of iron and fire. The terrors of incessant war and pestilence, grinding taxes, the visible decline of the Church, all made a vivid impression on the acute imagination of the time. Social unrest led to the revolts of peasants and artisans, which were so ferociously suppressed.

Disillusionment with life took the form of a ghoulish interest in death. Religious pictures of the passion of Christ became saturated with emotion and horror. Graveyards were a popular place of resort, while the "Dance of Death" became a favorite subject with artists and poets. All the terrifying and disgusting aspects of death were exhibited with perverted relish.

On the surface, life in Europe outside Italy seemed to be summed up in the crumbling of old ideas. Yet beyond the Alps, men were slowly laying the foundations for a new order of society which was to endure far longer than the ephemeral brilliance of the Renaissance. During the last half of the fifteenth century the kings of France, England, and Spain, who had been deprived of much of their power by the feudal reaction of the fourteenth century, recovered their authority and restored order in their countries. The solution of the political problem made it easier to deal with economic problems. Almost all classes benefited by the shift of trade "from an intermunicipal to an international basis." [2] Commerce between European states increased, and the great explorations financed by the kings of the West opened up new markets and new sources of raw materials. The shock caused by the growth of capitalism was mitigated by careful regulation of capitalism in the interest of the state. Even Germany, which had lagged behind the Western states, showed signs of political and economic revival in the last years of the fifteenth century.

Some historians have given all the credit for ending the social and moral anarchy of the later Middle Ages to the remarkable group of monarchs who came to power in the period after 1461. This seems an inadequate explanation. There were dozens of Italian princes who were as clever, as forceful and as unscrupulous as Louis XI of France, Ferdinand of Spain, and Henry VII of England. The Western kings succeeded where the Italians failed because they had something on which to build. Disastrous as the fourteenth and early fifteenth centuries had been, they had not annihilated medieval ideals in the countries beyond the Alps. The old ideals were slowly adapted to fit the new situation, and they gave a solid basis for the reorganization of society. The fact that large groups of people had the same objectives, and were willing to sacrifice immediate personal advantages to secure those objectives, made it much easier to restore order and good government.

One ancient ideal which was being revived in new forms was that of loyalty to the ruling dynasty. Civil wars throughout the West had convinced most men that submission to a hereditary ruler was the only guarantee of order. Obedience to the king's will was becoming the chief political virtue, and insistence on local or personal privileges the chief political vice. This belief had not yet taken on its theoretical form of divine right sovereignty, but it was only the theory which was lacking.

[2] W. E. Lunt, *History of England,* p. 287.

At the end of the fifteenth century kings were permitted to do whatever they thought necessary for the welfare of the state and challenges of their authority were considered impious. The men who worked out the theories of divine right and sovereignty derived their ideas from the actual practices of European monarchs after 1461.

Nationalism also reinforced the idea of loyalty to a hereditary ruler. Nationalism had been growing in Europe since the thirteenth century, and it existed in Germany and Italy as well as in the better organized countries of the West. But in Germany and Italy it remained a vague aspiration, since it could not be focused on any single individual or institution. In France, England, and Spain it could be concentrated and used for political purposes. Monarchy and nationalism, in those countries, were almost synonymous. The boundaries of the kingdom were the boundaries of the nation, and the king was the symbol of the nation. Union under the king had created common traditions, loyalty to the king had created common aspirations, and these are the basic elements in national feeling. The national monarchies were to dominate the history of modern Europe.

Finally, under the formalism and corruption of the late medieval Church, intense religious feeling still existed. The peoples of the North were not yet ready to abandon religion as a guide to life, or to make it a matter of festivals and revivals as the Italians had done. Christianity remained a powerful force beyond the Alps, one of the most effective means of securing social coöperation. The old ideal of a united Christendom was gone, but every one insisted that the new national monarchies must be Christian commonwealths. Since the Church was not giving much leadership, religious feeling sought new outlets in mysticism and in popular education. Mysticism has been much studied of late, but the word itself remains difficult to define. It may best be understood by what the mystics themselves have said. "The flight of the alone to the Alone"; "works in themselves are nothing, personal communion with God is everything." The clearest idea may be had from Thomas à Kempis' *Imitation of Christ*, the classic expression of fifteenth century mysticism, and a work which has been printed almost as often, and in as many languages, as the Bible:

> I will hear what the Lord God may say to me. Blest is the soul that hears its Lord's voice speaking within it, and takes the word of comfort from His lips. Blest are the ears that catch the throbbing whisper of the Lord, and turn not to the buzzings of the passing world; that listen not to voices from without, but to the truth that teaches from within. Blest are the eyes that, shut to outer things, are busied with the inner life. Blest are they who penetrate within, and more and more by daily use strive to prepare themselves to take the heavenly mysteries. And blest are they who try to

give their time to God, and shake them free from all the burden of the world . . . So, all is vanity, save loving God and serving Him alone.

In more prosaic terms: the mystic is one who has lost faith in reason, wholly or partially, and aspires, by faith, meditation, and prayer, either to unite his soul with God, or to feel intensely the presence of God.

Mysticism is intensely imaginative and introspective, and it is likely to find expression in many forms. It is also individualistic, and the mystic who has attained to the conviction of personal communion with God may feel that he is no longer bound by the commands of either church or state. All through the Middle Ages there were extravagant sects composed of those who felt themselves above law of all sort, what might be called the "lunatic fringe" of mysticism. In a second category might be put those who were so preoccupied with contemplation that their lives scarcely touched the existence of their fellow-men at any point. These "quietists" or "negative mystics" were also not uncommon, but they had little influence except through an occasional writing, such as the *German Theology*, a little manual on salvation through love and faith which had a profound effect on Luther. The most influential mystics of the Middle Ages, however, were those who remained in touch with the society around them and devoted the energy resulting from their conviction of the immediacy of God to the task of purifying current religious thought and action. A group of such men flourished in the fourteenth and fifteenth centuries in the Rhine Valley and particularly in the Netherlands. Their activities bore fruit in the shape of a vigorous educational and reform movement within the Church, but they also helped to pave the way for the Reformation. The spiritual father of this movement was Master Eckhart, who died in 1327. He was an accomplished scholar, but in mid-life he abandoned the intellectual approach to God and fell back on the faith and love so dear to the mystic. The important thing for us is that Eckhart, instead of leading a solitary life, was impelled to preach. That his speculative sermons had much meaning for most of his hearers may be doubted; certainly they now seem difficult to understand. His teachings did make a deep impression on a small group of men who were much preoccupied with the condition of their own souls and of the Church as a whole, and with these less abstruse thinkers mysticism became a force such as it had not been since the days of St. Francis.

Unorganized, the host of men who rebelled against the decline of spiritual feeling and the growing corruption apparent in the Church might have spent their energies to little avail. In the Netherlands, the movement focused in the Brothers of the Common Life, founded in the last quarter of the fourteenth century by Gerard Groot. Groot had been a lay preacher, and for many years his sermons on spiritual regeneration had drawn unprecedented crowds of hearers until the clergy, enraged by his attacks on their lax practices, enforced silence upon him. Then Groot began to meet a few of his more ardent disciples at the home of a friend, Florentius Radewyn, in Deventer. Shortly before Groot's death in 1384 these men decided to live together, sharing their goods in common and obeying an elected rector. Then a school was started and members began to preach. New adherents joined rapidly, and within a very few years the Brothers were famous throughout the Netherlands. All this sounds like the early history of the Franciscans and Dominicans, who had also striven by preaching and teaching to call men away from a religion of routine practice to one of sincere piety. The Brothers are, however, marked off from these earlier orders by two things. First of all, begging was prohibited; every member must earn his living. Whether this change was due to the disrepute into which the begging friars had fallen through their lax lives, or whether the commercial revolution was giving a dignity to work and making indigence seem contemptible, it is impossible to say; probably both elements influenced Groot and his followers. The second difference is much more important. The Brothers resolutely refused to make their society a part of the monastic system, or to take irrevocable vows. Each Brother led the common life while he lived in one of the "Brother Houses," but he was free to leave at will. Many members did join monasteries, though even then they usually joined the Austin Canons, the least regulated of all the orders, but the Brothers of the Common Life always remained a lay organization. Although the members were loyal Catholics and did not attack the monastic system, their resolve shows a dangerous divergence from the Catholic system. It exalted the lay mode of life and hence detracted from the peculiar sanctity of the clerical ideal, which had hitherto been regarded as the surest way to salvation. It was also an unconscious assertion of the intense individualism inherent in mysticism. The Brothers never taught anything which the Church condemned; they did, however, place much more emphasis on the individual than on the institution of the Church. The sacraments played a large part in their scheme, but only as aids to salvation; much greater emphasis was placed on the necessity of faith in God, and on love of God. From this, it was only a step to the assertion that the individual might, if he wished, attain salvation in his own way, even though this way lay outside the Church. By this exaltation both of the lay as against the priestly life, and of the individual as against the institution, mysticism in general, and the Brothers of the Common Life in particular, prepared men's minds for the Reformation.

During the fifteenth century the movement spread from the Netherlands into western and southern Germany, and the Brothers became the most famous schoolmasters in Europe. Some of their houses had an enrollment of over a thousand students, and one had over two thousand for a time. The extent to which thought in northern Europe was influenced by the society becomes apparent when we remember that nearly all the educated men in Germany and the Netherlands in the sixteenth century had either received their early training from the Brothers or from men who had themselves attended their schools. Both the impulse which impelled the Brother Houses to turn to teaching and the character of their teaching may be discerned from the *Imitation of Christ:* "Never read a word to seem more wise and learned . . . Read much, learn much, yet you must always come to one beginning—I [God] am He that teaches man knowledge."

Here we have the essential difference between the educational ideals which were rising in northern Europe and those of the Italian Renaissance. In Italy, learning was an end in itself, giving distinction and position to its possessor and serving as an aristocratic ornament. Vittorino's curriculum shows a broader conception, but he was an exception, and even he had emphasized the ideal of the polished gentleman. The education given by the Brothers was a means, not an end. The end was a pious life; education was essential so that the Christian might be in a position to understand his faith and be strengthened in that faith. Here again, the tendency to emancipate the individual from blind dependence upon the institutional Church is apparent, although the Brothers were unconscious of the form which that emancipation might, and later did, take. But education in the Netherlands was not merely reduced from an end to a means, it was also popular rather than aristocratic. The Brothers taught all, high and low alike, because every Christian needed a modicum of learning to lead a good and useful life, and every one, whether noble or baseborn, was equal in the sight of God. In the scores of books of pedagogy written by the Brothers, their innumerable translations of parts of the Bible into the vernacular, their grammars and their books of devotion alike, these two ideals of Christian democracy and utility are apparent.

Underneath a sordid and decadent exterior, therefore, extremely significant movements were taking place in northern Europe. The revival of strong monarchy, based on ideals which had wide popular support, created a framework within which social and intellectual progress was once more possible. At the same time the revival of mystical religious thought resulted in a partial regeneration of clerical morals and a strong recrudescence of Christian democracy. Without breaking completely from the medieval tradition, a new type of education was created which was less abstract than the old medieval scholasticism and better suited to the needs of the time. As these examples show, respect for medieval precedents, Christianity, and some regard for the needs of the common man characterized the new transalpine civilization, just as hostility to the Middle Ages, indifference in religion, and a narrowly aristocratic viewpoint characterized the civilization of the Renaissance. The contrast between the two regions is especially evident in their intellectual and artistic life. Thus, while the Italians were wrangling over rare manuscripts, the Germans were perfecting the art of printing from movable type. This invention, probably made by Gutenberg in the middle of the fifteenth century, seems to have been caused by the popular demand in Germany for religious works. Presses were established rapidly in other countries, but in Italy, even after Aldus Manutius had begun to print the classics, there was some disdain among the learned for printed books, partly because they were less beautiful than a well-written manuscript, partly because they made the spread of knowledge so easy. German and Dutch art shows the same democratic quality. The etchings, woodcuts, and engravings of Dürer and his lesser contemporaries, which today are eagerly sought by collectors, sold for almost nothing or were used as illustrations for cheap books, usually popular books of devotion. The northern attitude toward the classics is in striking contrast to that of Italy. In the fifteenth century classical studies began to spread over the Alps from Italy and were assimilated into the curriculum and into thought. But the classical cult never took hold as it had in Italy. In part, this difference may be attributed to the fact that the literature and thought of Greece and Rome always remained something foreign; the northerner naturally could not feel that he was the heir of, or even closely akin to, the ancient past. Even in Italy, however, the classics began to dominate thought only when medieval ideas had lost their vitality. In northern Europe, the Christian tradition still retained its hold, and the classics merely supplemented existing ideas, being bent to the service of an educational system with aims already clearly defined and too deeply rooted in the life of the time to be supplanted. We see, then, that although the fourteenth and fifteenth centuries were on the whole more dismal and unattractive north of the Alps than they were in Italy, the general gloom merely obscures significant political and intellectual achievements of the northern peoples. In the sixteenth and seventeenth centuries, Europe was to be distracted by religious and dynastic wars, but the impetus given in this earlier period was never wholly lost. If the elements which go to make up our modern civilization are analyzed carefully, it becomes apparent that the achievements of the northern nations were of more enduring vitality than those of the more superficially brilliant city-states of Italy.

LIST OF IMPORTANT DATES

1077   Henry IV at Canossa
1091   Completion of Norman Conquest of Sicily
1095   Council of Clermont
1098   Foundation of the Cistercian Order
1099   Capture of Jerusalem
1114   Foundation of Clairvaux
1122   Concordat of Worms
1140   St. Bernard persuades Council of Sens to condemn Abelard
c.1141   Compilation of Gratian's *Decretum*
1144   Fall of Edessa
1152   Death of Suger
1153   Death of St. Bernard
1164   Constitutions of Clarendon
1166   Assize of Clarendon
1170   Assassination of Thomas Becket
1176   Lombard League defeats Frederick Barbarossa at Legnano
1183   Peace of Constance between Barbarossa and Lombards
1187   Saladin captures Jerusalem
1191   Third Crusade recaptures Acre
1198–1216   Pope Innocent III
1204   Fourth Crusade takes Constantinople
1212   Battle of Las Navas de Tolosa, most of Spain freed from Moors
1213   Simon de Montfort defeats Albigensians at Muret
1214   Philip Augustus defeats Otto IV and rebellious barons at Bouvines
1215   Magna Carta
         Fourth Lateran Council
1221   Death of St. Dominic
1226   Death of St. Francis
1245   Frederick II deposed by Council of Lyons
1248–1254   Crusade of St. Louis to Egypt and Syria
1258   Provisions of Oxford
1265   Parliament of Simon de Montfort
1266   Charles of Anjou conquers Sicily
1268   Defeat and execution of Conradin
1270   Crusade of St. Louis to Tunis
1274   Death of St. Thomas Aquinas
1282   Sicilian Vespers
1291   Last Christian holdings in Palestine lost
1294–1303   Pope Boniface VIII
1296   Bull *Clericis laicos*
1297   Confirmation of the Charters by Edward I

1302   First French Estates-General
1303   Attack on Boniface VIII at Anagni
1305   Election of Clement V, beginning of Babylonian Captivity
1311   Lords Ordainer in England
1314   Battle of Bannockburn
1315   Swiss defeat Habsburgs at Morgarten
1321   Death of Dante
1324   The *Defensor Pacis* of Marsiglio of Padua
1327   Deposition of Edward II of England
1336   Death of Giotto
1346   Battle of Crécy
1348   The Black Death becomes epidemic in Europe
1356   Battle of Poitiers
1358   Peasant Rebellion (*Jacquerie*) in France
1360   Treaty of Calais (Brétigny)
1374   Death of Petrarch
1375   Death of Boccaccio
1376   The Good Parliament in England
1377   End of Babylonian Captivity
1378   The Great Schism begins
1381   Peasants' Revolt in England
1384   Death of Wycliffe
1399   Deposition of Richard II of England
1400   Death of Chaucer
1409   Council of Pisa
1414–1418   Council of Constance, end of Great Schism
1415   Execution of Huss
       Battle of Agincourt
1420   Treaty of Troyes
c.1429   Death of Masaccio
1429   Relief of Orleans by Joan of Arc
1434   Cosimo dei Medici "boss" of Florence
1440   Death of Jan Van Eyck
c.1450   Gutenberg prints his first books
1453   Constantinople falls to the Turks
1456   Death of Lorenzo Valla
c.1469   Death of Villon
1469–1492   Lorenzo dei Medici ruler of Florence
1485   Henry Tudor king of England
1492   Last Moorish territory in Spain conquered
       Columbus discovers America

GENEALOGICAL TABLES

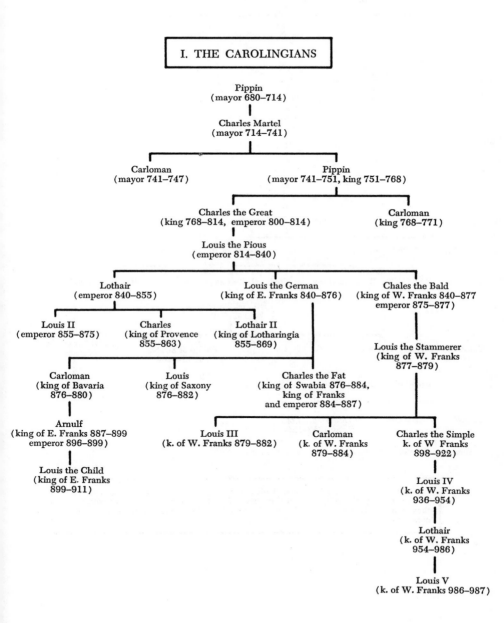

I. THE CAROLINGIANS

Pippin
(mayor 680–714)

Charles Martel
(mayor 714–741)

Carloman
(mayor 741–747)

Pippin
(mayor 741–751, king 751–768)

Charles the Great
(king 768–814, emperor 800–814)

Carloman
(king 768–771)

Louis the Pious
(emperor 814–840)

Lothair
(emperor 840–855)

Louis the German
(king of E. Franks 840–876)

Chales the Bald
(king of W. Franks 840–877
emperor 875–877)

Louis II
(emperor 855–875)

Charles
(king of Provence
855–863)

Lothair II
(king of Lotharingia
855–869)

Louis the Stammerer
(king of W. Franks
877–879)

Carloman
(king of Bavaria
876–880)

Louis
(king of Saxony
876–882)

Charles the Fat
(king of Swabia 876–884,
king of Franks
and emperor 884–887)

Arnulf
(king of E. Franks 887–899
emperor 896–899)

Louis III
(k. of W. Franks 879–882)

Carloman
(k. of W. Franks
879–884)

Charles the Simple
k. of W Franks
898–922)

Louis the Child
(king of E. Franks
899–911)

Louis IV
(k. of W. Franks
936–954)

Lothair
(k. of W. Franks
954–986)

Louis V
(k. of W. Franks 986–987)

567

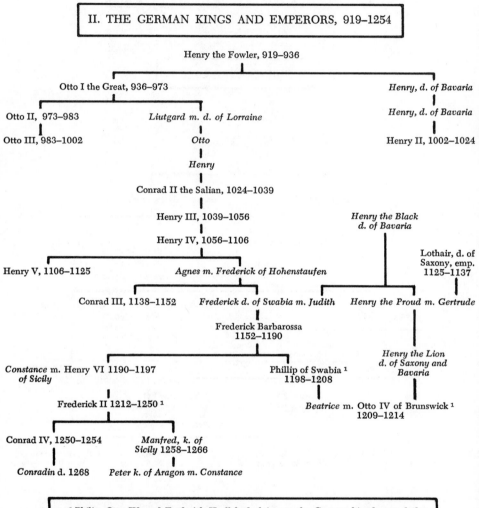

II. THE GERMAN KINGS AND EMPERORS, 919–1254

Henry the Fowler, 919–936

Otto I the Great, 936–973 — *Henry, d. of Bavaria*

Otto II, 973–983 — *Liutgard m. d. of Lorraine* — *Henry, d. of Bavaria*

Otto III, 983–1002 — *Otto* — Henry II, 1002–1024

Henry

Conrad II the Salian, 1024–1039

Henry III, 1039–1056 — *Henry the Black d. of Bavaria*

Henry IV, 1056–1106

Lothair, d. of Saxony, emp. 1125–1137

Henry V, 1106–1125 — *Agnes m. Frederick of Hohenstaufen*

Conrad III, 1138–1152 — *Frederick d. of Swabia m. Judith* — *Henry the Proud m. Gertrude*

Frederick Barbarossa 1152–1190

Henry the Lion d. of Saxony and Bavaria

Constance m. Henry VI 1190–1197 *of Sicily* — Phillip of Swabia [1] 1198–1208

Frederick II 1212–1250 [1]

Beatrice m. Otto IV of Brunswick [1] 1209–1214

Conrad IV, 1250–1254 — *Manfred, k. of Sicily 1258–1266*

Conradin d. 1268 — *Peter k. of Aragon m. Constance*

[1] Philip, Otto IV, and Frederick II all had claims to the German kingdom and the Empire during the early thirteenth century. The dates given are only approximate; they indicate the period in which the claimant had the support of most of the German princes.

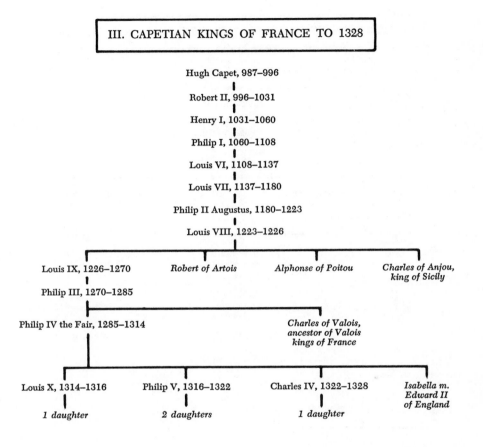

III. CAPETIAN KINGS OF FRANCE TO 1328

Hugh Capet, 987–996

Robert II, 996–1031

Henry I, 1031–1060

Philip I, 1060–1108

Louis VI, 1108–1137

Louis VII, 1137–1180

Philip II Augustus, 1180–1223

Louis VIII, 1223–1226

Louis IX, 1226–1270   *Robert of Artois*   *Alphonse of Poitou*   *Charles of Anjou, king of Sicily*

Philip III, 1270–1285

Philip IV the Fair, 1285–1314   *Charles of Valois, ancestor of Valois kings of France*

Louis X, 1314–1316   Philip V, 1316–1322   Charles IV, 1322–1328   *Isabella m. Edward II of England*

1 daughter   *2 daughters*   *1 daughter*

IV. CAPETIAN KINGS OF FRANCE OF THE VALOIS BRANCH

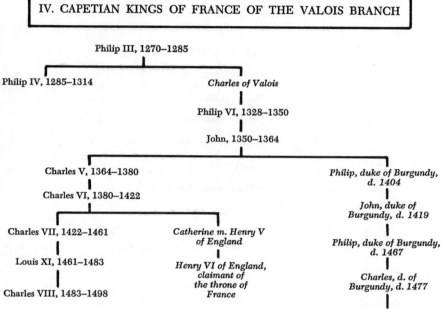

Philip III, 1270–1285

Philip IV, 1285–1314

Charles of Valois

Philip VI, 1328–1350

John, 1350–1364

Charles V, 1364–1380

Charles VI, 1380–1422

Charles VII, 1422–1461

Louis XI, 1461–1483

Charles VIII, 1483–1498

Catherine m. Henry V of England

Henry VI of England, claimant of the throne of France

Philip, duke of Burgundy, d. 1404

John, duke of Burgundy, d. 1419

Philip, duke of Burgundy, d. 1467

Charles, d. of Burgundy, d. 1477

Mary of Burgundy

V. NORMAN AND PLANTAGENET KINGS OF ENGLAND
TO 1377

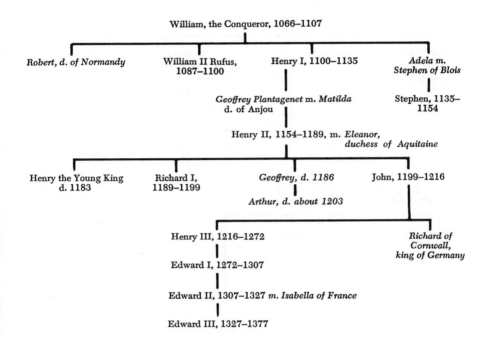

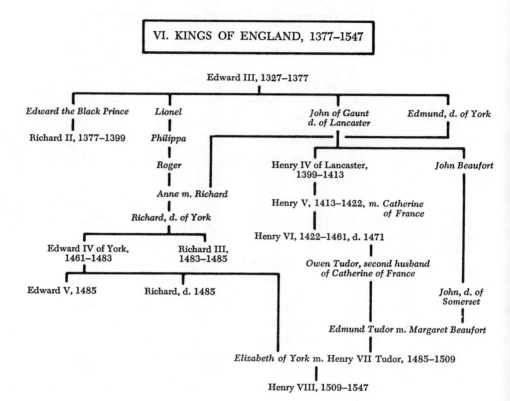

VI. KINGS OF ENGLAND, 1377–1547

Edward III, 1327–1377

Edward the Black Prince   *Lionel*   *John of Gaunt* *d. of Lancaster*   *Edmund, d. of York*

Richard II, 1377–1399   *Philippa*   Henry IV of Lancaster, 1399–1413   *John Beaufort*

Roger   Henry V, 1413–1422, *m. Catherine of France*

Anne m. Richard   Henry VI, 1422–1461, d. 1471

Richard, d. of York

Edward IV of York, 1461–1483   Richard III, 1483–1485   *Owen Tudor, second husband of Catherine of France*

Edward V, 1485   Richard, d. 1485   *John, d. of Somerset*

Edmund Tudor m. Margaret Beaufort

Elizabeth of York m. Henry VII Tudor, 1485–1509

Henry VIII, 1509–1547

SUGGESTIONS FOR READING

This is not a bibliography but a reading list. The books which are listed were selected, not for the specialist, but for the lay reader who would like more information about topics discussed in the text. A few important French works are cited; everything else is in English. Translations of source material are listed at the beginning of each section. These lists do not include all English translations of medieval texts and documents, but only those which have proved interesting and useful in classroom discussion. A full list of translations is provided by C. P. Farrar and A. P. Evans, *Bibliography of English Translations from Medieval Sources* (New York, 1946).

GUIDES AND ATLASES

L. J. Paetow, *Guide to the Study of Medieval History* (New York, 1931).

C. Gross, *The Sources and Literature of English History* (New York and London, 1915).

R. R. Palmer, *Atlas of World History* (Chicago, 1957).

W. R. Shepherd, *Historical Atlas* (New York, 1956).

GENERAL

F. B. Artz, *The Mind of the Middle Ages* (New York, 1954).

S. Baldwin, *The Organization of Mediaeval Christianity* (New York, 1929).

G. Barraclough, *The Origins of Modern Germany* (Oxford, 1947).

J. Bryce, *The Holy Roman Empire* (various editions).

Cambridge Economic History (Cambridge, 1941 ff.), Vols. I, II, and III.

Cambridge Medieval History (Cambridge, 1911 ff., 8 vols.).

R. W. and A. J. Carlyle, *A History of Mediaeval Political Theory in the West* (London, 1903–1936, 6 vols.).

F. Copleston, *Medieval Philosophy* (London, 1952).

A. C. Crombie, *Augustine to Galileo* (London, 1952).

E. R. Curtius, *European Literature and the Latin Middle Ages* (New York, 1953).

G. C. Crump and E. F. Jacob, *Legacy of the Middle Ages* (Oxford, 1926).

M. Deanesly, *A History of the Medieval Church* (London, 1925).

E. Gilson, *History of Christian Philosophy in the Middle Ages* (London, 1955).

H. Fisher, *The Medieval Empire* (London, 1898, 2 vols.).

F. Gregorovius, *History of the City of Rome in the Middle Ages* (London, 1894–1902, 13 vols.).

A. Harnack, *A History of Dogma* (London, 1896–1905, 7 vols.).

D. J. B. Hawkins, *A Sketch of Mediaeval Philosophy* (London, 1946).

J. E. A. Jolliffe, *The Constitutional History of England to 1485* (London, 1937).

D. Knowles, *The Evolution of Medieval Thought* (London, 1962).

K. S. Latourette, *A History of Christianity* (New York, 1953).

E. Lavisse, *Histoire de France* (Paris, 1901 ff.), Vols. II–IV.

H. K. Mann, *The Lives of the Popes in the Early Middle Ages* (London, 1902–1932, 18 vols.).

C. H. McIlwain, *Growth of Political Thought in the West* (New York, 1932).

Montalembert, *The Monks of the West* (London, 1896, 6 vols.).

C. R. Morey, *Mediaeval Art* (New York, 1942).

Oxford History of England (Oxford, 1934 ff.), Vols. I–IV.

H. Pirenne, *History of Europe* (New York, 1939).

——, *Economic and Social History of Medieval Europe* (New York, n.d.).

R. L. Poole, *Illustrations of the History of Mediaeval Thought* (London, 1920).

A. K. Porter, *Medieval Architecture* (New Haven, 1912, 2 vols.).

L. Salvatorelli, *A Concise History of Italy* (New York, 1939).

J. E. Sandys, *A History of Classical Scholarship* (Cambridge, 1921, 3 vols.).

H. O. Taylor, *The Mediæval Mind* (New York, 1925, 2 vols.).

J. W. Thompson, *Economic and Social History of the Middle Ages* (New York, 1928).

——, *Economic and Social History of the Later Middle Ages* (New York, 1931).

L. Thorndike, *History of Magic and Experimental Science* (New York, 1923 ff., 6 vols.).

M. de Wulf, *History of Medieval Philosophy* (New York, 1925).

COLLECTIONS OF SOURCES

R. Brentano, *The Early Middle Ages, 500–1000* (New York, 1964).

G. C. Coulton, *A Medieval Garner* (London, 1910).

——, *Life in the Middle Ages* (Cambridge, 1931).

D. C. Douglas, *English Historical Documents*, Vols. I and II (New York, 1953–1955).

Norton Downs, *The Medieval Pageant* (New York, 1964).

F. Duncalf and A. C. Krey, *Parallel Source Problems in Mediæval History* (New York, 1912).

E. F. Henderson, *Select Historical Documents of the Middle Ages* (London, 1896).

C. W. Jones, *Medieval Literature in Translation* (New York, 1950).

Bryce Lyon, *The High Middle Ages* (New York, 1964).

R. McKeon, *Selections from Medieval Philosophers* (New York, 1929, 2 vols.).

F. A. Ogg, *A Source Book of Mediæval History* (New York, 1907).

J. H. Robinson, *Readings in European History*, Vol. I (Boston, 1906).

J. B. Ross and M. M. McLaughlin, *The Portable Medieval Reader* (New York, 1949).

J. H. Scott, A. H. Hyma, and A. H. Noyes, *Readings in Medieval History* (New York, 1933).

C. Stephenson and F. G. Marcham, *Sources of English Constitutional History* (New York, 1937).

O. J. Thatcher and E. H. McNeal, *A Source Book of Medieval History* (New York, 1905).

Translations and Reprints from the Original Sources of European History (University of Pennsylvania, Philadelphia, 1894 ff., three series).

1. THE ROMAN WORLD IN THE FOURTH CENTURY

J. B. Bury, *History of the Later Roman Empire* (London, 1923, 2 vols.).

C. Dawson, *The Making of Europe* (New York, 1934).

E. Gibbon, *The History of the Decline and Fall of the Roman Empire*, ed. by J. B. Bury (London, 1896–1900, Vols. I–III).

T. Hodgkin, *Italy and Her Invaders* (Oxford, 1880–1890, Vols. I–II).

A. H. M. Jones, *The Later Roman Empire* (Norman, 1964).

F. Lot, *The End of the Ancient World* (New York, 1931).

H. Moss, *The Birth of the Middle Ages* (Oxford, 1935).

M. Rostovtzeff, *History of the Ancient World: Rome* (Oxford, 1931).

J. M. Wallace-Hadrill, *The Barbarian West, 400–1000* (London, 1952).

GOVERNMENT

Ammianus Marcellinus, *Roman History* (tr. by C. D. Yonge, London, 1902, by J. C. Rolfe, Cambridge, 1935).

R. Pound, *Readings in Roman Law* (Cambridge, 1914).

W. T. Arnold, *Roman Provincial Administration* (London, 1914).

J. B. Firth, *Constantine* (New York, 1905).

J. Maurice, *Constantin le Grand* (Paris, 1924).

T. Mommsen, *Roman Provinces* (London, 1909).

J. S. Reid, *The Municipalities of the Roman Empire* (Cambridge, 1913).

ECONOMIC AND SOCIAL CONDITIONS

S. Dill, *Roman Society in the Last Century of the Empire* (London, 1910).

M. Rostovtzeff, *Social and Economic History of the Roman Empire* (Oxford, 1926).

LITERATURE, EDUCATION AND ART

P. R. Cole, *Later Roman Education* (New York, 1909).

T. R. Glover, *Life and Letters in the Fourth Century* (Cambridge, 1901).

T. Haarhoff, *Schools of Gaul* (Oxford, 1920).

RELIGION

St. Augustine, *Confessions* (Everyman's Library and other editions).

——, *The City of God* (tr. by J. Healey, Edinburgh, 1909, 2 vols.).

Salvian, *On the Government of God* (tr. by E. M. Sanford, New York, 1930).

R. J. Deferrari, ed., *The Fathers of the Church* (New York, 1847 ff.).

P. Schaff and H. Wace, eds., *A Select Library of the Nicene and Post-Nicene Fathers* (series I, 14 vols., New York, 1886–1890; series II, 14 vols., New York, 1890–1900).

C. Bigg, *The Church's Task in the Roman Empire* (Oxford, 1905).

F. Cumont, *Oriental Religions in Roman Paganism* (Chicago, 1911).

L. Duchesne, *Early History of the Christian Church* (New York, 1902–1915, 2 vols.).

E. R. Goodenough, *The Church in the Roman Empire* (New York, 1931).

A. Harnack, *History of Dogma* (Vol. I, London, 1897).

F. Legge, *Forerunners and Rivals of Christianity* (Cambridge, 1915, 2 vols.).

G. Uhlhorn, *The Conflict of Christianity with Heathenism* (New York, 1908).

2. THE DECAY OF THE ROMAN WORLD IN THE WEST

For general reading on this topic, see the books listed under Chapter 1.

THE EARLY GERMANS

Jordanes, *Origin and Deeds of the Goths* (tr. by C. C. Mierow, Princeton, 1908).

Tacitus, *Germania* (Translations and Reprints, Vol. VI, no. 3, and other editions).

Cambridge Medieval History, Vol. I, Ch. 7.

F. B. Gummere, *Founders of England* (New York, 1930).

THE MIGRATIONS

J. B. Bury, *The Invasion of Europe by the Barbarians* (London, 1928).

Cambridge Medieval History, Vol. I, Chs. 9–15.

L. Halphen, *Les Barbares* (Paris, 1930).

C. J. H. Hayes, *Introduction to the Sources Relating to the Germanic Invasions* (New York, 1909).

P. Villari, *The Barbarian Invasions of Italy* (London, 1902, 2 vols.).

THE GERMANIC KINGDOMS

Bede, *Ecclesiastical History of England* (many translations).

The Burgundian Code (tr. by K. Fischer, Philadelphia, 1949).

Cassiodorus, *Letters* (tr. by T. Hodgkin, London, 1886).

Gregory of Tours, *History of the Franks* (tr. by O. M. Dalton, Oxford, 1927, and in part by E. Brehaut, New York, 1916).

Paul the Deacon, *History of the Langobards* (tr. by D. Foulke, Philadelphia, 1907).

Sidonius Apollinaris, *Letters* (tr. by O. M. Dalton, Oxford, 1915).

S. Dill, *Roman Society in Gaul in the Merovingian Age* (London, 1926).

T. Hodgkin, *Theodoric the Goth* (New York, 1891).

J. M. Wallace-Hadrill, *The Long-Haired Kings* (London, 1962).

THE CHURCH IN THE GERMANIC KINGDOMS

St. Benedict, *Rule* (tr. by F. H. Gasquet, London, 1908).

Boëthius, *The Theological Tractates* and *The Consolation of Philosophy* (ed. and tr. by E. K. Rand and H. F. Stewart, London, 1918). There is another translation of the *Consolation* by W. V. Cooper (New York, 1943).

St. Gregory the Great, *Dialogues* (tr. by E. G. Gardner, London, 1911).

————, *Letters* (*Library of Nicene and Post-Nicene Fathers*, series II, Vols. XII, XIII).

Jonas, *Life of St. Columban* (*Translations and Reprints*, Vol. II, no. 7).

L. R. Loomis, *The Book of the Popes* (New York, 1916).

Eddius Stephanus, *Life of Bishop Wilfrid* (tr. by B. Colgrave, Cambridge, 1927).

E. Brehaut, *An Encyclopedist of the Dark Ages* (New York, 1912).

J. B. Bury, *Life of St. Patrick* (London, 1905).

E. S. Duckett, *The Gateway to the Middle Ages* (New York, 1938).

F. H. Dudden, *Gregory the Great* (London, 1905, 2 vols.).

A. Harnack, *Monasticism* (London, 1901).

H. H. Howorth, *St. Augustine of Canterbury* (London, 1913).

P. de Labriolle, *History and Literature of Christianity from Tertullian to Boëthius* (New York, 1925).

M. Laistner, *Thought and Letters in Western Europe 500–900* (New York, 1931).

E. K. Rand, *Founders of the Middle Ages* (Cambridge, 1928).

H. O. Taylor, *The Classical Heritage of the Middle Ages* (New York, 1911).

H. Zimmer, *The Irish Element in Mediæval Culture* (London, 1913).

3. THE DECAY OF THE ROMAN WORLD IN THE EAST

JUSTINIAN'S REVIVAL

Procopius, *The Secret History* (tr. by R. Atwater, Chicago, 1927).

————, *History of the Wars* (tr. by H. B. Dewing, Loeb Library, London and New York, 1914–1928, 5 vols.).

J. Baker, *Justinian and the Later Roman Empire* (Madison, 1966).

C. Diehl, *Justinien et la civilisation byzantine au VIe siècle* (Paris, 1901).

P. N. Ure, *Justinian and His Age* (Harmondsworth, 1951).

See also the books listed under Chapter 6.

ISLAM AND THE ARAB CONQUEST

The Koran (tr. in Everyman's Library and elsewhere).

The Origins of the Islamic State (tr. of early Arabic accounts by P. K. Hitti, New York, 1916).

T. Andrae, *Mohammed, the Man and His Faith* (London, 1936).

T. W. Arnold, *The Caliphate* (Oxford, 1912).

B. Lewis, *The Arabs in History* (London, 1958).

D. S. Margoliouth, *Mohammed and the Rise of Islam* (New York, 1905).

W. Muir, *The Caliphate, Its Rise, Decline and Fall* (rev. ed. by T. H. Weir, Edinburgh, 1915).

————, *The Life of Mohammed* (rev. ed. by T. H. Weir, Edinburgh, 1912).

4. REVIVAL UNDER PIPPIN AND CHARLEMAGNE

J. Boussard, *The Civilization of Charlemagne* (New York, 1969).

S. C. Easton and H. Wieruszowski, *The Era of Charlmagne* (Princeton, 1961).

A. J. Grant, *Early Lives of Charlemagne* (London, 1907).

S. E. Turner, *Life of Charlemagne by Eginhard* (New York, 1880).

Willibald, *Life of St. Boniface* (tr. by G. W. Robinson, Cambridge, 1916).

Letters of St. Boniface (tr. by E. Emerton, New York, 1940).

G. F. Browne, *Alcuin of York* (London, 1908).

L. Duchesne, *The Beginnings of the Temporal Sovereignty of the Popes* (London, 1908).

E. S. Duckett, *Alcuin, Friend of Charlemagne* (New York, 1951).

H. Fichtenau, *The Carolingian Empire* (Oxford, 1957).

L. Halphen, *Charlemagne et l'empire carolingien* (Paris, 1947).

T. Hodgkin, *Charles the Great* (London, 1897).

Lavisse, *Histoire de France*, Vol. II, Pt. I.

5. THE COLLAPSE OF THE CAROLINGIAN EMPIRE

Lavisse, *Histoire de France*, Vol. II, Pt. II.

THE SUCCESSORS OF CHARLEMAGNE

J. Bryce, *The Holy Roman Empire*, Chs. 5–8 (various editions).

E. F. Henderson, *A History of Germany in the Middle Ages*, Chs. 6–8 (London, 1894).

R. S. Lopez, *The Tenth Century* (New York, 1959).

T. F. Tout, *Empire and Papacy*, Chs. 2–4 (London and New York, 1898).

P. Villari, *Mediæval Italy from Charlemagne to Henry VII*, pp. 1–75 (London, 1910).

THE NEW INVASIONS

G. W. Dasent, *The Story of Burnt Njal* (Everyman's Library and other editions).

W. Morris and E. Magnusson, *Saga Library* (London, 1891–1905, 6 vols.).

Mrs. Muriel Press, *The Laxdaelasaga* (London, 1899).

J. Sephton, *The Saga of King Olaf Tryggwason* (London, 1895).
———, *The Saga of King Sverri* (London, 1899).

H. Arbmen, *The Vikings* (New York, 1961).
S. A. Anderson, *Viking Enterprise* (New York, 1936).
J. B. Bury, *History of the Later Roman Empire,* Vol. II, pp. 11–24, 274–280, 331–338, 470–476; *History of the Eastern Roman Empire,* Chs. XI–XIII.
T. D. Kendrick, *History of the Vikings* (New York, 1930).
L. M. Larson, *Canute the Great* (New York, 1912).
C. A. Macartney, *The Magyars in the Ninth Century* (Cambridge, 1930).
P. Sawyer, *The Age of the Vikings* (London, 1962).
V. Thompson, *The Relations between Ancient Russia and Scandinavia* (Oxford, 1878).
G. Turville-Petre, *The Heroic Age of Scandinavia* (London, 1951).

FEUDALISM

Raoul de Cambrai (tr. by Jessie Crosland, London, 1926).
The Song of Roland (tr. by C. K. Scott-Moncrieff, New York, 1920; other translations also available).
Translations and Reprints, Vol. IV, no. 3.
All source collections have some material on this subject.

M. Bloch, *Feudal Society* (Chicago, 1961).
F. L. Ganshof, *Feudalism* (London, 1952).
C. Seignobos, *The Feudal Regime* (New York, 1902).
C. Stepsenson, *Feudalism* (Ithaca, 1942).
J. R. Strayer, *Feudalism* (Princeton, 1965).

THE MEDIEVAL VILLAGE

M. Bloch, *French Rural History* (Berkeley, 1966).
G. G. Coulton, *The Mediæval Village* (Cambridge, 1925).
N. Neilson, *Mediæval Agrarian Economy* (New York, 1936).
R. E. Prothero (Lord Ernle), *English Farming Past and Present* (London, 1936).
(See also vol. I., 2nd ed. of the *Cambridge Economic History.*)

THE CHURCH IN THE FEUDAL AGE

E. H. Davenport, *The False Decretals* (Oxford, 1916).
E. N. Johnson, *Secular Activities of the German Episcopate* (Lincoln, 1932).
H. C. Lea, *An Historical Sketch of Sacerdotal Celibacy* (New York, 1907, 2 vols.).
———, *Studies in Church History* (Philadelphia, 1883).
J. B. Russell, *Dissent and Reform in the Early Middle Ages* (Berkeley, 1965).

6. BRIDGES ACROSS THE DARK AGES

ARABIC CIVILIZATION

Arabian Nights (tr. by E. W. Lane, London, 1909, 3 vols. or other editions).
Benjamin of Tudela, *Travels* (tr. by Asher, London, 1840).

T. W. Arnold and A. Guillaume, eds., *The Legacy of Islam* (Oxford, 1931).
R. P. A. Dozy, *Spanish Islam* (London, 1913).
J. Hell, *Arab Civilization* (Cambridge, 1926).
P. K. Hitti, *History of the Arabs* (London, 1946).
G. von Grunebaum, *Medieval Islam* (Chicago, 1961).
W. M. Watt, *A History of Islamic Spain* (Edinburgh, 1965).

BYZANTINE CIVILIZATION

N. H. Baynes, *The Byzantine Empire* (London, 1926).
C. Diehl, *History of the Byzantine Empire* (Princeton, 1925).
————, *Byzantine Portraits* (New York, 1927).
————, *Byzantium: Greatness and Decline* (New Brunswick, 1957).
B. Diener, *Imperial Byzantium* (Boston, 1938).
J. M. Hussey, *The Byzantine World* (New York, 1961).
G. Ostrogorsky, *A History of the Byzantine State* (Oxford, 1956).
S. Runciman, *Byzantine Civilization* (London, 1933).
A. A. Vasiliev, *History of the Byzantine Empire* (Madison, 1928, 2 vols.).

THE REVIVAL OF THE WESTERN EMPIRE

Liudprand, *Works* (Chronicle of reign of Otto I, Embassy to Constantinople, etc., tr. by F. A. Wright, London, 1930).

G. Barraclough, *Medieval Germany*, Vol. I (Oxford, 1938).
J. Bryce, *The Holy Roman Empire*, Chs. 7–9.
H. Fisher, *The Medieval Empire*, Vol. I, Chs. 1–2.

7. THE REVIVAL OF WESTERN CIVILIZATION

THE RELIGIOUS REVIVAL

J. Evans, *Monastic Life at Cluny* (Oxford, 1931).
A. J. MacDonald, *Hildebrand, a Life of Gregory VII* (London, 1932).
G. Tellenbach, *Church, State, and Christian Society at the Time of the Investiture Contest* (Oxford, 1940).
J. W. Thompson, *Feudal Germany*, Chs. 1–7 (Chicago, 1928).
W. Ullmann, *The Growth of Papal Government* (London, 1955).

THE POLITICAL REVIVAL—FRANCE

Cambridge Medieval History, Vol. III, Ch. 5; Vol. V, Ch. 18.

Lavisse, *Histoire de France,* Vol. II, Pt. II.

Ch. Petit-Dutaillis, *Feudal Monarchy in France and England,* Chs. 1, 4 (London, 1936).

A. Tilley, *Medieval France,* Chs. 1–2 (Cambridge, 1922).

THE POLITICAL REVIVAL—ENGLAND AND SICILY

The Anglo-Saxon Chronicle (Everyman's Library and other editions).

Six Old English Chronicles (tr. by Giles, London, 1875).

The Laws of the Earliest English Kings (tr. by F. L. Attenborough, Cambridge, 1922).

Laws of the Kings of England from Edmund to Henry I (tr. by A. J. Robertson, Cambridge, 1925).

English Historical Documents, 1042–1189 (eds. D. C. Douglas and G. W. Greenaway, New York, 1953).

F. Barlow, *The Feudal Kingdom of England* (London, 1955).

E. Curtis, *Roger of Sicily and the Normans in Lower Italy* (New York, 1912).

D. C. Douglas, *William the Conqueror* (Berkeley, 1964).

C. H. Haskins, *The Normans in European History* (Boston, 1915).

L. M. Larson, *Canute the Great* (New York, 1912).

F. W. Maitland, *Domesday Book and Beyond* (Cambridge, 1897).

Ch. Petit-Dutaillis, *Feudal Monarchy,* Chs. 2, 3.

J. A. Robinson, *The Times of St. Dunstan* (Oxford, 1923).

F. M. Stenton, *Anglo-Saxon England* (Oxford, 1947).

————, *The First Century of English Feudalism* (Oxford, 1932).

THE ECONOMIC REVIVAL

R. S. Lopez and I. W. Raymond, *Medieval Trade in the Mediterranean World* (New York, 1955).

J. H. Mundy and P. Riesenberg, *The Medieval Town* (Princeton, 1958).

P. Boissonade, *Life and Work in the Middle Ages* (New York, 1927).

A. F. Havighurst, *The Pirenne Thesis: Analysis, Criticism and Revision* (Boston, 1958).

H. Heaton, *Economic History of Europe,* pp. 132–166 (New York, 1936).

R. Latouche, *The Birth of Western Economy* (London, 1961).

E. Lipson, *Economic History of England,* Vol. I (New York, 1915).

H. Pirenne, *Medieval Cities* (Princeton, 1925 and later editions).

————, *Belgian Democracies* (London, 1915).

C. Stephenson, *Borough and Town* (Cambridge, 1932).

J. Tait, *The Medieval English Borough* (Manchester, 1936).

8. THE LEADERSHIP OF THE CHURCH

THE EMPIRE AND THE PAPACY

Imperial Lives and Letters of the Eleventh Century (tr. by T. E. Mommsen and K. F. Morrison, New York, 1962).

The Correspondence of Pope Gregory VII (tr. by E. Emerton, New York, 1932).

Duncalf and Krey, *Parallel Source Problems*, pp. 29–94.

Henderson, *Documents*, pp. 361–409.

Otto of Freising, *The Two Cities* (tr. by C. C. Mierow, New York, 1928).

———, *Deeds of Frederick Barbarossa* (tr. by C. C. Mierow and R. Emery, New York, 1953).

B. Tierney, *The Crisis of Church and State* (Englewood Cliffs, 1964).

W. Butler, *The Lombard Communes* (New York, 1906).

Cambridge Medieval History, Vol. III, Chs. 10–12; Vol. V, Chs. 1–3.

D. J. Medley, *The Church and the Empire, 1003–1304*, Chs. 1–3 (New York 1910).

A. H. Mathew, *The Life and Times of Hildebrand* (London, 1910).

C. H. McIlwain, *Growth of Political Thought in the West*, pp. 149–221.

A. L. Poole, *Henry the Lion* (London, 1912).

S. Williams, *The Gregorian Epoch* (Boston, 1964).

The books listed under Chapter 6, section 2, and Chapter 7, section 1, contain material on this subject.

THE EARLIER CRUSADES

T. A. Archer, *The Crusade of Richard I* (New York, 1889).

Anna Comnena, *The Alexiad* (tr. by E. A. S. Dawes, London, 1928).

Duncalf and Krey, *Parallel Source Problems*, pp. 95–133.

Early Travels in Palestine (tr. by T. Wright, London, 1848).

Fulcher of Chartres, *Chronicle of the First Crusade* (tr. by M. E. McGinty, *Translations and Reprints*, 3rd series, Vol. I, Philadelphia, 1941).

P. K. Hitti, *An Arab-Syrian Gentleman and Warrior in the Period of the Crusades* (New York, 1929).

A. C. Krey, *The First Crusade* (Princeton, 1921).

Raymond d'Aguilers, *History of the Frankish Conquerors of Jerusalem* (tr. by J. H. and L. L. Hill, Philadelphia, 1968).

Translations and Reprints, Vol. I, no. 2 (*Urban and the Crusaders*); Vol. I, no. 4 (*Letters of the Crusaders*).

William of Tyre, *History of the Crusades* (tr. by A. C. Krey and E. W. Babcock, New York, 1942).

M. W. Baldwin, ed., *The First Hundred Years*, Vol. I of *A History of the Crusades*, ed. by K. M. Setton (Philadelphia, 1955).

E. Barker, *The Crusades* (London, 1923).

J. L. LaMonte, *Feudal Monarchy in the Latin Kingdom of Jerusalem* (Cambridge, 1932).

D. C. Munro, H. Prutz and C. Diehl, *Essays on the Crusades* (Burlington, 1903).

D. C. Munro, *The Kingdom of the Crusaders* (New York, 1935).

R. A. Newhall, *The Crusades* (New York, 1927).

L. J. Paetow, ed., *The Crusades and Other Essays Presented to D. C. Munro* (New York, 1928).

S. Runciman, *A History of the Crusades* (Cambridge, 1951–1954, 3 vols.).

W. Stevenson, *The Crusaders in the East* (Cambridge, 1907).

THE REFORM MOVEMENT IN THE TWELFTH CENTURY

St. Bernard, *Works* (tr. by S. J. Eales, London, 1889–1896, 5 vols.).

Guibert, Abbot of Nogent, *Autobiography* (tr. by C. C. S. Bland, New York, 1926).

The Chronicle of Jocelin of Brakelond (tr. by L. Jane, London, 1907; other translations also available).

F. A. Gasquet, *Some Letters of St. Bernard* (London, 1904).

L. Bouyer, *The Cistercian Heritage* (London, 1958).

G. G. Coulton, *St. Bernard, his Predecessors and Successors* (Vol. I of *Five Centuries of Religion*).

E. S. Davison, *Forerunners of St. Francis* (New York, 1926).

F. A. Gasquet, *English Monastic Life* (London, 1905).

D. Knowles, *The Monastic Order in England* (Cambridge, 1963).

H. O. Taylor, *The Mediæval Mind*, Vol. I, Chs. 16, 17, 18.

W. Williams, *St. Bernard of Clairvaux* (Manchester, 1953).

THE RENAISSANCE OF THE TWELFTH CENTURY

Abelard, *Letters* (tr. by C. K. Scott-Moncrieff, New York, 1926).

Walter Map, *Courtiers' Trifles* (tr. by F. Tupper and M. B. Ogle, Oxford, 1924. A translation by M. R. James is also available.)

Poole, *Illustrations of the History of Medieval Thought.*

John of Salisbury, *The Statesman's Book* (tr. in part by J. Dickinson, New York, 1927).

———, *The Metalogicon* (tr. by D. D. McGarry, Berkeley, 1955).

———, *Letters* (eds. W. J. Millor and H. E. Butler, Edinburgh, 1955 ff.).

J. A. Symonds, *Wine, Women, and Song: Mediæval Latin Students' Song* (London, 1884, and later editions).

H. Waddell, *Mediæval Latin Lyrics* (London, 1929).

H. Adams, *Mont-Saint Michel and Chartres* (Boston, 1922).

C. H. Haskins, *The Renaissance of the Twelfth Century* (Cambridge, 1927).

———, *The Rise of Universities* (New York, 1923).

———, *Studies in the History of Mediæval Science* (Cambridge, 1927).

H. Rashdall, *The Universities of Europe in the Middle Ages* (rev. ed. by F. M. Powicke and A. B. Emden, Oxford, 1936, 3 vols.).

T. G. Jackson, *Byzantine and Romanesque Architecture* (Cambridge, 1913, 2 vols.).

L. Thorndike, *History of Magic and Experimental Science,* Vol. II.

H. Waddell, *Peter Abelard* (New York, 1933).

———, *The Wandering Scholars* (London, 1927).

C. C. J. Webb, *John of Salisbury* (London, 1932).

9. THE RISE OF THE WESTERN MONARCHIES

Ch. Petit-Dutaillis, *Feudal Monarchy in France and England* (London, 1936).

ENGLAND

Giraldus Cambrensis, *Works* (tr. by T. Wright, London, 1913).

Ordericus Vitalis, *History of England and Normandy* (tr. by T. Forester, London, 1854, 3 vols.).

Roger of Hoveden, *Annals* (tr. by H. T. Riley, London, 1853).

Roger of Wendover, *Chronicle* (tr. by J. A. Giles, London, 1849, 2 vols.).

William of Newburgh, *Selections* (ed. by C. Johnson, New York, 1920).

William of Malmesbury, *Chronicle* (tr. by J. A. Giles, London, 1847).

J. C. Holt, *Magna Carta* (Cambridge, 1965).

J. E. A. Jolliffe, *Angevin Kingship* (London, 1955).

W. A. Morris, *The Constitutional History of England to 1216* (New York, 1930).

W. S. McKechnie, *Magna Carta* (Glasgow, 1914).

S. Painter, *William Marshal, Knight Errant, Baron, and Regent of England* (Baltimore, 1933).

———, *The Reign of King John* (Baltimore, 1949).

F. Pollock and F. W. Maitland, *The History of English Law,* Vol. I, Chs. 1–6 (Cambridge, 1923).

A. L. Poole, *From Domesday Book to Magna Carta* (Oxford, 1951).

F. M. Powicke, *The Loss of Normandy* (Manchester, 1913).

———, *Stephen Langton* (Oxford, 1928).

H. G. Richardson and G. O. Sayles, *The Governance of Medieval England* (Edinburgh, 1963).

L. F. Salzmann, *Henry II* (Boston, 1914).

G. O. Sayles, *The Medieval Foundations of England* (London, 1948).

W. Stubbs, *Historical Introductions to the Rolls Series* (London, 1902).

W. L. Warren, *King John* (London, 1961).

FRANCE

J. Evans, *Life in Mediæval France* (London, 1925).

F. Funck-Brentano, *The Middle Ages* (New York, 1923).

Lavisse, *Histoire de France,* Vol. II, Pt. II; Vol. III, Pt. I.

A. Luchaire, *Social France at the Time of Philip Augustus* (New York, 1912).

J. R. M. MacDonald, *A History of France,* Vol. I (New York, 1915).

A. Tilley, *Medieval France* (Cambridge, 1922).

W. Walker, *On the Increase of Royal Power in France under Philip Augustus* (Leipzig, 1888).

10. THE CHURCH STRUGGLES TO MAINTAIN ITS LEADERSHIP

INNOCENT III

Selected Letters of Pope Innocent III Concerning England (eds. C. R. Cheney and W. H. Semple, Edinburgh, 1953).

Cambridge Medieval History, Vol. VI, Chs. 1, 2.

A. Luchaire, *Innocent III* (Paris, 1905–1908, 6 vols., in French).

S. R. Packard, *Europe and the Church under Innocent III* (New York, 1928).

H. D. Sedgwick, *Italy in the Thirteenth Century,* Vol. I, Chs. 1–6 (Boston, 1912).

HERESY AND THE FRIARS

St. Bonaventure, *Life of St. Francis* (tr. by E. G. Salter, London, 1904).

G. G. Coulton, *From St. Francis to Dante* (extracts from the chronicle of the Franciscan Salimbene) (London, 1907).

St. Francis, *Writings* (tr. by P. Robinson, Philadelphia, 1906).

The Coming of the Friars to England and Germany (tr. by E. G. Salter, London, 1926).

The Legend of St. Francis by the Three Companions (tr. by E. G. Salter, London, 1905).

The Little Flowers and the Life of St. Francis (Everyman's Library).

The Lives of St. Francis by Thomas of Celano (tr. by A. G. Ferrers Howell, London, 1908).

R. F. Bennett, *The Early Dominicans* (Cambridge, 1937).

E. Hutton, *Franciscans in England* (London, 1926).

B. Jarrett, *Life of St. Dominic* (London, 1924).

J. Jörgensen, *St. Francis* (New York, 1912).

H. C. Lea, *History of the Inquisition* (New York, 1888, 3 vols.).

P. Mandonnet, *St. Dominic and His Work* (London, 1944).

S. Runciman, *The Medieval Manichee,* Cambridge, 1947.

P. Sabatier, *Life of St. Francis* (London, 1894).

E. Vacandard, *The Inquisition* (New York, 1908).

THE PAPACY AND THE HOHENSTAUFEN

W. F. Butler, *The Lombard Communes* (New York, 1906).

E. Kantorowicz, *Frederick II* (London, 1931).

D. J. Medley, *The Church and the Empire*, Chs. 6–10, 15.

T. C. Van Clive, *Markward of Anweiler and the Minority of Frederick II* (Princeton, 1937).

The books by Sedgwick, Thompson, Villari, and Barraclough, mentioned above, all contain material on this subject.

THE LATER CRUSADES

Joinville, *Life of St. Louis* (Everyman's Library, other translations available).

Philip de Novare, *The Wars of Frederick II against the Ibelins* (tr. by J. L. LaMonte, New York, 1936).

Robert of Clari, *Conquest of Constantinople* (New York, 1936).

Villehardouin, *The Conquest of Constantinople* (Everyman's Library).

A. S. Atiya, *The Crusades of the Later Middle Ages* (London, 1938).

E. J. Davis, *The Invasion of Egypt by Louis IX* (London, 1898).

D. C. Munro, "The Children's Crusade" in *American Historical Review*, XIX, 516–524.

K. M. Setton, R. L. Wolff, and H. W. Hazard, eds., *The Later Crusades* (Philadelphia, 1962).

See the general books on the crusades listed under Chapter 8, section 2.

THE EXPANSION OF CHRISTIAN EUROPE

Bernat Esclot, *Chronicle of the Reign of King Pedro III of Aragon, 1276–1285* (tr. by F. L. Critchlow, Princeton, 1928).

P. de Gayangos, *Chronicle of James I, King of Aragon, 1213–1270* (London, 1883).

The Lay of the Cid (tr. by R. S. Rose and L. Bacon, Berkeley, 1919).

W. W. Rockhill, *The Journeys of William Rubruk and John of Pian de Carpine* (London, 1900).

H. Yule, *The Book of Sir Marco Polo* (London, 1903). Other translations of Marco Polo's Travels are available.

———, *Cathay and the Way Thither: being a collection of mediæval notices of China* (London, 1866; revised ed., London, 1913–1915, 3 vols.).

C. R. Beazley, *The Dawn of Modern Geography* (London, 1897–1906), 3 vols.).

J. H. S. Birch, *Denmark in History* (London, 1938).

H. J. Chaytor, *A History of Aragon* (London, 1933).

H. B. Clark, *The Cid Campeador* (New York, 1897).

F. Dvornik, *The Making of Central and Eastern Europe* (London, 1949).

———, *The Slavs: Their Early History* (Boston, 1956).

V. O. Kluchevsky, *History of Russia*, Vol. I (London, 1911).

Karen Larsen, *A History of Norway* (Princeton, 1948).

F. H. H. V. Lützow, *Bohemia, an Historical Sketch* (London, 1909).

R. B. Merriman, *The Rise of the Spanish Empire,* Vol. I (New York, 1918).

A. S. Stomberg, *Sweden* (New York, 1931).

J. W. Thompson, *Feudal Germany,* Pt. II.

G. Vernadsky, *Ancient Russia, Kievan Russia, The Mongols and Russia* (three separate books, published in New Haven in 1943, 1948, and 1953 respectively).

INTELLECTUAL AND ARTISTIC ACTIVITIES

Henri d'Andeli, *The Battle of the Seven Arts* (tr. by L. J. Paetow, Berkeley, *Memoirs of the University of California,* Vol. IV, No. 1, 1914).

John of Garland, *Morale Scolarium* (tr. by L. J. Paetow, Berkeley, *Memoirs of the University of California,* Vol. IV, No. 1, 1927).

E. Lewis, *Medieval Political Ideas* (London, 1954, 2 vols.).

R. S. McKeon, *Selections from the Mediæval Philosophers.*

Thomas Aquinas, *Basic Writings* (ed. A. C. Pegis, New York, 1945, 2 vols.).

————, *Political Writings* (tr. A. d'Entrèves, Oxford, 1948).

H. Arnold and L. B. Saint, *Stained Glass of the Middle Ages* (New York, 1913).

A. Gardner, *Medieval Sculpture in France* (Cambridge, 1931).

E. Gilson, *The Philosophy of St. Thomas Aquinas* (Cambridge, 1924).

————, *Reason and Revelation in the Middle Ages* (New York, 1938).

————, *The Spirit of Mediæval Philosophy* (New York, 1936).

C. H. Haskins, *Mediæval Culture* (Oxford, 1929).

T. G. Jackson, *Gothic Architecture* (Cambridge, 1915, 2 vols.).

E. Mâle, *Religious Art in France in the Thirteenth Century* (London, 1913).

E. Panofsky, *Gothic Architecture and Scholasticism* (Latrobe, 1951).

G. Post, *Studies in Medieval Legal Thought* (Princeton, 1964).

H. Rashdall, *The Universities of Europe in the Middle Ages.*

O. von Simson, *The Gothic Cathedral* (New York, 1956).

H. O. Taylor, *The Mediæval Mind,* Vol. II, Chs. 28–34, 38–42.

P. Vinogradoff, *Roman Law in Medieval Europe* (Oxford, 1929).

11. THE GROWTH OF SECULAR INSTITUTIONS AND INTERESTS

THE GROWTH OF THE STATE IN FRANCE

Joinville, *Life of St. Louis.*

Lavisse, *Histoire de France,* Vol. III, Pt. II.

F. Perry, *St. Louis, the Most Christian King* (New York, 1901).

Petit-Dutaillis, *Feudal Monarchy,* pp. 233–271.

J. R. Strayer, *The Administration of Normandy under St. Louis* (Cambridge, 1932).

See the books on the history of medieval France listed under Chapter 9, section 2.

THE GROWTH OF THE STATE IN ENGLAND

Matthew Paris, *Chronicle* (tr. by J. A. Giles, London, 1852, 3 vols.).

C. Bémont, *Simon de Montfort* (tr. by E. F. Jacob, Oxford, 1930).
A. Gasquet, *Henry III and the Church* (London, 1905).
F. M. Powicke, *King Henry III and the Lord Edward* (Oxford, 1947, 2 vols.).
———, *The Thirteenth Century* (Oxford, 1953).
F. Thompson, *The First Century of Magna Carta* (Minneapolis, 1925).
R. F. Treharne, *The Baronial Plan of Reform, 1258–1263* (Manchester, 1932).

LAY SOCIETY IN THE THIRTEENTH CENTURY—THE NOBLES

C. C. Abbott, *Early Mediæval French Lyrics* (London, 1932).
Andreas Capellanus, *The Art of Courtly Love* (tr. by J. J. Parry, New York, 1941).
Aucassin and Nicolette (tr. by A. Lang, London, 1887; also in Everyman's Library).
C. Dickinson, *Troubadour Songs* (New York, 1920).
French Mediæval Romances (tr. by E. Mason, New York, 1911).
Guillaume de Lorris and Jean de Meung, *The Romance of the Rose* (tr. by F. S. Ellis, London, 1900, 3 vols.).
Old French Romances (tr. by W. Morris, London, 1896).
The Romance of Tristan and Iseult (tr. by H. Belloc, New York, 1927).
Tales from the Old French (tr. by I. Butler, Boston, 1910).
Walther von der Vogelweide, *Selected Poems* (tr. by W. A. Phillips, London, 1896).

H. J. Chaytor, *The Troubadours* (Cambridge, 1912).
R. C. Clephan, *The Tournament* (London, 1919).
W. S. Davis, *Life on a Medieval Barony* (New York, 1923).
M. W. Labarge, *A Baronial Household of the Thirteenth Century* (New York, 1965).
C. S. Lewis, *The Allegory of Love* (Oxford, 1936).
W. C. Meller, *A Knight's Life in the Days of Chivalry* (London, 1924).
C. W. C. Oman, *A History of the Art of War in the Middle Ages,* Vol. I, Book VI; Vol. II, Book VII (London, 1924).
S. Painter, *French Chivalry* (Baltimore, 1940).
S. Painter, *The Scourge of God: Peter of Dreux, Duke of Brittany* (Baltimore, 1937).
G. E. B. Saintsbury, *The Flourishing of Romance and the Rise of Allegory* (London, 1897).
J. H. Smith, *The Troubadours at Home* (New York, 1899, 2 vols.).
A. H. Thompson, *Military Architecture in England during the Middle Ages* (London, 1912).

LAY SOCIETY IN THE THIRTEENTH CENTURY—THE BOURGEOISIE

Legends and Satires from Mediæval Literature (tr. by M. H. Shackford, New York, 1913).

Reynard the Fox (various editions and translations).

P. Boissonade, *Life and Work in the Middle Ages.*

W. Cunningham, *Growth of English Industry and Commerce* (Cambridge, 1915).

C. Gross, *The Gild Merchant* (Oxford, 1890, 2 vols.).

E. Lipson, *Introduction to the Economic History of England,* Vol. I (London, 1929).

H. Pirenne, *Belgian Democracy* (London and New York, 1915).

————, *Economic and Social History of Medieval Europe.*

R. de Roover, *Money, Banking and Credit in Mediaeval Bruges* (Cambridge, 1948).

L. F. Salzmann, *English Industries in the Middle Ages* (London, 1923).

O. Walford, *Fairs, Past and Present* (London, 1883).

LAY SOCIETY IN THE THIRTEENTH CENTURY—THE PEASANTS

C. H. Bell, *Peasant Life in Old German Epics: Meier Helmbrecht and Der Arme Heinrich* (New York, 1931).

F. W. Maitland, *Select Pleas in Manorial Courts* (Selden Society, Vol. II, London, 1889).

Translations and Reprints, Vol. III, No. 5.

Walter of Henley, *Husbandry* (tr. by E. Lamond, London, 1890).

H. S. Bennett, *Life on the English Manor* (Cambridge, 1937).

M. Bloch, *Les caractères originaux de l'histoire rurale française,* Chs 1, 3.

The Cambridge Economic History of Europe, Vol. I, *The Agrarian Life of the Middle Ages* (Cambridge, 1941).

G. G. Coulton, *The Medieval Village* (Cambridge, 1926).

G. C. Homans, *English Villagers of the Thirteenth Century* (Cambridge, Mass., 1940).

A. Jessopp, *Coming of the Friars,* Ch. II (London, 1928).

E. Power, *Mediæval People,* Ch. 1.

J. E. T. Rogers, *A History of Agriculture and Prices in England,* Vol. I (Oxford, 1866).

P. Vinogradoff, *Growth of the Manor* (New York, 1905).

————, *Villeinage in England* (Oxford, 1892).

H. B. Workman, *John Wycliff* (Oxford, 1926).

12. THE CHURCH LOSES ITS LEADERSHIP

L. E. Binns, *Decline and Fall of the Mediæval Papacy* (London, 1934).

R. W. and A. J. Carlyle, *A History of Medieval Political Theory,* vol. V (London, 1928).

A. C. Flick, *Decline of the Mediæval Church* (New York, 1930, 2 vols.).

THE PONTIFICATE OF BONIFACE VIII

T. S. R. Boase, *Boniface VIII* (London, 1933).

F. Gregorovius, *History of the City of Rome*, Vol. V, Pt. II; Vol. VI, Pt. I.

H. C. Lea, *History of the Inquisition*, Vol. III, Chs. 1, 5.

THE GROWTH OF SECULAR LEADERSHIP
IN FRANCE AND ENGLAND

R. Fawtier, *Les Capétiens et la France* (Paris, 1942).

G. L. Haskins, *The Growth of English Representative Government* (Philadelphia, 1948).

E. Lavisse, *Histoire de France*, Vol. III, Pt. II.

F. W. Maitland, *Memoranda de Parliamento, Introduction* (London, 1893).

D. Pasquet, *Essay on the Origins of the House of Commons* (Cambridge, 1925).

J. R. Strayer and C. H. Taylor, *Studies in Early French Taxation* (Cambridge, 1939).

T. F. Tout, *Edward I* (London, 1893).

———, *History of England, 1216–1377* (London, 1905).

THE BABYLONIAN CAPTIVITY AND THE GREAT SCHISM

St. Bernardino, *Sermons* (tr. by A. Howe, London, 1926).

Johannes Herolt, *Miracles of the Virgin Mary* (London, 1928).

Jan Hus, *De Ecclesia: The Church* (tr. by D. S. Schaff, New York, 1915).

W. E. Lunt, *Papal Revenues in the Middle Ages* (New York, 1934, 2 vols.).

Marsilio of Padua, *The Defender of the Peace* (tr. by A. Gewirth, New York, 1956).

V. Scudder, *St. Catherine of Siena As Seen in Her Letters* (New York, 1926).

H. Workman and R. Pope, *The Letters of John Huss* (London, 1904).

L. E. Binns, *The Decline and Fall of the Medieval Papacy* (London, 1934).

M. Creighton, *A History of the Papacy*, Vols. 1–5 (London, 1919).

E. Emerton, *The 'Defensor Pacis' of Marsiglio of Padua* (Cambridge, 1920).

J. N. Figgis, *Studies of Political Thought from Gerson to Grotius* (Cambridge, 1923).

H. C. Lea, *History of the Inquisition*, Vol. II, Chs. 6–8; Vol. III, Chs. 1, 3, 4, 5.

C. H. McIlwain, *Growth of Political Thought*, pp. 233–363.

G. Mollat, *Les Papes d'Avignon* (Paris, 1912).

D. S. Muzzey, *The Spiritual Franciscans* (New York, 1907).

L. Pastor, *History of the Popes*, vols. 1–5 (London, 1891 ff.).

M. Spinka, *John Hus and the Czech Reform* (Chicago, 1941).

B. Tierney, *Foundations of the Conciliar Theory* (Cambridge, 1955).

W. Ullmann, *Origins of the Great Schism* (London, 1948).

H. B. Workman, *John Wyclif* (Oxford, 1926).

——, *The Dawn of the Reformation* (London, 1901).
J. H. Wylie, *The Council of Constance* (London, 1900).

13. THE FAILURE OF SECULAR LEADERSHIP

Cambridge Medieval History, Vols. 7, 8.
E. P. Cheyney, *The Dawn of a New Era* (New York, 1936).
E. Emerton, *Beginnings of Modern Europe* (Boston, 1917).
J. Huizinga, *The Waning of the Middle Ages* (London, 1927).
H. Pirenne, *Economic and Social History of Medieval Europe*, pp. 192 ff.
J. W. Thompson, *Economic and Social History of the Later Middle Ages* (New York, 1931).

THE DISINTEGRATION OF MEDIEVAL SOCIETY

F. Villon, *Poems* (various editions).

E. F. Chaney, *François Villon in His Environment* (Oxford, 1946).
F. A. Gasquet, *The Black Death of 1348 and 1349* (London, 1908).
A. E. Levett, *The Black Death on the Estates of Winchester* (Oxford, 1916).
B. N. Nelson, *The Idea of Usury* (Princeton, 1949).
B. H. Putnam, *Enforcement of the Statute of Laborers* (New York, 1908).
W. Sombart, *The Quintessence of Capitalism* (New York, 1913).
The books on economic and religious history listed just above, and those listed under Chapters 11 and 12, all contain material on this problem.

ENGLAND AND FRANCE IN THE FOURTEENTH CENTURY

Chaucer, *Canterbury Tales* (many editions).
Froissart, *Chronicles* (many translations).
William Langland, *The Vision of Piers Plowman* (London, 1922).
The Book of Margery Kempe (tr. by W. Butler-Bowden, London, 1936).

S. Armitage-Smith, *John of Gaunt* (Westminster, 1904).
H. L. Gray, *The Influence of the Commons on Early Legislation* (Cambridge, 1932).
V. H. H. Green, *The Later Plantagenets* (London, 1955).
Lavisse, *Histoire de France*, Vol. IV, Pt. I.
A. R. Myers, *England in the Later Middle Ages* (Harmondsworth, 1952).
C. W. C. Oman, *The Great Revolt of 1381* (Oxford, 1906).
C. Oman, *Art of War*, Vol. II, Book IX.
E. Perroy, *The Hundred Years' War* (London, 1951).
A. Steel, *Richard II* (Cambridge, 1941).
G. M. Trevelyan, *England in the Age of Wycliffe* (London, various editions).
T. F. Tout, *The Place of Edward II in English History* (Manchester, 1914).

ENGLAND AND FRANCE IN THE FIFTEENTH CENTURY

P. de Commines, *Mémoires* (London, 1900, and other translations).

J. Fortescue, *Governance of England* (Oxford, 1885).

T. D. Murray, *Jeanne d'Arc . . . being the story of her life as set forth in original documents* (New York, 1907).

The Paston Letters, ed. by J. Gairdner (London, 1904, 6 vols.) or *Selections from the Paston Letters,* ed. by A. D. Greenwood (London, 1920).

H. S. Bennett, *Chaucer and the Fifteenth Century* (Oxford, 1947).

O. Cartellieri, *Court of Burgundy* (New York, 1929).

P. Champion, *Louis XI* (New York, 1929).

A. B. Kerr, *Jacques Coeur* (New York, 1928).

J. F. Kirk, *History of Charles the Bold* (Philadelphia, 1864–1868, 3 vols.).

E. Lavisse, *Histoire de France,* Vol. IV, Pt. II.

F. W. Maitland, *Constitutional History of England* (Cambridge, 1911).

R. B. Mowat, *Wars of the Roses* (London, 1914).

C. Oman, *History of England 1377–1485* (London, 1906).

R. Putnam, *Charles the Bold* (New York, 1908).

R. Vaughan, *Philip the Bold* (Cambridge, 1962) and *John the Fearless* (New York, 1966), studies of two dukes of Burgundy.

THE EMPIRE, THE HABSBURGS, AND THE EAST

J. Bryce, *The Holy Roman Empire,* Chs. 13–15.

E. F. Henderson, *A Short History of Germany,* pp. 122–251.

Frederick G. Heymann, *John Zizka and the Hussite Revolution* (Princeton, 1955).

————, *George of Bohemia* (Princeton, 1965).

W. D. McCracken, *The Rise of the Swiss Republic,* Books 2 and 3 (New York, 1901).

R. B. Merriman, *Rise of the Spanish Empire,* Vols. I, II.

E. Pears, *The Destruction of the Greek Empire* (London, 1903).

W. Stubbs, *Germany in the Later Middle Ages* (London, 1908).

J. W. Thompson, *Economic and Social History of the Later Middle Ages,* Chs. 4–8, 15.

H. Zimmern, *The Hansa Towns* (New York, 1889).

14. THE END OF THE MIDDLE AGES

THE ITALIAN CITY-STATES

H. Baron, *The Crisis of the Early Italian Renaissance* (Princeton, 1955).

G. A. Brucker, *Florentine Politics and Society 1343–1378* (Princeton, 1962).

E. Emerton, *Humanism and Tyranny* (Cambridge, 1925).

R. de Roover, *The Medici Bank* (New York, 1948).

F. Schevill, *A History of Florence* (New York, 1936).

J. A. Symonds, *The Renaissance in Italy*, Vol. I, *The Age of the Despots* (London, 1926).

THE ITALIAN RENAISSANCE

Giovanni Boccaccio, *The Decameron* (many translations).

Baldassare Castiglione, *The Book of the Courtier* (Everyman's Library).

Benvenuto Cellini, *Autobiography* (tr. by J. A. Symonds, New York, 1924).

Dante, *Divine Comedy* (many translations).

Petrarch, *Secret* (tr. by W. H. Draper, London, 1911).

J. B. Ross and M. M. McLaughlin, *The Portable Renaissance Reader* (New York, 1953).

F. Schevill, *The First Century of Italian Humanism* (New York, 1928).

B. Berenson, *The Italian Painters of the Renaissance* (Oxford, 1930).

J. Burckhardt, *The Civilization of the Renaissance in Italy* (London, 1921).

W. K. Ferguson, *The Renaissance* (New York, 1939).

———, *The Renaissance in Historical Thought* (Boston, 1948).

A. C. Krey, *Florence, a City that Art Built* (Minneapolis, 1936).

F. J. Mather, *A History of Italian Painting* (New York, 1923).

J. H. Randall, *The Making of the Modern Mind*, Book 2 (Boston, 1926).

J. H. Robinson and H. W. Rolfe, *Petrarch, the First Modern Man* (New York, 1914).

J. A. Symonds, *The Renaissance in Italy*, Vols. 2–5 (London, 1926).

J. W. Thompson and others, *The Civilization of the Renaissance* (Chicago, 1929).

THE NORTHERN SOLUTION

W. R. Inge, *Light, Life and Love: Selections from* Eckhart, Tauler and Suso (New York, 1904).

Thomas à Kempis, *The Imitation of Christ* (many translations).

Theologica Germanica (tr. by S. Winkworth, London, 1907. Another translation is by T. S. Kepler, Cleveland, 1952).

R. W. and A. J. Carlyle, *A History of Mediæval Political Theory*, Vol. VI (Edinburgh, 1936).

J. M. Clark, *The Great German Mystics* (Oxford, 1949).

J. N. Figgis, *The Divine Right of Kings* (Cambridge, 1914).

A. Hyma, *The Christian Renaissance* (Grand Rapids, 1924).

R. M. Jones, *The Flowering of Mysticism* (New York, 1937).

E. Panofsky, *Early Netherlandish Painting* (Cambridge, 1953).

G. P. Winship, *Printing in the Fifteenth Century* (Philadelphia, 1940).

INDEX